The Bride and
the Dowry

The Bride
and
the Dowry

Israel, Jordan,
and the Palestinians
in the Aftermath
of the June 1967 War

AVI RAZ

Yale

UNIVERSITY PRESS

New Haven and London

Yale University Press books may be purchased in quantity for
educational, business, or promotional use. For information,
please e-mail sales.press@yale.edu (U.S. office) or
sales@yaleup.co.uk (U.K. office).

Set in Minion type by Westchester Book Group.
Printed in the United States of America.

Library of Congress Cataloging-in-Publication Data

Raz, Avi.
The bride and the dowry : Israel, Jordan, and the Palestinians
in the aftermath of the June 1967 War / Avi Raz.
p.   cm.
Includes bibliographical references and index.
ISBN 978-0-300-17194-5 (cloth : alk. paper)   1. Israel-Arab War,
1967—Influence.   2. Arab-Israeli conflict—1967–1973.   I. Title.
DS127.85.R39 2012
956.04ʹ6—dc23
2011049008

A catalogue record for this book is available from the
British Library.

This paper meets the requirements of ANSI/NISO Z39.48-1992
(Permanence of Paper).

10 9 8 7 6 5 4 3 2 1

"What could I do! Facts are such horrid things!"
Jane Austen, *Lady Susan*

"The past is never dead. It's not even past."
William Faulkner, *Requiem for a Nun*

Contents

List of Maps   *ix*
Prologue: Two Peoples, One Land   *xi*
Preface   *xiii*
Dramatis Personae   *xxv*
List of Abbreviations   *xxxii*

Introduction   1

ONE The Two Options: 5 June–Early July 1967   25

TWO The Jerusalem Syndrome: Late June–July 1967   53

THREE In Search of Docile Leadership: July–September 1967   79

FOUR The Right of No Return: June–September 1967   103

FIVE An Entity versus a King: September–November 1967   136

SIX A One-Way Dialogue: December 1967–January 1968   165

SEVEN Go-Betweens: February–Early May 1968   194

EIGHT The Double Game Redoubled:
Mid-May–October 1968   227

NINE "The Whole World Is Against Us": Epilogue   262

Notes   287
Sources and Bibliography   377
Index   417

Maps

1. The Middle East, 1967   xxxvi

2. The UN Partition Plan, 1947   9

3. Israel Following the Armistice Agreements, 1949   10

4. Israel and the Occupied Territories, 1967   11

5. Jerusalem Following the Annexation, 1967   52

6. The West Bank, 1967–68   106

7. The Allon Plan, 1968   246

Two Peoples, One Land

On a hot summer day in July 1967 Bashir Khayri, a young man from the West Bank town of Ramallah, rang the bell of a house in the Israeli town of Ramla. Founded in the beginning of the eighth century by the future Umayyad Khalifah Suleiman Ibn 'Abd al-Malik along the road connecting the port city of Jaffa with Jerusalem on the Judean hills, al-Ramlah was a vibrant Arab town until the first Arab-Israeli war in 1948. Then, also on a hot summer day in July, the Palestinian inhabitants of al-Ramlah, together with the people of the adjacent town of al-Lud, were forcefully driven out by the conquering Israelis. Six-year-old Bashir and his family were among the expellees who now became refugees. Nineteen years later and one month after the Israeli occupation of the West Bank in the Six Day War of June 1967, Bashir traveled from the family's new home in exile to see the old family house in al-Ramlah, built by his father in 1936 with the help of a Jewish architect friend. Dalia Ashkenazi, a young Israeli conscript, opened the door. Her parents were Holocaust refugees from Bulgaria who had been settled in the Khayri family house in what became the Israeli town of Ramla a few months after the expulsion of the Khayris. Dalia invited Bashir in, and a remarkable relationship developed between the Palestinian man and the Israeli woman. Their friendship survived more Arab-Israeli wars, two Palestinian uprisings, and Bashir's many years in Israeli prisons, followed by years of deportation for what the Israelis regarded as terrorism and he defined as resistance. Throughout the decades Dalia and Bashir maintained a poignant and frank dialogue about the conflict between their respective peoples. In 2004 Bashir reminded Dalia of their first meeting thirty-seven years before: "And since then," he said, "there have been more settlements, land confiscations, and now this wall—how can there be any solution? How can there be any Palestinian state? How can I open my heart, as you say?"

Dalia's reply captured the essence of the Palestinian-Israeli conflict: "We couldn't find two people who could disagree more on how to visualize the viability of this land," she said. "And yet we are so deeply connected. And what connects us? The same thing that separates us. This land."

The story of the unlikely link between Bashir Khayri and Dalia Ashkenazi-Landau was thoroughly investigated and engagingly told by the American journalist Sandy Tolan in *The Lemon Tree: The True Story of a Friendship Spanning Four Decades of Israeli-Palestinian Conflict* (London: Bantam, 2006). Bashir published his version of the relationship in a novel in the form of a series of unsent letters to Dalia, entitled *Khafaqat Dhakirah: Qissah*—Memory throbs: A story (Jerusalem: Markaz al-Ma'lumat al-Badilah, 1993). The quotations above were taken from Tolan, *The Lemon Tree*, 290–91, 294, respectively.

The house of the Khayri and Ashkenazi families was eventually turned by Dalia into a kindergarten for Palestinian children and a center for Arab-Israeli coexistence.

Preface

More than two decades ago, in a Tel Aviv bookstore, I stumbled upon a new book entitled *Shnat Shabak*—The year of the *Shabak*. I was intrigued. *Shabak* is the Hebrew acronym for Israel's General Security Service, the excessively secretive agency whose operations have always been shrouded in mystery. The book, written by David Ronen, a retired top-brass GSS officer, was about the activities of the GSS in the West Bank in the first year of its occupation in the Six Day War of June 1967. One passage in particular aroused my curiosity. The passage describes the GSS political contacts with prominent West Bank Palestinians in the summer and fall of 1967, and argues that many of the local leaders were willing to work for some kind of bilateral accommodation between themselves and Israel. The author concludes that the opportunity for a peace settlement was missed largely because of Israel's inchoate, occasionally inconsistent, policy.[1]

I was struck by this fascinating, hitherto unknown story. Being a journalist at the time, I interviewed David Ronen. In the interview he went even farther. During the Israeli-Palestinian dialogue, Ronen said, it had been agreed that Sheikh Muhammad ʻAli al-Jaʻbari, the magisterial mayor of Hebron, would be the prime minister of a new West Bank Palestinian state, and the only remaining decision was whether Hebron or Ramallah should be the seat of government.[2]

I was determined to pursue the matter more thoroughly. I am an Israeli, and the Arab-Israeli conflict concerns me deeply. My life has often been affected, and at times dominated, by the conflict. I fought in some of the Arab-Israeli wars and covered some as a journalist. Over the years, the knowledge I acquired of Israel's history, as well as my firsthand experience, has led me to question the official Israeli line that since its foundation in 1948 Israel has indefatigably extended its hand in peace to the surrounding hostile neighbors but has always been rejected. Since the late 1980s my doubts have been supported by archival-based studies on the first Arab-Israeli war of 1948 and the early years of the State of Israel. The passage in Ronen's book seemed also to undermine the traditional Israeli claim that there was no one to talk to on the Arab side in later years. In practical terms it offered a starting point for research which would challenge the generally accepted Israeli argument by examining the immediate aftermath of the June 1967 War in the light of the available historical evidence.

But soon my journalistic assignments abroad—first in the United States and then in the Soviet Union–becoming–Russia—and other professional and personal commitments compelled me to delay my inquiry. I returned to the subject a decade later as an academic, during my doctoral studies at the University of Oxford. By then many more relevant records had been declassified in Israeli, American, British, and United Nations archives, thereby providing invaluable ingredients for a fuller reconstruction of the past.

Early on I discovered that Ronen's narrative was inaccurate: the GSS contacts with West Bank leaders were in fact designed to transform as many of them as possible into collaborators.[3] But Ronen was correct in arguing that the Israeli government's approach frustrated the quest for a peace settlement with the West Bank Palestinians during the initial months of the occupation. However, the true story of the political maneuvering in the first formative years of the postwar era was far more remarkable. The Israeli search for Palestinian quislings was just one episode in what became a broader and complex effort to maintain the territorial status quo created by the military victory in the Six Day War. This effort, which involved King Hussein of Jordan as well as the West Bank political elite who were alike eager to reach a peaceful settlement with Israel, was mainly directed at the United States and amounted to a consistent foreign policy of prevarication. Its aim was to mislead the Americans into thinking that Israel was seriously trying to resolve the Arab-Israeli conflict.

This is in a nutshell what the present book is about. Its narrative and conclusions are the result of years of painstaking research, relying predominantly on many thousands of official records obtained from numerous archives on three continents. Some might argue that inevitably this work is colored by my Israeli background and by my emotional and practical involvement in the Arab-Israeli conflict. Indeed, no historical study can ever be objective. Any historical writing reflects the historian's personal convictions and prejudices, no matter how hard he or she may strive to cast them aside. In dealing with the Arab-Israeli conflict—still unresolved and raging—an Israeli historian faces an additional hurdle. The Israeli novelist A. B. Yehoshua addresses this issue in *The Liberated Bride*. The protagonist, a university professor of "Orientalism"—*mizrahanut,* Middle Eastern studies—maintains that Israeli scholars specializing in the Middle East

> are caught in a double bind. On the one hand, they are suspected by both the world and themselves of being unduly pessimistic about the Arab world because of Israel's conflict with it. And on the other hand, they are accused of unrealistic optimism because of their deep craving for peace. For the Israeli scholar, whether he likes to admit it or not, Orientalism is not just a field of research. It is a vocation involving life-and-death questions affecting our own and our children's future. . . . We are the Arabs' neighbors and even their hostages—participants in their destiny who are unavoidably part of what we study.[4]

Much of this is true. As I have conceded, I am not an indifferent bystander. Even when investigating events which took place four and a half decades ago, I have had difficulty detaching myself from the tragic present. Problems created or left unsettled during the early days of the June 1967 occupation later reemerged, sometimes assuming enormous proportions. The Jewish settlements in the occupied territories are an obvious case in point: to this day they constitute one of the principal obstacles to peace in the region. In producing this book, however, I have been inspired not by current events or by any political agenda, but by the empirical evidence alone. This point must be stressed because the study of the Arab-Israeli conflict is fraught with bias and propaganda, frequently disguised as academic work. As early as 1938 George Antonius, the Lebanese-born Palestinian historian, cautioned in *The Arab Awakening* that

> the most formidable obstacle to an understanding, and therefore to a solution, of the Palestine problem lies not so much in its inherent complexity as in the solid jungle of legend and propaganda which has grown up around it. To the ordinary tasks of a student dealing with the facts is thus added an obligation to deal with pseudo-facts and dethrone them from their illegitimate eminence. It is as much his duty to expose the fallacies as to assert the truth.[5]

These words remain valid today. On both sides of the Arab-Israeli divide are writers—including academics—who have abandoned responsible scholarship in favor of partisan polemics. As a result, even well-founded studies too often seem biased to apologists of one of the parties to the conflict who reject any criticism of their own side. Proving that a work is biased requires demonstrating that it is unsupported by reliable evidence; uncomfortable narrative and conclusions are not ipso facto biased. The archival and other sources this book brings to bear fully substantiate its version of events and arguments.

A Note on the Sources

Israel's foreign policy vis-à-vis King Hussein and the West Bank Palestinians following the Six Day War is an untold story. Even works on broader subjects relating to this study are exceedingly thin. This is a function primarily of the rules under which official documents in democratic countries such as Israel, the United Kingdom, and the United States are declassified, typically after thirty years. Only recently have scholars and writers been able to digest this indispensable historical evidence and to produce their works about the Six Day War and its aftermath.

Only two of these newly published books touch upon the themes discussed in the present volume. *1967* by Tom Segev does it in an unsystematic and superficial manner which does not add up to a coherent narrative. Although thoroughly researched, it lacks a meaningful argument.[6] Gershom Gorenberg's *The Accidental Empire* deals with Jewish settlement in the occupied territories during the first decade after the 1967 War, so its discussion of the main issues covered by this book is rather peripheral.[7] An earlier academic attempt to tackle the Israeli policy regarding the occupied territories during the period under review was a doctoral dissertation by Reuven Pedatzur, submitted in 1992 and later published in book form. Pedatzur, who conducted his research when many of the crucially relevant records were still inaccessible, argues that the Eshkol government was initially inclined to reach a settlement over the West Bank with the Palestinians, but after a few months replaced the "Palestinian option" with the "Jordanian option," opting to negotiate with King Hussein. This contention, based exclusively on Israeli sources, can now be dismissed.[8] All three authors are Israelis; none of them knows Arabic; and they did not consult Arab sources. Their volumes focus narrowly on the Israeli perspective while effectively ignoring the Arab side of the story.

There are, however, a significant number of secondary sources which pertain to the matters under discussion here. Contemporary statesmen, politicians, diplomats, army and intelligence officers, and state officials have published books relating to their personal experience. Israeli participants have been particularly prolific in this regard. Some of them dwelled on isolated episodes, while others purported to give a fuller view, based on recollection, diaries, privately obtained official documents, or even amateurish research. Carrying little scholarly weight, their work is nevertheless useful, for they bring valuable information and insights as to the wider context of this inquiry. The best example is Shlomo Gazit's *The Carrot and the Stick,* which treats extensively the first two years of military rule in the West Bank.[9] The author was a senior army officer who handled the occupied territories on behalf of Defense Minister Moshe Dayan. Gazit was privy to the decision-making process, including at cabinet level, and his book offers important data, based on confidential military and government records, some of which are still classified.

Yet this genre of literature is also replete with pitfalls, as vividly proven by the many self-congratulatory publications of Abba Eban, Israel's foreign minister at the time, which offer selective and occasionally untrue narratives.[10] Indeed, the writings of practitioners are as a rule biased because of the authors' affiliations, which can foster self-interested historical revisionism. Gazit's volume again serves as an illuminating example of the innate shortcomings of such sources. In *The Carrot and the Stick*, whose Hebrew original was published in 1985, Gazit concludes that the Israeli policy in the occupied territories during its initial period could be described as a success story.[11] In 1999, however, he published a second book which covers thirty years of Israel's military occupation, including the first two. "For many years I have wondered," writes the retired general, "was Israel's attempt to maintain an 'enlightened occupation' of the Territories doomed for failure from the start? Or did it fail because Israel's governments and its military apparatus did not stick to their original policy, and even contradicted it?"[12] Whatever the answer, one thing is clear: according to Gazit's new version, the "success story" was nothing but a failure.

Arab participants produced fewer personal accounts than their Israeli counterparts. Nothing has been written about the top-secret Hussein-Israel dialogue, and the few discussions of the contacts between the West Bank notables and the Israelis are out of context, sketchy, and distorted. The same is true with regard to other Arab authors. Most of them have avoided this highly sensitive issue. The idea of having a political dialogue with Israel, specifically with the aim of establishing a separate Palestinian state alongside the "Zionist entity," was totally unacceptable to the leaders of the resistance organizations outside the occupied territories, who rapidly turned into the real power in the Palestinian arena. This is probably why only a handful of Arab scholars mention the Palestinian-Israeli exchanges. Some of them even see these contacts as part of an alleged "Zionist conspiracy" to impose a one-sided Israeli solution.[13]

In short, the existing literature provides little credible substance on the subject at hand. Thus this study is chiefly based on primary sources in Hebrew, Arabic, and English, obtained from Israeli, American, British, and UN archives, and from individuals who possess relevant documents. Arab records, however, are unavailable. Most Arab countries have no national archives, and access to state papers is denied to researchers except for a privileged few. In the case of the Palestinians, records are virtually nonexistent. During the Palestinians' tragic history of defeat, dispersal, exile, and subjugation, much of their written

culture—libraries, archives, private holdings, and personal papers—
was plundered or expropriated by their conquerors, destroyed either by
the Israelis or by the Palestinians themselves in order to prevent the
occupiers from seizing it, or simply lost.[14] Many of the records that fell
into Israeli hands are held in sealed intelligence archives. The lack of
Palestinian documentation concerning the contacts with Israel in the
immediate aftermath of the June 1967 War is particularly understandable in view of the haphazard nature of the West Bank leadership due to
the Israeli ban on countrywide political organization. Moreover, discussion of any political settlement with the Israelis was then considered by
many Arabs as treason.[15]

On the face of it, the Israeli records of the contacts with the West
Bankers and King Hussein, as well as intelligence reports about the political developments in the occupied territories, fairly reflect the thinking
of the Arab side. After all, these were working papers, intended to furnish the policy makers with true accounts. However, intelligence reports
were based on data—not always accurate—gleaned from Palestinian
sources who often had their own reasons for sharing information with
their rulers. The minutes of the secret talks with the Arabs, and the related
memoranda, suffer from a different deficiency. Mainly composed by two
officials—Dr. Ya'acov Herzog, Prime Minister Levi Eshkol's confidant
who handled the channel of communication with King Hussein, and
Moshe Sasson, who was in charge of the political contacts with the West
Bank leadership—they unavoidably mirror the Israeli understanding of
the Arab interlocutors' positions, and even more so the writers' own.

This last point was acknowledged even by Sasson himself. During
a top-level consultation in May 1968 Sasson said that contrary to the
situation in the previous month, when it had seemed that the Palestinians were "close to being able to work out their strategy almost independently," now "the situation is almost the opposite. They are almost at
their lowest point." Defense Minister Dayan interrupted: "A month ago
I, Moshe Sasson, had a feeling and today *I, Moshe Sasson,* have the opposite feeling—this is how you should talk, because nothing has changed
with them [the Palestinians], but it is you that underwent a change." Sasson agreed: "Everything I say is my personal feeling."[16]

The copious material available in Israeli archives is clearly not sufficient for a comprehensive study dealing with the Arab-Israeli conflict,

for by its very nature it highlights the Israeli outlook, and it is often tinged with ideology. In view of the shortage of Arab primary sources, research at archives abroad is thus imperative.[17] The foreign missions in Israel and in Jordan, particularly the American and the British, followed the political scene in these countries closely; their reports, based on easy access to the very top in both states, are invaluable. Most useful are the dispatches sent by diplomats serving in the independent consulates general in Jerusalem (missions not subordinate to the embassies in Tel Aviv or Amman but answering directly to their respective foreign ministries), who were active in monitoring the Palestinian political currents and undercurrents, and in studying the viewpoints among the occupied West Bank political elite and society. What the West Bankers said to these diplomats—which sometimes was very different from what they told the Israelis—is essential for achieving a more precise and complete picture of the reconstructed past.[18]

Normally press articles can also be quite helpful in a historical inquiry, but here, again, the Arab side has little to offer. Newspapers in most Arab countries were state-controlled and subjugated to strict censorship or political conformity. Furthermore, the Arabic press in the occupied territories—including Arab Jerusalem—stopped appearing after the outbreak of the June War. The daily *Al-Quds* resumed its publication only a year and a half later, in mid-November 1968—toward the end of the period under review. The gaps in the documented material might be filled through diaries, interviews, and testimonies of contemporaries. As far as Palestinian historiography is concerned, oral history is essential.[19] However, most Palestinians have been reluctant to cooperate with Israeli researchers in general, and especially on such sensitive topics as the one covered by this study. Furthermore, oral history should be treated carefully regardless of ideological complications. Human recollection of events which took place three or four decades before can be misleading, and memories of politicians and officials quite often prove self-serving. But despite its subjective nature and deficiencies, oral history may provide what official documents do not record.

A Note on Terminology, Translation, and Spelling

The Arab-Israeli conflict has produced two opposing perspectives, each of which employs distinct terminology and rejects that of the other. The best illustration is the name of the territory which the conflict is about: *Filastin,* or Palestine, for the Arabs; *Eretz Yisrael,* or the Land of Israel, for the Israelis. I have attempted to avoid value-laden phrases whenever possible and opted for neutral ones instead. For example, I have referred to the first Arab-Israeli war—the War of Independence for the Israelis and *al-Nakbah* (the catastrophe) for the Arabs—as the 1948 War. On the other hand, I have used interchangeably the terms June 1967 War and Six Day War, even though the latter was coined by the Israelis and reflects their swift military victory, because Arabs too apply this expression occasionally.

Both sides also accept East Jerusalem as the name of the Jordanian sector of Jerusalem which Israel absorbed in the wake of the June 1967 War. Yet this study is concerned with the nexus between the people and the land, so I have found the term Arab Jerusalem more appropriate: in the late 1960s this section of the city was decisively Arab in both population and land ownership.[20] Moreover, the Arabs consider only the area which constituted Jordanian Jerusalem as East Jerusalem, whereas the Israelis regard as East Jerusalem the overwhelmingly larger annexed area which surrounds the prewar sectors of the city to the north, east, and south.

The territories Israel captured in June 1967 and controlled thereafter are universally designated as "occupied territories" except within Israel, where they are called "administered" or "disputed" territories. However, the juridical sphere is beyond the remit of this book; I have chosen the former phrase because these territories were controlled by military government and their Arab inhabitants were placed under an occupation regime. Similarly the West Bank is the internationally accepted definition of the region Israel seized from Jordan in June 1967 and is thus applied in this book, rather than Judea and Samaria, as Israel dubbed it shortly after war. In this case and some others the different expressions are indicated in the text.

For the sake of simplicity and clarity I have used the name Egypt instead of the United Arab Republic (UAR)—Egypt's official name between 1958 and 1971, including the time covered by this work. For the same reasons I have referred to the director of the Israeli prime minister's private office (*lishkat rosh ha-memshalah*) as the prime minister's "private secretary" so that readers would not confuse him with the director general of Israel's Prime Minister's Office (*Misrad Rosh ha-Memshalah*), which is in fact a ministry.

A number of the books and articles this study relies on or cites from were originally published in Hebrew or Arabic and subsequently translated into English. For the benefit of readers who do not know Arabic or Hebrew but may wish to consult these sources I have used their English versions—only, however, after comparing the translated text with the original. The examination revealed sometimes interesting discrepancies. The translations of all other non-English sources—including historical records—are mine unless otherwise specified.

Names, terms, and phrases in Arabic and Hebrew have been spelled in keeping with the conventional rules of transliteration but without the diacritical marks and accents (except the sign ' indicating the letter 'ayn in Arabic and 'ayin in Hebrew, and the sign ' for the Arabic hamzah). In certain cases, however, I have followed the commonly accepted English spelling. For example, King Hussein (instead of Husayn); Gamal 'Abd al-Nasser (Jamal 'Abd al-Nasir); Sheikh Ja'bari or Sharm al-Sheikh (Shaykh); Jericho (Ariha in Arabic and Yeriho in Hebrew).

Acknowledgments

There are a number of people and institutions that have contributed to the realization of this volume. My greatest debt of gratitude is to Professor Avi Shlaim, who has been tirelessly and generously supportive throughout my long journey, first as my doctoral supervisor and later as a colleague; and my dear friend Juliet Campbell, who has painstakingly read several drafts of my work, offering perceptive insights and wise editorial advice.

Heartfelt thanks go to the scholars who at different phases of my study devoted many hours to reading its drafts in their entirety. I am grateful to Dr. Louise Fawcett and Professor Yezid Sayigh (the examiners of my doctoral thesis), Professor Gershon Shafir, and Dr. Raffaella Del Sarto for their important suggestions and unfailing encouragement. Likewise, Dr. Yuval Ginbar, Dr. John Knight, and Dr. Andrew Novo provided me with invaluable feedback on individual chapters or passages; I thank them most warmly.

I am indebted to many other colleagues and friends whose advice and assistance have greatly benefited me and this project. They include Dr. Yossi Algazy, Professor Ami Ayalon, Professor Pamela Clemit, Dr. Hillel Cohen, Ran and Yaffa Dagony, Mastan Ebtehaj, David Fried-

...

man, Professor Israel Gershoni, Gershom Gorenberg, Professor Gur Huberman, Marga Lyall, Professor Avner Offer, Michal Pinkas, Professor Gabriel Piterberg, and Dr. Piet van Boxel.

The private papers of Moshe Sasson, Dr. Ya'acov Herzog, David Farhi, and a few others who wished to remain anonymous were crucial to this study. I am deeply grateful to Moshe Sasson (who died in 2006), Shira Herzog (Dr. Herzog's daughter), and Judy Farhi (Colonel Farhi's widow), and the unnamed sources for granting me access to these collections. I am equally in debt to Michael Shashar (who also died in 2006) for allowing me to consult his unpublished diary of his years in the Military Government of the West Bank. I thank David Ronen for permitting me to use the transcript of his interview with Victor Cohen of the GSS; Dr. Ami Gluska for providing me a copy of the unpublished manuscript Foreign Minister Abba Eban completed in 1969 and other useful material; and Professor Avi Shlaim for sharing with me the interviews he conducted and some of the primary sources he possessed.

I appreciate the willingness of the surviving contemporaries who very kindly agreed to give me their time and to share with me their recollections of events in which they played a role.

It is my pleasant duty to acknowledge the help I received from many archivists and librarians in Israel, the United Kingdom, the United States, and the United Nations. The list is too long to give in full, but special mention needs to be made of Sima Tocatly at Israel Cabinet Secretariat; Haim Gal, the curator of the Arabic press archive at the Moshe Dayan Center for Middle Eastern and African Studies (who died in 2011); and Regina Greenwell at the Lyndon B. Johnson Presidential Library, all of whom went out of their way to fulfill my many requests.

Acknowledgment of the tangible support that made this project possible is also in order. I owe much gratitude to the Rothschild Foundation Europe (London), the Lyndon Baines Johnson Foundation (Austin), the Anglo-Israel Association (London), AVI Fellowships (Geneva), and the Chaim Herzog Center for Middle East Studies and Diplomacy (Ben-Gurion University, Beersheba) for their generous research grants. I am much obliged to the University of Oxford (particularly the Department of Politics and International Relations) for promoting my project through several research funds.

On the production side I have been privileged to enjoy the skillful editing of Dan Heaton, senior manuscript editor at Yale University Press, who improved the quality of my prose; and the professionalism of my old friend and former colleague Yoram Neeman, who prepared the maps for this book with a deep sense of commitment and much care. I am indebted to both.

Last but not least is my gratitude to my sister Nurit in Tel Aviv, who voluntarily and efficiently served as a research assistant and helped me in so many other ways.

I dedicate this book to my late parents, Sarah and Issar, who instilled in me the thirst for learning and knowledge.

Dramatis Personae

Key Israelis

LEVI ESHKOL (1895–1969)
Prime Minister

Born Levi Shkolnik in a Ukrainian village near Kiev, Eshkol immigrated to Ottoman-ruled Palestine in 1914, at the age of nineteen. A veteran political activist in the Zionist Labor movement, Eshkol was elected to the Israeli parliament, the Knesset, in 1951 and served in the cabinet first as agriculture minister and later as finance minister. In 1963 he succeeded David Ben-Gurion as prime minister and defense minister. On the eve of the June 1967 War a political coup compelled him to cede the defense portfolio to Lt. Gen. (res.) Moshe Dayan. A compromiser by nature, Eshkol was reputed to be indecisive. Died in office.

MOSHE DAYAN (1915–81)
Defense Minister

Born to Zionist immigrants from the Ukraine in kibbutz Deganyah Alef, on the shores of the Sea of Galilee, Dayan grew up in the village of Nahalal in the Jezreel Valley. David Ben-Gurion's protégé, famous for the trademark black eye patch which he earned fighting with the British in Vichy-occupied Syria in 1941, Lieutenant General Dayan was chief of the General Staff, 1953–58, and the architect of Israel's retaliatory policy, which culminated in the Sinai Campaign of 1956. After retiring from the army, he entered politics and served in the cabinet as agriculture minister (1959–64), defense minister (1967–74), and foreign minister (1977–79). A controversial loner, he was considered a national hero until the 1973 Yom Kippur War debacle.

ABBA EBAN (1915–2002)
Foreign Minister

Born Aubrey Solomon Eban in Cape Town, South Africa, he grew up in the United Kingdom and studied classics and Oriental languages at the University of Cambridge. As a committed Zionist, Eban began his diplomatic career before the foundation of Israel in 1948. He served as ambassador to the United Nations, 1949–59, and simultaneously (from 1950) to the United States. In 1959 Eban entered politics and served in the cabinet as minister without portfolio, education minister, and deputy prime minister, until his appointment as foreign minister in 1966—a position he held until 1974. A prolific writer, Eban was mostly renowned for his oratorical skills in the service of Israel.

YIGAL ALLON (1918–80)
Cabinet Minister

Born in Kfar Tavor in the Lower Galilee. Commander of the *Palmah*, the prestate elite strike force, and following the foundation of Israel a general in the army, he led some of the most crucial battles of the 1948 War. After his retirement from the military Allon entered the political arena and was elected to the Knesset in 1955. In 1960 he took a brief timeout from politics to study at the University of Oxford. Upon his return he served in the cabinet as labor minister (1961–68), deputy prime minister and minister of immigrant absorption (1968–69); deputy prime minister and education minister (1969–74), and deputy prime minister and foreign minister (1974–77). Author after the Six Day War of the eponymous Allon Plan.

DR. YA'ACOV HERZOG (1921–72)
Director General of the Prime Minister's Office

Born in Dublin, Herzog immigrated to Mandatory Palestine in 1937, when his father, Yitzhak HaLevi Herzog, the chief rabbi of Ireland, was elected as chief rabbi in Palestine (later chief rabbi of Israel). Ordained as a rabbi himself, Herzog studied law and obtained a doctorate in international law. In 1948 he joined the Foreign Ministry and served as minister at the embassy in Washington (1957–60) and ambassador to Canada (1960–63). From 1963 onward Herzog handled the secret channel of communication with King Hussein. In 1965 he was appointed director general of the Prime Minister's Office and became Premier Eshkol's most trusted adviser. His brother Chaim was an army general, fleetingly the first military governor of the West Bank, and in later years became the sixth president of Israel.

MOSHE SASSON (1925–2006)
Prime Minister Eshkol's Representative to the West Bank Palestinians

Born in Damascus and grew up in Mandatory Palestine. Fluent in Arabic, Sasson served in the prestate intelligence service and in 1952 entered the foreign service. Shortly afterward, while based in Geneva, he was assigned to establish secret contacts with Arab leaders. His diplomatic and ambassadorial posts included Turkey (1961–67), Italy (1973–76), and Egypt (1981–88). His father, Eliyahu Sasson, was a cabinet minister (1961–69), and his brother-in-law, Avi'ad Yafeh, was Prime Minister Eshkol's private secretary.

DAVID FARHI (1936–77)
Military Government Adviser on Arab Affairs

Born in Tel Aviv, Farhi was a scholar specializing in the modern Middle East. In 1967, while working on his doctoral dissertation, he was also a teacher at the Hebrew University of Jerusalem with a bright academic future predicted. Following the Israeli occupation of the West Bank and Arab Jerusalem in the June War, Farhi was recruited by Defense Minister Dayan to the West Bank Military Government as an expert adviser on Arab affairs and was given the rank of major. Later he was promoted to lieutenant colonel, then full colonel. For one year (1974–75) he served as director general of the short-lived Information Ministry. Died tragically in 1977 at the age of forty-one.

Key West Bank Palestinians

SHEIKH MUHAMMAD ʿALI AL-JAʿBARI (1900–1980)
Mayor of Hebron

Born in Hebron and a graduate of al-Azhar University in Cairo with a degree in Islamic law. Mayor of Hebron between 1940 and 1976 under the British Mandate, Jordan, and the Israeli occupation. In December 1948 Jaʿbari presided over the Jericho Congress of Palestinian notables, which effectively legitimized the Jordanian annexation of the West Bank. He was appointed to the Jordanian *Majlis al-Aʿyan*, or Senate, several times and served intermittently as minister of justice, agriculture, and education in a number of Jordan's cabinets. Following the June 1967 War, Jaʿbari collaborated with the Israeli occupation authorities while advocating the establishment of a Palestinian state alongside Israel. Until the mid-1970s he was the unchallenged strong man of Mount Hebron.

HAMDI KANʿAN (1910–81)
Mayor of Nablus

Born in Nablus, Kanʿan was an industrial entrepreneur. Between 1950 and 1965 he was a board member and secretary general of the local chamber of commerce. From 1951 Kanʿan was a member of Nablus city council, and he became mayor in 1963. In late 1966, in the wake of the devastating Israeli raid on the West Bank village of Samuʿ, he was one of the Palestinian leaders who demanded that the Jordanian government arm frontline villagers. Following the Israeli occupation Kanʿan distinguished himself as a decisive leader of his city as well as a prominent player in West Bank politics, including the secret contacts with Israel. Kanʿan, who had friendly relations with Israel's Defense Minister Dayan, resigned as mayor in 1969.

ANWAR AL-KHATIB (1917–93)
Unofficial Representative of Jordan in the Occupied Territories

Born in Hebron, a lawyer by training, and Sheikh Jaʿbari's son-in-law. A member of Hajj Muhammad Amin al-Husseini's Arab Higher Committee during the British Mandate. Toward the end of the 1948 War he was appointed mayor of the Arab sector of Jerusalem until 1950. Elected to Jordan's *Majlis al-Nuwwab*, or Chamber of Deputies (1951–54), and later held various ministerial positions in Jordan's cabinets. In 1964 Khatib was nominated ambassador to Egypt, and in late 1966 he became the governor of the Jerusalem District. Under the Israeli occupation he was regarded as King Hussein's eyes and ears in the West Bank, although he gradually adopted more independent views. In 1991 Khatib was an adviser to the Jordanian-Palestinian delegation to American-backed peace talks with Israel.

RUHI AL-KHATIB (1914–94)
Mayor of Jordanian Jerusalem

Born in Jerusalem to a prominent family (unrelated to Anwar al-Khatib's), he received his higher education at Oxford and Cambridge. Upon returning to Jerusalem he became active in the Palestinian national movement. After the 1948 War he entered the hotel business. In 1951 Khatib was elected to the Jerusalem Municipal Council, and in 1957 he became mayor until Israel dissolved the Jordanian municipality in late June 1967, immediately after the annexation of Arab Jerusalem. In August 1967 Khatib was one of the founding members of the Jerusalem-based West Bank National Guidance Committee. A month later, when Israel deported Sheikh 'Abd al-Hamid al-Sa'ih, the committee's head, to Jordan, Khatib succeeded him—only to suffer the same fate in March 1968. He was not allowed back until 1993.

HIKMAT AL-MASRI (1905–94)
Unofficial Representative of King Hussein

Born in Nablus to a powerful notable family, Masri studied business and economics at the American University of Beirut (AUB) and was active in the 1936–39 Arab Revolt in Palestine. He was elected to Jordan's Chamber of Deputies (1950–57) and served as its speaker, 1952–53, after which he joined the cabinet as agriculture minister, 1953–54. Later he was appointed to the Senate (1962–71). Masri was a leading member of *Hizb al-Watani al-Ishtiraki* (National Socialist Party) in the mid-1950s; in 1964 he took part in the establishment of the Palestine Liberation Organization (PLO). Following the June 1967 War he was prominent in West Bank radical politics. Masri was among the few whom King Hussein regarded as his confidants in the occupied territories.

ANWAR NUSEIBEH (1913–86)
Unofficial Representative of King Hussein

Born in Jerusalem to a notable family, Nuseibeh studied law at the University of Cambridge and served as a judge in British-mandated Palestine. Shortly after losing a leg in the 1948 War, he took part in the short-lived, Egyptian-sponsored All-Palestine Government in Gaza as its secretary. Then he returned to Jerusalem and joined the Hashemite regime, serving in numerous capacities, including several terms in the cabinet; governor of the Jerusalem District; and ambassador to Britain. Under the Israeli occupation Nuseibeh emerged as one of the most prominent leaders in the West Bank. He was a member of the National Guidance Committee which was established in Arab Jerusalem in August 1967. While stressing that the Palestinian issue was the key to any peace settlement, he was considered by both Jordan and Israel as King Hussein's trusted representative.

ʿAZIZ SHEHADEH (1912–85)
Leader of the Palestinian Entity Movement

Born in Bethlehem, Shehadeh studied law in Jerusalem. In the 1948 War, after practicing law in Jaffa for twelve years, he became a refugee and was forced to flee to Ramallah. In 1949 Shehadeh attended the Lausanne Conference, organized by the United Nations Conciliation Commission, and on behalf of the Palestine Refugees Congress he advocated an independent Palestinian state alongside Israel. Following the June 1967 War, Shehadeh revived his effort for a Palestinian state coexisting in peace with Israel. He led a small movement which called for the establishment of a Palestinian entity in the Palestinian-inhabited occupied territories. A well-known lawyer, he was murdered near his Ramallah home in December 1985; a radical Palestinian guerrilla group claimed responsibility for the crime.

Key Jordanians
HUSSEIN BIN TALAL (1935–99)
King of Jordan

Born in Amman to the Hashemite family who are direct descendants of the Prophet Muhammad; a great-grandson of Hussein bin ʿAli, the Sharif of Mecca, who initiated the Arab Revolt against the Ottoman Empire in

1916. In 1951 Hussein witnessed the assassination of his grandfather, King 'Abdallah I, in Jerusalem; a medal he wore on his chest saved his own life. Hussein came to the throne at the age of seventeen after the brief reign of his father, King Talal, who was mentally ill. During his four and a half turbulent decades as an absolute monarch, he survived numerous attempts on his life. In 1963 he launched a secret face-to-face dialogue with Israel which culminated in the 1994 Jordan-Israel peace treaty.

ZAYD AL-RIFA'I (1936–)
King Hussein's Private Secretary

Born in Amman, the eldest son of former Prime Minister Samir al-Rifa'i, he was educated at Harvard University, where he studied political science and international law. Starting his career as a diplomat, he represented Jordan in Cairo, Beirut, and London, and at the United Nations. In 1964 he moved to the Royal Hashemite Court and worked closely with King Hussein, with whom he had a warm friendship formed during their school days. As the king's private secretary and confidant, he took part in many of the secret meetings between Hussein and Israeli leaders. In later years he served twice as prime minister (1973–76, 1985–89). His son Samir was until recently the family's third-generation prime minister of Jordan (2009–11).

Abbreviations

AEA	Abba Eban Center for Israeli Diplomacy Archive
C.G.	Commanding general
DefMin	Defense minister
DFP	The private papers of David Farhi
EMA	Eshkol Memorial Archive
FM	Foreign Ministry (of Israel)
FO	Foreign Office (of the United Kingdom)
ForMin	Foreign minister
FRUS	*Foreign Relations of the United States, 1964–1968*
GSS	General Security Service (Israel); *Shabak* or *Shin Bet*
ICS	Cabinet Secretariat (Israel)
IDFA	Israel Defence Forces Archive
IDP	*International Documents on Palestine*
ILPA	Israeli Labor Party Archive
ISA	Israel State Archives
JCP	Jordanian Communist Party
KFASC	Knesset Foreign Affairs and Security Committee
LBJL	Lyndon B. Johnson Library
MECA	Middle East Centre Archive
MK	Member of Knesset
MP	Member of Parliament
MSP	The private papers of Moshe Sasson

PAD	*Al-Watha'iq al-Filastiniyyah al-'Arabiyyah* [Palestinian Arab documents]
PLO	Palestine Liberation Organization
PM	Prime minister
PolMin	Police minister
PPI	Private papers, Israel
TMA	Tabenkin Memorial Archive
UKNA	United Kingdom National Archives
UNA	United Nations Archives
UNPR	United Nations public records
UNRWA	United Nations Relief and Works Agency
USNA	United States National Archives
YHP	The private papers of Dr. Ya'acov Herzog

The Bride and
the Dowry

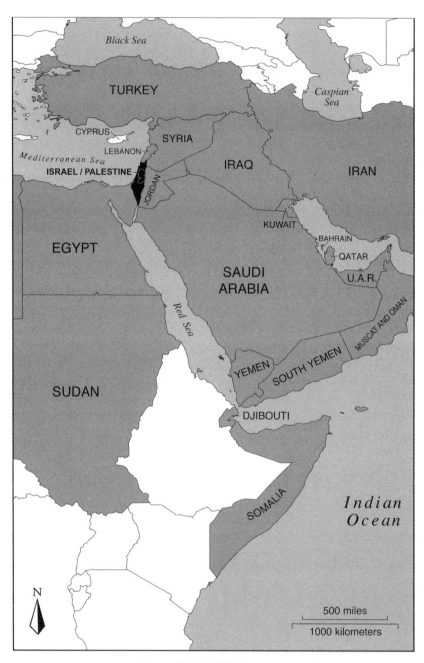

Map 1. The Middle East, 1967

Introduction

The year 1967 would go down in Israeli and Jewish history as *annus mirabilis,* prophesied Michael Hadow, the British ambassador in Tel Aviv, in the opening paragraph of his annual review. Not only was there the astonishing feat of the Israeli armed forces in the Six Day War in June, but also, after 2,000 years, a united Jerusalem had returned to Jewish authority.[1] The British diplomat neglected to mention the return of the entire *Eretz Yisrael,* or the Land of Israel, to Jewish authority following the conquest of the Palestinian-inhabited West Bank and Gaza Strip. Still, he was right: 1967 will go down in the annals—not only of Israel or the Jewish people but of world history as well—as the year that changed the Middle East and enabled Israel, for the first time since its foundation in 1948, to trade land for peace.

The June 1967 War left Israel with territory conquered from four Arab countries whose size was more than three times the state's prewar area: the West Bank, including Arab Jerusalem, was taken from Jordan; the Golan Heights were seized from Syria; Egypt lost the Sinai Peninsula and the Gaza Strip; and Saudi Arabia forfeited the tiny Island of Tiran.[2] "If the Arabs want their territory back they must pay the price of peace with Israel," Ambassador Hadow suggested.[3] But this meant that Israel too had to pay a price for peace—the renunciation of its territorial gains. Abba Eban, Israel's foreign minister, argued retrospectively that his government had accepted the trade-off formula. "Israel had cards to play," he said. "It held something which the Arabs wished to recover and which was therefore a basis for eventual negotiation. . . . The Arab position was that they wanted 100 percent of the [occupied] territories and would give zero percent of peace."[4] Or, as the Israeli official line has it, there was no one to talk to on the Arab side.

Indeed, Syria rejected any kind of accommodation with Israel, and Egypt was not ready in the aftermath of the June War to negotiate an accord with the Jewish state. Saudi Arabia used the United States to pressure Israel to give up the occupied island of Tiran.[5] But the two claimants to the West Bank and Arab Jerusalem—the West Bank Palestinian leadership and King Hussein of Jordan—were ready and eager to resolve the conflict with Israel directly. Both communicated their peaceful desire from the start of the occupation. They presented Israel with two competing options for a settlement. The West Bankers embodied what became known in Israel as the "Palestinian option," while the Hashemite Kingdom was considered the "Jordanian option." With the whole of Mandatory Palestine and more than half of the Palestinian people under its control, Israel was thus provided with a historic opportunity to defuse the Palestinian problem which lies at the heart of the decades-long Arab-Zionist conflict. However, it chose neither option.

Instead, the Eshkol government reacted evasively to Hussein's peace overtures, banned political organization in the occupied territories, and did its best to neutralize independent West Bank leaders while attempting to "nurture" pliant substitutes. The simultaneous contacts which Israel held with the Palestinians and Hussein were aimed mainly at fending off American pressure to negotiate with Jordan by misleading the United States into thinking that the government was weighing its options. But Israel's fait accompli policy indicated an intention which went far beyond a play for time. The cabinet hastened to annex Arab Jerusalem and secretly agreed to retain the Gaza Strip. Though persistently avoiding decision on the West Bank, Israel demonstrated its determination to keep the area or at least substantial parts of it: in the wake of the fighting some twenty West Bank villages and towns were destroyed, completely or partially; West Bankers were "encouraged" to flee eastward, across the Jordan River, and tens of thousands of the war refugees were later denied return to their homes; nascent Jewish settlement in the occupied territories was fervently fostered.

Israel desired the land without its population. As early as 7 June, the third day of the Six Day War, Defense Minister Moshe Dayan told Lt. Gen. Yitzhak Rabin, the chief of the General Staff, that the aim was to empty the West Bank of its inhabitants.[6] When the hostilities were over, Prime Minister Levi Eshkol coined a metaphor which adequately encapsulated the Israeli ambition. In the metaphor Israel's territorial conquests were a "dowry" and the Arab population a "bride." "The trouble is that the dowry is followed by a bride whom we don't want," Eshkol repeatedly said.[7]

In this book I shall investigate the policy and practice Israel applied in order to appropriate the dowry and divorce the bride during the twenty-one months immediately after the June 1967 War. This short period, whose starting point is self-explanatory, constitutes the critical and formative phase of the forty-five-year-long Israeli occupation, which still continues. The period ends with the death of Premier Eshkol on 26 February 1969. Though his successor, Golda Meir, maintained dialogue with King Hussein, the emphasis in the course of her reign was on security issues rather than a peace agreement.[8] Moreover, Premier Meir was not interested in a dialogue with the occupied Palestinians; after assuming office she cut off the political exchanges with the West Bank leadership.[9] February 1969 also marked the completion of a process whereby the Palestine Liberation Organization (PLO) was taken over by the resistance movement outside the occupied territories with Yasir 'Arafat's al-Fateh at the helm. This development ultimately turned the PLO from an insignificant body, largely controlled by Egypt, into an umbrella organization that became the sole representative of the Palestinian people and thereby rendered the West Bankers politically powerless. Additionally, in early 1969 Ambassador Gunnar Jarring, the United Nations peace envoy to the Middle East, recognized the futility of his efforts; consequently, his mission was suspended at the beginning of April. Finally, the War of Attrition along the Suez Canal, which broke out in March 1969 between Egypt and Israel, diverted much of Israel's attention to its southern front.[10] The start of 1969, then, was the end of the first chapter of the post-1967 era.

Throughout these twenty-one months, a major concern for Israel was not to alienate its friends in the West, particularly the United States. Until 22 November 1967 the Eshkol government fought hard to frustrate the adoption of any UN resolution demanding an immediate and unconditional withdrawal from the occupied territories. After the UN Security Council passed its ambiguous Resolution 242, which launched the Jarring peace mission, the main objective of Israel's foreign policy was to keep the mission afloat so as to avoid renewed discussion at the Security Council leading to a much stricter resolution than 242. At both stages the political support of Washington was essential. During the later period, in 1968, Israel also had another pressing goal: persuading the Americans to allow the sale of fifty state-of-the-art F-4 Phantom fighter-bombers. Israel desperately needed the planes after losing 20 percent of its air force in the war, and France refused to deliver the fifty Mirage fighter jets Israel had already paid for.

In the following chapters we shall see the diplomacy of prevarication that Israel applied for fear of forfeiting the all-important American backing. The Israelis considered the indecision regarding the fate of the West Bank and the play for time as "tactics," but in fact their successive resolutions and other moves coalesced into a clear, solid strategy which amounted to a foreign policy of deception.

In the first four chapters I explore the initial three months of the period under review. Some of the most significant decisions and measures were taken between June and September 1967 and they crucially shaped the things to come. A glaring example is the annexation of Arab Jerusalem, which was presented by Israel as an administrative "municipal fusion." Another is evident in the civilian settlements in the occupied territories, which Israel falsely claimed to be "military strongpoints." Those early steps affected the Israeli approach vis-à-vis the West Bank Palestinians and Jordan's King Hussein during the remaining eighteen months of the Eshkol government. In the next four chapters I examine the double game whereby Israel held secret contacts with the West Bankers on the one hand and Hussein on the other with the aim of preserving the territorial status quo. The Israelis demanded that the king acknowledge their "historical association" to the Land of Israel which allowed them, so they argued, to settle anywhere in the West Bank—including the parts which Jordan might eventually recover.

The ninth and final chapter offers an epilogue and conclusions. My main argument is that Israel preferred land to peace and thus deliberately squandered a real opportunity for a settlement with its eastern neighbors. The Americans were not fooled by Israel's foreign policy of deception. But despite possessing the necessary levers to exert influence on Israel, Washington did not use them. The United States provided uninterrupted political support and arms to Israel.

The Winners, the Losers

The June 1967 War was a great historical watershed in many respects. The conquest of vast Arab lands by Israel caused a significant change in the nature of relations between the Arab states and Israel. Egypt, Syria, and Jordan were no longer mere enemies of the Jewish state because of their declared objection to its existence in the region. Having lost territories to Israel, each had its own, separate score to settle—for the sake of which they effectively abandoned their often proclaimed commitment to fight for the Palestinian cause. A more critical change was brought about by the Israeli seizure of the West Bank and the Gaza Strip. The borders which had kept apart the Palestinians of the West Bank, of the Gaza Strip, and within Israel (the "Israeli Arabs") were removed. As a result, Israel—whose population in 1967 was 2.77 million (2.38 million Jews and 393,000 non-Jews, mostly Palestinian Arabs)—now controlled more than 1.4 million Palestinians: according to a census conducted in September 1967, 600,000 Palestinians lived in the West Bank, 66,000 in Arab Jerusalem, and 356,000 in the Gaza Strip.[11]

The calamity the Palestinians suffered in the *Naksah*—literally "setback," the Arab defeat in June 1967—was threefold. First, they were deprived of what was left of Palestine after the *Nakbah* (catastrophe) of the 1948 War. Second, the war set in motion another huge wave of refugees. In November 1967 the number of those who had fled the occupied territories or were effectively driven out was estimated by the Israelis at 210,000.[12] Third, about half of the Palestinian people found themselves under Israeli occupation. True, the Palestinians have never enjoyed independence or self-rule. In the twentieth century alone they were governed by Ottoman Turks, British, Jordanian Hashemites, royalist and revolutionary Egyptians, and Israelis. In the words of the writer Said Aburish, none of these alien powers was responsive to local custom and need, but the degree of estrangement from the occupying powers differed substantially. Turkey was Muslim and religiously accommodating; Britain was mostly a caretaker regime sanctioned by the League of Nations; and Jordan and Egypt were Muslim and Arab. Israel, however, was radically different. Not only religiously, culturally, socially, and politically, but most important because of its claim on the very source of the existence of the people: their land.[13]

The loss was no less painful to King Hussein, who pretended to speak for the Palestinians because they constituted about half of his subjects. The West Bank comprised around half of the inhabited territory of his kingdom, half of its industrial capacity, and a quarter of its arable land. It contained valuable water resources, and it contributed nearly 40 percent of its gross domestic product. Most devastating was the fall of the Old City of Jerusalem—the third sacred site in Islam and the jewel in the Hashemite crown—into Jewish hands. In addition to its symbolic significance, Arab Jerusalem was a primary source of revenue from tourism, together with the West Bank towns of Bethlehem and Hebron. The disastrous outcome of the war had a profound impact on Hussein. As a result of a strong sense of personal responsibility, the young monarch was in an emotionally disturbed state and suffered mood swings between resignation and fatalism on one hand and, on the other, sober realism in dealing with the bitter consequences of the defeat.[14]

In Israel the territorial conquests that resulted from the military victory provoked messianic passions which swamped the traditional relatively moderate approach of the Zionist movement's mainstream. This growing fervor led to a convergence between religious and secular Jewish nationalism. Many of Israel's leaders were enthusiastic about extending Israeli sovereignty over what they perceived as parts of their historic homeland. Nonetheless, they were aware that this could create a "demographic danger," jeopardizing the Jewish majority within Israel and thereby its nature as both a Jewish and a democratic state. The desire to prevent such demographic danger was a fundamental principle in Israel's strategic thinking. These two desiderata—the wish to hang on to the newly acquired territories and the unwillingness to increase the Arab population of the state—acted as magnetic poles, often pulling Israel's approach vis-à-vis both Jordan and the Palestinians in conflicting directions. The fear of the demographic danger, coupled with the will to retain the coveted land, also impelled the Israelis to carry out a number of top-secret programs designed to encourage the Palestinians—primarily the 1948 refugees residing in the Gaza Strip—to emigrate.

A widespread panic, fed by threats and bloodcurdling rhetoric from Arab capitals, dominated Israel during the three weeks of the "waiting period," 15 May–5 June, which preceded the Six Day War. The army generals and many of the decision makers did not feel that there was an existential danger to Israel, although they feared a high number of casualties if war broke out.[15] The Israeli economy lurched to a standstill because of the general mobilization of the army reserves, which constituted the backbone of the country's combat force. Emerging triumphant from the war, the Israelis insisted on preventing the recurrence of a similar situation. They demanded direct negotiations with their Arab neighbors aimed at obtaining peace treaties to replace the armistice agreements in effect since 1949. After nineteen years of independence Israel was determined to use the war's outcome to attain recognized and secure borders that would be very different from the provisional Green Line demarcations that Foreign Minister Abba Eban described as Israel's "nightmare map."[16]

"We said openly that the map will never again look as it did on 4 June 1967," Eban stated to a German weekly in an interview. "I am not exaggerating when I say that for us it [the prewar map] has something of the memory of Auschwitz."[17]

Most Arab governments, however, rejected all Israeli preconditions, which for them spelled additional degradation after the humiliating military rout in June. But there were two exceptions, the biggest losers of the war: the West Bank Palestinians and King Hussein of Jordan. The overtures by the West Bankers and Hussein, which began even before the guns of the Six Day War fell silent, and the ensuing talks between Israel and both parties during the following twenty-one months, are at the core of this study.

The Israeli contacts with the Palestinians occurred in four phases, each meant to serve a different purpose, but none intended to develop into genuine negotiations. In June–July 1967 the Israeli aim was to survey the political thinking of the West Bank elite. Between November 1967 and January 1968 an extensive round of talks was designed to exploit Hussein's fear of a separate Palestinian-Israeli settlement and to force him to the bargaining table with low expectations. In the subsequent months, as Israel's foreign policy of deception evolved, prominent West Bankers were used as go-betweens to deliver diversionary messages to the king. Finally, in the summer of 1968 Israel attempted to obtain Palestinian endorsement of the occupation of the West Bank by creating an Arab civil administration devoid of power and run by local collaborators.

The secret dialogue with Hussein included face-to-face meetings between the king and senior Israeli representatives, such as the foreign minister and the deputy prime minister. The dialogue was character-ized by the king's repeated efforts to extract from Israel its peace terms and the evasive response he was repeatedly given by his Israeli inter-locutors. When, in September 1968, increasing American pressure compelled Israel to stop beating around the bush, it offered Hussein a peace plan which was never approved by the cabinet and, more signifi-cant, was presented in the knowledge that the plan was totally unac-ceptable to him.

Background and Setting

Before delving deeply into the aftermath of the June 1967 War, it may help to recall the circumstances of the main players before the conflict erupted.

In 1905, only eight years after the inception of political Zionism, Nagib Azoury, a keen Arab nationalist, observed the emergence of two similar yet opposed movements in the Arab provinces of the Ottoman Empire: "These are the awakening of the Arab nation and the latent effort of the Jews to reconstitute the ancient kingdom of Israel on a very large scale. The two movements," Azoury predicted, "are destined to fight one another continuously, until one prevails over the other."[18] Forty-two turbulent years later, the United Nations attempted to resolve the bloody dispute between these two bitter rival movements. On 29 November 1947 the General Assembly adopted a resolution which called for the partition of Palestine into two states—one Jewish and one Arab (Palestinian).[19] The Partition Plan allocated 55 percent of Manda-tory Palestine's approximately 10,400 square miles to the Jews, who at the time made up only about a third of the total population and owned less than 7 percent of the land. The rest of the country was granted to the Arab state, for the remaining two-thirds of the inhabitants.[20] Jeru-salem was to become an international zone. The Jews accepted the Par-tition Plan, but the Arabs rejected it outright. Wishing to prevent its

Map 2. The United Nations Partition Plan of 29 November 1947

Map 3. Israel following the 1949 armistice agreements with
Egypt, Lebanon, Jordan, and Syria

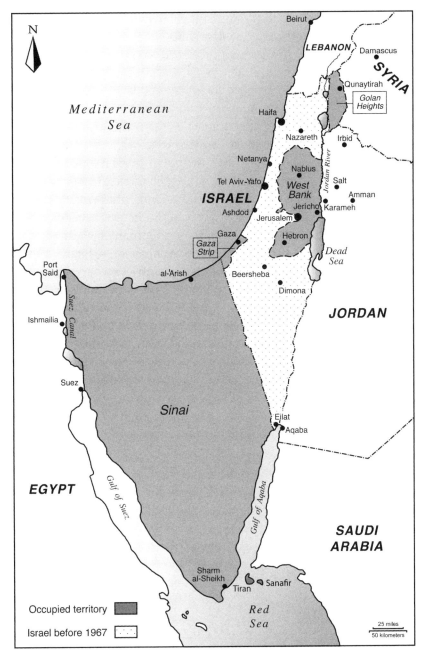

Map 4. Israel and the territories it seized in the June 1967 War

implementation, the Palestinians immediately launched guerrilla attacks against Jewish targets. The first Arab-Israeli war erupted.[21]

Israel's victory in the war caused the territory of the proposed Palestinian state to shrink—there remained just the hilly area west of the Jordan River, now controlled by Jordan and later dubbed the West Bank (less than 2,300 square miles), and a much smaller strip of land alongside the Egyptian border, known as the Gaza Strip (140 square miles). Jerusalem, located on the western edge of the West Bank, was divided between Jordan and Israel. The Jordan-Israel Armistice Agreement, signed on 3 April 1949, determined the boundaries of the West Bank, known thereafter as the Green Line. Under the armistice agreements with the Arab states, the territory of the State of Israel increased to 77 percent of Mandatory Palestine. In 1950 Jordan officially annexed the West Bank and granted its Palestinian inhabitants, many of them refugees, Jordanian citizenship. Only two countries recognized the annexation: the United Kingdom and Pakistan. But by signing the Armistice Agreement with Jordan in April 1949 Israel too recognized de facto the annexation of the West Bank by the Hashemite Kingdom.[22] Nevertheless, following its capture by Israel in 1967, the legal status of this region became a matter of deep controversy: whereas the Israelis claimed that the territory was "administered," not "occupied," since it had been annexed illegally by Jordan, the Arabs considered it occupied land.[23]

The 1948 War produced some 700,000 refugees—more than half of the entire Palestinian population. Many of them fled out of fear and panic, but many others were driven out by the Israeli conquerors, to ensure the Jewish nature of the newly born State of Israel.[24] The bulk of the uprooted and dispossessed Palestinians found refuge in the West and the East Banks, the Gaza Strip, and other neighboring countries, where they have maintained their Palestinian identity and the desire to return to their lost homes. In dozens of squalid camps, where hundreds of thousands of displaced people were cramped in miserable conditions, the Palestinian refugee problem arose and mushroomed. It constituted a festering wound which henceforth dominated the Arab-Israeli conflict. In December 1948 the UN General Assembly adopted a resolution that called upon Israel to allow refugees wishing to return to their homes to do so, and to compensate those who chose not to return for their property.[25] The Israeli government, which had agreed months before to bar repatriation of Palestinians, defied the resolution.[26] Between 1948 and 1967, the number of the refugees and their descendants rose sharply; it is estimated that the refugee population almost tripled to 2 million.[27]

The second Arab-Israeli war broke out in 1956. With Britain and France, Israel attacked Egypt in late October in what was subsequently dubbed by the Israelis as the Sinai Campaign and by the Arabs as *al-'Udwan al-Thulathi,* or the Tripartite Aggression. Within four days Israeli forces took control of the Gaza Strip and the entire Sinai Peninsula, including the Straits of Tiran. Immediately after its swift victory Israel was faced with immense pressure from both the United States and the Soviet Union to withdraw. It complied four months later, only after the United States had pledged that any attempt to block the free passage of Israeli shipping through the straits—as the Egyptians had done before the war—would be regarded by Washington as a *casus belli,* to which Israel could respond in self-defense. Ten years later, on 22 May 1967, President Gamal 'Abd al-Nasser of Egypt ordered the revival of the Tiran blockade, thereby annulling Israel's main achievement of the 1956 war. The American assurances proved futile, and Israel went to war on 5 June for the third time in its short history.[28] When the dust of the fighting settled, the 1956 lesson was very much on the Israelis' mind. They were determined that what had happened then should not be repeated now: Israel should accept nothing less than full peace with its Arab neighbors, and in the meantime it must brace itself against anticipated international pressure.

From the late 1950s the Middle East states had been engaged in what Malcolm Kerr defined as the Arab Cold War.[29] By the summer of 1967 the inter-Arab bickering in the region had been overshadowed by the global Cold War between the Eastern block and the West. The Soviet Union and the United States had been long involved in the Middle East as patrons of many of its countries and suppliers of armaments and military aid, but the third round of full-scale Arab-Israeli hostilities in June 1967 brought about a momentous change in the superpowers' involvement. In May that year the Russians fed President Nasser false reports about Israeli troops massing along the Syrian border, thereby triggering the Egyptian leader's belligerent moves which eventually caused the war that nobody wanted. For their part, the Americans acted hesitantly and ambiguously during the crisis. On 3

June the Israelis chose to think that the red light president Lyndon
Johnson had given them a week before had changed to an amber one;
they took it as green, and two days later Israel launched its strike. As a
result of the crushing defeat and the loss of weaponry, Egypt and Syria
became much more dependent on Moscow than previously, and Soviet
penetration of the region deepened significantly. Abandoned by France—
hitherto its main source of fighter planes—Israel came to rely much more
heavily on Washington.[30] Within a few months, concluded a contemporary Western observer, the Soviets achieved the political polarization of
the Middle East which the Americans had hoped to prevent.[31] This development had a profound impact on the Arab-Israeli conflict and the attempts to resolve it.

Another consequence of the 1967 War was that the Arab-Israeli
conflict proceeded on two levels: the interstate conflict between Israel
and the neighboring Arab countries, and the intercommunal conflict
between Israel and the Palestinians. In essence, the origin of the conflict
was a clash between two national movements—Jewish nationalism, or
Zionism, and Arab nationalism, which had started in Ottoman-ruled
Palestine toward the end of the nineteenth century and later developed
specifically into Palestinian nationalism. In the late 1930s the Arab
states intervened in the conflict politically on the side of the Palestinians, and in 1948 they intervened militarily. Between 1948 and 1967, the
Palestinian issue, effectively reduced to a refugee problem, often served
competing Arab governments in their rivalries. After June 1967, however, the involvement of the Arab states in the conflict was no longer
primarily in support of the Palestinians but aimed at the recovery of
the territories they had lost in the fighting. Yet the Palestinian question
remained the heart of the Arab-Israeli dispute.

Al-Fateh—a reverse acronym of *Harakat al-Tahrir al-Watani al-
Filastini,* or the Palestinian National Liberation Movement—was established in 1959, and the PLO was created in 1964. Proclaiming that the
Palestinian people had an exclusive right to Mandatory Palestine, both
organizations were committed to armed struggle against Israel—to the
destruction of the State of Israel—to implement this right. But numeri-
cally and politically their power was rather modest. It was the *Naksah* of
1967 which resuscitated the Palestinians' consciousness regarding their
homeland and their distinct national identity. Following the Arab de-

feat in the June War, the Palestinians emerged as an independent factor. The PLO, al-Fateh, and other militant groups rapidly gathered
strength and influence. The Palestinian *fida'iyyun*—Arabic for self-
sacrificing commandos—mostly resorted to terrorism against civilian
targets inside Israel. But the disproportionate Israeli reprisals contributed in no small measure to the growing popularity of the fida'iyyun
among their brethren and in the Arab world.

Conventional wisdom has it that any solution to the Palestinian
problem which fell short of a Palestinian state (or "entity") comprising
the entire land of Mandatory Palestine was at that stage anathema
to the Palestinians as well as to the Arab leaders. Indeed, a two-state
compromise was broadly unacceptable. Yet in late 1966, following a
devastating Israeli raid on the West Bank village of Samu' that ignited
large-scale unrest and riots against King Hussein and his regime, some
leading West Bank figures decided to declare the creation of a Palestinian state in their area.[32] Moreover, shortly after the war in June several
al-Fateh leaders, including Khalid al-Hasan, Faruq Qaddumi, and
Kamal 'Udwan, saw an opportunity to set up an autonomous Palestinian entity in the newly occupied West Bank and Gaza Strip. Although
they stressed that this entity would not compromise or negotiate with
Israel, the idea met with strong opposition from other members of the
leadership; nonetheless, it dominated leadership thinking and behavior
for at least a year.[33] As we shall see, a number of personalities in the West
Bank openly and strongly advocated the establishment of a Palestinian
state alongside the State of Israel in the immediate aftermath of the war.

The Actors

As negotiating parties Israel, the West Bank Palestinians, and King
Hussein were strikingly unequal. In Israel's contacts with the West
Bankers one side was a government with all the might and the elaborate apparatus of state authority, while the other was an unorganized
group of individuals. In addition, the two interlocutors were a country
and a community, a regional power and a civilian population, occupier
and occupied. Hussein was the ruler of a sovereign kingdom, but his
defeat, with its territorial, military, political, economical, and psychological effects, put him in a much weaker position than the Israelis. The

latter used to scorn the Jordanian monarch. Deriding his youth and his small stature, they referred to him in their internal discussions as *Yanuka* (infant), "the little king," or simply "Hussi."

King Hussein, conversely, respected the Jews. Before the June 1967 War he and Israel had been the best of enemies. As early as 1963 Hussein had initiated a secret dialogue with his Jewish neighbors which ended three decades later in a bilateral peace accord. In a series of clandestine meetings the king and Israel reached an understanding on a number of issues and effectively established a peaceful coexistence. The young monarch—he was twenty-eight years of age in 1963—personally handled the crucial political and foreign affairs issues of his kingdom. His talks with the Israelis were kept a closely guarded secret even from his successive prime ministers and foreign ministers. Only a handful of trusted confidants were privy to these contacts. On the Israeli side the official who handled the secret channel of communication with Hussein was Dr. Ya'acov Herzog, former ambassador to Canada and from 1965 the director general of the Prime Minister's Office. In 1963 and 1964 Herzog met the king three times in London, and he accompanied Foreign Minister Golda Meir to another rendezvous with "Charles"—the Israeli code name for King Hussein—in Paris in September 1965.[34]

The Israeli raid on the village of Samu', south of Hebron, on 13 November 1966 shattered Hussein's trust in Israel and seriously damaged Jordanian-Israeli relations. The foray was a large-scale operation in response to the killing of three Israeli soldiers by a land mine the previous day. The mine had been planted by Syrian-sponsored al-Fateh saboteurs, but Israel chose to retaliate against Jordan. The attack resulted in the death of twenty-one Jordanian soldiers and the injury of thirty-seven, in addition to the destruction of 118 houses in the village. In the king's view the attack signaled an Israeli intention to capture the West Bank.[35]

Six months later, on 30 May 1967—when the countdown to war was gathering momentum—Hussein flew to Cairo and signed a mutual defense pact with Egypt's President Nasser, his archrival. Hussein signed the pact mainly because he feared for the survival of his regime. Following Nasser's belligerent moves from mid-May onward, Arab nationalism and eagerness to go to war against Israel swept the Middle East, including Jordan. Though aware that the Arabs were not ready for battle, Hussein realized that he must swim with the tide.[36] The pact placed his army under the command of an Egyptian general.[37] Shortly after Israel launched its war against Egypt, Jordanian artillery fatefully started shelling Israeli targets.

When the fighting was over, many Israeli leaders wrote off Hussein as a highly expendable commodity because they could not forgive the king for taking part in the war. They felt that he had betrayed them. "In his attack on us Hussein acted like Mussolini when he stabbed France in the back shortly after the German invasion. Hussein showed that he is not trustworthy," said Minister Yigal Allon in a press interview in February 1968.[38] Even when realpolitik finally prevailed and the Israelis embarked on a secret parley with the king, they still insisted that he must pay a price for his behavior in June 1967: "War had its consequences," Allon told him point-blank in September 1968.[39]

But Washington thought differently. The US position was that the West Bank should be returned to Jordan with minor, reciprocal border modifications. A few days after the war had ended the Americans considered the "Palestinian option": Secretary of State Dean Rusk entertained the idea of self-determination for the West Bank Palestinians with autonomous status for the region.[40] But this was only a fleeting thought. Both the White House and the State Department maintained that the Palestinian option was not desirable. They believed that such an entity would not be viable. More important, pro-Western Hussein—reportedly on the Central Intelligence Agency's payroll for more than two decades—was a US ally.[41] While remaining more committed to Israel, the Americans had a sense of duty toward the king. President Johnson and his administration repeatedly assured the king that he would regain the land he had lost in the war.

Jordan was almost five times the size of Israel within its pre-June borders, but less populated: before the losses of the West Bank and Arab Jerusalem, Jordan's inhabitants numbered barely 2 million.[42] The captured region, relatively small in size, was the most significant one in terms of population and value. Hussein felt a deep obligation to retrieve it. He was an autocratic ruler, occasionally ruthless, but foreign leaders and diplomats as well as his Israeli interlocutors always found him well mannered and refined. In the secret rendezvous with the Israelis, Hussein time and again faced obstinacy and chicanery, but he never lost his temper. He left the role of the "bad cop" to Zayd al-Rifa'i, his loyal private secretary, who accompanied him in most of the meetings which followed the 1967 debacle and who handled this channel of communication on the king's behalf.[43]

Israel entered the crisis which led to the June hostilities after more than a year of deep economic recession, with unemployment reaching a record high and public morale a record low. For the first time since the foundation of the state, emigration exceeded immigration. Depressed and angry, the Israelis lost faith in their leadership. As the situation deteriorated and war with Egypt seemed unavoidable, frustration gave way to fear. Levi Eshkol, who in 1963 had succeeded David Ben-Gurion, the resolute founding father of Israel, as prime minister and defense minister, was regarded as indecisive, weak, and inept as a wartime leader. A political coup forced him to give up the defense portfolio—a personal blow from which he never recovered. On 1 June 1967 a "National Unity Government" was formed by the inclusion of three additional cabinet members: former Chief of Staff Moshe Dayan from *Rafi*—a Ben-Gurion loyalists' splinter of the ruling *Mapai*—as defense minister, and Menachem Begin and Yosef Sapir from the right-wing *Gahal,* as ministers without portfolio.

A few months later the British ambassador in Tel Aviv described the government as "a collection of disparate forces, lacking firm direction on internal problems and now further divided by multifarious opinions on how to cope with the occupied territories and the elusive peace with the Arabs."[44] Indeed, some cabinet members, firmly believing in the idea of "Greater Israel" (*Eretz Yisrael ha-Shlemah,* literally, the Whole Land of Israel), demanded the annexation of the occupied territories and primarily the West Bank; others viewed such a move as dangerous and were ready to cede most of the captured lands; and the rest teetered between these two extremes. Many ministers were in the habit of making political statements which betrayed the schizophrenic nature of the government. The enlarged cabinet survived notwithstanding until the death of its head in February 1969. The reason is twofold. First, it simply avoided crucial decisions; in the words of Ambassador Hadow, it was easier to show unity in intransigence.[45] Second, many important issues were discussed not in the cabinet but by the inner circle of the top political echelon.

In 1967 the Alignment, comprising Mapai and *Ahdut ha-'Avodah,* was the dominant political force in Israel's coalition government. In January 1968 the two parties, together with a third, Rafi, merged into the

Israeli Labor Party.[46] The Political Committee of the Alignment (until the merger) and of the Labor Party (thereafter) was the forum before which delicate matters were brought for deliberation and decision, with the aim of presenting the cabinet with a unified position, thereby ensuring its adoption. The committee's members were the Alignment/Labor ministers and a handful of influential politicians outside the government. Meetings were held irregularly, and decisions were normally taken by consensus. In addition, critical political and military moves were frequently determined at informal gatherings of senior statesmen and selected officials. In most cases these discussions involved Premier Eshkol, Defense Minister Dayan, Foreign Minister Eban, Minister of Labor and later Deputy Prime Minister Yigal Allon, Eshkol's adviser Dr. Ya'acov Herzog, and Gideon Rafael of the Foreign Ministry. Moshe Sasson, who was in charge of the political contacts with the West Bank elite as the prime minister's representative, was invited when matters regarding the occupied Palestinians were on the table.

There was no love lost between the participants in these intimate consultations, however. Eshkol, seventy-two in 1967, was unable to forgive Dayan for taking over the Defense Ministry; Dayan despised Eshkol and urged that he vacate the premiership as well; Eban argued that Dayan endangered the government's moderate line; Dayan, fifty-two, and Allon, forty-nine, wanted to see the "old guard" go, but at the same time they competed with each other over the succession. (Cambridge-educated Eban, fifty-two, was also considered part of the old guard, if not altogether an outsider.) Yet all shared a common distrust of "the Arabs" and harbored deep prejudice toward them. Dayan, who unlike Eshkol and many among the old guard maintained regular contacts with Arabs and spoke Arabic, went as far as claiming that for the Arabs "the idea of liquidating us is a matter of faith."[47] Disdain for the Arabs was widespread among the Israelis. For example, Maj. Gen. Aharon Yariv, chief of the Military Intelligence, talked on one occasion about an inherent "fundamental flaw in the Arab person's character." The Arabs, he said, were *drek*—Yiddish for rubbish or shit—and would remain that way.[48]

Whereas Israel had a democratically elected government and Jordan was ruled by an absolute sovereign, the political leadership of the indigenous Palestinians in the occupied territories—now placed under military government—was undefined and fluid. In the Gaza Strip the

potential leadership class, which had been suppressed by the Egyptian
military rule, failed to emerge after the Israelis took control of the area.
The vacuum was soon filled by guerrilla cadres who adopted armed
struggle.[49] In the context of political dialogue this state of affairs mattered little to the Israelis, who were determined to keep the Strip without the 1948 refugees.[50] According to the census Israel conducted in the
occupied territories in September 1967, about half of the 356,000 Palestinians living in Gaza—175,000 persons—resided in refugee camps; the
real number was definitely higher.[51] However, Arab Jerusalem, annexed
by Israel immediately after the war and formally incorporated into the
Jewish sector of the city, remained an indispensable part of the West
Bank and the hub of the occupied Palestinians' political activity. Unlike the Gaza Strip, the West Bank and Arab Jerusalem had an active
political elite which provided the local population with leadership, but
most of its members were part of the Jordanian establishment.

These men represented prominent families of the "urban notables" class (a'yan), whose influence and power derived from their historical status and wealth. From the Ottoman days through the British
Mandate, the notables had been acting as intermediaries between the
foreign rulers of the land and the population, in a well-rooted pattern
known as the politics of notables. This practice was based on the notables' having the ear of the dominant authority on the one hand and influence over the people of their localities and the immediate surroundings
on the other.[52] By 1948 the power of the a'yan families had diminished,
yet they continued to perform a mediating role between the central
government in Amman and wider society. Under the Hashemites
the notables served as cabinet ministers, members of the Senate and the
Chamber of Deputies, district governors, ambassadors, mayors, and so
on. These positions preserved the notables' authority and prestige, and
endowed them and their cronies with material rewards.[53]

There were also radical activists in the West Bank who were members of political opposition organizations that had been suppressed
under the Jordanian regime: al-Ba'th (the Revival), al-Qawmiyyun al-
'Arab (the Arab Nationalists), al-Ikhwan al-Muslimun (the Muslim
Brotherhood), and the Jordanian Communist Party. Many among
them were in the liberal professions and relatively young—in their thir-
ties and forties—who had studied at Arab universities, mainly in Cairo
and Damascus, during the revolutionary period of the 1950s and had

been deeply affected by a combination of nationalist and extreme ide-
ologies.[54] Israel was their demon.

The Israelis opted to work with the traditional leadership and existing officialdom. West Bank mayors and councilors were allowed to
retain their positions, and the municipalities continued to function as
before; in fact, the mayors' powers were increased. The notables, including most of the mayors, were also chosen by the Israelis as interlocutors for the political exchanges with the occupied Palestinians.[55]
When asked to what extent his Palestinian interlocutors represented
the West Bank population, Moshe Sasson replied: "It was not about
representation. This was not a democracy. I met people of status."[56] These
notables, whose authority was limited to their respective communities,
were divided by personal, sectarian, and local rivalries. Many among
them had economic interests in Jordan, and dependence on Amman
thus swayed their political views. Attempting to preserve his influence
in the land he had lost in the war, King Hussein channeled funds to
his loyalists there. The Jordanian money helped the West Bank traditionalists forget their grievances over the discriminatory policy of the
Hashemite regime against the Palestinians and their region. Quite a
few, however, still perceived President Nasser as the supreme leader of
the Arab world. In time, and by no small measure thanks to Israel's
attitude, a growing number of traditionalists inclined toward the resistance movement outside the occupied territories.

The First Shot

On the morning of 5 June 1967, at 08:10, the regular programming of
Kol Yisrael, Israel's state radio, was interrupted by an official announcement from the army spokesman:

> Since this morning heavy battles have been taking place in
> the southern region between Egyptian armored and air forces
> and Tsahal [the Israeli army] forces which advanced to stop
> them. The Egyptian forces opened an air and land offensive
> this morning. Egyptian armored forces advanced towards the
> Negev at dawn, and our forces went out to meet them. At the
> same time a large number of Egyptian jets were seen on ra-
> dar screens approaching the coasts of our country. A similar

effort was made in the Negev region. The Israeli Air Force
went out to meet the enemy, and an air battle developed which
is continuing even at this minute.[57]

None of this was true. No Egyptian tanks had moved toward the Negev
at dawn, nor had Egyptian aircraft approached Israel's territory. It was
Israel that had started the war by launching a meticulously preplanned
aerial attack on Egyptian air bases less than half an hour before the
broadcast of the announcement. Because of stark warnings from friend
and foe—including the United States, Britain, France, and the USSR—
not to fire the first shot, the Israelis had been looking for a pretext to
justify their assault.[58] On 1 June, for example, Chief of Staff Rabin and
some of his generals had considered staging a mock shelling of an Israeli settlement to create a false pretext for going to war against Egypt.[59]
    The substance of the official announcement was approved in a
consultation headed by Premier Eshkol on the eve of the war.[60] Shortly
after the fighter planes had begun striking Egypt, Israel's ambassador to
the United Nations telephoned the president of the Security Council
and told him that Israel was responding to "a cowardly and treacherous"
attack from Egypt.[61] Foreign Minister Eban repeated the claim in a
press conference with foreign correspondents sometime later, and kept
the lie alive in his speech before the UN Security Council the next day.[62]
Initially the fabricated story confused President Johnson and his administration, though they suspected that "the Israelis probably kicked
this off."[63] Within a few hours their suspicion became certainty.[64] When
the war was over, Eban nevertheless stressed in the cabinet that it was
extremely important that Johnson should think that Israel had responded
to an Egyptian assault.[65] The Israelis thus attempted to maintain their
false version in the days to come.[66] Eban himself reiterated it when he addressed the UN General Assembly on 19 June.[67]
    In his pioneering analysis of lying in international relations, John
Mearsheimer argues that leaders regard lying as a useful tool of state-
craft. They tell interstate lies when they believe that the lies serve national
interests, and they do so more often in wartime than in peacetime.
Such lies occasionally make good strategic sense, even when they are
told to an ally.[68] Indeed, Israel might have had valid reasons for lying as
to who started the hostilities in June 1967—either to maintain the fog of
war for military purposes or in an effort to prevent serious diplomatic

damage and risk to its arms supply. The latter point was particularly relevant because of the firm demand of France's President Charles de Gaulle that Israel must not be the first to shoot.[69] Because France was a major arms supplier, particularly of the frontline Mirage fighter jets, de Gaulle's warning carried much weight. But it would be difficult to justify Israel's subsequent foreign policy of deception whose aim was—as will unfold in the following chapters—to preserve the territorial status quo of 10 June at the expense of a peace settlement.

The Two Options

5 June–Early July 1967

Shortly after Israeli jets started blasting the Egyptian Air Force on its runways on the morning of 5 June 1967, Israel Defense Minister Moshe Dayan stated in a radio address to the nation, "Soldiers of Israel, we have no aims of conquest. Our purpose is to bring to naught the attempts of the Arab armies to conquer our land and to break the ring of blockade and aggression which threatens us."[1] Soon afterward Foreign Minister Abba Eban echoed Dayan's declaration in a press conference in Tel Aviv. "The policy of Israel's government does not include any intention of conquest," he said.[2] At noon Prime Minister Levi Eshkol assured President Lyndon Johnson in a personal message: "We seek nothing but peaceful life within our territory, and the exercise of our legitimate maritime rights." Eshkol made the same promise in a note to USSR Premier Aleksey Kosygin.[3]

Less than three days later, by the morning of 8 June, the inhabitants of the West Bank and the Gaza Strip found themselves under Israeli military control. Not having taken any part in the fighting, they were astounded by the rout of the Arab armies and by the occupation of their areas. By all accounts, the Palestinians were in a state of shock. Their sense of humiliation and despair notwithstanding, a large number of West Bank leaders realized in the wake of the defeat that a new situation had arisen, and with it new prospects: after seventeen years as Jordanian citizens, they could now become Palestinians again—and turn

the Palestinian problem, a humanitarian issue since 1948, back into a
national one. Those members of the West Bank political elite who sought
to seize the opportunity included prominent officials of the Jordanian
regime. But by the end of the war, overwhelmed by the stunning battlefield victory and the territorial acquisitions that came with it, Israel's
leadership already considered the West Bank and the Gaza Strip "liberated" and was having second thoughts about its pledges of 5 June.

The Palestinian Option Presents Itself

As early as Saturday, 10 June—the last day of the war—'Aziz Shehadeh, a
fifty-five-year-old Christian lawyer from Ramallah, approached the Israelis with a written plan for peace negotiations between Israel and the
Palestinians in both the West Bank and the Gaza Strip, aiming at establishing an independent Palestinian state. Shehadeh, no friend of the
Hashemite regime, was a 1948 refugee from Jaffa and a veteran political maverick: he had been one of the representatives of the Palestinian
refugees at the Lausanne Conference, organized by the UN Conciliation
Commission, in the spring of 1949, and had advocated then an independent Palestinian state on the basis of the UN Partition Resolution of
November 1947. Eighteen years later, on 8 June 1967, Shehadeh repeated
the same idea when Moshe Sasson, an Israeli Foreign Ministry official
who had also taken part in the Lausanne Conference, hurried to the just-
occupied Ramallah to pay him a courtesy visit.[4] The next day Shehadeh
discussed the subject in more detail with two Israeli intelligence officers.

The two officers were Lt. David Kimche, an official of the Mossad,
Israel's Institute for Intelligence and Special Operations, who chose to do
his reserve duties with the Military Intelligence's "political department,"
in charge of psychological warfare, and his friend Capt. Dan Bavly, a Tel
Aviv accountant who found himself at the beginning of the war "unemployed" by his own reserve infantry brigade and thus gladly accepted
Kimche's invitation to join him on his assignments.[5] On Friday, 9 June,
Kimche's task was to reactivate the Ramallah radio station. While the
two Israelis were in Ramallah, when the Jordanian official responsible for
the radio station could not be found, it was suggested by Daud al-'Isa, a
Palestinian journalist who accompanied them, that they meet "an interesting man" in the meantime; that man was 'Aziz Shehadeh.

Shehadeh told his guests that Israel must take advantage of the geopolitical change resulting from the removal of the Hashemite regime from the West Bank and establish without delay a Palestinian state, compatible with the UN Partition Resolution of 1947. When Kimche commented that the 1947 borders were no longer realistic and that the only possible basis for a settlement could be the 4 June Green Line demarcation, Shehadeh explained that he was only positing a starting point for negotiations. He undertook to give the names of roughly forty persons recommended for a Palestinian constituent assembly, indicating a dozen of them as suitable members of the proposed Palestinian government. Shehadeh insisted that his ideas were shared by many of his compatriots and agreed to put them in writing.

A day later, Saturday, 10 June, Kimche and Bavly returned to Shehadeh's house, accompanied by his friend Muhammad Tawfiq al-Yahya of Nablus, also a lawyer and former member of a Palestinian delegation at the Lausanne Conference. Shehadeh kept his promise: he handed the Israelis a two-page document, typed in English by his sixteen-year-old son Raja. The paper read:

A. Negotiations to be conducted between inhabitants of the Western Bank of Jordan and the Gaza Strip along the following lines:

    1. The formation of an independent Palestine State to be admitted as a member state in the United Nations.

    2. The territorial limits of the Palestine State shall be along the lines of the 1947 Partition Scheme with such necessary modifications as may be agreed upon by further negotiations and subject to the stipulations mentioned herein after.

    3. The Old City of Jerusalem surrounded by the ancient walls shall be under the joint sovereignity [sic] of the state of Israel and Palestine and ruled in accordance with a special agreement to secure free access to all Holy Places.

    4. The Capetal [sic] of the Palestine state shall be the Arab section of Jerusalem.

5. The Palestine State shall be provided with a port on the Mediterranean Sea linked by a corridor as may be agreed upon by further negotiations.

6. Economic and non aggression treaties shall be concluded between the two states.

7. The independence and territorial boundaries of the Palestine State shall be guaranteed by the United Nations[.]

8. Subject to any agreement as may be reached between the two States under the economic treaty referred to in para. 6 above; all rights of Palestinians in movable and immovable properties existing at the termination of the mandate in both states shall be settled by mutual agreement. In case of despute [*sic*], however, such rights shall be settled in accordance with the principles layed [*sic*] down in the U. N. resolution of Dec. 12, 1949.[6]

B. The Israeli Government shall give written assurances that the above proposals are acceptable in principle and may be considered as a working scheme towards a final and peaceful solution of the Palestine problem in particular and the establishment of good relations with the Arab States in general.

C. When such assurances are given, attempts should be made to form a preliminary committee to call for a general assembly in order to adopt the necessary resolutions.[7]

Shehadeh and Yahya assured the two Israelis that some of the eight points included in the first article did not reflect their own thinking and were drafted merely as a "bait" intended to lure the Palestinian extremists to join in.[8] The second half of the document suggested that the preparatory committee should hold a meeting in Nablus, at the house of Deputy Mayor Hajj Ma'zuz al-Masri, a wealthy businessman, on Friday, 16 June. A supplementary paper, in Arabic, contained a tentative list of fifty-seven West Bank personalities as recommended members of the committee.[9] The Israeli authorities were to allow two of them, Walid al-Shak'ah and Dr. 'Abd al-Majid Abu Hijleh, both from Nablus, to travel to Gaza in order to secure the names of that region's representatives at the meeting. The Shehadeh document emphasized the need to act fast and in the utmost secrecy.

Shehadeh's list lacked some names of influential West Bankers, including religious leaders. Particularly conspicuous was the omission of Anwar Nuseibeh, one of the most prominent figures in the West Bank. Several names on the list were of people of lesser stature and importance. Moreover, because of the curfew and cutting of telephone lines, Shehadeh had not been able to consult all of those whose names appeared on the list. His scheme was crude, rudimentary, and even somewhat naïve. Yet it was a significant initiative for two reasons. First, it brought to the fore a bold Palestinian readiness for the then "treacherous" idea of a separate settlement with Israel, and thus for a two-state solution. Second, on the Israeli side the plan generated a process of political contacts with the Palestinian leadership in the occupied territories. Though the Israeli authorities did not respond to Shehadeh's outline and timetable, Kimche was consequently commissioned by the Military Intelligence chief to conduct a survey of political trends among the West Bank leadership. Even Assistant Defense Minister Zvi Tsur, with whom Kimche and Bavly met on 11 June, encouraged them to continue meeting Palestinian representatives, in spite of his deep doubts about the political feasibility of implementing Shehadeh's scheme.[10] In carrying out their assignment, the two junior but well-connected officers used the list of names Shehadeh had given them.

Hamdi Kan'an, the mayor of Nablus, disclosed in late 1968 that on the third day of the occupation he had been approached by two Israeli army officers, who suggested to him the establishment of a Palestinian state. According to Kan'an, he had rejected the idea outright and immediately afterward summoned the city council and notables, informed them of the Israeli proposal, and warned against its dangers.[11] Kimche, however, contended that he and Bavly never proposed anything to any of the Palestinians they had met. "In our talks, we stressed that our aim is only to listen to their views, and that we have no intention to raise any suggestions at this stage," he claimed in his second report of 13 June. "But we emphasized that a totally new situation has been created, and under no circumstances would a return to the pre-war situation be possible."[12] In their book, published in 1968, Kimche and Bavly endorse an *Economist* article which explained that the purpose of their mission was "to test the response of well-known groups and personalities to the idea of creating an autonomous Palestinian state, having federal bonds with Israel."[13] A Foreign Ministry document reveals that the two Israelis did suggest to their interlocutors that Palestinian leaders in the West Bank should request the creation of an "independent Palestinian unit" on a limited part of the West Bank, with Israeli responsibility for its security.[14]

Relying on Kimche's accounts, the director general of the Foreign Ministry recommended permitting the assembly of the Palestinian preparatory committee in Nablus on 16 June, outlined in Shehadeh's plan, and asked the foreign minister to discuss the matter with the prime minister.[15] The available records do not reveal whether this recommendation was taken up, but the 16 June Nablus gathering never happened.

Kimche and Bavly, who met Kan'an, recorded in their report that he argued first for the return of the West Bank to Jordan, then began gradually to support the idea of an independent state.[16] Kan'an might have had his reasons for publishing his own version of the encounter. The two Israelis, on the other hand, were unfamiliar with West Bank society, politics, and culture; neither of them was fluent in Arabic, so they conducted their talks in English or Hebrew or through a translator. These factors, coupled with their overenthusiasm, might have led them to a deep yet unfounded conviction that a settlement with the Palestinians was within reach. Little wonder, then, that already on 14 June, after meeting only fifteen West Bankers—and not necessarily the most prominent ones—Kimche and Bavly and two other Mossad officers attached to Military Intelligence headquarters drafted a detailed proposal for the immediate establishment of a Palestinian state by Israel. In the informal fashion characteristic of Israel in those days, they sent the document to the prime minister, the defense minister, and several other top decision makers.[17]

During their weeklong assignment Kimche and Bavly held talks with thirty Palestinians, including eight from Jerusalem, ten from Nablus, five from Ramallah, and others from Tulkarm, 'Anabta, Bethlehem, Hebron, and Jericho; they made "preliminary contacts" with seven more Jerusalemites.[18] These Palestinians represented a wide range of political leanings and affiliations—from radical Pan-Arabists, fervent nationalists, and Communists to pro-Hashemites and traditionalists. The overall impression of the Israeli surveyors was that most of their interlocutors did not want the West Bank to be returned to Jordan. Although there was no consensus on the form a desirable solution would take—some advocated an independent state, others preferred an autonomous entity—there was broad agreement about the need to come to terms with Israel and to make a lasting peace with the Jewish state. Fearing Jordanian retaliation, they declared their utter refusal to enter into negotiations before receiving official Israeli assurances that the West Bank would never be returned to Jordan under any circumstances. Most important, almost all of them wished to be allowed to convene in the near future in order to discuss freely and openly the fate of the West Bank.[19]

Similar ideas were recorded separately by Maj. Rafi Sutton, a commander of an intelligence-collection unit based in Jerusalem. During the first days of the occupation Sutton held a series of conversations with eleven West Bank dignitaries, including Antoun 'Atallah of Jerusalem, a former foreign minister of Jordan, and the mayors of Hebron and Jericho. The men fiercely criticized the Arab states for mishandling the Palestinian problem and asked for a meeting of West Bank leaders and accredited Israeli representatives in order to conclude a final bilateral Palestinian-Israeli agreement, in the shape of either a federation or a confederation. Salah 'Abdu, the mayor of Jericho, undertook to convene a conference in his hometown to undo the outcome of the December 1948 Jericho Congress, which had effectively conferred on Jordan's King 'Abdallah the legitimacy for the annexation of the West Bank. Sheikh Muhammad 'Ali al-Ja'bari, the influential mayor of Hebron, had presided over the Jericho Congress of 1948. Sutton, according to his published account, apprised his superiors of the Palestinian overtures; the information was passed on to Defense Minister Moshe Dayan.[20]

A desire for Israeli authorization for a meeting of West Bank notables was widespread in the West Bank in the early days of the occupation.[21] Reports reached King Hussein of Jordan and his prime minister, Sa'd Jum'ah, almost instantly on the willingness of "certain Palestinians in the West Bank" to make peace with the Israelis and of support for a separate Palestinian entity, incorporating the West Bank.[22] "There is some evidence that Palestinians in Nablus, Tulkarm and some other West Bank towns are prepared to accept Israeli occupation and possibly subsequent absorption by Israel," cabled the British ambassador in Amman.[23] In Jerusalem another British diplomat discerned "a feeling among Palestinians that they should be left to work out their own destiny apart from the Arabs."[24] The American consul general in Jerusalem also summarized the prevailing mood in the West Bank, based on visits and talks by him and his staff during the first week of the occupation; his account conformed to the findings of the Israeli survey: "Few Christians or Muslims have indicated a desire to return to [the] former *status quo*. More stress [the] need for lasting and peaceful solution." He found, however, that the most common proposal was that the West Bank and the Old City of Jerusalem should be internationalized under UN control.[25]

The West Bankers' yearning for reconciliation was reportedly conveyed directly to Israel's chief of staff, Lt. Gen. Yitzhak Rabin. While in Nablus a couple of days after the end of hostilities, Rabin and some of his officers accepted an invitation to visit Rashad al-Nimr, a former Jordanian cabinet minister, at his home. Several traditional leaders from the Nablus region were also present. Nimr, fifty-eight, a Jewish agriculture high school graduate and fluent in Hebrew, told Rabin that the Palestinians wished to live in peaceful coexistence with Israel; they sought a free Palestine, comprising the West Bank and the Gaza Strip, with Arab Jerusalem as its capital. Israel, he suggested, should therefore withdraw all its forces from the Palestinian occupied territories. This episode was reported two decades later in a New York Arabic weekly, based on information from the Palestinian side. The writer concluded the story by quoting Rabin as saying that he had delivered the message to Premier Eshkol.[26]

It would appear that Sheikh Ja'bari, the erstwhile loyal Hashemite, was the first to speak publicly about the need for Palestinian-Israeli cooperation in an attempt to reach a peace settlement. Ja'bari told an Israeli reporter on 16 June that he was ready to go to Amman in order to mediate between Israel and Jordan.[27] A couple of days later he repeated to Israeli and foreign journalists what he had expressed previously to Kimche and Bavly: the Israeli government should convene the leaders of the West Bank as well as the leaders of the Palestinian citizens of Israel; an elected committee of twelve would then consult the Israeli, Jordanian, and other Arab governments about the prospects for peace; according to its findings, a plan for peace negotiations would be drawn up by the assembly on the basis of the 1947 Partition Resolution, with some border adjustments. The Palestinian state, federated with Israel, would be demilitarized.[28] The mayor of Hebron, then, introduced a new element into the already complex problem, by incorporating the "1948 Arabs"—namely, the Palestinians who after the 1948 War had stayed in what became the State of Israel and had as a result acquired Israeli citizenship.

Unlike Ja'bari, his son-in-law Anwar al-Khatib, the Jordanian governor of the Jerusalem District, remained a loyal Hashemite. He was devastated by the Arab defeat and the subsequent Israeli occupation. Khatib "appeared shaken and to have lost all of his overbearing and rather truculent manner which he often displayed to western members [of the] Jerusalem Consular Corps," noted the American consul general.[29] Like Ja'bari, Khatib volunteered to mediate between Israel and Jordan. He asked to be permitted go to Amman as the head of a small Palestinian deputation, to deliver Israeli suggestions to the king and to describe to him the frame of mind prevailing in the West Bank. Khatib was confident of a positive reception.[30]

Even though an Israeli Foreign Ministry official found Anwar al-Khatib responsive to the idea of forming a national Palestinian government, Khatib never committed himself to the "Palestinian option."[31] He merely asked the Israelis, including Maj. Gen. (res.) Chaim Herzog, to allow him to organize a meeting of Palestinian notables which would elect an executive committee, empowered to represent the West Bankers' interests. Herzog, the first military governor of the West Bank, was dismissed for his incompetence on 15 June after just one week in office and was assigned instead by Dayan to handle the political contacts with the Palestinians.[32] He granted Anwar al-Khatib the requested permit and asked him to prepare a list of 120 participants in a West Bank general assembly.[33] Palestinian political activists were indeed eager to convene; but the conference, set to take place at Al-Hamra movie theatre on Salah al-Din Street, was canceled at the last minute by order of the highest authority.[34]

Nevertheless, the Palestinians did hold small gatherings to discuss their future options. Ruhi al-Khatib, the mayor of Jordanian Jerusalem and a fervent Palestinian, who himself entertained at that time the notion of a Palestinian-Israeli federation, disclosed to a British diplomat that meetings "between thinkers" were taking place in Anwar Nuseibeh's house.[35] Cambridge-educated, fifty-four years old, and the son of a leading notable Jerusalem family, Nuseibeh was cabinet secretary to the short-lived All-Palestine Government, established in Gaza in September 1948, and later held senior positions with the Jordanian regime, including cabinet membership, the governorship of the Jerusalem District, and ambassadorship in London. Nuseibeh was perceived as a pro-Hashemite, yet he too preferred the "Palestinian option"—or, rather, an "Israeli option." Shortly after the war Nuseibeh even attempted to persuade the PLO to negotiate a two-state solution with Israel.[36]

On 16 June, Anwar Nuseibeh intimated to a British diplomat his interest in the concept of confederation and said that if only Palestinians could move freely, "some ideas might be developed."[37] Nuseibeh believed that the local West Bank leadership was capable of reaching a peace settlement with Israel, if Israel could be magnanimous at the negotiating table.[38] Old Jerusalem, he maintained, must be the Arab state's capital.[39] Even after the Israeli annexation of Arab Jerusalem—which created, as we shall see, a profound change in the West Bankers' attitude—Nuseibeh still adhered to the idea of a separate settlement. "Anwar is of the opinion that there should be an autonomous Palestinian entity, in some form of economic union with Israel," wrote Professor P. J. Vatikiotis, the renowned British historian of the Middle East, who met his old friend Nuseibeh in Jerusalem during a visit in July.[40]

In fact, Nuseibeh tried to take the initiative in mid-June by approaching the military governor of Jerusalem, Col. Shlomo ("Chich") Lahat. According to Lahat's deputy, Lt. Col. Shmuel Albeq, who was present at the meeting, Nuseibeh said: "I come to you on behalf of the Palestinian people, as their representative. I propose that you [Israel] will strike a deal with us and establish an Arab Palestinian state." Like other Palestinians before him, Nuseibeh referred to the 1947 Partition Resolution as a starting point for negotiations. Lahat told Albeq later that he had delivered the proposal to his superiors, including Dayan, but received no information regarding its fate.[41]

On the evening of 18 June, Nuseibeh assembled a group of about twenty prominent Palestinians, mostly from the Jerusalem region, at his home for a meeting with General Herzog. The group included Anwar al-Khatib, Ruhi al-Khatib, and other well-known dignitaries.[42] It was Nuseibeh's idea to invite the Israeli general and to have an open discussion with him about possible political solutions. As a curfew was in force from early afternoon until morning, Herzog arranged the necessary permits for the invitees to attend the meeting. Before the general's arrival the conversation between the Palestinians present turned into rather candid self-examination and soul-searching. "I cannot understand how this [the defeat] could have happened to us," Mayor Khatib said.

One of the radical nationalists reacted: "It happened because for twenty years we have been building up a regime and destroying a nation—the Palestinians—while on the other side they have been building a state, not a personal regime. Now everybody can see the results."[43]

According to Herzog's version, some of the young leaders continued to blame the old-timers for the calamities that had befallen the Palestinians. David Kimche, who accompanied Herzog, told of an elderly former member of the pre-1948 Arab Higher Committee who said that the only solution for the Palestinian problem was the liquidation of the Zionist state and reported the angry reaction of a younger doctor: "You talk as if you were living on the moon." The doctor went on to say that it was time for the Palestinians to tackle the problem of living together with the Jews in a realistic and constructive manner, as the alternative was more wars, more refugees, and more suffering.[44] Some of the notables suggested the implementation of the 1947 Partition Resolution, and a few others talked about a binational state, in which Jews and Arabs could live side by side.[45] Herzog responded bluntly to both ideas by saying that those who raised them were completely detached from reality. Nothing came out of the meeting, but it was another demonstration of West Bank Palestinians' determination to embark independently on a political road leading to a peaceful settlement with Israel.

The West Bankers' overtures did not escape the world's attention. One press report, published in a British daily on 20 June, broke the news that the Palestinians "are engaged in forming a Representative Council . . . which will negotiate directly with the Israelis for a Palestinian settlement."[46] The correspondent who dispatched this report from Jerusalem was Jon Kimche, whose source was undoubtedly his Israeli brother David. David Kimche was adamant about creating a Palestinian state. On the same day he met Dr. Ya'acov Herzog, the director general of the Prime Minister's Office and Levi Eshkol's most trusted adviser, and demanded that "within 48 hours Israel will declare the West Bank a Palestinian state."[47] In Washington, Undersecretary of State Eugene Rostow informed the Soviets and the British about a "flow of reports at various levels" in recent days concerning a growing interest among the Palestinians in cutting a separate deal with Israel.[48] The British Foreign Office, which already knew about this from its own sources, analyzed the prospects for such an accommodation in a briefing paper prepared for the cabinet.[49] On 27 June, shortly before he met

King Hussein, President Lyndon Johnson was advised of "the possibility of an autonomous Arab State on the West Bank, federated with Israel, and of comparable status for the Gaza Strip."[50]

News about Palestinian-Israeli contacts also reached Arab capitals, where they were regarded as ominous. In mid-June, Amman
Radio broadcast a strong denunciation of what was described as Israel's
attempts to solve the Palestinian problem through the cooperation of
West Bank Palestinians, as if the problem were a local matter and not
a pan-Arab one. Prime Minister Jum'ah announced that cooperation
with the Israeli enemy would be considered high treason and that perpetrators would be punished severely.[51] Al-Thawrah, the Syrian regime's
mouthpiece, warned on 24 June against an Israeli scheme to establish a
Palestinian state in the West Bank which would absorb the Palestinian
refugees and make peace with Israel.[52] All these Arab alarm calls, warnings, and threats were based on hard facts and confirmed that many
leading West Bankers were indeed serious in their readiness to do business with the Israelis.

Ordinary Palestinians were also of the opinion that the aftermath
of the war offered them a new opportunity for an independent state of
their own. This was reflected in letters sent by West Bankers when postal
service in the occupied territories was resumed, and became clear to
the Israeli authorities as they carried out a strict screening process and
censorship of Palestinian mail.[53] A military survey during the first two
weeks of the occupation of the political mood in Nablus—the most
radical city in the West Bank—concluded that the people were eager for
an independent Palestine. But they rejected the idea of an Israeli satellite
West Bank state and suggested instead a confederation of Israel and Jordan including the West Bank, or of Israel, Jordan, and Palestine.[54]

What discouraged the Palestinian notables who favored negotiating
with Israel was the lack of Israeli commitment not to return the West
Bank to Jordan. Their demand for such assurances became more imperative in view of the explicit Jordanian threats.[55] Evidently the ball was in
Israel's court, but Israeli policy makers kept it there, ignoring the consequences of delaying their response. Indeed, Anwar al-Khatib, together
with Tiyasir Kan'an, a Jerusalem judge, exploited the Israeli political silence to meet with Palestinian leaders, first in Nablus and then in Hebron,
in an effort to persuade them against a separate settlement with Israel.
They should wait, Khatib explained, because it seemed that Hussein

would make peace with Israel; but peace would be possible only if Israel withdrew from the West Bank.[56] Recycling his rejected idea of electing an executive committee empowered to represent the West Bankers' interests, Khatib also intended to convene a committee of ten for that very purpose. Apart from him, Judge Tiyasir Kan'an and former Foreign Minister Antoun 'Atallah were mentioned as members of the committee.[57]

Still, the atmosphere in the West Bank during the days of the nascent occupation was generally conducive to Palestinian-Israeli political contact. In the words of Evan Wilson, then US consul general in Jerusalem, the West Bankers felt that they had backed the wrong horse for nineteen years and they wanted no more of Nasser or Hussein.[58] Even the journalist 'Abdullah Schleifer, an American Jew who had converted to Islam and was sympathetic to the Arabs, acknowledged that during the first couple of weeks after the war a pro-Israeli sentiment prevailed in the West Bank.[59] Adopting the later Palestinian stance of unwillingness to negotiate with Israel, Schleifer writes: "Were the Israelis not so ill-mannered and land lecherous among a people of exquisite politeness and reasonable jealousies, they would have harvested a convention hall of prominent Arab quislings late that June."[60]

A student of the Arab-Israeli conflict may wonder whether the Palestinian leadership in the West Bank was capable of delivering on its intentions. This is a legitimate question, to which no unambiguous answer can be offered. Undoubtedly, however, the Palestinian elite was much freer of external constraints at this early stage than later on, when the resistance movement outside the occupied territories grew stronger. At any rate, the Israelis had every reason to ask this question before entering into any negotiations with the Palestinians under their rule. But there was a more burning question to be answered by Israel first: did it really want the Palestinians to deliver? The answer was far from unequivocal.

Waiting for the Arab Phone Call

Israel did not want to fight on more than one front. Therefore, shortly after the start of the lightning attack against Egypt, an Israeli message of assurance-cum-warning was conveyed to King Hussein through three separate channels: "We are engaged in defensive fighting on the Egyptian sector, and we shall not engage ourselves in any action against Jordan, unless Jordan attacks us. Should Jordan attack Israel, we shall go against her with all our might." But the message arrived too late and went unheeded. The Arab forces on the Jordanian front, under the command of an Egyptian general since 1 June, had already started shelling the Israeli part of Jerusalem and other targets in central Israel.[61] In the early afternoon Jordanian infantry troops took Government House, the UN headquarters in Jerusalem, which was situated in a demilitarized zone on the Jordanian side of the line dividing the two parts of the city and which was off-limits to both Jordan and Israel. Though the Jordanian attack seemed a precursor of an all-out offensive, Israel still attempted to avoid fighting its eastern neighbor. In yet another message, Hussein was told that should Jordan cease firing and evacuate Government House, Israel would be prepared to guarantee recognition of the 1949 armistice line as its border with Jordan through the United Nations and an unnamed friendly country, presumably the United States.[62] Hussein fatefully did not accept, and consequently lost the entire western region of his kingdom.

"Even if we seize the Old City and the West Bank, we would eventually be forced to withdraw from them," an apprehensive Eshkol told his generals, in the presence of Defense Minister Dayan and Labor Minister Yigal Allon, on 5 June, the first day of the war.[63] Two days later the Israeli prime minister began using an entirely different language, speaking about the "liberation" of the Old City of Jerusalem and the West Bank.[64] "There were matters that had remained as if they were a cause of mourning for generations to come. . . . Generations have not yet passed and all those matters have been repaired. All the defects have been repaired," Eshkol stated in the first cabinet session after the ceasefire, on 11 June.[65] He was referring to an expression coined by his predecessor and now political foe David Ben-Gurion, who had defined the government's September 1948 rejection of his proposal for the capture of the West Bank as a cause of "lamentation for generations to come" (*bekhiyah le-dorot*).[66] The euphoric mood, which instantaneously replaced the fear and the somber atmosphere that had prevailed in Israel since mid-May, was best summed up by Dayan, who announced at the Air Force's victory ball: "We are now an empire."[67]

The Israelis were drunk with victory. A Foreign Ministry official told American diplomats that as a result of the unexpected acquisition of the West Bank, "some people [in the cabinet] were losing their heads. They were saying now that we have this territory [and] we ought to annex it."[68] But even in those heady days the Israeli policy makers knew that the spoils of war, specifically the West Bank and the Gaza Strip, came with a liability. As early as 8 June, the fourth day of the war, Eshkol said at a party forum: "We will have to devote thought to how we shall live on this land without giving up what we have [just] conquered, and how we'll live with such a [great] number of non-Jews. But we won't do this today."[69] When the war was over, the prime minister spelled it out much more clearly: "We won the war and received a nice dowry of territory, but it came with a bride whom we don't like."[70] This phrase, which the premier reiterated numerous times in slightly different versions, reflected Israel's subsequent twin driving ambitions: the desire to keep as much of *Eretz Yisrael* as possible and to get rid of as many Arabs as possible, first and foremost Palestinian refugees.[71] Whereas the former aim was to emerge in the course of time, the latter, defined as the "demographic danger," was discussed openly from the start.

Israel, then, faced a dilemma. Its leaders recognized that they must determine the future of the occupied territories quickly. The decision took on added urgency because of ominous diplomatic developments in the broader context of the Cold War. On 13 June, Soviet Foreign Minister Andrei Gromyko sent a letter to UN Secretary General U Thant, demanding that an emergency special session of the General Assembly be at once convened to consider the situation and to adopt a resolution designed to bring about an immediate Israeli withdrawal behind the armistice lines of 1949.[72] Four days later the emergency special session opened. In Washington, a special committee of the National Security Council, which had been set up by President Johnson on 7 June to provide high-level crisis management during the fighting, was assigned to establish the US postwar policy.[73] The task at hand was dealing with the Russian démarche at the United Nations. This required McGeorge Bundy, the committee's executive secretary and special consultant to the president, to ascertain the Israelis' plans. If the Americans were to side with the Jewish state in the forthcoming battle at the United Nations, as expected, the Israelis needed to convey their ideas for a Middle East settlement without delay.[74]

The American demand prompted hectic deliberations in the top echelon of the Israeli government. The decision-making process was significantly influenced by the painful recollection of the Sinai Campaign of 1956, when Israel's armed forces had swiftly captured the entire Sinai Peninsula and the Gaza Strip. Prime Minister Ben-Gurion had then declared that the island of Tiran—which dominates the entrance to the

Gulf of Aqaba—would be restored to "the third kingdom of Israel," only to succumb two days later to pressure from the United States and the Soviet Union to withdraw from all the occupied territories completely.[75]

While the policy makers weighed their options, officials in various branches of the government were quick to draft plans to solve the Palestinian problem. Already on 8 June a number of experts on Arab affairs and senior officials from the Prime Minister's Office, the Foreign Ministry, and the General Security Service (GSS, also known as Shabak or Shin Bet) were summoned by Dr. Ya'acov Herzog, the director general of the Prime Minister's Office and Eshkol's right-hand man, to discuss ideas for a "political solution." The group favored the establishment of a Palestinian state consisting of the East Bank and the remainder of the West Bank "after annexing the parts which are vital for securing our borders." Since the scheme required the removal of King Hussein, who enjoyed "a strong Anglo-American backing," the officials suggested as an alternative the creation of a Palestinian state in the remnants of the West Bank alone.[76]

An unsigned document found in a Foreign Ministry file summarizes the proposals submitted to the policy makers:

1. To annex not the entire West Bank but only parts which have security or historical significance, such as the Old City of Jerusalem, Latrun, and the Qalqilyah area;
2. To establish a Palestinian state that would include the West Bank and Trans-Jordan, tied to Israel in a military, political, and economic treaty. This would involve the overthrow of Hussein;
3. To annex the Gaza Strip, empty of its refugee inhabitants, who would be transferred to the Palestinian state;
4. To incorporate the Old City of Jerusalem immediately into New Jerusalem.[77]

More proposals came from the army. On 9 June, Col. Shlomo Gazit, chief of Military Intelligence's Research Division, composed an analysis paper that suggested the establishment of an independent Palestinian state in both the West Bank and the Gaza Strip. Gazit submitted the document to the prime minister and the defense and foreign ministers, in addition to his immediate superiors.[78] Two days later Col. (res.) Yuval Ne'eman, a physics professor who had been called up during the war to serve in the General Staff as a special aide for intelligence and special liaison, drafted a proposal which envisaged, among other features, an autonomous Palestinian state federated with Israel and with no common border with any Arab country.[79] The concept of allowing the West Bankers to establish an autonomous Palestinian entity was also raised and supported by some army generals.[80]

In an interdepartmental brainstorming session on 12 June, Foreign Minister Abba Eban's main concern was "what Bundy should be told about our thoughts regarding the future."[81] Eban presented two alternatives: returning the West Bank to Jordan or establishing a Palestinian entity. Maj. Gen. Meir Amit, chief of the intelligence agency Mossad, recommended the formation of a working group that would consider the possibility of setting up a Palestinian state. According to the available accounts of this meeting, none of the others offered a clear, direct response.[82] One of the participants was Shlomo Hillel, deputy director general of the Foreign Ministry. He seems to have been the only official who rejected any version of the Palestinian option. On the same day, Hillel recommended in writing that Israel annex the West Bank and the Gaza Strip, "permanently or temporarily." His letter to Eban reveals that one of the other ideas broached was a partial annexation of the West Bank and a return of the rest to Jordan.[83]

On 16 June, in a meeting at Defense Minister Dayan's office, Gen. Rehav'am Ze'evi, assistant head of the General Staff Branch, discussed the initial impression that emerged from the Kimche-Bavly survey of political thinking among the West Bank elite, including the proposal of David Kimche and his intelligence associates to establish a Palestinian state immediately. Ze'evi argued that the West Bankers' readiness to reach a political settlement with Israel should be exploited without delay. He thus offered a plan of his own: setting up a Palestinian state in parts of the West Bank—mostly the northern region—that would be closely affiliated with Israel. Ze'evi suggested further to name the Palestinian state Ishma'el, apparently after Abraham's first son, traditionally considered the father of the Arab peoples.[84]

All these plans had a couple of common denominators. The most obvious one was that they were one-sided, with no consideration of Palestinian wishes or interests. Second, they reflected the understanding that Israel should not, indeed could not, rule such a great number of Palestinians directly. The authors of these schemes saw a golden opportunity to solve the refugee problem that had haunted Israel since its birth. Some of them believed that a separate arrangement with the West Bankers would also serve as a proper punishment to King Hussein for going to war with Israel. Like the Palestinian initiatives and suggestions discussed above, the Israeli officials' proposals reached the very top of the policy-making machinery. However, none of them received any response, and it is safe to conclude that none was ever discussed seriously, if at all.[85]

In his autobiography Dayan explains that all the plans he received were based on what he considered as an unrealistic assumption that Israel, by virtue of its victory and the Arabs' defeat, was free to determine its borders as it wished and to decide unilaterally the fate of the Palestinians who came under its rule.[86] Perhaps, except that Dayan ignored the West Bankers' willingness to discuss their future and, more significant, the Israeli refusal—particularly his own—to allow their leaders to convene for that purpose. Anwar al-Khatib's offer to assist the Israelis in restoring the administration in Arab Jerusalem and the West Bank is a case in point. The former governor of the Jordanian Jerusalem District approached General Herzog on 9 June; Herzog, who mistakenly interpreted the overture as a proposal to set up a central Arab administration subordinate to the Israeli military, was excited by the idea, but Dayan did not approve, explaining that there was a danger that Ahmad al-Shuqayri, the PLO leader, might take control of such a central administration.[87] Dayan thus concluded the 16 June discussion at his office by saying that there was no point in permitting the local leadership to convene until the framework and the substance were prepared.[88]

After the war Dayan enjoyed the image of the great victorious hero, and subsequently he became the most powerful politician in Israel. He believed that Israel should retain the Palestinian-inhabited occupied territories without giving the population Israeli citizenship. "We want a Jewish state like the French want a French state," he said in television interviews on 9 June.[89] In the following days, Dayan posited several ideas for implementing his thinking in the West Bank. One was to grant the West Bankers autonomy; another was to establish a Palestinian state subjugated to, or confederated with, Israel.[90] Apparently the notion of autonomy was his favorite, but as Maj. Gen. Uzi Narkiss, then the commanding general of the Central Command, remembered it, when he proposed Palestinian autonomy in the West Bank, "Dayan almost threw me out of the room."[91] Toward the end of June the defense

minister unsuccessfully attempted to apply Israeli law in the West
Bank—a step which, had it been approved by the cabinet, would have
been tantamount to annexation.[92]

Dayan's most significant statement, however, was made in a BBC
interview on 12 June. In response to a question about Israel's next move,
Dayan said: "We are awaiting the Arabs' phone call. We ourselves won't
make a move. We are quite happy with the current situation. If anything
bothers the Arabs, they know where to find us."[93] Some prominent Palestinians considered Dayan's condescending declaration an indication
of Israel's unwillingness to make peace. According to Maj. Rafi Sutton,
the eleven notables with whom he was in contact about a separate settlement with Israel regarded Dayan's statement as the death knell of their
initiative.[94]

The Cabinet's 19 June Resolution

On the whole, the fundamental Israeli line following its victory was
that the war's outcome created a radically different situation, with new
possibilities for Israeli-Arab relations and the prospects of peace; under
no circumstances would Israel return to the status quo ante of 4 June.[95]
This stance was pronounced by Premier Eshkol in closed meetings as
well as in public, including from the podium of the Knesset.[96] Washington, meanwhile, urged Israel to translate its undefined position into
concrete peace terms. To that end, the cabinet held a series of serious
discussions, first in an informal debate of its leading members and advisers at the prime minister's residence on 14 June, then in deliberations
of the Ministerial Committee for Security Affairs on 14 and 15 June,
and finally in three prolonged plenary sessions, on 18 and 19 June.

In the informal debate Foreign Minister Abba Eban advocated an
active peace policy, whereas Dayan argued that because the Arabs were
still in a state of shock, the time was not ripe for peace moves.[97] At the
Ministerial Committee for Security Affairs, however, Dayan proposed
to offer King Hussein peace, based on the Jordan River as the border
between the two countries. During a "transition phase," while "seeking
a long-range constructive arrangement," the military regime in the West
Bank would remain in place. The "long-term arrangement" would allow
the inhabitants self-rule without granting them Israeli citizenship,
and the security and foreign affairs of the area would continue to be

Israel's responsibility. The other members of the committee abstained from making clear recommendations regarding the West Bank.[98]

The committee's recommendation and Dayan's counter-recommendation were brought before the cabinet's plenum.[99] The ministers were unable to reach a decision as to the future of the West Bank. Most of them rejected the notion of full annexation but supported the concept of the Jordan River as Israel's border. Dayan repeated his plan for self-rule, and Labor Minister Yigal Allon discussed in broad terms what would soon take shape as the Allon Plan: annexation by Israel of the Jordan Valley and Mount Hebron, thus creating a densely populated Palestinian enclave which might ultimately be granted independence. Some floated the idea of a Palestinian "canton." Only a handful of ministers were ready to contemplate negotiations with King Hussein that would lead to the return of the West Bank to the Hashemite Kingdom. Eventually the cabinet resolution avoided any concrete decision concerning the West Bank and declared only "to defer the discussion of the position regarding Jordan."[100] The decision not to decide (as it was later described by Minister Menachem Begin) reflected the deep divisions within the government on this fundamental subject.[101] The discussions also revealed the general mood with regard to a related and no less crucial issue, namely, the refugee problem, in particular the refugees residing in the Gaza Strip. Israeli cabinet ministers were eager to see this problem solved outside Israel's borders.

From the outset, the policy makers were adamant about keeping the occupied Gaza Strip. As early as 8 June, Golda Meir, the secretary general of Mapai, the ruling party, stated in a meeting of the Alignment's Political Committee that she was for retaining the Gaza Strip and "getting rid of its Arabs."[102] Defense Minister Dayan expressed a similar view before the war had ended and immediately afterward.[103] Indeed, Cabinet Resolution 563 of 19 June determined that "According to the international border, the Gaza Strip is located within the territory of the State of Israel."[104]

During the cabinet discussions Eshkol mentioned more than once the "four hundred thousand Arabs" living in Gaza and said that they should be settled in Arab countries: in Iraq, for example, in return for the Iraqi Jews who had been absorbed into Israel during the state's early years. But being realistic and pragmatic, Eshkol suggested transferring as many Arabs as possible from the Gaza Strip to the West Bank. Yigal Allon was firmly against any settlement of more Arabs in the West Bank.

"I am for [their] emigration across the sea, and this should be handled in the most serious manner, and not only with regard to refugees; I am prepared to encourage emigration of non-Jews in general." Some ministers mentioned Australia and Canada as possible destinations for the Palestinian refugees, and Allon, who thought that Arab countries would be better for resettlement but at the same time realized that no Arab state would allow this to happen, suggested the Sinai Peninsula, not only the Al-'Arish region, as the designated territory for the refugees' resettlement. Only one cabinet member, Justice Minister Ya'acov Shimshon Shapira, indicated that as the refugees were in territories occupied by Israel, it was Israel's exclusive responsibility to solve their problem.

The Ministerial Committee for Security Affairs recommended relocation of Palestinian refugees to Iraq, Syria, Algeria, Morocco, Jordan, and other states but also suggested that Israel, with the Great Powers' assistance, should explore the possibilities of resettling refugees in occupied Sinai and the West Bank.[105] The cabinet, however, chose to "defer the discussion of ways to settle the refugee problem."[106] In his meeting with US Secretary of State Dean Rusk two days later, Foreign Minister Eban attempted to present the indecision in a more promising fashion. He said that the "Israelis wondered whether some [Gaza refugees] could not be settled elsewhere, e.g. [the] northern part of Sinai, 'central Palestine,' or [the] West Bank of Jordan."[107]

With regard to Egypt and Syria, Resolution 563 was on the face of it forthcoming and bold. It proposed peace agreements based on the international borders "and the security needs of Israel"—which arguably meant the return of Sinai and the Golan Heights to Egypt and Syria, respectively—in exchange for full demilitarization of these areas; guarantee of freedom of navigation in the Straits of Tiran, the Gulf of Aqaba, and the Suez Canal, and guarantee of overflight rights in the Straits of Tiran and the Gulf of Aqaba; and guarantee of noninterference with the flow of water from the sources of the Jordan River.[108] In fact, the formulation "based on the international border and the security needs of Israel" was intended to allow Israel to keep some parts of the occupied Sinai Peninsula and Golan Heights. A ten-member cabinet committee, headed by Prime Minister Eshkol and assigned to draft the final version of the resolution, struggled hard to ensure that the resolution's wording would make the option for border modifications implicit but not explicit.[109]

The minutes of the cabinet sessions which ended with the adoption of Resolution 563 clearly show that the discussion was aimed at defining the position Israel should present to the Americans regarding the occupied territories in the secret bilateral talks that were about to commence.[110] The resolution was kept a closely guarded secret even from Chief of Staff Rabin, who learned about it from highly classified cables he read months later at the Israeli embassy in Washington, after he had shed his uniform and been appointed ambassador to the United States in early 1968.[111] Foreign Minister Eban, on the other hand, was specifically authorized by the resolution—the text of which was communicated to him in New York—to convey in confidence to US representatives Israel's terms for withdrawal from Egypt's Sinai and Syria's Golan. Eban, who was attending the emergency special session of the UN General Assembly, met Secretary of State Rusk in New York on 21 June. In his autobiography Eban claims that Rusk and his colleagues could hardly believe their ears when he outlined the magnanimous Israeli proposal, which he later described as "the most dramatic initiative ever taken by an Israeli government before or since 1967, [which] had a visibly strong impact on the United States." Eban continues, "A few days later replies came back through Washington stating that Egypt and Syria completely rejected the Israeli proposal. Their case was that Israel's withdrawal must be unconditional."[112] This account made Israel's search for peace seem convincing.

Numerous scholars and writers, including many Israelis, drew on Eban's account to argue that the Israeli government conveyed the 19 June resolution to the United States so that Washington would pass it along to Egypt and Syria, which in their turn rejected the generous peace offer outright.[113] However, nothing in the resolution suggests such an intention. Moreover, neither the American record of the Rusk-Eban meeting nor the cable sent by Eban to Premier Eshkol immediately afterward mentions any explicit or implicit Israeli request to communicate a proposal to Egypt and Syria. Furthermore, contrary to Eban's claim that Rusk was astonished, the American document mentions only the secretary's perfunctory comment that "it was helpful to have these preliminary thoughts."[114] Eban himself wrote in his contemporary report: "Rusk listened to our thoughts as to peace with Egypt and Syria. He didn't respond."[115] There is also no confirmation from Arab sources that Egypt and Syria received a conditional Israeli offer of withdrawal through the State Department in late June 1967.[116] "No such proposal reached us," insisted Salah Bassiouny of the Egyptian Foreign Ministry in an interview three decades later.[117]

Isma'il Fahmi, a diplomat at the United Nations in 1967 and the foreign minister of Egypt between 1973 and 1977, said that he had been told about the Israeli idea by Rusk only in 1968.[118] By then, the Israeli government had long since effectively retracted the 19 June resolution.

Abba Eban's tale is nothing but a fiction, and the most compelling piece of evidence to prove this came from Eban himself. On 24 May 1968, during a high-level discussion at Premier Eshkol's office, the foreign minister referred to the 19 June resolution and the motives which led to its adoption: the cabinet, he said, had intended to give the Americans something which would motivate them to thwart the Soviet drive for a UN resolution demanding an unconditional Israeli withdrawal from the occupied territories. According to the cabinet resolution, Eban continued, he was authorized to impart its substance *only* to the Americans.[119] Eban reiterated the same explanation behind the closed doors of the Foreign Affairs and Security Committee of the Knesset a few days later.[120] In his second autobiography, *Personal Witness*, which was published in 1993, Eban refrains from claiming that the 19 June resolution had been promptly conveyed to Egypt and Syria and immediately rejected by them; Eban's new version argues that the announcement of the three "no"s of the Khartoum Arab Summit—no peace with Israel, no recognition of Israel, no negotiations with Israel—on 1 September 1967 (see chapter 5), was "a direct answer to the Israeli proposal of June 19."[121] In short, the 19 June resolution was not a generous offer at all but a diplomatic maneuver to win over the one international player that really mattered to Israel—the United States.[122]

The Jordanian Option Presents Itself

The indecisiveness of the cabinet about the fate of the West Bank and the preferable partner in future negotiations—King Hussein or the Palestinians—resulted from real concerns about Israel's security, primarily because of its vulnerable narrow waist (a little more than nine miles wide) at the densely populated center of the country. The debates on 14–15 and 18–19 June did not reflect a passion for expansionism per se, although some ministers, notably Begin, were clearly driven by ideological considerations about "Greater Israel." Another theme which emerged from the deliberations was the perceived threat to the Jewish nature of the State of Israel—the "demographic danger," which underlay the desire to transfer the Gaza Strip's Arab inhabitants elsewhere when absorbing Gaza into the Jewish state. Yet the government's inability to decide emanated not only from strategic, political, and ideological disagreements between its members but also, at least in part, from personal rivalries, particularly between the two leading figures—Prime Minister Eshkol and Defense Minister Dayan.

Eshkol, who on the eve of the war had been forced to relinquish the Defense portfolio in favor of Dayan, held a grudge against his successor. The prime minister reluctantly accepted his advisers' recommendation to congratulate the defense minister, in addition to the chief of staff and the army's generals, for the military victory, in his speech before the Knesset, having at first angrily refused.[123] A week after the end of hostilities, when an old friend recommended that Eshkol should immediately recognize publicly the Palestinians' right for self-determination and for a state of their own alongside the State of Israel, he demurred colorfully: "If I reach out a hand, and no hand is returned in peace, then *Abu Jildah* [Eshkol's derogatory nickname for Dayan] and the *terrorist* [Begin] will give me *a-petsale* [Yiddish: a slap] that will knock me off my chair. And who'll replace me? You already know."[124]

Evidently this was the main reason for Eshkol's decision to handle the political issues regarding the occupied territories, including contacts with Arab personalities, on his own, and to leave the defense minister with the responsibility for day-to-day life and security in those areas. The prime minister informed Dayan unequivocally of his decision on 19 June.[125] Dayan was unhappy with his reduced role.[126] The next day he signed a notice of appointment of an "Advisory Team on Political Matters Concerning the West Bank, the Gaza Strip, and the Syrian Plateau," answering to the defense minister and assigned, among other tasks, "to monitor opinion current[s] among the leadership, population, and various religious groups." In fact, the Advisory Team, whose members were Gen. Chaim Herzog, David Kimche, and two representatives of the Foreign and Interior Ministries, had already been formed a few days earlier, but it never carried out its remit.[127] Following his determination to take exclusive charge of the political issues, Eshkol established another committee, subordinate to him, to explore "the political standpoints of the West Bank and the Gaza Strip," including contacts with their inhabitants.[128] Consequently, Dayan dissolved his team.[129] Two members of Eshkol's new team, which came to be called the Committee of Four, were also members of Dayan's group: General Herzog, now representing the defense minister, and David Kimche on behalf of the Mossad. The other members were Moshe Sasson and Shaul Bar-Haim of the Foreign Ministry. Dr. Ya'acov Herzog, the director general of the Prime Minister's Office and General Herzog's brother, was appointed to supervise the committee's work and to preside over its meetings. However, he was unable to carry out these duties in the coming week.

On 26 June, Herzog traveled to Britain for eight days. On that day Eshkol assured a concerned Israeli citizen, who had sent him a letter proposing to set up a Palestinian-Arab entity, "Your suggestions coincide with one of the possible solutions to these problems, and we are examining them thoroughly. . . . We are now maintaining contacts with the Arab notables in the West Bank and are trying to assess the viability of a Palestinian entity."[130] The other possible solution was dealing with the Hashemite Kingdom. Indeed, the Committee of Heads of the [Intelligence] Services (*Varash*), assigned to guide the Committee of Four, discussed during its meeting on 30 June both the contacts with Palestinian leaders and the prospects of negotiating with King Hussein.[131] The aim of Herzog's trip was to pursue the latter option; he was on his way to see King Hussein in a secret meeting concealed even from Defense Minister Dayan.[132]

The available documentation does not reveal who prompted the meeting, but it is plausible that the initiative came from Hussein, who was eager to retrieve the land he had lost in the war. There is some evidence that the king approached Israel through the British immediately after the war.[133] The Israelis too desired a dialogue with Hussein. On 7 June, the third day of the war, when Hussein pleaded for a ceasefire through the United States and the United Kingdom, Israel responded with a firm demand for direct talks "about anything," and Eshkol instructed Herzog and another Foreign Ministry official to establish contact with the king.[134] A fortnight later Washington offered to mediate between Jordan and Israel, and on 25 June, Eshkol told Eban to stress Israel's insistence on direct talks with Jordan.[135]

The next day, on hearing that Hussein had gone to the United Nations in New York, Herzog flew to London "under adequate cover" and "on instructions from the Prime Minister" in the hope of establishing contact with Hussein there on the king's way back from America.[136] It seems unlikely that a senior official such as Dr. Herzog would spend six days in a foreign capital, waiting, without any prearrangement.[137]

Be that as it may, on the evening of 2 July, three weeks after the fighting had ended, the king of Jordan and the Israeli premier's envoy met for one hour and thirty-five minutes. The two had already met secretly several times in recent years.[138] Like all but one of their past four encounters, this meeting took place at the house of King Hussein's Jewish physician, Dr. Emanuel Herbert, in St. John's Wood in London.

According to Herzog's fifteen-page report, which is the only available primary source, most of the conversation dwelled on the circumstances leading to the war. The king's mood, the Israeli official observed, suggested sadness and fatalism rather than anger and bitterness. Only late in the meeting did Herzog finally ask, "What of the future?" The king replied that the Arab summit conference which he was trying to set up would decide what course the Arabs would take. "If it is peace," Hussein said, "it will have to be peace with dignity and honour." Herzog remarked that the king had yet to tell him officially that he was ready to enter into peace negotiations with Israel. "So long as he did not say so, I could not discuss details of peace settlement." Herzog stressed that he had been sent unofficially to clarify the king's thoughts, yet he shared with Hussein what he described as his own personal view about peace: an economic union between Jordan and Israel, leading to a confederation, with a joint effort to settle the refugee problem. He then volunteered to sum up the king's position: if Hussein were not to succeed in achieving a united Arab line for peace at the summit, he would feel free to act unilaterally in relation to Israel. "Charles [Hussein] nodded agreement," Herzog noted in his account. They parted after deciding to resume contacts following the summit.[139]

During the long discussion neither the Palestinians nor the issues of the West Bank or Jerusalem were mentioned. In any case, Israel, the victor who claimed to seek peace, did not suggest anything concrete to the defeated king. When Julian Amery, a British politician who maintained good relations with the Jordanian monarch, inquired on the day of the meeting about Israel's conditions for peace, Herzog instructed the Israeli ambassador in London to tell Amery that only when Hussein agreed to enter into negotiations would the Israeli government decide on the conditions for settlement.[140]

The Arab phone calls Dayan had expected came without delay—first there was a local call from the occupied territories, and soon afterward Jordan rang. Though King Hussein's agreement to negotiate with Israel was pending until an Arab summit took place, he clearly pronounced his desire to resolve the conflict peacefully. Israel now had two options on the table to choose from: a Jordanian option in addition to the Palestinian option which the West Bankers had already presented to their occupiers.

Thus far Israel's leaders had taken no initiative concerning the future of the Palestinian/Jordanian issue. ʿAziz Shehadeh's peace proposal, which had yielded a cursory survey of political opinions, produced at the executive level several recommendations and schemes advocating the Palestinian option. None of these unilateral ideas had a realistic chance of being acceptable to the Palestinians, but none was discussed in earnest by the Israeli policy makers anyway. Even the magnanimous peace offer embodied by the cabinet resolution of 19 June was never offered to Egypt and Syria, and was merely a diplomatic exercise.

In late June Israeli diplomats assured London and Washington that their government's policy was to reach a settlement with Hussein if possible, and that Israel was willing to make a "pretty favorable deal" with the king if he accepted the idea of peace.[141] At the same time, Premier Eshkol launched another round of talks with the Palestinian leadership, intending to study, yet again, the political viewpoints of its members. The simultaneous pursuit of two mutually exclusive options might suggest that Israel was exploring both in order to reach a decision. This approach would soon develop into a calculated double game, but at this stage it reflected the government's hesitation and confusion: faced with two actual options, Israel deferred decision.

Yet the territorial appetite which the policy makers had been developing from the start of the occupation had already been manifested in political action: the cabinet secretly decided that the Gaza Strip was part of the State of Israel, and it openly annexed the Arab part of Jerusalem. As we shall see, the latter step served as a powerful deterrent to many of the West Bankers who had advocated a separate accommodation with Israel. But as far as Defense Minister Dayan was concerned, what mattered were the "ideal borders" Israel gained in the war.[142] He was not alone. Though the bride was unwelcome, the dowry was irresistible.

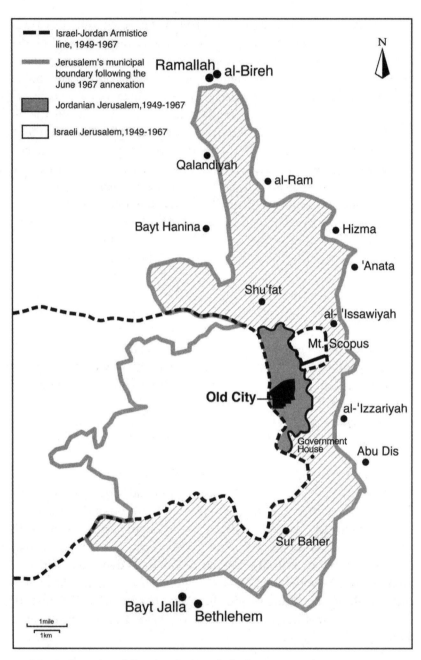

Map 5. Jerusalem following the Israeli de facto annexation in June 1967

T · W · O

The Jerusalem Syndrome

Late June–July 1967

The annexation of Arab Jerusalem was the first concrete demonstration of the growing Israeli wish to have the dowry without the bride. On 11 June, less than twenty-four hours after
the final ceasefire had taken effect, the cabinet agreed to annex
the Arab part of Jerusalem.[1] The decision was carried out on 27 June by
swift passage in the Knesset of three laws which deliberately did not
mention Jerusalem or use the term "annexation." But this was annexation in all but name. The annexed area was twelve times bigger than the
municipal territory of Jordanian Jerusalem. It encompassed, wholly or
partially, the lands of twenty-eight Palestinian villages, and also covered
areas which had been included within the municipal limits of al-Bireh,
Bayt Jalla, and Bethlehem. The boundaries had been demarcated so as to
include the minimum possible number of Arab inhabitants, and the
method by which the annexation was legislated freed Israel from the
need to grant the 70,000 Arab residents of the annexed area Israeli citizenship.[2] Some cabinet ministers even called for the eviction of the Arab
population from Jerusalem. They further recommended immediately
proclaiming the Old City as "abandoned property" and its entire population as "absentees." The idea was not accepted.[3]

What Israel did was against international law.[4] Even Justice
Minister Ya'acov Shimshon Shapira, who stated in the Knesset that "the
eastern part of Jerusalem" had been "liberated" from foreign rule by

the Israeli armed forces, said in the cabinet: "We set about Jerusalem with our eyes open and contravened the Geneva Conventions in the most blatant way."[5] Aware of this breach and fearing diplomatic fallout because of great sensitivity to the issue of Jerusalem worldwide—especially when the UN General Assembly was still debating the Soviet demand for Israel's immediate and unconditional withdrawal from the occupied territories—the Israeli government naïvely attempted to conceal its true intention and the significance of its decision. Legislators were asked by the leaders of the ruling coalition parties to refrain from making grandiose speeches in the Knesset debate, and ministers pleaded with local journalists to downplay their reporting on the legislation process and its import.[6] Israel's diplomatic missions abroad were instructed by the Foreign Ministry to minimize the two laws that effected the annexation of Arab Jerusalem, to highlight the third, which provided for the protection of the holy places, and to characterize the Israeli move as "municipal fusion" aimed at activating the essential services in the Arab part of the city.[7] In New York, Foreign Minister Abba Eban told his British counterpart George Brown on 21 June that "the Israel government only intended to do at practical level those things which would unify the city without annexing it."[8]

In fact, the annexation of Arab Jerusalem, particularly the small walled area known as the Old City, was the one issue on which there was almost a consensus in Israel, it being the ancient capital of the Jewish people and the object of Jewish yearning throughout centuries in the Diaspora.[9] "We have reunited divided Jerusalem, the dismembered capital of Israel," Defense Minister Moshe Dayan proclaimed on 7 June, standing beside the Western Wall (ha-Kotel ha-Ma'aravi)—the remnant of the wall which surrounded the ancient Jewish Temple and the most sacred site in Judaism—just hours after it had been taken. "We have returned to our most holy places; we have returned and we shall never leave them."[10] A day later Premier Eshkol was already talking about resettling Jews in the Old City.[11] The extension of Israeli sovereignty over the Arab part of Jerusalem was meant to last forever. The cabinet made the decision in spite of anticipated strong international disapproval, taking no notice of the objections of Washington, London, and other friendly capitals. United Jerusalem was a fait accompli, Eshkol said unequivocally when former Vice President Richard Nixon, who came to see him on 23 June, asked whether the issue was still negotiable.[12]

It was impossible to hide a move of such magnitude, and all Israel's efforts to misrepresent the annexation of Arab Jerusalem as bureaucratic or technical steps were doomed to failure. Washington pressured Foreign Minister Eban to say at the United Nations that the Israeli act was not annexation but "municipal administration by the occupying power."[13] On 29 June, Eban addressed the General Assembly and claimed that the Israeli legislation was intended "to assure for the inhabitants of all parts of the city social, municipal and fiscal services."[14] Unconvinced, the General Assembly called on Israel a few days later "to rescind all measures already taken and to desist forthwith from taking any action which would alter the status of Jerusalem."[15] The cabinet refused to budge. "The term 'annexation' . . . is out of place," Foreign Minister Eban insisted in a letter to UN Secretary General U Thant the next day. "The measures adopted relate to the integration of Jerusalem in the administrative and municipal spheres."[16] In a cable to Premier Eshkol, Eban cautioned that it would now be impossible to talk about "temporary steps" in Jerusalem.[17]

Before the war Arab Jerusalem was the hub of the West Bank. The Israeli annexation separated the city from the rest of the country. This spelled disaster for Bethlehem, a town of 14,500 in 1967, located just five miles to the south. Jerusalem was Bethlehem's historical source of livelihood, and many of its inhabitants had properties there. Hundreds of prominent residents petitioned the Israeli government several times to "maintain the present situation of Bethlehem with regard to Jerusalem," and not detach their town from Jerusalem.[18] The petitions were ignored. Despite the biblical significance of Bethlehem, the Israelis—determined to limit the number of Palestinians inside the annexed area—excluded the town. In a press conference in August, Defense Minister Dayan disparagingly dismissed the Bethlehem requests, saying that Jerusalem was a unique issue and that the fate of no other part of the West Bank would be determined by the wishes of "the shopkeepers who live there."[19] At the same time, the petitions were represented by Israeli officials and media as the signatories' pleas for their town to be annexed by Israel.[20] Israel's ambassador to the United Nations addressed the Security Council on a Bethlehem petition: "Surely this is an indication of what the real views of the local Arab inhabitants are on the situation in Jerusalem."[21] In fact, the real views of the West Bank Palestinians were very different.

Under the Partition Resolution of 1947, Jerusalem was to become a *corpus separatum*, or separated body, administered by a trusteeship council acting on behalf of the United Nations.[22] By agreeing to the Partition Resolution, the executive of the Jewish Agency endorsed the creation of *corpus separatum*. But in the course of the events of 1948, the leaders of the newly born State of Israel abandoned the idea, and eventually the city was divided between Jordan and Israel. In December 1949 the Israeli cabinet decided to make the Jewish part of Jerusalem the seat of government; that is, the capital of Israel.[23] In contrast, the Hashemite regime, attempting to "Jordanize" the West Bank and to enhance the stature of Amman as the kingdom's capital, deliberately reduced the political-administrative position of Arab Jerusalem even below the status of a second Jordanian capital, as requested by its mayor in the early 1950s, 'Arif al-'Arif.[24]

Nevertheless, the Palestinians were passionate about al-Quds—Jerusalem's Arabic name, meaning the Sanctity. The fall of the Old City in the June 1967 War was for the Palestinians a devastating blow. "They have lost the apple of their eye, Jerusalem, their spiritual capital"—so the British consul general in Jerusalem encapsulated the prevailing mood in one of his dispatches to London.[25] Jerusalem is the third-holiest city in Islam, after Mecca and Medina. It is the site of *al-Haram al-Sharif* (the Noble Sanctuary), comprising al-Aqsa Mosque and the Dome of the Rock (the Jews' Temple Mount). For Christian Palestinians, too, the city is religiously significant. Beyond the spiritual sphere, Jerusalem had worldly importance for the West Bank Palestinians—politically, economically, and culturally. Even the most moderate Palestinians under Israel's occupation refused to accept the annexation of al-Quds to Israel.

This was reflected from the outset of their contacts with the Israelis.[26] Ruhi al-Khatib, the mayor of Arab Jerusalem under Jordan, described the annexation as part of a well-prepared plan to Judaize Jerusalem, going back to the first Zionist Congress in 1897.[27] He warned an Israeli army officer that no rapprochement between Israel and a Palestinian entity would be possible after a unilateral Israeli act regarding Jerusalem.[28] Following the annexation, Anwar al-Khatib, the former Jordanian governor, said that until the arbitrary move he had believed that the Israelis were sincere in wanting to negotiate with the Palestinians, but was now disillusioned.[29] The Knesset's decision was ample proof of Israel's intention to create facts on the ground and dictate its terms. Israel, he concluded, was not looking for peace.[30] Still, the West Bank notables did not abandon their desire to resolve the conflict peacefully. But as the American consul general in Jerusalem observed, the more the Israelis strengthened their grip on the Old City, the more disenchanted the Palestinians became about the prospects for a separate settlement.[31] The Israelis learned firsthand about this shift of mood through the talks the Committee of Four held with West Bank leaders immediately after the annexation of Arab Jerusalem.

The Committee of Four

Formally the Special Interministerial Committee for Political Contacts in the Occupied Areas came into being on 4 July 1967, when Prime Minister Eshkol sent a letter of appointment to five officials, instructing them to follow the "guidelines which have been given to you orally." The five men were Dr. Ya'acov Herzog, the director general of the Prime Minister's Office; Gen. Chaim Herzog, the defense minister's representative; Moshe Sasson, who headed the Foreign Ministry's Armistice Department, which became redundant following the war; Shaul Bar-Haim, the director of the Foreign Ministry's Middle East Department; and David Kimche on behalf of the Mossad.[32] Dr. Herzog, then still in London, was not expected to take part in the committee's work, only to supervise it. In fact, the committee had been established in June and had already started to carry out its mission. The first meetings with Palestinian notables were held on the very day the prime minister sent his letter of appointment. According to Moshe Sasson, the four members of the active committee split into two teams: one comprised himself and Bar-Haim, both fluent in Arabic; the other included the two native English speakers, Chaim Herzog and Kimche. Only the first team conducted a series of talks with Palestinian dignitaries.[33]

Sasson prepared an organizational scheme which stressed that the committee's aim was solely to listen to the Palestinian interlocutors; hence its members must refrain from expressing any views concerning a possible solution. But in order to encourage the West Bankers to be outspoken, it should be made clear to them that Israel had no intention to withdraw from the occupied territories; thus their fate depended exclusively on the government's decision. Finally, the Palestinians should be asked not to discuss their political future with anyone other than the committee's members, particularly not with the press.[34]

Contrary to the improvised manner in which the Kimche-Bavly talks had been carried out in mid-June, serious preparations were made

for the new round of meetings. In response to Sasson's request, the
Foreign Ministry's Research Department furnished him with a list of
prominent West Bankers, along with their profiles. The Research Department also provided Sasson with a short preliminary outline of the
West Bank's political structure. The paper argued that many West
Bank politicians had higher education, mostly from the American University of Beirut (AUB), "which was known for its Arab nationalistic
atmosphere," and adhered to those beliefs. Yet their affiliations spread
across the full range of the political spectrum. Some of them were
members of the PLO and its Palestinian National Council (PNC), but
PLO membership did not guarantee fervent nationalism any more than
nonmembership disproved such convictions. "A salient feature of the
political activity of West Bank personalities is *opportunism*," the outline continued, giving three examples of West Bank figures who had
completely changed their political postures and replaced one political
home with another.[35]

The paper was rather sketchy and general, but thanks to the
background material most of the West Bankers whom Damascus-born
Sasson and Baghdad-born Bar-Haim met were indeed prominent Palestinians. Between 4 and 12 July they held twenty-three meetings with
twenty-five men from Jerusalem (five), Ramallah (seven), al-Bireh (one),
Nablus (three), Hebron (five), and the Jericho area (four). Nine of the
twenty-five were former cabinet ministers; five others were current or
former members of Jordan's Chamber of Deputies; six were current
or former mayors; and others were high-ranking officials, including district governors and ambassadors. On the whole, they represented the
traditional, pro-Hashemite West Bank elite. Only two were conspicuous exceptions to the rule: Ibrahim Bakr, a lawyer from Ramallah and
a Communist; and Kamal Nasir from Ramallah, an al-Ba'th activist.
Many other influential dignitaries and leaders, moderates and radicals
alike, were not approached by the two Israeli officials.[36] Little wonder,
then, that the majority of the West Bank leaders who were interviewed
advocated a peace settlement between Israel and Jordan. Still, the overall opinions expressed were more nuanced and complex.

Most striking was the desire to make peace with the Jewish state.
No fewer than twelve of the Palestinians, including the radicals Ibrahim
Bakr and Kamal Nasir, talked explicitly and emphatically about the ne-
cessity to resolve peacefully the Arab-Israeli conflict. The same view

was implied by others too. The recent war had sobered the Palestinians, some of the notables admitted. "There is no room for more wars between Israel and the Arabs," asserted Hikmat al-Masri, a senator from Nablus and former cabinet minister and speaker of the Chamber of Deputies. At the same time, however, the Palestinian interviewees stressed the need for an honorable and just settlement. Those two terms, "honor" and "justice," were repeated time and again. "The Palestinians want peace and to live in peace," Anwar Nuseibeh explained, "but only if the solution is an honorable one; not a victor-vanquished settlement." In other words, Israel should not seek a settlement which would humiliate the Arabs; Israel must be magnanimous. A number of the dignitaries emphasized solution of the refugee problem as an imperative, suggesting that this could be achieved by generous compensation. "The refugees would choose to be compensated rather than returning [to their previous homes]," Mayor Ja'bari of Hebron predicted.

As noted, most of the Palestinian interlocutors recommended the return of the West Bank to King Hussein's rule. During the previous twenty years a fully integrated state had been created, Bakr, Nasir, and Masri argued. The banks of the Jordan River had become closely linked—economically, socially, and culturally—and the West Bankers would never agree to be cut off from Jordan and the Arab world. Not all who advocated resumption of the Hashemite sovereignty were Jordanian patriots. "The return of the [West] Bank [to Jordan] would not require any special status for the land or the Palestinians," former Minister Rashad al-Khatib from Hebron said. "The Palestinians will take control of Jordan anyway, in the course of time." In practical terms, many dignitaries urged the Israeli government to negotiate a settlement with Hussein.

Mayor Nadim al-Zaru of Ramallah disclosed that a group of notables had met with former Governor Anwar al-Khatib and agreed that the king should be consulted about the position they should take. He should even be pressured to enter into peace negotiations with Israel, based on the return of the West Bank to Jordan and some border modifications in favor of the Arabs. 'Isa 'Aql, a member of the Chamber of Deputies from Ramallah, added that Anwar al-Khatib "and the like" had advised prominent West Bankers not to commit themselves to any "anti-Jordanian" or "anti-Arab" solution in their dealings with the Israeli officials.[37] Khatib seems to have been acting in concert with the Hashemite court. An American diplomat reported from Jordan in mid-July that King Hussein had sent word to Khatib, asking him to come to Amman for discussions on laying the groundwork for a settlement. Not receiving a reply, the king requested American assistance in persuading Israel to let West Bank notables cross over for consultations with him.[38]

Zaru's and 'Aql's accounts of Anwar al-Khatib's maneuvering were confirmed by Daud al-'Isa, the Jerusalemite journalist who had effectively initiated the first contact between Kimche and Bavly and 'Aziz Shehadeh. 'Isa gave Sasson and Bar-Haim a glimpse of the behind-the-scenes deliberations the Palestinian leaders had held in preparation for their meetings with the two Israelis. The notables, 'Isa confided to Sasson and Bar-Haim, were fearful of being accused of treason at the imminent Arab summit and had attempted to formulate an agreed position for the contacts with the Israelis.

Two of the most experienced and respected statesmen in the West Bank, Anwar Nuseibeh and Antoun 'Atallah, recommended a comprehensive solution to the Arab-Israeli conflict. 'Atallah, a bank director and former foreign minister, argued that Israel should begin its quest for a settlement with the wider circle—the Arab world as a whole—and then narrow it in accordance with the difficulties it might encounter. To this end Israel should use any source of influence in the Arab world. The settlement he envisaged was a triple confederation—Israel, Jordan, and the West Bank. Nuseibeh saw President Gamal 'Abd al-Nasser of Egypt as the key to any Arab-Israeli settlement; Nasser, he said, should be the chief negotiator on behalf of the Arab states. It was incumbent upon the West Bank Arabs to persuade Nasser to come to the negotiating table; if he did not agree to do so, then Jordan should take the lead. Only if Hussein also declined should a bilateral settlement between Israel and the West Bankers be negotiated, with the Palestinians serving as a bridge between Israel and the Arab states. In the latter case, the settlement should be based on the UN Partition Resolution of 1947, with necessary changes in favor of Israel to reflect developments since 1947.[39] Nuseibeh commented that he would not object to total annexation of the West Bank by Israel, on condition that the integrated state be called Palestine and have a Lebanese-style system of government, which would provide an agreed ratio of seats in government and allocation of such key offices as president, prime minister, and so on. Both Nuseibeh and 'Atallah undertook to act openly for a peaceful resolution.

Of the twenty-five interlocutors only one, Mayor 'Abd al-Jawad Saleh of al-Bireh, demonstrated an unrelentingly extremist position. He was open and blunt about his feelings toward the Israelis. When Saleh first met the military governor of his area, he stated that he hated the Israelis, he was still fighting them, and he wished to see them leave soon.[40] In the conversation with Sasson and Bar-Haim, Saleh said that Mandatory Palestine must become an undivided country again, with an Arab majority. The Palestinians, the mayor continued, did not want a truncated state in the West Bank. While the only source for what the Palestinians said during this round of talks is the series of the rather concise memoranda composed by the two Israelis—which inevitably reflect their understanding and preferences—'Abd al-Jawad Saleh later presented a view from the other side. In an article published in 1978 Saleh describes a meeting he had with Moshe Sasson which took place during "the first days of the occupation." According to his own account, he told the Israeli official that as a mayor his responsibilities were confined to municipal matters; he therefore refused to discuss his political thinking. Yet he eventually stated: "The solution is—either we [Palestinians] or you [Israel]; there is no third choice." Saleh's testimony is, however, problematic. First, he does not mention the presence of Shaul Bar-Haim, Sasson's partner. Second, he describes Sasson as an adviser to *ra'isat al-wuzara*—Arabic for a female prime minister. But Golda Meir became Israel's prime minister almost two years later, in March 1969.[41]

Seven dignitaries expressed explicit, unequivocal objection to the idea of an independent Palestinian state in the occupied territories. It would never be viable, Ibrahim Bakr and Kamal Nasir insisted, and Nadim al-Zaru added that because the Arab world would not recognize such a state, it would be completely isolated. Some were ready to contemplate a Palestinian state if all the other options were exhausted. 'Isa 'Aql, the only one to support the idea unreservedly, claimed that those who were against it and called for the return of the West Bank to Jordan, did so only because they were not certain about Israel's intentions; they feared an Israeli withdrawal which would put them at risk when the Hashemites took over. 'Aziz Shehadeh, who had actively advocated the establishment of a Palestinian state, told Sasson and Bar-Haim that following the annexation of Jerusalem, an independent state was inconceivable.[42] Therefore he inclined to the idea of a Palestinian-Israeli confederation, which would allow the Palestinians access to Jerusalem and would incorporate Jordan at a later stage.

For the Palestinian notables the question of Jerusalem seemed the most acute stumbling block in the pursuit of a peaceful accommodation. Some of them did not mince words. Anwar Nuseibeh said that the annexation of Jerusalem infuriated him. It destroyed almost any prospect for a settlement; he for one would never support an agreement that recognized the annexation, and no Muslim would ever accede to a settlement which put the Islamic holiest sites under Israeli control. Anwar al-Khatib pledged that if the annexation was final, he would emigrate. Jalil Harb, former mayor of Ramallah and one-time cabinet minister, warned that the hitherto political war between the Arabs and Israel would now turn into an Islamic holy war.[43] The two secular activists, Ibrahim Bakr and Kamal Nasir, who also stressed the absolute need for al-Aqsa Mosque to be in Arab hands, pointed to the extent of the annexation, which went far beyond the boundaries of the Jordanian Jerusalem. For many West Bankers this was a clear demonstration of Israel's expansionist intentions.

Sasson and Bar-Haim were aware that the opinions they elicited might be prejudiced by the desire of their Palestinian interlocutors to please them.[44] After all, the two sides to these talks—representatives of a people under occupation on the one hand, officials on behalf of the occupying power on the other—were by no means equal. Even the venue of most of the meetings—the local Military Government headquarters—served as an unpleasant reminder of this inequality. In an attempt to get reliable information about the West Bank leadership's internal deliberations and inner thinking, the two Israelis deputized the journalist Daud al-'Isa as their agent and sent him to meet as many dignitaries as he possibly could.[45]

'Isa carried out his secret assignment on 11 and 12 July. According to his written account, he talked to mayors, judges, lawyers, merchants, workers, and ordinary passersby in Jerusalem, Ramallah, Nablus, Tulkarm, 'Anabta, Bethlehem, Bayt Jalla, and Hebron. "The majority of the people want peace in the land," he reported. They expected King Hussein to strive for peace. Some, however, had different views. In Nablus and in Hebron it was suggested that a Palestinian state should be set up, comprising both the West Bank and the Gaza Strip, but even the people who floated this idea feared that such a state would in fact be controlled by Israel. Others proposed a one-state solution—the state of Palestine—in which Jews and Arabs would live together under a Lebanese-style regime. The Palestinian refugees should return to Palestine and Jewish immigration should cease, so that Jews would become a minority. The focal point of 'Isa's account was the dire economic situation in the West Bank following the war. This, he cautioned, might lead to despair and unrest.[46] Despite the journalistic nature of the report, it confirmed what Sasson and Bar-Haim had been told by two dozen prominent Palestinians: the West Bankers were anxious to resolve the Arab-Israeli conflict and to achieve peace.

On 18 July, Shaul Bar-Haim shared the gist of his and Sasson's findings with an American diplomat. There had been a shift in the political opinion in the West Bank, he said. The shock caused by the defeat had worn off; the West Bankers had realized that the Arab states and, incredibly, the Arab governments were still standing. Consequently, many prominent political figures who had favored an autonomous Palestinian entity under Israeli tutelage had changed their mind. Now they said that Israel should try to come to an agreement first with at least one Arab country regarding the disposition of the West Bank. If this failed, then they would find "Israeli Palestine" the only real alternative.[47]

A two-page summary Sasson and Bar-Haim drafted offered a somewhat different conclusion. The document, partly adopting Daud al-'Isa's accounts and arguments almost word for word, maintained that "the 'Jordanian-Israeli solution' is favored by most of the notables. . . . The overwhelming majority insists that Israel should first exhaust every possibility for a peace settlement with Jordan." Here, again, the change in the West Bankers' thinking was attributed to the wearing off of the initial shock and to the severe economic difficulties. The staggering impact on the Palestinians of the annexation of Arab Jerusalem was completely ignored.[48] Furthermore, Sasson and Bar-Haim, who favored the Jordanian option, seem to have allowed their personal inclination to influence the position they represented to their Palestinian interlocutors. Anwar al-Khatib wrote to Sa'd Jum'ah, Jordan's prime minister, that Israeli Foreign Ministry officials had told him that if King Hussein would negotiate with Israel, not only would he be given back the West Bank, but the Israelis would be willing "to discuss" Jerusalem.[49]

In his exchange with the American diplomat, Bar-Haim indicated the probable effect the Palestinian uncertainty about Israel's ultimate intentions had on their position. For David Kimche, another member of the Committee of Four, there was no uncertainty about the crucial role of the government's indecision. In a letter to his journalist brother Jon, sent on 17 July, Kimche wrote that the Palestinians were quick to sense that Premier Eshkol was not interested in a prompt solution and that they adjusted their attitude accordingly. "No one speaks any longer about the establishment of a Palestinian state as an immediate target as was so common two or three weeks ago. . . . For the word has been passed round that, by agreement with the Israelis, King Husain is coming back and will rule again over the West Bank." David Kimche went on to say that Moshe Sasson and General Herzog, his co-members of the Committee of Four, actually welcomed this change of mood as an encouraging step toward peace: "Understandably, the West Bankers take this as a confirmation of an Israeli deal with Husain."[50]

Three days later, however, on 20 July, Kimche joined his committee colleagues in unanimously recommending the prime minister to strive urgently "to reach an immediate peace accord with Hussein."[51] This accord should be based on either triple confederation (Israel, Jordan, and the West Bank) or an Israeli-Jordanian condominium in the West Bank; some border adjustments and demilitarization of the West Bank; an Israeli-Jordanian defense pact; and a formula which would allow the Jordanian monarch to carry the title Defender of the Holy Sites of Islam in Jerusalem. Most important, Hussein must give his unqualified consent to a joint solution to the refugee problem through compensatory payments and through resettling the refugees on both banks of the Jordan River. The Gaza Strip should be annexed to Israel, empty of its refugees, who would be transferred to the East or the West Bank. Until peace with Jordan was achieved, the West Bank should remain under direct Israeli rule. The committee proposed a civilian, centralized regime in place of the Military Government, for the latter signified occupation and provisional circumstances, whereas the former "would indicate to the inhabitants of the [West] Bank that Israel has definitively decided not to withdraw from the [West] Bank." The creation of a Palestinian state, or an Arab "canton" with a special political status, seemed to General Herzog, Sasson, Bar-Haim, and Kimche undesirable "at this stage." Israel, they argued, should hold on to the West Bank and keep it as a bargaining chip for achieving peace with Jordan, as well as a designated area for "final liquidation" (*hisul sofi*) of the refugee problem. They also recommended a "discreet and strenu-ous effort to encourage Arab emigration across the sea," although they did not pin much hope on the success of such an endeavor.[52]

The recommendations, drafted by Sasson and Bar-Haim, could hardly be seen by the Palestinians as honorable and just.[53] On the whole, the West Bankers favored a Jordanian-Israeli settlement, but only after the Israeli government had declined to respond seriously to their overtures aiming at a separate Palestinian-Israeli deal. In fact, this is what the members of the Committee of Four had reported before com-posing their final paper: the shift in the Palestinian thinking had been influenced by the lack of a clear Israeli policy, coupled with pressures from Jordan.[54] Some Palestinians, as we have seen, were disenchanted by Israeli measures and attitudes. Thus the Jordanian option seemed inevitable to Palestinians who felt that Israel had led them to believe that the Hashemite regime was about to return. What had already been sug-gested in the cabinet—"relocation" of Arab refugees by transferring them to the West Bank, the East Bank, and even beyond the sea—was now endorsed by the Committee of Four. The committee did not ad-dress the West Bankers' grievances regarding Jerusalem. It offered them instead indefinite occupation in a civilian guise.

The committee's suggestions were never discussed by the cabinet or in any other policy makers' forum.[55] On 27 July the Committee of Heads of the [intelligence] Services (*Varash*), assigned to guide the Com-mittee of Four, effectively approved the recommendations.[56] The follow-ing day Dr. Ya'acov Herzog noted in his diary that in the morning he had handed "the various papers of the Sasson group," along with other re-lated documents, to Avi'ad Yafeh, Eshkol's private secretary, who prom-ised to read them to the prime minister on their way from Jerusalem to Tel Aviv.[57] This entry in Herzog's diary is the last recorded official refer-ence to the Committee of Four's work.

King Hussein's Démarche

The Israeli government was united on three basic political objectives: direct peace negotiations with the Arab states, free passage through the Straits of Tiran and the Suez Canal, and retention of Jerusalem and the Gaza Strip. Otherwise the policy makers disagreed on almost every-thing, including the methods for achieving their goals, and particularly

on the future of the West Bank.[58] Prime Minister Eshkol himself toyed
with both the Palestinian and Jordanian options. On 8 June he told Harry
McPherson, President Johnson's special counsel, that Israel "could con-
ceive a 'protected state'—neither Jordanian nor Israeli—in the West
Bank lands, managed by international authorities."[59] In early July, Eshkol said in an interview with the French daily *Le Monde* that he could
envisage a demilitarized Palestinian entity in the West Bank, which
would comprise urban centers such as Nablus, Jenin, Qalqilyah, and
Jericho, with the Jordan River as its eastern border. Israel would give
the Palestinians access to the sea and would offer them economic, commercial, and even cultural links.[60] "If they eventually want representation in the UN, I wouldn't mind," Eshkol asserted at a meeting of the
Alignment's Political Committee which was held on the same day he
was interviewed. "I've begun with an autonomous region; if it turns out
that this is impossible, they would get independence."[61] In both the interview and the party forum, Eshkol talked about his desire to resettle
the Gaza refugees in the West Bank or preferably elsewhere. One week
later, however, on 14 July, the prime minister said that Israel was prepared to negotiate with King Hussein, and in a cabinet session on 30
July he broached the possibility of returning the West Bank to Jordan
while maintaining a "security border" along the Jordan River.[62]

Foreign Minister Abba Eban was against granting the Palestinians
autonomy in the West Bank. He held that such autonomy was bound to
develop into a demand for independence which the United Nations,
after admitting so many mini-states, was sure to favor. As a result, Israel
might end up with a fourteenth Arab League state more hostile than
the other thirteen. Eban thus advocated the return of a large part of the
West Bank to Jordan in exchange for a peace settlement.[63] In contrast,
Defense Minister Moshe Dayan believed that the Jewish state had a
rightful claim to *Eretz Yisrael*, or the Land of Israel (namely, the former
Mandatory Palestine), and it ought to redraw the existing map accordingly. Martin Van Creveld, Dayan's biographer, argues that he intended
to retain the West Bank; only how this was to be done was unclear.[64]

In mid-August, Dayan presented to the cabinet a plan he had
been contemplating for some time, to establish what he defined as five
"fists" along the north-south watershed of the West Bank ridge. The area
on both sides of the watershed was the most densely inhabited in the
West Bank, containing four-fifths of the West Bank population. Dayan

suggested that these "fists"—large army barracks surrounded by civilian settlements—should be located near the major Palestinian cities of
Jenin, Nablus, Ramallah, and Hebron, and should be connected by a grid
of roads to Israeli territory inside the Green Line.[65] The cabinet approved
only the building of five permanent military bases on the West Bank
ridge.[66]

Labor Minister Yigal Allon, Dayan's political rival, submitted to
the government on 26 July the plan he had already presented in broad
terms during the cabinet deliberations leading to the 19 June resolution.
The Allon Plan proposed that Israel should annex a six- to ten-mile-
wide thinly populated strip of land along the Jordan River and the
Mount Hebron region including the Judean Desert, while relinquish-
ing the main populated areas of the West Bank to local Palestinian autonomous rule. What the Allon Plan envisaged was, in fact, a Palestinian
enclave in the northern part of the West Bank, completely surrounded
by Israeli territory.[67] The plan was never put to a vote or seriously discussed by the cabinet.[68]

"There is plurality of thinking in Israel," Foreign Minister Eban
informed US Secretary of State Dean Rusk and Undersecretary Eugene
Rostow on 15 July. "Some advocate a Palestinian solution. . . . Others
doubt this is feasible or desirable and urge a Jordanian solution. Israel,"
Eban concluded, "needs an internal decision on whether to seek a Jordanian or Palestinian solution."[69] Less than an hour later, in a separate
meeting with Rostow, the foreign minister already knew that the school
of thought likely to predominate was the one that corresponded to his
own views: "Current [Israeli] thinking supported a return of the West
Bank to Jordan with Jordan being given rights with respect to the Mos-
lem holy places in Jerusalem," he said.[70] Israel's attitude was best summarized by its ambassador to Washington, Avraham Harman, who
told American officials that there were two alternative policies: an active one, of searching for a settlement; and a passive one, of letting the
pressure of the situation operate on the Arab world. Israel, he said, opted
for passivity.[71]

This American-Israeli exchange was not academic. It was conducted in the context of a top-secret Jordanian démarche which Washington endeavored to facilitate. On 12 July, King Hussein revealed to the
American and British ambassadors in Amman separately that he was
ready to make a bilateral settlement with Israel. The Jordanian monarch

believed that the Israeli position was solidifying and that the longer he
waited to act, the less chance he had of getting an acceptable agreement.
Hussein said that he had discussed the matter with Egypt's President
Nasser, who had not objected to the move. The king wanted to know
what the Israelis might do vis-à-vis Jordan if he agreed to a settlement.
Jordan, the king indicated, would have to get back substantially all it had
lost in the war, including the Jordanian sector of Jerusalem.

Secretary of State Rusk regarded Hussein's initiative as a courageous "first important breakthrough toward peace" after the June hostilities. He sent an urgent message to Foreign Minister Eban in New
York and instructed Ambassador Walworth Barbour in Tel Aviv to
convey that message immediately to Prime Minister Eshkol, urging the
Israelis to respond positively and without delay. Rusk specifically advised Israel "to make the broadest kind of gesture possible with respect
to Jerusalem . . . that would in effect explicitly interpret as interim the
administrative arrangements recently placed in effect with respect to
that city."[72]

The Israeli policy makers were aware through an intelligence
source of the green light Nasser had given Hussein to strike a deal with
Israel when the two leaders met in Cairo on 11 July.[73] Hussein saw Nasser
in Cairo on his way back to Jordan from the UN General Assembly in
New York and his meeting with Dr. Herzog in London. Nasser agreed to
Hussein's move on condition that there should be no peace treaty and
no direct negotiations.[74] Nevertheless, the Israeli reaction to the king's
peaceful overture was far from enthusiastic. In a meeting with Ambassador Barbour on 14 July, Premier Eshkol said that he welcomed the
overture from Hussein, although he saw nothing new or surprising in
the king's readiness to negotiate. The prime minister felt, however, that
it was too early for Israel to make concessions. Barbour noted that Eshkol was considerably agitated by the tenor of Rusk's message that Israel
should yield on Jerusalem and indicate willingness to modify the unification of the city. Israel, Eshkol said, was prepared to accept Hussein as
guardian of the Muslim holy places in the Old City, but refused to announce that the steps taken in Jerusalem were "interim."[75]

A somewhat more refined "quick oral reply" to Rusk's approach
on behalf of Hussein was delivered that day by Foreign Minister Eban.
He told American diplomats in New York that Israel's response was
positive, and that the government was ready to enter into discussions

with Jordan at a convenient time and place. Eban offered no concrete Israeli ideas about a settlement, however. When Arthur Goldberg, the American ambassador to the United Nations, asked him whether he could specifically say that the "administrative measures" taken in Jerusalem were interim, Eban retorted that if he did, the "government in Tel Aviv would become interim."[76]

Reports from Amman showed widespread support in Jordan for a settlement with Israel.[77] Jordan's director of *al-Mukhabarat al-'Ammah* (General Intelligence) told American diplomats shortly before Hussein's meeting with Nasser on 11 July that the initial numbness of defeat was giving way to frustration and bitterness, and that people were ready to clutch at any straw—even a separate peace with Israel.[78] On 20 July the British embassy in Amman observed that "King Hussein appears to have begun his campaign to secure Jordanian public support for a policy of negotiating a settlement with Israel."[79] Hussein saw merit in the idea that he should seem to respond to a call by Jordanian Palestinians to negotiate, and that this call could be engineered through a gathering of leading personalities from the occupied West Bank as well as the East Bank. In fact, the king had already taken steps to make this happen. On 16 July, Hussein disclosed to a British diplomat that he had recently received prominent West Bankers, who had agreed to call for him to try to get back the West Bank, if necessary by negotiation with Israel.[80] At this stage Hussein was optimistic about a settlement with the Jewish state. "Soon the West Bank will be returned to Jordan," he forecast to three members of the Executive Committee of the PLO whom he met shortly after his initiative had been launched.[81]

Jerusalem was the crux of any Jordanian-Israeli accommodation. Israeli sovereignty over Jordanian Jerusalem was unacceptable to Hussein. He told British and American diplomats that if the Israelis were determined to exclude Jerusalem from the discussions and insisted that the return of Arab Jerusalem was a nonstarter, then there was no point in his entering into negotiations. The king added that he would be surprised to find the Israelis ready to sacrifice all prospects for a settlement solely in order to maintain their claim to Jerusalem.[82] "It is becoming increasingly clear that it is the return of Jerusalem that they [the Jordanians] are after and that the West Bank is of secondary importance," concluded British Ambassador Philip Adams.[83] But Israel was no less adamant about the annexation of the Old City. Ambassador Barbour, who was called to Washington for urgent consultations, repeated what he had heard from Eshkol before his departure: united Jerusalem under Israeli control was indispensable, and any return to a divided city, as Hussein demanded, was out of the question.[84] Michael Hadow, Britain's ambassador in Tel Aviv, found the Israelis passionately intransigent about Jerusalem and was convinced that nothing would budge them.[85] Citing a still-classified source, the CIA reported in mid-July that "the Israelis are emotional to the point of being irrational (*meshuga*) over the Old City, so its absorption cannot be reversed."[86] A more accurate translation of the Hebrew word *meshoga'* is "crazy" or "insane." The Israeli stance led Secretary of State Rusk to predict that "the issue of Jerusalem will certainly be the most difficult feature of the negotiation, perhaps the breaking point."[87]

In contrast to its policy on Jerusalem, Israel had no agreed position concerning the West Bank. The Israeli response to Hussein's démarche was thus negative as far as Jerusalem was concerned and evasive regarding the West Bank. During the Hussein-Herzog secret meeting at the beginning of the month the Israeli emissary had said that he could not discuss the details of a peace settlement as long as the king did not tell him officially that he was ready to enter into peace negotiations (see chapter 1). Now, after Hussein had conveyed his willingness to negotiate, the Israelis still refrained from talking substance. They simply had nothing to say. Instead, Israel played for time. Its envoys offered a host of excuses for the government's indecision. Israel was uncertain about Hussein's seriousness, they said; the king could no longer be regarded a reliably moderate figure after attacking Israel on 5 June; there were doubts whether the survival of the Hashemite regime was to Israel's advantage; and Foreign Minister Eban went so far as to claim that some people in Israel were considering whether the best tactic would not be to make a separate negotiation with Egypt's Nasser the priority.[88]

Was Hussein really the "great and only hope?" Eban asked rhetorically when he received Ambassador Barbour on 4 August, more than a week after the demise of the king's initiative. He then reiterated the Egyptian argument, wondering whether there might not be a greater opportunity to negotiate with Nasser in his political weakness.[89] Nothing in the historical evidence suggests that negotiations with President Nasser were feasible then, or that the idea was raised by Israeli policy makers. In fact, Eban himself had placed Jordan first on Israel's settlement priority list in his meeting with Rusk in mid-July; Egypt was mentioned second.[90] Nasser certainly was not ready to negotiate. Yet Eban was quite open about his approach when he met British Foreign Secretary George Brown in London on 23 July, as recorded by the latter:

> Eban told me that the readiness he had indicated to negotiate separately with Jordan arose merely from the position Israel had always taken up, that she was ready to talk to anyone at any time. . . . There was no firm Israeli government decision about the terms that could be offered to Hussein, nor even whether it was in Israel's interests to negotiate seriously with him at all.[91]

The United States was formally informed on 18 July that the Israeli government was "carefully examining all the alternatives for a Jordan settlement. . . . It will have a definite position in about two weeks." Minister Ephraim Evron, who conveyed this message upon his return to Washington from Israel, added a personal observation: it would take the Israelis some time to recover from the euphoria and grip the difficult real problems that lie ahead.[92]

The Americans thus deferred the delivery of Israel's response to Hussein. In the meantime they tried to set up a secret meeting between the king and representatives of the Israeli government. Records of this episode are scant, but the few available Israeli and American sources show that the rendezvous, arranged by the Central Intelligence Agency through the Mossad representative in Washington, was scheduled to take place in Switzerland in late July. The CIA told the Israelis that Hussein—desiring to retrieve Arab Jerusalem and the West Bank—wanted to hear the Israeli position "before he burned the bridges with the rest of the Arabs." From New York, Eban cabled his wish to represent Israel, together with Dr. Ya'acov Herzog, in the meeting with the king. But Prime Minister Eshkol felt that it would be unwise to send a cabinet member—either Eban or himself—as long as Israel had nothing conclusive to tell Hussein. Besides, he wanted to consult Eban upon his return from New York, and perhaps other key politicians, before moving forward. The Israelis, moreover, were against US involvement in the meeting for fear of American pressure on behalf of Jordan. Dr. Herzog, who handled the secret channel of communication with Hussein, suggested advising the king that if he wished to talk with Israel, he should use the existing channel. Consequently it was decided, on Wednesday, 19 July, to tell Washington that Premier Eshkol was out of town and unable to respond until his return the following week. A day later the CIA informed Israel that the meeting was off, without explaining why. The Mossad representative in Washington learned later from James Jesus Angleton, the chief of counterintelligence at the CIA, who was also in charge of the agency's "Israeli desk," that the State Department had reached the conclusion that there was no choice but to let Hussein talk with the Israelis without intermediaries.[93]

As the days rolled on, King Hussein was getting nervous about the delay in the answer he had been expecting since 12 July.[94] On 21 July, Hussein was talking explicitly about a peace settlement with Israel which would include exchange of diplomatic representatives.[95] The Israelis, however, were now telling the Americans that they were not ready for serious talks with Jordan, only for initial feelers. McGeorge Bundy, special consultant to the president, informed Johnson of the Israelis' hardening position. In his memorandum he observed "their edginess about the Jordanian negotiations, their increasing interest in solutions that would not return the West Bank to Jordan, and the evidence of political jockeying among their leaders (each tougher than the other)." Bundy regarded a Jordanian-Israeli settlement as an American strategic goal that would not be achieved without US pressure on Israel. He advised the president to consider whether Israeli access to American weapons should be linked to a settlement with Jordan: We are the people with the carrot but also with the stick, he wrote.[96]

The stick was not used, and American diplomatic pressure on Israel was to no avail. Though realizing that the prospects for a settlement were far from promising, Washington could no longer wait. On the evening of 25 July, Ambassador Findley Burns saw King Hussein and delivered the evasive Israeli response, as drafted by the State Department and approved by President Johnson. The Jordanian monarch reacted with deep disappointment, saying that he must now rethink his position. Bitter, he remarked that the United States had made its agonizing choice and had chosen Israel. According to Prime Minister Saʿd Jumʿah, Hussein was very depressed after the meeting. Two days later, when the American ambassador came for another audience, the king's mood improved and his mind was made up. It was not at present feasible to pursue the idea of a bilateral agreement with Israel, he said, because his security situation was too weak for the risks involved and because the Jerusalem problem looked insoluble.[97]

King Hussein's initiative effectively offered Israel "land for peace"—a formula soon to be enshrined in UN Security Council Resolution 242 (see chapter 5). Israel chose to miss the opportunity. The "definite position" it promised Washington on 18 July to establish "in about two weeks" never took shape. Instead, Israel resorted to delaying tactics which later developed, as we shall see in the following chapters, into a foreign policy of deception. In the scholar Nigel Ashton's view, "The strategy of prevarication was appealing not only because it avoided domestic problems, but also because Israel . . . was in no hurry to sacrifice its territorial gains."[98] Foreign Minister Eban provided an appropriate postscript to this episode. "It would be logical for the Jordan Government to indicate . . . a willingness to discuss a peace treaty with us," Eban said in a press conference in Jerusalem in mid-August. But, he claimed, no offer to negotiate came from Jordan or any other Arab country.[99]

Ban on Political Organization

The West Bank political elite was not privy to the international diplomatic maneuvering around King Hussein's initiative or to the Israeli government's internal debate concerning the fate of their occupied region. The Palestinian notables were also oblivious of the Committee of Four's unheeded recommendation that Israel should negotiate a peace accord with Jordan. Although the recommendation was one-sided and meant to serve Israel's interest, in formulating it the committee took account of what it had heard from its twenty-five Palestinian interlocutors. The committee ignored, however, the West Bankers' main motive for advocating a Jordanian-Israeli settlement, which was to rid themselves of the Israeli occupation. Indeed, journalists' soundings of West Bank opinion after the annexation of Jerusalem did not entirely correspond to the Committee of Four's findings. The return of the Hashemite regime, which had ruled for two decades with a heavy, even brutal hand, was not an ideal for many. According to these reports, the West Bankers rejected the concept of an independent state but aspired to exercise their right of self-determination; they demanded the return of the occupied territories to their rightful owners—their inhabitants.[100]

A number of prominent Palestinians attempted to translate these local political wishes into practical language.

One such initiative took place in early July. 'Aziz Shehadeh again, accompanied by 'Abd al-Nur Janho, a wealthy businessman from Ramallah, and five other dignitaries from Ramallah and Bethlehem, requested a meeting with Maj. Gen. Uzi Narkiss, the commanding general of the army's Central Command. In this capacity Narkiss was the titular military governor of the West Bank. Shehadeh, the spokesman of the group, proposed a withdrawal of Israeli forces from the environs of Ramallah, Bethlehem, and Jericho, followed by devolution of domestic affairs to the local inhabitants; foreign, security, and fiscal responsibilities would remain in Israeli hands. This would be considered an experiment. If successful, it would be expanded to the entire West Bank. The idea of experimental autonomy appealed to General Narkiss, and he put it before the defense minister. "Dayan almost threw me out of the room," Narkiss recalled. Explaining his rejection, Dayan said that the scheme would inevitably lead to a Palestinian state, which was to him an utterly undesirable outcome.[101]

While the initiative of the seven dignitaries could be dismissed as not representing the majority of the West Bank leadership, dozens of West Bankers, including some of the most prominent politicians, stood behind another political endeavor which took place around the same time. On 9 July, Muhammad Nasir al-Din Bashiti, a businessman from Sho'afat, a Jerusalem suburb, called on Col. Raphael Vardi, the chief of staff of the Central Command and the de facto military governor of the West Bank, in his Military Government headquarters office in Arab Jerusalem. Bashiti told Vardi that he came on behalf of Anwar Nuseibeh and eighty-two other notables, to request permission to hold a conference to discuss the political future of the West Bank. The list of eighty-three names Bashiti gave Vardi included those of leading members of the West Bank elite: Nuseibeh, Antoun 'Atallah, Anwar al-Khatib, Ruhi al-Khatib, Tiyasir Kan'an, and Walid al-Shak'ah, to name just a few. 'Aziz Shehadeh was also on the list, as well as Muslim and Christian religious leaders. Most conspicuous among them was Sheikh 'Abd al-Hamid al-Sa'ih, the president of the Islamic Court of Appeal. It is likely that the initiative of the eighty-three was motivated by the political talks conducted by Sasson and Bar-Haim: the talks might have led the Palestinians to believe that Israel was genuinely interested in resolving the political future of the West Bank. In any event, Vardi responded that no assembly would be permitted before the matter was considered by the Israeli authorities. The next day he requested instructions from Chief of Staff Rabin.[102]

Anwar Nuseibeh claimed a few days later that Bashiti had put his name on the list without consulting him first.[103] However, Michael Shashar, the Military Government's spokesman, recorded in his diary that Nuseibeh himself came on 11 July to see Vardi about the proposed conference. He told the Israeli officer that Jerusalem should be internationalized and the West Bank—including Beersheba within Israel's prewar Green Line (the Arab town of Bi'r al-Sab' until 1948, thereafter the Israeli city of Be'er Sheva)—should become a Palestinian canton.[104] According to Vardi, Bashiti gave him a letter in which the West Bank notables explained that they wished to discuss whether they should opt for the return of the Hashemite regime or for an independent Palestinian "system." Since this was a purely political matter, the letter was passed on to Dr. Ya'acov Herzog at the Prime Minister's Office. Following a deliberation headed by Herzog, and possibly with Eshkol's approval, it was decided to reject the dignitaries' appeal, and they were informed accordingly.[105] With the hindsight of two decades, Vardi felt that the Israeli denial had negative repercussions for Israel: "Probably as a reaction to this refusal, the Jerusalem religious and political leadership began moves toward independent political action against the wishes of both Israel and Jordan," he said, referring to the eruption of civil disobedience in the West Bank in late July.[106]

As we have seen, all Palestinian requests to convene for the purpose of discussing political matters were rejected. Even a letter from an Israeli official, Moshe Sasson, asking Defense Minister Dayan whether an assembly of West Bank leaders should be allowed, went unanswered.[107] Dayan objected to any Palestinian political activity. "What for?" he snapped when Housing Minister Mordekhai Bentov challenged his position. "Do you wish them to convene and decide that they don't want us? I don't need such a resolution."[108] The ban on political organization became a strict formal policy. Nonpolitical association, including social clubs such as Rotary or Lions, were not permitted to gather, either.[109]

Raphael Vardi, then the de facto military governor, explained thirty-five years later the logic behind the sweeping prohibition: "We concluded that any kind of meeting would eventually turn into a political one. The extremists would take control and consequently the decisions reached, or statements announced, would be extreme. The easiest way to deal with that was, then, to ban any assembly, political or otherwise."[110] Shlomo Gazit, who served as staff officer at Dayan's office in charge of handling the occupied territories and in late 1968 became the first coordinator of government operations in the occupied territories, added retrospectively: "Military administration and free and democratic political activity cannot coexist; this would be a contradiction in terms."[111] And so, while a government propaganda pamphlet boasted in early 1969 that the "Arabs in Judea and Samaria [the biblical names adopted by the Israeli authorities for the West Bank] enjoy rights of political organization, freedom of speech and discussion," a military injunction in effect from late August 1967 interdicted any political activities in the occupied territories. An offender could be jailed for up to ten years.[112]

Israeli occupation authorities attempted to prevent Palestinian leaders from even talking to the press. As early as 20 June, Colonel Vardi instructed the military commanders in the West Bank "to advise" the Arab notables that if they did not cease contacts with journalists, their position "might be harmed."[113] Vardi was following an order from Chief of Staff Rabin, who had been approached about this by Dayan.[114] Elyashiv Ben-Horin, the Foreign Ministry's representative in the West Bank, endeavored to justify the logic behind this attitude to his colleagues, while demanding that no foreign correspondent would be brought together with an Arab notable without his prior approval: because of the ongoing survey of Arab public figures' thinking, Ben-Horin said, it was imperative "to protect" the notables from being "burned" by exposure to the press.[115] In fact, Defense Minister Dayan wanted to forbid foreign and local journalists from entering the West Bank altogether, explaining that the local leaders had begun competing with one another to prove their Arab nationalist bona fides. This edict was countermanded only after high-level intervention by the Foreign Ministry.[116] In addition to forbidding press interviews by Palestinian dignitaries, the Committee of Four recommended against contacts between notables and representatives of Israeli political parties.[117] Ultimately, however, all governmental and military attempts to isolate the West Bank elite failed.

Had the ban on political organization been formulated by the occupation authorities, it might have been regarded as the product of narrow-minded military thinking. But the restrictions on political activity in the occupied areas were dictated by government policy and recommended by some of the officials involved in the actual contacts with the West Bankers. The ban contradicted the declared intention of Israeli leaders to consult the inhabitants of the occupied territories about the political future of their land. For example, Defense Minister Dayan told the mayors of Ramallah and al-Bireh and their councilors in October 1967, "If you wish to bring an end to the military regime, please establish a delegation and let's talk."[118] Dayan's aide Shlomo Gazit claimed in January 1970 that the Military Government was telling the inhabitants of "the territories" that it was their duty to decide which political solution would be best for them.[119] But how could the West Bank Palestinians make such a decision, based on open and unfettered discussion, if they were not allowed to convene? Gazit himself admits: "It was hard to explain Israel's refusal to allow any free political organization or activity."[120]

By the end of July, Israel was left with a single option—the Jordanian one. The shift in the West Bank leadership's thinking rendered the Palestinian option theoretical. The Committee of Four attributed the shift to the lack of a clear Israeli policy and pressure from Jordan. A senior Foreign Ministry official suggested that fear of Hussein's eventual return to the West Bank caused the Palestinians' change of heart.[121] Another Foreign Ministry official alerted Dayan to the linkage between Israel's actions and the West Bankers' political mood. The official, Moshe Sasson, cited, among other examples, the destruction of West Bank villages and the growing problem of the Six Day War refugees who, with some Israeli "encouragement," were streaming eastward to Jordan.[122] Although all these explanations were undoubtedly valid, the single most significant factor was the "Jerusalem syndrome"—the emotional attachment of all concerned to the Old City.[123] Beyond the religious, historical, and cultural aspects of the Israeli control of Arab Jerusalem, the annexation signaled to the Palestinians Israel's ominous political intentions.

"Jerusalem syndrome" also contributed to the failure of King Hussein's peace initiative. The initiative transformed the Jordanian option into a realistic opportunity for a bilateral settlement. Israel effectively rejected this opportunity by claiming that the government was unable to formulate its peace terms. Yet on 30 July the divided cabinet agreed to maintain the ceasefire lines of 10 June until directly negotiated peace treaties were signed with the neighboring Arab states. Two days later the Knesset endorsed the cabinet's new line.[124] Conditioning Arab-Israeli peace on direct negotiations constituted a hardening of the Israeli position. It was the first formal retreat from the cabinet's 19 June resolution, which seemed to offer Egypt and Syria "land for peace." Inside the occupied West Bank, while unrest was mounting, the Israelis were looking for leaders who would lean more toward Israel.

In Search of Docile Leadership

July–September 1967

From the beginning of the occupation Defense Minister Dayan was convinced that a Palestinian uprising was a matter of time. The day after the war he advised one of his underlings to tour the West Bank "before the revolt begins!"[1] The occupied territories were Dayan's responsibility. His pessimistic prognosis, coupled with the lessons he drew from the American experience in Vietnam, led him to formulate a policy of indirect rule, or "invisible administration," under which "an Arab can be born, live and die in the West Bank without ever seeing an Israeli official." The "open bridges" that allowed the Palestinians from early July 1967 onward to resume trade and, to a lesser extent, travel between the two banks of the Jordan River, constituted an essential element of Dayan's policy. The declared purpose of this policy was to minimize any potential points of friction between the occupiers and the occupied and to reinforce the return to normal life. Dayan, who did not anticipate any political resolution in the foreseeable future, wanted "business as usual" in the occupied territories.[2]

Dayan's policy was designed to facilitate a trouble-free occupation. But the annexation of the Old City by Israel in late June provoked Palestinian unrest, beginning in Arab Jerusalem, from which, paradoxically, Israel had unilaterally lifted the military regime. The unrest was fomented by local dignitaries and political activists, with others in the rest of the West Bank soon following suit. Israel, which sought the cooperation of the Palestinians under its occupation, was striving to subdue any political activity in the occupied territories and concurrently attempting to mold a submissive second-tier leadership.

Operation Sadducees

The Military Government's proclaimed policy was strictly to avoid making use of Palestinian quislings, or collaborationist leaders, whose authority with the local population derived from their loyalty to, and the protection of, the Israeli authorities.[3] In truth, however, Israel pursued this very objective from the start of the occupation. Throughout the preceding nineteen years Israel's policy with respect to its Arab minority (until 1966 under restrictive military government) had been to cultivate an alternative leadership of lesser stature that, in return for privileges and personal favors, would cooperate with the government.[4] Now Israeli policy makers and officials—wishing to neutralize independent-minded Palestinian leaders and to influence others through material rewards—intended to employ similar methods in the occupied territories.[5] As early as 16 June, in a meeting at Dayan's office, Gen. Rehav'am Ze'evi, assistant head of the army's General Staff Branch, argued that there was no chance that the current Arab leaders would cooperate with Israel. Therefore, he suggested, Israel should cultivate a secondary echelon of local leadership, one that would be willing to accept minimal conditions for a peace settlement with Israel.[6] The Committee of Four also recommended "nurturing" West Bank leaders, in part by granting them favors.[7] In the committee's final report to the prime minister this recommendation was repeated and expanded: "We shall cultivate desirable renowned Arab leaders, and will use some of them for implementing our policy in the [West] Bank, as well as our political activity in the Arab world in general and in Jordan in particular."[8]

The West Bank Committee—an extended interdepartmental body comprising high-ranking officials, which had been meeting at the Prime Minister's Office during the initial period of the occupation—went even farther. On 11 July the committee decided to set up a special structure in charge of "supervising and nurturing the Arab leadership in the West Bank." Yosef Harmelin, the GSS chief, was appointed as the coordinator, and the other designated members were Shaul Bar-Haim (Foreign Ministry), David Kimche (Mossad), Shmuel Toledano (the prime minister's adviser on Arab affairs), and Gen. Chaim Herzog (Defense Ministry).[9] Five days later, during an advisory committee's meeting presided over by Eshkol, former GSS chief Amos Manor proposed organization of a group of Palestinian notables expected to demand peace. Consequently Dr. Herzog told Manor that he would suggest that Harmelin include him too in the "supervisory body."[10] Harmelin, however, felt that instead of creating a "nurturing mechanism," it would be better to let his agency handle the matter. After all, the GSS had been a key player in the Arab arena inside Israel until 1967 and had gained plenty of experience. In its meeting on 19 July the West Bank Committee adopted Harmelin's position, provided that this project be carried out in close coordination with the Foreign and Defense Ministries. Dr. Herzog added that the concept of peace should be instilled in the consciousness of the West Bank notables; "Harmelin would take care of that."[11] The next week, following the first serious expressions of Palestinian resentment and civil disobedience, Moshe Sasson urged Foreign Minister Eban to expedite creation of the GSS's supervisory body "and to establish without delay the nurturing structure which was decided upon."[12]

Old habits die hard. Israel resorted to the same methods which had been applied before the war with regard to its Palestinian citizens. Permits to travel to the East Bank were issued in the early days of the occupation "to reward certain [West Bank] individuals," and permits to visit Israel were granted "in some cases" to West Bankers "according to a policy of reward and punishment."[13] The "reward approach" particularly targeted influential persons. For example, David Kimche reported to his superiors in mid-June that Sheikh Ja'bari, the mayor of Hebron, had requested Israel's help in facilitating the return of some members of his family from the East Bank. "This could be used to pressure him," Kimche noted.[14] The Foreign Ministry strove to allow Anwar Nuseibeh's sons, who were in London, to visit their parents in Jerusalem. "We need Nuseibeh's good offices and arranging a visa would be helpful to us," argued Teddy Kollek, the mayor of Jerusalem, in a cable to Israel's ambassador in the United Kingdom sent through the Foreign Ministry.[15] There was no real need to pressure Ja'bari, and favoritism seemed unlikely to work in the case of Nuseibeh. Thus the efforts to buy the goodwill of the notables went beyond these individual cases and turned into a comprehensive effort. It was decided to "lend" monthly or one-time sums of money to dignitaries—specifically former members of the Jordanian cabinet and members of Jordan's legislature—who despite their wealth suffered from a lack of ready cash. The Middle East Department of the Foreign Ministry was assigned to prepare a list of potential beneficiaries.[16]

The most ambitious venture in this regard was executed by the GSS. Harmelin put Victor Cohen, head of the GSS Interrogation Branch and fluent in Arabic, in charge of this endeavor, code-named *Mivtsa' Tsdokim* (Operation Sadducees), which was directed at all those who belonged to the West Bank political elite. The assignment was to establish relationships with mayors, former Jordanian cabinet ministers, senators, members of the Chamber of Deputies, religious leaders, and all other kinds of local politicians, and turn as many of them as possible into "pro-Israelis," who would cooperate with the authorities and promote Israeli interests. The purpose was, in Cohen's own words, to create quislings.[17]

With a generous budget for dispensing material benefits and "good time," Cohen began his contacts with Palestinian notables. Essentially, Cohen suggested to each of his targets, You scratch our back and we'll scratch yours (in colloquial Palestinian Arabic, *id ibtighsil id*, literally: one hand washes the other); we'll take care of your *personal* interests—and your public ones as well, if you wish, but first and foremost your own private interests—and you'll take care of our political interests.[18] For instance, Cohen told Mayor Hamdi Kan'an of Nablus that the return of the ten or so peasants who cultivated his arable lands in the Jordan Valley, now left unattended because of the peasants' flight to the East Bank during or immediately after the war, could be arranged. Then the Israeli added a not too subtle hint indicating that the mayor was expected to reciprocate. He further suggested that they should lunch at the Tel Aviv Hilton in a few days. Kan'an agreed. Subsequently they started to meet regularly. According to Cohen, Kan'an never rejected his overtures; on the contrary, he said, the Palestinian dignitary was quite forthcoming. So was Sheikh Ja'bari, "who was limitlessly ready to cooperate with us. In fact, he was corrupt."[19] The GSS officer concluded: "They all went for it," with the exception of the intellectuals—mostly journalists and writers from Jerusalem—who were radical nationalists. He described the traditional, pro-Hashemite politicians as a "rotten class."

Nothing in Victor Cohen's account, however, indicates that the Palestinian dignitaries delivered favors of substance. This is not to say that they did not have personal interests, or that they refused to enjoy certain privileges and rewards bestowed upon them by the Israelis. But they may never have had any intention of giving anything in return. As the Israelis had their own agenda, so did the Palestinians. Furthermore, sometimes collaboration is in the eye of the beholder. For acting Military Governor Raphael Vardi, 'Aziz Shehadeh and others who shared his views were "quislings," whereas Cohen regarded Shehadeh as neither a corrupt political leader nor a radical nationalist; "he stood somewhere in between."[20] Cohen genuinely believed that in time the operation could have been successful: "There was an opportunity to mold a docile leadership." Thus he was alarmed when one day, on the eve of an important debate at the United Nations, he was ordered by Yosef Harmelin to arrange public statements in favor of Israel by West Bank leaders. Cohen explained to the GSS chief that once these leaders went public with their support of Israeli interests, they would be "burned" and useless. Their cooperation should be clandestine, he insisted.

It is not clear whether Harmelin accepted Cohen's position, but Operation Sadducees ended three or four months after its inception because of the "wars of the Jews," as the Shabak man put it. General Narkiss asked Victor Cohen to carry out his assignment in cooperation with the Military Government, as if he were a staff officer. Cohen could not make good his promises to the Palestinians—such as arranging the return of people from the East Bank, travel permits, and so on—without the collaboration and approval of the Military Government. Therefore he accepted Narkiss's suggestion. Soon afterward, however, he realized that the Military Government people were unhelpful to such a degree that they torpedoed his mission.

Victor Cohen felt that the demise of Operation Sadducees, in October or November 1967, was the result of Defense Minister Dayan's objection to any dealings with quislings. Given that the order to execute the project reportedly had come from the prime minister, one could argue that the Eshkol-Dayan rivalry played a role in its failure.[21] But in mid-October, Dayan himself approved the idea that "key men" among the West Bank Palestinians should be appointed to various administrative positions "with the purpose of cultivating alternative leadership."[22]

Operation Sadducees was launched when the Palestinian unrest, which had been simmering since the end of June, was reaching boiling point. The annexation of Arab Jerusalem, followed by the Committee of Four's futile round of talks and the ban on political organization, augmented the frustration resulting from the occupation. Around 23 July, Moshe Sasson cautioned Foreign Minister Eban that the positions of many West Bank notables had dangerously shifted since the talks held by the Committee of Four during the first half of the month, becoming overtly hostile.[23] The Israeli attempts to enlist local politicians as collaborators—hardly a recipe for a just peace settlement—could only aggravate the situation. 'Aziz Shehadeh, ever eager to bring about a Palestinian-Israeli accommodation, acknowledged in mid-July that "the honeymoon between [the] occupiers and [the] occupied was over."[24]

The 24 July Assembly

An ominous harbinger of the Palestinians' radical change of mood appeared immediately after the annexation of Arab Jerusalem. A leaflet, circulated in the Old City and signed *Al-Nidal al-Sha'bi al-Quds* (The popular struggle, Jerusalem), warned against any cooperation with the Jews.[25] In the following days a few more leaflets were distributed, including one signed *Abna' al-Quds al-Ahrar* (The free sons of Jerusalem) and another which the Israelis suspected was issued by members of the Jordanian Communist Party (JCP). These leaflets also cautioned against "more than the necessary" collaboration with the Jews.[26] The JCP was the only political group which managed to maintain an organizational network in Arab Jerusalem despite being constantly hunted by Jordan's security services.[27] But it was not responsible for any of those leaflets; the Communists had more ambitious plans for resisting the Israeli occupation. Their preparations started in earnest with the arrival in Jerusalem of one of their leaders, Na'im al-Ashhab, in late June.

Ashhab, a thirty-eight-year-old Jerusalemite, infiltrated the West Bank from Jordan. He had been imprisoned for his Communist activity ten months before and on 16 June had been taken from his East Bank jail to a meeting in Amman with Gen. Muhammad Rasul al-Kilani, chief of Jordan's General Intelligence. Kilani told Ashhab that the situation in the West Bank was very grave since some of the traditional leaders had begun wooing the Israelis. Pinning his hopes on the Communists' skills in clandestine activity, the general asked Ashhab to cross over into the occupied territory. Ashhab responded that he would go to the West Bank not because of Kilani's request but because he believed it was his conscientious duty. When he got to Jerusalem, Ashhab contacted prominent politicians with the urgent aim of stopping the huge outflow of Palestinians to Jordan by establishing a national guidance committee. Ashhab and his Communist associates saw the looming specter of a repetition of the Palestinian flight and expulsion of 1948. However, the Jerusalem leaders chose to wait. Ruhi al-Khatib, the mayor of the Jordanian sector of Jerusalem, said that "quiet" was necessary for the time being.[28]

Following the Knesset legislation whereby Israel absorbed the Old City, the Jordanian municipality of Arab Jerusalem ceased to exist. Military government over Arab Jerusalem was abolished, and government ministries and the municipality of the Israeli part of Jerusalem assumed responsibility for the Old City affairs. As stated in a classified military document, the purpose of this move was "to reflect the political fact of the annexation of [Arab] Jerusalem."[29] On 29 June Military Government officers unceremoniously informed Mayor Ruhi al-Khatib and his councilors that their municipality had been dissolved. Khatib, who during the preceding three weeks had cooperated faithfully with the Military Government in bringing life back to normal, felt bitter and humiliated by the hasty and undignified manner of this dissolution, as did his councilors.[30] Nevertheless, Khatib remained ready to work with the Israelis for the good of Jerusalem. On 20 July he asked two Israeli officials who came to see him to deliver this message to Mayor Teddy Kollek.[31] But Khatib's willingness to cooperate did not include any actions that might be construed as legitimizing the Israeli occupation and the annexation of Arab Jerusalem.

Khatib and seven members of the city council thus announced their refusal to join the municipal council of Israeli Jerusalem and to create thereby a municipal council of the unified city. "The mere discussion of the question of joining the Jerusalem Municipal Council under the Israeli rule proclaimed by the Israeli authorities constitutes an official recognition by us of the principle of the annexation of Arab Jerusalem to the Israeli-occupied part, an annexation which we refuse to accept as a fait accompli," they stated on 22 July in declining the invitation of the Israeli official who had summoned them.[32] The American consul general speculated that in addition to the points of principle which they put forward in support of their stand, the eight notables might have been influenced by fear of reprisals against collaborators, promised in the leaflets that had been circulated in recent weeks.[33] That may have been a factor, but in any case, within forty-eight hours the "quiet" that Ruhi al-Khatib had recommended was over, and civil disobedience broke out in the West Bank.

The opening salvo was fired on 24 July. A group of prominent Palestinian leaders gathered at the hall of the Islamic Court of Appeal in Jerusalem. They were convened by Sheikh ʿAbd al-Hamid al-Saʾih, the president of the court, in the wake of a long series of discussions about what had been regarded as Israeli interference in Islamic religious affairs and the Islamic legal system. Yet only five of the participants were religious leaders; the majority were politicians and members of the nonreligious elite, even including a Communist—Ramallah lawyer Ibrahim Bakr. The group drafted a statement addressed to the military governor of the West Bank, in which they not only protested against the Israeli infringement on Islamic matters but also stressed in no uncertain terms that Arab Jerusalem was "an integral part of Jordan," and that its annexation by Israel was "null and void." They demanded that the annexation resolution be rescinded and that intervention in Islamic religious issues stop. Finally, the group proclaimed itself *Al-Hayʾah al-Islamiyyah,* the Islamic Council, in charge of Islamic affairs in the West Bank, including Jerusalem, "until the termination of the occupation."

Twenty signatures appeared on the document, written under a letterhead which read "The Hashemite Kingdom of Jordan." Former Governor Anwar al-Khatib led the list, followed by Mayor Ruhi al-Khatib, the five senior Muslim functionaries, and other eminent men, representing the Jordanian establishment as well as Jordan's opposition activists belonging to al-Baʿth, al-Qawmiyyun al-ʿArab, the JCP, and the PLO. Nowhere in the long, legalistic text did the terms "Palestine" or "Palestinians" appear. In fact, the signatories committed themselves to Jordanian sovereignty over the West Bank and Arab Jerusalem. In establishing the Islamic Council they opted to resuscitate a body which had been created by the British Mandate authorities in 1922 and headed by Hajj Muhammad Amin al-Husseini, the Grand Mufti of Jerusalem. Designed to allow the Muslims to handle their religious matters under the sovereignty of a non-Muslim ruler, this body was dissolved by the British in 1937 in response to the Arab Revolt. The rejuvenated council appointed Sheikh ʿAbd al-Hamid al-Saʾih as its chief, and the memorandum it drafted was promptly delivered by hand to foreign consuls and correspondents.[34]

According to Sari Nusseibeh's autobiography, published in 2007, his father, Anwar, took part in establishing the Islamic Council and envisioned it "as a representative institution that could give a voice to the people under the new occupation."[35] At the time, however, Anwar Nuseibeh himself tried to belittle the significance of the 24 July assembly. Originally, he told US Consul General Wilson, the intention was only to express nonacceptance of the Israeli takeover of the Old City. Nuseibeh, who had been invited to the gathering but did not go, described the conference as merely a "private meeting [of] community leaders determined [to] place on record their objection to [the] Israeli exercise of sovereignty in [the] Old City." Had he gone, Nuseibeh said to a Military Government officer, without elaborating the reasons for his absence, he would have signed the petition. The press, he complained to the American diplomat, had "greatly exaggerated [the] matter."[36]

Dr. Ya'acov Herzog, the director general of the Prime Minister's Office, was also unhappy with the press coverage. He asked Israeli journalists "to play down" the whole affair and instructed his subordinates to respond with "no comment" to foreign press queries about the matter.[37] Nevertheless, the *New York Times* correspondent in Jerusalem reported that the 24 July assembly "developed into the first political demonstration against Israeli control since the end of the recent war," and the Israeli press went even farther, describing the notables' statement as an "anti-Israeli petition" and a display of rebelliousness.[38] Both Nuseibeh and Dr. Herzog were, of course, fully aware of the true import of the Palestinian move, and the Israelis viewed it very seriously. The notables' statement was a disturbing addition to the blunt rejection of the Arab Jerusalem councilors of participation in a unified municipality, the refusal by most of the West Bank judges to return to the bench, and other manifestations of unrest, including indications of West Bank teachers' intention not to open the school year at the end of the summer break.[39] Upon receiving the manifesto—copies of which were also sent to the prime minister and to the minister of religious affairs—Herzog convened an emergency meeting of the interdepartmental West Bank Committee.

In the meeting, held in the afternoon of 25 July and attended by the directors general of the Prime Minister's Office and the Foreign Ministry, the GSS chief, the de facto military governor of the West Bank, and a few other officials, it was agreed to separate the practical religious matters from the "secular" political ones, including the establishment of the Islamic Council. An effort was proposed to come to terms with the Muslim leaders regarding the Islamic issues, such as the Israeli demand to censor the al-Aqsa mosque Friday sermon (*khutbah*). The participants in the discussion effectively accepted that quite a few of the Arabs' practical complaints were well founded. For example, the 24 July statement argued that the censorship of the Friday sermon resulted in the deletion of many passages, including verses of the Qur'an. The functionary who carried out the censorship was Ya'acov Yehoshu'a, head of the Muslim Affairs Department at the Ministry of Religious Affairs. "He did not like the Arabs," conceded Minister of Religious Affairs Zerah Warhaftig in his memoirs. "Perhaps he was somewhat rigid in censoring the *Mufti*'s sermons during the initial period [of the occupation]." On the other hand, a consensus formed in the meeting that strict steps should be taken against the political aspects of the statement and other expressions of discontent. The high-ranking officials suggested "selective arrests among those behind the various occurrences, together with a search for an appropriate explanation." Further, "suitable steps" were recommended "to take care of" some of the notables' property, "as a warning and deterrence to others." [40]

In the following days the subject was hectically deliberated in various top-level forums, including the cabinet. Although the steps taken by the West Bankers were political or passive, the prime minister warned at a meeting of the Alignment's Political Committee on 28 July: "We tried [to approach the Palestinians in the occupied territories wearing] kid gloves, but it turns out that under the '*abayah* [a traditional Arab cloak-like garment] a knife is being sharpened." Eshkol went on to say that the government would start using a strong hand against certain individuals in the West Bank, prominent ones among them. [41] Essentially, all the panels endorsed the initial proposals, with minor modifications. The main concern revolved around how Israel should best react; the available records reveal no serious discussion about what had triggered the Palestinian moves. Premier Eshkol suggested that the "problem" resulted to a large extent from lack of clear political security guidance and poor coordination between the government ministries and the security organs. [42] Evidently he and the others failed to comprehend what the unilateral annexation of Arab Jerusalem, coupled with the overall Israeli attitude thus far, signaled to the Palestinians about Israel's future aims.

Yet Chief of Staff Yitzhak Rabin felt that the manner in which the contacts with the Palestinians had been handled since the beginning of the occupation was utterly flawed and most injudicious. He admitted that the Israeli authorities knew very little about "what was happening on the Arab Street," that is, in Arab Jerusalem and the West Bank. On 31 July, one day after the government had decided to exile for a period of three months "up to 5 men" from among the twenty signatories of the 24 July statement, General Rabin told the members of the General Staff that the policy as he understood it was not to establish a Palestinian leadership but rather to nullify it. "The desire is to fragment (le-forer) the leadership. To neutralize [it] by exile and arrest, and to work on what could be influenced, using reward and punishment, economic pressure, and so on."[43] Indeed, the ministerial committee, whose recommenda- tion to exile "up to 5 men" was eventually adopted by the cabinet, did not mention any names. Clearly, this was meant to be a stark warning to the entire Palestinian elite, and thus it did not make much difference who was selected to be made an example of.

There was one exception, however. The Israelis regarded Anwar al-Khatib, the influential former governor of the Jerusalem District who headed the signatories, as the mastermind behind the unfolding unrest and suspected him of acting upon instructions from Amman. Conse- quently, they were determined to teach him a lesson. According to Chief of Staff Rabin, some "experts"—presumably GSS men—suggested ar- rests of Palestinian leaders of lesser stature while not touching Anwar al-Khatib; "on the contrary, [they advised,] visit him at his home many times and drink coffee [with him]," so as to make the West Bankers sus- pect him of collaborating.[44] The idea was not accepted. In a note con- taining a list of "candidates for arrest," scribbled on 25 July, David Farhi of the Military Government indicated next to Khatib's name: "An order from above" (hora'ah mi-lema'lah). At the bottom of the note Farhi added: "As for Khatib: our recommendation—exile him to Israel."[45]

On 31 July, at the crack of dawn, Khatib and three other nonreli- gious figures—the Ba'th activist 'Abd al-Muhsin Abu Mayzar, the for- mer member of Jordan's Chamber of Deputies and PLO activist Dr. Daud al-Husseini, and the Communist Ibrahim Bakr—were ar- rested. Shortly afterward they were transferred to their places of exile: respectively Safed, Tiberias, and Hadera inside Israel, and Jericho in the occupied Jordan Valley. A fifth candidate, the former Jordanian

deputy and PLO activist Ishaq al-Dazdar, was not found at his home
when the police came to arrest him and thereby escaped exile in the
Israeli city of Ashdod.[46] In accordance with the government resolution,
Israeli officials informed first Khatib and later Sheikh Sa'ih that the Islamic Council was an illegal body and that the government of Israel did
not recognize it. Sheikh Sa'ih was given "friendly advice" by two Military Government officers "to consult his colleagues, to stay in touch
with us, and to consider their future steps in a favorable spirit."[47]

Some Muslims decried the steps taken against Anwar al-Khatib to
Israeli officials, arguing that Khatib had been striving to bring about a
peaceful accommodation.[48] As if to prove them right, Khatib, from his
place of exile in Safed, reportedly urged the Palestinians to cooperate
with the Israelis. Moreover, when a school strike broke out a few weeks
later, Khatib insisted that his son, a student at a private institution who
intended to show solidarity with his fellow Arabs, attend classes.[49] Hikmat al-Masri, one of Nablus's most eminent leaders, also declared that
"there is no excuse for noncooperation especially if Israel is permitting
the continued observation of the Jordanian law here."[50] The appeals of
Khatib and Masri were not heeded, however. In Jerusalem, representatives of the Chamber of Commerce and Muslim leaders deliberated
boycotting Israelis and starting what was described as a civil disobedience campaign; near Nablus, handwritten leaflets were found exhorting
readers "to wage war against the Jews"; more petitions were signed and
fervent declarations were made, asserting noncooperation with the occupation authorities.[51] Israeli policy makers had attempted to pacify the
Palestinian public and suppress what they regarded as manifestations
of disobedience or even fledgling insurgency by arresting and exiling a
handful of prominent leaders. "Extract the tooth and you extract the
pain with it," advised Defense Minister Dayan, using an Arab adage.[52]
But he and his associates managed to achieve the complete opposite.

The 24 July manifesto and the swift Israeli response generated a
flood of statements, letters, and petitions flaunting opposition to Israel's
occupation, protesting against the attitude of the occupiers, and expressing identification with, and approval of, the twenty signatories and their
arguments.[53] These remonstrations were signed by notables and ordinary citizens, organizations of professionals and trade unions, clergy
and women's associations, and were sent from Jerusalem, Nablus, Jenin,
Ramallah, al-Bireh, Tulkarm, Bethlehem, Hebron, and countrywide; they

were addressed to the military governor of the occupied area, Sheikh Sa'ih, King Hussein, and the secretary general of the United Nations. By mid-August some 600 Jerusalemites and West Bankers, many of them leading dignitaries representing a far greater number of people, had signed at least one such public petition or declaration. Most of the statements of protest found their way to the other side of the Jordan River, whereupon they were broadcast on Amman Radio and appeared in *al-Dustur* or another Jordanian newspaper. Some even made it to Syrian, Lebanese, and other Arab media organs. They lent full support to the Islamic Council and its head, Sheikh Sa'ih, and carried an identical theme: Jerusalem is an integral part of the West Bank, and the West Bank is an integral part of the Hashemite Kingdom of Jordan; the annexation of Arab Jerusalem is illegal; the occupation should be ended.

A cursory reading of the texts reveals that the wording of many of them is almost identical. Evidently there was a guiding mind behind this wave of protest.[54] In a military governors' conference, held on 11 August, Col. Raphael Vardi noted, "These are petitions of the entire West Bank professional and intelligent class," identical in shape and content, and orchestrated by "a central hand."[55]

The National Guidance Committee

A central hand required the Palestinian political elite to put aside their political differences and personal rivalries for the sake of an effective resistance to the Israeli occupation. This was not easy. On 6 August the Communists distributed mimeographed leaflets, signed "The Committee for Defense of the Arabism of Jerusalem," which called for a general strike on the following day from morning to evening, so that "your resounding cry will be heard in the whole world." While teams of small boys and young members of the JCP carried the message orally to shopkeepers, Mayor Ruhi al-Khatib went from one store to another, asking the merchants to disregard the call for strike because it was a Communist initiative. Nevertheless, the strike was complete: on 7 August, all shops were closed, buses and taxis stopped running, and many officials did not show up at work.[56]

On the afternoon of the strike day, the Communist leader Na'im al-Ashhab called on Sheikh 'Abd al-Hamid al-Sa'ih, the head of the newly created Islamic Council. The two men discussed the imperative need to unite all forces and to form a leadership that would provide guidance to the confused Palestinians under occupation. The meeting led to the establishment in mid-August of the semi-clandestine National Guidance Committee (*Lajnat al-Tawjih al-Watani*), with Sheikh Sa'ih again as its head. The other eight members of the committee were Mayor Ruhi al-Khatib; Anwar Nuseibeh, former cabinet minister, governor of Jerusalem, and ambassador; Antoun 'Atallah, a bank director and former foreign minister; Sa'id 'Ala' al-Din, a lawyer and former cabinet minister; Kamal al-Dajani, a lawyer; Judge Tiyasir Kan'an; Dr. Nabih Mu'ammar, the medical director of al-Maqased hospital; and Na'im al-Ashhab. A number of prominent leaders were not included because of the objection of some of the National Guidance Committee's founders; most salient among those excluded was Anwar al-Khatib.[57]

Similar committees were soon set up in Nablus, Ramallah and al-Bireh, Tulkarm, and Hebron, and a number of their members took part in the discussions of the Jerusalem National Guidance Committee.[58] Two representatives of trade unions in Jerusalem also joined. The growing number of participants in the meetings of the Jerusalem committee increased the danger of its being exposed and raided by Israel's security services, and also made quick adoption of decisions more difficult. A five-man bureau was thus created, whose members were Sheikh Sa'ih, Nuseibeh, Sa'id 'Ala' al-Din, Dr. Mu'ammar, and Ashhab. According to Ashhab, the committee's immediate priorities were to supervise the education system and to persuade the Jerusalemites and West Bankers not to leave the occupied territories but to stay put.[59]

"The . . . committee is guiding the Palestinian people and officialdom as to the position they should take vis-à-vis [the] authorities," reported David Farhi of the Military Government a week after the National Guidance Committee had been set up, upon learning about its establishment from a Palestinian contact. "These days it considers the issue of education in Jerusalem."[60] More generally, however, the committee was intended to exhibit a solidified front in face of the Israeli occupation, to lead the civil disobedience, and to coordinate acts of resistance and remonstration. Because quite a few of its members came from the ranks of the traditional elite and the former Jordanian establishment, the National Guidance Committee was unavoidably pro-Hashemite. But contrary to Israel's claims, it was not a Jordanian creation; it was a genuinely local Palestinian initiative. In the words of Emile Sahliyeh, a

Palestinian scholar, both the National Guidance Committee and the Islamic Council "were attempts by the West Bank urban elite to create structures that would give political expression to the interests of the local populace."[61]

Israel was determined to break the spirit of defiance. The occupation authorities reacted vigorously to the general strike on 7 August with arrests, the closure of four shops, and revocation of the license of an Arab bus company.[62] These acts were misdirected, Hasan Tahbub, the head of the Jerusalem *Waqf* (Islamic endowment) administration, told David Farhi: "There was a need to hurt the *zu'ran* [Arabic for ruffians] who had enforced terror. Instead you hurt the notables." Tahbub's "zu'ran" were youngsters who had threatened reluctant traders to participate in the strike. "You don't know how to operate," said another Palestinian dignitary, Deputy 'Isa 'Aql, censuring the steps taken by the Israelis. 'Aql argued that the occupiers should have responded forcefully against the agitators.[63] Doubtless there were Palestinians who had little sympathy with the civil disobedience, and pressure had been applied by activists to "encourage" dissenters to conform. Nevertheless, the authorities' retaliation inspired a general Arab response contrary to Israel's expectations. The entire West Bank was now seething, with a reinvigorated spate of petitions, pronouncements, and protests.

One such appeal was sent to King Hussein by twenty prominent residents of the Bethlehem region. According to one of the signatories, Senator Edward Khamis of Bayt Jalla, the group had planned to urge the Jordanian monarch to negotiate with Israel for a final settlement, but then feared that this would expose its members to danger from "extreme elements."[64] They therefore contented themselves with a "conventional" text which, in the opinion of an American diplomat, did not go beyond the usual assertion of the illegality of Israel's occupation of the West Bank and the annexation of Arab Jerusalem, and reiteration of charges of harsh measures. Nevertheless, shortly after Amman Radio broadcast the appeal's substance and the names of its senders, nine of the signatories—among them two members of Jordan's parliament and four physicians—were arrested.[65] Another four Bethlehem men were arrested a few days later for petitioning the UN secretary general to put an end to the Israeli occupation. This petition, copies of which were sent to King Hussein, Sheikh Sa'ih, and the Israeli military governor, was signed by fifty notables of Bethlehem. David Farhi described the petition as "very serious" because of its substance and because of the address-ees.[66] The Israelis' tough response belied Defense Minister Dayan's claim that Israel's policy allowed the Arabs living in the occupied territories "to work against us by political means and to express their criticism in speech and in writing."[67]

The overall mood in the West Bank, as reflected in the myriad pe-titions and written declarations, favored a return to Jordan rule. Many honestly felt that the Hashemite regime was the lesser of two evils; the fact that the government in Amman continued to pay its former em-ployees in the occupied territories their salaries also helped maintain loyalty for the regime. In mid-August some eighty of the most promi-nent members of the West Bank elite—including Anwar Nuseibeh, An-toun 'Atallah, Hamdi Kan'an, and Hikmat al-Masri—addressed a strong statement to the "Arab People," which was sent to King Hussein and duly broadcast on Amman Radio. In addition to the routine rejection of the occupation of the West Bank and the annexation of Arab Jerusa-lem, the text included a "resolute and emphatic" condemnation "of all attempts to establish a Palestinian entity under whatever name or in whatever form."[68] Before the petition was completed, David Farhi had learned from his ever-eager informant Bishop Capucci that Sheikh Sa'ih was behind it.[69] The next day Farhi and Victor Cohen of the GSS visited Sa'ih and told him unequivocally that "the State of Israel would not tol-erate acts of incitement and attempts by certain people to send letters to certain kings." Such an act, they added, would be considered a contact with the enemy, for which the punishment was very severe.[70]

The statement was sent in defiance of this warning, and the un-rest continued, even gathering momentum. Threatening calls demand-ing that citizens refuse to pay taxes and other Israeli levies, and that they boycott Israeli products, increased significantly.[71] Dozens of lawyers from Jerusalem, Ramallah, Nablus, and Hebron convened in the Old City and decided not to appear in Jerusalem or West Bank courts; 50,000 Jordanian dinars (equivalent to 50,000 sterling pounds), sent by the Am-man Bar Association, was divided among the attorneys in the occupied territories.[72] The Israeli insistence on revising the West Bank school cur-riculum and banning or censoring 78 of 134 textbooks brought another wave of angry protests and petitions proclaiming the Jordanian identity of the occupied area. The objection was particularly strong in Arab Jeru-salem, because the Israeli authorities demanded assimilation of the public schools of the annexed sector of the city into the existing Israeli-Arab educational system and enforcement of its curriculum. Teachers all over the occupied region pledged to strike against arbitrary Israeli interference.[73]

The declared purpose for scrutinizing the Jordanian textbooks was to purge them of incitement against, or defamation of, the State of Israel, Zionism, and the Jews. But the actual censorship targeted also basic historical, cultural, and religious facts and values, including Qur'anic verses.[74] It was primarily intended to obliterate any mention of Palestine and Palestinian identity.[75] On 16 October, in a meeting in Nablus between the local Education Committee and representatives of the Military Government and the Education Ministry about the Israeli-revised curriculum and textbooks, the Israelis informed the Nablus side that "the Palestine question" was excluded as a separate subject from the educational program. Dr. Qadri Touqan, the principal of a teacher-training college and former foreign minister of Jordan, wondered why the subject could not be taught without a textbook, as long as the presentation was confined to the objective historical facts. One of the Israeli officials replied that the Palestine question was "a delicate subject and related to political problems." Teachers, he added, should not be put in uneasy situations. The official went on to argue that the history curriculum included a brief review of the history of the region, "and this [was] absolutely enough."[76]

The growing manifestations of civil disobedience gave the lie to Israel's pretense of introducing an "enlightened occupation" and shattered the Israeli claim of achieving the cooperation of the Arab population. Publicly, Defense Minister Dayan appeared indifferent to Palestinian passive resistance. "If they want to write protests or close their shops or schools, let them! I am not interested," he stated offhandedly in a press interview.[77] In reality, however, the Military Government, on Dayan's instructions, reacted furiously. For example, steps were taken to confiscate a number of West Bank school buildings—two or three "at the first stage"—and use them for army purposes in order "to deter the local population from continuing the school strike."[78] Two education inspectors in Arab Jerusalem, who had allegedly incited teachers to boycott schools, were put in administrative detention; after a month, Dayan authorized a two-month extension of their incarceration.[79] Nablus, which was the only West Bank city to respond fully to the call for a general strike on 19 September, was chosen by Dayan to endure a "punitive campaign" consisting of no fewer than thirteen severe sanctions. "The philosophy underlying the response was to break Nablus economically, to hit its residents in the pocket and undermine their self-esteem," explained Shlomo Gazit, Dayan's aide at the time.[80]

The Palestinians could not fail to interpret many of Israel's actions as attempts to hold on to the occupied region and to present them with faits accomplis—in addition to the annexation of Arab Jerusalem, the intervention in Islamic religious affairs and in the school curriculum were cases in point—without any consideration of their historical, national, or religious sensitivities, desires, and needs. Raphael Vardi, the de facto military governor of the West Bank in 1967, effectively acknowledged in 1989 that the Palestinians had had good reasons to fear unwarranted Israeli meddling in their education, culture, and social and religious life.[81] Vardi argued further that the curriculum issue turned into a political bone of contention between Premier Eshkol and Education Minister Zalman Arrane on the one hand, and Defense Minister Dayan on the other hand. Dayan strongly objected to the Education Ministry's insistence on what the journalist Amos Elon described as "converting West Bank children to Zionism."[82]

The West Bankers made every effort to inform international bodies of their predicament, thereby exasperating the Israelis even more. Thus when Ambassador Ernest Thalmann of Switzerland arrived in Jerusalem in the second half of August as a special representative of the UN secretary general, assigned to investigate the situation following the annexation, Israeli officials attempted unsuccessfully to impede his mission and to prevent him from talking freely with Palestinian personalities.[83] Fourteen notables, including Sheikh Sa'ih and some moderates such as Anwar Nuseibeh, Antoun 'Atallah, and Ruhi al-Khatib, requested to meet him in a long letter detailing Israel's repressive actions.[84]

There was a thin line which most West Bankers resolutely refused to cross—turning the civil disobedience into a violent insurgency.[85] Israeli intelligence learned from its sources about some initiatives to set up armed underground movements to fight the occupation. One such motion, for a clandestine armed group to be named *Jabhat al-'Umal* (The workers' front), was put forward but rejected in a meeting of Communist activists in early September. Sheikh Sa'ih, who as the head of the National Guidance Committee led the civil disobedience, was firmly against the establishment of a combatant organization. Addressing a group of "fervent Muslim nationalists" (as they were described in an Israeli intelligence report) from Jerusalem who came to ask his moral and financial support for such an endeavor, he warned that it would be impossible to defeat Israel by means of belligerent resistance from within, and that fighting was the Arab states' task.[86] A leaflet urging the West Bank Palestinians to cooperate with the resistance organizations explicitly demanded that they should avoid hurting "enemy civilians," and seven West Bank mayors appealed to their citizens not to resort to violent means as a way of achieving patriotic aspirations.[87] Indeed, when cadres belonging to guerrilla groups based outside the occupied areas infiltrated the West Bank during the summer of 1967 and initiated an armed struggle through terror attacks, they were crushed by the Israelis and ended up in complete failure after barely four months, largely due to the noncooperation of the West Bankers.[88]

King Hussein welcomed the civil disobedience. His crushing defeat in the war had made him feel that his days on the throne were numbered. The eruption of civil disobedience on the other side of the river led the king to believe that he could hold his position longer than had been originally thought.[89] West Bank leaders and government officials in Amman maintained contacts, and the Hashemite regime, dispossessed of a territory it considered its own, supported noncooperation of its citizens in the West Bank with the occupation authorities. No hard evidence was found to substantiate the Israeli claim that Jordan had been orchestrating the resistance, but the Israeli government persistently accused Jordan of inciting the unrest in the occupied territories, even using this allegation as a pretext to frustrate the return to the West Bank of the June War refugees (see chapter 4). Israel's spokesmen produced unconvincing testimonies to this effect: predominantly West Bankers' petitions and proclamations which had been broadcast over Amman Radio.[90] The American consulate general in Jerusalem investigated the matter but could not find any corroboration for the claim that Amman had been behind the petitions, statements, and letters dispatched by the West Bankers.[91]

Resentful of Israel's rule, the West Bankers needed no outside encouragement to express their grievances and anxieties. Almost everything Israel did, every step or measure taken, further inflamed the occupied Palestinians, and alienated even those moderates who still harbored hopes for achieving a peaceful settlement, with or without Jordan. This atmosphere of defiance was inspired in some cases by blunt intimidation from extremists, and consequently even non-radical Palestinians felt compelled to join in with petitions and declarations of their own. According to the American investigation of the "incitement" accusation, a number of petition signatories, notably from Bethlehem and Ramallah, argued that they could not be caught *not* petitioning when everyone else had done so. Others pointed to the conditions of political uncertainty, which called for hedging one's bets, and thus even some of those against a return of the Hashemite rule chose to subscribe publicly to the opposite viewpoint.[92] They too endured the tough Israeli reaction.

Operation Excrement 2

In early September 'Aziz Shehadeh publicly launched the movement for the creation of a Palestinian entity in the West Bank and the Gaza Strip. His initiative met with strong opposition (both the movement and the counter-reaction it sparked will be discussed in chapter 5). On 18 September the National Guidance Committee called a one-day general strike for the following day, on the occasion of the opening of the UN General Assembly in New York, to protest the occupation and Israel's efforts "to create a Palestinian entity at bayonet point." Leaflets were circulated in Arab Jerusalem and other West Bank urban centers, but the strike was supported fully only in Nablus, and scarcely at all in Jerusalem and the rest of the occupied area.[93] This was the National Guidance Committee's second call for strike in a space of a month; the first, set for 21 August to coincide with the arrival of UN envoy Thalmann in Jerusalem and limited to the Old City, had failed completely—at least in part due to the merchants' fear of the heavy police and paratrooper forces who patrolled the commercial districts.[94] Nevertheless, the Israeli authorities regarded the September strike as the last straw. They decided to arrest and banish Sheikh Sa'ih, whom they considered principally responsible for the civil disobedience.[95] Unlike the internal expulsion of the four notables in late July, whose places of exile had attracted many Palestinian visitors, Sheikh Sa'ih was deported to the East Bank—the first of a very long list of deportees to suffer this fate.[96]

The actual expulsion, code-named *Mivtsa' Peresh 2* (Operation Excrement 2), took place in the early hours of 23 September.[97] On his way to the Allenby Bridge, Sheikh Sa'ih argued that what had been hap-pening in the occupied territories was of Israel's own making. "All the manifestations of resistance expressed by the inhabitants of the [West] Bank and Jerusalem came about as a result of the proclamation of the annexation of Jerusalem by Israel," he told an Israeli police ranking of-ficer who accompanied him. He suggested further that Israel could have avoided "the problem" had it annexed Arab Jerusalem in stages, step by step, without attracting so much attention. "The annexation of no other part of the [West] Bank would have created such an objection as the annexation of Jerusalem did," he added.[98]

Sheikh Sa'ih's argument was endorsed by Shlomo Gazit, then the military staff officer in charge of handling the occupied territories on behalf of Defense Minister Dayan. In his hindsight analysis, Israel's an-nexation of Arab Jerusalem served as a catalyst for the civil disobedi-ence and determined the timing of the first protest actions.[99] Raphael Vardi, then de facto military governor of the West Bank, who years later shared this view, also blamed the Israeli rejection of the request of the eighty-three leading notables to convene in mid-July.[100] Another pene-trating explanation was offered in a contemporary letter sent by Police Minister Eliyahu Sasson, an expert on Arab affairs, to Prime Minister Eshkol in mid-August. Sasson wrote that the Palestinians, upon hear-ing Amman urging them to become a thorn in Israel's flesh, had ex-pected the Israeli government to reveal its intentions and plans for the future of the occupied territories, but the discordant cabinet failed to give them any credible answer.[101]

When the brewing Palestinian unrest was first discussed by the cabinet on 27 July, the ministers seemed to grasp the seriousness of the situation. They decided to set up a ministerial committee to deal with "the internal security problems arising from the danger of civil disobedience (*meri ezrahi*) in East Jerusalem and the West Bank."[102] Later on, however, the Israelis found it difficult to acknowledge the sig-nificance of the Palestinian resistance to their rule. As if they were in a state of denial, they refused to define the unrest as "civil disobedience." In the General Staff debate on the new developments on 31 July, the gen-erals chose to talk about displays of noncooperation which did not in-volve the entire population. General Ariel Sharon avoided any definition and simply said, "The Arabs should be treated with a firm hand. This is elementary."[103] In the following weeks the disturbances grew stronger, but Avraham Ahituv, who ran the activities of the GSS in the occupied territories, still maintained in mid-August that what was happening did not amount to civil disobedience. "There are personalities—and I am not saying leaders—various personalities who are trying to perpetrate acts of resistance," he argued, adding that those efforts lacked an organizational common denominator.[104]

Defense Minister Dayan agreed. So far, he curtly stated, there was no disobedience.[105] The occupation policy was a success, he proudly told an American diplomat a few days later. For him, the Palestinian strikes and the manifestos were merely a nuisance, and "in [the] absence of any indigenous leadership," he saw no real fears for the future.[106] According to Dayan's daughter, "Frictions, strikes, clashes, and demonstrations he regarded as local incidents, rather than representing a large and deeper dissatisfaction."[107] As late as the end of September, Dayan offered a rosy picture to the readers of *Life* magazine: "The abortive attempts at 'revolt' and the incidents of non-cooperation are isolated episodes. In the West Bank, life is normal, ordered and peaceful. . . . It is difficult to start a revolution unless the conditions are appropriate."[108] Three days before the article was published, however, the defense minister finally recognized the true nature of the rebellious actions in the West Bank. "The disobedience has gathered strength," he reported behind the closed doors of the Foreign Affairs and Security Committee of the Knesset. Dayan described Sheikh Sa'ih as the man who had orchestrated the disobedience, which was, he argued, an integral part of the guerrilla terror campaign.[109]

One day after Sheikh Sa'ih's expulsion, the Islamic Council convened to elect Sheikh Hilmi al-Muhtasib, a member of the Islamic Court of Appeal, in his stead. In order not to anger the Israeli authorities, it was agreed that Sheikh Muhtasib would refrain from intervening in political matters and engage himself solely in religious affairs.[110] Sa'ih's political hat, as the head of the National Guidance Committee, was entrusted to Ruhi al-Khatib.[111] The former mayor of Arab Jerusalem, who had expressed his readiness to cooperate with the Israeli authorities for the good of his city's people even after the unilateral annexation and the unceremonious abolishment of his municipality, was now recruited to lead the noncooperation and civil disobedience. A telegram expressing "deep regret and strong objection" to the expulsion of Sheikh Sa'ih was hastily drafted and sent to Prime Minister Eshkol, but following Sa'ih's banishment defiance began to recede.[112] The spate of civil disobedience soon gave way to a yearlong hibernation.

A contemporary Palestinian commentator concluded that in addition to Israel's harsh measures there were other reasons why the unrest in the West Bank during the first few months of the occupation did not develop into full-scale and prolonged civil disobedience. Among them were the weakness of the traditional leadership and its detachment from the ordinary city dwellers; the collaborative stance adopted by Sheikh Ja'bari, the influential mayor of Hebron; and the absence of leadership in the rural areas.[113] Another Palestinian scholar ascribes the failure of the civil disobedience to the lack of organizational capability and economic self-reliance of what he calls "the national movement."[114] An American expert on the Israeli occupation during this period stresses that the locally initiated political action was not supported by effective international pressure. Even the Arab regimes, still stunned by their June defeat, stayed on the sidelines.[115]

Be that as it may, the Israelis seemed to succeed in pacifying the unruly West Bank, at least for a while. But in the process they gave the already disillusioned Palestinians every reason for alarm about their intentions. The occupiers did not bother to distinguish between instigators and those who yielded to threats. They overlooked the tightrope— stretched between previous and potentially future Jordanian rule at the one end, and Israeli military control at the other—on which the West Bankers had been carefully treading, especially during the initial period of the occupation, when the situation and the prospects were so volatile and precarious.

Seeking a pliant West Bank leadership, Israel strove to do away with strong-minded men. It often acted indiscriminately and heavy-handedly against political figures to make an example of them or because they did not toe the official line. With trouble-free occupation as their primary goal, the Israelis alienated the notables who still desired a peaceful settlement. Indeed, the Israeli approach to both the Palestinian political elite and King Hussein clearly shows that Israel was not committed to either the Palestinian or the Jordanian option. But while this attitude reflected the wish to hold on to the Palestinian-inhabited land, the picture is still incomplete without looking at its other constituent—the people living on this land. As we shall see in the next chapter, Israel sought to disrupt the nexus between the people and the land by encouraging the people to depart the occupied territories and, more significant, by preventing tens of thousands of "new refugees"—who had fled the area during the war or immediately afterward and were stranded in makeshift shelters in the East Bank—from returning to their homes in Arab Jerusalem and the West Bank. The fear of Na'im al-Ashhab and other West Bank leaders of a reprise of the 1948 catastrophe—*Nakbah*—was not entirely without foundation.

The Right of No Return

June–September 1967

The exodus of Arab inhabitants from the territories seized by Israel in the six days of fighting was enormous. These new refugees were designated *nazihun* by the Arabs and "displaced persons"—which means the same thing—by the United Nations, in order to distinguish them from the "old refugees" of 1948.[1] In fact, many were both. According to an investigation conducted by Nils-Göran Gussing, a special representative of the UN secretary general, some 200,000 people crossed the Jordan River from the West Bank to the East during the war or immediately afterward; about 93,000 of them were 1948 refugees, registered with the United Nations Relief and Works Agency (UNRWA), who now became refugees for the second time. Additionally, between 85,000 and 110,000 persons fled the Syrian Golan Heights, including 17,000 UNRWA-registered 1948 refugees. Another 35,000 people from the Gaza Strip or Sinai moved across the Suez Canal into Egypt; 3,000 of them were UNRWA-registered refugees.[2]

Unlike the 1948 War there were no mass expulsions in June 1967. Many residents fled their homes, as people in war zones always do; some left because of fears fed by the memories of what had happened in 1948. But Israeli troops also played a role in the outflow by applying various methods intended to induce the Palestinians to leave. While nothing in the available records indicates that the Israeli cabinet initiated the Arab flight from the occupied territories, there is plenty of evidence that Israeli decision makers, including the army's top brass, welcomed wholeheartedly the mass outward movement.

"We certainly hoped that [the West Bankers] would flee, as in 1948," stated Maj. Gen. Uzi Narkiss, the commanding general of the Central Command.[3] On 6 June, the second day of the war, Defense Minister Dayan instructed Chief of Staff Rabin to allow anyone wishing to depart the West Bank to do so.[4] The next day, on hearing that many Tulkarm inhabitants were escaping from their town, Dayan expressed his satisfaction. He ordered the armor brigade operating in the area to slow down while keeping the roads open. Dayan believed that this would help lower the Arab population in the West Bank, which would in turn spare Israel difficult problems.[5] The aim, he told Rabin on the morning of 7 June, was to empty the West Bank of its inhabitants.[6] General Narkiss thus delayed the conquest of Jericho, a city located near the Allenby Bridge, so that the West Bankers could cross over to the East Bank unhindered.[7] In the evening, shortly after the attack on Jericho had started, General Rabin instructed Narkiss to refrain from dynamiting the Jordan bridges "in order to ease the emigration" of West Bank residents.[8] A week after the war had ended, when the estimated number of those who had fled the West Bank was only 100,000, Minister Eliyahu Sasson shared his sense of gratification with his cabinet colleagues.[9] A few days later Dayan expressed similar feelings of delight, and added: "I hope they all go. If we could achieve the departure of three hundred thousand without pressure, that would be a great blessing. If we could achieve hundreds of thousands from Gaza crossing with UNRWA approval, we would be blessed."[10]

The Destruction of Border Villages

Shortly after the occupation of Bethlehem on 7 June, British journalist David Pryce-Jones witnessed an army loudspeaker van announcing that the city population should take the road to Jericho—that is, toward the Jordan River—"or face the consequences."[11] Sister Marie-Thérèse, a French nun who reached Bethlehem two days later, also recorded in her diary that Israeli vehicles were circulating and broadcasting in Arabic that residents had "two hours to leave your houses and flee toward Jericho and Amman; if not, your houses will be bombarded."[12] Senior UN officials in Jordan believed that a pattern of expulsion was emerging.

They collected evidence from new refugees arriving in Amman about other places in the West Bank where Israeli soldiers, using loudspeakers, warned the inhabitants: "You have two hours to leave. After that we cannot guarantee your safety."[13] Although the Israeli government took no policy decision to expel Palestinians from the occupied territories, there were military efforts to push the West Bankers eastward. These efforts, described later as "local initiatives," were not local at all. Evidently concerted, they primarily targeted Palestinian villages and towns near the 1949 Armistice Green Line. The task was entrusted to the psychological operations unit of the Intelligence Branch. Small psyops squads with vehicles with loudspeakers were attached to the fighting brigades in the West Bank.[14]

On 6 June one of the squads reported to Col. Ze'ev Shaham, the commander of brigade no. 5, which operated in the northern region of the West Bank. Shaham sent the squad to Qalqilyah, a small town located on the Green Line at the eastern end of Israel's narrow waist, which had just been taken by the combat forces.[15] Once there, they went directly to Mayor Hussein Sabri and told him that the residents must leave at once because the Iraqi air force was going to bomb the town. Mayor Sabri was given a prepared note in Arabic to this effect and was driven through the town in a jeep equipped with a loudspeaker to make the announcement.[16] About half of Qalqilyah's 14,000 inhabitants had already fled to the mountains following the retreat of the Jordanian troops; now the town was emptied of the other half. Some were told to assemble at the mosque, where they found buses to take them to the Jordan River.[17] Many others were simply driven away and attempted to find shelter in the Nablus area, some twenty miles to the east. "We were forced to leave," a Qalqilyah woman said in Nablus a day later. "The Israelis—they brought everyone to the mosque and ordered us to get out of the town. Immediately."[18]

Colonel Shaham's orders, which came down from the army "senior command" on behalf of General Narkiss, were, according to Shaham's own account, "plain and unambiguous: the town was to be cleared of its inhabitants and razed to the ground." Shaham was in no doubt that the directive had the defense minister's authorization.[19] Indeed, on the evening of 8 June—two days after Qalqilyah had been taken—Dayan instructed Chief of Staff Rabin "to lay into the houses of Qalqilyah" [*le-hakhnis le-vatei* Qalqilyah].[20] Shaham carried out his assignment

Map 6. The West Bank, 1967–68

faithfully: once the townsfolk had been sent away, the area was sealed and the systematic dynamiting of the buildings began. More than 40 percent of Qalqilyah's dwellings—some 850 houses—had been demolished and many more had been badly damaged before the operation was stopped by political intervention.[21] Strong diplomatic pressure and international outcry forced the Israeli cabinet on 25 June to allow the people of Qalqilyah to return to the ruins of their town.[22] Not all of them went back; faced with the harsh conditions of destitution, some gave in: Jordan's ambassador to the United Nations reported that five busloads of Qalqilyah residents had been driven into the East Bank on 20 June alone.[23] Those who did return discovered that the destruction had been followed by looting.[24] Consequently quite a few decided to cross over to Jordan.[25] Israel strove unsuccessfully to conceal the expulsions and the destruction. But its spokespersons' endeavors to argue that the devastation had occurred in the heat of battle and that the population had left voluntarily also failed to convince world opinion.[26]

The strategically significant Latrun Salient, controlling the access to Jerusalem from the coastal plain in the west, was taken by Israeli troops in the early hours of 6 June. Immediately thereafter Col. Baruch ("Borka") Bar-Lev, General Narkiss's second in command, requested approval from the army high command for the demolition of Bayt Nuba, one of the three villages in Latrun. The request was denied forthwith; shortly afterward Chief of Staff Rabin explicitly prohibited the destruction of Bayt Nuba and the other two villages, 'Imwas and Yalu.[27] In the meantime, however, the 7,000 or so inhabitants of the villages were ordered to leave without delay. "Where shall we go?" asked Hasan Ahmad Hasan Abu Ghosh of 'Imwas. "Go to Jeddah," one of the soldiers responded, and his comrades in arms started shooting over the peasants' heads.

The villagers plodded along the hilly road leading to Ramallah, about twenty miles to the east, with military escorts in cars behind them. The next day Dayan was informed by General Narkiss that the Latrun people had "fled." He was pleased: "Good thing they ran in the right direction and not towards Tel Aviv." A week later, when the fighting was long over, the villagers were instructed through loudspeakers to go back. So they did, only to be stopped at roadblocks surrounding Latrun, where they were told that their villages had been turned into a closed military area; entry was prohibited, and anyone trying to proceed would be shot.

Before leaving for Ramallah again, many of them watched from afar the start of the methodical demolition of their homes. Altogether, 1,464 houses were bulldozed: 375 in 'Imwas, 539 in Yalu, and 550 in Bayt Nuba.[28]

"Even if a cease-fire were forced upon us," General Narkiss recounted in his memoirs, "even if we were obliged to withdraw to the Green Line, I was determined [then, on 6 June] that the Latrun enclave, that years-old thorn in our flesh, would never be returned."[29] At the time, however, Narkiss gave a different explanation. When Yosef Ohman, who had witnessed and photographed the destruction of 'Imwas, met the general in nearby kibbutz Harel a week later and asked why it was done, he replied: "We squared an old account from 1948."[30] Narkiss was referring to the successive Israeli attempts to capture Latrun from the Jordanian Arab Legion in the 1948 War, which cost the lives of scores of Israeli soldiers and all ended in failure. Either way, 'Imwas, Yalu, and Bayt Nuba were wiped off the face of the earth, apparently in defiance of Rabin's order but with the post factum endorsement of Israel's cabinet and the retroactive blessing of the prime minister. In Latrun "we corrected what needed to be corrected," Eshkol stated on one occasion; "we settled [the issue of] Latrun in the way [such issues] are settled in a war," he elaborated on another.[31]

Mayor 'Abd al-Jawad Saleh of al-Bireh argues that the Israeli military governor asked him to persuade the Latrun refugees to leave for Jordan; he refused.[32] Saleh and his Ramallah counterpart, Mayor Nadim al-Zaru, told an American diplomat that the majority of the dispossessed villagers accepted the Israeli offer of a free bus ride to the Allenby Bridge.[33] Forty-nine hundred of the Latrun population crossed the Jordan River; the remaining 2,100, reported an UNRWA official at the end of August 1967, stayed with friends or in makeshift shelters, but mostly in the open air under trees in four mountain villages just east of Latrun.[34]

As in the case of Qalqilyah, the Israeli government did its utmost to hide the Latrun affair. For months, the area remained tightly sealed by military orders signed by General Narkiss.[35] These efforts at secrecy were doomed to failure, however, not least because of a handful of Israelis who were appalled by what had happened there.[36] Once again Israeli officials gave false explanations for the annihilation of the Latrun villages.[37] Unlike in the aftermath of Qalqilyah, the cabinet banned the return of the people of Latrun.[38] Their fields and orchards were given to adjacent Israeli kibbutzim and agricultural settlements; Dayan ruled that the Military Government would pocket the proceeds of the harvest and fruit picking.[39] With the defense minister's approval, a Jewish settlement was established on the lands of Bayt Nuba on the last day of 1969, a military *Nahal* outpost (*he'ahzut*) which later turned into a civilian village called Mevo Horon.[40] Most of the rest of the area became a big recreation park which was built in the early 1970s.

The final ceasefire of the war, on 10 June, was followed by busy days for the Israeli wreckers. On Monday, 12 June, soldiers told the 2,500 people of Zeita, a village on the Green Line some five miles north of Tulkarm, to abandon their homes; then they systematically tore down about one-third of the buildings—sixty-two dwellings were leveled and thirty-eight severely damaged, including the mosque, a clinic, an UNRWA milk station, and a school. An American diplomat reported that the destruction caused the death of one person and injury to two others. After the villagers were permitted to return to the rubble, the Israeli commander explained to Zeita's *mukhtar,* or village headman, that the order to destroy had come "from higher up."[41]

The previous day, 11 June, Israeli troops operated in the southern region of the West Bank. They entered Bayt 'Awa, southwest of Hebron and close to the Green Line, and ordered the 2,500 inhabitants to take two loaves of bread each and go to the hills surrounding their settlement. Within two hours the soldiers started to demolish the houses, using dynamite and bulldozers. Ninety percent of the 400 structures were razed and the farmers' belongings inside them destroyed. In addition, the majority of the standing wheat crop was burned. A neighboring hamlet, Bayt Mirsim, received an even more meticulous treatment that day: it was completely flattened, and its entire population of 500 was rendered homeless. They all were allowed back to the ruins from the hills a week or so later.[42] A Military Government's spokesman, asked by Swedish journalists in late July about the demolition of Bayt 'Awa and Bayt Mirsim, was ordered by his superiors to lie: "I receive[d] a directive 'from above' [*mi-gavo'ha*] to say that the houses had been blown up *during* the fighting, due to a clash with al-Fateh men."[43]

There were more incidents of destruction by Israeli troops in West Bank villages, including Sourif, Hablah, al-Burj, Bayt Illo, Kharas, Idna, Shweikah, Badras, Ya'bed, Taybeh, and al-Nabi Samwil.[44] The common feature of all the bulldozed places was that they were border settlements, and the main purpose of their destruction was to obliterate the Green Line, to draw the map anew. In some cases, however, there was another reason—revenge; a desire to settle bloody scores from the 1948 War. The case of the three villages of Latrun was not an isolated one.

In Sourif, a village in the Hebron District adjacent to the Etzion Block, the order was given directly by General Narkiss to Col. Eliezer Amitai, the commander of brigade no. 16, and revenge appears to have been the only motive. According to Amitai, on 8 June, after his brigade had taken the entire southern region of the West Bank without a fight, Narkiss approached him and said that Sourif should be "removed." Both officers were veterans of the *Palmah,* the prestate elite strike force, and it was clear to Amitai that Narkiss wished to avenge the death of the *lamed-heh*—a platoon of thirty-five *Palmah* men who had been at-tacked and killed near Sourif in January 1948. The brigade commander felt uneasy about the order, which was conveyed to him orally and rather casually, and demanded to have it in writing.[45] In an official debriefing that took place shortly after the war, Amitai reported succinctly and matter-of-factly what happened next: "Towards sunset the unit reached Sourif. The inhabitants were driven away from their home [*sic*] by an intelligence squad [equipped] with loudspeakers, and about 15 houses were dynamited. [Then] the unit proceeded to the Etzion Block."[46] Sis-ter Marie-Thérèse, the French nun, visited Sourif four weeks later and recorded in her diary that one resident had been shot dead because he did not leave quickly enough.[47]

Hundreds of houses were ruined in the West Bank after the hos-tilities had ceased, and thousands of Palestinians lost their homes and properties. All these acts of destruction were war crimes: the Hague Regulations of 1907 and the Fourth Geneva Convention of 1949 prohibit any kind of demolition which is not required by military necessity.[48] Evidently Defense Minister Dayan had a different view. In a gathering of the army General Command Staff in September he referred to the de-struction spree, saying that it had been motivated by "Zionist inten-tions" which he fully shared.[49] In his autobiography, however, Dayan defines the razing of Qalqilyah and the two villages near Hebron as "punitive actions"—he does not elaborate the reasons—decided upon by local commanders and, in the case of Bayt ʿAwa and Bayt Mirsim, intended to drive away their Arab residents.[50] Yet it is highly unlikely that those responsible for the havoc were junior "local commanders." A destruction campaign of such magnitude, with a similar pattern of demolition and eviction applied simultaneously in different border villages throughout the West Bank, must have been sanctioned by at least the commanding general of the Central Command. Indeed, two of the main culprits were General Narkiss and the chief of staff of the Central Command, Col. Baruch ("Borka") Bar-Lev.

Five months before he died in December 1997, Narkiss offered a candid account to an oral history project in which he listed some of the villages he had instructed to be razed, and related the reasons. The list included "lots of dwellings" of 1948 refugees in the Jericho area. In the early days of the occupation, Narkiss said, "I could do whatever I wanted, and indeed I did." By his own admission, the obliteration of the three villages of Latrun, and of Bayt 'Awa, Bayt Mirsim, and Sourif, was motivated in part by the bitter memories of 1948 and meant as retribution; in other places, including Qalqilyah, Tulkarm, and the big refugee camps near Jericho, Narkiss—expecting that the occupied West Bank would soon be returned to Jordan—had attempted to create irreversible facts on the ground. Quite proudly he stated that the decision to eradicate those settlements was his alone. Chief of Staff Rabin was unaware of Narkiss's orgy of destruction. On 13 June, when Rabin finally discovered what was happening, he ordered it to stop, and threatened Narkiss with a commission of inquiry.[51]

Yet Narkiss's blatantly unauthorized actions, which continued on a smaller scale, enjoyed the defense minister's acquiescence and, at least in the case of Qalqilyah, were done on Dayan's orders. According to Shlomo Gazit, who from August 1967 worked very closely with Dayan, the "initial policy . . . was clear and unambiguous; once demolition and evacuation of residents had been decided upon, no resettlement was to be permitted in the same locality." This policy, Gazit continues, remained in force until Dayan decided to reverse it after meeting some of the uprooted refugees.[52] Gazit's account implies that the "initial policy" was Dayan's. The defense minister, who had at one stage stated that blowing up houses was "incompatible with the orders given," nevertheless rejected the idea of prosecuting the perpetrators.[53] He assumed full responsibility for the havoc, and even untruthfully told UN envoy Gussing that it was he who "had ordered the destruction of the damaged villages [of Latrun] for strategic and security reasons since they dominated an important strategic area."[54]

Dayan acknowledged that "the Palestinians on the West Bank had not taken part in the war. . . . Whether or not they had wanted this war, it had not been their war after all."[55] But neither this nor the suffering of the newly displaced West Bankers he had seen had any bearing on his attitude, for the devastation was aimed first and foremost at imposing faits accomplis. This course of action coincided with Dayan's expressed thinking that the aftermath of the June War called for a new map of Israel.[56]

Prime Minister Eshkol, always cautious about possible international repercussions, had greater qualms than Dayan. Housing Minister Mordekhai Bentov of the left-wing *Mapam* party relates that upon hearing from a reservist member of his kibbutz that "horrendous things are being done on the [Jordanian] front"—including expulsions and destructions in Qalqilyah and elsewhere—he immediately conveyed the information to Eshkol. The premier was "astounded," says Bentov; he ordered that these actions stop at once.[57] Eshkol also rebuffed representatives of Israeli settlements near Qalqilyah who begged him to be allowed to demolish the buildings that were still standing in the partially destroyed town.[58] When the issue of the Jewish Quarter in the Old City was discussed on 14 June, Eshkol decided to postpone the eviction of the Arab residents in order to avoid "negative impact" abroad on the eve of the emergency special session of the UN General Assembly.[59] Yet both Eshkol and Dayan shared the same desire to establish facts on the ground and to reduce the Arab population under Israel's control. Regardless of their direct responsibility, Eshkol, Dayan, and almost every other member of Israel's political elite, were all too ready to embrace the consequences of Narkiss's wanton destruction.

The liquidation of Harat al-Magharibah, the Moroccan quarter immediately adjacent to the Wailing Wall, which was carried out in the dead of night on 10–11 June without government approval, is a case in point. Eight centuries old, the quarter was *waqf* (Islamic endowment) property that included two small ancient mosques, a few other historic sites, and many dwellings.[60] The initiative to level the quarter came from the military governor of Arab Jerusalem, Col. Shlomo ("Chich") Lahat, who sought a way to accommodate the tens of thousands of worshipers

expected on the eve of the Jewish holiday of Shavu'ot. Teddy Kollek, the
mayor of the Israeli part of Jerusalem, strongly supported the idea, and
General Narkiss authorized its execution. Justice Minister Ya'acov Shimshon Shapira told Kollek that he was not sure about the legal aspects, but
added: "Do what has to be done, and the God of Israel will help thee."
Defense Minister Dayan learned about the demolition only after the operation was already under way; he did not stop it. One hundred thirty-
five hovels, inhabited by some of the poorest people in the Old City, were
knocked down; the roughly 650 residents were given a couple of hours'
notice to vacate. One of them, an elderly woman, died that night in the
ruins of her home. The historic buildings were also destroyed.[61]

On the morning of 11 June, when the war was over and Harat al-
Magharibah ceased to exist, the Israeli cabinet was discussing "the status
of unified Jerusalem." Most ministers, including Premier Eshkol, were
unaware of what had happened to the quarter during the night. The
prime minister mentioned one of several unsuccessful Jewish attempts
to acquire the area between 1887 and 1919, and raised the idea of bull-
dozing the quarter and relocating its dwellers. He wondered whether
such an action required legislation, but ultimately concluded: "I understand that we all agree that even if there is no fighting it is possible to demolish a few houses with bulldozers by military order so that there will be
a plaza next to the Western Wall."[62] In the early afternoon the cabinet
arrived in the open plaza that had been created overnight. The ministers were dumbfounded by the change, but only Minister of Religious
Affairs Zerah Warhaftig, a jurist by training, commented that what had
been done was unlawful. "Perhaps . . . ," Chaim Herzog, the weeklong
military governor of the West Bank, responded retrospectively in his
memoirs, "but the area was completely clear in time for the mass pilgrimage."[63] The evicted Palestinians found temporary shelter with relatives, in empty school buildings, and in ruins in the Old City, and were
belatedly given meager compensation.[64] Shlomo Lahat, who had initiated the effacement of their homes, insisted thirty-four years later that
they accepted their removal "in good spirits."[65]

Free One-Way Bus Service to the River

Not many buildings were destroyed in Tulkarm, a Palestinian town
of 25,000 about 1,000 yards from the Green Line. Here Israeli soldiers

rounded up the terrified population from their homes and drove them in buses and trucks down to the Jordan River. "Now go to Hussein, go to Nasser," the soldiers said, according to a Tulkarm schoolteacher who added: "They took all the young men away."[66] Hilmi Hanoun, the mayor of Tulkarm, told an American diplomat that neighboring villages were also evacuated and that Israeli troops forced many residents across the Jordan.[67] 'Anabta, six miles east of Tulkarm, was one of these villages. It was seized by a company belonging to brigade no. 5 whose commander, as we have seen, had readily obeyed the order to level Qalqilyah. On 7 June the company commander, Maj. (res.) Ra'anan Lurie, was instructed to expel the village's people. Buses were already waiting to transport them to the river. Lurie refused, and another officer carried out the task. Many of the deportees from the Tulkarm area, including from 'Anabta, had been eventually dropped on the main road close to Nablus and were allowed to return to their homes a few days later, but others ended up in the East Bank.[68]

Several Israeli commanders felt that the immediate aftermath of the fighting offered them a unique opportunity to change the demography of the West Bank in Israel's favor. "Tonight or never," Colonel Shaham, the commander of brigade no. 5, told Major Lurie when the latter argued that expulsion of Palestinians would stain Israel's name. "Otherwise," Shaham went on, "we'll be stuck with them forever."[69] This was also the thinking of Yigal Allon, a cabinet minister and former army general. Allon, who on the eve of the June hostilities had proposed a war plan which included transfer of hundreds of thousands of Palestinian refugees across the Suez Canal into Egypt, was displeased with the manner in which the army conquered Hebron. The city was captured without a fight. "Is this the way to take Hebron?" Allon asked rhetorically in a private meeting in late 1967. "Two cannon shots on Hebron and no 'Khalili' [Arabic for Hebronite] would have remained there."[70]

New refugees arriving in Amman said that they had been forced at gunpoint to cross the river.[71] Palestinians from border villages in the northern region of the West Bank told stories similar to those from Tulkarm and 'Anabta. Evidently there was a pattern of expulsion reflecting an overall scheme to clear the Green Line area of its Arab population.[72] In the southern region Israeli fighter planes caused a stampede across the Jordan when, on the second day of the war, they bombed and strafed the large complex of the three refugee camps around Jericho—

'Aqbat al-Jaber, 'Ayn Sultan, and Nu'aymah—ostensibly while targeting an advancing Iraqi brigade. According to eyewitness accounts, napalm was used. Ninety percent of the camps' 53,000 inhabitants eventually fled, and the majority of Jericho's townsfolk followed suit.[73]

Thousands of West Bankers left during the hostilities or immediately afterward with no direct Israeli inducement. Panic-stricken, they escaped either because of the natural human fear of war and what might follow it, for economic or family reasons, or because they did not want to live under Israeli occupation. Rumors about the havoc in Arab Jerusalem, Qalqilyah, Latrun, and the other destroyed villages were swiftly spread throughout the West Bank by the long columns of refugees trudging eastward, and they accelerated the rush to the other side of the river.[74]

During the first days of the occupation Israelis went about in the West Bank announcing over loudspeakers that anyone was free to stay or leave.[75] Kol Yisrael, Israel's state radio, broadcast a similar message, addressed to "any inhabitant of the West Bank area living in Jerusalem and its surroundings": those wishing to cross into Jordan had only to register their names with the military governor.[76] "In the light of past history this can only be interpreted as pressure on the Arab population to leave," the British foreign secretary instructed his ambassador in Tel Aviv to tell Foreign Minister Eban, referring to the mass exodus of Palestinian refugees in 1948.[77] An Israeli Foreign Ministry official, sharing his own personal view privately with an American diplomat, agreed: in the circumstances, he intimated, such a message "tended to be encouragement to leave." He said that he personally had vetoed broadcasts of that announcement on Kol Yisrael's Arabic service.[78]

The Israelis also provided transport to the Jordan River gratis. The idea was conceived when Anwar al-Khatib, the Jordanian governor of the Jerusalem District, pleaded with General Herzog on 9 June "to facilitate means of transport for a large number of Jordanian nationals who [are] in the West Bank and would like to be reunited with members of their family in Amman."[79] What Khatib had in mind was a few dozen Jordanian officials and family members of Arab diplomats stranded in Jerusalem because of the war. Seizing the opportunity, Herzog not only granted Khatib's request but undertook to arrange a free bus route from the Damascus Gate in the Old City to the Jordan bridges for anyone wishing to go.[80] This way, writes a contemporary observer, Herzog hoped to thin out the Arab population of Jerusalem.[81] The one-way bus line, supervised by Col. Shlomo Lahat, began to operate on 11 June. Two days later Herzog boasted in an interview with an American journalist that buses were leaving every thirty or forty minutes.[82] General Narkiss, Herzog's superior, who subsequently assumed credit for the whole enterprise, said that a similar service was made available to residents in other West Bank towns; the word about it had been spread through local individuals and bodies with countrywide contacts. All the buses carried a sign in Arabic which read: "To Amman for free."[83]

All the while the world was watching with growing apprehension: the Palestinian refugee problem, which had been created in the 1948 War, was now about to be redoubled. On 19 June, when US President Lyndon Johnson set out the five principles of peace in the Middle East, "justice for the refugees" was listed second. Johnson expressly mentioned the new refugees of the Six Day War:

> A new conflict has brought new homelessness. The nations of the Middle East must at last address themselves to the plight of those who have been displaced by wars. . . . There will be no peace for any party in the Middle East unless this problem is attacked with new energy by all, and certainly, primarily by those who are immediately concerned.[84]

As far as the new refugees of 1967 were concerned, the main responsibility lay with Israel. On 14 June the UN Security Council unanimously passed a resolution calling upon Israel "to facilitate the return of those inhabitants who have fled the areas [where military operations took place] since the outbreak of the war."[85]

Indeed, after the dust of the fighting had settled, many Palestinians who had crossed over to the East Bank wished to go back. By order from Defense Minister Dayan, they were not allowed to do so.[86] "The further they moved from their towns and villages the greater became obstacles to their return," observed a Jewish American scholar who visited the area during the very first days of the occupation. "The nearer they came to the Jordan River, the more encouragement they received from Israeli soldiers on the spot to keep moving until they reached the other side of the river."[87] Washington urged Israel to allow a reverse flow of refugees. President Johnson and Secretary of State Dean Rusk saw no justification for mounting an expensive relief operation to provide temporary shelter in the East Bank "while refugee camps in the Jericho area, with housing and facilities built up over years, remain practically empty" because of the flight of their inhabitants to the East.[88] Yet the Israeli defense minister had different ideas. On 23 June, Dayan met an UNRWA representative in Jerusalem and asked whether the agency would consider a transfer of 1948 refugees from Gaza to its vacated camps in the West Bank "on a purely voluntary basis." A separate approach was made to the director of the UNRWA camps near Jericho about resettling the Gaza refugees there. UNRWA rejected the idea outright.[89]

Dayan's move not only attested to the eagerness to empty the Gaza Strip of its 200,000 or more 1948 refugees, but also indicated the Israeli determination not to allow a return of new refugees who had crossed to the East. At a press conference in Tel Aviv on 25 June, Dayan confirmed that permission would not be given to the main bulk of the new refugees. Asked why he opposed the return, Dayan replied: "Why should we [let them in]? We are two and one-half million Jews here, and the last contact that we had with these people was that they wanted to destroy us. That was just 20 days ago, if you recall."[90] The decision to prevent those who had crossed to the East Bank from coming back was approved at cabinet level—presumably by the Ministerial Committee for Security Affairs—sometime during the first two weeks of the occupation. On 25 June the cabinet voted against a motion to allow the new refugees to return within a month.[91]

In the cabinet Dayan informed his colleagues of the bus service to the river. "In two days' time, the whole of Jerusalem will become Jewish," he said ebulliently. During the past few days, Dayan went on, 600 persons had left daily from Jerusalem and its environs, and an additional 400 from other places. "It adds up to approximately 1,000 a day," Dayan concluded, "this is terrific."[92]

By mid-June television screens and the front pages of newspapers around the globe had become increasingly dominated by heartbreaking scenes of Palestinian refugees, loaded with hefty bundles, walking heavily under the scorching summer sun of the Jordan Valley toward the river's fords, then scrambling over the wreckage of the dynamited bridges. Israel faced scathing accusations of driving them out. To counter these allegations Israeli spokespersons argued that anyone exiting the occupied area had to sign a paper stating that he or she was leaving voluntarily.[93] General Herzog, the initiator of the bus operation, was exceptionally active and creative in the desperate efforts to deny that Israel was exercising any pressure on the Palestinians to go. In a statement issued on 14 June, Herzog claimed that the Military Government's announcements regarding the freedom to depart from the West Bank had been primarily directed at "the Jordan Legion soldiers, who threw off their uniforms, went into hiding and now desired to rejoin their families," and also at other East Bankers wishing to return home.[94] "There had not been and will not be any evacuation of inhabitants of towns near the old demarcation line," Herzog asserted in a briefing for foreign military attachés.[95]

In his memoirs, published three decades later, Herzog bragged that as a result of the free transport offered to the West Bankers, "approximately 100,000 people crossed over to the East Bank."[96] On 16 June 1967, however, a day after he had been relieved of his duties as the military governor of the West Bank, Herzog said in a second public statement that "only several hundreds" had been transferred by the free bus service to the river.[97] Similarly, he told a United Press International correspondent that "only several hundreds" were leaving daily. Shortly afterward the UPI journalist came to the Allenby Bridge and asked an Israeli sentry there how many people had crossed to the other side that day. "Four thousand," the soldier replied. "Fortunately," reported an Israeli Foreign Ministry official who escorted the correspondent, "he [the soldier] did not speak English, so while translating [his reply] I removed one zero." Before this journalist met the deputy military governor of Jericho, his Israeli minder had brought to the officer's attention "the line taken by General Herzog regarding the numbers" of West Bankers crossing to the East.[98]

All this was to no avail: nobody was convinced. "It would be [a] great tragedy if the refugee problem was re-created," warned Secretary of State Rusk when he met Foreign Minister Eban in New York on 21 June.[99] That day, Undersecretary of State Nicholas Katzenbach instructed the US ambassador in Tel Aviv immediately to approach the Israeli government and ask it to halt the exodus from the West Bank. "In particular," he wrote, "we would suggest [that the] Israeli authorities show less zeal in facilitating speedy departure of persons who indicated such desire." Katzenbach also mentioned some very simple steps that could, if applied, stop the refugee stream to the East Bank.[100] But General Narkiss was unwilling to relent; he refused to end the free bus service to the river and asked not to be pressured in this regard, as "he considers the matter beneficial to the future handling of [Arab] Jerusalem."[101] Simply put: the fewer Arabs the better.

In New York, Israel was fighting the diplomatic war on the UN front, striving to prevent a resolution which demanded an unconditional Israeli withdrawal from all the territories seized during the hostilities. Because of the horror stories in the mass media about the terrible suffering of the new refugees, "mounting international resentment began to cast a shadow over the sympathy Israel had enjoyed in the hour of its triumph." As early as 14 June, Gideon Rafael, Israel's ambassador to the United Nations, warned at an informal consultation headed by Premier Eshkol that "the world, especially our friends, would not tolerate the creation of a new Palestine refugee problem. Any action which could be interpreted as the encouragement of a second exodus would arouse strong anti-Israeli feeling."[102] A week later Israeli representatives abroad started sending desperate calls to Jerusalem.[103] Even Finance Minister Pinhas Sapir—who had telephoned General Narkiss twice a day to enquire, "How many [West Bankers] left today? Is the [West] Bank becoming empty?"—cautioned Premier Eshkol from London that world opinion was moving against Israel. "It is imperative to publish the correct facts and to embark on an information campaign (*hasbarah*) and counter-propaganda."[104]

The term *hasbarah* has always been the ultimate magic device for Israeli policy makers, capable of cleansing any wrongdoing: indeed a panacea for any blunder, political, military, or otherwise. This time, however, Foreign Minister Eban felt that the question was not how effective the Israeli *hasbarah* was, but whether there was any wisdom in the government's policy, which had not been explained. Israel, he cabled Eshkol, was perceived by the nations of the world and the Jews of the Diaspora as "devoid of humane and moral foundation." Eban asked the prime minister to bring the matter before the cabinet.[105] The following day the cabinet discussed the issue and agreed to make "vigorous *hasbarah* efforts" to clarify that the outflow of refugees was voluntary and mainly for economic reasons. Furthermore, in the future, any West Banker wishing to leave would have to produce a document signed by the mayor or *mukhtar* of his or her locality, confirming a voluntary departure.[106]

In a letter repeating the cabinet decision Avi'ad Yafeh, Eshkol's private secretary, remarked: "The government of Israel does not encourage

[Palestinians to leave], but puts itself at the [West Bank] citizens' disposal."[107] Michael Comay of the Foreign Ministry advised his minister at the United Nations that "Our declared policy is that we will not interfere with those wishing to cross and will not force people to remain under our rule against their will." His urgent telegram went on: "It should be remembered that they are Jordanian subjects"; it was only natural, Comay seemed to imply, that they would go to the eastern province of their country.[108] Clearly, government officials like Yafeh and Comay— even if they were ignorant of what was really going on and believed that all those tens of thousands of West Bankers were streaming eastward willingly—displayed an utter lack of empathy toward the new refugees' misery. Most insensitive was General Herzog, who cynically "pointed out that the refugees from 1948 who fled this time . . . lost nothing by leaving; they exchanged one set of camp conditions for another."[109] In fact, Herzog was echoing a similar statement made earlier by Dayan. At his 25 June press conference the defense minister said that many of those who crossed the river were "landless refugees who had nothing to lose" because they would continue to receive their UNRWA rations in Jordan.[110]

Michael Comay was at least honest enough to acknowledge that the hard facts did not leave much room for *hasbarah*. In his cable to Eban, Comay also acknowledged, "It is our calculated policy not to allow passage in the reverse direction," from the East Bank back to the West.

Licking its war wounds, defeated and impoverished, Jordan was unable to cope with such a gigantic influx of *nazihun,* or displaced persons. Many found refuge with relatives or friends, yet a great many more were in desperate need of sanctuary and basic sustenance. Eleven tented camps were set up by the government, but scores were housed, at least during the initial period, in public buildings, schools, and mosques, or found shelter under trees or in the open air.[111] The Hashemite Kingdom cried out for help. It even reportedly attempted to stop the flow of refugees by forbidding commercial vehicles, which had been carrying people from the main crossing point to the capital, to approach the river. Jordan's ambassador to the United Nations, himself a Palestinian from the Gaza Strip, thought that his government should march all new refugees to the river and on into the West Bank in order to expose Israel to world public opinion.[112] Amman Radio appealed to the West Bankers to stay put. It also threatened to blacklist anyone cooperating with the Israelis. Undersecretary Katzenbach held that the radio warnings contributed to the exodus, but conversations with new refugees, conducted by American diplomats and UNRWA officials, turned up no evidence to confirm this. The appeals, Jordan's ambassador in London explained, were aimed not at ordinary people or at junior government officials but at the political elite who might make a separate deal with Israel.[113]

The unfolding human tragedy, coupled with fear for the survival of King Hussein, Washington's longtime ally, and his pro-Western regime, drove the Americans to intensify their pressure on Israel.[114] Foreign Minister Eban became increasingly fearful that this might affect the outcome of Israel's diplomatic campaign at the General Assembly. "The public is bombarded with frequent news reports from Israel about expulsions of civilians from the West Bank," he wrote in an alarming cable to Eshkol on 29 June. "This weakens our position in world opinion and among friendly governments." After listing a number of other erroneous Israeli moves and instances of unacceptable behavior, he exclaimed: "Since the foundation of the State there has never been such a grave prospect to the creation of which Israeli deeds contributed so immensely." He insisted on action, including a move "to stop the expulsions" and to "slow down the flight and block it altogether." Eban demanded an urgent cabinet meeting to discuss his review of the situation.[115]

The cabinet convened that day and later issued a statement reiterating its previous decision, which made departure from the West Bank conditional on producing a written endorsement from the local authority.[116] However, Palestinians newly arriving in the East Bank from different parts of the occupied area told American diplomats who went down to the bridges from Amman that they had not been told to get such a document or been asked to present one before crossing.[117] This was corroborated by Housing Minister Mordekhai Bentov's firsthand account, following a visit to the Allenby Bridge after the relevant resolution had been adopted.[118]

The cabinet's statement also included a strong denial that any Palestinians had been expelled or encouraged in any way to emigrate from the West Bank. But Dr. Ya'acov Herzog, Eshkol's senior adviser, had recorded what the defense minister told the government several days before: "[The military] is continuing to apply pressure by way of night searches and all sorts of oppressive acts [negisot], 'so that they [the Arabs] will take the hint.' "[119] Indeed, diplomatic dispatches and press stories kept reporting nightly shouts in Arabic, mostly through loudspeakers, calling on the Arab residents of Jerusalem to leave the city; in addition, West Bankers were reportedly being terrorized by shots fired aimlessly or over their heads, usually at night.[120] In 'Anata refugee camp, near Jerusalem, Israeli soldiers searching for hidden weapons staged a mock execution; consequently, the camp's residents, some 500 families, contemplated moving to the East Bank. Consul General Wilson said that he had heard of similar incidents.[121]

Defense Minister Dayan reported in the cabinet on 6 August on the intimidation of hundreds of new refugees—including women and children—who had crossed the Jordan River from the East Bank, attempting to return home. Israeli soldiers had violently forced some of them to turn back. Dayan described these incidents as "shocking," and Foreign Minister Eban, in a letter to Premier Eshkol, called for a stop to "these 'shocking' actions."[122] His appeal went unheeded. Unwilling to allow any return of West Bankers from the East, Israeli troops regularly ambushed those attempting to cross back over the river. On 11 September, Mayor Salah 'Abdu of Jericho told a British diplomat that 100 people from his region alone had been killed by the Israelis as they tried to cross the Jordan from the East. "This may well be true," the diplomat commented, and he alluded to other cases of the same nature.[123] The dead, Mayor 'Abdu complained a month later, were buried without any record.[124]

"We killed civilians," General Narkiss confessed in a press interview in 1988. "How many were killed? I can't tell you [for sure], but certainly several dozen."[125] Col. Eliezer Amitai, who was in charge of the ambushes along the southern sector of the Jordan River, was also unable to tell how many returning refugees were killed by his troops; "many dozens," he said in an interview in 2007. "It was tough, very tough," Amitai muttered repeatedly.[126] According to an army document, by mid-September 146 "infiltrators" had been shot dead, including two women and four children; the real number was undoubtedly higher. Several were injured, and more than 1,100 were seized and sent back to the East.[127] In September an Israeli soldier gave a bloodcurdling account of the military practice which he had witnessed in late July and early August:

We were given an order to shoot to kill with no early warning. Indeed, shots of this kind were fired every night at men,
women, and children, even during moonlit nights when we
could identify the people crossing [the river]. That is, distinguish between men, women, and children. In the mornings
we searched the area and, by explicit order from the officer
present, killed the living, including those who hid [or] were
wounded (again: women and children among them). After
the killing we covered the corpses with earth, and sometimes left them [lying] in the terrain until a bulldozer came
to cover them with earth.[128]

On 13 September, following a letter to Premier Eshkol from soldiers complaining that they had been ordered to kill women and children crossing the Jordan, the issue was brought before the Ministerial
Committee for Security Affairs. Chief of Staff Rabin argued that under
the standing orders soldiers were to shoot people trying to cross the
river at night, unless they identified them as women or children. In the
daytime, the soldiers were to shout a warning, and if the infiltrators
did not stop, they were to fire shots in the air. Foreign Minister Eban
suggested instructing the soldiers to shoot to wound, not to kill.[129]
General Rabin saw no reason to change the orders by which refugees
trying to sneak back should be fired upon. Dayan supported Rabin's position; "He [Dayan] was not too impressed by the number of the dead,"
remarked Yisrael Li'or, Eshkol's military aide-de-camp. Eshkol and some
other cabinet members firmly demanded an end to this unnecessary
bloodshed.[130]

Nevertheless, Israel stated publicly in October that persons attempting to cross the ceasefire line from the East Bank at night would
be shot on sight.[131] In December, Mayor Hamdi Kan'an of Nablus told
an American television correspondent that Israeli troops had killed 150
refugees attempting to return to the West Bank. All had been buried in
one big pit dug by a bulldozer. Military censorship suppressed the story.[132]
Some six months later, in a meeting with Dayan, Kan'an mentioned the
killing in July and August 1967 of 14 Palestinians, among them a number of youngsters, who had been trying to go across the Jordan to the
West Bank. The defense minister responded: "Are you surprised that a

Zahal [Israel's army] patrol shot people trying to cross the Jordan at night when a state of war exists between Israel and Jordan?"[133]

Israel's decision makers, divided as they were on almost every issue, subscribed to one shared guideline: it would be most advantageous to have as few Arab inhabitants as possible in the occupied territories in general and in the Gaza Strip—intended to be annexed to the State of Israel—in particular.[134] About 3,000 men were expelled from Gaza after the end of the hostilities; Israel argued that they were members of the PLO's Palestine Liberation Army. In early July an UNRWA officer visited their place of refuge in al-Tahrir province north of Cairo and heard from them that many did not belong to the PLA. Nearly 50 of them, in fact, were UNRWA employees, and hence barred from the PLA.[135] Decades afterward, Maj. Gen. (res.) Moshe Goren, the first military governor of the Gaza Strip and northern Sinai after the June War, revealed that he had received the order to expel Palestinians from Gaza from Maj. Gen. Yesha'yahu Gavish, the commanding general of the Southern Command, in the presence of Defense Minister Dayan. Lt. Col. (res.) Yitzhak Moda'i, then the military governor of the city of Gaza and in later years a cabinet minister, said that the Palestinian deportees were mostly young men who had been selected by the GSS, Israel's security service.[136] Subsequently an ironfisted policy was applied in the Strip by the occupation forces in order to drive the Gaza refugees out.[137] Special efforts were also exerted in Arab Jerusalem to ensure an absolute Jewish majority in the unified city. Mayor Ruhi al-Khatib writes that about 5,000 people—7 percent of the overall population, mostly 1948 refugees—fled the city as a result of the brutal attitude of the Israeli conquerors.[138] According to the International Committee of the Red Cross, roughly 7,000 refugees left the greater city area.[139]

On 2 July, facing the danger of an unfavorable resolution under which the UN General Assembly might demand an immediate and unconditional withdrawal from the occupied territories, the Israeli cabinet gave in to the increasing pressure from Washington and other friendly governments, and from its own representatives on the diplomatic front line. With eleven in favor and seven against, the cabinet authorized the return of the displaced West Bankers from the East Bank; Premier Eshkol was one of the seven nays.[140] A senior army officer admitted to a British diplomat that the decision had been taken in part to counter the adverse publicity Israel had been receiving concerning the West Bankers' exodus.[141] King Hussein was nevertheless pleased and expressed his gratitude for the ruling during his secret meeting with Dr. Herzog later that day.[142] Little did he know.

Operation Refugee

The cabinet's decision permitted West Bankers who crossed to the East between 7 June and 4 July to go back no later than 10 August, provided that they constituted no security risk. The Israeli bureaucratic machine set about executing the decision. While waiting for details of how Israel proposed to implement the return program, code-named *Mivtsa' Palit*—Operation Refugee—Jordan's Interior Minister Radhi 'Abdallah hoped that at least 140,000 of the displaced persons would go back.[143] Laurent Matri, the Red Cross representative in Israel, offered a far more realistic—hence pessimistic—view: the return of just 100,000 people might take six to ten months; the thirty days allowed by Israel for the return scheme would not be adequate.[144]

Israel's leaders were, of course, wholly conscious of this fact. Their "gesture of goodwill," as the cabinet's decision was presented by official spokespersons, had been forced upon them, but they did not want the Palestinians who had fled to come back. Premier Eshkol told the Alignment's Political Committee on 7 July that the grand total of Arabs in the West Bank, the Gaza Strip, and Israel was 1.5 million, "and that is why I was not enthusiastic about the idea of bringing back refugees within one month." Habitually Eshkol embellished his statement with his favorite metaphor regarding the "demographic threat": "We won the war and received a nice dowry of territory, but along with a bride whom we don't like."[145] In mid-July Labor Minister Yigal Allon also explicitly expressed the wish that the new refugees remain in the East Bank.[146]

Little wonder, then, that the Israelis were rather sluggish about the arrangements concerning Operation Refugee. The British felt that the return of the refugees to the West Bank was subjected to "bureaucratic obstruction," as Foreign Secretary Brown put it to Israel's ambassador in London.[147] Observing from the East Bank as the Red Cross representatives shuttled back and forth across the Jordan, endeavoring to bridge the procedural issues between Jerusalem and Amman, the *Guardian* correspondent Harold Jackson dispatched a bitter article on Israel's "on-again-off-again tactics," which were "nearly incomprehensible except in terms of unfeeling real-politik."[148] When Israel finally delivered its proposed scheme to Jordan through the Red Cross in mid-July, it was unacceptable to both. Thus new refugees awaiting their return in harsh conditions had to wait—and suffer—longer. "The important thing is that people flow and not just papers," Assistant Secretary of State Lucius Battle wrote to Secretary Rusk.[149] Rusk instructed Ambassador Barbour in Tel Aviv immediately to tell the Israeli government that a delay in getting the repatriation started would appear as reneging on its promise.[150] From UN headquarters in New York Foreign Minister Eban cabled a similar message to Eshkol.[151]

The main obstacle was the application form which each head of family was required by Israel to fill out. The problem was not with any of the questions but with its heading. The bickering over the letterhead lasted three weeks. The first batch of forms was transmitted to Jordan on 17 July with a heading in Hebrew, Arabic, and English that read: "State of Israel, Ministry of Interior; Application for Permit to Return to the West Bank." The Jordanians refused to accept this form. They pointed to the fact that the draft questionnaire which they had approved did not carry the "State of Israel" letterhead. More important, the heading gave the impression that the West Bank was now part of Israel and that Jordan was dealing directly with Israel. Israel expressed its "dismay" at the Jordanian refusal to distribute the forms. An Israeli official claimed that the printing of official documents with this heading by the Government Printer was simply routine and it was done inadvertently in this case. Israel nevertheless refused to cut off the "inadvertent" letterhead or to replace it with the Red Cross symbol.[152]

Red Cross and UNRWA officials, the State Department, and many foreign diplomats pushed hard for the obvious solution: a triple heading which would mention the State of Israel, the Hashemite Kingdom of Jordan, and the Red Cross. Jordan accepted. Israel demanded direct contact between delegates of the two states in order to settle the practical arrangements for the return program, including the letterhead. Jordan accused Israel of using a humanitarian issue for political purposes, but eventually agreed to a low-level meeting at the Allenby Bridge, provided that Israel agreed to the triple heading. Israel, however, insisted on a mid- to high-level encounter before reaching its decision on the letterhead question. US Ambassador Barbour rushed to "make a presentation" to the Israeli government. The American pressure helped: one hour later Israel backed down.[153]

The meeting took place on the Israeli-occupied side of the bridge on 4 August. Israel was represented by Yosef Tekoah, deputy director general of the Foreign Ministry, and Jordan by Dr. Yusif Zahni, the secretary general of Jordan's Red Crescent. Tekoah accepted the triple heading but refused to include the Red Cross sign. So another Israeli-Jordanian meeting was scheduled for 6 August, and only then did Tekoah withdraw his objection to the Red Cross emblem. Roland Troyon, the Red Cross representative in Jordan, who had viewed the Israeli attitude as "harassment and petty obstructionism," soon found additional justification for this feeling: when the new application forms arrived in Jordan a few days later, they lacked the Red Cross symbol. The Israeli explanation maintained that a two-color form would have taken too long to print. Troyon was adamant that the symbol be printed by hand.[154]

The whole questionnaire saga might seem like a farce, had there not been tens of thousands of West Bankers languishing in the East Bank. Israel and Jordan accused each other of obstinacy and of making political issues of insignificant formalities. Both were right: each argument could have been turned against the respective accuser. Yet Jordan was correct with regard to the political gains Israel had in mind when it insisted on direct contact at the bridge. One of Israel's paramount demands ever since its military victory in June was for direct negotiations with the Arab states. So Foreign Minister Eban hastened to reap the political fruits of the Allenby Bridge meetings. In a press conference in Jerusalem on 14 August he spoke about a "direct agreement between Israel and Jordan" on the arrangements concerning the return of the new refugees. "This agreement," he went on, "has its instructive quality. It was a direct encounter between Israeli and Jordanian representatives that brought about this agreement."[155]

Because of the protracted haggling, the 10 August deadline set by Israel for Operation Refugee in the beginning of July was about to expire without any actual return, except for some 150 "special hardship cases" who had been allowed back on 18 July for propaganda purposes.[156] Thus on 6 August the cabinet pushed back the deadline to the end of the month.[157] The interdepartmental Execution Committee cautioned that the extended deadline would still not allow the bulk of the new refugees to be repatriated.[158] But Foreign Minister Eban knew better. He told the foreign press on 14 August: "We think the time between now and the 31st of August is sufficient." It had taken very little time for the West Bank refugees to go across, Eban added, so the decision to stay or to come back could also be taken quickly.[159]

The distribution of the application forms began on 12 August. Throughout Jordan dozens of registration centers were set up and, according to Jordan, by the end of the month some 40,000 applications covering about 170,000 persons were transmitted to Israel for approval.[160] The Israeli figures were smaller—only 33,000 applications for 112,250 people—but regardless, Israel had no intention of readmitting such a large number of Palestinians into the occupied territories.[161] Israel informed all concerned that it was ready to receive returnees at the rate of 3,000 a day.[162] The operation started on 18 August, so the return had to be completed within twelve working days (no return was to take place during the Jewish Sabbath). Basic arithmetic will show that Israel was willing to let in no more than 36,000 new refugees.

In fact, Premier Eshkol was hoping for far fewer. "One thing is clear to me," he told the Alignment's Political Committee on the very day Operation Refugee began. "We cannot increase the Arab population in Israel. . . . At this moment no one knows how to find a way out from the gesture we wanted to make in agreeing to the return of the refugees from Jordan. . . . I expect and hope that this will end up with 15–20 thousand."[163] Significantly, the prime minister was referring to the West Bank as part of the State of Israel. According to Ambassador Barbour, who had served in Israel since 1961 and was intimately familiar with the country's politics, Eshkol and other "old Zionists" in the cabinet were unwilling to have large numbers of refugees return because of the possibility that the ceasefire line along the Jordan River might become Israel's permanent border, and thus the additional Arab population would stay permanently in the State of Israel.[164]

When Operation Refugee got finally under way on 18 August, the number of persons who crossed to the West was much smaller than that authorized by Israel. Jordan argued that this was a result of procedures followed by the Israelis: each day, usually in the afternoon, they handed over the approved applications for return on the next day, leaving the Jordanian authorities twelve hours or less to contact those on the list—who were dispersed between several localities and camps—and to transport them to the crossing point. In many cases it was impossible to reach the designated people on such short notice; in other instances the approved returnees were unable to make it to the bridge in time. In still other cases, families refrained from going back because one or more of their members—frequently the breadwinner—were not approved for return.[165]

Yet the decisive factor in reducing the inflow to a relatively negligible figure was the Israeli strictness in vetoing the return of residents of Jerusalem and its environs including Bethlehem, the Jericho area, and UNRWA refugee camps throughout the West Bank. These were the largest groups who had registered for return. According to UNRWA's director in Jordan, almost the entire population of the three big refugee camps near Jericho, some 50,000 persons, applied for repatriation and were ready and eager to go back. None was allowed to do so. Only 3,000 of the 93,000 UNRWA-registered refugees who had crossed to the East were cleared by Israel; the agency's commissioner general said that they were from the Nablus area. His deputy informed the US consul general in Jerusalem that only 1 of the 5,000 Old City inhabitants was readmitted. The American diplomat knew of 14 returnees out of the 30,000 Greater Jerusalem area refugees; their applications had been approved because they gave addresses outside the region.[166] Eshkol's "lack of enthusiasm" about bringing the refugees back was indeed translated into a practical policy.

The United States stressed the high importance it attached to the objective of enabling all bona fide West Bank residents, including the 1948 refugees, to repatriate.[167] But Israel did not listen. Its policy regarding Jerusalem was to keep the number of Arab inhabitants in the city as low as possible, and certainly not to increase it.[168] As far as the 1948 refugees were concerned, the traditional Israeli position held that Israel bore no responsibility for the refugee problem and that a solution should be found outside Israel's borders. The cabinet—which for the time being declined to annex the Gaza Strip, largely because of its huge 1948 refugee population, and invested much effort in encouraging the Gaza refugees to emigrate—had no intention to allow any 1948 refugees back. The official in charge of Operation Refugee confirmed to a foreign journalist that the 1948 refugees were not considered eligible for return, and so did Chief of Staff Rabin.[169]

Attempting to ward off international accusations of hindering the return of the new refugees, Israel resorted to a counterattack, putting

the blame on Jordan. On 7 August, one day after Israel and Jordan concluded the procedural agreement, Jordan's chairman of the Higher
Ministerial Committee for Refugees, Finance Minister 'Abd al-Wahab
Majali, stated: "Every refugee should return there to help his brothers to
continue their political action and remain a thorn in the flesh of the
aggressor until the crisis has been solved."[170] In the words of a British
journalist, the Israelis were lucky to have such a quotation handed to
them.[171] The Foreign Ministry briefed Israel's diplomatic missions that
there was "a long delay by Jordan over the nature of official forms to be
filled out by refugees. In the meantime Jordan launched a campaign of
inciting returnees to become a spearhead of subversion against Israel."[172] Foreign Minister Eban went even farther, claiming that the
government of Jordan "would like them [the returnees] to fulfill a ter-
roristic role" by waging a guerrilla war against Israel, thus compelling
Israel to be stringently vigilant about security screening.[173] Minister
without Portfolio Menachem Begin demanded that the cabinet rescind
its Operation Refugee resolution. Eshkol objected, but the cabinet
agreed not to extend the return period beyond the end of the month.[174]
An Israeli diplomat in London suggested to the Foreign Office that his
government deserved some praise for still going ahead with the return program despite Jordan's incitement of the Palestinian refugees,
while an American diplomat reported from Jerusalem that as the date
for the beginning of Operation Refugee drew near, Israeli officials and
press stressed the danger of readmitting a large number of potential fifth
columnists to Israeli-held soil.[175]

In Amman, US Ambassador Findley Burns raised the incitement
issue with King Hussein and Premier Jum'ah several times. He warned
them that stimulating Arab resistance in the West Bank could inhibit
both the new refugees' desire to return and Israeli willingness to allow
them back. Furthermore, it could offer a pretext for evacuating Arabs
from the West Bank: "There are certain people in Israel who have hinted
[that] they would like Israel to retain the West Bank for *Lebensraum* [liter-
ally 'living space,' a term used by Nazi Germany to justify its expansionist
policy] and security reasons." The king and his prime minister acknowledged that any agitation would be undesirable for Jordan. Jum'ah told
Burns that he had been annoyed by Majali's "thorn in the flesh" expression and had personally ordered that this phrase be neither published

nor broadcast. On 10 August he summoned all the press and radio personnel and instructed them to say nothing which might be interpreted as stimulating civil disobedience in the West Bank. He also told them to minimize news reports of dissidence in the occupied area. American monitoring of the Jordanian media indeed indicated that the coverage of what was happening in the West Bank was factual and almost identical to reporting in Israel. "We detect no incitement," Ambassador Burns concluded.[176] After two weeks, during which Israel continued to complain incessantly about Jordan's "violent campaign of incitement," Undersecretary Rostow rejected the Israeli claim: the US government, he wrote on 25 August, was satisfied that instigation from the East Bank had been muted in recent weeks.[177]

As the final repatriation date approached and the number of returnees remained low, the United States, Britain, the UN secretary general, the Red Cross, UNRWA, and others exerted mounting pressure on Israel to extend the deadline. Israel refused to budge. As early as 16 August, two days before the beginning of Operation Refugee, Dr. Herzog acknowledged that it would be impossible to justify ending the return program on 31 August, and he therefore suggested abolishing the scheme altogether: making a peace offer to Hussein—inevitably on Israel's terms—or demanding that he publicly pronounce an end to the incitement in the West Bank; so long as the king accepted neither, Israel would not readmit any of the new refugees, save for family reunion. "Thus," Herzog said, "we would prevent the return of tens of thousands." Eshkol, however, chose to go ahead with the program in the hope that a way would be found to limit the repatriation to a small-scale family-reunion scheme.[178] Now, despite forceful international criticism, the Israelis simply reiterated the incitement charge and pointed to Jordan's alleged incompetence in facilitating the repatriation operation, meanwhile ignoring the real stumbling blocks in the way of the intended returnees: the ban on the return of UNRWA-registered refugees and residents of Jerusalem, Bethlehem, and Jericho; the short notice given to approved applicants; and the separation of family members.

Some of the Israeli excuses were ludicrous. London Ambassador Aharon Remez, for example, told British Foreign Secretary George Brown on 30 August—when civil disobedience in the West Bank was at its height—that the West Bankers themselves did not want Israel to allow

the return of a "disruptive element which would disturb the present tran-
quility of life" in the occupied area. The Israeli arguments and excuses were universally rejected. Brown warned Remez that because
of its rigid position Israel would lose friends.[179] Secretary of State
Rusk delivered particularly strong messages to Israel. The sudden cut-
off of the return program, he wrote on 23 August, "would have severe
repercussions . . . and leave Israel in a very difficult position." Two days
later Rusk ordered Barbour to tell the Israeli government that by insisting on the 31 August deadline it would lay itself open to the accusation
that it—not Jordan—was playing politics with a humanitarian issue.[180]

    In fact, this was precisely what Israel was doing, according to
Avi'ad Yafeh, Eshkol's private secretary. In early September, at a dinner
given by *New York Times* correspondents in Jerusalem at which an
American diplomat was also present, Yafeh wondered whether the Israeli government did not have the right to use the refugees as a political
weapon, since the Arabs had been using them that way for so many
years. Yafeh went on to say that of course Israel did not want any of the
refugees under its control and welcomed a reasonable opportunity to
cut off the return from the East. Unrepatriated, Yafeh concluded, the
West Bankers constituted a means of pressuring Hussein toward recognition of Israel.[181] Another explanation for Israel's attitude was offered
by David Farhi, a Hebrew University scholar who had been recruited
to the Military Government because of his expertise on Arab affairs.
When an American diplomat estimated that at least 100,000 new refugees desired to repatriate, Farhi smiled wryly and said that if such a
number returned, "they would destroy us." Arab leaders, Farhi added,
still talked of driving the Jews into the sea.[182]

    In the cabinet session on 27 August, after Eban reviewed the
diplomatic pressure regarding the deadline, the ministers decided to
allow two additional weeks, but only for "no-show" cases—those who
had already been approved for return but had for whatever reasons not
yet crossed back. The cabinet resolution also endorsed a decision taken
by a special ministerial committee three days earlier to issue no more
than 6,000 additional permits to return. At first the government intended to avoid publicity for its decision to extend the deadline, and the
resolution specifically instructed Eban to delay by a day or two inform-
ing the Americans about the new development.[183] But following a harsh

letter from Rusk to Eban, sent immediately after the expiration of the deadline, the 27 August resolution was made public, although with no mention of the length of the extension.[184]

Rusk's letter was indeed alarming: "The sympathy which the American people have for Israel would be weakened," he warned, "and with it the ability of the U.S. Government to take [a] constructive position on Israel's behalf."[185] Still, the Israeli policy makers, determined to diminish the Palestinian population under Israel's control, refused to yield further. At most, Israel was willing to donate materials for the construction of housing in the East Bank for the West Bank refugees whom they refused to readmit; in October, the cabinet approved a donation of 1 million Israeli pounds (equivalent then to $333,000 US).[186]

UNRWA's director in Jordan estimated at the beginning of September, after Operation Refugee ended, that the number of new refugees in the East Bank was 192,000.[187] Only about 14,000 actually returned to their homes in the West Bank.[188] At the same time the outflow eastward continued at the rate of several hundred a day: 10,226 West Bankers and 4,512 Gazans crossed into Jordan during August alone. Their combined number was higher than the number of the Operation Refugee returnees.[189] Those who left the West Bank after 4 July were forbidden to come back; they left nevertheless because of various economic and social reasons, coupled with the strict measures applied by the occupation authorities and, particularly in Gaza, due to the Israelis' unsubtle "encouragement" to leave.[190] The international community kept demanding that Israel allow all the June War refugees to repatriate.

Foreign Minister Eban, back in New York for the annual UN General Assembly, was unable to cope with the pressure. In a cable to Eshkol, Eban defined the cabinet's policy regarding the return of the new refugees as "niggardliness" and desperately insisted on an Israeli gesture: "After we had been fortunate with the flight of 350,000 [persons] from the administered territories," Eban wrote, Israel's friends—including all the Jewish leaders who had spoken with him—found it very difficult to understand why the cabinet refused to consider the return of 20,000 or 30,000 people, "of which a large number would leave within weeks anyway."[191] A few days earlier Eban had endeavored to soothe his party comrades' concerns about the "demographic danger." "The number of those who leave is much higher than of those who return," he told them. "Therefore, the cabinet believes that if 20,000 or 30,000 of them should return, this would be a political problem, not a demographic one."[192]

Contrary to Eban's claim, however, the cabinet did not subscribe to this belief. The government had reluctantly authorized a restricted family reunion program, but the vast majority of the displaced West Bankers had to remain in the East Bank.[193] Their return could take place only within the framework of a final and definitive solution to the whole Arab-Israeli conflict, Premier Eshkol told UK Ambassador Hadow in mid-October.[194] Eban, the Jewish state's most eloquent spokesman even on issues he personally opposed, reportedly promised King Hussein in 1969 that Israel would resettle the 1967 West Bank refugees "as soon as agreement had been reached on secure boundaries."[195] Four years on, Defense Minister Dayan also made the resolution of the new refugee problem contingent on a comprehensive settlement with the Arabs.[196]

"A guilty conscience and the dictates of self-interest are masked behind the defiant attitude of self-righteousness," wrote Ambassador Hadow on Israel's policy in his annual review for 1967. He concluded the dispatch by asserting that it was becoming increasingly hard to detect the humanism and humanitarianism so evident in the Jewish people in its exile.[197] Indeed, following the end of the hostilities, the conquering troops had demolished Arab villages, expelled their inhabitants, and rendered some 20,000 West Bankers homeless.[198] The occupation forces had pushed Palestinians to cross to the East Bank, and in some cases had forcefully driven them out; but most significant, Israel was preventing the great majority of those who had fled or had been expelled from returning to their homes. This was a "retroactive transfer"—an expression coined as early as May 1948, just after the State of Israel had been founded, by Yosef Weitz, one of the main proponents of cleansing the land from its native Arabs, a concept euphemistically known as "transfer."[199]

Whereas in 1948 the return of 700,000 refugees would have been to a State of Israel whose Jewish population barely exceeded 650,000, the new refugees of 1967 wished to go back to their homes in the occupied territories. Israel's attitude, then, clearly attested to its resolve to keep the West Bank, and Operation Refugee was nothing but an attempt to obscure this. "To this day," wrote the historian Gabriel Piterberg in 2001, "what structurally defines the nature of the Israeli state is the return of Jews and the non-return of Arabs to Palestine."[200]

The West Bank leadership followed the whole new refugee affair very closely and with growing resentment. In its statements and petitions the political elite denounced the destruction and expulsions by Israel, called for the repatriation of the *nazihun,* or displaced persons, and demanded that those who had been banished from border villages be allowed back to their destroyed settlements. "Various measures have been used in attempts to induce the inhabitants to leave the country and to prevent them from returning to their homes," read one of the petitions, signed in mid-August by more than eighty notables.[201] In their view, the manner in which Operation Refugee was handled reflected Israel's true intentions and exposed its hypocrisy.[202] The disillusionment was now complete. Yet the Palestinian elite, perhaps paradoxically, was not ready to give up hope of finding a political settlement, even if it meant dealing directly with Israel.

An Entity versus a King

September–November 1967

The emergency special session of the UN General Assembly adjourned on 21 July without producing a resolution demanding that Israel withdraw from the lands it had conquered during the June hostilities. Foreign Minister Abba Eban was jubilant. "A favorable impasse has been created," he told his party's leaders at the end of July. Eban suggested maintaining the diplomatic impasse by avoiding a cabinet decision regarding the West Bank.[1] But as the summer of 1967 drew to a close, the scene for the political struggle over the fate of the occupied territories shifted again farther from the disputed area, first to the Sudanese capital Khartoum and later to the UN headquarters in New York. In both venues the paramount goal of most of the international community was to make Israel pull back. Israel attempted to sidestep such a demand by the United Nations, and refused to acknowledge the moderate tone that emerged from the summit conference of the Arab League in Khartoum. A no less crucial aim of Israel's foreign policy was to evade negotiations with King Hussein. The hitherto ignored Palestinian option offered Israeli policy makers an escape route.

A Turning Point in Khartoum

The driving force behind the Khartoum Summit was King Hussein of Jordan. Hoping to regain his lost lands through a peaceful settlement

with Israel, Hussein concluded immediately after the defeat in June
that the Arab heads of state must convene and discuss the course they
should now take. The efforts he invested in convincing his fellow Arab
rulers to hold a conference finally bore fruit. The summit opened on 29
August and lasted four days; only Syria, entrenched in its extreme position, refused to attend. The joint communiqué issued at the end of the
conference on 1 September showed that realpolitik had prevailed: the
Arab leaders resolved to employ political and diplomatic means in
order to "eliminate the consequences of the aggression"—to restore the
prewar borders. The Israelis, however, pointed to the three "no"s included in the summit's resolutions—"no peace (*sulh*) with Israel, no
recognition of Israel, no negotiations with Israel"—as an unequivocal
proof of Arab animosity and intransigence.[2]

The three "no"s had been proposed by Ahmad al-Shuqayri, chairman of the PLO, and were largely incorporated in the resolutions to
satisfy his firm demand.[3] Muhammad Heikal, President Gamal 'Abd
al-Nasser's confidant, describes them as "a way of putting a brave face
on defeat and papering over inter-Arab differences."[4] When Nasser returned to Cairo from Khartoum, he told his information minister that
"no peace with Israel" meant "no peace treaty." A treaty, Nasser explained,
would constitute recognition of the Arab defeat. "I cannot negotiate
now," he said, "but this doesn't mean that I am not going to negotiate
forever."[5] The three "no"s notwithstanding, the Arab leaders, who up
until then had been determined to consider only belligerence toward
Israel, realized at Khartoum that in the circumstances they should seek
a political settlement. Evidently they had come a long way since their
first summit in Cairo in January 1964 in which the main decision had
effectively called for "the final liquidation of Israel."[6]

As recognized by contemporary Western observers, the Khartoum decisions heralded a significant turning point in the Arab approach. President Lyndon Johnson, for example, told British Foreign
Secretary George Brown that he believed in the genuineness of the new
mood of moderation displayed by the Arabs at Khartoum, while at the
same time he felt that the Israeli attitude was hardening.[7] The British
Foreign Office agreed: "The Khartoum Conference produced a welcome
and encouraging climate of moderation among the Arab states."[8] Lacking military might to match Israel's for the foreseeable future, President
Nasser and his Arab colleagues opted, albeit grudgingly, to embark on

a diplomatic path. Such a new course, with the dynamics involved, could have led to a real breakthrough in resolving the Arab-Israeli conflict. Muhammad Mahjub, Sudan's premier and a key player at the summit, says in his memoirs that the Khartoum resolutions were the first step toward an eventual negotiated settlement.[9]

Israel, whose intelligence services managed to obtain the verbatim text of the in-camera deliberations at Khartoum, was fully aware of this sea change in the Arab attitude.[10] Maj. Gen. Aharon Yariv, Israel's chief of Military Intelligence, informed the Knesset Foreign Affairs and Security Committee that it had been decided at the summit to go for a "political solution."[11] In an informal discussion at Foreign Minister Eban's residence, Dr. Ya'acov Herzog, Prime Minister Eshkol's closest adviser, maintained that whatever the Israeli public interpretation of the Khartoum resolutions might be, they marked Arab progress toward peace.[12] Abba Eban seemed not to share this view and suggested that due to the inclination of the world press to characterize the Khartoum resolutions as moderate, the government of Israel must expose them as extreme. Referring to the "no recognition" segment of the resolutions, Eban quipped: "The main question now is not whether Hussein recognizes the State of Israel, but whether Israel recognizes Jordan."[13]

A few weeks later, however, Eban was more candid. "I fear," he said behind the closed doors of the Knesset Foreign Affairs and Security Committee, "that any readiness of the Arabs to accept things which they refused to accept in the past might lay waste to the front which we have formed [at the United Nations]."[14] Available records show that Israel's policy makers feared Arab moderation. Following the discussion in the cabinet of the Khartoum Summit, Dr. Herzog confided to his diary that the Arab rejection of the idea of peace negotiations did not disappoint or frustrate the Israeli leadership. It was becoming increasingly evident that the longer the status quo prevailed, the better it was for Israel: there was no serious threat of renewed hostilities, "and in the meantime we hold on to the territories and have time to think, plan and maybe even to act."[15]

Thus Israel hastened to exploit the three "no"s of Khartoum as a pretext to further toughen its political stance. The cabinet's reaction took shape in a public government statement which said that because of the three "no"s, Israel would "strengthen its position in view of the vital needs of its security and development," and would not budge from the

June ceasefire lines. This revised policy was adopted by the cabinet on 17 October and ratified by the Knesset on 13 November.[16] Between these two dates the cabinet—wholly mindful of the ongoing deliberations at the United Nations—in special sessions on 7 and 8 November drafted another, stricter resolution which was not made public but instructed Foreign Minister Eban promptly to transmit its content to the American government: "Israel," it read, "considers that the determination of agreed and secured boundaries between itself and its neighbors can *only* be achieved in the framework of peace treaties."[17] Both decisions put together spelled a further retreat from the cabinet's 19 June resolution, which had manifested an ostensible Israeli readiness to withdraw to the international borders with Egypt and Syria in return for peace (see chapter 1).

The Israeli cabinet backed away from the 19 June resolution for the first time as early as 30 July by making Arab-Israeli peace conditional on direct negotiations (see chapter 2). The 17 October decision, which stated that Israel would "strengthen its position in view of the vital needs of its security and development," portended the Israeli government's intention not to relinquish all its territorial conquests and to establish Jewish settlements on them. The 8 November resolution explicitly excluded any accommodation with the Arabs not arrived at through direct negotiations and formalized by contractual accords. Furthermore, in contrast to the 19 June resolution, whose text referred to the international border as the basis for peace treaties with Egypt and Syria, the new resolution did not mention the international borders at all. "For your information," Eshkol cabled Eban at the end of October, "I doubt whether the cabinet would approve today the precise decision of 19 June."[18]

In what appears to have been a symbolic endeavor to demonstrate its new tack, the cabinet decided that henceforth Israel's maps—produced by the governmental Survey Department—would not feature the armistice lines of 1949 (dubbed the Green Line) but would show only the ceasefire lines of the June 1967 War, which encompassed the entire Land of Israel—the State of Israel, Jordan's West Bank, and the Gaza Strip—in addition to Syria's Golan Heights and Egypt's Sinai Peninsula. There was a fear, however, that the new map might contribute to diplomatic fallout in New York. The decision thus provided that the new map should not be published until the end of the current session of the UN General Assembly.[19]

The symbolic act of removing the prewar borders from the official map was accompanied by a much more tangible step—the beginning of building Jewish settlements in the occupied territories. Pressure from various circles to settle Jews in the "liberated lands" had already begun during the war in June. The first settlement was established in the Golan Heights barely one month later, in mid-July, without formal government authorization but with the strong support of Labor Minister Yigal Allon, who funded the settlers—members of Upper Galilee kibbutzim—using his ministry's special budget for work projects for the unemployed.[20] In the wake of the Khartoum Summit, the government felt that it was time to embark on a planned settlement project in the Golan, the West Bank, and Sinai.[21] The issue was discussed in the cabinet several times. On 10 September, Justice Minister Ya'acov Shimshon Shapira alerted his colleagues to the international illegality of civilian settlement in occupied territories.[22] Shortly afterward Theodor Meron, the legal counsel to the Foreign Ministry, likewise advised Foreign Minister Eban and Premier Eshkol's private secretary that civilian settlement in the occupied territories would contravene the Fourth Geneva Convention.[23] Notwithstanding the breach of international law, the cabinet on 10 September approved a number of settlements in the Golan and northern Sinai.[24] Two weeks later, on 27 September, the first West Bank settlement was set up in the Etzion Block, between Bethlehem and Hebron.[25]

The settlers were religious Jews motivated by nationalistic zeal. Most of them were child survivors of the original Kfar Etzion, one of the four kibbutzim which had been built during the 1940s in the Etzion Block, an area allocated by the UN Partition Resolution of November 1947 to the proposed Arab state. In mid-May 1948, after a four-month Arab siege, the Jewish settlements fell. Dozens of the settlers were massacred and others were taken prisoners of war by Jordan's Arab Legion.[26] The new settlement, now in the occupied West Bank, was founded without prior formal approval of the cabinet. On 24 September, Premier Eshkol merely informed the cabinet that a he'ahzut (settlement) would "soon" be established in the Etzion Block. He added that the establishment of another settlement, in the Jordan Valley, would be considered during the coming month.[27] Eshkol's announcement received much publicity and triggered diplomatic criticism, followed by desperate dispatches from Israel's envoys abroad.[28] Most notable among them was Foreign Minister Eban, who attended the UN General Assembly in New

York. In an urgent cable to Jerusalem, Eban reminded the government that it had been agreed to build settlements if need be, but without making any announcement. Eshkol's announcement, he concluded, "damages us here."[29]

A week later the cabinet attempted to avert foreign condemnation by passing the following secret resolution: "Settlements whose establishment has already been decided upon (in the [Golan] Heights, the Etzion Block and Sinai) will be, until further resolution, in the framework of the *Nahal* or a military-agricultural settlement."[30] *Nahal,* a Hebrew acronym for Fighting Pioneer Youth, was a military framework which combined service in a combat unit with civilian service in a newly founded agriculture settlement. The cabinet resolution was intended to allow Israel to claim that the Jewish settlements in the occupied territories served military purposes and thus did not violate the Fourth Geneva Convention. The army's high command was told by the defense minister's office that "as a 'cover' for the purpose of [Israel's] diplomatic campaign," the new settlement in the Etzion Block should be presented as a *Nahal* military settlement and the settlers should be given the necessary instructions in case they were asked about the nature of their settlement.[31] Similar orders were issued regarding the Golan settlements.[32] The Foreign Ministry directed Israel's diplomatic missions to translate *he'ahzut* as "strongpoint" and to emphasize its alleged security importance.[33]

Kfar Etzion was a civilian kibbutz from the very start.[34] Neither its settlers nor the Golan settlers were ready to take part in their government's charade.[35] The enthusiastic Israeli press did not play along either, leaving—as a State Department briefing paper recorded—"no doubt that the settlements were there to stay."[36] This was precisely the Israeli intention, as confirmed publicly by many Israeli leaders. The Etzion settlement and the many more settlements to come were designed to prevent territory from being returned to any Arab rule.[37]

When the Americans, distrustful of Israeli disingenuous explanations regarding the new settlements in the occupied territories, received through Abba Eban the cabinet resolution of 8 November, they could only conclude that this was "a prescription for 'instant peace' entirely on Israel's terms." Assistant Secretary of State Lucius Battle described the resolution as a "profoundly disturbing development" that should be viewed in the context of "growing Israeli territorial appetite."[38] This grave allegation was effectively acknowledged by none other than Prime

Minister Eshkol. Referring to public statements—including his own—
during the June War and immediately afterward, in which Israel had assured the world that it did not seek territorial gains, Eshkol stated in
closed meetings: "In the early days we said that we were not going [to
war] in order to occupy lands, . . . but I argue that *a priori* is not the same
as *a posteriori*."[39] Already in mid-August Eshkol virtually confessed to
the Alignment's Political Committee that the cabinet was constantly
changing its "formulae" regarding the occupied territories: "And he saw
that it was good," the prime minister added, paraphrasing a verse from
the Creation story in Genesis.[40] Defense Minister Dayan bluntly asserted
at a party rally in August that Israel must ensure "living space"—an expression shockingly reminiscent of Adolf Hitler's infamous *Lebensraum*—to deter "adventurous Arab leaders," and that therefore it must
not return to the prewar borders.[41] When Secretary of State Rusk reminded Eban of Israel's June pledges, the foreign minister "simply
shrugged his shoulders and said, 'We've changed our minds.'"[42] And so,
long before the end of 1967, Israel was seen by even its staunchest ally, the
United States, as taking a hard line.

The Palestinian Entity Movement

The Khartoum Summit accepted that priority should be given to the
recovery of the West Bank, including Arab Jerusalem, over the rest of
the occupied Arab territories. King Hussein stressed at the conference
the danger that Israel's measures in the West Bank might drive some
of the inhabitants to negotiate the creation of a Palestinian government
that would collaborate with Israel. He read a letter to that effect which
he claimed had been sent to him by Anwar al-Khatib, his former governor of the Jerusalem District. President Nasser unreservedly supported
Hussein's plea: Sinai, Nasser said, can wait; the West Bank cannot.[43] In
fact, shortly after the end of the hostilities Nasser had given the Jordanian monarch a green light to do whatever he deemed necessary—even
to go as far as to terminate the state of belligerency with Israel—in order
to retrieve his conquered region, so long as he refrained from direct
negotiations and signing a separate peace treaty with the Jewish state.[44]
The Israeli intelligence learned about this almost instantly.[45]

  The West Bank political elite were of course oblivious to the green
light that had been given to Hussein. Before the summit they had nur-

tured high hopes of general Arab endorsement of a reasonable peace plan. At Hussein's behest several notables had even helped in persuading Nasser to convene the summit.[46] Although the West Bankers' request to be represented at Khartoum had been denied by the Israelis, they were encouraged by the news about the recommendations of the preparatory conference of the Arab foreign ministers in Khartoum in early August.[47] A month later, following the summit, their hopes for a quick solution were shattered; it became clear that the occupation would be a prolonged one. An American diplomat in Jerusalem reported that many Palestinians were further depressed by the apparent failure of the summit to produce a plan for an accommodation.[48]

Military Government soundings immediately after the summit corroborated Hussein's stark warning at Khartoum that the West Bankers might collaborate with their occupiers. The survey found that many Palestinians believed that they had been abandoned by the Arab rulers; a number of them argued that they should therefore take their lot into their own hands and start negotiations with Israel about setting up an independent Palestinian government, or even to discuss annexation by Israel. "We, the Arabs of Palestine, must secure a satisfactory settlement with Israel," an unnamed notable was quoted in a press article as saying. The GSS, Israel's internal security agency, reported in early September that the deep feeling of disappointment at the outcome of the summit led Muslim and Christian inhabitants of Arab Jerusalem to feel that they should come to terms with the occupation, establish contacts with the Israeli authorities, and get on with their daily life. A number of dignitaries assembled in Arab Jerusalem to discuss these ideas.[49]

It is unclear whether the lawyer 'Aziz Shehadeh, the political maverick from Ramallah, took part in the Jerusalem gathering. But it was he who in the wake of the Khartoum Summit set in motion a prolonged and intensive debate among politically conscious West Bankers about the pros and cons of a separate Palestinian solution. On 6 September, Shehadeh, together with former Ramallah Mayor Bulus Saba, joined the district's military governor when the latter hosted a group of Israeli journalists at his office. Shehadeh told the reporters that a considerable number of prominent Palestinians throughout the West Bank—politicians, professionals, and businessmen—had been meeting recently to discuss the formation of a movement that would work for the establishment of a Palestinian entity in the West Bank. He did not

dwell on the specifics of the envisaged entity but indicated that Arab
Jerusalem must be part of it. Israeli leaders, Shehadeh complained, had
been talking about peace with the Arab states while ignoring the Palestinians. He claimed that more than half of the West Bankers were in
favor of his views.[50]

Shehadeh's last point was undoubtedly an overstatement. The
civil disobedience orchestrated by the pro-Hashemite National Guidance Committee was then still raging, and the overall mood in the
West Bank favored return to Jordanian rule.[51] Still, quite a few local
dignitaries were inclined to go it alone. Most prominent among them
was Hebron's influential mayor, Sheikh Muhammad 'Ali al-Ja'bari, who
openly talked about self-reliant political endeavors in press interviews
and with foreign diplomats. He even strove to mobilize the Gazans behind the concept of an independent Palestinian state.[52] There were others,
predominantly members of the Christian minority, who attempted
to round up backing for the so-called Palestinian option. Muhammad
Darwish, for instance, a Muslim from Bayt Jalla, drafted a manifesto
calling for a congress of the West Bank leadership to revoke the decision of the Jericho Conference of December 1948 which had given
Jordan the legitimacy to annex the West Bank, and to deliberate the
foundation of a Palestinian state.[53] In fact, the journalists who recorded
Shehadeh's comments in Ramallah met a few hours later in Bethlehem
with Ayub Musallam, a former mayor and cabinet minister, and Mayor
Elias al-Bandak, and learned that they effectively backed Shehadeh's
nascent movement.[54]

Like Shehadeh, Musallam addressed the newsmen at the local military governor's office. In both cases the choice of venue was most unfor-
tunate, for it gave rise to the suspicion that the Israeli government was
behind the Palestinian entity initiative.[55] Available documentation does
not substantiate this allegation; quite the contrary. On the heels of Shehadeh's statement, the Israeli interdepartmental Coordinating Committee rejected a proposal to encourage the emergence of moderate political
movements in the occupied territories to counterbalance the "extreme
national elements." At the time, such activity was not desirable, the committee concluded; maybe in the future, particularly once the government
had formed a policy concerning the fate of the territories.[56]

As we have seen—and shall see further—such a policy was never
formed. The so-called moderates and their ideas were equally ignored

by Israel. All the same, Foreign Minister Eban—an avowed opponent of the Palestinian option—presented the declared desire for an independent state to Secretary of State Rusk as one of the options considered by Israeli policy makers. "[The] Mayor of Hebron, for example, has evidenced interest perhaps because he sees an opportunity to exert leadership in a sovereign new state," Eban told Rusk in a meeting in New York in late September. "Gleam of sovereignty among leaders in [the] West Bank is similar to attitudes evident in communities in Cyprus. This [is] only an incipient movement, but some 'state personality' could emerge on [the] West Bank."[57]

By mid-September, Shehadeh's initiative became the topic of the day in every political circle throughout the occupied territories and was vehemently debated. Many expressed opposition or reservations. Some adopted a practical attitude: as reported in a GSS document, a group of notables in Arab Jerusalem—Anwar Nuseibeh was one of them—concluded a series of deliberations by agreeing that it was inadvisable openly to approach the Israeli authorities about the establishment of a Palestinian government in the West Bank because they would be humiliated in the likely event that the Israelis did not respond.[58] "The question is whether Israel recognizes the Palestinians," an unidentified prominent Palestinian remarked poignantly.[59] The Military Government's weekly report for mid-September affirmed that due to the uncertainty regarding Israel's intentions, the "entity movement" lacked momentum. Furthermore, the ambiguity over the future of the West Bank reinforced the extremists.[60]

Nevertheless, the proponents of the Palestinian option were virulently attacked from both banks of the Jordan River. In Amman, Prime Minister Sa'd Jum'ah accused the West Bankers who were "collaborating with the enemy in establishing a buffer state" of high treason; he strongly implied that Sheikh Ja'bari was one of them. A Jordanian official described the mayor of Hebron as "an agent, a hireling and a tool in the hands of the foe." Amman radio and the local press repeated the charges and directed similar ones against 'Aziz Shehadeh.[61] The newly formed underground National Front in the Gaza Strip and its organ, *Al-Muqawamh* (the Resistance) vilified Shehadeh and his followers and violently condemned the idea of creating a "feeble Palestinian entity under the protection of the occupation authorities' bayonets."[62] In Arab Jerusalem members of the National Guidance Committee decided to denounce Ja'bari for his recent statements concerning collaboration with Israel.[63] Shehadeh himself revealed to an American diplomat that he had been threatened by both Amman and the West Bank.[64] Toward the end of the month Mayor Hamdi Kan'an of Nablus warned Shehadeh to stop talking about a Palestinian state.[65] A French journalist who returned from Nablus intimated to a Military Government official that Kan'an had mentioned Ja'bari to him and said—while drawing his hand across his neck—"soon he will be slaughtered."[66]

Ja'bari, Shehadeh, and the others who constituted the nascent "entity movement" found themselves in a Kafkaesque situation: they were seriously accused on the one hand of being Israel's lackeys, while on the other Israel ignored their thinking. The charges of betrayal directed at them were unsubstantiated. Sheikh Ja'bari, for instance, proposed that a twelve-man executive committee, elected by a conference of 2,000 Palestinian delegates and empowered to speak on behalf of the Palestinian people, should open negotiations with Israel as well as the neighboring Arab states on a peace settlement.[67] Clearly there was nothing "treacherous" about this scheme. What triggered the campaign by Amman and its faithful in the occupied territories against the supporters of the entity idea was the fear that they might sabotage Jordan's efforts to recover the West Bank and Arab Jerusalem.

Aiming to overwhelm the entity movement, the pro-Hashemites initiated an "Interim National Covenant" (Al-Mithaq al-Watani al-Marhali), proclaiming the West Bank an inseparable part of Jordan and deploring any attempts to establish a Palestinian entity. The covenant, signed by 129 prominent West Bankers, eminent Muslim and Christian clergy, and representatives of various associations, reflected consensus among widely varying political creeds. Its text appeared in a few Arabic newspapers and was also broadcast on Damascus and Baghdad radios in early October. It is not clear, however, whose brainchild it was. A Palestinian source says that the charter's text was drafted in a gathering which took place at an unspecified venue on an unspecified date. The Communist leader Na'im al-Ashhab claims that it was the Communists' effort. The introductory notes in the Lebanese daily Al-Hayat reveal that the document was submitted for publication by the PLO bureau in Beirut. Israel's GSS argued that a new radical organization collaborated with the "Jordanites" in producing the covenant. Accord-

ing to this intelligence account, following the setback to the National
Guidance Committee—resulting from the expulsion of it head, Sheikh
Sa'ih, on 23 September—a new Political Front was formed in the West
Bank for the purpose of resisting the occupation. Hikmat al-Masri, a
former Jordanian cabinet minister and speaker of the Chamber of Deputies, was the person behind this organization, which was composed of
members of the Communist and al-Ba'th parties, the Arab Nationals
(al-Qawmiyyun al-'Arab), and the PLO; like Masri, all the other main
activists were natives of Nablus.[68]

Despite the commitment to the unity of the two banks, the covenant most certainly antagonized King Hussein because it also expressed dissatisfaction with the prewar regime and called for a more
democratic one, giving the Palestinians equal opportunities, including in the military. It may be that at least the radical sponsors of the
document aspired to "Palestinianization" of Jordan. Additionally, the
covenant demanded that Jordan adopt an "independent foreign policy" comprising "positive neutrality and nonalignment." This implied
a policy more sympathetic toward the USSR than the hitherto close
ties with the United States and the West.

Some names were conspicuously missing from the long list of the
covenant's signatories. Most noticeable was the absence of Anwar al-
Khatib, who had returned to Jerusalem from his exile in Safed (see
chapter 3) just before the text was composed.[69] Khatib was regarded by
many as King Hussein's man in the West Bank, but the positions he
enunciated now tended to fluctuate. While still in Safed—eager to end
his distressing and costly exile—he had voiced an idea which he must
have believed to be to Israel's liking: a federated Arab-Israeli Palestine.
Even if Israel preferred a settlement with Hussein, Khatib said, it must
be sought through the Palestinians. "Don't look to Washington or London, or to Cairo or even Amman," he pleaded with the Israeli policy
makers via a press interview. "Look here, to Nablus, Jerusalem, and Hebron."[70] He reiterated his conviction that the West Bank should form a
political system separate from the East Bank and not subject to Hussein's rule in a meeting with Rustum Bastuni, an Arab citizen of Israel
and former member of Knesset, who visited him in Safed on 9 September. If the Israeli authorities would permit, Khatib told Bastuni, he
would be ready to resume political activity—but only in a framework

directed at the creation of some sort of a Palestinian entity, closely
linked to Israel. Many West Bankers endorsed this concept, he said, including Anwar Nuseibeh.[71]

Upon his return to Jerusalem, however, when Khatib was asked to
put his money where his mouth was, he displayed a rather reluctant attitude. When ʿAziz Shehadeh and the journalist Mahmoud Abu al-Zuluf
visited him, they invited Khatib to join the entity endeavor and suggested sending a delegation to the United Nations to speak on behalf of
the Palestinians. Khatib rejected the idea, arguing that such a move was
premature, that a deputation must be empowered by a general Palestinian congress, and that Israel would not permit it.[72] A few days later, in a
meeting with Major Farhi of the Military Government, Khatib reverted
to an Israeli-Jordanian solution to the West Bank problem.[73]

Anwar Nuseibeh's name did not appear on the covenant's signatories list, either. Nuseibeh—perhaps the most distinguished figure in the
occupied territories and a former Jordanian cabinet minister, district
governor, and ambassador—offered the notion of a unified Arab-Jewish
state with a central parliament. Such a binational state, he argued, would
solve the problem of Jerusalem. Nuseibeh disclosed to a US diplomat
that he had shared his thoughts with some Israelis, including members
of Knesset, but none had discussed the matter in an official capacity. He
viewed an autonomous Palestine entity as a better option than the existing situation but regarded it as his least preferred option.[74] Others were
attracted to the prospect of creating a binational state in Palestine,
among them Dr. Rashid Nashashibi, who nonetheless signed the covenant.[75] Evidently the volatile political situation drove quite a few to
hedge their bets.

Mayor Hamdi Kanʿan of Nablus struggled to belittle the calls for a
separate Palestinian-Israeli settlement. In a meeting with Major Farhi
in mid-October, Kanʿan acknowledged that some segments of the leadership in Jerusalem and Hebron were indeed ready for an independent
solution, but these people were of a lesser stature than the Israelis believed. Kanʿan said that the leadership of Nablus, without exception,
wanted the return to Jordanian rule—in order to preserve the Arab
nature of the West Bank and to avoid disconnection from the Arab
world—and a lasting peace between reunited Jordan and Israel. True to
Israel's policy of seeming indifference to the political currents in the

occupied territories, Farhi refrained from even asking Kan'an any clarifying questions.[76]

Hilmi Hanoun, the mayor of Tulkarm, who appeared to incline to the concept of a Palestinian entity independent of Amman, revealed in a press interview that a group of West Bank mayors meeting in Nablus in late October had all agreed to drop the idea for the moment because they did not want to be isolated from the Arab world. Their projected state, he said, should have to be approved by the Arab League.[77] A British diplomat in Jerusalem thus advised the Foreign Office in London that the entity movement had subsided, as some of its supporters had grown lukewarm about the feasibility of its ambitions.[78] The reports of the movement's demise were greatly exaggerated, however.

Around that time, 'Aziz Shehadeh and his associates completed a long series of discussions with many West Bank leaders and drafted a political program which expounded their thinking, including the practical steps required for its realization. The paper was distributed among dignitaries whose cooperation was sought. It suggested convening a congress of Palestinian representatives "from every province and district" of Palestine, which would establish a national council charged with electing a national assembly. This assembly would represent the Palestinian people before the Arab world and internationally; endeavor to reach an agreement with the Arab League and the Arab leaders on a unified plan for "saving the situation from deterioration"; demand that the United Nations recognize the Palestinian people's right of self-determination; and negotiate with the "parties concerning the Palestinian problem," but only if this would lead to an "honorable, favorable outcome." The outcome would then be brought before the Palestinian people for ratification in a referendum. Signed "The Preparatory Committee of the Palestinian National Council," the typewritten document carried no names, but press reports pointed to Sheikh Ja'bari as one of its main instigators.[79]

Shehadeh and his group of ardent Palestinian separatists used in their program the Arabic term *qawmi* for "national"—which suggests all-Arab nationalism—while the authors of the Interim National Covenant, whose text embodied pan-Arab sentiments, chose the word *watani,* which refers to the attachment to one's native land, or patriotism. The word choices were doubtless intentional, designed to blur the distinct nature of each platform and make each appeal to a wider constituency.

The evolving controversy over the two opposing orientations, the Jordanian option and the Palestinian option, climaxed in a stormy meeting of Ramallah and al-Bireh dignitaries which took place in Ramallah's city hall in mid-October. The meeting was convened to protest against the wanton murder of two local public works employees by two Israeli border guards following a minor road accident near Ramallah on 9 October.[80] The only source for what occurred in that gathering is the apparently slanted account of 'Abd al-Jawad Saleh, the radical mayor of Al-Bireh, which was written a decade later. According to Saleh, proponents of the entity movement diverted the discussion from the tragic crime to the burning political issue at hand: electing a local advisory committee as a first step toward setting up a national body entrusted with founding the Palestinian entity. The proposal provoked a heated debate. The objectors, led by Saleh, accused their opponents of collaborating with the occupation authorities. In response, 'Abd al-Nur Janho, a staunch follower of Shehadeh's entity initiative, said—while pointing to the handgun he was carrying—that anyone opposing the local committee once it was legally elected would be taken care of appropriately. Eventually, Saleh says, he managed to gain the backing of the majority of the conferees. Shehadeh, Janho, and a third person, 'Izzat Karman, left the assembly hall without anybody following them.[81]

Nablus, branded "the very furnace of Mahometan bigotry" in the nineteenth century, has remained the most radical city in the West Bank ever since.[82] Its leadership continued vigorously to lead the opposition to the entity initiative. Dr. Hamdi al-Taji al-Farouqi, a Ramallah physician, tried unsuccessfully to patch up the breach between 'Aziz Shehadeh and the Nablus politicians.[83] The latter prepared a manifesto expressing their objection to a separate solution, and in addition resolved to meet Shehadeh, Anwar Nuseibeh, and Anwar al-Khatib in order to persuade them to cease any activity directed toward the establishment of a Palestinian state. Their main argument was that such a state would exclude Arab Jerusalem, whereas a Jordanian-Israeli settlement would compel Israel to make concessions regarding the Holy City. The meeting was held at Anwar al-Khatib's home in Jerusalem on 30 October. Israeli and Palestinian sources relate that Shehadeh promised to refrain from further activity so long as Nablus did not agree to cooperate with the entity movement, while the Nablus delegates—among them Hikmat al-Masri, Qadri Touqan, and Walid al-Shak'ah—undertook to study the entity idea and in the meantime to shelve their manifesto. They also decided to send an envoy to Cairo to seek President Nasser's advice.[84]

Dr. Farouqi—described by Major Farhi as a "lone wolf" who had been persecuted by the Jordanian regime for his involvement with the Ba'th party—did not favor the return of the Hashemite regime. But he differed from Shehadeh and his group on the course that should be taken in order to achieve the desired political entity. He thus drafted his own plan, calling it "The Proposed Palestinian State." At the end of October he began sending copies of the plan to some 500 West Bankers, and also to rulers and influential people in the Arab world—including Egypt's President Nasser, Syria's President Atasi, and the PLO's Shuqayri—whose support he wished to gain. Unlike the Shehadeh-Ja'bari paper, which avoided any talk about the nature of the entity, the five-page document drawn up by Farouqi offered in some detail the contours of the envisioned state, which was to be established by consent of the Arab governments or, should they object, by approval of the Palestinian people in a referendum. Its borders would follow the lines of the UN Partition Resolution of 1947, with Arab Jerusalem as the capital. For the first five years the infant Palestinian state would be under the nominal auspices of the Arab League and the practical supervision of the United Nations. Farouqi stressed the need to maintain good neighborly relations with Israel, yet in the long preamble of his plan he expatiated on the expansionist and aggressive character of the Jewish state. Farhi reported that some Arab Jerusalemites held that Farouqi deliberately chose what was described as an apologetic tone to preempt accusations from nationalist quarters.[85]

Reconstructing the past—always a complex and uphill pursuit—is even more precarious when the available records are almost exclusively Israeli intelligence reports based on informants' accounts. After all, Palestinian sources had their own agendas, their own reasons for relating information to their occupiers. The information they offered was not always true or accurate, and accounts received from different Palestinian contacts were sometimes mutually contradictory. In the absence of independent Palestinian evidence, the emerging picture regarding the political scene in the West Bank during the months under review here is far from complete. But two major political currents can be identified as developing in the occupied area: one favored a reunion with Jordan, and the other argued for a separate accommodation. It is also clear that the Israeli authorities maintained a watchful eye but did not interfere or strictly enforce the ban on political organization.[86] More important, they refrained from reacting to any of the proposals or ideas put forward by the Palestinians. A response would have entailed a decision concerning the future of the occupied territories, something that the government of Israel wished to avoid.

Jordan had a completely different perception of the situation. The American ambassador in Amman reported in early November that the Hashemite regime regarded the recent talk about an entity as having been stimulated by the Israeli government, "which was seeking to use as spokesmen opportunistic 'nobodies' among [the] West Bankers whom none would follow."[87] Jordan's newly appointed prime minister, Bahajat al-Talhuni, stated disparagingly in a television interview that "Israel's endeavors to create a Palestinian state cannot succeed" in the face of the West Bankers' rejection of this scheme.[88] In reality, however, Amman had become perturbed by the bustling activity in the West Bank stirred up by discussion of a separate entity. On 11 October, after his government deliberated the issue for five hours, Premier Talhuni instructed Jordan's ambassador in Washington to approach Secretary of State Rusk urgently and demand that the United States apply pressure on Israel to rescind its support for the creation of a Palestinian state.[89] As we have seen, Amman's assumptions were unfounded. Yet Israeli policy makers, under increasing American pressure to negotiate a settlement with King Hussein, realized that the entity movement which worried the Jordanian monarch so much offered them useful leverage if negotiations with him were to take place.

The Palestinian Alternative Stratagem

The fall months of 1967 were spent in reinvigorated diplomatic endeavors to produce an acceptable UN resolution about the aftermath of the war. "The main thing now is to get through the regular [General] Assembly safely," Foreign Minister Eban said in the cabinet on 10 September.[90] The battlefield, however, was no longer the General Assembly but the Security Council. Israel sought relentlessly to block wording demanding a total pullback from the territories it had captured in June.

Eban candidly disclosed in a confidential forum on 20 October that Israel's first preference was no UN resolution at all; the second was a resolution concerning merely procedural matters; and the third a resolution in which principles, if mentioned at all, would be obscure. He then traveled to the United States; according to Donald Neff—relying on a detailed State Department research paper—Eban and his ambassador to the United Nations, Gideon Rafael, exerted "threats and assurances," particularly directed at the Americans, to ensure vague language regarding the question of withdrawal.[91]

On 23 October the Israeli foreign minister arrived in Washington for a series of top-level talks, including with President Johnson. The Americans' incessant attempts to learn from Eban what his government wanted produced only recurrent statements that Israel would never return to the 4 June lines. As for the new lines, Eban said that the cabinet had not decided how different they should be. Instead, he time and again volunteered to outline the conflicting viewpoints within the government.[92] The loquacious Eban "turned aside discussion of thorny issues and talked out the clock," Walt Rostow reported to the president.[93] The Americans still insisted on hearing something of substance. Eban yielded to pressure just before his meeting with Johnson: he told Undersecretaries Nicholas Katzenbach and Eugene Rostow that Israel territorial requirements vis-à-vis Jordan could be satisfied with only "small security adjustments."[94]

This was untrue, according to Abba Eban himself. In an unpublished manuscript about the Six Day War, completed in 1969, Eban says that between the summer and the fall of 1967 the Israeli thinking had "moved to broader perspectives. . . . Demilitarization arrangements would not be sufficient without territorial change in several areas. . . . *Substantive* changes of the previous lines would be necessary if peace were to be secure."[95] In truth, the Israeli cabinet was not prepared to concede anything as far as the West Bank was concerned. The moderate stance Eban presented in Washington thus angered many in Jerusalem. Minister of Information Yisrael Galili demanded that Premier Eshkol instruct Eban to avoid any talk that might even remotely imply an Israeli readiness to relinquish the West Bank. A resolution declaring the Jordan River as Israel's eastern border, Galili concluded, was inevitable.[96] Eshkol's chief adviser wrote a cable rebuking Eban on behalf of the prime minister and stressing that it had been decided long ago that only when the other side was ready to negotiate would the cabinet discuss its position.[97]

The Americans, who accepted Eban's words at face value, were pleased. Expecting King Hussein in Washington in early November, they had urged Israel to allow progress toward a settlement with Jordan. The foreign minister's pledge was the basis on which President Johnson promised Hussein the return of the West Bank to his rule within six months.[98] There was indeed ample room for optimism: upon arrival in the United States the young monarch revealed to his hosts that he and President Nasser had on 17 October decided to declare an end of belligerency with Israel; to recognize the right of every state in the area to live in peace and security; and to open the Suez Canal and other international waterways to Israeli navigation. These concessions were conditioned on Israel withdrawing its forces from the occupied territories, accepting the end of belligerency, and cooperating in finding a permanent solution to the refugee problem.[99] The Jordanian-Egyptian agreement was effectively confirmed by President Nasser in a meeting with Robert Anderson, an unofficial American envoy, on 2 November.[100]

Jordan and Egypt, then, proposed a peaceful coexistence with the Jewish state. The State Department lost no time in breaking the good news to Israel. Hussein means business, US Ambassador Arthur Goldberg informed Eban on 4 November, and gave him a full account of the king's proposal. He also indicated Nasser's concurrence. The foreign minister was neither surprised nor impressed. He told Goldberg that the Israeli embassy in London had already cabled him that the king was saying similar things there, but with the addition that Israel should "restore [the] June 4 situation." Eban asserted that this distinction was "crucial."[101]

In fact, the Israelis were alarmed. They had learned from several other diplomatic sources about the Hussein-Nasser agreement and the consequent readiness of the king to strike a deal with them.[102] The new development meant that the moment of truth was imminent, but they were not prepared for it. A cable Premier Eshkol sent to Eban in New York on 12 November was explicit: the reports on Hussein's talks in the United States, he wrote, uncovered the wide gulf between Israel and America regarding the future of the West Bank and perhaps of Jerusalem too. The prime minister went on to say that the prevalent hypothesis in Jerusalem assumed that Israel would manage to survive the General

Assembly—would escape a UN resolution—and would try afterward to formulate a substantive policy concerning the occupied territories; the prime minister asked the foreign minister whether this hypothesis was still valid. Evidently Eshkol feared it was not. In Dr. Herzog's assessment, Hussein was likely to use his peaceful proposals to get the United States and the United Nations to lean heavily on Israel. To Herzog's dismay, Eshkol betrayed in a public speech that through intermediaries Hussein—whom the Israeli leader scornfully nicknamed "the Flying Dutchman" for his many trips abroad—had expressed his willingness clandestinely to meet with Israel's representatives. In his cable to Eban, Eshkol relayed that the cabinet had decided that morning to launch a publicity campaign against Hussein's "propagandist moves" because—in the premier's words—"it is necessary to rebut his feigned 'moderation.' . . . It is necessary to stress that [the] Arab rulers are [using him] to deceive the West."[103]

The anti-Hussein campaign began without delay. Available records show that the campaign was premeditated. Some two months before, Galili appointed a three-member "working group" of senior officials to design the Israeli *hasbarah* (propaganda) against the settlement-seeking king. On 2 October one of the group's members circulated a detailed three-page proposal on how "to refute Hussein's positive image in world opinion, especially in the West, in order to support the foreign and security policy of the Government of Israel" during the period the UN General Assembly was in session. The paper suggested that Hussein be described as an aggressor who shared the desire to liquidate Israel.[104] On 12 November, the day the cabinet decided to launch the anti-Hussein campaign, the Foreign Ministry instructed its missions in the United States, Britain, West Germany, France, and Italy to discredit King Hussein's ostensibly moderate and constructive statements. Despite the king's peace initiative in July, which had been effectively rebuffed by Israel (see chapter 2), the Israeli diplomats were to say that Hussein was unwilling to recognize Israel or to coexist with it, and that he refused to meet Premier Eshkol. The Israeli emissaries were also told to encourage Jewish organizations to speak publicly along these lines.[105] That day the Israeli consulate general in New York issued a statement accusing Hussein of hypocrisy and "remarks verging on racism."[106] Though Eban cautioned Eshkol that the nature of the campaign against Hussein should take account of potential implications for Israel's relations with the United States, the negative propaganda continued. On 18 November the American embassy in Amman confirmed that "the Israelis are persisting in their campaign against Hussein."[107]

The campaign did not put a stop to the pressure the Israelis dreaded. In fact, the Americans had been exerting pressure on both Israel and Jordan for quite some time. However, so long as King Hussein did not restate his intention to talk, Israel was able not only to disregard the pressure but also to present itself in the diplomatic arena as eager to meet the king at the negotiating table. Moreover, the Israeli message for Hussein was unequivocal and blunt: time was not in his favor; he would therefore be well advised to stop dragging his feet. In order to make this message more convincing, Eban played, yet again, the Palestinian card. In his meeting with Undersecretaries Katzenbach and Rostow he stressed that the passage of time was a significant factor with respect to a settlement with Jordan. He claimed further that "provisional arrangements" with the Palestinian leadership had been contemplated in Israel, leaving a final settlement in abeyance.[108] Shortly afterward, when Eban was received at the Oval Office, he reiterated the same argument: "There are many Arabs on the West Bank who ask why we do not make a deal with them. . . . We are not encouraging this posture on their side, but Hussein ought to know that this is what many of them think. He should decide soon if he does not want the position to crystallize." In other words, Eban told the president that Israel had a real alternative to the king—the West Bank Palestinians—so Hussein should hurry up, or else.[109]

There was a serious flaw in Eban's ruse: it did not account for Hussein's readiness to negotiate. Four days before he saw President Johnson, Eban had told the Knesset Foreign Affairs and Security Committee that the king's tactics were to try to find out through numerous middlemen what Israel's peace terms were without committing himself to negotiations. Israel, Eban continued, always responded by saying that it would satisfy Hussein's curiosity in full at the negotiating table.[110] In reality, however, Israel was unable to do so because there had been no decision regarding the Palestinian-inhabited territories.[111] As Dr. Herzog put it candidly when a State Department official inquired whether Israel had any contingency planning for negotiations with the Arabs: "None had gone on since July because the issues involved were so sensitive that discussion within the [cabinet] might well bring about the fall of the war cabinet [the National Unity Government]."[112] The Palestinian alternative was used simply to convince the Johnson administration that Israel was weighing its options. But following Hussein's new diplomatic overture, negotiations with Jordan—and exposure of Israel's empty rhetoric—seemed unavoidable. Israeli policy makers sought a way to repel this danger and to place Israel in an advantageous position once negotiations got under way. Thus they maintained the Palestinian alternative—but now as a ploy directed at the Jordanian monarch.

Eban had already broached the idea before the Foreign Affairs and Security Committee when he speculated that contacts with the West Bankers could prod Hussein toward a settlement.[113] Labor Minister Yigal Allon also saw merit in dialogue with Palestinians in the occupied territories because in his opinion it might encourage Arab governments to come to the negotiation table for fear of a separate deal with "the Arabs of the Land of Israel."[114] But the main proponent of this stratagem was Defense Minister Dayan. In November, during a meeting with leaders of the Movement for the Whole Land of Israel—an organization formed by prominent Israeli public figures and intellectuals weeks after the war demanding the government to keep all the occupied lands—Dayan disclosed his wish to find West Bankers who would be willing to cooperate with the government in determining the fate of their region in order to reduce international pressure on Israel.[115] The defense minister elaborated his thinking in internal discussions. Dr. Herzog recorded several instances in late October and early November in which Dayan suggested holding talks with both Hussein and the Palestinians simultaneously. Dayan believed that when a meeting with the king took place, he should bluntly be told that the West Bankers "were not in his pocket"; and by negotiating with them, he added, Israel would undermine Hussein's standing in the West Bank.[116]

In a discussion about economic policy in the occupied territories at his office on 10 November, Dayan expressed his consternation that Hussein had been turning into the West's chosen darling. Israel, he argued, needed a "maneuvering option"; it must create a "'positive' alternative" to Hussein as an interlocutor. Dayan pointed to the "movement for an independent Palestinian state"—the Palestinian entity movement—as such an alternative. Contacts with this movement would enable Israel to claim that there were West Bankers who wished to cut a deal with Israel. "Hussein is scared to death of this," he said. The meeting was called primarily to deliberate a comprehensive program aiming to "encourage" Palestinians to emigrate. Dayan passionately desired to push the Palestinians out, but because of the importance he attached to the "alternative" concept, he ordered his subordinates to refrain from applying economic pressure on the inhabitants of the occupied territories lest the alternative evaporate with their emigration.[117] A week later, at a plenary session of the interdepartmental Coordinating Committee, the defense minister restated the necessity of an alternative to Hussein.[118]

Dayan was right that Hussein was fearful of the creation of a Palestinian state: the king expressed his apprehension in his talks in Washington and London, and the Israelis were duly informed.[119] Undoubtedly this was one of the motives that drove them to launch a new round of talks with the West Bank leadership. On 12 November, Eshkol chaired a consultation session in his office, which he opened by asserting the need to examine the likelihood of a movement for an independent state in the West Bank, and to determine which Palestinian leaders Israeli cabinet members—perhaps even the prime minister himself— should meet. Eshkol proposed setting up a small ministerial committee under his chairmanship, comprising the defense, foreign, and police ministers, to handle the project. Dayan agreed, suggesting the organization of separate, uncoordinated groups of West Bankers to demand an independent state, thus constituting an alternative to Hussein.[120] Dayan thought that the Gaza Strip Palestinians should also be organized in order "to [put] pressure on Hussein."[121] Premier Eshkol, who in October already had begun weighing the idea of contacts with the Palestinian political elite, appointed the Foreign Ministry official Moshe Sasson, a former member of the Committee of Four (see chapter 2), as coordinator of the new ministerial committee; in practice, Sasson, a native Arabic speaker, was entrusted with carrying out the talks with the Palestinians.[122] His letter of appointment, signed by the prime minister later that day, stated that his assignment would last between three and six months.[123]

Meanwhile, Israel received more evidence from the United States regarding Hussein's declared intention of rapprochement, and there were also other indications to that effect. Top-echelon figures seemed to have been convinced. "In his heart he wants peace with Israel," Dr. Herzog assured Premier Eshkol on 7 November. "Had we withdrawn, he certainly would have signed peace [with us]."[124] Herzog, who maintained the secret channel of communication with the Jordanian monarch, knew through his clandestine contacts that Hussein wanted to talk with his Jewish neighbors. The king said so to the British politician Julian Amery in Amman in late September, and again to Dr. Emanuel Herbert, his Jewish physician and main intermediary with the Israelis, in London on 1 November.

During October other sources informed the Israelis about Hussein's wish to hold a high-level meeting—preferably with General Dayan, possibly with Eshkol, but definitely not with Eban, whom the king regarded as bereft of independent thinking—in order to find out whether a Jordanian-Israeli settlement was achievable. After long and extensive deliberations the Israeli policy makers decided against such an encounter, for a number of reasons, not least among them personal motives, particularly on Eban's part. The decisive factor, though, was Israel's inability to tell the king anything of substance. Nevertheless, Dr. Herzog traveled to London on 1 November for a prearranged meeting with Hussein, initiated by the latter, and felt relieved when Dr. Herbert told him that Hussein had decided at the last moment to cancel. "Apart from asking whether he [the king] was ready to negotiate, I actually had nothing to say to him," Herzog noted in his records.[125] Yet the two men saw each other when Hussein made another stopover in London on his way back from the United States eighteen days later.

Although available records do not reveal how this meeting came about, it is safe to assume that the king initiated it. He and Herzog met at Julian Amery's home on 19 November for nearly two hours. The Israeli told Hussein that Premier Eshkol and Foreign Minister Eban had asked him to convey a message of goodwill. He had been instructed, Herzog continued, to inquire whether the king had reached a decision about direct negotiations with Israel, leading to a peace treaty. In response, Hussein outlined the position he had presented to the Americans, based on his 17 October understanding with Nasser. Herzog said that this was not good enough: what the king was proposing was effectively an armistice agreement of the kind that had not been honored during the past twenty years, whereas Israel would accept nothing less than a peace treaty arrived at through direct negotiations. Herzog then lectured Hussein about the historical association of the Jews with the Land of Israel and claimed that the root of the Arab-Israeli problem lay in the Arab refusal to acknowledge this. When the Arabs agreed to direct negotiations, Herzog concluded, this would attest to their acknowledgment of "our right to our country." Smiling wistfully, Hussein asked: "What were the limits of the land?"

As we shall see, the "historical association" with biblical *Eretz Yisrael* was a key Israeli concept. It meant that Jews had the inalienable right to settle anywhere in the West Bank. Herzog, however, did not explain the import of the phrase in so many words. He told Hussein only that "even the minimalists [in Israel] emphasized security and historical association" and asserted that "this was not expansionism."

The king, on the other hand, wanted the West Bank back. He agreed that direct negotiations should be official and public, but said he would not be able to negotiate with Israel without the consent of his fellow Arab rulers. However, if the people of the West Bank approached him, he would be free to enter into negotiations with Israel on his own and without seeking agreement of the other Arab states. But he must know in advance the Israeli position. Herzog reminded his interlocutor that he had been sent merely to discuss the king's preparedness for direct negotiations. What he said next was intended to emphasize the polyphonic, confused thinking of his government. Some Israelis, Herzog said, insisted that the present situation should continue unchanged; others felt that in order to achieve peace Israel should negotiate with Jordan; still others maintained that Jordan had no right whatsoever to the West Bank and that negotiations should be held with the Palestinians. Hussein replied that he had sent a message to the West Bankers to hold on. "If you wish to make propositions about the area, I should consider them, but I must receive a reply about the Western Bank."

At this point the Israeli emissary resorted to the "Palestinian alternative." He said that some West Bankers wanted the restoration of the king's rule, but there were others who desired to become part of Israel, and others again craved an autonomous Palestinian entity. Is your position regarding the West Bank rigid? Herzog asked. "My position is not rigid," Hussein answered. "It is flexible, but I have my rights. I want to know your position." He repeated several times in the course of the conversation his plea that Israel not be obstinate, and indicated that the issue of Jerusalem might upset all hope. Before parting, when Herzog summarized their talk, Hussein said that he beseeched Israel not to recognize a separate Palestinian entity. Herzog asked the king whether he wished to include this plea in the summary as a stipulation, and Hussein told him that he did. The two men met again at Dr. Herbert's house the following day; Herzog recapped their previous discussion, and Hussein approved his account.[126]

So the king spelled it out: he would accept Israel's precondition for direct negotiations. Hussein was sincere, and the Israelis knew it. Before he told Dr. Herzog that he would negotiate with Israel if the West Bankers approached him, he had taken steps to make it happen. Mayor Nadim al-Zaru of Ramallah disclosed to the local military governor in early November that Amman had asked the West Bank notables to organize a petition demanding that the king reach a peace settlement with Israel if the Security Council discussions came to naught.[127] Once again, the ball was in Israel's court. It was incumbent upon the Israelis to set out their proposals regarding a settlement with Jordan and the future of the West Bank. They did not bother. Instead, the Israelis chose to seek the best bargain they could get from either Hussein or the West Bankers.

Defense Minister Dayan explicitly outlined this attitude in another discussion of the contacts with the West Bank leadership which took place at Premier Eshkol's office a day after the Hussein-Herzog meetings. Israel, Dayan said, wanted peace and direct negotiations, and it did not want an additional million Arabs in the country. "We are ready to buy peace from whoever is willing to offer it. . . . If Hussein wants peace we will deal with him. Should the Palestinians want this we may deal with them. Moreover, it is in our interest that Hussein should not appear as the only claimant to the [West] Bank." Dayan therefore suggested "nurturing" the Palestinians, both for tactical reasons vis-à-vis Hussein and perhaps even as a substitute to the king. Furthermore, the pro-Hashemite West Bankers should be encouraged, as well as the proponents of a separate solution. Police Minister Eliyahu Sasson concurred: encouraging the rival factions simultaneously would provide Israel with more room for maneuver. Prime Minister Eshkol approved the divide-and-rule strategy. The meeting adjourned with an agreement to allow the Palestinians to consult with King Hussein, President Nasser, or any other leader outside the occupied territories about their position. As for Israel's position, the participants accepted the following guideline, again proposed by Dayan: Israel would demand peace and direct negotiations; all the rest was "secondary" and would be discussed at the negotiating table.[128]

Israel, then, only refined the "Palestinian alternative" ploy by permitting the West Bankers to see the king, thereby driving home even
harder the implicit message to Hussein: he should forget about recovering the entire territory he had lost in the war and hurry to the negotiating table with much lower expectations. Quite cynically the Palestinians
of whatever political inclination were cast for this tactical purpose,
though the Israelis kept their options open, ready to make a deal with
them rather than with the king. For what really mattered to the policy
makers—motivated by either security, historical, religious, ideological,
or messianic considerations—was keeping as much occupied territory
as possible with as little Arab population as possible under Israeli rule.

It was "simple arithmetic," said Premier Eshkol in a public address on 22 November while explaining why his government did not
decide what to do with the occupied territories. "Had we had here four
[or] five millions of Jews it would have been easier to decide." He reminded his listeners that the Palestinian citizens of the state—within
the pre-June borders, that is—amounted to "eleven or twelve percent"
of the overall population of 2.77 million. Eshkol's words could be interpreted only as an apologetic excuse for not annexing the West Bank
and Gaza Strip, because the 1 million or so Palestinians who lived there
would undermine the "demographic balance" of Israel. The inhabitants of Nablus and Jenin, the prime minister stated, were "numerous
as olives"; he then further illustrated the argument with his habitual
adage of the fat territorial dowry Israel had won in the war, followed by
a bride—the Palestinians—"whom we don't want." Eshkol stressed that
the "security border" of Israel must be the Jordan River.[129]

On that day, 22 November, the UN Security Council finally adopted a unanimous resolution concerning the aftermath of the June
War. The British-sponsored text, which has become known as Resolution 242 and turned into the cornerstone of all the attempts to solve the
Arab-Israeli conflict to date, emphasized the inadmissibility of the acquisition of territory by war but fell short of demanding a total Israeli
withdrawal; its English version called for a "Withdrawal of Israel armed
forces from territories"—not *the* (or *all the*) territories—"occupied in
the recent conflict." The exclusion of the definite article "the" was intentional, born of Israeli insistence, British ingenuity, and American
backing.[130] Years later Secretary of State Dean Rusk explained that the
purpose of omitting the article "the" was "to permit minor adjustments

in the western frontier of the West Bank, for demilitarization measures in the Sinai and the Golan Heights and for a fresh look at the future of the city of Jerusalem. Resolution 242 never contemplated the movement of any significant territories to Israel."[131]

The resolution was not what Israel wanted or what the Arabs wished for, but the deliberate "constructive ambiguity" its wording created was used by both sides to argue for their respective positions. The Arabs pointed to the lack of an explicit call for contractual peace with Israel, whereas the Israelis insisted that the withdrawal clause allowed them to keep parts of occupied territories. Significantly, Resolution 242 ignored the core of the Arab-Israeli conflict: nowhere in the text was the term "Palestine" or "Palestinians" mentioned. The only indirect allusion to the Palestinians was in a brief subsection that affirmed the necessity for "achieving a just settlement of the refugee problem." Lord Caradon, Britain's ambassador to the United Nations and the author of the final draft of 242, argued retrospectively that the resolution did not speak of Palestinian self-determination because "we all took it for granted that the occupied territory would be restored to Jordan."[132]

Despite its vagueness and flaws, Resolution 242 enshrined the overriding principle of the exchange of land for peace. Operatively it requested the secretary general of the United Nations to send a special representative to the Middle East to "promote agreement and assist efforts to achieve a peaceful and accepted settlement" of the conflict. Soon afterward Dr. Gunnar Jarring, Sweden's ambassador to the Soviet Union—whose appointment as the special representative had been decided even before the adoption of 242—began his Sisyphean peace mission. Saved from an unequivocal resolution demanding an immediate and unconditional withdrawal, Israel had now to prevent renewed discussion at the Security Council leading to a much stricter resolution than 242. The "Palestinian alternative" ruse was one way of achieving this goal.

So far the Israeli stratagem seemed to be working. On 30 November, King Hussein told the British ambassador in Amman: "There will have to be negotiations [with Israel] with or without a U.N. umbrella."[133] The American consul general in Jerusalem reported that the Palestinian reaction to Resolution 242 ranged "from unrealistic optimism to profound skepticism," yet all his contacts agreed that the resolution was a necessary first step toward peaceful settlement and withdrawal of the occupying forces.[134] In unruly Nablus, Mayor Hamdi Kan'an endeavored—according to an Israeli intelligence paper—to convince the city notables that the West Bank Palestinians should take an active part in the search for a solution, because their fate was in the hands not of the United Nations but of Israel.[135] Even US Ambassador Walworth Barbour in Tel Aviv was caught up in the sanguine mood. When Moshe Sasson informed him about his new assignment, the seasoned diplomat rosily prophesied: this "may be a significant change in Israeli relationships with [the] West Bank Arab leaders."[136] And so, the stage was conveniently set for Israeli-Palestinian talks. Only the Israelis had other ideas, or, it may be argued, did not have any ideas at all.

A One-Way Dialogue

December 1967–January 1968

Moshe Sasson's terms of reference as the "Prime Minister's Representative for Political Contacts with Arab Leaders in Jerusalem, the [West] Bank, and Gaza" were indefinite and broad: Israel demanded peace and direct negotiations and was willing to make a deal with the highest bidder; all the rest was left to his discretion. Sasson's interpretation of his task was to find out whether "the Palestinians *in Israel*" could play a role "in the political events" and, if necessary, "to activate them."[1] The forty-two-year-old Foreign Ministry official was an opinionated man with a distinct perception of the Arab psyche. He held that the leadership under occupation must be told what to do rather than being consulted.[2] On 17 November 1967, five days after formally assuming his new job, Sasson stated that the West Bankers should depend on Israel alone, and he thus suggested isolating the West Bank from the East in order to diminish its dependency on Jordan. Defense Minister Dayan, who believed that Israel needed to maintain all potential lines of communication with Jordan, dismissed his proposal forthwith.[3] A day later Sasson told the American ambassador in Tel Aviv that he did not have any preconceived ideas regarding a general political framework, and that he intended to carry out his assignment on a case-by-case basis.[4] Indeed, the first few talks with Palestinian figures—which had taken place even before Sasson's formal appointment—seem to have been directionless, some of them involving Arab interlocutors of insignificant stature.[5] But in view of the government's "Palestinian alternative" tactic, Sasson soon focused on the entity movement—its adherents as well as its opponents.

Negotiating the Negotiations

The West Bank notables who advocated a Jordanian-Israeli settlement accused 'Aziz Shehadeh and his group of opportunism in seeking personal material benefits.[6] Conversely, the separatists made similar allegations about their rivals. Because Nablus leaders had economic interests in Amman, Shehadeh argued, they acted upon its directives. It appeared, he said, that they were instructed to silence the entity movement.[7] Major Farhi of the Military Government was also informed by a Palestinian contact that Nablus's efforts to stifle the movement had been ordered by King Hussein.[8] Shehadeh's henchman 'Abd al-Nur Janho, an opulent Ramallah businessman who knew Hussein from their school days in England, was assigned by the group to soothe the king's concerns.

On 27 November Janho related to Sasson that he had met Hussein in Paris in late October and told him that the movement did not oppose the king; quite the contrary. However, the West Bankers felt that the present situation could not go on unchanged, and that the only way out was a peaceful settlement with Israel. If the king was afraid or unable to take this road, the Palestinians were not and could do so. Janho gave Hussein a copy of the political program which had just been drafted by Shehadeh and his associates (see chapter 5). The king's response, Janho claimed, was uncompromising: he was determined to retrieve Arab Jerusalem and every single square inch of the land he had lost in the war, and indicated that the Egyptian armed forces were fast regaining their strength. His ambassador to France who accompanied him was more precise and demanded that the West Bankers resist the occupation the same way the *Maquis* had in Nazi-occupied France. Hussein was unwilling to negotiate a settlement with Israel, Janho inferred, and without the West Bank he would turn into a hard-liner.[9]

The reliability of Janho's account is doubtful. Neither the language he attributed to the king nor the substance of his alleged response was compatible with Hussein's personal demeanour and political thinking. Janho's main goal was to convince Sasson that the entity proponents were ready for action—namely, negotiations with Israel—and that the movement was gaining backing from more and more West Bankers, including such influential personalities as Anwar Nuseibeh and An- toun 'Atallah. As we shall see, this too was untrue. Still, Janho and 'Aziz Shehadeh, who was also present at the meeting, said that in addition to Israeli recognition their group needed political and material support in order to increase its influence. In accordance with the government's policy line, Sasson told the two men that they should limit their ambi- tions to a peaceful solution arrived at through direct negotiations, without going into any specifics. He instructed them to arrange per- sonal meetings between their followers and himself. Thereafter, the movement's official appeal to the government of Israel—to be approved by him beforehand—should be drafted in a clandestine conference in which he would also take part. The Israeli record indicates that Sheha- deh and Janho acquiesced.[10]

Obviously, Sasson aimed at converting the entity movement into an Israeli-controlled puppet organization. Anwar Nuseibeh, who saw through his intention, cautioned that Israel might use the group as a political tool for its own ends. Shehadeh and Janho conferred with Nuseibeh immediately after the discussion with Sasson. Nuseibeh said that it was inconceivable to negotiate a peace settlement without any prior knowledge of its general outline. He argued that a Palestinian initiative could take place only if Israel accepted the following six basic principles:

- The UN Partition Plan of 1947 as a starting point, modi- fied as necessary in the light of security and political re- quirements;
- Jerusalem as the capital of the two states, run by two sepa- rate municipalities with a joint council;
- the Gaza Strip as part of the Palestinian state;
- all UN resolutions regarding the refugee problem as fur- ther underlying principles;
- the right of return of any refugee or Palestinian who so wished;
- Palestinian ratification of the settlement in a referendum.

In a meeting with Sasson on 30 November, Nuseibeh reiterated these tenets. The Arab world, he said, would not accept a Palestinian state made of "remnants of the [West] Bank." If, however, Israel contemplated a viable Palestinian state, the Arab world would welcome such a country. Which would it be? The answer depended entirely on Israel's intentions, Nuseibeh concluded.[11]

Janho, too, insisted that the state the entity movement envisaged must be viable. He and his comrades manifestly toed Nuseibeh's line. Janho, Shehadeh, and 'Isa 'Aql—a member of the Chamber of Deputies from Ramallah—called on Sasson that day and told him that they refused to be manipulated or exploited by Israel. They were practical men, Janho explained, and knew full well that Israel would never revert to the 1947 Partition Plan or agree to repatriation of Palestinian refugees; the solution they sought would leave the Palestinians only with the West Bank and the Gaza Strip. But it must appear as if both parties accepted partition as the basis of the settlement. Otherwise the Palestinians would be condemned as traitors. The three entity activists asked Sasson to transmit their proposal and arguments to Prime Minister Eshkol, with the assurance that a positive response would give their movement the power to carry the West Bank.

Sasson, however, would have none of this. Israel, he reminded his guests, demanded that the Arab states enter into direct peace negotiations before it revealed its concept of a future settlement. This requirement was all the more valid in the case of the Palestinians under occupation who did not constitute a government or represent a state and, most important, could not bring about an accommodation with the neighboring countries. By Sasson's own account, he was blunt and offensive. He advised Shehadeh, Janho, and 'Aql to abandon any illusions about the 1947 Partition Plan even as an ostensible starting point. Moreover, Sasson said that he would not even take a copy of Nuseibeh's six points away with him. The only basic question, he stressed, was whether or not their group desired a peace whose substance and particulars would be determined at the bargaining table. Sasson made it abundantly clear that if negotiations were to take place, they would involve two unequal parties, the victorious occupier and the vanquished. Nonetheless, the three Palestinians asked him to reconsider their wish to communicate their message to Levi Eshkol.[12]

Sasson saw the prime minister later in the evening to report on his talks with the West Bankers. On the entity movement the terse record of the forty-five-minute meeting merely mentions the difficulties which the proponents of a Palestinian state had been facing. Presumably Sasson did deliver their message, including Nuseibeh's six principles—after all, he had included them in his memorandum of the conversation—but the document does not reveal Eshkol's reaction or his further instructions.[13] Yet when Sasson received Shehadeh on 5 December, his attitude was even tougher than before. Shehadeh argued that the obscure Israeli "peace and direct negotiations" formula deterred many West Bankers from orderly political activity because they suspected that it was nothing but a tactical maneuver intended to trick the Arab world by bringing the Palestinians to the negotiating table. Sasson retorted sharply that he did not know on whose behalf Shehadeh was speaking: "Who are the Palestinians? They differ in their views, and I don't see [even] two [West Bankers] who share the same opinion." He demanded that Shehadeh provide him with a list of those who were willing to negotiate with Israel. The men on the list and their standing would then be evaluated; if they were deemed unrepresentative, Israel would regard the list as unsatisfactory. In any event, until Sasson received such a list, his government sadly must consider that there were no independent-minded Palestinians ready to work realistically for a solution.[14]

Although Sasson greatly exaggerated the dissension, there was some truth in his remark about the varied viewpoints among the West Bank leadership. In the beginning of December, after the prime minister's representative had conducted about twenty discussions, the political elite in Arab Jerusalem and Ramallah set up an advisory committee (*lajnah istishariyyah*) with the purpose of ensuring a unified position toward Premier Eshkol's envoy. The committee ruled that those who met Sasson must adhere to the principles of the National Covenant, which proclaimed Arab Jerusalem and the West Bank inseparable parts of Jordan (see chapter 5). Hence any political settlement would need to be negotiated between King Hussein and the government of Israel. Despite this, Moshe Sasson felt that the men he saw gave their own personal views.[15]

By mid-December, Sasson had held thirty-five meetings with thirty-three West Bankers.[16] On the whole, all of them wished for a peaceful solution and expressed disappointment at Israel's refusal to propose anything beyond the refrain "peace and direct negotiations." The predominant theme was that the conflict should be resolved through the Arab leaders—either Egypt's Nasser or the Jordanian monarch.

Anwar al-Khatib offered the good offices of the Palestinian leadership in transmitting Israel's basic concept regarding a settlement to Hussein, without which—he insisted—the king would find it difficult to enter into direct negotiations. Undoubtedly Khatib acted upon Amman's directives: Sasson learned that on the heels of their conversation the former Jordanian governor of the Jerusalem District dispatched a secret envoy to King Hussein with the following oral message: "They talked with me. Proposed nothing. [They] asked whether [we] were willing to convince Jordan to negotiate peace without preconditions. Awaiting instructions."[17] Similarly, Amman's fingerprints were all over a suggestion put forward by Hamdi Kan'an. The mayor of Nablus offered to send a delegation of West Bank notables to the East Bank demanding that Hussein make peace with Israel, and asked Sasson to furnish the delegation with the general terms of Israel's practical thinking. Not surprisingly, Sasson refused. He also rejected the request to permit a countrywide conference that would elect the members of the proposed deputation, telling Kan'an that he favored a single envoy, not a delegation.[18]

The Israeli representative, rigidly interpreting his government's vague guidelines, showed an exceptionally inflexible attitude. Clearly there was not much point in pursuing the talks when literally every idea was bound to bump into Sasson's "rejection front." But the Palestinians were not creative, either. Whereas the entity movement called for the establishment of an independent Palestinian state, the pro-Hashemite politicians from Jerusalem and Ramallah propounded no practical plan beyond volunteering to serve as intermediaries between Israel and Jordan. Time, however, was not in their favor. The Israelis were in no hurry whatsoever, while the West Bankers desired anxiously to rid themselves of the occupation.

It was Nablus's notables who initiated an attempt to break the deadlock. In late November six of the town's most prominent men gathered for a discussion in which one of them, Walid al-Shak'ah, broached the following scheme: Israel should transfer the internal administration of the West Bank affairs to its inhabitants as an interim step toward a peaceful settlement; Israeli troops should leave the occupied territories, creating the impression that the Palestinians ran their affairs without any pressure from the occupier. Subsequently Palestinian leaders residing outside the West Bank would be invited to return. The representatives of the Palestinian people and their leadership would then determine their future—whether to establish an independent state or to return to Jordan's rule—yet their first decision would call for peace with Israel. All but one were in favor of this crude plan. On 29 November, Shak'ah and Hikmat al-Masri separately communicated it to Sasson. Masri stressed that the plan was in line with President Nasser's recent speech in which he had stated that the "Palestine cause . . . belongs to the people of Palestine." Significantly, neither Shak'ah nor Masri mentioned Jerusalem or the Gaza Strip.[19]

As it happened, the proposal of the Nablus dignitaries coincided with a new Israeli approach designed by the defense minister. In mid-November, Moshe Dayan instructed the Military Government to create a quasi-Arab civil administration in the West Bank by turning overall administrative matters over to local hands and granting the West Bankers "maximum autonomy in running their affairs." Within a few weeks most of the Israeli civilian staff officers operating on the district level were replaced by Palestinian civil servants.[20] But Israel pulled out only its civil officials; the troops stayed put and the Military Government maintained rigorous supervision of all the administrative issues. Dayan's intention was to integrate the occupied territories into Israel, primarily in the economic sphere. Israel's policy, he told his subordinates, should be based on the premise that the West Bank was part of Israel.[21] This was definitely not what the Nablus leaders had suggested. Notwithstanding, in a report to the prime minister, Moshe Sasson argued that their idea could be developed into a "de facto canton" whose borders would be secured by Israel. He added that "the independent Palestinians of Ramallah"—presumably 'Aziz Shehadeh and his group—supported the idea wholeheartedly.[22]

Sasson's elaborate seven-page report seems an honest account of his discussions with three dozen West Bank personalities during the previous five weeks. The paper says that the majority of the interlocutors saw Israel as an uncompromising, expansionist country, which aspired to retain the entire occupied territories while reducing the number of their inhabitants. They believed further that Israel wanted to impose a peace settlement upon the Arab states by virtue of its military might and battle victories. Without exception, all sought to learn what Israel's plans were and expressed frustration at its unresponsiveness. Sasson identified four principal political currents prevailing among the West Bank elite: the first rejected any peace settlement; the second favored an Arab-Israeli settlement, preferably with King Hussein; the third demanded a Palestinian state; and the fourth, which he regarded as an "interim solution," backed the Arab administration scheme that was conceived by the Nablus notables. He portrayed the Communists and the members of the Ba'th party as rejectionists, arguing that they pretended to favor a settlement only to stay in the loop and thereby be in a position to push the moderates toward extremism. Conversely, many prominent leaders viewed the idea of an independent state as their second choice, should the attempts to reach a settlement between Israel and the Arab states fail.

In an accompanying letter Sasson advised Premier Eshkol to pursue the "Palestinian alternative" tactic by orchestrating pressure from pro-Hashemite West Bankers on Hussein to negotiate with Israel, so that the king could claim a peaceful solution on behalf of the Palestinians at the forthcoming Arab summit. In this context Sasson stressed the need to "restrain" the radical Communists and Ba'thists, and also suggested the deportation to Jordan of Ruhi al-Khatib, the former mayor of Arab Jerusalem who now headed the National Guidance Committee, in the hope that this move might impair the Jerusalem leaders' unity. Finally, Sasson requested guidance as to the entity movement and the Nablus dignitaries' Arab administration scheme.[23]

Leadership under a Two-Front Attack

The idea of deporting prominent Palestinians had been in the air for quite some time. In early December the Israeli authorities arrested the Communist leader Fa'iq Warrad at his home in Ramallah, and shortly afterward he was deported to Jordan. Warrad asserted later that he had been exiled because of the circulation of a plan he had written on behalf of the Communist Party which called for the recognition of the State of Israel based on the UN Partition Resolution of 1947.[24] Defense Minister Dayan, however, gave the Knesset the excuse that Warrad, a Ramallah native, "had entered the region unlawfully."[25] A few days later the Ministerial Committee for Security Affairs approved a recommendation by the military to expel two other Ramallah residents—the Communist Ibrahim Bakr and the Ba'th activist Kamal Nasir.[26] Bakr had already suffered a forced exile in late July, when the Israelis had banished him to Jericho for three months in retaliation for the emerging civil disobedience in the West Bank (see chapter 3). But the new expulsion was to beyond the ceasefire lines and for an indefinite period of time. Code-named *Mivtsa' Peresh*—Operation Excrement—3, it was carried out on 20 and 21 December.[27] Unlike in the Warrad case, the Israelis were now explicit about their true motives. The Foreign Ministry official Shaul Bar-Haim told the American consul general in Jerusalem that Bakr was removed because he and "elements around him" had been intimidating Palestinians disposed to cooperate with Israel. The deportation, he said, was a punitive step intended to reassure "more cooperative Palestinians."[28]

In his report to the prime minister of 15 December, Moshe Sasson said that the Communists and Ba'thists were openly persecuting the supporters of the entity movement. Sasson relied on what he had heard from Shehadeh and his acolytes. For example, 'Izzat Karman accused Ibrahim Bakr, Kamal Nasir, and a few other Communists and Ba'thists of endeavoring to set up a "workers' front" in order to organize strikes and intimidate the moderates.[29] Shehadeh himself told Sasson that he had been summoned to a meeting with Ruhi al-Khatib, Anwar al-Khatib, Antoun 'Atallah, and the Anglican *Mutran* (Bishop) Najib Quba'in at the latter's home in Jerusalem on 8 December and had been warned to cease his political activity. The threatening message, Shehadeh told Sasson, had been agreed upon by a larger group of Jerusalem and Ramallah leaders, including Ibrahim Bakr.[30] Evidently the Palestinian disagreements and inter-rivalries engendered useful information for the Israelis, which they were quick to translate into action. A GSS intelligence paper reported that many in Ramallah viewed the expulsion of Bakr and Nasir, as well as the arrest of two other activists, as measures taken against those who opposed the creation of a Palestinian state on which Israel was determined.[31]

Shortly after midnight on 29 December the residence of Dr. Hamdi al-Taji al-Farouqi in Ramallah was attacked by bazooka fire. Farouqi advocated a Palestinian state, although he was not an integral part of the entity movement (see chapter 5). There were no casualties and the house was only slightly damaged, yet the single rocket sent the entire entity movement into a deep hibernation. Al-Fateh took responsibility for the assault, which was the culmination of a series of threats directed at those who were considered, according to the Palestinian writer 'Isa al-Shu'aibi, an undesirable "alternative leadership" in the West Bank. An American diplomat reported from Jerusalem that 'Aziz Shehadeh had received death threats before Bakr and Nasir were deported, and the Israeli journalist Ehud Ya'ari revealed that a "death sentence" had been pronounced against Sheikh Muhammad 'Ali al-Ja'bari, the mayor of Hebron.[32]

'Aziz Shehadeh sensed that the bazooka attack, stirring memories of the inter-Palestinian terror during the Arab Revolt of 1936–39, had a deterrent effect on the people.[33] Indeed, some other disturbing incidents occurred. Muhammad Darwish of Bayt Jalla complained to Sasson about a plan to assassinate him, of which he allegedly learned from an anonymous letter.[34] Whereas Darwish was reputed by many to be a collaborator, Mayor Hamdi Kan'an of Nablus was deemed a loyal nationalist. But he too received threatening letters demanding he stop making so-called treacherous statements disgracing the Palestinians.[35] A shot was even reportedly fired at the car of Nadim al-Zaru, Ramallah's radical mayor, and the electrical system of his vehicle was tampered with.[36]

Israel did not condone these ominous provocations, but they certainly served its overarching aim to eliminate the Palestinian leadership in the occupied territories, or at least to cripple it. As early as 31 July, Chief of Staff Rabin told his generals that the government policy as he understood it was to neutralize the leadership by various means, including exile.[37] In the following months the military considered the fate of the West Bank mayors, who constituted the backbone of the local leadership. Ultimately, it recommended the removal of Mayor Zaru and his ultraradical colleague from adjoining Al-Bireh, Mayor 'Abd al-Jawad Saleh, from their positions. Apparently political considerations preempted this move.[38] It may be argued that the deportation of Bakr and Nasir and the intended dismissal of Zaru and Saleh were measures directed against extremists. But the de facto exile of the temperate Antoun 'Atallah clearly demonstrated that there was more to it than that.

'Atallah, a bank director in Jerusalem and former foreign minister of Jordan, traveled to Amman in mid-December for another round of the prolonged indirect negotiations between Israel and Jordan about reopening the Arab banks in Arab Jerusalem and the West Bank, which had been closed since the war. While in Jordan he was sworn in as a senator. The reappointment of 'Atallah to the Senate was no surprise to Israel: 'Atallah himself had discussed it openly in a press interview pub-

lished almost a month before he was sworn in.[39] But when the news of
his oath of allegiance to King Hussein was broadcast that evening on
Amman Radio, the Israeli reaction was swift: by order of Defense Minister Dayan, 'Atallah was banned from returning home. Premier Talhuni, pleading for the United States to intercede, argued that 'Atallah
could serve as a useful bridge to bring about a Jordanian-Israeli peace
settlement.[40] The Israelis agreed; 'Atallah was a "rather moderate fellow,"
they informally told US Ambassador Barbour in Tel Aviv.[41] But they
refused to rescind the banishment order, even after 'Atallah sent an
apology to the Israeli government. Col. Shlomo Gazit, Dayan's aide,
claimed that Israel was unable to reverse the decision because the
Arabs would consider this "an Arab victory."[42] A Foreign Ministry
functionary delivered the Israeli official position to an American diplomat, adding: "The man behaved in an extremely provocative fashion
with no real justification."[43] The reason given by Dayan to the Knesset
for the exile of 'Atallah, as well as the deportation of Bakr, Nasir, and
Sheikh Sa'ih, went much farther: "Hostile activity, which amounts to a
security risk."[44] However, a fortnight before the exile an Israeli intelligence
circular said that 'Atallah, together with Anwar Nuseibeh, supported a
separate Palestinian solution.[45] "'Atallah's banishment," concluded the
British consul general in Jerusalem, "will further weaken the local Palestinian leadership."[46]

Available evidence suggests that this was precisely what the Israelis intended. As we have seen, Moshe Sasson unsuccessfully attempted
to convert the entity movement into an Israeli-controlled puppet organization, but the bazooka rocket that hit Farouqi's house dealt a lethal
blow to the group. As for the pro-Hashemite leadership, the aim was to
use them in prodding King Hussein to negotiate a settlement on Israel's terms.[47] In consequence, those who proved to be unresponsive to
pressure or manipulation became redundant and had to be disposed
of. Numerous writers, former practitioners as well as scholars, have
indeed inferred that Israel's motive for deporting Palestinian political
activists was the desire to deprive the inhabitants of the occupied territories of their leadership, thereby suppressing their spirit of resistance
and steadfastness.[48] Defense Minister Dayan himself alluded to this
goal in a confidential forum in late September.[49] At any rate, a new development, coinciding with the deportation of Ibrahim Bakr, Kamal

Nasir, and Antoun ʿAtallah, allowed Israel to pursue its policy line vis-
à-vis Hussein.

A West Bank Delegation to the Arab Summit

Following the adoption of Resolution 242, Egypt initiated a new Arab
summit conference, scheduled for 17 January 1968 in Rabat, Morocco.
King Hussein, eager to recover his lost territory, resolved to enlist the
West Bankers to help him face Arab intransigence at the summit. In
mid-December he and Prime Minister Bahjat al-Talhuni each received
Mayor Hamdi Kanʿan in Amman. Kanʿan was asked to arrange a delegation of West Bank dignitaries to attend the Rabat conference. Its
designated task was twofold: to emphasize the urgent need for a quick
solution and to push for a moderate position, as Hussein felt that the
occupied Palestinians would be more persuasive in this respect than he
could. Both the king and Kanʿan were fearful of a separate Palestinian-
Israeli settlement, particularly if the summit should take a tougher
line against Israel. The Israeli "Palestinian alternative" stratagem
proved successful again. Upon his return to the West Bank, Kanʿan
embarked on a series of contacts with Palestinian politicians in the occupied territories—including the Gaza Strip—with the purpose of setting up an agreed deputation. Meanwhile, Anwar al-Khatib attempted
to convince Sasson that it was in Israel's interest to tolerate such a delegation. It would deny Ahmad al-Shuqayri, the PLO's chairman, his
pretense of representing the Palestinian people, Khatib argued in his
meeting with Sasson on 22 December. The inflexible Sasson expressed
reluctance. But Defense Minister Dayan had already decided to endorse a Palestinian delegation to the Rabat summit, so Sasson yielded.[50]

When the Ministerial Committee for West Bank Affairs convened on 24 December, Dayan forcefully argued for the delegation. As
defense minister he was preoccupied with the growing guerrilla operations of al-Fateh and other Palestinian organizations from across the
Jordan River. The Palestinian representatives, he told the committee,
would assert at the summit that they, not the Jews, were the ones who
suffered from al-Fateh actions because of the harsh Israeli retaliatory
measures inside the West Bank—which included the blowing up of
houses. They would contend further, Dayan went on, that the Israelis
were savage; that being occupied by them was insufferable. Still, their

basic argument would be that a peace settlement was imperative. Foreign Minister Eban concurred: these delegates would curse Israel yet at the same time would say that they wanted peace, not war. Premier Eshkol raised the question whether representatives of the Gaza Strip should be permitted to join the delegation. Again, Dayan was all for it. The government was determined to keep the Gaza Strip within Israel's boundaries, he reminded his colleagues, but wished its refugee inhabitants to leave. "They should be settled elsewhere, and elsewhere means chez Hussein"; however, without Hussein's consent, the Gazans would not be settled in Jordan. In Dayan's thinking, the Israeli determination to empty the Gaza Strip of the greater part of its populace not only linked the two occupied Palestinian-inhabited regions but also required responsiveness to Hussein's wishes. Accordingly, the committee approved a Palestinian delegation to the summit without meddling in its makeup, which could include members from Gaza. This decision allowed indefinite deferral of the discussion of the Nablus notables' proposal for Arab self-rule. The soon-to-be-paralyzed entity movement was not mentioned at all, and the meeting adjourned without any further instructions regarding talks with the West Bank leadership.[51]

Three days later Sasson called on Anwar al-Khatib to inform him of the government's decision. Khatib gleefully welcomed the news. He thought that granting the West Bankers a free hand in electing their representatives would fly in the face of those who argued against a delegation because it would be perceived as an Israeli pawn. Khatib suggested that it would be helpful if the Palestinians could know of Israel's ideas for a solution. Sasson retorted that their determination not to go to Rabat on Israel's behalf required them to appear at the summit without any Israeli proposals. Khatib also said that the delegation should be endorsed by at least fifty West Bank leaders. In response, Sasson reiterated that political gatherings were forbidden.

Consultations, however, were tolerated. Such a political consultation had taken place two days previously at Ruhi al-Khatib's home in Jerusalem. Anwar al-Khatib was also present, as well as Hamdi Kan'an, who vigorously endeavored to promote the summit deputation initiative. Kan'an had sought to include Ibrahim Bakr and Kamal Nasir in the delegation, but their recent banishment appeared to foil his intention. Ruhi al-Khatib, the head of the National Guidance Committee, and other participants in the meeting strongly opposed the delegation

idea on the grounds that Israel's approval of its departure would undermine its standing at the summit. Instead, they proposed that the
three deportees—Sheikh 'Abd al-Hamid al-Sa'ih, Bakr, and Nasir—
should join the Jordanian delegation to the summit on behalf of the
West Bankers. This position, in defiance of Hussein's wishes, refutes
the Israeli allegation that the National Guidance Committee was a
Jordanian-controlled body. Eventually the majority agreed to send a
memorandum to the government of Jordan on these lines. A few days
later Shehadeh met Sasson and claimed that the exiled Antoun 'Atallah
would also take part in the Jordanian delegacy.[52]

In accordance with Dayan's strict policy of preventing the emergence of national leadership in the West Bank and with Israel's divide-
and-rule strategy, Sasson stressed that a delegation assembled by Hamdi
Kan'an would enjoy no exclusivity or be considered by Israel as a representative group; others, too, would be allowed to go to Rabat if they so
wished.[53] Ironically, the objections of such prominent notables as Ruhi
al-Khatib to a West Bank deputation had the same implications—its
members would be unable to claim at the summit that they spoke in the
name of the West Bank as a whole. In the GSS assessment, personal considerations involving inter-Palestinian rivalries and prestige lay behind
the negative stance of Ruhi al-Khatib and like-minded dignitaries: a
successful return of the delegation from Rabat with tangible achieve-
ments might strengthen Kan'an's position and influence, and hence diminish their own.[54]

Some politicians rejected the idea for more substantial reasons.
Most prominent among them was Anwar Nuseibeh, who told Shehadeh that there was no point in arriving at the summit without any political plan or suggestions. He would support a delegation to the summit
only if its members had the courage to proclaim willingness to negotiate a settlement with Israel. Alas, this would not happen, Nuseibeh
said. Such a delegation therefore would simply frustrate any further
Palestinian course of action, something that King Hussein indeed desired, but which should not be permitted to occur.[55]

On 8 January 1968, after all efforts to induce Syria and Saudi Arabia to attend the summit failed, the Rabat conference was postponed.
Consequently the delegation issue became academic. Available records,
exclusively Israeli, suggest that the objectors to the delegation had the
upper hand. This was also Dayan's understanding, which he duly shared

with the Knesset Foreign Affairs and Security Committee. He further inferred that the West Bankers wanted to negotiate a settlement with Israel.[56] In an analysis paper for the prime minister, Moshe Sasson described the whole affair as "the first serious attempt at a local Arab political initiative since the war," but concluded that the West Bank leadership was unable to play a significant role in the Middle East political setting for the time being. He argued that a change depended, among other factors, on "nurturing suitable leadership."[57] Both Dayan and Sasson avoided any acknowledgment of Israel's responsibility for the failure to assemble a West Bank delegation to the summit. Sasson's critical report listed numerous factors that in his view had contributed to the leadership's poor performance and immobility, most of which were well founded. But he intentionally left out the most crucial one—Israel's obstinate refusal to allow any political organization in the occupied territories. Denied political institutions or any kind of countrywide organization, the Palestinians were left with local, sectarian, petty politics, which time and again proved futile.

Furthermore, one Israeli official handled the political contacts with the Palestinians almost singlehandedly. Regardless of his qualities and personal preferences, such a sensitive and intricate undertaking should have been carried out by a team, closely guided and supervised by policy makers. The paper trail clearly reveals the impromptu nature of the whole operation. Characteristically, no systematic process existed for decision making, with brainstorming experts submitting alternative courses of action for the policy makers to weigh and choose from.[58] Indeed, when the Arab summit was postponed, thereby putting an end to the delegation initiative, Premier Eshkol met with President Johnson at the latter's ranch in Texas, and Sasson was left with no instructions for further dealings with the West Bank elite. In Eshkol's absence, the Ministerial Committee for the West Bank Affairs did not convene.[59] Thus the Nablus proposal for Arab self-rule, which had been put on hold because of the intended delegation to the summit, remained suspended.

As we have seen, Defense Minister Dayan favored an administrative autonomy for the West Bankers, believing that this would allow Israel to have it both ways: to appear as if it were moving toward a settlement with the Palestinians while in practice still retaining the conquered lands. However, the GSS—which answered to the prime minister—interpreted the Nablus scheme rather differently. Avraham Ahituv, who ran the agency's activities in the occupied territories, identified the proposal with the opposition to the delegation. Appearing before the Knesset Foreign Affairs and Security Committee, Ahituv argued that for those who objected to the delegation, Israel's consent to its departure indicated its wish to negotiate a settlement—but a settlement diametrically opposed to the one they desired, which was a canton within Jordan. Ahituv insisted that Israel profited from the non-departure of the delegation.[60] The GSS position, then, was at odds with the security establishment's policy. Obviously this state of affairs ensured steady progress toward a cul-de-sac.

Eban's Dossier Diplomacy

The GSS interpretation coincided with a new Jordanian initiative to break the deadlock. In mid-January, King Hussein solicited US and British support for the following idea: Israel would withdraw from the West Bank, and Jordan would resume civil administration in the area while its military forces remained in the East, pending a settlement of outstanding issues such as boundaries and refugees. Hussein told the American ambassador in Amman that prominent West Bankers and East Bankers whom he had sounded out about the plan unanimously agreed that it was worth trying. A couple of days later the US embassy learned that the king had authorized the UN peace envoy Gunnar Jarring to discuss the proposition with the Israelis, provided he secured Israeli agreement that their government was ready to announce its acceptance of Resolution 242. From its adoption on 22 November, Israel had adamantly avoided explicit acceptance of the resolution. But after a few more days Hussein decided to shelve his proposal. So long as the Israelis were not prepared to state their acceptance, he said, there was no point in taking any initiative.[61]

It would take Israel another three months to express a halfhearted acceptance of Resolution 242.[62] In the meantime Foreign Minister Eban contrived a canny scheme to circumvent his government's refusal to convey anything of substance. As he related in mid-January behind the closed doors of the Knesset Foreign Affairs and Security Committee, there was a danger that Jarring would give up his mission in despair and the Arabs might go back to the United Nations, seeking an unambiguous resolution. Such a revised resolution could only be worse for Israel, Eban stressed; it would probably demand an Israeli withdrawal from the occupied territories as a first step. To preempt this eventuality, Israel flooded the UN envoy with procedural suggestions, particularly a lengthy itemized "agenda for negotiations." As expected, Egypt and Jordan, insisting on an Israeli commitment to a pullback, rejected the agenda outright, thereby serving Eban's goal: Israel, he explained to his fellow legislators, had been compiling a dossier of the numerous proposals and schemes it put forward through Jarring, while the Arabs had been merely offering rejections. Eban's remarkable presentation betrayed the Israeli attempt to avoid the real issues at hand. It also reflected Eban's awareness that his diplomatic approach fooled neither the Arabs nor Jarring. But anticipating a future international debate about who was responsible for the lack of progress toward peace, Eban believed that for tactical reasons Israel must multiply its proposals and thicken its "dossier." This was also important in the short run, he added, for maintaining the support of the United States and other friendly governments.[63]

With Eban's "dossier diplomacy" and the "Palestinian alternative" scheme, Israel's peacemaking strategy started to take the shape of a consistent foreign policy of deception, which was maintained throughout the following months and years. Eban, the architect of this approach, claimed retrospectively that peace was unattainable between June 1967 and the Yom Kippur War of October 1973 because the humiliation the Arabs felt as a result of the defeat in the Six Day War "made them almost incapable of negotiating." Eban's words were at odds with the historical facts, namely, King Hussein's many peace overtures and expressed desire to negotiate a settlement with Israel. Building on this misstatement nevertheless, Eban elaborated on the doctrine he had pursued as foreign minister:

> Some people said, what is the use of making proposals that you know the Arabs will not accept? Whereas my orientation would have been, not to ask whether the Arabs would accept something, but whether the enunciation of something would help Israel outside the Arab world. Once you make the Arab response the criterion for formulating Israeli political attitudes, you are really reduced to hopelessness and to sterility. I thought we should not give them the honor

of deciding what our policies toward them should be. We should have been looking at the non-Arab world, and not the Arab world itself. Also, we could have played the Jarring Mission in a much more prolonged way, even if it was degenerating into a tactical exercise. Some of my colleagues did not understand that even a tactical exercise fills a vacuum.[64]

Resolution 242 and the Jarring mission were indeed viewed by the Israeli leaders in the context of the government's relations with Washington. More specifically, Israel's main concern after the adoption of 242 on 22 November was American arms supply and political backing. In a memorandum drafted in late 1967, Lt. Gen. Yitzhak Rabin, the designated ambassador to Washington, set Israel's objectives vis-à-vis the United States as he understood them. The first objective was to ensure that Israel was provided with its "defense requirements," including financial support to cover arms purchases; another was to coordinate the policies of the two governments regarding a Middle East political settlement "or at the very least, preventing the emergence of too wide a disparity in policies."[65]

Prime Minister Eshkol was scheduled to meet President Johnson in early January, and top on his agenda was Israel's request for fighter planes, predominantly fifty F-4 Phantom fighter-bombers—the most advanced war machine of the time.[66] Israel was in urgent need of aircraft after losing forty planes in the war—roughly 20 percent of the Jewish state's air power.[67] France, Israel's supplier of fighter planes before the war, had announced an arms embargo on the Middle East on the eve of the hostilities and had refused to deliver the fifty Mirage fighters Israel had already ordered and paid for.[68] Eshkol knew, however, that the American agenda was quite different, that President Johnson would insist on hearing from him concrete ideas about Israel's intentions regarding the occupied territories and peace settlements with its Arab neighbors. "Some say that he [Johnson] likes to ask nasty questions, [and] I need to know how to respond," Eshkol told a group of army generals whom he consulted on the fate of the West Bank in early December.[69] Suddenly, six long months after the war, the question of Israel's future borders became pressing.

In fact, shortly after the war Premier Eshkol felt that Israel must determine its position vis-à-vis the West Bank: "No decision—evasion is also a decision," he warned the members of the Alignment's Political Committee in mid-August.[70] What prevented a decision was not only the sharp difference of opinion on substance within the cabinet, but also—perhaps even more—the belief of some leading policy makers that Israel would be better off without such a resolution. This view was prompted by either tactical considerations or sheer hubris. The latter was best represented by former Foreign Minister Golda Meir, the secretary general of the ruling Mapai party and Eshkol's future successor. "Why should we say anything?" she rhetorically asked at a previous meeting of the Political Committee. "There is no pressure on us. Let Hussein talk, he is under pressure."[71] Some time later, in a discussion at the parliamentary Foreign Affairs and Security Committee, Meir vowed to cut out her tongue before admitting the need to return the occupied territories. She suggested counting on the Arabs who by refusing to negotiate with the Jewish state over the years "had never disappointed" Israel.[72] Foreign Minister Eban, on the other hand, was a firm believer in *takhsisanut*—a Hebrew term frequently used by him apparently to indicate "tactics," though in reality it meant "deviousness." In late July, when Eban rejoiced at the "favorable impasse" which had been created in the diplomatic arena, he explained in a party forum his objection to deciding what to do with the West Bank by arguing that such a resolution would not remain secret and that consequently the United States and the Soviet Union would unite in pressuring Israel.[73] There were many options, he told a British diplomat, and it might well be that the only decision reached would be to keep all of them open.[74]

Playing for time was clearly the name of Eban's game. He and many other government officials were confident that time was on Israel's side. Early on, Secretary Rusk instructed Ambassador Barbour in Tel Aviv to convey to the Israelis Washington's strong dissent from this view.[75] The Israelis were not impressed. But with Eshkol's summit meeting with Johnson fast approaching, and with the urgent need to replenish Israel's military arsenal, time was viewed differently, certainly by the prime minister. "I have demanded several times that the cabinet reach a decision about our future plans as to the occupied territories and peace terms," he reminded his foreign minister in mid-November, "so that we would be able, inter alia, openly to discuss [these matters] with the Americans." Eshkol insisted that the issue must be dealt with seriously upon Eban's return to Jerusalem from abroad.[76]

Thus the month of December was spent in strenuous efforts to define a position that aircraft-hungry Israel could stomach and the Americans would find satisfactory. Yet with the passage of time since the war it had become a mission impossible. As early as August, Ambassador Barbour perceived a rising swell of popular feeling that Israel must keep the occupied territories indefinitely or even forever.[77] The nascent Movement for the Whole Land of Israel, whose leaders included some distinguished public figures and intellectuals, enjoyed increasing public support and was turning into a powerful and influential pressure group.[78] In December, Barbour's observation was corroborated by Avi'ad Yafeh, Eshkol's private secretary: within the cabinet, Yafeh informed Israel's ambassador in Washington, the viewpoint had been growing stronger over time that retaining as much of the "administered territories" as possible was imperative on historical and security grounds.[79] The expression Yafeh used—"administered territories" (*shtahim muhzakim*, literally "held territories")—officially replaced the hitherto "occupied territories." Many officials and army officers went a step farther and applied the phrase "liberated territories." In December the government also instructed that the term "West Bank" should be replaced by "Judea and Samaria"—the biblical names of the region.[80]

These symbolic but meaningful changes were accompanied, yet again, by practical and more far-reaching steps. On the eve of his departure for America, Premier Eshkol gave the go-ahead to the establishment of two new Jewish settlements in the West Bank: one at the northern tip of the Jordan Valley, on lands belonging to "absentees"—new refugees whose return was denied by Israel—and the other at the southern end. It was also decided to examine the establishment of two more settlements along the Jordan Valley.[81] The formal cabinet resolution, adopted a month later, specifically instructed that there should be no publicity.[82] The two settlements were founded surreptitiously in February 1968 and manned by *Nahal* conscripts. They were disingenuously represented as army barracks.[83] By December 1969 the northern one, Meholah, became a civilian *moshav*, or cooperative agriculture settlement; Kalyah in the south was turned into a kibbutz in May 1974.[84]

Lt. Gen. Haim Bar-Lev, who succeeded Rabin as chief of staff at the turn of 1967, disclosed in a confidential forum that the army had its doubts about settlements bereft of military significance, such as Kalyah.[85] But settlements in the occupied territories, disguised as military *Nahal* outposts, were meant to serve a different purpose altogether; they were built in areas designated to remain under Israel's sovereignty. In the fall of 1967 Dayan made this very clear to his ministry's new head of the Youth and *Nahal* Department, and added that the economic viability of any proposed settlement should also be considered.[86] By February 1968, twenty-four applications to settle in the occupied territories had been submitted to the authorities, and only seven of them were rejected because of economic infeasibility or shortage of intended settlers.[87]

The plans to settle Jews in the Jordan Valley made the Arab population of the area unwelcome. A well to supply water for the settlement of Meholah was drilled with the full knowledge that it would adversely affect half a dozen wells and springs used by two neighboring Palestinian villages, Bardalah and Tall al-Bayda. A steadily increasing decline in the output of these villages' water sources began within two years.[88] In early December the Israeli army removed the non-nomadic Bedouin tribe al-Nusayrat from its small village of mud huts and tents near Jericho. Between 150 and 300 members of the tribe, mostly able-bodied men, crossed to the East Bank. Israel cited security reasons for the removal of the Bedouins and claimed that those who had left the West Bank did so voluntarily. The Palestinians and the Jordanians insisted that the men were trucked to the Allenby Bridge and expelled at gunpoint. A British diplomat concluded that the Israeli action was part of a policy of creating a cordon sanitaire along the Jordan River. In his opinion, so was the destruction the previous month of al-Jiftlik, a small town of 6,000 a few miles north of the Damya Bridge.[89] It appears, however, that these actions were not unrelated to Israel's settlement ambitions.

The town of al-Jiftlik was built after the 1948 War by Palestinian refugees who earned their living by tilling the fertile farmland in the Jordan Valley. Most of al-Jiftlik's residents fled to the East during or immediately after the fighting in June, but between 50 and 100 families stayed. In early November 1967 the Israeli army entirely demolished the 800 dwellings of the town. Rendered homeless and prevented by the army from returning to work their fields, they found shelter in a nearby village. In less than a month this village and other "abandoned" villages in the region were bulldozed, too. The official Israeli explanation was that the empty houses were a hazard to security and to health: they served as centers for guerrilla infiltrators from Jordan, affording them cover and storage for weapons; and that they were breeding places for rats and disease.[90] But a letter to Premier Eshkol, dated 18 September—seven weeks before al-Jiftlik was leveled—reveals that at the army's request the Settlement Department of the Jewish Agency was examining the feasibility of establishing two settlements in the al-Jiftlik area.[91]

The Cabinet Decides Again Not to Decide

The Israeli fait accompli policy puts the cabinet indecision in a distinctive perspective. It was not so much that the divided government was unable to determine the future of the West Bank as that there was no real inclination to do so. Neither annexation nor concession seemed conceivable: the former would be very likely to imperil the American support Israel depended on, and the latter became increasingly difficult because it meant giving up parts of the "promised land" which arguably guaranteed Israel's security. Eshkol, however, feared confrontation with President Johnson. Dr. Herzog, his confidant, later admitted to worries before Eshkol's journey that he might return home without the West Bank.[92] The prime minister was desperate for a solution.

In early December, Eshkol sought advice from a group of the army generals.[93] His opening remarks betrayed unyielding but confused thinking. The Jordan River, he said, must be Israel's security border, and Israeli forces should be placed on the north-south ridge running along the West Bank, where the great majority of the population lived. The prime minister said that they could be Jordanian citizens and the military would not interfere in their daily life. Adding Arabs to Israel's population, Eshkol emphasized, was out of the question. In other words, he coveted the territory without responsibility for its inhabitants. This was absurd, as Eshkol himself acknowledged: King Hussein, whose consent was a sine qua non for such an arrangement, would never agree to it. The prime minister was generously willing to throw in the king's private properties in the West Bank—a few villas and a small plot of land—in addition to granting Jordan access to a Mediterranean port and bestowing upon Hussein the status of Guardian of *al-Haram al-Sharif*. But being a seasoned and realistic politician, Eshkol knew that he could not have a face-to-face meeting with Hussein only to tell the king to forget about his occupied territory. The prime minister confessed that the one thing he dreaded was direct negotiations with the Arabs—he would not know what to say to them. Eshkol thus wondered whether

Israel should be content with some border changes—namely, annexing a relatively small portion of the West Bank—although it might entail an increase of Israel's Arab residents, or, as he colorfully put it, "it might cost us Arabs." Eshkol threw this quandary to the generals.

Chief of Staff Rabin thought that the only conceivable option was a demilitarized Palestinian state in the West Bank, closely linked to Israel. Eshkol interjected, saying that his objection to this idea had been growing daily, "but I haven't told anybody yet." This was indeed a sea change in Eshkol's thinking. During the war and immediately afterward Eshkol talked about the establishment of a Palestinian state in the West Bank.[94] In mid-August he assured the acclaimed Jewish-French intellectual Raymond Aron that Israel would grant the West Bankers independence if they so desired.[95] As we have seen in the preceding chapter, just three weeks previously Eshkol had launched talks with the West Bank leadership to examine the feasibility of a Palestinian state. There is nothing in the historical evidence to explain his rapid disavowal of his erstwhile preference. Perhaps Eshkol had toyed with the idea so long as a Palestinian state was an abstract notion, and abandoned it when he felt that it might materialize. It also appears that what the Israeli leader had envisaged was more of a Bantustan than a state. Thus he expressed shock when Assistant Defense Minister Zvi Tsur supported Rabin's viewpoint, arguing that a Palestinian state was desirable for at least tactical considerations and that it should also include the Arabs in the Gaza Strip. This would engender a Palestinian entity, Eshkol exclaimed, which would soon attain representation at the United Nations. He then invoked the danger of irredentism as another argument, and warned that a West Bank state would allow the 200,000 or so new refugees of the June War to return to their homes. Undoubtedly Premier Eshkol wished to have as few Arabs as possible not only under Israel's sovereignty but also in its vicinity. Or, rather, he inadvertently unmasked yet again his wish to annex the entire territory to the State of Israel.

Defense Minister Dayan, who was present at Eshkol's discussion with the generals, did not take part in the debate. Three weeks later Eshkol urgently solicited his ideas as to "secured and recognized" borders on all three fronts.[96] Dayan's response was given at a meeting of the Ministerial Committee for Security Affairs two days later. He insisted on retaining the Sinai Peninsula and the Golan Heights, but was ready to accept the prewar Green Line as the "political border" between

Israel and Jordan if King Hussein agreed to the following conditions:
Israeli military and civilian presence on the West Bank ridge; relocation
of 200,000 refugees of 1948 from the Gaza Strip to the East Bank; and
the right of Jews to travel and settle anywhere in the West Bank. The last
proviso was in fact an explicit enunciation of Dr. Herzog's concept of the
Jewish "historical association" (see chapter 5). In addition, Hussein
should accede to Israel's control over Arab Jerusalem. Realizing that the
king would reject all four demands, Dayan expressed strong objection
to Israeli withdrawal from any part of the West Bank. A withdrawal
from the West Bank, he said, could lead to more withdrawals on the
other fronts.[97]

As part of the feverish preparations for the Johnson-Eshkol
summit, the General Staff of the military, on the orders of the government, held lengthy discussions about Israel's future borders on 27 and
31 December.[98] The same subject was also thoroughly debated by the
Ministerial Committee for Security Affairs on 20 and 26 December.
When the cabinet convened on 31 December, its members focused on
whether Israel should react to the American pressure for negotiations
with Hussein about the return of the West Bank, wholly or partly, to
the king's rule. A consensus to reject a Palestinian state emerged but
the ministers, again, were unable to reach a decision on the fate of the
occupied territories and the government's peace terms. They thus resolved not to decide. For the third time since the war the cabinet preferred the ambiguity of deferral to the clarity of decisiveness: in the first
two instances, on 19 June and in August, it simply avoided any decision;
now the cabinet concluded that it should decide "in due course."[99]

Explaining the indecision, Foreign Minister Eban told his party's
secretariat two days later that he and his cabinet colleagues felt that
a substantial discussion was premature because "we don't have an Arab
partner."[100] On that very day, however, Eban informed the Knesset Foreign Affairs and Security Committee of Hussein's recent overtures. The
cabinet considered them, Eban said, and agreed to avoid any explicit reaction. The prime minister would say only that if negotiations with Jordan took place, the agenda might include the border issue.[101] In fact, the
cabinet authorized Eshkol to speak to President Johnson along the lines
of its inflexible resolution of 8 November (see chapter 5), and effectively
annulled the 19 June resolution (see chapter 1).[102] Thus, despite the official
claim, it was the Arabs rather than Israel who did not have a partner.

When Eshkol and his retinue arrived at President Johnson's ranch in Texas, they learned that Israel's boundaries were indeed the focus of the Americans' attention. The US leadership demanded to hear what the prime minister was unable to say. "We must . . . know what kind of Israel we would be expected to assist," Johnson insisted. Eshkol could only reply that Israel was not ready to return to the prewar lines. The final borders, he stated, reciting the Israeli mantra, should be determined in direct negotiations between Israel and the Arabs. By Eshkol's own admission, his hosts refused to buy this. The prime minister later recalled Johnson jokingly teasing him: "You want a country that lives in peace. You want [a] piece of this and [a] piece of that." Though the president was hospitable and the atmosphere during the two-day summit was informal and congenial, there was no doubt about American displeasure with the Israeli attitude.

Referring to the main objective Israel hoped to achieve at the summit, Johnson said that "peace was not to be saved by 27 or 50 new planes. Much more was required, including positive moves toward a peaceful settlement." He and his men stressed that time was not on Israel's side because the Soviets would exploit delays to deepen their penetration into the Middle East. A month before the summit Undersecretary of State Nicholas Katzenbach had advised Johnson to "avoid further substantial US arms commitments until we know more about the chances for a negotiated settlement" between Israel and Jordan. Dean Rusk now took a tougher approach. In a personal exchange with Dr. Herzog, the secretary of state bluntly warned that if Israel should face a Soviet threat following the persistence of its inflexible policy, the administration "would not go to the Congress"—namely, would not rush to Israel's rescue. Nonetheless, Eshkol returned home with an agreement for all the A-4 Skyhawk jets he had asked for, and with a promise to consider favorably Israel's request for Phantoms. Unlike Secretary Rusk, whom Eshkol considered as being tough on Israel, President Johnson was after all very sympathetic to the Jewish state.[103]

The joint communiqué that was published at the end of the summit did not mention any new American aircraft sales to Israel. Palestinians in the occupied territories, reported the US consul general in Jerusalem, initially greeted the news with guarded optimism. But press articles, particularly in Israeli newspapers, soon convinced them that President Johnson had promised their occupiers more support than the official statement indicated.[104] With the indefinite postponement of the Rabat summit, many West Bankers were now disillusioned about the prospect that the Arab world might bring about their deliverance. The Jarring mission thus seemed the only real opportunity for a solution, and they pinned their hopes on the UN peace envoy.

In December the newly established advisory committee of the political elite in Arab Jerusalem and Ramallah assigned to a small panel the task of composing a memorandum for Jarring. The document was meant to outline the position of the mainstream Palestinians under occupation in accordance with the National Covenant of October: a reunion with Jordan, and an appropriate Palestinian representation in the kingdom's political regime. A month later a rough draft of the memorandum was transmitted for approval to Nablus leaders. However, the text was based on the 1947 Partition Resolution. According to the last piece of evidence in this imperfect jigsaw, dated 22 January, the intention was to use the memorandum only to balance the viewpoint of the Shehadeh group or Ja'bari, if they sent Jarring a petition of their own.[105] It should be noted that the available records concerning this matter are scarce, sketchy, and evidently conflicting. Nevertheless, it is clear that in the beginning of 1968 the Jarring mission predominated the West Bankers' thinking. If a change of heart about the advisable Palestinian line did indeed occur, it could be attributed to their expressed realization that the mission should run its course. In the words of Anwar Nuseibeh, Resolution 242 transferred the issue to the governments involved; hence the Jarring peace efforts largely denied the Palestinians any active role in the endeavors to resolve the conflict.[106]

All this was recorded by Moshe Sasson. During the fortnight of Eshkol's journey abroad, Sasson continued his talks with West Bank politicians, going through the motions without a defined aim. The paper trail shows that what the Israeli official heard was more of the same: again, he was assured by many of Hussein's eagerness to negotiate a settlement with Israel; again, the vast majority of the interlocutors implored his government to disclose its conditions for peace. Israel cared about neither issue. Quite apart from the cabinet's decision not to decide, the Jordanian monarch was written off by most prominent policy makers. In a meeting with the British ambassador a few days after Eshkol's return, Foreign Minister Eban expressed disdain for Hussein and said that whether or not the king stayed on the throne was immaterial to Israel, because the key to peace lay in Cairo, not in Amman.[107] Labor Minister Yigal Allon, a self-confessed anti-Hashemite at the time, regarded the Jordanian regime as unstable and "interim." A few months after the war—presumably in January 1968—Allon met Julian Amery tête-à-tête in London. The British politician assured Allon that he was speaking on behalf of King Hussein and endeavored in vain to convince him that Israel should prefer a settlement with Jordan to a Palestinian solution. Allon did not even bother to report what he had heard.[108] Similarly, Moshe Dayan—who characteristically abandoned previous positions for new ones—explicitly and publicly rejected a separate peace with Jordan. Like Eban, the defense minister gave precedence to the Egyptian front.[109]

As we have seen, it was Dayan who had advocated vigorously the "Palestinian alternative" stratagem, whereby talks with the West Bank leadership would be designed to compel Hussein to accept peace on Israel's terms. Perhaps the king's refusal to be coerced into such a settlement inspired the adverse Israeli attitude toward him. The Israeli attitude, in turn, proved Hussein right for getting cold feet about his latest peace initiative in mid-January. And, more important, it was probably one of the reasons why Sasson was not given any new guidelines regarding his contacts with the West Bankers.

Ignoring the unflinching desire of King Hussein to negotiate a settlement and his unremitting overtures since the end of the war, Dayan stated openly that the only Arabs prepared to negotiate with Israel were the Palestinians.[110] Even so, Israel was unwilling to negotiate with them. By Sasson's post factum admission, he was expected to discover some way of using the West Bank as a "political lever" for securing a settlement. In doing so, Sasson told Ambassador Barbour, he had not been attempting to encourage any particular solution, which to his mind would depend on influences extraneous to the West Bank. Since the postponement of the Rabat Arab summit, Sasson went on, the West Bankers—realizing that a quick solution by outside forces was "a phantasmagoria"—had been thinking of taking matters into their own hands.[111] In his concluding report to the prime minister—which interestingly offered no recommendations—Sasson made the same point unequivocally: people who only a month before had been against any local initiative, he reported, clearly had begun to change their minds.[112]

This was untrue. By late January 1968 Sasson had held seventy-two meetings with sixty Palestinian personalities; his report was intended to summarize the three-month round of these talks. Yet an examination of the individual minutes of the talks reveals that the great majority of the political elite did not support an independent initiative, certainly not at that juncture. At best, they were ready to act as intermediaries between Israel and the Arab world, particularly King Hussein.[113]

The significance of Sasson's inaccurate claim that the Palestinians were changing tack is twofold. First, the prime minister was misinformed. Second, it attests to the selective, incomplete nature of Sasson's reporting. Undoubtedly some issues were not recorded by the Israeli official. Conspicuously absent is the internal struggle within the Palestinian arena, culminating in the removal of Ahmad al-Shuqayri, the vociferous chairman of the PLO, and the appointment of Yahya Hammudah in his stead.[114] The introductory paragraph of Sasson's final review described the background against which the contacts had been held, including "the changes in the PLO's leadership."[115] But the individual memoranda do not reflect the forced resignation of Shuqayri, the founding father of the PLO, on 24 December.

Shuqayri's dismissal marked the beginning of a process whereby the PLO was transformed from a lightweight organization, created by the Arab League and effectively dominated by Egypt, to an independent body, encompassing most of the Palestinian guerrilla groups and run by them, and giving the Palestinian people a political voice. Obviously it was impossible to foresee this development in full in December 1967, but the PLO crisis did occupy the attention of the West Bank political elite.[116] Thus it is astonishing that the prolonged inter-Palestinian struggle was not cited in the Sasson talks or was discussed but not recorded. The only recorded references to it are 'Aziz Shehadeh's comment, quoted by Sasson, that the appointment of the Communist Hammudah was a Soviet victory over the pro-Chinese leaning of Shuqayri, and indirect allusions by two other dignitaries to the same appointment, both arguing that the new PLO chairman was a moderate who believed in coexistence and rejected terrorism.[117] The available historical evidence suggests that the PLO upheaval was not debated at cabinet level, either. Given the Israelis' preoccupation with al-Fateh and their persistence in depicting the PLO and other resistance organizations as diabolical, this was equally odd, indicating a political myopia.

Sasson's final report also omitted the insistence of his interlocutors that peace between the Arabs and Israel would require a fair solution to the problem of refugees—both the 1948 refugees and the 1967 new refugees. Anwar Nuseibeh defined it as a "basic element" of any settlement.[118] The government of Israel was also eager to resolve the refugee problem, but had totally different ideas about the nature and the methods of the solution. Whereas what the Palestinians had in mind was the implementation of the right of return, sanctioned by numerous UN resolutions since 1948, the Israelis were willing to allow the Palestinians only the right of departure. At this particular point in time, however, Israel was preoccupied with much more pressing issues. One was international pressure to move on the Jarring peace mission, and another was the escalating Palestinian guerrilla warfare from across the Jordan River. The policy makers believed that the West Bank leadership might be helpful on both issues, and a new round of talks with the Palestinians began. Enter the prime minister.

S · E · V · E · N

Go-Betweens

February–Early May 1968

O
n 5 February 1968 Premier Eshkol successively received two
Palestinian politicians in his office. The first was Ayub Musallam of Bethlehem, a former mayor, member of Jordan's
Chamber of Deputies, and cabinet minister, who carried
limited political weight outside his constituency and was "warm in his
praise of the Military Government."[1] The second guest, the maverick
'Aziz Shehadeh, was well connected countrywide but ineffective in attracting influential West Bankers to his Palestinian entity enterprise.
The attainable documentation does not reveal why these two men were
chosen to see the prime minister or how the idea of holding this series
of talks came about. According to Moshe Sasson, it was he who toward
the end of January advised Eshkol to meet a number of notables.[2] A few
of them indeed desired to talk directly with the Israeli leader, but the
prime minister's interlocutors were handpicked by Sasson, and it appears that some had to be persuaded.[3]

In their talks with Eshkol, Musallam and Shehadeh did not tell the
prime minister anything he had not heard before through Sasson. Both
argued that Israel should allow the Palestinians to determine their own
political future. Musallam stressed the need to solve the refugee problem,
and Shehadeh cautioned that several dignitaries were skeptical about
Israel's sincerity, suspecting that the Israelis merely wanted to use the
Palestinians to pressure King Hussein. The memoranda of the conversa-

tions do not record what Eshkol said.[4] By contrast, a third meeting at the prime minister's office, which took place the next day, was quite significant—not on account of what was said in the course of the discussion but because the visitor, the heavyweight politician Anwar Nuseibeh, was designated by the Israelis to serve as a secret emissary to the Jordanian monarch.

Exchanges across the River

The failure to establish underground bases inside the West Bank during the first months of the occupation prompted the Palestinian resistance organizations, notably al-Fateh and the Popular Front for the Liberation of Palestine (PFLP), to use the eastern Ghor, or Jordan Valley, as a launching pad for their armed struggle against Israel. The guerrilla attacks increased considerably in early 1968, exacting a heavy toll on Israel.[5] Many of these operations by *fida'iyyun* (Arabic for self-sacrificing commandos) were aimed at civilian targets and defined by foreign observers and the world press as terrorism. Although Israel had proved itself a regional power that had recently routed three Arab armies and conquered lands more than three times its own size, these assaults, paradoxically, made the Israelis feel in their element—restoring the self-image of a tiny and feeble nation surrounded by vicious and omnipotent enemies, whose very existence was endangered. Inevitably the guerrilla warfare became the uppermost concern for the policy makers. Yet the subject was not raised at all during the hour-long discussion Eshkol held with Anwar Nuseibeh, although four days later the latter delivered to King Hussein an Israeli message regarding this very issue. Possibly the prime minister wished to figure Nuseibeh out before assigning him as a go-between.

The dialogue was dominated by the Jerusalem question. Nuseibeh stressed that Israel's fait accompli policy—measures such as the de facto annexation of the Arab sector and the recent requisition of 838 acres of land outside the Old City—a quarter of which was privately owned by Palestinians—had a negative effect on the prospect of peace. Eshkol, undoubtedly aware that his comments would soon reach Hussein, accused the king of breaching a bilateral understanding and of not keeping his word by attacking Israel in June. He nevertheless was ready to allow him sovereignty over the Islamic holy places in Jerusalem, including Jordan's

flag above them. Nuseibeh was unsatisfied. The Israelis were developing a voracious territorial appetite, he said later while recounting the
conversation to an American diplomat, and he wondered whether they
would ever give up anything. He added, however, that Eshkol did not
seem particularly interested in Arab populated districts except Jerusalem. Nuseibeh's impression was that the Israeli premier was willing to
cede most of the occupied territories.[6]

On 8 February, two days after the Eshkol-Nuseibeh talk, a mine
planted by fida'iyyun exploded in a kibbutz in the Beisan Valley, south
of the Sea of Galilee, inside the prewar border with Jordan, killing three
Israeli farmers and a Swiss volunteer and wounding two others. Israel
reacted instantly and forcefully, triggering a lethal artillery duel with
Jordanian army units across the ceasefire line. Subsequently, Israel suffered three more fatalities and eleven injured, all of whom were soldiers. Israeli fighter planes struck guerrilla and military targets in the
eastern Ghor, causing heavy casualties in a refugee camp.[7] As had happened so often in the past, recent and remote, Jordan paid dearly for
Palestinian wrongdoings. The Hashemite armed forces were under orders, and indeed tried, to prevent the guerrillas from crossing over to
the West Bank, but many low-ranking commanders and ordinary soldiers defied these orders and assisted the irregulars by providing information on Israeli deployment and fire cover.[8] Aware that Hussein
considered the fida'iyyun's operations detrimental to his kingdom's
interests, the Israelis decided to demand his immediate cooperation in
containing the guerrillas.

Thus Anwar Nuseibeh arrived in Amman on 10 February with a
typed Israeli message for the king, suggesting a secret meeting of Israel's
and Jordan's chiefs of staff. Although couched in a non-threatening tone,
the message blamed the Jordanian army for starting the latest artillery
exchanges and for refusing to prevent militants' infiltration into the
West Bank. Hussein was asked to respond promptly. The king remarked
that the Israelis had been endeavoring for quite some time to arrange
bilateral meetings, and he would not mind a meeting at Col. Muhammad Daud's level. Daud was Jordan's representative on the Jordanian-
Israeli Mixed Armistice Commission, which had ceased functioning
since the war. Nuseibeh interpreted Hussein's choice as a precautionary
measure: should the secret contacts be revealed, he could argue that
they were merely a continuation of Daud's prewar routine.[9]

The Israelis regarded Colonel Daud—later fleetingly a prime minister—as a "very small and stale fish," but nonetheless did not rule out talks with him.[10] Hussein urgently summoned Daud to return from sick leave in New York.[11] However, Daud did not show up at the rendezvous which was set for 12 February on the Allenby Bridge; he was still in America, recovering from an ear operation. The Israelis dismissed the Jordanian explanation for Daud's absence as untrustworthy and deemed it "useless" to have a discussion with his deputy, who came tardily to the bridge in his stead. They conveyed to the Americans their resentment of the "negative Jordanian response to a serious and genuine Israeli initiative."[12]

Meanwhile, the situation along the ceasefire line escalated fast. On 15 February gunplay in the Beisan Valley turned into a fierce ten-hour battle. Israeli fighter planes struck hard, deep into Jordan's territory, and extensively up and down the Jordan Valley. Scores of Jordanians, mostly civilians, were killed or wounded.[13] Within the next few days the eastern Ghor was emptied of its inhabitants, the majority of whom were new and old Palestinian refugees. They fled eastward to the highlands, thereby becoming displaced for the second or the third time. According to official estimates, only 8,700 people out of some 75,000 remained in the Ghor.[14]

"The exodus of substantial numbers of refugees from the Valley was a net security gain for Israel," said Michael Michael, director of the Research Department at Israel's Foreign Ministry.[15] Another senior Foreign Ministry official, Shaul Bar-Haim, insisted that it had been Hussein's policy to keep the ceasefire line in a constant state of turmoil for internal and inter-Arab reasons. A similar allegation was made by Avi'ad Yafeh, Eshkol's private secretary. This was a false accusation. As Ambassador Barbour told Bar-Haim, the American embassy in Amman was in no doubt that the king, who gave every indication of his desire to come to a peaceful accommodation with Israel, was doing everything possible to control terrorism against it.[16] In a radio broadcast in the wake of the 15 February fighting, Hussein called for an end to what he described as providing Israel with excuses to hit Jordan, and a day later his interior minister reinforced the message by publicly warning of punitive measures.[17] The Israelis, however, maintained that their aggressive response on 15 February had driven the king to reverse his policy.

Curbing the guerrilla activity required a degree of Jordanian-Israeli collaboration. Yet in view of Israel's unrelenting demand for face-to-face bargaining with its Arab foes, coupled with the deadlock in the Jarring mission, it was quite clear that the Israelis had a more far-reaching goal in mind. Ambassador Harrison Symmes in Amman suggested that they aspired to hold meetings with some senior Jordanian officer who would give these contacts the appearance of "summit talks" or "direct negotiations." This was precisely what the Jordanians wished to avoid at that stage, Symmes reported.[18] The State Department, perturbed by the dangerous situation in the Jordan Valley, strongly urged a rendezvous at a high level, preferably between officers of general rank. Simultaneously, Israel was firmly advised to withdraw its objection to the presence of a UN officer in such a meeting.[19] But Amman refused any communication above Colonel Daud's level. Premier Talhuni informed Symmes that he had instructed Jordan's ambassador to the United Nations to send Daud back "even if he is dying."[20]

Moreover, Talhuni, who recognized the need for clandestine discussions with Israel going beyond security matters, told Symmes of the encouragement he had given to Jerusalemites he saw recently—namely, Nuseibeh—to continue their dealings with Israeli officials. When he met Jarring on 14 February, the premier asked the UN peace envoy to transmit to Israel Jordan's proposal to invoke the services of "responsible Palestinians" to discuss the respective positions of the two governments. Talhuni mentioned two potential emissaries: Anwar Nuseibeh and another person—presumably Hikmat al-Masri—whom he regarded as less acceptable. The proposal had already been relayed by Anwar Nuseibeh. Upon returning from his 10 February mission to Amman, Nuseibeh reported to Sasson that both King Hussein and Premier Talhuni had suggested that he and other West Bank leaders should negotiate with Israel on Jordan's behalf. Jarring delivered Talhuni's proposal to Abba Eban on 19 February.[21] The next day the foreign minister received Nuseibeh at his official residence in Jerusalem.

Eban, who frequently played fast and loose with the truth in his self-serving writings and speeches, argues that at the end of their talk Nuseibeh volunteered to acquaint King Hussein with their exchange.[22] The Israeli record of the conversation shows, however, that Eban opened the meeting by saying that "an extremely distinguished personage of international stature"—Jarring—believed that Nuseibeh could play an important role in the pursuit of an Israeli-Jordanian accord. Nuseibeh expressed his readiness to carry out any assignment he regarded as honorable. Eban then asked him to transmit a seven-point message to Hussein; the only point worth mentioning was the third, which stated that Israel wished to be "a compact country with a distinct Jewish character." The message also contained the assertion that advance toward a settlement required a tranquil "border," meaning ceasefire line. The rest was the usual Israeli rhetoric, including the hackneyed argument that Israel saw no point in determining its peace plan until an Arab partner came forward. Nuseibeh emphasized that any peace settlement should have Egypt's consent and the Palestinians' support. The Palestinians, he said, should be the starting point; Israel must recognize their existence and the necessity to solve their problem. Eban, an avowed opponent of the Palestinian option, did not respond. Instead, he noted that he and Prime Minister Eshkol constituted the "strong moderate" faction in the government, but they needed some Arab concessions "to feed to the hungry hard-liners in the cabinet." When Nuseibeh reported this to Hussein, the king shrugged and asked: "What can I do?"[23]

Nuseibeh's audience with his monarch took place on 24 February, four days after the meeting with Eban. As the records clearly demonstrate, this episode was a rerun of all previous episodes in the unending futile saga of the direct and indirect contacts Hussein had had with Israel since the war and a preview of the contacts to follow: Israel was demanding direct negotiations while avoiding the substance, and the king was articulating his desire to resolve the conflict but insisting on knowing Israel's terms. So Hussein repeated the message he had conveyed a fortnight before. What kind of Israel should he recognize, he had asked the Israelis via Nuseibeh on 10 February: Israel of the 1947 boundaries, Israel of the 4 June 1967 borders, or Israel of the current lines? Now he told the Jerusalemite emissary that there was no problem in concluding a just settlement with Israel, but he was still waiting to hear its ideas about such a settlement in order to appraise the prospects for progress.[24]

The Israeli leadership had no inclination to satisfy Hussein's wish, as amply evidenced by a debate at a meeting of the Labor Party's Political Committee on 27 February. Labor Minister Allon and Defense Minister Dayan clashed over their opposing ideas about the future of the West Bank: Dayan favored holding the densely populated north-south ridge running along the occupied region, while Allon insisted on keeping the Jordan Valley in its entirety. More specifically, Allon demanded the establishment of twenty-five Jewish settlements in the Valley, emphasizing that the recent escalation of guerrilla activity provided Israel with an "excellent pretext" to define these settlements as a "security deployment." Premier Eshkol sided with Allon. Settlements, although not necessarily as many as twenty-five, should be established without delay "because history should be made quickly," he said, and the few Arabs still living in the western Ghor must be concentrated in just one "very nice" village. Eshkol, indecisive as ever, preferred a settlement with Jordan to the establishment of a Palestinian entity ("Why do I need another Arab state?"), but decided to avoid further discussion concerning the Allon-Dayan disagreement, and to maintain the status quo "because there is nothing better than the way things are developing now." At the same time, however, he reiterated yet again his fears of the day when Israel would meet the Arabs at the negotiating table. The Political Committee effectively ratified the eight-month-old decision not to decide.[25]

A day later Foreign Minister Eban told the British ambassador that the government had stepped up contacts with Hussein through prominent West Bankers, aiming to persuade the king that Israel would be generous in the negotiations once these were embarked upon.[26] Israel's strategy, elaborated a less refined Foreign Ministry official in a conversation with American diplomats, was to keep up every available pressure on Hussein until he realized that there was no option but to settle with the Jewish state.[27] Since it was abundantly clear to the Israelis that Hussein had realized precisely that point long ago, their attitude could only be construed as a firm attempt to coerce him into direct negotiations without letting him know what to expect—and perhaps even as a signal that he should not expect much. Some West Bankers refused to participate in the Israeli charade. Musa Nasir of Ramallah, for example, a former foreign minister of Jordan, who had also been approached by the Israelis as a possible go-between to Amman and had declined, said he would accept such an assignment only if they "unofficially whisper[ed]" to him what they were prepared to offer.[28] Undoubtedly the sole key to progress was an Israeli disclosure of its fundamental proposals, as Eshkol, Eban, and others acknowledged time and again in internal discussions. In early December, Eban told the Knesset Foreign Affairs and Security Committee that he did not believe Israel, facing international charges of obstinacy and rejectionism, would be able to get through 1968 without presenting its terms for peace.[29] But as Israel remained unable or unwilling to formulate its ideas, its insistence on open and direct negotiations was clearly a ploy to gain time.

Nonetheless, the Israelis assigned the blame for the impasse to the Arabs. On 26 February, Premier Eshkol received Hikmat al-Masri and Walid al-Shak'ah of Nablus. The Israeli record reflects a dialogue of the deaf; the Jordanian weekly *Akhbar al-Usbu'* described the meeting in its 17 May 1968 issue as a "stormy exchange." Ignoring Jordan's persistent pleas to discuss an agreement, Eshkol told the two Nablus notables that the main political difficulty resulted from the "Arab obduracy not to negotiate with Israel."[30] As if to prove him wrong, an oral message from Premier Talhuni arrived in Jerusalem a couple of days later, stating unequivocally at the very beginning: "Jordan wants a peace settlement with Israel." The message was delivered by the Jerusalemites Salim al-Sharif, Raja al-'Isa, and Daud al-'Isa in a meeting with Sasson upon their return from Amman. In the message, Talhuni conveyed Jordan's encouragement of bilateral contacts with Israel through West Bank leaders, saying that they should take an active part in the quest for a solution. Talhuni also disclosed the intention to appoint some prominent Palestinians to key positions in his cabinet.[31] In the words of King Hussein, it was essential that anyone who negotiated "for Palestine" should carry weight on the West Bank. Hussein told the British ambassador that he therefore intended to include one or two West Bank politicians in a new cabinet to be formed shortly.[32]

Jordan and Israel, then, were both taking advantage of the occupied Palestinians to promote their respective interests. Their goals were diametrically opposed, however. Whereas Israel's aim was to stall the political process for fear of its inevitably unfavorable territorial outcome, Jordan's was to accelerate it in order to recover the kingdom's lost land. Pretending to appear in the Arab world to be speaking on behalf of the Palestinian people, Hussein sought to give his government a Palestinian flavor by appointing West Bankers as cabinet ministers and possibly giving one of them the premiership. He could then argue that this government was empowered to solve the Palestinians' problem in any way it deemed fit, and that he was bound to accept its decision.

Anwar Nuseibeh believed that the king genuinely meant this. Together with Hikmat al-Masri, Nuseibeh was summoned to Amman, and both were offered ministerial posts when they met Hussein on 12 March. The two men turned the offers down. Their bleak assessment of progress led them to conclude that their appointment to the cabinet would be of no avail because Israel was dodging an unambiguous acceptance of Resolution 242 and refusing to state its minimum bargaining position. According to a secondhand account, Nuseibeh and Masri also made their consent to go along with the scheme conditional on endorsement by an Arab summit or Nasser's written approval. Nuseibeh told American and British diplomats in Amman that he could do more good by remaining in Jerusalem and helping to maintain a semblance of an Arab presence there. Back in Jerusalem he frankly imparted to Sasson his reservations about Hussein's idea of forming a Palestinian cabinet and making it responsible for resolving the conflict. There was another, more personal reason for Nuseibeh's negative attitude: bearing in mind the Israeli reaction to Antoun 'Atallah's swearing in as a senator (see chapter 6), he feared a similar denial of reentry to the West Bank if he assumed a governmental office.[33]

Given Nuseibeh's balanced, down-to-earth attitude, his membership in the Jordanian cabinet could have been beneficial to Israel. By banishing 'Atallah in December, it appeared four months later, Israel had shot itself in the foot. Very soon things would get even worse.

A Pyrrhic Victory in Karameh

In February 1968 al-Fateh's leader Yasir 'Arafat sent an armed man from the organization's main base in Karameh, Jordan, to murder 'Aziz Shehadeh and his follower 'Abd al-Nur Janho, "who are preaching for the establishment of a Palestinian government." The assassin was fingered and arrested within days after he had entered the West Bank.[34] Available records suggest that Shehadeh and Janho were not informed about the attempt on their lives. Apparently the Israelis did not attach much importance to the homicidal plot against these two Palestinians, whose entity movement was dormant at the time. The Israeli security establishment was then much more concerned about, and growing increasingly impatient with, fida'iyyun activity directed at Israeli civilians.

The guerrillas kept launching hit-and-run forays into Israel and Israel-controlled territories from Jordanian soil, notably mining rural byways and public roads. The Israeli army considered responding in kind. "We had frequently asked ourselves whether it would be expedient to lay, say, 200 mines [in the eastern Ghor] so that the local population would put pressure on the Fateh," Chief of Staff Bar-Lev divulged in a confidential forum in March. Bar-Lev said in effect that the idea of resorting to state terrorism was shelved because most of the civilian inhabitants of the Ghor had fled the area.[35] But apparently it was not. On 9 April, a day after reports from Amman that three Jordanian soldiers had been killed when their vehicle ran over a mine laid by the Israelis inside Jordan, Bar-Lev said on Israel's state radio: "Counterterrorist activity cannot be excluded, although it would not be a reply par excellence."[36] The US State and Defense Departments were thus resistant to an Israeli request to purchase 400,000 American-made antipersonnel mines for its new defense system along the Jordan. The Americans feared that the mines might be used for countermeasures in the East Bank.[37] Defense Minister Dayan and Lieutenant General Bar-Lev agreed, nevertheless, to turn the eastern Ghor into what the latter called "a wasteland" and the former "a graveyard."[38]

By and large, Israeli military thinking was dominated by the traditional doctrine of retaliatory raids, whose staunch sponsor was Dayan. On 6 March, following an intelligence review of al-Fateh's buildup in the East Bank and Hussein's helplessness in this regard, Bar-Lev suggested to the Ministerial Committee for Security Affairs an attack on the main al-Fateh base in Karameh, a small and now almost deserted town with an adjacent refugee camp some four miles east of the Allenby Bridge. Dayan asked the committee to approve the operation in principle, with timing subject to developments. Foreign Minister Eban objected, expatiating on the anticipated diplomatic fallout from the incursion, and won the committee's support. Dayan's reasoning that a bus full of children would one day hit a mine planted by al-Fateh failed to persuade the decision makers, but in less than a fortnight it proved to be an accurate prophecy.[39]

On 18 March a bus on a high school outing detonated a mine on the Arava Road near Eilat. Two adults were killed and twenty-eight others, mostly students, were injured. Within hours the ministerial committee reconvened and approved the operation it had rejected on 6 March; this time Eban did not object. In Amman, remembering bitter past experience such as the devastating raid on the West Bank village of Samuʿ in November 1966 (see introduction), Hussein dreaded a Pavlovian Israeli reprisal. He feared, moreover, that Israel might seize the opportunity to occupy additional territories in the East Bank in order to consolidate its grip on the West Bank, which in his view the Jewish state was adamant in holding on to for religious and cultural motives.[40] Attempting to pre-empt this, Hussein hastily authorized Colonel Daud's overdue rendez-vous with his Israeli counterpart. Daud had returned to Jordan at the beginning of the month but for some reason was so far barred by the king from going to the Allenby Bridge. More significant, Hussein sent an urgent message to Israel through the Americans in which he expressed "shock and regret" at the bus incident and gave personal assurances that his government was doing its utmost to apprehend the perpetrators and bring them to justice. Washington also urged Israel to stay its hand.

Hussein's plea, which arrived in Jerusalem on the morrow of the attack, elicited a resentful response from Eshkol for mentioning only the latest occurrence. However, the prime minister promptly brought the new development to the ministerial committee's attention. In the dis-cussion Eshkol favored putting the operation against Karameh on hold, while Dayan scorned Hussein's message and pressed to go ahead with the approved plan. Furthermore, the defense minister hoped for an "Arab military intervention"—Jordanian or Iraqi—thus betraying his wish to expand the operation beyond the declared aim of dealing a heavy blow to the Palestinian guerrillas. Dayan's desire to involve Jordan in the combat appears particularly bellicose in light of the fact that the kingdom's army had refrained from intervening in the exchanges of fire during the previ-ous weeks—as confirmed, for example, by Minister without Portfolio Menachem Begin.[41] Apparently Dayan's position prevailed.[42]

The next day, 20 March, the United States increased its pressure on Israel to exercise restraint. The preparations for a large-scale operation had been observed by the Americans as well as the Jordanians and the fida'iyyun. It was clear that a military action was imminent. The Ameri-cans stressed that a reprisal would be self-defeating and seriously preju-dicial to the hopes for a peaceful settlement.[43] An additional push came from Ambassador Jarring. That day, the UN envoy visited Amman and found there a tense atmosphere and widespread anticipation of an Is-raeli offensive. Premier Talhuni asked him to assure the Israelis that "everything possible would be done to control terrorist activities." Con-sequently, Jarring let Jerusalem know of his wish to come at once. Because the raid was scheduled to begin at dawn on the following day, his meeting with Eban was deliberately set for several hours afterward.[44]

Meanwhile, however, the diplomatic burden impelled Eban to change his mind again, and he vigorously called for a suspension of the attack. The government might have heeded the calls for a postponement had it not been for the near-fatal injury of Defense Minister Dayan in a cave-in during one of his illegal amateurish archaeological excavations outside Tel Aviv in the afternoon. Delaying the operation, Eshkol said in an informal discussion, would be disastrous because it would create the impression that the state depended on one person alone. Evidently the prime minister sought to demonstrate that he was no less decisive than and equally combative as his political archrival.[45] Domestic politics, then, dictated Israel's foreign policy and military deeds yet again.

In the final, nocturnal debate of the ministerial committee Eban continued his intense efforts for a deferral. By concentrating forces on the ceasefire line, he argued, Israel had already "brought Hussein to his knees." The foreign minister warned against a further deterioration of Israel's already tense relationship with the United States if the raid were carried out. He alluded to a stern American representation made the previous day by senior White House official Harold Saunders to an Israeli diplomat. In Eban's telling, Saunders had asserted that the president could not recall a single case of Israel's having accepted an American appeal during the previous six months. According to Saunders's own account, Washington felt that the Israelis believed they had the United States "in their pockets" and therefore could easily ignore its requests and suggestions.[46] There was now a danger, Eban went on, of losing the longed-for Phantom jets.

Subsequently Eshkol broached the idea of demanding that either Hussein immediately declare publicly his readiness to make peace or Johnson supply the Phantoms in return for calling the operation off. No one present was recorded as commenting on this incredible suggestion of blackmailing the highly supportive American president.[47] Eshkol's highly unusual idea of a shady bargain with the US president in order to get the Phantoms was not an isolated case. A few months later Eshkol stunned American diplomats by implying that he might consider signing the Treaty on the Non-Proliferation of Nuclear Weapons (NPT) in return for the Phantoms.[48]

Just before midnight, at zero hour minus six, the Ministerial Committee for Security Affairs decided by a majority of one to approve the incursion. In Washington, President Johnson made a last-ditch effort to prevent the assault and sent a personal message to Premier Eshkol, strongly advising him "in the interest of both our countries" against it. The message arrived in Tel Aviv belatedly and was delivered when the battle was already in full swing.[49] A short while after the pre-planned operation began, Ambassador Barbour was told by an Israeli official that this was not a "reprisal" but a vital "improvised action." Barbour's first reaction was: "Oh, my God!"

Operation *Tofet* (Hebrew for inferno) was executed by a massive force of 1,300 troops, including the elite airborne brigade, an armor brigade, and other auxiliary units, with 75 tanks, 120 half-tracks, and the aerial support of 360 sorties.[50] There were only 300 al-Fateh irregulars in and around Karameh, yet they were well prepared and fought back hard.[51] Jordanian artillery and armor joined in the fighting, too. The Israelis destroyed many dozens of buildings in Karameh and about 40 Jordanian tanks, and killed, wounded, and captured hundreds of Palestinian guerrillas, Jordanian soldiers, and civilians. But this was a pyrrhic victory. Israel suffered heavy losses: 31 dead and about 90 wounded. One of its fighter planes was shot down. Moreover, the invading force left behind 3 bodies, 4 tanks, 2 armored personnel carriers, and other armaments. Some of it was later boastfully paraded in the streets of Amman.[52] The troops failed to apprehend al-Fateh's leader Yasir 'Arafat, who allegedly escaped the battleground shortly after the fighting began.[53]

Most important, the operation did not achieve its primary objective. Though Premier Eshkol hastily bragged in the Knesset during the battle that the Israeli forces had "purged the terrorist nests and destroyed their bases," within a day Karameh was swarming again with armed cadres.[54] Attacks mounted from Jordan continued with scarcely a pause, culminating within a week in the killing of four more Israeli civilians whose car hit a guerrilla-laid mine in the Beisan Valley.[55] Israel reacted with an aerial attack on Jordanian positions and lost a plane. In daylong firing in the Ghor, one Israeli was killed and eight were wounded.[56]

The image of the invincible Israeli military was shattered in Karameh. The battle was no Arab military triumph, says the Palestinian scholar Rashid Khalidi, yet it has been narrated as the heroic "foundation myth" of the commando movement, a symbol of the Palestinian resistance.[57] Overnight, writes Yezid Sayigh, another Palestinian pundit, the battle turned into a resounding political and psychological victory in Arab eyes.[58] Although most of the damage the Israelis endured was inflicted by the Jordanians, the fida'iyyun took pride in standing up to the mighty Israeli army and celebrated the *karameh*—Arabic for dignity—their defiance earned them. Karameh went down in Palestinian history as their Stalingrad.[59] The PLO activist Nabil Sha'th maintained retrospectively that on 21 March 1968 it had dawned on the Palestinians for the first time that liberation was feasible; this was, he said, the day when the Palestinian revolution was truly born.[60]

In the West Bank, the results of the fighting produced much jubilation. In a conference of military governors a few days after the operation, the governor of Hebron described the shining eyes with which the city's dwellers greeted the news, and the governor of Nablus talked about expressions of malignant pleasure at the Israeli bungle. Other governors said that the battle of Karameh boosted the prestige of both King Hussein and al-Fateh.[61] There were also palpable consequences for the Palestinian-Israeli confrontation. The fight immediately inspired thousands of highly motivated young men to join al-Fateh and other resistance groups. The considerable growth of these organizations, particularly al-Fateh, gave a weighty impetus to the process, which ended less than a year later in their complete takeover of the PLO.[62] At the same time, it further diminished the power of the West Bank traditional elite, and thus accelerated the shift of Palestinian leadership from the *dakhil*, or the "inside" of the occupied territories, to the *kharij*, the "outside." Before long, this would render the Israeli "Palestinian alternative" stratagem redundant. But not yet.

The Palestinian Option Revisited

Since its inception, observed Roger Owen, Israel had been a "warfare state" conducting its relations with the neighboring Arabs almost exclusively by force and by threat of force.[63] This practice came with a price. In the inferno of Operation *Tofet* it was Israel who was badly burned. Instead of weakening the fida'iyyun, the botched Karameh reprisal served them as a recruiting sergeant. The Security Council unanimously condemned Israel, saying that the operation was carried out "in flagrant violation" of the UN Charter and the ceasefire resolution.[64] Foreign Minister Eban described in the cabinet the overall international reaction as "complete shock"; Israel's best friends were unable to accept the disproportion between the action and what had triggered it. "We told you so!" Washington furiously scolded the Israelis, according to Eban's account.[65] Even the much-desired emigration from the occupied territories, notably the Gaza Strip, dwindled significantly because of the precarious situation the Karameh escapade created in Jordan.[66]

Although the Israeli policy makers were disillusioned, their subsequent moves showed inconsistency and confusion. Before the raid Israel had demanded Israeli-Jordanian military liaison, yet Colonel Daud was rebuffed when he finally arrived at the Allenby Bridge for a prearranged meeting on 21 March while the combat was still raging. The presence of General Bull of the United Nations, who accompanied Daud, was the reason given for the snub.[67] A day later, however, Eshkol and Eban endeavored to bring about through the United Nations a "frank exchange between representatives of both sides on practical measures for avoiding further deterioration"; they urgently invited UN envoy Jarring to Jerusalem and asked him to convey that message to King Hussein without delay.[68] Meanwhile, Israel attempted to excuse the attack on Karameh by presenting it as coming to Hussein's rescue in his uphill struggle against the terrorists.[69] An Israeli diplomat told Undersecretary Rostow: "[The] medicine had been strong but [the] King was now on [the] road to recovery."[70] But Abba Eban—who had forcefully objected to the raid—formulated a revised position: it did not matter who perpetrated an act of aggression against Israel; whether it was al-Fateh or the Jordanian army, Israel settled scores with the country from which the attack was launched. "We should blur this"—Eban went on, referring to the fact that the guerrilla attacks against Israel were executed by Palestinian commandos—"and say that Jordan did not keep the ceasefire agreement."[71]

Eban's statement revealed a new Israeli tack vis-à-vis Hussein. In a way, the king played into Israel's hands. In a press conference two days after the raid he was asked whether the declared number of civilian victims included fida'iyyun. "Possibly," the monarch replied, "but the truth is that the inhabitants of Karameh put up a courageous resistance. It is difficult to distinguish between a fida'i and someone else. We may reach a stage when everybody becomes fida'i, and it might happen soon."[72] Taken out of context, the last sentence was flaunted as proof of the king's support of the guerrilla movement—a preposterous charge, given the obvious threat the fida'iyyun posed to the stability of the Hashemite regime, if not to its very existence. At most, Hussein attempted to appropriate some of the upsurge in the fida'iyyun's popularity in the wake of Karameh. The king was unable to overpower the guerrillas, and the Israelis knew it.[73] Nevertheless, Israeli diplomats used the incessant Palestinian terrorism as a pretext to talk about overthrowing Hussein.[74] Secretary of State Rusk expressed Washington's growing consternation at the "continuing evidence that elements in [the Israeli government are] seriously considering [the] possibility of toppling Hussein as means of somehow improving [the] current situation for Israel." He stressed that the preservation of the Hashemite regime was "a major US interest."[75]

Israel's change in attitude was accompanied by an apparent espousal of the Palestinian option. The Israelis viewed Hussein as very weak and thus wondered whether only the Palestinians could take the lead. In a conversation with the White House official Harold Saunders on 29 March the Israeli diplomat Ephraim Evron said that perhaps it was about time for his government to begin thinking "again" seriously about a separate Palestinian entity.[76] This orientation coincided with attempts by West Bank proponents of a separate solution to revive the idea. While Sheikh Ja'bari made statements to this effect, 'Aziz Shehadeh sought American support.[77] Even such Nablus hard-liners as Hikmat al-Masri, despairing of the likelihood of any Arab-Israeli settlement, began to incline toward a "local approach."[78] Shehadeh raised with Sasson what he described as the growing tendency in Nablus to subscribe to his thinking. The Israeli official advised him to encourage this trend "slowly, cautiously, but also persistently."

This first traced instance of overt Israeli advocacy of the entity movement was in fact nothing but the "Palestinian alternative" ruse in disguise. The cat was out of the bag when Shehadeh endeavored to find out about Israel's political intentions. As expected, Sasson dismissed his request. What mattered, Sasson argued, was that the West Bank notables should resolve "to put their hand in ours" and decide with the Israelis on the best solution—be it a local one or a settlement either with Hussein or with Nasser. Shehadeh feared that the Israelis intended to take advantage of the Palestinians to advance a bilateral settlement with

Jordan. Nonetheless he accepted Sasson's line, provided the Israelis pledged not to desert the Palestinians along the way as they had done at the Lausanne Conference in 1949.[79]

Sasson and Shehadeh soon discovered that an independent Palestinian solution meant different things to different people. Upon his return to Nablus from Beirut via Amman at the end of March, Walid al-Shak'ah told first Sasson and Maj. David Farhi and later Shehadeh and Judge Tiyasir Kan'an that he was empowered by both the leaders of the PLO and al-Fateh to examine with the government of Israel its preparedness to allow the establishment of a Palestinian state. Shak'ah informed his Israeli interlocutors of his intention to seek President Nasser's blessing for the initiative, adding that he preferred not to go to Cairo empty-handed; information about Israel's basic position regarding an accommodation was needed. In the light of the Antoun 'Atallah precedent, Shak'ah also felt that his return to the West Bank should be solemnly guaranteed. On the actual plan he said only that following the withdrawal of Israel's troops and Military Government from the occupied territories, the Palestinian leaders of the *kharij* would arrive in the West Bank and the Gaza Strip to discuss self-determination and a peaceful settlement with Israel. King Hussein would not be consulted, and his army would not be allowed into the West Bank. This schematic outline was in fact the Nablus plan, which had been conceived in late November (see chapter 6) and broached by Shak'ah and Hikmat al-Masri in their dealings with the Israelis on several occasions. Only now the program had, according to Shak'ah, the endorsement of the leadership of the major Palestinian organizations. Shak'ah asked 'Aziz Shehadeh to use his good contacts with Defense Minister Dayan and Prime Minister Eshkol—through Sasson—to advance the initiative. Shehadeh acquiesced; in a meeting with Sasson he stressed that the Palestinian move, aiming at a peaceful settlement based on a Palestinian state alongside Israel, brought both parties to a decisive historical juncture.[80]

Neither the existing literature nor non-Israeli records corroborate what seems to be a dramatic about-face in the position of the Palestinian organizations that hitherto regarded a two-state solution as anathema. Whether Shak'ah misunderstood the intentions of his al-Fateh and PLO interlocutors, misinterpreted them, or even made the whole thing up has no bearing on the present discussion, because the Israelis did not doubt the initiative and acted upon it. In fact, Sasson had already tried to establish clandestine links with the PLO. Apparently he did it on his own, prompted by accounts of Chairman Yahya Hammudah's moderate position. The latest report came from the Jerusalemite ʿAli al-Sharif, who met Shuqayri's successor in Amman in February. Sharif said that Hammudah had assured him of the PLO's policy to restrain the guerrilla activity and to seek a political solution.[81] Sasson asked Shehadeh to probe whether Hammudah would agree to some sort of a parley between the PLO and Israel. Hammudah replied via a middleman in a written chit: "Affirmative under certain conditions." The conditions were not specified, and Shehadeh undertook to pursue the matter further.[82]

Shakʿah's initiative on behalf of al-Fateh and the PLO gave the issue some urgency. On 6 April, Sasson reported the new development to Dayan. The defense minister, still hospitalized, reacted with a flat rejection. Al-Fateh was engaged in terrorism, he said, and as long as it held a gun against the Israelis' temple, Israel would not respond to its overtures. Dayan explicitly mentioned only al-Fateh, but he clearly referred to all Palestinian organizations, including the PLO, without making any distinction among them. There was no rush, Dayan added. "We should have the opportunity to kill them. The way to deal with them is by killing them." Dayan's position was subsequently approved by the prime minister.[83]

From his hospital bed Dayan devised a revolutionary concept of his own: the West Bank Palestinians should take matters into their own hands and assume control of Jordan. "Not Amman should rule Nablus, but Nablus should rule Amman," he told Mayor Hamdi Kanʿan, who came to visit him on 31 March. His approach fell short of an open call for a coup in Jordan, but only just. In the conversation with Kanʿan and later in a discussion with Sasson and two of his aides, Dayan put his idea in the context of the struggle against al-Fateh. He believed the West Bankers to be readier to make concessions than Hussein; once they controlled Amman, Israel would be able to reach a settlement with them through negotiations "under the king's aegis."[84] When Sasson updated Dayan on the recent exchanges, including Anwar Nuseibeh and Hikmat al-Masri's talks with Hussein and Talhuni about constituting a "Palestinian government" in Jordan, the defense minister was pleased. With the Palestinians, he said, "the cards are falling our way." He pressed hard for strengthening Israel's contacts with the occupied Palestinians rather than with the Palestinian leaders in Beirut, and said that having a "common language" with them was of utmost importance.[85] Again, Dayan's stance promptly earned Eshkol's approval.[86]

Foreign Minister Eban's main concern was the deadlocked Jarring mission. On 27 February he reiterated to the Knesset Foreign Affairs and Security Committee his fear of renewed discussion of the Middle East crisis at the United Nations because, he said, it could only produce a clearer resolution than 242, hence a worse one for Israel. Eban added that Israel was now required to exercise flexibility—tactical rather than political—and mentioned in this regard his "dossier diplomacy" ruse (see chapter 6).[87] Three weeks later, in another appearance before the same forum, Eban stressed that Israel was engaged in a "tactical-political campaign. It is not about peace." In both cases the Hebrew word he used for "tactical" was *takhsisit;* as we have seen, Eban had avidly advocated *takhsisanut,* or prevarication, in devising Israel's postwar foreign policy. The committee's members knew little about the ongoing secret contacts with King Hussein and were unable to challenge what the foreign minister told them next. No Arab county wanted to make progress toward peace, Eban claimed, thus Israel was exerting itself to diminish international pressure and putting the blame for the impasse on the Arab side.[88] In practical terms what Eban said meant unceasing diplomatic activity, no matter how futile, to make it appear as if Israel was strenuously endeavoring to achieve peace. Without "certain activity in search for peace," he wrote in mid-April to Ambassador Rabin in Washington, time was not in Israel's favor.[89]

Since the war Israel had been speaking with more than one voice. Foreign Minister Eban alone was now speaking with two. Echoing the new Dayan-Eshkol position, which seemingly embraced the Palestinian option, he emphasized on 4 April at a party forum the important role the occupied Palestinians should play in promoting an Arab-Israeli settlement, and suggested an end to talk about Hussein. Instead, he said, Israel should talk about Jordan and what might happen in the East Bank, "and it doesn't matter whether it is a Hashemite king today or a republican prime minister tomorrow."[90] Concurrently, however, Eban followed the opposite course. When Hikmat al-Masri requested to see him about 242, Eban grabbed the opportunity to use Masri to transmit a message to King Hussein and President Nasser. Masri had been told in Amman that if Israel would announce its unqualified acceptance of Resolution 242 and its willingness to implement it, Jordan would agree to negotiate under Jarring's auspices. He asked to see Eban in order to learn the precise Israeli position. Masri also mentioned his intention to meet both Hussein and Nasser soon.[91]

Eban received Hikmat al-Masri at his residence on 4 April. As the Israeli record shows, Eban dominated the conversation, confirming yet again Saul Bellow's observation: "He is not a listener."[92] His message included the conventional rhetoric about Israel's insistence on direct negotiations and obscure assurances regarding the government's preparedness to consider border and security issues in a positive manner. There was nothing new in what he said, and the whole episode might have been dismissed as another example of Eban's adherence to diplomacy for the sake of diplomacy had it not been for two additional caveats. The first was an openly belligerent threat: Eban stated that because of the fida'iyyun's activities a settlement must urgently be reached; if a settlement was not achieved during April, Israel would resort to force. The second point supplemented the first and mirrored the rivalries within Israel's top political echelon. Eban argued that the Israeli politicians were losing control, and that if peace was not achieved by the end of that month, the army—he undoubtedly meant Dayan and the military establishment—would gain the upper hand. Eban indicated that the message was intended for Hussein and Nasser's ears only, and was very anxious that Masri should deliver it to the king before the latter's departure for Cairo on 6 April.[93]

Eban, then, presented the leaders of Jordan and Egypt with an ultimatum—direct negotiations now, or we will attack. Available records provide no indication that the ultimatum was sanctioned by the cabinet or authorized by the prime minister. Hikmat al-Masri did not find Eban's message important enough to consider it urgent. Nevertheless, he duly delivered the Israeli threat to King Hussein, who in turn conveyed it to President Nasser.[94] Neither ruler reacted. Appearing before the confidential Foreign Affairs and Security Committee of the Knesset on 9 April, Eban did not mention the ultimatum. Instead, he disclosed the use the government was making of a handful of "very impressive" West Bank politicians as go-betweens. Recently, Eban said without divulging any details, the prime minister and he had had "very comprehensive discussions" with these men, who constituted a new channel of communication with Hussein.[95] Two weeks later Eban told the committee that there had been many contacts between "the leaders of Palestine"—namely, the

West Bank political elite—and the Jordanian government about a settlement. The Palestinians, he said, had been putting pressure on Amman and even on Cairo. Some of the leaders favored Hussein, while others desired an independent state. But the West Bank Palestinians, Eban concluded, were the only Arabs working for a settlement, thereby preventing a complete political stalemate.[96]

His inconsistent or even contradictory conduct notwithstanding, Eban clearly preferred a settlement with Jordan to the Palestinian option, and sought to exploit the West Bankers as a way of exerting leverage on Hussein.[97] Ironically, Eban not only confirmed ʿAziz Shehadeh's suspicions but also used the same wording. By and large, however, the Israeli thinking in the immediate aftermath of the Karameh raid focused on the occupied Palestinians. In another exchange with Harold Saunders of the White House staff, Israeli Minister Ephraim Evron elaborated on his government's inclination. He asserted that Hussein was unable to negotiate a settlement without Nasser's consent, and that feelings of Palestinian separatism had been growing stronger in the West Bank. He thus wondered again whether Israel should negotiate with the Palestinians and let them determine their own relations with Jordan. Evron suggested further that the policy makers' intention was to introduce a substantial modification in the prewar armistice line by pushing it eastward at least as far as the ridge that runs down through Nablus past Jerusalem and Hebron. Saunders estimated that the coveted area amounted to between 15 and 25 percent of the West Bank region.[98]

Everything Evron said was effectively substantiated by his prime minister. On 9 April, when Moshe Sasson informed him that the West Bank leaders were pushing hard for an answer about Israel's readiness to go for a "Palestinian settlement" with them, Eshkol was responsive to the approach but miserly on substance. The Palestinian leaders, he said, should be told that Israel would sit along the Jordan River and on the north-south ridge. On the remainder of the West Bank they could establish some sort of an independent state, with a parliament of their own but with no army, thus saving security costs. The truncated Palestinian state would be granted a linking corridor to Jordan and access to the Mediterranean Sea. Israel might even consider a tripartite federation which would include itself, Jordan, and the Palestinian state. Eshkol made negotiations with the Palestinian leaders conditional on their mandate to speak on behalf of the whole population of the West Bank, and recommended that they hold a conference for that purpose. Sasson did not bother reminding him of the ban on any political organization in the occupied territories, but pointed out that no Palestinian would ever accept his proposal without Arab Jerusalem as the capital of the state. Eshkol reacted sharply: Jerusalem was out of the question.[99]

With or without Jerusalem, Eshkol's outline was pie in the sky. Dayan, however, pragmatically attempted to put the ball in the Palestinians' court. Back in his office in mid-April, he received Mayor Hamdi Kan'an of Nablus and 'Aziz Shehadeh, at the former's request. The joint démarche corroborated Shehadeh's claim that Nablus had been coming around to his approach. More fluent in English than Kan'an, Shehadeh opened the political discussion by reiterating the question about the government's intentions, which Israel had been doggedly avoiding all along. If there was common ground for negotiations, he said, the West Bankers would send a representative delegation to the bargaining table. Dayan was unable to offer a straight answer. He told his guests that negotiations were within the prime minister's bailiwick and, moreover, the divided cabinet would not make a decision on negotiations before it was forced to do so. Dayan posed instead a series of six questions meant to convey his personal views. The first three concerned whether the Palestinians were prepared to make real contractual peace (*sulh*) with Israel—separately or in conjunction with Hussein—including resolution of the refugee problem. The other three were not really questions but statements: an Israeli-Palestinian settlement was possible only if the United States supported it; no Israeli government would ever agree to any change in the status of Israel-ruled Jerusalem; Israel would never return to the prewar border which allowed Jordanian guns to shell urban centers and to cut the country in half.

Dayan described himself as one of the moderates within Israel's cabinet, because he was unwilling to naturalize the West Bankers as Israeli citizens. He wanted a Jewish state with a Jewish majority. Therefore only a nominal number of refugees would be allowed to return to their homes, for Israel needed every piece of land in order to increase the Jewish population. Kan'an asked why Gaza was not mentioned. In an evasive answer designed to conceal the intended annexation of the Strip, Dayan claimed that the fate of Gaza depended on which entity Israel ultimately negotiated with. He added, however, that the government did not envisage the region returning to Egyptian rule or becoming part of Jordan. When Shehadeh raised the issue of Jerusalem and wondered why Israel would not allow the Arab sector of the city to be the capital of the Palestinian state in the same way that the Palestinians recognized the Jewish sector as Israel's capital, Dayan came up with an imaginative idea: 'Izariyyah, biblical Bethany and now a small town just outside the Old City, or even Ramallah, could be developed by building into sections of Jerusalem, and thereby serve as the Palestinian capital. The defense minister then brought King Hussein into the picture. He said that "certain Arab rulers" whom he did not wish to name had approached Israel about its terms for a settlement. In response, Israel had asked whether they would accept significant changes in the pre-June border, but had not received a positive reply. Dayan's story, which has no recorded foundation, clearly unmasked his territorial aspirations.

Armed with plentiful wishful thinking, Shehadeh regarded Dayan's position as promising sufficient grounds for further contacts, ideally leading to a separate Palestinian state. Major Farhi noted that Shehadeh—until recently an outcast and even branded a traitor by Nablus radicals—was excited by his new self-perceived status as chief negotiator. As such, Shehadeh asked whether the significant territorial changes mentioned earlier would be one-sided, and attributed much weight to Dayan's insincere response: "not necessarily." Hamdi Kan'an, on the other hand, felt that the overall attitude of the defense minister was rigid and left the meeting pessimistic. Indeed, Dayan had not been forthcoming at all. Toward the end of the discussion he added a seventh question, demanding to know on whose behalf the West Bank representatives were authorized to speak—the majority of the Palestinians or Jordan? Israel, he stressed, would not talk substance with individuals.[100]

Nonetheless, Dayan's questions and dictates were debated in depth by Nablus leaders in the coming days. On 19 April they informed Shehadeh of their conclusions. Nablus replied with an unqualified "yes" to making real peace, sealed in a treaty which enjoyed US approval, and agreed that a final settlement should entail the resolution of the refugee problem. Their answers to the two remaining points, Jerusalem and borders, were more nuanced. Border modifications, they suggested, should be reciprocal, Jerusalem should stay undivided but with shared sovereignty, and both issues should be discussed in detail at the negotiation table. Nablus leaders argued, however, that in order to appoint a negotiating team they required a clearer idea about Israel's territorial thinking, including the future of the Gaza Strip and Palestinian access to the Mediterranean Sea. They obliquely addressed the question of for whom they spoke by saying that once the "authorized local leadership" reached an understanding with Israel regarding peace, attempts would be made to obtain approval of the Palestinians abroad and the Arab states; in case of failure, the West Bankers would go it alone. The overall favorable reaction of Nablus was buttressed by additional behind-the-scenes information which Shehadeh readily shared with Farhi.[101]

Dayan believed that the West Bankers were the only Arabs ready to talk peace with Israel despite knowing that a settlement would involve major territorial changes. In a political stocktaking on 18 April he even assured those present that the Palestinians were going through "a process of sobering up" concerning the most difficult issue of Jerusalem. Obviously, Shehadeh was not alone in succumbing to wishful thinking. The defense minister also expressed objection to overthrowing King Hussein and occupying Amman, thereby reconfirming that such ideas had been seriously considered in government circles.[102] Upon receiving the Nablus response, Dayan held that it was in Israel's interest to pursue the Palestinian course. He promptly urged Eshkol to do so, arguing that the discussions should be conducted by the Prime Minister's Office in accordance with clear guidelines. Therefore, Dayan concluded, he regarded his own part in this endeavor as finished.[103]

Eshkol took up the gauntlet. On 24 and 25 April he met Judge Tiyasir Kan'an and former Governor Anwar al-Khatib, respectively, and discussed a potential settlement in broad terms.[104] However, he adopted a different line with each of his interlocutors, apart from one point: Eshkol firmly asserted that the return of no Palestinian refugee, new or old, would be permitted—even to the occupied territories. There is not enough room for them, he told Tiyasir Kan'an, adding that Jews should stop being a minority. The refugee problem, Eshkol emphasized, must be resolved on a regional basis. In his exchange with Anwar al-Khatib he was more explicit: "The refugees should be settled outside [Israel-controlled territories]. In Iraq." Khatib reacted with deep disappointment. He reminded the prime minister that the Jews had suffered banishment and knew what it was to live in exile. "If Israel wants peace," Khatib insisted, "don't say: 'they should go to Iraq.'"

Eshkol's objection to the repatriation of refugees also had a more topical motivation. He told Tiyasir Kan'an that he did not want the West

Bankers to seek the consent of their brethren in the *kharij* to a settlement with Israel because it would inevitably raise the issue of return. The general outline Eshkol suggested to Kan'an was far less generous than what he had contemplated a fortnight before. Then he had talked about "some sort of an independent state," with a parliament of its own; now he merely offered "some sort of autonomy" in the inhabited region of the West Bank and mentioned no Palestinian legislature. In his meeting with Anwar al-Khatib, Eshkol had said that Israel did not want the populated parts of the West Bank, "but there are unpopulated areas [there]"—indicating his government's desire to keep them permanently. With Khatib, who was regarded as King Hussein's eyes and ears in the West Bank, Eshkol talked about negotiations with Jordan. Khatib proposed that authorized West Bankers should bargain on behalf of Hussein, as the king was unable to engage in open negotiations. Moshe Sasson recommended a joint Jordanian-Palestinian delegation, and Avi'ad Yafeh, Eshkol's other adviser, floated the name of former Prime Minister Wasfi al-Tall as leader of the team. "I too thought of Wasfi al-Tall," Khatib concurred. It was up to Eshkol to decide whether to accept Anwar al-Khatib's proposal. Khatib expected to hear from the prime minister within twenty-four to forty-eight hours.

Because of the scarcity of Palestinian sources it is worth giving Anwar al-Khatib's side of the story. His contemporary version of the exchange with the Israeli prime minister ignored the debate about Jordanian-Palestinian negotiations with Israel. He told an American diplomat that Eshkol—who struck him as a good-hearted man, "not crafty like so many Israelis," but weak—made no specific proposals but asked whether there could not be some sort of arrangement for the "administration" of the West Bank, since there did not seem to be much prospect for peace.[105] In his memoirs, published two decades later, Khatib writes that the Israeli premier inquired whether he could speak on behalf of Jordan. Khatib said he could not, yet if there was an opportunity for peace talks, he was willing to present the matter in Amman. Eshkol promised to contact him within two days for further discussion but never did.[106]

Conversely, Tiyasir Kan'an was expected to respond to the suggestion of a meeting between Eshkol and fifteen to twenty prominent West Bankers with the purpose of conveying the prime minister's ideas. Kan'an's first reaction was negative. He contended that such a gathering was pointless if Eshkol intended to say what he had just told him, and stressed that concrete proposals were needed. "There are no other details," Eshkol retorted impatiently. "The West Bankers should decide what they want—[a settlement] with Jordan or autonomy. The armistice lines are dead. Perhaps in the future there will be a basis for a confederation." Despite this inflexible attitude, Kan'an agreed to think about the invitation and to offer a considered reply.

A week later Tiyasir Kan'an informed Sasson and Farhi that he could not accept. Reiterating the reasons he had specified to Eshkol, Kan'an said that there was no point in a group meeting with the premier unless an official scheme for a solution was to be presented there.[107] This position was formulated by the West Bank notables after careful deliberations. According to Mayor Hamdi Kan'an, Tiyasir's cousin, the notables felt that seeing Eshkol would be dangerous in view of Israel's habit of exploiting such opportunities for propaganda purposes. The consensus was that when Eshkol had something to offer, he should pass it to one or two dignitaries, who in turn would circulate it among the rest for consideration.[108] All the while Anwar al-Khatib waited in vain for Eshkol's decision about secret negotiations with Wasfi al-Tall. The lack of response was interpreted by Khatib and others as evidence of Israel's unwillingness to reach a settlement.[109] Oddly enough, Sasson accused the Palestinian leadership of acting as Jordanian agents—as if his government was not using them as emissaries to Amman and, moreover, playing a double game whereby they juggled with the Palestinian option and the Jordanian one.[110] Now it was time for the latter.

The Jordanian Option Revisited

The month of April was not exclusively reserved by the Israelis for exploring the Palestinian course. In addition to the West Bank go-betweens they maintained another confidential channel of communication with Hussein. A high-level meeting with the king was set up via this channel. Golda Meir had believed that there was no escape from an Eshkol-Hussein summit, but eventually Foreign Minister Eban was assigned the task.[111] The meager accessible paper trail sheds little light on how the meeting came about and does not disclose who took the initiative. But it is evident that Israel's top policy makers held a number of discussions in which the line to be taken with the Jordanian monarch was formulated.

An unsigned two-page document outlining the approach instructed the Israeli representative to assure Hussein of the government's continuous encouragement of the Palestinians to work both covertly and overtly for an Israeli-Jordanian settlement; as long as negotiations took place and progressed, the status of the West Bankers would not be determined. This last point was meant perhaps to sugar the pill which followed: the final border would be "substantially different" from the prewar line, and unified Jerusalem would remain under Israeli sovereignty. As for the occupied territories that Israel was willing to cede, not only did the paper say nothing, but the clause which suggested telling the king that a decision had not been reached was crossed out.[112] The Labor Party's Political Committee and the cabinet approved the secret rendezvous and the agreed position.[113]

Hussein and Eban met on 3 May at the home of Dr. Emanuel Herbert, the king's Jewish doctor, in London. The king was accompanied by Zayd al-Rifa'i, his trusted private secretary, and the Israeli foreign minister was joined by Dr. Ya'acov Herzog, Eshkol's chief political adviser who handled the "Hussein channel." Eban opened by emphasizing that he had come not to negotiate or to make commitments but to seek answers to two questions: first, could the king reach a contractual peace with Israel, independent of his neighbors? Second, what could the king do to stop the terrorist activities launched from his country against Israel? The ensuing conversation never reached the second question. The guerrilla attacks were discussed by the chiefs of staff of the two countries in a separate meeting in London a few days later. Jordan's Gen. 'Amer Khammash asked his opposite number to limit Israel's reactions to al-Fateh targets and to avoid hitting the Jordanian army. General Bar-Lev replied that this was unworkable.[114] Hussein and Eban's exchange dealt only with the first question about a separate peace accord. "It is not impossible," the king said, but he added a crucial question of his own: "Can you not tell me what kind of a settlement you would be prepared for?"

The Israeli record shows that Eban's response occupied about one half of the three-hour discussion. His initial remarks reiterated the usual elusive position that the Israeli government saw no reason to take a binding decision before believing that the subject was actual. He then detailed the three competing approaches held in Israel—annexation of the West Bank; a settlement with the West Bankers; and a negotiated peace with Jordan. In order to pressure Hussein, Eban claimed that many Palestinians had been urging Israel to choose the Palestinian option, either because of reservations about the Hashemite regime or due to their conviction that the king would not negotiate. When he finally arrived at the Jordanian option, it appears that Eban's lecture went beyond his guidelines. He said that the significant changes to the 4 June lines would be motivated by security considerations and "historical association"—a definition which could be applied to the entire West Bank. Specifically, Eban mentioned the Jordan Valley as an area vital for Israel's security, but he also talked about army bases in the heart of the West Bank. In essence, Eban presented Hussein with a mélange of the Allon and the Dayan plans.

Apart from one interjection, indicating that military encampments could be allowed only on the basis of reciprocity, the king refrained from any reference to the substance. Instead, he stated that Jordan and Israel should begin negotiations, either under Jarring's auspices or privately. Rifaʿi, who feared that Hussein's response might leave Eban with the impression that his ideas were acceptable, emphatically called them all proposals "for Arab surrender, not for agreement." Jordan's starting point, he stressed, would be the 4 June lines with minor, mutual changes, including Jerusalem. Rifaʿi dismissed the Palestinian option as a pipe dream. Israel might make a deal with some secondary figures, he said, but all the prominent West Bank leaders sided with the king and maintained contacts with Amman; they would not dare act against the regime. Furthermore, they had been discussing a local settlement with Israeli officials only to prevent Israel from consolidating its grip on the West Bank. Herzog observed that contrary to November 1967, when Hussein had been afraid of a separate Palestinian-Israeli settlement (see chapter 5), he and Rifaʿi now seemed fully confident that no such a danger existed.

Before they parted, the king said, "There should be further contact between us." Although he remained ignorant of Israel's starting point, Hussein assured Eban that he aimed at a bilateral peace accord, but he indicated that more effort to win Egypt's approval was required to allow open negotiations to take place.[115]

Cairo's consent was necessary because President Nasser had rescinded the green light he had given Hussein in the summer and the fall of 1967 to negotiate a separate deal with the Israelis (see chapter 5).

Nasser's about-face was spurred by three Israeli decrees, promulgated
in late February, the effect of which was that the occupied areas were no
longer regarded as "enemy territory," and the Allenby Bridge was designated as an official point of entry into, or exit from, the State of Israel.
Albeit the decrees were purely administrative and lacked political purpose, Egypt, Jordan, and other Arab states interpreted them as intended
to change the status of the occupied territories and to annex them de
facto to Israel.[116]

Herzog learned later that the meeting with Eban had discouraged
Hussein, though the king still harbored hopes of making some headway
at the UN headquarters in New York. Eban also felt that no real progress
had been made. So Herzog initiated follow-up discussions with Rifaʻi.
In the first, on 5 May, the two officials covered the same ground more
frankly and in more detail. In the second, on the following day, Rifaʻi
informed Herzog of a dispatch from Cairo which had been received
in the interim. Presumably reporting on Premier Talhuni's talks in the
Egyptian capital, the message related that Nasser saw no point in negotiating with the Jewish state because he did not believe that Israel would
implement Resolution 242, give up Arab Jerusalem, relinquish the Gaza
Strip, and return to the 4 June lines. On the day of the Hussein-Eban
dialogue, Nasser had secretly received Hikmat al-Masri, who told him
that Eshkol and Eban, whom he had met recently, had said that they
were ready to make concessions which the Arabs would not expect—
provided Egypt agreed to negotiate with Israel.[117] Obviously, the Egyptian president was not convinced. Indeed, Eban and Herzog had effectively
affirmed in their discussions with Hussein and Rifaʻi at least three of
Nasser's four predictions. Nonetheless, at Jordan's insistence, Nasser
promised to instruct his UN ambassador to take part in the first stage
of the talks under Jarring's auspices, which would include one meeting
between Jarring and the representatives of Jordan and Egypt, another
between Jarring and Israel's delegates. Rifaʻi told Herzog that at the second stage, a Jordanian-Israeli face-to-face discussion would take place.
The Egyptians would stay away; Nasser maintained that once he agreed
to take part in such a meeting, the Israelis would have won the June 1967
War politically as well. The Israelis learned about the go-ahead Nasser
had given Jordan through several other international sources.[118]

The disagreements between Herzog and Rifaʻi, primarily over Jerusalem, seemed irreconcilable. Even when the two men appeared to

reach an understanding, it was based on Israeli deception. Rifaʻi said yes when Herzog inquired whether Jordan would settle the Gaza Strip refugees on its territory as part of a peace arrangement, but the latter was deliberately concealing Israeli determination not to allow their settlement in the West Bank, only in the East. For his part, Rifaʻi raised the issue of the new refugees languishing in makeshift camps in Jordan since the war and said that as a gesture of goodwill Israel should permit them to return to their homes in the West Bank, particularly those who lately had been evacuated from the eastern Ghor as a result of Israeli shelling. Herzog promised to bring the request to the attention of his prime minister and foreign minister.[119] In his blow-by-blow oral report to the cabinet, Herzog stressed that the meeting with Hussein reconfirmed what Israel had known all along—the king desired peace. Herzog indicated that as early as July 1967 Hussein had resolved to make peace with Israel and that he had persistently been working to achieve this goal ever since: in November, the king had tried to circumvent the binding three "no"s of Khartoum through the West Bank Palestinians; now he pinned all his hopes on Jarring.

In the debate that followed Herzog's presentation, quite a few ministers argued that from what they had just heard there was no need to make any decision and there was nothing to tell the Jordanians. Premier Eshkol agreed to wait a while—"a week or two"—saying, "It's not urgent." At the same time, he expressed deep concern that President Johnson might learn through Jarring and U Thant of Hussein's unequivocal readiness to negotiate a settlement. Israel, Eshkol knew, would bear the brunt of Washington's displeasure if it refused to respond. But he was also aware that peace talks would force his cabinet to make the decision it had so strenuously tried to avoid. "I've said it more than once," the prime minister reminded his colleagues: "I fear the day when we have to sit face to face and conduct negotiations." The reason for Eshkol's apprehension was obvious to Hussein, who clearly saw through the Israelis' motives: there was a growing conviction in Jordan and Egypt, the king told Britain's Foreign Secretary Michael Stewart just three days after his meeting with Eban, that Israel was not interested in peace and intended to hang on to the territories it occupied, including Arab Jerusalem. Evidently Eshkol and his cabinet were caught between hammer and anvil. They chose, yet again, not to decide.[120]

It can be argued with some cogency that a cabinet resolution, particularly if it gave up large parts of the West Bank, would have led to the breakup of the National Unity coalition, and even to a split within the ruling, newly reunited Labor Party. But deeds speak louder than words, and Israel's actions suggest that it repeatedly shied away from making a decision for an entirely different reason. In the spring of 1968, while evading Hussein's appeal for direct negotiations as well as the Palestinians' initiatives—despite of all its grandiloquent promises of generosity at the bargaining table—Israel was busy with its traditional fait accompli practices. Special emphasis was put on accelerating the Judaization of Arab Jerusalem, including the construction of housing projects for Jews and requisition of Arab-owned real estate. Attempting to escape denunciation by the Security Council and international condemnation, Eshkol gave instructions to avoid any publicity about the building spree in Arab Jerusalem.[121] For the same reason the cabinet decided to maintain low-key celebrations of the first "Jerusalem Liberation Day" on 26 May.[122]

Ruhi al-Khatib, the former mayor of Arab Jerusalem, who had headed the National Guidance Committee since the deportation of Sheikh 'Abd al-Hamid al-Sa'ih in September (see chapter 3), undertook to coordinate the struggle of landowners whose properties were expropriated. He also vigorously objected to Israeli attempts to take control of the strictly Arab, privately owned Jerusalem District Electricity Company, and was vocal in asserting the illegality of the annexation of Arab Jerusalem. Consequently, he was forced to follow his predecessor: on 7 March, Khatib was unceremoniously expelled to Jordan.[123] Defense Minister Dayan claimed that he had given the order because of Khatib's "subversive activity and incitement to violent actions against the Israeli rule."[124] His exile marked a further emasculation of the independent-minded leaders of the occupied Palestinians.

The government craved Jewish settlement outside Jerusalem in specific areas but suffered from a tight budget and a lack of willing settlers.[125] Yet in mid-April, against the cabinet's policy but with secret help from some of its members, notably Yigal Allon, the most contentious and troublesome settlement began in the Arab city of Hebron. A group of ultranationalistic observant Jews rented rooms in a local hotel, pretending to celebrate the Passover but refusing to leave when the holiday was over. Instead of evicting the lawbreakers, the indecisive government made a deal with them whereby they moved to the local Military Government compound until the Jewish suburb of Kiryat Arba' could be built for them east of the city in 1971. "What could we have done?" Premier Eshkol asked apologetically in a confidential forum, "Instruct the police to remove *Jews* from Hebron? This is all we need." Foreign Minister Eban confessed that the whole affair disgraced Israel abroad, and Eshkol agreed; nevertheless, the government gave its tacit post factum approval to the wildcat settlement.[126]

On the first anniversary of the occupation, the British journalist Harold Jackson found that the "prospects for any real advance towards a Middle Eastern settlement seem remoter than ever." The hope of flexibility of the previous summer had been replaced by the certainty of rigid impasse, Jackson wrote. The Israelis, oblivious to their growing isolation, "were steadily hardening their attitude about what is actually negotiable. Not the Old City of Jerusalem; . . . nor the Syrian Heights and Gaza Strip. Bits of Sinai, maybe. The West Bank conditionally."[127] In fact, the Israeli policy makers were looking for a way to have their West Bank cake and eat it too.

Minister without Portfolio Yosef Sapir shared with American diplomats in Tel Aviv what he described as his private ideas which he claimed not to have discussed with anyone: since peace was not possible at least for the time being, Israel should think in terms of intermediate solutions. "We do not believe him for a minute," Ambassador Barbour reported undiplomatically, explaining that similar concepts had been kicking around the Israeli government for quite some time. Based on an exchange he had had a fortnight before with Avi'ad Yafeh, Eshkol's private secretary, Barbour believed that the Israelis were seriously contemplating local autonomy in the West Bank. Yafeh had recognized the undesirable reactions that endowing the West Bankers with increased administrative powers might provoke in the Arab world, but he relished the attractive features of the scheme: "It would remove some of the stigma Israel bears as an occupying power," he said.[128]

Rather than negotiating peace with King Hussein, the Israelis favored an Arab civil administration under their own rule which would give the appearance of Palestinian autonomy. "I would prefer the dowry without the bride," Eshkol told a group of intellectuals from the Hebrew University of Jerusalem in a closed gathering, using his tired metaphor.[129] In the circumstances, he regarded a restricted autonomy as the best possible way to fulfill his wish. Yet Israel was unable to ignore the American demand to negotiate with Hussein, ever eager for a peaceful settlement. The solution was typical Eshkol: pursuing both paths.

The Double Game Redoubled

Mid-May–October 1968

B y mid-1968 the prevailing perception in the world was, according to Foreign Minister Abba Eban, that the Arab-Israeli conflict involved a sheep and a wolf—and Israel was not the sheep.[1] Even friendly Europe, Eban said, believed that Israel was interested not in achieving peace but in maintaining the status quo.[2] The Americans, Israel's most steadfast supporters, felt the same and advised the Eshkol government to concentrate on its deteriorating global image.[3] "Tell Israel they better work out a peace plan," President Johnson snapped in late February, when he was informed of the Israelis' claim that they were losing their air superiority and thus needed 100 more fighter planes.[4]

Increasingly apprehensive, the policy makers realized that something had to be done, and quickly. Although it was the twilight of the Johnson administration, the Israelis could not afford to alienate the president while their request for Phantom fighter-bombers was still pending.[5] Getting those Phantoms was Israel's paramount goal. Eban once went so far as to suggest that the prime minister listen to the United States rather than to UN peace envoy Jarring, "because he doesn't produce Phantoms nor does he deter the USSR."[6] Yet Eban and his colleagues were also fully aware that the collapse of the Jarring mission would inevitably beget a renewed discussion of the Arab-Israeli conflict at the Security Council. This, they feared, would result in the ambiguous Resolution 242 being superseded by a firm and unequivocal resolution demanding that Israel withdraw unconditionally from all the territories it had occupied in June 1967. These two considerations dictated Israel's immediate approaches to both King Hussein and the West Bankers.

The Birth of the Modus Vivendi Project

On 17 May the *Times* of London published an unsigned article proposing re-creation of a Palestinian community in the West Bank and the Gaza Strip under temporary international custodianship.[7] The writer was Dr. Cecil Hourani, a British national of Lebanese-Christian origin who had served President Habib Bourguiba of Tunisia as a political adviser until recently; but the author of the idea was his friend Musa al-'Alami, an eminent veteran Palestinian politician, who after the 1948 War had established a farm for Palestinian orphans near Jericho. The outbreak of the 1967 War caught 'Alami outside the West Bank, yet he declined a personal invitation from his old acquaintance David Ben-Gurion to come back lest Israel—which denied repatriation to tens of thousands of new refugees—use his own return as propaganda. In the fall of 1967, reviving an unheeded scheme he had propounded in 1948, 'Alami submitted a memorandum to the secretary general of the United Nations detailing a plan to place the occupied territories, emptied of Israeli forces, under UN trusteeship for a period of five years. During this time Palestinians outside Palestine, including refugees, would be encouraged to return, and political, economic, and other institutions would be developed; at the end of the guardianship period the inhabitants would determine their political future in a plebiscite. Since October, 'Alami and Hourani had been endeavoring in vain to promote this plan in British and American diplomatic circles in London, Washington, and New York.[8]

The French consul general in Jerusalem who advocated a similar concept in the West Bank was more successful. The diplomat, Baron Christian d'Halloy, argued in his discussions with Palestinians that the plan enjoyed the Vatican's blessing. He reportedly won over some influential politicians, including such prominent Nablus leaders as Walid al-Shak'ah, Hikmat al-Masri, and others. As we have seen in chapters 6 and 7, Nablus leaders agreed in late November on a scheme which Shak'ah and Masri floated several times in their dealings with the Israelis without getting any response: withdrawal of the occupying forces from the West Bank, followed by transfer of the civil administration to the inhabitants of the region as a provisional step toward a peaceful settlement. No UN trusteeship was mentioned, but from what Bishop Capucci told Israeli officials in late February, it appears that the Nablus blueprint was inspired by Baron d'Halloy's thinking.[9] In May, when the West Bank leadership despaired of any prospect of a political solution through the Arab states and felt that the Jarring mission was leading nowhere, the idea of a transitional administration under UN auspices gained momentum. An extensive debate developed in the West Bank, specifically in its northern region, including Arab Jerusalem. Among the many supporters of the scheme were Anwar Nuseibeh and Anwar al-Khatib. Hikmat al-Masri failed to secure Jordanian endorsement of the plan, but President Nasser told him that he did not object. Dr. Hourani's unsigned article in the *Times* appeared, then, at an opportune moment. Photostats of the piece were distributed throughout the area and it was widely read.[10]

"Israel never paid any attention to this article," Foreign Minister Eban told Anwar Nuseibeh on 4 June.[11] A week later, however, on hearing that Musa al-'Alami's request to spend a fortnight in his farm near Jericho had been promptly approved by Defense Minister Dayan, Premier Eshkol was displeased. His letter to Dayan, in which he argued that the decision on a visit of a personality of such stature should have been taken by himself or by the Ministerial Committee for Security Affairs, indicated that Eshkol might have wanted 'Alami's application to be rejected. At this stage an attempt to set up an Arab civil administration was already under way. Apparently the prime minister feared that 'Alami's visit, although intended to be private and without publicity, could jeopardize the Israeli effort. Dayan dismissed Eshkol's complaints.[12] But neither he nor any of the policy makers had any intention of removing Israel's troops from the occupied territories or of allowing any foreign power—let alone the United Nations—to take control over the West Bank and the Gaza Strip.

The West Bank leadership knew this. Well informed and realistic, the Palestinian politicians were under no illusion that a plan such as 'Alami and Hourani's would ever be accepted by the Israelis. Because no Palestinian records exist, one can only surmise why so many sensible

West Bankers subscribed to the unachievable UN trusteeship idea. It is obvious that they passionately desired to rid themselves of the Israeli occupation. It is also clear that the majority of them favored the return of Jordanian rule. The ʿAlami-Hourani plan offered a solution to the former and did not negate the latter. Perhaps some of them believed that the adoption of a scheme which appeared to be balanced and just would bring about international pressure on Israel. Yet it is most likely that after losing hope they were simply clutching a ready straw.

The despair of the Palestinians was fed by the Israeli attitude, as the Israelis themselves acknowledged. In a discussion about the situation in the occupied territories at Dayan's office on 3 May, and later in a written memorandum, Major David Farhi of the Military Government described the feeling among prominent West Bankers, particularly those who had met the prime minister and other Israeli leaders, as "bitter disappointment" at the lack of response to their proposals and ideas. Mayor Hamdi Kanʿan, Farhi said, had expressed regret for approaching the Israelis about a political accommodation. Kanʿan and his colleagues interpreted the Israeli behavior as unwillingness to reach a peaceful settlement. Farhi warned that in the circumstances the West Bank leaders might resort to civil disobedience and could even reverse their hitherto negative stance on terrorism.[13] At the behest of Dayan a copy of Farhi's memorandum was made available to members of the cabinet.[14] Farhi's disturbing assessment was soon corroborated by Moshe Sasson. In a discussion at the prime minister's office on 21 May, Sasson talked about the Palestinians' about-face: their April readiness to negotiate with Israel had almost disappeared since, he said.[15]

Worse still, not only were the Palestinians' suggestions ignored, but press reports about their meetings with the Israelis appeared in Arab newspapers. Consequently, the West Bank political elite, especially those who had met Eshkol, were accused by their brethren and by Jordan of advocating severance of the West Bank from the East. In order to clear themselves, the anxious notables held a number of gatherings in Nablus and Jerusalem which produced a statement denouncing any attempts to establish a Palestinian entity and adhering to the Interim National Covenant of October 1967 that proclaimed the West Bank an inseparable part of Jordan (see chapter 5).[16] And so, by failing to react, Israel forfeited the will to engage in a political dialogue of the

northern half of the West Bank, at least for the time being. Prominent
West Bankers from the south seemed to be much less involved, but the
most powerful figure among them, Mayor Ja'bari of Hebron, attended a
gathering at Anwar Nuseibeh's home, where it was decided to publish
a manifesto condemning the occupation of Arab Jerusalem. However,
Ja'bari refused to sign the declaration and left before the meeting adjourned. Referring to the Jordanian regime, he later told an Israeli journalist: "I'm not prepared to follow orders from the outside."[17]

As we have seen, Sheikh Ja'bari had been publicly arguing for a
separate settlement with Israel from the beginning of the occupation.[18]
In late April he was given the opportunity to put his ideas to the Israeli premier in person.[19] No record of the Eshkol-Ja'bari conversation is accessible, but its existence and essence can be verified by, and
reconstructed through, a number of contemporary references to the
meeting.[20] It appears that Ja'bari asked Eshkol to create an Arab civil
administration in the West Bank with himself as governor. According to the available evidence, Ja'bari told the prime minister that he
was ready to enter into negotiations with Israel. Eshkol wanted to know
what kind of backing he had. The sheikh claimed to enjoy the support
of Bethlehem and Ramallah—some 100,000 to 150,000 people—and
added that the number would be bigger if he was granted the Gaza
Strip as well. The refugee inhabitants of Gaza, the would-be ruler of
the Strip argued, should emigrate to the East Bank. As for Jerusalem,
Ja'bari requested unimpeded access to *al-Haram al-Sharif.* In a letter
to Ja'bari, sent a short time after their rendezvous, Eshkol expressed
his confidence that they would have more opportunities to continue
the discussion of their "common interests and goals" in the same positive spirit.[21]

With Ja'bari's ideas in mind, Eshkol convened the secret, semi-
official Political Contacts Committee on 21 May. This was the first in a
series of top-level debates about the two most pressing questions Israel
faced—the negotiations with King Hussein and the talks with the West
Bankers. Although the Contacts Committee, in charge of supervising
the contacts with the Palestinian leadership, was dealing with the latter, the former was also in the air. Ultimately it was decided to pursue
the exchanges with the Palestinians with the aim of achieving a modus
vivendi and examining practical proposals "for an enlargement of the

administrative autonomy" in the West Bank. The reasons for the decision were varied, however. Eban pointed to the diplomatic gains that
contacts with the West Bankers would bestow upon Israel, and Dr.
Herzog spelled it out: they would buy Israel time. Dayan, on the other
hand, argued that no Arab partner would accept Israel's minimum terms
for peace, and since the Palestinians and the Israelis were destined to
live together, an effort for coexistence must be made. Eshkol favored
negotiations with both Hussein and the Palestinians, and Police Minister Eliyahu Sasson urged taking advantage of the West Bankers so as to
keep two alternatives open. Thus it was also agreed to continue "groom-
ing" prominent personalities such as Anwar Nuseibeh, Hikmat al-Masri,
Hamdi Kan'an, and Anwar al-Khatib with the intention of using their
good offices as go-betweens on the Hussein channel. Concurrently the
economic integration of the occupied territories into Israel should be
strengthened "in order to increase the Palestinians' dependence on Israel." The official summary of the discussion attempted to synthesize the
different arguments into coherent guidelines. Given the explicit determination to keep all the options open—the Palestinian option, the Jordanian
option, and both options simultaneously—it was a mission impossible.[22]

A week later, on 29 May, a second high-level debate took place at
the prime minister's office. The participants this time were Ministers
Dayan, Eban, and Allon, and three high-ranking officials—Dr. Herzog,
Gideon Rafael, and Avi'ad Yafeh. Eshkol opened by presenting the issue at hand. "What do we do further with the Arabs?" he said. The
premier was honest enough to admit, "We don't really know what we
actually want." On the agenda was Hussein's wish for a follow-up summit with the Israelis, yet inevitably the Palestinian issue was also mentioned. Dayan elaborated his thinking on a de facto integration of the
occupied territories into Israel and recommended cultivating "a pro-
Israeli leadership among the Palestinians." Whereas Dayan's approach
was based on his conviction that negotiations with both Hussein and
the Palestinians would produce nothing, coupled with his desire to
keep the occupied territories, Eshkol was concerned with the "demographic danger." "Crush me with a mortar," he said, "and I wouldn't
know how to swallow another million Arabs in this country. By doing
so we would liquidate ourselves." Yet Eshkol and Dayan were in agreement that the question about what exactly Israel should say to its West
Bank interlocutors was still open.[23]

The accepted concept of modus vivendi was rather vague. Eshkol's conversation with Nasser al-Din al-Nashashibi on 27 May indeed attested to the lack of any clear program. Nashashibi, a member of a notable Jerusalem family, was a prominent journalist in Egypt with close relationships with many Arab leaders, notably Nasser; in 1966 he was appointed ambassador-at-large for the Arab League. At the close of a monthlong visit to the occupied territories, during which Nashashibi met many of the area's leaders, Eshkol was interested to hear his observations. The West Bankers felt that Israel gave precedence to a deal with Hussein and neglected them, Nashashibi said. He asked the premier point-blank whether he supported a settlement with the Palestinians. In his reply Eshkol pronounced readiness to grant the Palestinians autonomy with responsibility for religious affairs, education, and commerce, yet his comments were still ambiguous and even somewhat elusive. Eshkol said nothing about a real peace deal with the West Bankers, and did not rule out the Jordanian option. When Nashashibi volunteered to convey a message to President Nasser on the prime minister's behalf, Eshkol responded: "I have nothing to tell him."[24]

What helped the Israelis shape their thinking as to how to translate the modus vivendi concept into practical terms was a secret scheme concocted by Sheikh Ja'bari and Wadi' Di'mas, a well-respected Jordanian senator from Bayt Jalla. Their plan, which Di'mas imparted to Sasson in strict confidentiality on 28 May, consisted of two layers, one overt and the other covert. Under the first, intended for public consumption, once all efforts for a peaceful settlement failed, the Palestinians would demand to run their civil affairs themselves until the Palestine problem was solved, insisting that they could no longer be subjected to military rule. In reality, however, they would work out with the Israelis the establishment of a Palestinian "canton" subordinated to the Military Government. The canton would include Hebron, Bethlehem, and neighboring Bayt Jalla and Bayt Sahour ("the triple B's"). Ja'bari and Di'mas excluded the northern region of the West Bank because they did not believe that Nablus would go along with the scheme. Di'mas explained that in view of Israel's intention to annex chunks of the West Bank, the remainder of the area could not become a viable state, and in any case it would be considered by the Arab world a traitor satellite. He and Ja'bari therefore favored a canton, or cantons, which would allow de facto peace with Israel.[25]

According to Moshe Sasson's retrospective account, he advised the prime minister on 20 May that the time was ripe for the establishment of Arab civil administration in the West Bank, and Eshkol reacted favorably.[26] A week later the Ja'bari-Di'mas outline provided the Israelis with the much-needed key to move ahead with their modus vivendi enterprise. The Palestinian scheme was effectively translated by Israel into an initiative designed to serve its own objectives.

The Stillborn Arab Civil Administration

On 3 June the Political Committee, the Labor Party's most important forum, deliberated the next steps regarding King Hussein, and in the process tacitly endorsed Eshkol's wish concurrently to follow the Palestinian track. The specific objectives of this track were formulated in separate discussions Moshe Sasson held with the defense minister and the prime minister on 7 and 9 June, respectively. Eshkol authorized Sasson not to negotiate with the Palestinians but only to examine the feasibility of negotiations and to lay the foundations for them, should they take place. The instructions, similar to the 21 May guidelines, expressly indicated that Israel's goal in negotiations with the Palestinians would be "to freeze the current situation while giving the Palestinians more autonomy in running their internal affairs"—but only in the West Bank; Jerusalem and the Gaza Strip were not included. Israel, then, clearly sought to maintain the occupation under a different cloak. Sasson's approach was particularly rigid. At the discussion with Dayan he insisted that success depended on finding ways to "neutralise" antagonistic personalities capable of frustrating the operation, while encouraging sympathetic leaders through financial incentives. Sasson, who incessantly grumbled about Jordan sustaining its influence in the West Bank by lavishly funding the traditional leadership, in fact proposed that Israeli money should replace Jordanian cash for the purpose of buying Palestinian collaboration. The record does not reflect any objection from Dayan.[27]

Sasson reiterated the suggestions in a meeting with Eshkol on 20 June. Only five days had passed since he embarked on the new endeavor, but Sasson already felt that the contacts with the West Bankers would not bear fruit. True to his conviction that Arabs should be told what to do rather than be consulted, he advocated Israeli unilateral

action: presenting the occupied Palestinians with an Arab civil administration as a fait accompli. His account and recommendation to the prime
minister were based on three talks with a single person—'Aziz Shehadeh. Attempting to play it safe, Sasson chose Shehadeh, the avid cham-
pion of a Palestinian entity, as his starting point. Indeed, Shehadeh
viewed the Israeli move on the civil administration plan as a historical
decision of the first order. Sasson got him to sound out Anwar Nuseibeh
and Walid al-Shak'ah. Reporting back, Shehadeh confirmed what Sasson had already known from the horse's mouth: Nuseibeh not only
supported the idea of self-rule but had even discussed it with unnamed
officials in Amman during his recent visit there and had received a
wholly encouraging response. This would soon prove to be a fatal misjudgment. At any rate, both Nuseibeh and Shehadeh held that a local
civil administration should apply to Arab Jerusalem and the Gaza Strip
as well. Shak'ah's reaction, however, was totally negative. He stressed
that the Nablus plan rested on the principle of Israel's withdrawal, which
was missing from the Israeli outline. After listening to Sasson's blow-
by-blow presentation, Eshkol rejected his advice to go ahead unilaterally. Insisting on obtaining the Palestinians' cooperation, he instructed
Sasson to respond affirmatively should the West Bankers ask to organize a negotiating delegation.[28]

The divide between the West Bank's radical north—including
Arab Jerusalem—and the moderate south was amply clear.[29] Sasson
realized that his efforts should be restricted to the southern region of
the West Bank, or "Judea" in the Israeli postwar parlance. Between 23
and 28 June he conducted a series of discussions with Mayor Ja'bari of
Hebron, Senator Wadi' Di'mas of Bayt Jalla, former Minister Ayub Musallam of Bethlehem, Mayor Elias al-Bandak of Bethlehem, and Shehadeh. Essentially, Sasson was orchestrating one-on-one talks between
Ja'bari and the others, with the aim of developing a consensus on the
establishment of a civil administration in the south. Though inspired
by the Ja'bari-Di'mas idea, this was an Israeli initiative, but Di'mas accepted Sasson's request to introduce it as his own endeavor. Ja'bari needed
no persuasion; in fact, he made his consent conditional on presenting
the scheme as a Palestinian demand which Israel accepted, rather than
as an Israeli enterprise. This way, he said, the personalities involved could
boast that it was their achievement and avoid the risk of denunciation
as traitors. Ja'bari also demanded that the Arab civil administration

answer to the military governor of the West Bank and not to the various Israeli ministries; otherwise, it would be perceived as annexation.
These terms, conveyed through Di'mas and Shehadeh, were acceptable
to Sasson. However, when he went down to Hebron to discuss the next
moves with Ja'bari, the mayor insisted that the civil administration
should cover the whole West Bank and that he, Ja'bari, must be appointed
the civil governor of the area. He did not mind a gradual implementation of his version of the scheme, but he stated that until he had the
prime minister's approval he would do nothing to further it.[30]

Ja'bari's lust for power was to be his downfall. When Di'mas and
Musallam came to see the sheikh again to persuade him to content himself with a civil administration in the south, they found Ja'bari day-
dreaming about ruling over the entire West Bank from King Hussein's
palace, still under construction, at Tall al-Ful near Jerusalem. Consequently, they withdrew their readiness to subordinate the Bethlehem
area to Hebron. In a meeting with Sasson on 1 July, Di'mas and Musallam proposed instead three separate administrations: one in Hebron,
another in Bethlehem, and the third in Jericho. They added that since the
Bethlehem District was predominantly Christian, it should not be the first
to have a civil administration. The two men gave Sasson a draft petition
on behalf of "the regional mayors and notables" which requested, among
other provisions, the substitution of the Israeli Military Government with
an Arab civil administration (*idarah madaniyyah 'Arabiyyah*).[31] So in addition to the south's split from the north, it was now split between the
Hebron and Bethlehem districts.

The new development was promptly brought before the Contacts
Committee on 3 July. Ja'bari's demand was rejected and Bethlehem's
approach was approved. The logic behind the ruling was best articulated by Dayan. He maintained that it was in Israel's interest to replace
the current regime, imposed on the West Bankers, with a new regime
which would not be very different except that it would enjoy the inhabitants' endorsement in a bilateral agreement. Thus Israel should not act
unilaterally and must consider the Palestinians' wishes. Dayan argued
further that it would be absurd to subjugate Bethlehem to Ja'bari's control because Bethlehem and its leaders were far more civilized than
Ja'bari. "There are people there who are absolute Europeans," he said.
In contrast to Dayan's ethno-anthropological observations, Police

Minister Eliyahu Sasson, who had known Jaʻbari from the days before
the foundation of Israel, was unambiguously precise. He described the
sheikh as corrupt and infinitely greedy. This was what Wadiʻ Diʻmas
had told Moshe Sasson more than once. The decision makers clearly
disapproved of Jaʻbariʻs personality, but they still did not rule him out.
Eshkol dwelled on the political profit he believed would result from
having Jaʻbari as a local governor: first, "it might serve as a catalyst"
regarding Hussein. Second, it would enable Eban to tell Hussein and
Jarring that "something is moving." That is to say, Jaʻbari's appointment
would put pressure on Hussein and deceive Jarring. The premier was
also driven by another motive. Obsessed with the desire to rid the Gaza
Strip of its refugees, he hoped to settle some 10,000 refugee families in
the Hebron area. "It is important to us that those Arabs leave Gaza,"
Eshkol said, so he did not care whether Jaʻbari would be "a big boss or a
smaller boss with little bosses around him."[32]

When Sasson conveyed the Contacts Committee's decision to
Jaʻbari on 7 July, the mayor was visibly displeased. But he eventually
agreed to settle for the Hebron District alone, provided that he be
regarded outwardly as the governor of the southern region. Jaʻbari
also inquired about his powers as governor and mentioned the need
to have a secret slush fund at his disposal. Sasson replied that all these
matters would be discussed in due course and that Jaʻbari should proceed to draft a petition in the name of the area's notables, addressed
to the prime minister, requesting the establishment of a civil administration. Later that day Sasson briefed Diʻmas, Musallam, and Elias
al-Bandak on the conclusion of his meeting with Jaʻbari. Diʻmas and
Musallam consented to formal subordination to the mayor of Hebron; Bandak refused.[33] This hitch was temporarily overcome on 10
July, when Jaʻbari informed Sasson that he had dropped his plea for
token rule over Bethlehem. He gave the Israeli official a handwritten
draft petition which was short and sycophantic but clear and forthright.[34]

The text was minutely examined by the top echelon of the Israeli
government. First, the justice minister, a trained lawyer, studied the
paper carefully. Then, in a special session of the Contacts Committee
on 12 July, the premier, four of his senior ministers, and a handful of
high-ranking advisers spent at least an hour on rewriting Jaʻbari's

letter, deleting some expressions and adding others; they even took the trouble to correct the style. The revised text was hardly any different in terms of substance. But this farcical episode was a further proof that the effort to set up a puppet Arab civil administration was an Israeli project. Dayan insisted that the powers of the civil administration must be determined meticulously before implementing the scheme, so that the West Bank partners to the plan could never argue that they did not understand what the Israelis meant. Eshkol agreed. Moshe Sasson, however, urged the decision makers to act briskly for fear that leaks about the Israeli-Palestinian contacts might induce pressure from "hostile elements"—Jordan and Nablus.[35]

Sasson's caution was proven well founded almost instantly. At best it was naïve to think that the contacts could remain confidential for long. Instructions given to the military censorship by the Contacts Committee to suppress all news reports on the subject were to no avail. The story broke as early as 16 July in *Al-Ittihad,* the Arabic organ of the Israeli Communist party Rakah.[36] Although not wholly accurate, the article played a part in the eventual failure of the initiative. Nablus was privy to the talks even earlier. Its leaders discussed the matter on 13 July in a gathering reportedly attended also by the mayors of Bethlehem and Bayt Jalla, Elias al-Bandak and Jabara Khamis, respectively. Conflicting intelligence reports and Ayub Musallam's account given to Sasson in a tête-à-tête revealed that Mayor Hamdi Kan'an of Nablus made vigorous efforts to frustrate the Israeli plan. Shortly after the discussion in Nablus he traveled to Bethlehem and in two consecutive meetings with all the leaders of the district, including active proponents of the civil administration plan such as Di'mas and Musallam, he forcefully argued against it. Seeing through Israeli motives Kan'an said that the scheme was intended to serve Israel's interest by enabling it to argue that some political progress toward a settlement had been made. Kan'an also fiercely attacked Ja'bari ad hominem. This turn of events caused another split in the southern region—this time within the ranks of the Bethlehem area itself—so much so that Wadi' Di'mas, who was identified with the endeavor more than anyone else, announced that he would not sign the petition for a separate civil administration in the Bethlehem District. His excuse, that as a Jordanian senator it would be best for him to stay behind the scenes, was viewed by many as abandonment of the project.[37]

It took a while before the Israelis learned about these inauspicious developments. In the interim Defense Minister Dayan was hopeful. On 14 July, at a consultation headed by the prime minister to prepare for the imminent visit of two American envoys, he suggested telling them that there was a good chance to reach a settlement with the West Bankers which would provide a modus vivendi. "I am optimistic in this regard, really optimistic," he stated.[38] He was not the only one. Eshkol authorized Dr. Herzog, his confidant, to approach Lord Rothschild in London with the aim of involving the Jewish benefactor's Hanadiv Fund in economic projects in and around Hebron. The decision makers resolved to give the district preferential treatment once the civil administration was established there in order to signal to other districts that joining in would be to their advantage. Rothschild promised to consider the Israeli request.[39]

Meanwhile, the military bureaucracy, which had been working assiduously on translating Dayan's guidelines into a practical blueprint, in mid-July produced a detailed seven-page document. Explaining the political goals of the self-rule scheme, the drafters of the paper said that among its purposes was to show Amman that Israel had a Palestinian option for a settlement. The authors proposed the creation of two or three civil administrations in the West Bank. Each of their heads was to be given the title *Mohafiz* (governor) in Arabic and *Ha-Memuneh ʿal ha-Mahoz* (district commissioner) in Hebrew. Apart from a title his powers would be nominal: the lengthy small print clearly revealed that the Arab governor would be completely subservient to, and dependent on, the occupation authorities.[40] This was intentional. When the Contacts Committee convened on 17 July to review the document, Dayan stated categorically: the idea was to allow Jaʿbari to feel "[as] a king in the army" ([*ke-*]*melekh ba-Gdud*—Job 29:25) while in practice he would have to refer all matters to the Military Government. Jaʿbari would rejoice at this, Dayan promised his peers, claiming that it was doubtful whether the Hebron leader wanted more. Eshkol, stressing the Israeli interest in setting up more than one administration in the West Bank in order to hinder attempts to boycott it, argued for encouraging the Bethlehem District to go along with the plan.[41]

Hence Sasson focused now on the "triple B's." On 21 July he successively saw the three mayors. Bayt Jalla's Jabara Khamis accepted enthusiastically; Bayt Sahour's Nikola Abu ʿItah consented reluctantly; and

Bethlehem's Elias al-Bandak was rather evasive but did not object.[42] A day later, however, the trio called on Ja'bari, and they all agreed to delay any decision until Israel familiarized them with the powers it would grant the local governors. A few hours earlier, in a meeting with Sasson, Ja'bari had endorsed the revised version of the draft petition and demanded a fat salary for the job of governor in addition to his wage as mayor. When Sasson inquired how in his opinion Jordan would react to the implementation of the plan, Ja'bari suggested a strong military response by Israel's air force if Amman took practical steps, such as blocking passage on the bridges connecting the two banks. Sasson sensed nonetheless that Ja'bari had become lukewarm about the scheme. He was right. On the following day Ja'bari decided to support a Palestinian civil administration only if it encompassed the West Bank as a whole. He sent a special messenger to his Bethlehem, Bayt Jalla, and Bayt Sahour colleagues with a draft letter to that effect, addressed to the prime minister and intended to be signed by the four mayors.[43] Ja'bari later ascribed his change of heart, which he claimed was the result of Sasson's question, to fear of a negative Jordanian response.[44]

The modus vivendi project was starting to crumble, but the Israelis were still unaware of it. Furthermore, the cabinet—excluding the five members of the Contacts Committee—was kept in the dark. The subject was first broached at the Ministerial Committee for Security Affairs on 17 July and received mixed reactions. A subcommittee, appointed to study the matter in depth, convened on 23 July. Dayan, eager to integrate the West Bank into Israel, emphasized the benefits Israel might gain through a civil administration headed by Ja'bari, including the establishment of a Jewish settlement near Hebron with the sheikh's approval. Eshkol assured the ministers that the powers Ja'bari would possess as governor would be negligible, and echoed Sasson's repeated cautions against foot-dragging that might thwart the operation. But Ministers Menachem Begin and Yisrael Barzilai were unconvinced. Because of their opposition to the initiative, the premier said that he was forced to bring the issue before the next plenary session of the cabinet on 28 July. This was not to happen. Within a day Sasson's assessment that Jordan knew of the scheme and did not object was proven dead wrong.[45]

On the evening of 24 July, Radio Amman aired on its 9 o'clock newscast a statement by Prime Minister Bahjat al-Talhuni which strongly rebuffed Israeli attempts to establish "a local Arab government that will administer the towns and villages of the West Bank under the control of the occupation authorities." In an unsubtle warning Talhuni expressed full confidence that no West Bankers would cooperate with the enemy's scheme.[46] The Jordanian announcement was reinforced by a news article in the Amman weekly *Akhbar al-Usbu'* two days later.[47] The newspaper also carried an editorial threatening Ayub Musallam and any other "collaborator" with "death to the traitors."[48] Apparently the weekly's source was Ribhi Mustafa, a West Banker and former Jordanian official, who was against the civil administration plan and refused to take part in it. With a Military Government travel permit he went to Amman and allegedly disclosed the scheme to Talhuni and others.[49]

The new turn of events dealt a lethal blow to the Israeli project. By the end of the month Wadi' Di'mas and Ayub Musallam, both key players in the affair, and Mayor Jabara Khamis, an ardent supporter, effectively acknowledged this.[50] So did the Israelis: one of Dayan's top aides described the scheme as "put on ice," and Dayan himself told the Knesset Foreign Affairs and Security Committee that "for now, the matter is dead."[51] Recognizing its failure, the defense minister instructed Sasson to shelve the civil administration program, subject to the prime minister's approval. Although Eshkol did not raise the issue in the cabinet as intended, he still harbored hopes: maybe Nablus would turn receptive after all, or perhaps Sheikh Ja'bari—whom the premier was due to meet shortly—"would regain his courage if we let him squeeze another something out of us."[52]

In fact, it was Eshkol who tried to squeeze something out of Ja'bari when they met on 12 August. The sheikh pleaded for a unilateral move: Israel, he said, should establish the Arab civil administration in the whole West Bank by simply appointing governors and without consulting the leadership. He recommended, moreover, that Sasson should falsely assure the candidates for governorship positions that they would enjoy all the powers the military governors now had. Explaining that Israel sought to introduce the scheme by mutual agreement, the premier undertook to have Sasson look for "distinguished and serious men" in the north who might agree to play a part in it. Yet Eshkol was much more interested in securing Ja'bari's cooperation in resettling tens of thousands of Gaza refugees around Hebron. The mayor insisted that there was not enough

water in the area or enough room; he mentioned the enormous tracts of
land the Israelis had already appropriated in 1948. Eshkol kept pressuring Ja'bari relentlessly. He promised industrial and agricultural development and pledged that land for the refugees would be purchased for
good money. Ja'bari, equally unrelenting, struggled strenuously to avoid
the subject.[53]

The efforts to sway Nablus resulted in a resounding fiasco. In his
talks with Walid al-Shak'ah, Hamdi Kan'an, and Hikmat al-Masri in
early August, Sasson heard a host of reasons for their negative attitude.
Nationalistic and bitter, the Nablus leaders reminded the Israeli official
of his government's persistent silence regarding the Palestinians' overtures and its refusal to recognize the West Bankers as a political partner.
They considered the civil administration plan as "a clever ruse aimed at
convincing world opinion that the West Bankers were living comfort-
ably and normally, side by side with the Israelis, operating what [Israel]
would depict as a free Palestinian Government." A modus vivendi, they
said, would not provide the Palestinians with identity but would blunt
their political senses instead. Jordan might decide to boycott Nablus
economically, and this would spell disaster. Most important, the Israeli
initiative did not address the West Bankers' foremost predicament—
the occupation. The only choice they saw was between a solution and
an occupation, with nothing in between. Moreover, Arab Jerusalem
should never be excluded. Nablus's rejection was endorsed in a gathering of notables on 8 August.[54]

The last rites for the civil administration project were read in
Nablus two days later, in a conference of all West Bank mayors, except
three. Ja'bari was the most conspicuous absentee. He had known about
the assembly a week earlier and through Sasson had demanded that
Israel prevent it, saying: "There is no room for political activity under
military rule."[55] The assembly took place notwithstanding, with the
local military governor's approval. Its outcome was interpreted by the
GSS, Israel's internal security service, as reinforcing Hamdi Kan'an's
position in his campaign against Ja'bari.[56] The gathering produced a
strong manifesto, demanding an end to the occupation and reunion of
the West Bank with the Hashemite kingdom. Drafted by Kan'an and
Qadri Touqan and signed by twenty mayors from all parts of the West
Bank and seven other dignitaries, the petition was sent to Defense

Minister Dayan on 26 August.[57] Brig. Gen. Raphael Vardi, the military governor of the West Bank, considered the mayors' statement a reaction to the civil administration scheme.[58] The blunt message and the un-equivocal language drove Dayan to advise the prime minister to circu-late the letter among the members of the Ministerial Committee for Security Affairs; Eshkol complied.[59] Dayan also ordered punitive mea-sures in retaliation for the petition with the intention of undermining Kan'an's position: a suspension of travel permits for Nablus residents wishing to go to the East Bank, save in emergency cases.[60]

This was further evidence of Israel's unwillingness to tolerate independent-minded West Bankers. The whole modus vivendi effort clearly demonstrated that the policy makers sought a docile Pales-tinian leadership that would serve Israel's purposes. An Arab civil administration could have been a significant first step toward an Israeli-Palestinian accommodation, had the occupying power intended to al-low the occupied genuine self-rule with able, honest people. But the civil administration the Israelis had in mind was a sham. Devoid of power and completely subjugated to the Military Government, its aims, according to Premier Eshkol, were threefold: first, to create a false im-pression that the government was negotiating a functional settlement with the West Bankers; second, to fend off international pressures and thereby gain Israel time; third, to apply pressure on Jordan to adopt a pliable approach.[61]

Furthermore, the actor chosen by the Israelis to play the lead role in the scheme was a person whom they knew to be venal, avaricious, and tyrannical. Following strikes and demonstrations in the West Bank on the first anniversary of the occupation, this man, Sheikh Ja'bari, re-buked the Israelis for not paying heed to his earlier advice to use an iron fist in the West Bank.[62] On another occasion he suggested that Israel dynamite Hikmat al-Masri's factories so that the Nablus leader would stop actively opposing the civil administration plan.[63] Ja'bari once told Sasson that he expected Israel "to clear the way for him of his opponents."[64] He even fingered a Palestinian resistance activist, enabling his arrest.[65] His personality and attitude notwithstanding—or perhaps because of them—the Israelis were determined to crown Ja'bari as a regional governor despite the expressed objections of many of his fel-low West Bankers.

In hindsight some Israelis acknowledged the contribution of the Ja'bari factor to the failure of their initiative. But top on their list was Talhuni's warning.[66] There was also some self-criticism about the sluggishness of the Israeli decision making which arguably allowed the interference of Jordan and Nablus. Sasson even condemned what he regarded as a lenient approach toward Palestinian opposition, notably that of Nablus. Yet much of the responsibility for the debacle was directed at the Palestinian leadership. Ignoring the ban on country-wide political organization, Sasson described the leaders as fragmented, even atomized, and suffering from the same defects that had cost the Palestinians so dearly throughout their struggle against Israel: corruption was rife; many politicians were motivated by individual interests, many more by local, sectarian, or personal controversies and rivalries.[67] Much of this was undoubtedly true but the fact remains that Israel was looking not for fair-minded nationalist representatives of the Palestinians but for lackeys. Ultimately, however, the modus vivendi affair only strengthened the radical leaders of the north.

Since the battle of Karameh in March there had been a growing tendency among the West Bank leadership, especially in the northern region, to take seriously the position of the Palestinian resistance organizations outside the occupied territories, particularly al-Fateh. During this period these organizations had been involved in a power struggle with the PLO. Eventually they got the upper hand; when the fourth session of the Palestinian National Council (PNC), the legislative body of the PLO, convened in Cairo in mid-July, about half of its seats were allocated to members of the organizations. The new makeup of the PNC signaled a further significant step in the transformation of the PLO into the representative institution of the Palestinian people. A more immediate change was reflected in the firm, uncompromising resolutions adopted by the PNC, including a revision of the Palestinian National Charter. For example, article 9 of the amended charter asserted: "Armed struggle is the only way to liberate Palestine. Thus it is a strategy, not tactics." The PNC resolutions referred to both the 'Alami-Hourani plan and the civil administration scheme. They totally denounced the ideas of establishing "a spurious entity" alongside Israel, creating an international custodianship framework for the occupied territories, or setting up "an agent Palestinian Arab administration." The PNC proclaimed any supporter of these concepts an enemy of the Palestinian people and the Arab nation.[68] For the West Bank political elite the PNC warning undoubtedly carried no less threatening weight than Prime Minister Talhuni's.

An Offer Hussein Could Not But Refuse

Jordan's opposition to the civil administration scheme was conveyed to Israel at the highest level. At a secret meeting in London on 24 August, in the presence of Hussein, Zayd al-Rifa'i, the king's confidant, assured Ya'acov Herzog that the Israeli efforts would not succeed. Without mentioning that the plan had already failed, Herzog disingenuously replied that he would have expected the king and Rifa'i to be interested in the transfer of the administrative duties of the military governors to the Arab mayors. Rifa'i retorted that they understood Israel's true motive and that it would not work. Herzog concluded by claiming that Israel had borne in mind Hussein's plea of November 1967 not to recognize a separate Palestinian entity (see chapter 5).[69] Indeed, the Israelis had no intention of allowing the West Bankers anything of the kind. But whereas they did attempt to establish an Arab civil administration in order to create an appearance of political progress on the Palestinian track, they were not prepared to make Hussein an offer that would be acceptable to him.

The historical evidence overwhelmingly shows that the Israeli leadership was in no doubt that the king desired an honorable peace settlement, that he was willing to negotiate with Israel directly, and that he expected to hear the Israeli terms. Instead of reaching the long overdue and crucial decision on the West Bank, the Israelis deliberately opted to present Hussein with an unreasonable proposal.[70] This was the Allon Plan, which envisaged the annexation of a strip of land six to ten miles wide along the Jordan River, as well as the lion's share of the West Bank's southern region, thereby turning the heavily populated area of the West Bank into an Arab enclave. Originally the plan called for a Palestinian autonomous regime in that enclave (see chapter 2), but the revised version of mid-1968 suggested Jordanian rule with a connecting corridor to the East Bank. Incredibly, Premier Eshkol became aware of the fact that the Allon Plan would incorporate no less than one-third of the West Bank into the State of Israel only after seeing the small map that the American weekly *Time* published in late June 1968, shortly after the plan had been leaked to the press.[71]

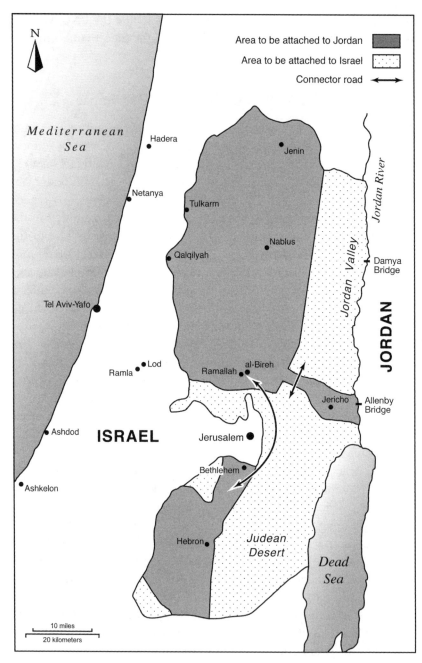

Map 7. The Allon Plan, 1968

The Allon Plan had made a bad impression in the United States, Minister Menachem Begin reported to the cabinet upon returning from his visit there in June.[72] William Scranton, the former governor of Pennsylvania, who in late 1968 was sent on a fact-finding mission to the Middle East by President-elect Richard Nixon, warned Yigal Allon that American public opinion might construe the plan as an expression of Israel's expansionist intentions and that the Arabs would argue that it was a cunning "trick" aimed at settling the Jordan Valley first and annexing the rest of the West Bank later.[73] Allon's reply indicated his desire to retain the entire West Bank if Israel could "get away with it."[74]

In fact, few Israeli policy makers believed that the Jordanian monarch would ever consider the Allon Plan as a basis for negotiations. Premier Eshkol said that he would be surprised if King Hussein would go along with it, and Defense Minister Dayan stated categorically that there was no chance he would.[75] Even the author of the plan, Yigal Allon—now the deputy prime minister—confessed privately that his brainchild was only a subterfuge: "No Arab would ever accept the plan and nothing will come of it, but we must appear before the world with a positive plan."[76] Allon gave a similar explanation to his protégés, the Jewish settlers in Hebron: "Jews have to be smart. No Arab will ever accept this plan," he told them.[77] Allon never abandoned his original idea of an "autonomous Arab unit" unbreakably connected to Israel— rather than returning the densely populated area of the West Bank to Jordan—so as to create *Eretz Yisrael shlemah,* or a whole Land of Israel, with full Israeli control and a Jewish demographic majority.[78]

In their internal discussions the Israelis were candid about the motives behind their doomed approach. Eshkol mentioned the longed-for Phantoms and the danger of international sanctions against Israel, and said that he favored the Hussein channel because this was what America—Israel's supplier of fighter planes—wanted. Eban, who ceaselessly boasted about his *takhsisanut*—which amounted to deviousness rather than simple maneuvering—in handling Israel's foreign policy, did not mince words: the government was engaged not in a peace process, he told the Labor Party's Expanded Political Committee on 3 June, but in a tactical political struggle designed to maintain the status quo and to avoid "all kinds of calamities" such as foreign political intervention. Only contacts with Hussein could save Israel from this, Eban argued. He therefore strongly advocated "a futile discussion" with the Jordanians "which should last weeks and months." Golda Meir, soon to be prime minister, agreed that negotiations with Jordan should be dragged out for as long as possible, and suggested putting the king in a position that would make him go home to think long and hard about how to solve the refugee problem and how to pacify the border. She objected to the Allon Plan as the starting point of the negotiations and suggested instead the annexation of the Palestinian-inhabited western part of the West Bank's northern region. By then Eshkol, because of the "demographic danger," opposed any border modifications along the Green Line, with the exception of the Latrun Salient, whose villages had long been obliterated following the expulsion of their residents (see chapter 4). He thus dismissed Meir's idea, saying it was senseless.

Eban wasted no time in applying *takhsisanut* by initiating unnecessary moves. On 4 June, Ambassador Rabin informed State Department officials in Washington that Hussein was ready for a peace treaty through secret, direct negotiations under cover of the Jarring mission, and that President Nasser had given him a green light to strike a deal with Israel.[79] That day Eban met Anwar Nuseibeh in Jerusalem and claimed to have been wondering what kept Jordan from moving forward with its contacts with Israel. Was Jordan waiting for a green light from Egypt? Eban asked. He, of course, knew the answer, for it had been conveyed by Rifa'i to Herzog in early May (see chapter 7) and indeed was as Rabin told the Americans. Nuseibeh, however, was unaware of this and volunteered to help. Seizing the opportunity, Eban got him to ask Hussein what had been preventing Jordan from making progress.[80] The foreign minister was not really interested in promoting substantive and genuine negotiations with Jordan. Rather, his purpose was to build up the pretense to the Americans and Jarring that the contacts with Jordan were serious. "So long as the Powers believe that we have independent contacts—it holds off Jarring and America," he argued in late May at a high-level consultation headed by Premier Eshkol.[81]

Upon his return from Amman on 12 June, Anwar Nuseibeh unsurprisingly reaffirmed the response that was already known. He also reported that the king expected to regain all the territory he had lost in the war but did not object to demilitarization of the West Bank and reciprocal border modifications.[82] A week later, when Herzog met Rifa'i in London on 19 June regarding the next Jordanian-Israeli summit, the latter broached the Allon Plan, of which he had learned from the press, and said that it was unacceptable to Jordan.[83]

Although he should have expected it, Eshkol was nevertheless irritated by the Jordanian rejection of the Allon Plan. On hearing Herzog's report, the prime minister said that the whole effort vis-à-vis Hussein should be stopped. Eban disagreed. Eshkol backed down eventually but refused to be personally present at the summit. He said at a meeting of the Contacts Committee on 3 July that "in such a situation, a prime minister cannot go," meaning that as premier, perceived as speaking on behalf of the government, he was unable to attend because of the lack of a cabinet decision.[84] As with the Arab civil administration project, the cabinet was still in the dark about the Hussein channel. After reaching a consensus to propose the Allon Plan as the minimum West Bank territory Israel would settle for, those in the know time and again debated whether the matter should be brought before the cabinet and resolved against it for fear of an internal political crisis.[85] They spent many more hours on the question of who should join Eban and Herzog at the next meeting with Hussein. There was little talk about substance, however, even after Jordan's refusal to consider the Allon Plan had become abundantly clear. Instead, the decision makers resorted to more *takhsisanut*. The visit of Ambassador George Ball, the new permanent representative of the United States to the United Nations, and Assistant Secretary of State Joseph Sisco in mid-July furnished them with an opportunity which they readily seized.

The visit was part of an orientation trip for Ball. At the initiative of Premier Eshkol or Foreign Minister Eban, Allon gave Ball and Sisco a thorough presentation of his plan. Years later Allon bragged about the admiration the plan had elicited from his guests and claimed that the usually reserved Ball had called it "an ingenious plan."[86] An American diplomat recorded, however, that Ball and Sisco considered it useless even as a bargaining position, but for the sake of politeness they commented only that they doubted whether King Hussein would be able to agree to the proposal.[87] Eban told Ball and Sisco that though the Allon Plan was not endorsed by the cabinet, it should be viewed as a possible model for achieving greater security without Israeli domination of the Arab population. He stressed that Hussein should overcome his inhibitions about negotiating with Israel and that it was necessary to "give Hussein a push" in this respect. Eban suggested that the Americans convey to the king a detailed message which promised that in a "real peace settlement" he would retrieve a great deal of what he had lost in June 1967, although not all.[88] Eshkol went even farther. Authorizing Ball to tell Hussein that in return for peace Israel would be prepared to give him back the West Bank with minor modifications, he depicted the king as a changeable leader and pledged that a day would come when he, as prime minister, would face his cabinet with a decision about the West Bank.[89]

As we have seen, both Eshkol and Eban were aware that the envisaged modifications were anything but minor. Three weeks previously Eban himself had stressed in a letter to Eshkol that Israel's case was based on the premise that there was a "substantial territorial, security and political difference between the 4 June lines and the recognized and secure boundaries" which Resolution 242 called for.[90] Eban, moreover, talked about significant changes to the 4 June lines when he met Hussein on 3 May (see chapter 7). But their message to Hussein was intended for the United States, not for the king. In contrast, Dayan was forthright with Ball and Sisco. He expressed pessimism about the prospects of reaching a settlement with Jordan because in his view Hussein was unable "to deliver the goods, and the goods is peace." Dayan stated, however, that since most of the Gaza Strip refugees should be settled in the East Bank, Israel needed the cooperation of Jordan.[91]

At any rate, the Israeli message, drafted by Eban, was promptly transmitted to Amman and received a chilly reaction. According to a British diplomat's evaluation, the Jordanians suspected an Israeli tactical gambit to escape responsibility for carrying out Resolution 242. Foreign Minister 'Abd al-Mun'im al-Rifa'i told Ball and Sisco that the message was too general and too vague to justify much comment. Obviously, Jordan's desire to hear specific details of substance was still unfulfilled. "The trouble is [that] the Israelis never get down to earth with us," Zayd al-Rifa'i, King Hussein's right-hand man, told Ambassador Symmes in early August. He said that Israel would be surprised by how receptive Jordan would be to realistic proposals for a bilateral settlement.[92]

The Americans immediately passed Rifa'i's comments on to Eban through Ambassador Barbour in Tel Aviv on 8 August. As if the Allon Plan had not already become public and had not already received an unequivocal rejection from Amman, the Israeli foreign minister emphatically claimed that his government had concrete ideas about a settlement which should be disclosed directly to the Jordanians, either privately or in Jarring's presence.[93]

King Hussein, who saw nothing new or exciting in the Israeli communication either, displayed concern at what he regarded as the hard-line aspects of some of its points.[94] He was not the only one to observe a hardening in Israel's attitude. Ambassador Ball concluded from the talks he had conducted during his Middle East tour that Hussein desperately wanted a settlement whereas Israel, unless compelled to move by events or external pressure, was quite ready to live indefinitely with the situation of neither peace nor war.[95] Even Ball's predecessor, Arthur Goldberg, a pro-Israel Jew—"our Goldberg," as Eshkol referred to him fondly—upon leaving his post at the United Nations in June suggested that the Americans lean on the Israelis to bring about an acceptable compromise. In a paper sent to the president and the secretary of state Goldberg argued for Israel's return to the 4 June 1967 lines with small changes.[96]

Nevertheless, the Americans believed that Ball and Sisco had succeeded in getting Israel to adopt a less rigid approach. Thus they lost patience when it became clear that the Israelis had gone back on what they had told the two senior diplomats just three weeks before. Ball and Sisco's understanding was that Israel was prepared to have exchanges of real substance with Jordan through Jarring. Yet Eban told Ambassador Barbour in Tel Aviv and Jarring in London on 8 and 9 August, respectively, that the generalities he had conveyed to the Jordanians were all they would get until a direct Israeli-Jordanian meeting. Furthermore, when Barbour mentioned the enormous efforts put into military action against al-Fateh's assaults and wondered whether Israel was prepared to take the same risks in the search for peace, Eban argued that the parallel was not valid because the Israeli endeavors on the peace front got no reactions from the other side. The White House official Harold Saunders reacted angrily. "The flexibility we thought Ball found in Jerusalem was just a sop the Israelis threw us," he wrote in a blunt memorandum to the president's Special Assistant Walt Rostow. "I think we ought to arrange a small explosion. If we let them get away with this without more than a passing comment, we can write off now most of the progress Ball achieved."[97]

Consequently, Secretary of State Rusk instructed Barbour to press Eban hard on the need for flexibility and responsiveness to Jordan's request for specifics.[98] Barbour saw Eban on 20 August. Facing American fury, Eban denied any retraction of what had been said to Ball and Sisco but acknowledged Jordanian willingness to hold joint meetings with Israel in the presence of Jarring. He promised that "Jordan will know more about our concepts regarding a settlement" before the opening of the forthcoming UN General Assembly.[99]

The Israelis feared that alienating the United States might not only return the Middle East issue to the Security Council and jeopardize their request for Phantoms but could also drive the Americans to take an independent initiative in order to circumvent the deadlocked Jarring mission. Eban and his advisers thus considered letting President Johnson into the secret of Israel's direct contacts with King Hussein so as to regain his confidence.[100] In a handwritten letter to Ambassador Rabin, Eban said that "Menasheh"—the Israeli code name for Arthur Goldberg—had strongly advised against the move. Had Washington known of these high-level direct contacts, it would have been more trusting of Israel, the former American ambassador to the United Nations said. But he warned Eban that "Issachar"—the Israeli code name for Johnson—was loose-tongued (*patpetan*), and his administration was in love with paperwork. A leak, which was very likely, would seriously damage future contacts with Jordan. Eban also reiterated his conviction that it was essential to hold continuous direct contacts with the king as a means of preventing diplomatic fallout. Dayan, Eban wrote, favored "clarification talks" rather than negotiations, but he, Eban, felt that there was nothing to clarify without a decision to return some West Bank territory to Hussein.[101]

The Triumph of the Failed *Takhsisanut*

While maintaining secret contacts with Amman through the Hussein channel, Israel was also striking at targets in Jordan in what were intended to be reprisals for fida'iyyun attacks launched from the East Bank. These two conflicting approaches were closely intertwined, however. On the Hussein channel, Ya'acov Herzog traveled several times to London during the summer months to discuss with Zayd al-Rifa'i the arrangements for the next Jordanian-Israeli summit. In August he saw the king himself for that purpose. Yet these talks were also used to deliver stark Israeli warnings about al-Fateh terrorism, which included the shelling of civilian settlements in the Beisan Valley.[102] Hussein was incapable of completely suppressing the irregular activities and insisted that the Israelis should not expect him to do what they were equally unsuccessful in achieving.[103] Although Israel knew full well that the king was too weak to control the fida'iyyun, it refused to recognize his efforts.[104] More significant, Israel's massive retaliations not only were disproportionate and more harmful to Jordan than to the Palestinian guerrillas, but they also endangered, or at least impeded, the political dialogue about a settlement. Even if this was not intentional, it certainly served the Israeli primary goal of playing for time.

On 4 June a daylong exchange of fire across the Jordan River culminated in a heavy aerial bombardment by Israeli jet fighters of positions around Irbid, a small town some eleven miles east of the ceasefire line whose population of 15,000 had swollen to between 70,000 and 100,000 as a result of the recent flight of the eastern Ghor's inhabitants. Three Israeli civilians were killed that day and 10 were injured, whereas the Jordanian side suffered 34 fatalities and 134 wounded—mostly civilians.[105] Anwar Nuseibeh, who had on the same day accepted Eban's aforementioned futile mission to Hussein, decided to delay his trip because of the inevitably tense atmosphere in Amman created by the devastating Israeli attack.[106]

On 4 August waves of Israeli aircraft pounded what was described as a terrorist command center near the city of Salt, seventeen miles northwest of Amman, for three hours. Thirty-seven people lost their lives—only fourteen of them were al-Fateh men—and dozens more were injured. Four ambulances were also hit. By chance Yasir 'Arafat's tent was burned, but al-Fateh's leader escaped again unharmed: he had left the base fifteen minutes before the assault. According to Israeli sources, quoted by the *New York Times,* the airstrike had a political purpose: to warn Jordan "that it was playing a dangerous game by harboring and supporting the saboteurs."[107] The attack drove Zayd al-Rifa'i to cancel his imminent meeting with Herzog, scheduled for 8 August. He cabled Dr. Herbert, the Hussein channel's middleman, about his decision, explaining that "when guns of napalm and other kinds of bombs and rockets have begun again to rain destruction and death on our people," he felt obliged "to postpone all plans until a more opportune time presents itself."[108]

The Security Council strongly condemned Israel for yet another "flagrant violation" of the UN Charter and the council's previous resolution regarding the Karameh incursion in March. The new resolution was adopted unanimously, with the support of the United States.[109] Israel's Minister of the Interior Hayyim Moshe Shapira, expressed understanding of the Americans' reservations about the Israeli attitude. Morally, he said in the cabinet on 18 August, the Israeli behavior was inexplicable.[110] Ambassador Rabin once told the Knesset Foreign Affairs and Security Committee that whenever Israel had made complaints about its civilian casualties, the American dismissive response had been: you do the same, and much more.[111]

King Hussein, who according to Jarring was shocked by the attack on Salt, pointed out a more practical aspect of Israeli policy. The raids on Karameh and Salt solved nothing, he told Herzog on 24 August, and only made al-Fateh stronger. The king's meeting with the Israeli official demonstrated, however, his unflinching desire to pursue the political track with his Jewish foes despite his awareness that they were simply stringing him along. Hussein's biographer Avi Shlaim attributes the determination of the king to fear and hope: fear that the extremists in Israel would gain the upper hand and try to overthrow him or even capture more land in the East Bank; and hope that ultimately Israel would make peace with Jordan on the basis of the prewar border. Shlaim's discussion highlights fear as Hussein's driving force, whereas I believe that the hope he harbored, however unrealistic, of reasoning with the Israelis was his decisive motive.[112]

Undoubtedly the king's hopes were reinforced by repeated American assurances that he would regain his lost territory. Thus he was not deterred when Herzog reiterated that the Allon Plan was Israel's preferred peace proposal or when Herzog explained that the Israeli claim for "historical association" with the occupied lands included the right of Jews to settle anywhere in the West Bank, regardless of sovereignty. Indeed, Rifa'i reemphasized that the Allon Plan was totally unacceptable to Jordan and that the 4 June lines were its starting point. But despite the wide gulf between the positions of the two countries, Hussein resolved to go ahead with the Jordanian-Israeli summit. The king pleaded with the Israelis, hinting that he might be toppled: "Make up your minds. Will it be easier for you to yield to the extremists when they are in power than to yield now?"[113]

Hussein's plea went unheeded. Premier Eshkol accepted Herzog's formula that no cabinet decision concerning the West Bank should be taken so long as "the other side does not suggest any kind of negotiations," because such a decision would split the Israeli nation into two camps. Defense Minister Dayan was also against making such a resolution. Moreover, when Herzog reported that Rifaʻi had quoted Eban's statement to Ball—namely, that Israel would relinquish most but not all of the West Bank—Eshkol exclaimed: for saying such things the foreign minister should be dismissed. Herzog reminded the prime minister that he too had made similar statements to foreign visitors, but Eshkol retorted that Israel would cede nothing unless it retained its military presence along the Jordan River.[114]

In early September, Eban sent Anwar Nuseibeh on another go-between mission to Hussein. No record is available of the mission's nature or of the content of Eban's message, except for the king's response. In addition to yet another expression of his willingness to hold a bilateral meeting at the United Nations under Jarring's auspices, Hussein asked Nuseibeh to tell the Israelis that eventually Jordan and Israel would have to live together, so it would be best if they arrived at coexistence of their own free will rather than being faced with a settlement imposed by external forces.[115] Eban repeated Hussein's message in the cabinet on 16 September without disclosing the direct contacts Israel had had with Jordan since the May summit. He also said little about Israel's objectives regarding these contacts.[116] Yet four days later, at a meeting of the Labor Party's Political Committee, whose members were in the loop, Eban was open and clear.

The summit, now scheduled for 27 September in London, was just a week away. Its purpose, Eban said, should be one follow-up meeting after another, simply to keep the contacts going. Tactically, he continued, this was the only way to save Israel from heavy international pressure— by making President Johnson believe that Israel was having contacts with the Arab ruler "entrusted with the so-called Palestine problem." Eban tenaciously adhered to the same old tune of *takhsisanut*. So did Golda Meir. She stressed "with a red pencil" that the meeting with Hussein should take place only as *takhsis* (Hebrew for tactics or trick). Dayan objected to such an approach and warned that Hussein, who expected to hear specific ideas, might tell the Americans that "the Jews are trying to deceive the world in this regard." Eshkol wanted Dayan to join Eban at the summit and together, armed with some proposal—apparently the Allon Plan—to present Hussein with Hobson's choice. Dayan refused to go, but he failed to convince his fellow members of the Political Committee: their vague conclusion regarding what should be said to Hussein reflected the Allon Plan.[117]

Instead of Dayan, Premier Eshkol decided that Deputy Prime Minister Allon would join Eban and personally present his plan to the king, but as his own and not on behalf of the government. On 24 September, Eshkol briefed the cabinet in general terms about the next high-level meeting with Hussein, saying that its aim would be merely to clarify whether there was a basis for future peace negotiations with Jordan. Hence the government was not required to make a decision over the West Bank. The cabinet endorsed Eshkol's statement.[118] So, in addition to being yet another decision not to decide, this meant that Israel's representatives to the summit would effectively cover the same ground that had already been discussed in early May. This approach was pursued in the face of unrelenting American pressure on Israel to move beyond generalities and get to the nuts and bolts. Until this was done, peace would not be attainable, Secretary of State Rusk said flatly in a tough conversation with Ambassador Rabin on 18 September. "It was not enough to chant 'Peace,'" Rusk insisted.[119] A week later, in another discussion with Rabin, Walt Rostow, the president's special assistant, referred to the thorny Jerusalem problem, quoting Israeli Assistant Defense Minister Zvi Tsur, who had said: "We can't give Hussein enough in Jerusalem for him to live with." When Rabin argued that Israel would give Hussein a role in the Islamic holy places, Rostow replied that this was not good enough.[120]

Israel was unwilling to give Hussein enough elsewhere, either. When its representatives, Allon, Eban, and Herzog, met the king and Rifa'i at Dr. Herbert's home on 27 September, they followed their prepared scenario and presented the Allon Plan in a sketchy manner, without betraying the extent of the land Israel intended to keep. Eban claimed that the recently published map of the plan was distorted and inaccurate. "The precise delineation of the substantial change must be negotiated," he said. Toward the end of his characteristically long speech, Eban also used the "Palestinian alternative" stratagem and warned Hussein: "If the opportunity is lost it would be a tragic error, especially for Jordan. In Israel, people would cease to believe in the possibility of a new peace structure. We should have to face and solve the problem of our relations with the Palestinian Arabs independently of Jordan." This was an empty threat which did not impress the king. Hussein told the Israelis that he saw "some difficulties" in their proposals and needed time to consider them. But it was not hard to foresee his rejection. Indeed, it came one day later through Rifa'i, who met Herzog and dictated to him the king's response. The most significant passage read: "The [Allon] plan itself is wholly unacceptable since it infringes Jordanian sovereignty. The only way is to exchange territory on the basis of reciprocity." On Jerusalem the statement said that Jordan would recognize the right of Israel in the Jewish holy places but nothing more. In reference to the Israelis' emphasis on the overriding importance of their state's security, the message argued that Jordan's security must be taken into account as well.[121]

Hussein expected to have an Israeli reply before setting up the time and place for the next top-level meeting. Eban instructed Herzog to express "amazement" at the king's response, "which was entirely outside the context of what had been discussed."[122] Although Hussein did not shut the door on further talks, the chasm between the viewpoints of Israel and Jordan now seemed unbridgeable. This did not bother Eban much. The foreign minister was more preoccupied with the imminent struggle he anticipated at the United Nations over Israel's failure to accept unreservedly the 242 Resolution and specifically its implementation. Furthermore, fear had been developing in Israel that a joint American-Soviet accord to bring about an imposed settlement in the Middle East might undermine Israel's political and security aims.[123]

Two days after the summit and just before he left London for the UN General Assembly in New York, Eban was concerned with ensuring the success of his takhsisanut. His handwritten letter to Eshkol is quite revealing. For the time being, he advised the premier on 29 September, Israel "should focus on the tactical (ha-takhsisit) aim of securing the continuation of the contacts [with Hussein]." Eban then went on to say that he would look for ways to guarantee that "Issachar"—President Johnson—knew that a substantive contact with "Charles's government" had taken place and that Hussein was offered an honorable way out of his predicament. The king, Eban said, "should be pressured to adopt a realistic attitude and not to miss the moment." The rest of the letter betrays the foreign minister's apprehension of a diplomatic rout at the United Nations, and the concluding paragraph puts his advice regarding Hussein in its true context. "Our fate at the [General] Assembly depends on Issachar and the kind of support he is willing to give us."[124]

Eban took the necessary steps to win Johnson over. On 30 September, immediately upon arriving in New York, he met Secretary of State Rusk and told him that the Jordanians had received a detailed conceptual picture of what Israel wanted, which, so he boasted, most of the world would consider magnanimous. Without saying it explicitly, Eban left a clear impression that he was referring to a direct dialogue with Jordan.[125] The president was promptly informed of this.[126] Johnson also received a nine-page letter from Eshkol, dated 29 September, which Walt Rostow summarized for him as follows: "The UAR doesn't want peace; please don't get in bed with the Soviet Union on the Middle East; the Israelis are trying to do something with Jordan; please give us the Phantoms."[127] The latter plea was granted: on 9 October the president finally decided to supply Israel with the coveted fighter-bombers.[128] But Johnson was not convinced that Israel was trying seriously to achieve a settlement. In the reply to Eshkol's letter he said that real peace could not be exclusively built "on the walls of a fortress—or under the umbrella of air power—or behind a nuclear shield. . . . I must urge you to resist those who find it easier to risk Israel's future on today's expanded boundaries than to reach out for real peace."[129]

The Americans had consistently held the position that the West Bank should be returned to Jordan with minimal boundary rectifications, for which Jordan should be compensated. This is what King Hussein had been told in November 1967 (see chapter 5) and, on Rusk's instructions, the same assurances were given to him again on 9 November 1968.[130] When Undersecretary of State Katzenbach conveyed this message to Rabin and expressed concern at the indications that Israel sought a settlement involving territorial acquisitions, the ambassador said that Israel's security requirements dictated territorial changes. Rabin also claimed that the stance outlined by Katzenbach represented a shift in the US stand.[131] American officialdom, far less conciliatory toward Israel than its president, reacted with impatience to the Israeli arguments. Harold Saunders of the White House staff sharply reminded an Israeli diplomat that the administration had never agreed to Israel's border schemes, but that the Israelis had never taken the Americans seriously: "They just turned off their hearing aids."[132] In a report to the president, Walt Rostow used these very words, and added: "We can't afford to go along with their [the Israelis'] bazaar haggling if we're going to have any chance of peace."[133] Harsh words indeed, but they were not followed by action.

This indulgent American attitude remained unchanged despite the increasing signs of Israel's insistence to cling to its military conquests. The government resolution of 19 June 1967 is a case in point. On that day the Israeli cabinet had secretly decided to relinquish the occupied Egyptian and Syrian territories and return to the international borders in exchange for peace. Although the resolution was adopted as a diplomatic maneuver (see chapter 1), it was a binding one. Shortly afterward, however, the government gradually retreated from its seeming bold line by adopting a series of decisions departing from the original text as well as by deeds. The Americans, who had been informed about the 19 June resolution, never used it as a political weapon against Israel's growing intransigence and refrained from leaking it, apparently for fear of Soviet and Arab pressure on Washington, even after the Israelis formally abrogated it.[134] On 31 October 1968 the cabinet adopted a top secret resolution which explicitly replaced the 19 June 1967 resolution. It decided that peace with Egypt required changes to the international border. The Gaza Strip would "obviously" stay within Israel's limits, and Israel would maintain its control over Sharm al-Sheikh with "territorial continuity to the State of Israel."[135] The distance between Sharm al-Sheikh, at the extreme south of Egypt's Sinai Peninsula, and Eilat, at the extreme south of Israel, is 200 miles.

The new resolution was soon communicated to Washington.[136] The Americans were furious. In a meeting with Ambassador Rabin, senior White House officials Walt Rostow and Harold Saunders bluntly said:

> We've told you the US position *ad nauseam*—you have to give the West Bank back, you have to give Hussein a role in Jerusalem, a "Polish corridor" to Sharm el-Sheikh doesn't make sense. When Allon was here, we told him what we thought of his plan. If the Israelis aren't tired of hearing this, we'd be glad to say it again, but we think they've known all along what our position is if they've been listening.[137]

Yet American consternation at the new development and at overall Israeli policy had no practical follow-up. Instead, Israel was about to receive fifty

Phantoms and, by and large, continued to enjoy America's staunch support.

It may be argued that Israel's double game failed. After all, the scheme to create a semblance of a Palestinian civil administration ended in fiasco, and the disingenuous contacts with Hussein fooled neither the king nor the Americans. All concerned clearly read the Israelis' intentions. But in more than one sense the Israeli *takhsisanut* did achieve its goal. There was a follow-up meeting with Hussein, and then another one and yet a third. They all led nowhere, but earned Israel what its leaders really wanted—time.[138] In late October, Dr. Herzog concluded that the recent contacts on the Hussein channel gained the government two crisis-free months on the UN front, yet he felt that this "tactical move" would soon fizzle out.[139] The Israeli policy makers, however, did not let go. Further attempts were made to resuscitate the defunct civil administration project. In mid-October, Moshe Sasson approached Anwar al-Khatib and apparently other Palestinian politicians about the plan, only to face a firm rebuff.[140] Efforts to convince the international community that Israel strove to make peace with its Arab neighbors also continued unabated, in the same ways as before.

Addressing the General Assembly on 8 October, Abba Eban presented what he described as a nine-point peace plan, which was bereft of any new ideas but was packaged in a more appealing wrapping. According to Eban himself, the speech was intended to win better world opinion.[141] Golda Meir took much pleasure in Eban's speech. "When the foreign minister doesn't want to say [something] he uses many words," she praised him at the Knesset Foreign Affairs and Security Committee three days later. Referring to the Israeli precondition that the Arab states must declare their readiness to make peace with Israel, Meir added: "True, the foreign minister said something [about this in his speech] to confuse the enemy." She particularly commended Eban and the government for their triumph in keeping alive the useless Jarring mission, thereby preventing harsh resolutions against Israel at the United Nations.[142] Golda Meir, then, paid tribute to Israel's foreign policy of *takhsisanut,* which she and others deemed fruitful.

And there was more. In an effort to persuade U Thant that abandonment of the Jarring mission would be a "tragedy," Eban told the UN secretary general on 5 October that contacts with Amman were being conducted "through key Jordan cabinet members now in Israel-held territory and 'other channels.'" No such cabinet members existed.[143] Moreover, despite repeated Jordanian rejections, the Allon Plan was all the Israeli leaders were ready to offer Hussein—hoping that he would decline it. In the words of Eshkol: "If we give a finger, they would want the entire hand if not the whole head."[144] So Israel kept it all.

"The Whole World Is Against Us"

Epilogue

On 1 September 1968 the Israeli cabinet passed a secret resolution entitled "Lily North" (*Havatselet Tsafon* in the original Hebrew) that authorized "preliminary preparations in Deganyah," which included paving roads to the local cemetery and building parking lots there.[1] "Lily" is the Israeli code name for a state funeral, and Deganyah Bet was Prime Minister Eshkol's old kibbutz. Remarkably, six months before he passed away, the government—with Eshkol himself presiding—was planning the funeral of its incumbent head. Indeed, these were the dying days of Levi Eshkol. Although doggedly hidden from the public, the premier's fast deteriorating health was known to his inner circle. In the fall of 1968 Golda Meir was told by one of her party's elders that Eshkol was a goner and that she should succeed him. The seventy-one-year-old semiretired politician agreed. She took office shortly after Eshkol died on 26 February 1969.[2]

The rise to power of the imperious and obstinate Meir may seem to many like the end of whatever prospect the Palestinian option might have had, because the new prime minister believed that there was no Palestinian people. "There was no such a thing as Palestinians," she insisted. "It was not as though there was a Palestinian people in Palestine considering itself as a Palestinian people and we came and threw them out and took their country away from them. They did

not exist."[3] She claimed further that the "Palestinian entity"—a fundamental and time-honored concept in the Palestinian political ideology—
was a "hundred percent made-in-Israel": an invention of certain Jewish
Israelis, some of whom Meir considered disloyal.[4] These views earned
Meir much notoriety, but in fact Eshkol—reputedly a moderate—
essentially thought the same way.

He claimed that when Palestine had fallen into the hands of the
Arabs, "the hills became denuded, the valleys turned into malarial
swamps, the coastal plain was reduced to sand dunes. The land stood
all but empty. . . . It was the arrival of the Jews that attracted Arab immigrants."[5] In the late nineteenth century, Eshkol told an American
senator, when the modern Jewish return to the Land of Israel had begun, there had been "no more than ten or twenty thousand non-Jews in
the whole area."[6] And in an interview with the American weekly *Newsweek,* published only a fortnight before he died, Eshkol said: "What are
Palestinians? When I came here there were 250,000 non-Jews—mainly
Arabs and Bedouins. It was desert—more than underdeveloped. Nothing. It was only after we made the desert bloom and populated it that
they became interested in taking it from us."[7]

In fact, Palestine in the early twentieth century was by no means a
wilderness. Hundreds of villages dotted the land, large parts of it were
covered with citrus and olive groves, and its towns enjoyed vibrant commercial life. When Eshkol first arrived in Palestine in 1914, the country's
population—excluding Bedouins—totaled some 689,000, of whom only
60,000 were Jews; and at the start of the 1880s the number of inhabitants—
excluding Bedouins—had been about 470,000.[8] The Palestinians in the
occupied territories, however, were less concerned with Eshkol's igno-
rance than with what they saw as further evidence that their Jewish occupiers still adhered to the old Zionist notion of Palestine as "a land
without a people for a people without a land."[9] The prime minister's denial of reality apart, his statements and arguments vividly showed that a
Palestinian option did not exist even during his reign.

Israel and the Palestinians

Bernard Lewis rightly argued that the West Bank Palestinians were unable to form a coherent general leadership or to formulate a decisive
policy while the Israeli occupation continued.[10] The main reason for

this, which Lewis failed to mention, was Israel's approach toward the West Bank leaders. The Israelis treated them only as a means to an end—either for retaining the occupied West Bank through some functional arrangement, or for pressuring King Hussein to yield to Israel's terms. The occupiers sought "cooperation" from the occupied—namely, a submissive attitude which would allow them a trouble-free occupation—and did not view the West Bankers as genuine partners to bona fide negotiations. Thus, countrywide political organization was banned in the occupied territories and independent-minded figures were neutralized by arrest and exile. While repeatedly claiming publicly that they did not want quislings, the Israelis strove to "cultivate" or "groom" pro-Israel leaders—a euphemism for collaborators. Inevitably, this approach led to the emasculation of the political elite in the West Bank at a time when the local leadership could have played an important role in achieving an Arab-Israeli accommodation.

For their part, the West Bank leaders did not rise to the challenge. They were divided by personal, local, and sectarian rivalries, and quite a number among their ranks were motivated by self-interest. Hence they were susceptible to enticement and influence, which both Jordan and Israel were quick to exploit. With few exceptions, the West Bank dignitaries followed the traditional "politics of notables"; none could muster the courage to initiate an audacious political effort vis-à-vis Israel. By and large, they satisfied themselves with the role of go-between, leaving the job of resolving the conflict to King Hussein, President Nasser, or UN peace envoy Jarring. Against the occupation—their most excruciating predicament—they fought mainly by the conventional methods of manifesto, petition, and protest. They did not even consider the option of armed resistance.

The Palestinians outside the occupied territories were rather weak at the beginning of the period under review. In the summer of 1967 the PLO was an insignificant organization and the guerrilla groups, notably al-Fateh, were still limited in number and appeal. But despite their many setbacks at the hands of the Israelis in the subsequent months, the fida'iyyun—wholly committed to an armed struggle against the "Zionist entity"—rapidly gathered strength and influence. This process was enhanced by Israel's aggressive policy of disproportionate reprisals. Such was the Karameh raid in March 1968, which according to

Sari Nusseibeh helped al-Fateh's leader Yasir 'Arafat gain full control over the PLO in February 1969.[11] By then, the fida'iyyun enjoyed soaring popularity and support for their defiance in the Arab world, regardless of their terrorist actions. Israel's behavior, then, not only enfeebled the largely moderate West Bank leadership but also invigorated the belligerent resistance organizations.

These two converse trends and their impact were well demonstrated in late 1968, when Walid al-Shak'ah of Nablus put to Moshe Sasson a far more daring version of his unheeded proposal of March 1968. Shak'ah suggested negotiations between Israel and a representative West Bank delegation about an independent Palestinian state with the prewar lines as a starting point. This extraordinary initiative clearly reflected the West Bank radicals' deep despair at the failure of the Arab states, the world community, and Jarring to remove the occupation. Shak'ah added optimistically that he should first go to Amman in order to seek the backing and guidance of the Palestinian leaders outside the occupied territories. Prime Minister Eshkol agreed. However, the heads of the resistance organizations flatly rejected the idea, and forbade the West Bankers to negotiate with Israel. Shak'ah and his associates acceded.[12] The Palestinians living in *al-dakhil,* or the inside of the occupied territories, unequivocally acknowledged now that the center of gravity had shifted to *al-kharij,* or the outside.

In 1969 there were still some key Israelis who myopically belittled al-Fateh and the Palestinian guerrilla movement as a whole, regarded them as Arab governments' marionettes, and predicted their eventual demise. Foreign Minister Eban was one of them.[13] Others, more realistic, recognized the recently acquired significance of the fida'iyyun and their increasing influence over the Palestinians in the occupied territories. In mid-January 1969 Defense Minister Moshe Dayan told the British ambassador in Tel Aviv that "the only real [Palestinian] leaders who command any respect were the Fatah [*sic*]. The Israel Government would do well to take into account that Abu Ammar [*sic;* Yasir 'Arafat's nom de guerre] was the only Palestinian leader it would be worth their while to do a deal with."[14] In fact, Dayan had already initiated steps to establish contact with 'Arafat. In December 1968 he offered a captured al-Fateh fighter his freedom if he would go to Abu 'Amar and convey that he, Dayan, wanted to meet him in order to talk peace. Apparently the prisoner did not take the suggestion seriously and refused to go. Upon hearing the story from Dayan, the Nablus poet Fadwa Touqan volunteered to carry out the mission. But 'Arafat, whom she saw in Beirut in early 1969, was unwilling to meet the Israeli defense minister.[15] So the unceasing Israeli claim that there was no one to talk to on the other side was finally vindicated, at least as far as the non-collaborating Palestinians were concerned, but lack of communication was of Israel's own doing.

These two episodes also attest to the inconsistent and frequently contradictory moves of the Israeli government. Premier Eshkol did not turn down the proposal to negotiate the establishment of an independent Palestinian state, and even acquiesced in Shak'ah's consultations with fida'iyyun chiefs, though he was determined to deny the West Bankers statehood. Dayan, who in April 1968 had rejected the idea of a parley with al-Fateh, saying that the way to deal with the fida'iyyun was by killing them (see chapter 7), was now attempting to have a tête-à-tête with his archenemy. It was inconceivable that Eshkol would embark on such negotiations, and even more so that a Dayan-'Arafat rendezvous would take place. So why did Eshkol, Dayan, and their colleagues act the way they did in these and similar cases? There is no explanation for this irrational conduct, except that Israel's record during this period—as well as the preceding and succeeding periods—was replete with conflicting statements and actions. Furthermore, Israel chronically suffered from the lack of long-range thinking, coherent strategy, and systematic decision making; crucial decisions were often taken on a whim or a hunch.

Yet the policy makers were very consistent and persistent about what they regarded as Israel's vital interests.

Israel and Its Motives

The publicly announced Israeli consensus in the aftermath of the Six Day War was that there would be no return to the prewar situation; that the armistice agreements with the neighboring Arab states should be replaced by peace treaties; and that peace treaties should be arrived at through direct negotiations. The unavowed controlling consideration of the government was the desire to retain as many of the occupied lands as possible with as few Arab inhabitants as possible. As far as the West Bank and the Gaza Strip were concerned, Israel aspired to sever the nexus between the land and the people who lived on it. The government took action on both these interconnected issues.

It is widely accepted that the National Unity coalition and the decision makers within the ruling Labor Party were divided over the fate of the occupied territories. Thus the cabinet avoided formulating its precise peace terms in binding resolutions and effectively decided not to decide. Yet toward the end of the Eshkol administration there was an agreement to keep Arab Jerusalem, the Golan Heights, and Sharm al-Sheikh together with a connecting 200-mile-long strip of land along Aqaba Bay, the Gaza Strip, parts of Sinai, and significant portions of the West Bank. Arab Jerusalem was promptly annexed by Israel under the pretense of "municipal unification," and Jewish settlements were built in other regions of the coveted land, mostly under the guise of "military strongpoints." The government permitted this despite knowing that it breached international law.

Precedence was given to the Judaization of Arab Jerusalem. Shortly after the war hundreds of acres were expropriated in the annexed area for building housing projects for Jews.[16] By January 1969 ten Jewish settlements had been established with the government's blessing in the Golan Heights, two in Sinai, and five in the West Bank, including the most contentious settlement in Hebron.[17] That month the cabinet secretly approved seven to nine new settlements in the Golan, Sinai, and the Jordan Valley.[18] Only budget constraints and a scarcity of would-be settlers limited the pace of expansion. The humble beginning notwithstanding, the settlement enterprise manifestly signaled the Israeli intention not to relinquish these territories. While refusing to draw a peace map, Israel effectively demarcated its new frontiers by fait accompli.

This was a love story: the Israelis fell in love with the Arab lands they occupied in the war. In the words of Abba Eban, "Many Israelis who had begun by regarding the captured territories as cards to play at a peace table ended up by falling in love with the cards and embracing them so tenaciously as to eliminate their bargaining value."[19] There were different motives for the Israeli infatuation. Some were ideological and religious: messianic ardor, generated by the stunning June 1967 victory and the following euphoria, affected many—observant and secular Jews alike—and was translated into a new hastily tailored political theology.

A major concern of the largely pragmatic political elite was, however, the state's security.

Ever since the foundation of Israel in 1948, the thinking of its leaders on national security started from the premise that their tiny country was engaged in a struggle for its very survival. At the root of this perception lay the traumatic memory of the Holocaust. Given the impossibly long and serpentine armistice lines of pre-June 1967 Israel, its narrow waist, and the proclaimed hostility of the surrounding Arab neighbors, the obsessive search for security was understandable. The rout of three Arab armies in the Six Day War turned Israel into a regional power overnight. But this profound change was not accompanied by a corresponding shift in the mindset of most of its political and military leaders, either hawks or doves. They were not prepared to give up the "strategic depth" with which the war conquests had endowed their state.[20]

Close examination of the internal discussions of the Israeli policy makers reveals, however, that there was more to it than mere security considerations. In often contradictory ways, the so-called "demographic danger"—the fear of even slightly undermining the overwhelming Jewish majority within the State of Israel—had always been given a high priority. After the Six Day War it began to be applied to the occupied territories as well. Abba Eban, for example, objected to augmenting the number of Arabs living in Israel by the inclusion of the West Bank inhabitants, asserting that there was a limit to the amount of arsenic the human body could absorb. In response to those who questioned the morality of his attitude, Eban said that any Arab who wished to live in an Arab state was free to do so.[21] Levi Eshkol rejected the idea of settling the 1948 refugees in the occupied territories and insisted that the refugee problem should be solved elsewhere. From the Knesset podium he stated: We are not allowed to place a time bomb in Israel.[22]

This was not the first time, or the last, that the prime minister referred to the occupied territories as part of the State of Israel, thus betraying his desire to hang on to them. But their Palestinian inhabitants were undesirable to Eshkol and his associates. After Arab Jerusalem, the Gaza Strip was top of Israel's list of lands designated for annexation. As early as 19 June 1967 the cabinet decided that "the Gaza Strip is located within the territory of the State of Israel."[23] When, on 19

November 1968, King Hussein suggested that Jordan should get the Gaza Strip in exchange for letting Israel have certain small areas in the West Bank, Deputy Prime Minister Yigal Allon rejected the idea and said, "The Israelis are falling in love with Gaza." Allon then added, "Gaza is a historical place." The king, who wanted access to the Mediterranean, also believed that placing all the Palestinians under one umbrella would be politically advantageous for all concerned.[24] The Israelis were ready to give Hussein access to a Mediterranean port and all the occupied Palestinians—but not the Gaza Strip itself.

Yet the Israeli government refrained from formal annexation of the Gaza Strip, mainly because of the region's large Palestinian population— some 330,000 persons in July 1968, of whom about 200,000 were 1948 refugees.[25] In September 1967 Foreign Minister Eban told Arthur Goldberg, US ambassador to the United Nations, that Israel would like to have the territory of the Gaza Strip without the inhabitants but did not see how that could be achieved.[26] Israel attempted nevertheless to empty the region of its people. From the very start of the occupation strenuous efforts were exerted by various branches of the Israeli government—the military, the Foreign Ministry, the Mossad, and others—to make the Gazans leave. These efforts predominantly targeted the 1948 refugees: the Israelis did not want the refugee problem in their lap. Claiming that Israel bore no responsibility for the creation of the refugee problem, they insisted that the issue should be solved by the international community; Premier Eshkol reluctantly agreed to share up to 10 percent of the costs.[27]

Mass expulsion and forced "transfer" were out of the question under the world's watchful eye. The methods used ranged from making life in Gaza unbearable to an organized project designed to encourage emigration. The former included ruling with an iron fist and keeping the standard of living very low. The latter, personally supervised by the prime minister, relied on financial incentives.[28] Despite the niggardly inducements, by mid-1968 some 40,000 refugees left the Strip, mostly for the East Bank.[29] But Jordan, already overwhelmed with tens of thousands of the displaced new refugees from the West Bank, decided at the end of July 1968 to stop admitting old refugees from the Gaza Strip.[30] So Israel increased its attempts to boost emigration of Gazans to such non-Arab countries as Brazil and other South American states, as well as Canada and Australia, but with little success.[31] "I still don't know how to get rid of them [the Arabs of Gaza]," Premier Eshkol lamented in October 1968.[32]

The Israeli drive to reduce the Palestinian population in the West Bank took a more indirect form, largely by denying repatriation to new refugees and persons who had happened to be outside the area during the war. Fortunately for the Israelis, thousands of Palestinians left the West Bank in the months that followed the war exodus. In most cases they did so of their own volition for various reasons, not least unwillingness to live under military occupation. Yet there was ceaseless international pressure on Israel, specifically from Washington, to permit the return of those wishing it. Thus the government introduced a family reunion scheme in late 1967, but as in the case of Operation Refugee (see chapter 4), the Israelis had no intention of tolerating a mass inflow. The scheme explicitly excluded the inhabitants of Arab Jerusalem and effectively barred the reentry of UNRWA-registered refugees and men between the ages of sixteen and sixty. Landowners were not allowed back, either, because there were plans to build settlements on properties belonging to "absentees." By the end of 1969 only 11,000 Palestinians out of about 30,000 applicants had actually returned.[33] Not very many returned under this scheme in later years, either. At any rate, the efforts to encourage Palestinian emigration and to prevent a reverse movement clearly attested to the Israeli desire to cling to the occupied territories—that is, to much more sparsely populated territories.

On the whole, the Israeli attempts to thin out the West Bank population failed. Shortly after the *Naksah* of June 1967 the Palestinians adopted a political strategy called *sumud,* Arabic for steadfastness, to defy the occupation. One of its core tenets was to stay on their land at all costs. And stay on the land most of them did.

Israel and King Hussein

The Eshkol government chose not to agree on Israel's peace terms. The so-called "generous peace offer" to Egypt and Syria, embodied in the cabinet resolution of 19 June 1967, was merely a political maneuver aimed at winning Washington over and was never offered to Cairo or Damascus. Shortly after adopting the resolution, the cabinet began gradually to retreat from it, taking a series of decisions departing from the original text until annulling it altogether on 31 October 1968. When the new

Prime Minister Golda Meir presented her government to the Knesset in mid-March 1969, she praised the former cabinet for not setting Israel's conditions for peace, claiming that "wisdom and responsibility" dictated this approach "so long as there is no sign from the other side about its readiness to reach peace."[34]

Meir's statement was untrue on two counts. First, King Hussein had time and again communicated to Israel his unwavering desire to make peace. Second, the decision not to decide, particularly regarding Jordan, had nothing to do with the alleged lack of any "sign from the other side." Yossi Beilin, a political scientist and senior politician within the Labor Party until 2003, argues in a book published in 1985 that between the Six Day War of June 1967 and the Yom Kippur War of October 1973, the Eshkol and Meir governments avoided crucial political decisions—including bold moves regarding the occupied territories—because the leaders of the ruling Labor Party feared that such decisions would split their ranks.[35] The Labor leaders were indeed anxious to preserve party unity and thereby to maintain its—and their—ruling position, but the reason for avoiding those decisions was far more fundamental.

It was rooted in the Israeli insistence on the Jewish "historical association" with biblical *Eretz Yisrael*. The concept of the historical association dominated the thinking of the decision makers. Deputy Prime Minister Yigal Allon, the author of the Allon Plan, whose 1968 version offered King Hussein two-thirds of the West Bank in return for peace, described his perception of the historical association in the expanded edition of his book *Masakh shel Hol* (A curtain of sand), published in late 1968. Israel, he argued, must adhere to its historical right to the Land of Israel as a moral, national, and political value. When the government determined the secure borders of the state by incorporating territories which Israel had not controlled before the Six Day War, the move should not be regarded as annexation or as morally wrong. Allon held that Jordan had no legitimate right—either historical or political—to claim sovereignty over the West Bank.[36]

The expression "historical association" was coined by Dr. Ya'acov Herzog, who handled the secret channel of contacts with King Hussein and had Premier Eshkol's ear. In his discussions with Hussein and Zayd al-Rifa'i, the king's confidant, Herzog stressed the import of the idea. For example, on 22 August 1968 he explained to Hussein what the Jewish historical association meant in practical terms: "settlement as of right for Jews [*sic*] throughout the Western Bank and free access to all places therein."[37]

Israel was in no doubt that an Arab-Israeli peace settlement would never be achieved without surrendering most if not all the occupied territories. In the immediate aftermath of the June 1967 War such a settlement was anyhow unlikely in the cases of Syria and Egypt: the former intransigently stuck to a rejectionist attitude vis-à-vis Israel; the latter, despite its declared acceptance of Security Council Resolution 242 and seeming cooperation with UN peace envoy Jarring, was not ready to make real peace with Israel. Jordan was a different matter because of King Hussein's eagerness to resolve the conflict and his concept of total peace for total withdrawal. Yet the land he had lost and demanded back in return for peace was the land that the Israelis coveted most due to its national, historical, and religious significance. Their best offer was an attempt to have it both ways: granting King Hussein a limited sovereignty over parts of the West Bank, while preserving the privilege to settle there and come and go as they pleased.

The saliency given to the historical association with the entire Land of Israel as a political argument suggests that the overriding Israeli motive had little to do with security. Furthermore, the historical association, coupled with the use of the disingenuous Allon Plan as a peace proposal to Jordan, indicates that the Israeli approach was guided by a strong reluctance to part with what the Israelis named Judea and Samaria. What distinguished the so-called moderates from the extremists was their reasonable style, which lacked the fire and brimstone so frequently used by the fervent enthusiasts for Greater Israel. But regardless of their pragmatic attitude and milder rhetoric, these "moderates"—with Prime Minister Eshkol in the lead—were hardly less passionate about the newly acquired lands. A telling piece of evidence is Eshkol's recurrent use of the metaphor of the bride and the dowry: the premier was always complaining about the unwanted bride—the Palestinian inhabitants of the occupied territories—but never about the rich territorial dowry that came with her. "We need the land," Eshkol stated from the podium of the Knesset in August 1968, in reference to the occupied territories and specifically the West Bank.[38]

In a study of the Eshkol government's policy on the occupied territories, published in 1996, Reuven Pedatzur argues that Israel was at first inclined toward the Palestinian option but in early 1968 abandoned this attitude in favor of the Jordanian option. As the historical evidence clearly shows, this argument is unfounded.[39] The Palestinian option was never regarded seriously by the Israeli leaders. Instead, they first concocted the "Palestinian alternative" stratagem, whose immediate purpose was to pressure Hussein (see chapter 5), and later attempted to create an Arab civil administration, devoid of power and run by collaborators (see chapter 8). 'Aziz Shehadeh, who led the ineffective "entity movement" in the West Bank, believed that Israel was actively against the idea of a Palestinian entity because it realized that the Palestinians' appeal for political rights in accordance with the UN Partition resolution of 1947 was more powerful and convincing than any demand by an Arab state to restore the 4 June 1967 lines.[40] However, the real reason for the Israeli attitude was entirely different. Playing for time, the Israelis simply used the contacts with the West Bankers to support their claim to the Americans that they were weighing their options. They used the contacts with King Hussein for the same purpose.

The Israeli position on Jerusalem alone rendered the Jordanian option unrealistic. Moreover, the Allon Plan was proposed to Hussein as Israel's peace terms not only in anticipation of its rejection but even after Jordan had refused repeatedly and unequivocally to consider it. And, as if this was not enough, the Israeli representatives emphasized that these peace terms were informal and reflected just one of three prevailing schools of thought in the government; the other two did not envisage a settlement with Jordan. They said that should Hussein accept the offer, an effort to achieve cabinet endorsement would be made.

In short, Israel did not take the Jordanian option seriously either. King Hussein certainly had every reason to talk about the three faces of Israel, as he often did. According to Hussein, the first face represented extremism, the wish to dominate not only the occupied territories but also other parts of the Arab homeland; the second looked to the destruction of Jordan and settlement of the Palestinian question by the creation of a West Bank satellite; and the third was a moderate face, seeking a peaceful accommodation with the Arabs. Occasionally, the king argued, one of the three faces overshadowed the others, depending, among other factors, on the international situation and world opinion.[41] But what Hussein failed to recognize was that all these faces masked one policy line: *takhsisanut,* deception.

This is not a learned analysis or a sophisticated interpretation but the naked truth about the Israeli foreign policy as articulated by Abba Eban—a self-proclaimed moderate. Eban explicitly recommended holding a "futile discussion" with the Jordanians "which should last weeks and months," and a never-ending series of meetings with King Hussein in order to deceive US President Lyndon Johnson into thinking that direct contacts regarding a bilateral settlement were taking place in good faith. The purpose of this exercise was—again, by Eban's own admission—to deflect international pressure and maintain thereby the territorial status quo.[42] "Prevarication," noticed Nigel Ashton, King Hussein's biographer, "remained the favoured Israeli strategy. If Hussein could at least be kept in play in the peace process, the Americans would be discouraged from launching any peace initiative of their own which might require much greater concessions from the Israeli government."[43] The Israeli policy makers readily adopted Eban's approach of takhsisanut.

It may be argued that neither King Hussein nor the West Bank Palestinians were genuinely ready to make peace with Israel in the late 1960s. But in the first place, there is nothing in the historical record to corroborate such an argument. If this were the case, the wise course would have been to call Hussein's and the West Bankers' bluff by responding affirmatively to their respective overtures. The crucial point, however, is that Israel's policy makers never doubted the peaceful intentions of either Hussein or the West Bank leaders. Israel resorted to a deceitful foreign policy precisely because the government was convinced that the king of Jordan and the West Bankers meant what they said regarding an accommodation with Israel.

It was naïve to think that the Israeli duplicity could continue unnoticed. Hussein explicitly described it in a written statement which he handed to Governor William Scranton, President-elect Richard Nixon's special emissary to the Middle East, during their meeting on 8 December 1968:

> For whatever reason, Israel is not truly serious in negotiating settlement with Jordan. . . . It is quite clear to me that Israel had adopted a transparent and cynical policy of using the excuse of alleged negotiations in an attempt to prevent or delay any possible pressure from outside, and thus—because of in-

ternal differences—to avoid having to make any decisions of the terms of the final settlement.[44]

Shortly afterward Secretary of State Dean Rusk also wondered "whether the Israelis sought to lull us into inactivity by assuring us repeatedly of progress being made in these [covert] talks [with Jordan]."[45] Four months later, during yet another pointless secret meeting in London on 25 April 1969, Hussein put it to Dr. Herzog with unwonted bluntness. The king said that he had heard at the United Nations and in Washington that Israel was using the bilateral talks with Jordan to placate international concern regarding a settlement, and that "you [the Israelis] are cheating the world." Referring to the possibility that the four Great Powers might summon Arab and Israeli representatives to New York, Hussein bitterly asked Herzog whether Israel would try to avoid these discussions as well on the pretext of being engaged in a direct clarification process with the Jordanians.[46]

In fact, none of Israel's duplicitous decisions, actions, and statements worked. None of Israel's friends believed that the annexation of Jerusalem was a mere administrative measure, that the Jewish settlements in the occupied territories were real frontline strongholds, or that Operation Refugee was truly intended to allow a mass repatriation of the "new refugees" of the June War. John Mearsheimer argues that interstate lying is not prone to backfire, and if it does, it is unlikely that the target state would retaliate. But Mearsheimer's discussion does not provide a fitting answer to the Israeli case.[47] Israel enjoyed impunity in Washington despite its persistent foreign policy of deception, which damaged American interests while being dependent on diplomatic support and the supply of arms from the United States. So why did Washington acquiesce? The explanation lies at the very heart of the Johnson administration.

Israel and Washington

Moshe Dayan was honest enough to admit that basically Israel wanted peace but did not want to give up territory. The hawkish and influential defense minister refused to take part in his government's line of *takhsisanut,* but his own peace ideas, as conveyed with astonishing frankness to the British ambassador in Tel Aviv in January 1969, were much more drastic. Dayan thought that by the early fall of 1969 the Arabs might decide to have another go at Israel. He rather hoped this would happen, Ambassador Michael Hadow noted, because in Dayan's view the occupation of Amman and Damascus would mean a final peace settlement with the Jordanians and the Syrians. Dayan went on to say that Israel would have to occupy Cairo as well, "but only for a week." Thereafter the Suez Canal would become Israel's frontier with Egypt, and he did not care much whether Egypt made peace with Israel or not.[48] Insisting that Jews had the right to settle anywhere in the Land of Israel, Dayan maintained that coexistence should be imposed on the Palestinians. In a meeting with the Nablus poet Fadwa Touqan he illustrated his thinking with the following elaborate simile:

> The situation between us today is like the complex relationship between a Bedouin man and a girl he has abducted against her will. But once they have children, the children will recognize the man as their father and the woman as their mother. The original act of abduction will mean nothing to them. You Palestinians, as a nation, do not want us today, but we will change your attitude by forcing our presence upon you.[49]

Dayan's remarkable words reflected the widespread Israeli hubris in the wake of the 1967 triumph which eventually led to the traumatic Yom Kippur War in October 1973. "The Israeli public," observed Yeshayahu Leibowitz, one of Israel's most incisive sages, "were overcome by the intoxication of national pride, military arrogance, and fantasies of the glory of messianic deliverance."[50] As acknowledged retrospectively by Maj. Gen. Meir Amit, the Mossad chief until mid-1968, Israel was swept by feelings of megalomania.[51]

Israel desperately needed to be saved from itself in those heady days, and only the United States possessed the necessary levers of influence. However, Washington did not use these levers, despite its awareness of, and anger over, Israel's maneuvering. True, the defeat of Egypt and Syria—both Soviet clients who were equipped with Soviet weapons— brought Israel directly into the Cold War, and the Americans were unsettled by the steadily deepening penetration of the USSR into the Middle East following the hostilities. The Israelis incessantly harped on the Communist threat in their dealings with America. But this argument was irrelevant in the case of pro-Western Hussein: the United States was expressly committed to the restoration of his curtailed kingdom. The dominant explanation for Washington's passivity is the growing involvement in its own war in Southeast Asia. Preoccupied with the worsening situation in Vietnam, the Johnson administration was unable to deal decisively with the Arab-Israeli conflict. According to the senior White House officials Harold Saunders and Walt Rostow, the administration passed the responsibility for negotiating a settlement within the framework of Security Council Resolution 242 to UN peace envoy Gunnar Jarring, limiting the American role to "active diplomatic support" of the Jarring mission.[52]

There was another reason for the impunity Israel was granted by Washington—the personal attitude of President Johnson. "Johnson was our president, [president] of [the] Jews," Premier Meir said in May 1969 while comparing him with Richard Nixon, his successor. Traditionally, American Jews tended to vote for the Democrats; thus Meir stated that "we"—Israel through its Jewish advocates in America—had had more powerful influence with Johnson the Democrat than it now had with Nixon the Republican.[53] Furthermore, although US foreign policy decision making goes beyond the compass of this study, it is safe to conclude that Johnson's approach vis-à-vis the Arab-Israeli conflict was not motivated by electoral or pragmatic calculations alone.

Shortly after Johnson took office following the assassination of President John F. Kennedy in November 1963, he told a visiting Israeli diplomat, "You have lost a very great friend. But you have found a better one."[54] The new president, says the political scientist Steven Spiegel,

reinforced Kennedy's relationship with Israel. . . . Johnson cemented a more intimate connection between Jerusalem and Washington. Like [President Harry] Truman, Johnson had a biblically based religious background that reinforced his sympathy toward Israel. . . . Johnson tended to see the Israelis fighting the Arabs as a modern-day version of the Texans struggling with the Mexicans.

Some of President Johnson's oldest and best friends were Jews and loyal supporters of Israel. His administration was filled with sympathizers of Israel, including Vice President Hubert Humphrey, Undersecretary of State Eugene Rostow, and Ambassador Arthur Goldberg, to name just a few. Many of them were Jewish. Johnson, moreover, developed a personal friendship with Minister Ephraim ("Eppie") Evron, the number two at the Israeli embassy in Washington.[55] Joseph Califano, the president's chief domestic adviser, once told an Israeli official that Johnson genuinely liked Jews "because they can be trusted."[56]

In his memoirs Lyndon Johnson openly articulates his admiration for the Jewish state. "I have always had a deep feeling of sympathy for Israel and its people, gallantly building and defending a modern nation against great odds and against the tragic background of Jewish experience." He describes the Israelis as "living in a harassed and beleaguered fortress." The eighteen-page chapter Johnson devotes to the June 1967 War shows his strong backing of Israel and distorts basic facts regarding the Arab-Israeli conflict. The Palestinians are totally absent from his narrative; in the fleeting mention of the refugees the former president refers to them as *Arab* refugees.[57]

Muhammad Heikal, President Nasser's confidant, provides a colorful vignette illustrating what the Arabs saw as Johnson's pro-Israel bias. Relying on a cable allegedly received from Muhammad al-Kony, Egypt's ambassador to the United Nations, Heikal says that following the Arab defeat in June, Johnson invited a number of Arab ambassadors to a meeting at the State Department. The president arrived with his dog Beagle, and instead of addressing the ambassadors he talked to the dog:

> Listen, Beagle, to a story about a bad man who got into a fight with his good neighbor, believing that the good neighbor was unable to answer back. But the good neighbor, Beagle, gathered all his strength, hit the bad man with a strong fisticuff and knocked him down.
>
> He was right to do so, don't you think, Beagle?
>
> Why are the bad person's friends now making complaints to others?
>
> What's your opinion, Beagle?[58]

Heikal's incredible tale about Johnson's allegory of "bad man" Egypt, "good neighbor" Israel, and the Arab states as "the bad man's friends" is not corroborated by any recorded evidence. But regardless of its dubious veracity (for starters, Johnson had a number of beagles but none of the dogs he had in 1967 was called Beagle), the story clearly reflects the image of the Johnson administration and the president himself in Arab eyes as far as the Arab-Israeli conflict was concerned. This image was not without foundation. Yet Johnson believed that the Israelis would have to reach out and help construct a basis for the dignity of their humiliated neighbors.[59]

They did not. In addition to their foreign policy of deception, the Israelis adopted a foreign policy of defiance, with excessive belligerence frequently directed at the wrong targets and rebounding adversely on Israel.

One good example is the attack on Karameh. Another is the raid on Beirut airport at the end of 1968. On 26 December two gunmen from the Popular Front for the Liberation of Palestine (PFLP) attacked an Israeli El Al airliner as it prepared to take off from Athens airport. They killed one passenger and wounded a young female flight attendant.[60] Within thirty-six hours, on the pretext that the two terrorists had arrived in Athens from Lebanon, Israel retaliated against Beirut international airport. The Ministerial Committee for Security Affairs approved the destruction of three or four aircraft of Arab airlines, but the Israeli commandos who raided the airport dynamited thirteen passenger planes, including one leased from Ghana Airways.[61] There were no casualties, but the damage was enormous. Defense Minister Dayan nevertheless expressed anger that the airport itself had remained intact.[62] Prime Minister Eshkol later said that the raid was "a kind of public information activity"— pe'ulat hasbarah—which had had an impact on Lebanon, other Arab states, and the Palestinian guerillas.[63]

The Israeli foray provoked unprecedented shock and outrage around the globe. The UN Security Council unanimously condemned Israel in very strong terms. France imposed a total embargo on arms sales to Israel, thus adding spare parts for the Mirage fighter jets Israel possessed to the fifty embargoed Mirages already paid for.[64] The disproportionate assault on Beirut airport furthered the steady decline in Israel's international standing that had begun with the occupation and the government's overall behavior in the wake of the June 1967 War. By early 1969 even a right-wing member of Knesset acknowledged that the world now regarded Israel as a "belligerent, racist, occupying and repressive power who is annexing territories which do not belong to it."[65] Under Golda Meir it got worse. "We are now Israel's *only* major friend in the world," President Nixon remarked in February 1973. Frustrated with the Middle East stalemate, he went on to say:

> I have yet to see *one iota* of give on their [the Israelis'] part—conceding that Jordan and Egypt have not given enough on their side. This is the time to get moving—and they must be told that *firmly*. . . .
>
> The time has come to quit pandering to Israel's intransigent position. Our actions over the past have led them to think we will stand with them *regardless* of how unreasonable they are.[66]

But Israel did not budge. In early September 1973, on the eve of general elections, the ruling Labor Party adopted a plan which in Avi Shlaim's view "provided a powerful boost for the policy of creeping annexation": it called for reinforcing existing Jewish settlements in the occupied territories and for building new ones.[67] Labor's slogan for the elections boasted, "Our situation has never been better." In October the Israelis paid dearly for their exuberant self-confidence and political myopia.

1969 and Beyond

After the death of Premier Eshkol in late February 1969, Israel faced a bleaker situation than during the first twenty-one months of the postwar era. Its new leader, Prime Minister Golda Meir, was far more inflexible than her predecessor; the Palestinian resistance movement, now loosely gathered under the umbrella of the PLO, was more effective and daring; and King Hussein of Jordan was becoming increasingly weak because of the threat the fida'iyyun groups presented to his regime. They established a state within a state in Jordan, thus challenging the sovereignty of the Hashemite Kingdom and the very survival of the king. The ceasefire line along the Jordan River was the scene of frequent exchanges of fire. Palestinian terrorist activity targeted Israelis in the occupied territories, inside the State of Israel and abroad. The Israelis responded with tougher retaliations and countermeasures. Greater numbers of Palestinian houses were blown up by the occupation authorities, and many more Palestinians were exiled from their homeland. Support for the guerillas grew significantly among the West Bankers, traditional leaders included. The PLO gradually acquired the dominant influence in the West Bank and the Gaza Strip. At the Suez Canal intermittent shooting and shelling developed into a full-scale War of Attrition, which lasted a year and a half and exacted a heavy toll on both sides. Much blood—Israeli, Palestinian, Jordanian, and Egyptian—was spilled in the aftermath of the June 1967 War. Many of the victims were innocent civilians. There was little security for the Israelis or for their Arab neighbors. The prospect of peace seemed more remote than ever.

Another major war, longer and more painful than the Six Day War, was needed for Israel to start moving toward peace. On 6 October 1973 President Anwar al-Sadat, Nasser's successor, in tandem with Syria, launched an all-out offensive against Israel with the limited goal of breaking the political deadlock. Israel emerged militarily victorious, though the Arabs were by no means routed. Politically, Sadat was the winner because he achieved his objective. After the hostilities Israel accepted an interim agreement with Egypt, similar to what Sadat had proposed and Israel had rejected in early 1971. The 1971 proposal required Israel to withdraw its troops some twenty miles eastward to allow reopening of the Suez Canal. By 1982, following Sadat's peace initiative of 1977 and the ensuing peace accord in 1979, Israel had returned to Egypt every square inch of the Sinai Peninsula, including Sharm al-Sheikh.

A peace treaty between Israel and Jordan was signed in October 1994, with the Jordan River as the recognized international border. But this did not resolve the question of the West Bank, from which King Hussein had announced Jordan's disengagement in July 1988. Israel, then, made peace with the East Bank alone. There was hope that Israel was on the road to a peace settlement with the Palestinians as well, in the wake of the mutual recognition of Israel and the PLO in September 1993 and the subsequent historic handshake of Prime Minister Yitzhak Rabin and Chairman Yasir 'Arafat on the White House lawn. In 1970 and 1971 the Israelis had watched with much satisfaction the expulsion of the fida'iyyun organizations from Jordan, and in 1982 they had invaded the PLO's new base in the Lebanese capital Beirut so as to push the PLO even farther away. Now they agreed to allow the PLO—hitherto demonized by the Israelis and branded "two-legged beasts"—to repatriate and to establish a Palestinian Authority with limited power in the occupied territories.[68]

The Israeli volte-face was considerably influenced by the *Intifadah,* or uprising, of the West Bank and Gaza Strip inhabitants which broke out in December 1987. While forcefully dealing with a large-scale and prolonged insurgency, Israel realized that the Palestinians under its control were no longer ready to tolerate repressive military occupation. Though the June 1967 War had catapulted the Palestinians onto center stage, Israel had refused to recognize their emergence as an independent political factor—a nation with a legitimate claim to statehood. It took more than three decades of occupation and five years of Intifadah for Israel to concede its momentous mistake.

However, the Israeli-Palestinian peace process failed, and in 2000 a second, much bloodier Intifadah erupted. A serious study of the peace process and its collapse awaits sufficient historical perspective and access to the relevant official records. But it is already clear that the failure is largely rooted in the pattern set by the Israeli government during the early days of the occupation. While Washington insisted that Israel should return to the pre–June 1967 War borders, the Israeli aim was—in the explicit words of Premier Levi Eshkol—to retain the "maximum of territory."[69] This line was pursued by subsequent governments. It was underpinned by Jewish settlement in the occupied territories, which the Eshkol government had instigated early on. The settlement construction in the West Bank never stopped; in fact, it increased sharply after the Israeli-Palestinian peace process had got under way. Ehud Olmert, Israel's prime minister between 2006 and 2009, stated in 1988 that the "policy of expanding Jewish settlements in Judea and Samaria . . . was designed to block any possibility of pressure for Israel to withdraw from those areas."[70] It took Olmert another two decades of intensive building of settlements to acknowledge the inevitable territorial price the Israelis must pay for peace.[71]

On 6 June 1967, the second day of the Six Day War, Abba Eban said at the UN Security Council that "men and nations do behave wisely once they have exhausted all other alternatives."[72] Eban reiterated the same aphorism in articles and speeches in later years, always referring to the Arabs. He and his government colleagues never thought of themselves in this context. Only when Eban was no longer a member of the cabinet did he admit privately that "the [Israeli] government sometimes makes the right decisions but not before trying every other possibility."[73] Indeed, throughout the four and a half decades that followed the June 1967 War, it has been Israel that has time and again proved the validity of Eban's maxim.

The policy toward the Gaza Strip is yet another glaring example of a fatal mistake that took Israel nearly forty years to correct. As we have seen, the Eshkol government decided to retain Gaza, and subsequent governments built civilian settlements there. This blunder was not corrected until the premiership of Ariel Sharon, one of the prime movers of the Israeli fait accompli approach and the godfather of the settlement project. In the summer of 2005 Sharon finally yielded to the intolerable cost—in blood, money, and international reputation—of keeping this tiny, poor, and densely populated province and of maintaining the security of a few thousand Jewish settlers who lived lavishly in twenty-two settlements in the midst of 1.4 million destitute Palestinians.

To be sure, Sharon had no intention of giving up "Judea and Samaria." In fact, the so-called Disengagement from the Gaza Strip was designed to freeze the political process, thereby preventing the establishment of a Palestinian state and maintaining the geopolitical status quo in the West Bank.[74] Yet an increasing number of the more realistic Israelis have recognized that the conflict with the Palestinians cannot be resolved unless Israel accepts what the whole world has been saying from day one of the occupation: Israel must return to the pre–Six Day War lines with minor and reciprocal modifications. In 2002 the Arabs offered what Israel had called for from its foundation in 1948: an end to the Arab-Israeli conflict, recognition of Israel, peace agreements, and normal relations—in exchange for withdrawal from all the territories occupied in June 1967, a just solution to the refugee problem in accordance with UN Resolution 194, and the establishment of an independent Palestinian state in the West Bank and the Gaza Strip, with Arab Jerusalem as its capital.[75] This far-reaching peace initiative was crafted by Saudi Arabia, adopted by the twenty-two-member Arab League at its summit in Beirut in March 2002, and reaffirmed at the Riyadh Summit of the Arab heads of state in March 2007. In Israel none of the governments since 2002—Sharon's, Olmert's, or Netanyahu's—has ever discussed the Arab peace offer.

Despite high-sounding proclamations about the desire to make peace with the Arabs, whenever a prospect of reconciliation was on the table, Israel has been immobilized by fear of what it would entail. 'Aziz Shehadeh, who led the Palestinian entity movement, wrote in 1969: "Immediately after June 1967 a golden opportunity was offered to the Israel Government to achieve a peaceful settlement. . . . The Israeli leaders wavered and did not grasp the importance of this offer." Shehadeh concluded: "The seed of peace that was planted immediately after the Six Day War has thus been trampled upon by forces both within and without the country."[76] But Israeli leaders kept maintaining that no Arabs were willing to negotiate a peaceful settlement with Israel. As late as 1975 Yisrael Galili, who served in the cabinet from 1963, went so far as to claim that "there was not a single occasion when the government of Israel refused to respond to an Arab initiative."[77] However, a number of prominent contemporary officials and observers—including a cabinet minister and an army general—argued retrospectively that in the aftermath of the 1967 War, Israel missed an opportunity for a settlement with both Jordan and the Palestinians, particularly the latter.[78]

Indeed, it was not the Arabs who never missed an opportunity to miss an opportunity—as Eban's often-cited quip suggests—but the Israelis, who persistently and deliberately squandered every opportunity for a settlement. They changed tack only when doing so was inescapable. King Hussein's pithy summary was that "Israel can have either peace or territory, but not both." Abba Eban, who quotes this observation in his 1993 memoirs, goes on to say that it was "not far from being a universal international consensus."[79] But it was Eban who a quarter of century before had carried out Israel's foreign policy of *takhsisanut,* or deception, designed to serve as a political cover-up for the effort to gain time while staying put in the occupied lands and creating a fait accompli.

This study has focused on Israel's policy and practice in the aftermath of the June 1967 War, and some readers might feel that its conclusions, which are especially critical of Israel, are not even-handed. But it should be borne in mind that the parties to the conflict were unequal. There were the victorious occupiers on the one hand and the vanquished and the occupied on the other, and the former held all

the cards. They were aware of international resentment but did not
care. A popular song which came out in 1969 appropriately captured
the Israeli collective spirit:

> The whole world is against us
> Never mind, we'll overcome
> . . . .
> And everybody who's against us
> Let him go to hell.[80]

Notes

Preface

1. David Ronen, *Shnat Shabak: Ha-Heʿarkhut bi-Yehudah ve-Shomron, Shanah Rishonah* [The year of the *Shabak*: The deployment in Judea and Samaria, first year] (Tel Aviv: Misrad ha-Bitahon—ha-Hotsaʾah la-Or, 1989), 31–32.

2. Avi Raz, "The *Shabak* Man," *Sofshavuʿa* (*Maʿariv* weekend magazine, Tel Aviv), 13 April 1990.

3. See chapter 3, the section headed "Operation Sadducees."

4. A. B. Yehoshua, *The Liberated Bride,* trans. Hillel Halkin (London: Peter Halban, 2003), 514. The terms "Orientalism" and "Orientalists" as used in the translated version of Yehoshua's novel have nothing to do with Edward Said's critical concept of Orientalism.

5. George Antonius, *The Arab Awakening: The History of the Arab National Movement* (London: Hamish Hamilton, 1938), 386–87.

6. Tom Segev, *1967: Israel, the War and the Year that Transformed the Middle East* (London: Little, Brown, 2007). The original Hebrew edition was published in 2005.

7. Gershom Gorenberg, *The Accidental Empire: Israel and the Birth of the Settlements, 1967–1977* (New York: Times Books, 2006).

8. Reuven Pedatzur, *Nitshon ha-Mevuʾha: Mediniyut Yisrael ba-Shtahim le-ahar Milhemet Sheshet ha-Yamim* [The triumph of bewilderment: Israel and the territories after the Six Day War] (Tel Aviv: Bitan and Yad Tabenkin, 1996); Reuven Pedatzur, Hashpaʿatam shel "Mitbahei Hahlatah" bi-Kviʿat Mediniyut ha-Bitahon ha-Leʾumi: Memshelet Eshkol ve-ha-Shtahim, 1967–1969 [The influence of "decision kitchens" on the formation of national security policy: The Eshkol government and the territories, 1967–1969], Ph.D. diss., Tel Aviv University, 1992.

9. Shlomo Gazit, *The Carrot and the Stick: Israel's Policy in Judaea and Samaria, 1967–68* (Washington, D.C.: B'nai Brith Books, 1995). The book is based on the writer's 400-page autobiographical master's dissertation, Gibush ha-Mediniyut u-Dfusei ha-Irgun ba-Shtahim ha-Muhzakim (Dagesh ʿal Yehudah ve-Shomron, 1967–1968) [The consolidation of policy and organization patterns in the administered territories (Emphasis on Judea and Samaria, 1967–1968)], Tel Aviv University, 1980. Quite a number of "sensitive" passages in the dissertation and all the footnotes, including the references, have been omitted from the book.

10. For a striking example of such a false account see the discussion of Israel's "generous peace offer" of 19 June 1967 in chapter 1, in the section headed "The Cabinet's 19 June Resolution."

11. Gazit, *Carrot and the Stick,* 291.

12. Shlomo Gazit, *Trapped Fools: Thirty Years of Israeli Policy in the Territories* (London: Frank Cass, 2003), 333. The book first appeared in Hebrew in 1999.

13. A notable example is ʿAli al-Khatib, "The Political Orientations in the Occupied Land and the Different Positions Regarding the Zionist Enemy's Plot to Establish Civil Administration in the [West] Bank and the [Gaza] Strip" [in Arabic], *Shuʾun Filastiniyyah* 55 (1976), 61–68. Khatib, the former editor of the Jerusalem Arabic daily *Al-Shaʿb,* was deported by the Israeli authorities from the West Bank in 1974. Not only is his account extremely biased and lacking in details or supporting evidence, but it is also quite inaccurate.

14. See Saleh ʿAbd al-Jawad, "Why Cannot We Write Our Contemporary History without Using Oral History? The 1948 War as a Case Study" [in Arabic], *Majallat al-Dirasat al-Filastiniyyah* 64 (2005), 43–48.

15. The absence of Palestinian documentation is well demonstrated by the fact that even Palestinian studies dealing with the occupied territories use almost exclusively Israeli and foreign sources. A telling example is provided by the minutes of a meeting between the Israeli defense minister and two West Bank personalities in mid-April 1968, which appear in a Palestinian volume of selected documents: they are, in fact, an Arabic translation of the Israeli record. See chapter 7.

16. Minutes, Consultation on the issue of Arabs in the administered territories, 21 May 1968, A/7921/4, Israel State Archives, Jerusalem (ISA). Emphases in the original.

17. For the subjective nature of the Arab-Israeli conflict-related material held in Israeli archives and the need to make maximum use of foreign archives see Yehoshua Porath, "On the Writing of Arab History by Israeli Scholars," *Jerusalem Quarterly* 32 (1984), 33–34.

18. Moshe Sasson sensed that what his West Bank interlocutors were telling him and other Israelis was different from what they were saying among themselves; Sasson's comments in minutes, Knesset Foreign Affairs and Security Committee (KFASC), 9 February 1968, A/8161/10, ISA. The American consul general in Jerusalem, however, found the Palestinian elite mercurial. "About the time the observer decides he has a fair

comprehension of the main streams of Palestinian thought," he reported, "along comes a new voice which must be heard if not necessarily believed." Campbell, Jerusalem, 24 July 1968, POL 18 ISR, RG59, Central Files 1967–69, United States National Archives, College Park, Maryland (USNA).

19. See, for example, 'Abd al-Jawad, "Why Cannot We Write Our Contemporary History without Using Oral History?"; Thomas M. Ricks, "Memoirs of Palestine: Uses of Oral History and Archaeology in Recovering the Palestinian Past," in *Archaeology, History, and Culture in Palestine and the Near East: Essays in Memory of Albert E. Glock*, ed. Tomis Kapitan (Atlanta: Scholars Press, 1999), 23.

20. See Rashid Khalidi, "The Future of Arab Jerusalem," *British Journal of Middle Eastern Studies* 19, no. 2 (1992), 137.

Introduction

1. Michael Hadow, Israel: Annual Review for 1967, 22 January 1968, FCO/17/468, United Kingdom National Archives, Kew, London (UKNA).

2. The island of Tiran is strategically located at the entrance of the Straits of Tiran, which separate the Gulf of Aqaba and the Red Sea. Before the war the Saudis allowed Egypt to use the island to block the passage of Israeli shipping, thereby creating a *casus belli* for Israel.

3. Hadow, Israel: Annual Review for 1967.

4. Abba Eban, *The New Diplomacy: International Affairs in the Modern Age* (London: Weidenfeld and Nicolson, 1983), 223–24.

5. See, for example, memoranda of conversation: President Johnson et al. and Prime Minister Eshkol et al., 7–8 January 1968 (sessions I and III), *FRUS*, vol. 20, *Arab-Israeli Dispute, 1967–1968* (Washington, D.C., 2001), 79–87, 95–99.

6. Shimon Golan, *Milhamah be-Shalosh Hazitot: Kabalat ha-Hahlatot ba-Pikud ha-'Elyon shel Tsahal be-Milhemet Sheshet ha-Yamim* [A war on three fronts: The decision-making by the IDF's Supreme Command in the Six Day War] (Tel Aviv: Ma'arakhot, 2007), 258.

7. The quotation is from Eshkol's speech at the Kibbutzim Union's conference, 22 November 1967, A/7920/7, ISA.

8. See Avi Shlaim, *Lion of Jordan: The Life of King Hussein in War and Peace* (London: Allen Lane, 2007), 300–310.

9. Moshe Sasson, *Le-lo Shulhan 'Agol* [Without a roundtable] (Or Yehudah: Sifriyat Ma'ariv, 2004), 11. Sasson was the official who handled these talks on behalf of Eshkol.

10. Some writers date the start of the War of Attrition from July 1967, while others argue that it erupted in September–October 1968. Though artillery duels and other military clashes between Egypt and Israel did indeed occur intermittently from July 1967 onward, it was in March 1969 that Egypt launched a large-scale offensive which President Gamal 'Abd al-Nasser dubbed *Harb al-Istinzaf* (war of attrition).

11. For Israel's demographic statistics see Dov Friedlander and Calvin Gold-scheider, *The Population of Israel* (New York: Columbia University Press, 1979), 30, table 2.1; for the 1967 census in the West Bank and the Gaza Strip see Press Release, 1967 Census, Done by the Central Bureau for Statistics for the IDF Head-quarters, First Review, 3 October 1967, A/7921/3, ISA; for Arab Jerusalem see memorandum by Ben-'Amram, Census in East Jerusalem—September 1967, 22 November 1967, A/7920/8, ISA.

12. Memorandum by Col. Shlomo Gazit, Total Exiting to the East of the Jordan, 20 November 1967, enclosed with Chaim Yisraeli to Cabinet Secretary, 21 November 1967, G/6304/1074, ISA. Chapter 4 offers an extensive discussion of the new refugees.

13. This passage borrows heavily from Said K. Aburish, *Children of Bethany: The Story of a Palestinian Family* (London: I. B. Tauris, 1988), 163.

14. Shlaim, *Lion of Jordan,* 252–54; Kamal Salibi, *The Modern History of Jordan* (London: I. B. Tauris, 1993), 222.

15. See Yigal Allon, oral history interviews, second meeting (26 March 1979), A/5001/19, ISA.

16. Interview with Abba Eban, *Washington Post,* 6 March 1969. For example, article V(2) of the Egyptian-Israeli General Armistice Agreement (signed in Rhodes on 24 February 1949) reads: "The Armistice Demarcation Line is not to be construed in any sense as a political or territorial boundary, and is delineated without prejudice to rights, claims and positions of either Party to the Armistice as regards ultimate settlement of the Palestinian question." Ruth Lapidoth and Moshe Hirsch, eds., *The Arab-Israel Conflict and Its Resolutions: Selected Documents* (Dordrecht: Martinus Nijhoff, 1992), 74–81.

17. Interview with Abba Eban, "Die Sackgasse ist Arabisch" [The dead-end street is Arab], *Der Spiegel* (Hamburg), 27 January 1969.

18. Nagib Azoury, *Le Réveil de la Nation Arabe* (Paris: Plon-Nourrit, 1905), v.

19. Resolution 181 (II): Future government of Palestine, 29 November 1947, A/RES/181 (II) (A+B), United Nations Public Records (UNPR).

20. Walid Khalidi, *Before the Diaspora: A Photographic History of the Palestinians* (Washington, D.C.: Institute for Palestine Studies, 1984), 305.

21. The most recent and comprehensive study of the 1948 War is Benny Morris, *1948: A History of the First Arab-Israeli War* (New Haven: Yale University Press, 2008).

22. Aharon Klieman, "Israeli Diplomacy—Continuity and Change," in *Ha-Sikhsukh ha-'Arvi-Yisre'eli: Gormim, 'Imutim, Sikuyim* [The Arab-Israeli conflict: Causes, confrontations, prospects], ed. Eytan Gilboa and Mordechay Naor (Tel Aviv: Misrad ha-Bitahon—ha-Hotsa'ah la-Or, Matkal / Ktsin Hinukh Rashi, 1981), 57.

23. For a discussion of three basic approaches to the legal status of the occupied territories see Menachem Hofnung, *Democracy, Law, and National Security in Israel* (Aldershot: Dartmouth, 1996), 218–21.

24. For a thorough and updated study on the causes of the Palestinian refugee problem see Benny Morris, *The Birth of the Palestinian Refugee Problem Revisited,*

2nd ed. (Cambridge: Cambridge University Press, 2004). Arab and Israeli estimates of the number of refugees differ significantly. See, for example, Baruch Kimmerling and Joel S. Migdal, *The Palestinian People: A History* (Cambridge: Harvard University Press, 2003), 154.

25. 194 (III): Palestine—Progress Report of the United Nations Mediator, 11 December 1948, A/RES/194 (III), UNPR.

26. Morris, *Birth of the Palestinian Refugee Problem Revisited,* 309–40.

27. Mohamed Hawary, "Between the Right of Return and Attempts of Resettlement," in *The Palestinian Refugees: Old Problems—New Solutions,* ed. Joseph Ginat and Edward J. Perkins (Brighton: Sussex Academic Press, 2001), 34.

28. See Michael B. Oren, *Six Days of War: June 1967 and the Making of the Modern Middle East* (New York: Oxford University Press, 2002), 11–12; Avi Shlaim, *The Iron Wall: Israel and the Arab World* (London: Allen Lane, Penguin, 2000), 239–41. For a thorough discussion of the origins of the Six Day War see Oren, *Six Days of War,* 33–169.

29. Malcolm H. Kerr, *The Arab Cold War: Gamal 'Abd al-Nasir and His Rivals,* 3rd ed. (Oxford: Oxford University Press, 1971).

30. Charles Smith, "The Arab-Israeli Conflict," in *International Relations of the Middle East,* ed. Louise Fawcett (Oxford: Oxford University Press, 2005), 222–27; Avi Shlaim, "The Middle East: The Origins of Arab-Israeli Wars," in *Explaining International Relations since 1945,* ed. Ngaire Woods (Oxford: Oxford University Press, 1996), 226–28; William B. Quandt, *Peace Process: American Diplomacy and the Arab-Israeli Conflict since 1967* (Washington, D.C.: Brookings Institution, 1993), 48.

31. Winston Burdett, *Encounter with the Middle East: An Intimate Report on What Lies Behind the Arab-Israeli Conflict* (London: Andre Deutsch, 1970), 344.

32. Samir A. Mutawi, *Jordan in the 1967 War* (Cambridge: Cambridge University Press, 1987), 81. Mutawi argues that this intention was one of the reasons why Prime Minister Wasfi al-Tall swiftly moved to dissolve the Parliament and impose martial law.

33. Yezid Sayigh, *Armed Struggle and the Search for State: The Palestinian National Movement 1949–1993* (Oxford: Clarendon, 1997), 155. See also Abu Iyad, *My Home, My Land: A Narrative of the Palestinian Struggle* (New York: Times Books, 1981), 138. In his discussion, Salah Khalaf (Abu Iyad), one of al-Fateh's top leaders, disparagingly refers to the proposed entity as a "mini-state" (*duwailah*).

34. Shlaim, *Lion of Jordan,* 195–200, 207–9, 212–15, 217–18, 220–22.

35. Ibid., 223–28; Sayigh, *Armed Struggle and the Search for State,* 138.

36. Shlaim, *Lion of Jordan,* 236–37.

37. See Oren, *Six Days of War,* 127–32; 161.

38. "'Our posture is unbeatable'," *Jewish Observer and Middle East Review,* 9 February 1968. See also Hadow, Israel: Annual Review for 1967, FCO/17/468, UKNA.

39. Meeting with Charles, on September 27th, 1968, in London (15.30–17.0 p.m), Ya'acov Herzog papers (YHP).

40. Notes of a Meeting of the NSC [National Security Council] Special Committee, 14 June 1967, *FRUS*, vol. 19, *Arab-Israeli Crisis and War, 1967* (Washington, D.C., 2004), 478–80; Dean, Washington, to FO, 29 June 1967, FCO/17/503, UKNA. See also Quandt, *Peace Process*, 521–22, n. 18.

41. Bob Woodward, "CIA Paid Millions to Jordan's King Hussein," *Washington Post*, 18 February 1977. See also Shlaim, *Lion of Jordan*, 146–48. Hussein's latest biographer argues, however, that Woodward's story was sensationalized, inaccurate, and misleading; Nigel Ashton, *King Hussein of Jordan: A Political Life* (New Haven: Yale University Press, 2008), 190–92.

42. According to World Bank surveys, the population of Jordan in 1965 was estimated at 1.962 million, and in 1970 (including the occupied territories) at 2.299 million. Gad G. Gilbar, *Population Dilemmas in the Middle East: Essays in Political Demography and Economy* (London: Frank Cass, 1997), 68, table 4.1. Given the loss of the West Bank and Arab Jerusalem in 1967 and the ensuing influx of the war refugees, estimating the kingdom's population on the eve of the war at around 2 million seems reasonable.

43. This paragraph relies mostly on Shlaim, *Lion of Jordan*.

44. Hadow, Israel: Annual Review for 1967, FCO/17/468, UKNA.

45. Hadow, Tel Aviv, to Foreign Secretary Brown, The Second Arab/Israel War, 1967—the Aftermath: Political, 20 November 1967, PREM/13/1624, UKNA.

46. The history of the political system of Israel is a complex saga of myriad splits of existing parties, establishment of new ones, reunifications, and ad hoc alliances. See Asher Arian, *The Second Republic: Politics in Israel* (Chatham: Chatham House, 1998), 103–40.

47. Minutes, meeting between Ball et al. and Dayan et al., 16 July 1968, A/7044/5, ISA.

48. Gen. Aharon Yariv's comments, General Staff meeting, 21 August 1967, 206-117/1970, Israel Defense Forces and Defense Establishment Archive, Tel ha-Shomer (IDFA).

49. See Ahituv's comments in minutes, KFASC, 17 August 1967, A/8161/8, ISA; "The Palestinians as a Political Factor Today," a Military Intelligence review paper, June 1971, File 12-4, Box 54, Record Group 15 (Galili), Tabenkin Memorial Archive, Ef'al (TMA); 'Abd al-Qadir Yasin, *Tajribat al-Jabhah al-Wataniyyah fi Qita' Ghazzah* [The experience of the National Front in the Gaza Strip] (Beirut: Dar Ibn Khaldun, 1980), 11–33; Sayigh, *Armed Struggle and the Search for State*, 168.

50. See, for example, Eban's comments as reported in Goldberg, New York, 23 September 1967, *FRUS* 19: 834–38; Eshkol's comments in minutes, KFASC, 2 July 1968, A/8162/1, ISA.

51. Press Release, 1967 Census, Done by the Central Bureau for Statistics for the IDF Headquarters, First Review, 3 October 1967, A/7921/3, ISA.

52. For the concept and practice of the politics of notables see Albert Hourani, "Ottoman Reform and the Politics of Notables," in *Beginnings of Modernization in the*

Middle East, ed. William R. Polk and Richard L. Chambers (Chicago: University of Chicago Press, 1968), 41–68. Hourani was influenced by Weber's ideas regarding administration by notables. See Max Weber, *Economy and Society: An Outline of Interpretive Sociology* (Berkeley: University of California Press, 1978), 289–92.

53. See Mark Heller, "Politics and Social Change in the West Bank since 1967," in *Palestinian Society and Politics,* ed. Joel S. Migdal et al. (Princeton: Princeton University Press, 1980), 185; Issa al-Shuaibi, "The Development of Palestinian Entity-Consciousness," part II, *Journal of Palestine Studies* 9, no. 2 (1980), 61; Jamil Hilal, *Takwin al-Nukhbah al-Filastiniyyah: Mundh Nushu' al-Harakat al-Wataniyyah al-Filastiniyyah ila ma ba'da al-Qiyam al-Sultah al-Wataniyyah* [The formation of the Palestinian elite: From the rise of the Palestinian national movement until after the foundation of the National Authority] (Ramallah: Muwatin, al-Mu'assasah al-Filastiniyyah li-Dirassat al-Dimmuqratiyyah, 2002), 31–33.

54. Moshe Shemesh, *The Palestinian Entity, 1959–1974,* 2nd (rev.) ed. (London: Frank Cass, 1996), 167–68.

55. As confirmed by Shlomo Gazit, Raphael Vardi (the first military governor of the West Bank), and Moshe Sasson. For Gazit see David Pryce-Jones, *The Face of Defeat: Palestinian Refugees and Guerrillas* (London: Quartet, 1974), 100; for Vardi and Sasson see interviews, 9 December 2002, Tel Aviv, and 20 November 1996, Jerusalem, respectively.

56. Interview with Moshe Sasson (1996).

57. Ruth Bondy, Ohad Zmora, Raphael Bashan, eds., *Lo 'al ha-Herev Levadah: Ha-Sipur ha-Mufla 'al Gvurat 'Am Yisrael ve-Nitshono be-Milhemet Sheshet ha-Yamim* [Not by the sword alone: The miraculous story of the heroism of the Israeli people and its victory in the Six Day War] (Tel Aviv: A. Levin Epstein, 1968), 79.

58. See Golan, *A War on Three Fronts,* 170, 175, 182, 183. On warnings against starting a war, see, for example, Dayan's comments in minutes, KFASC, 13 June 1967, A/8161/7, ISA.

59. Golan, *A War on Three Fronts,* 144.

60. Eitan Haber, *Hayom Tifrots Milhamah: Zikhronotav shel Tat-Aluf Yisrael Li'or, ha-Mazkir ha-Tsva'i shel Rashei ha-Memshalah Levi Eshkol ve-Golda Meir* [Today war will break out: The reminiscences of Brigadier General Yisrael Li'or, military aide de camp to Prime Ministers Levi Eshkol and Golda Meir] (Tel Aviv: 'Edanim, 1987), 221–22.

61. Oren, *Six Days of War,* 198.

62. *Davar* (Tel Aviv), 6 June 1967; Statement to the Security Council by Foreign Minister Eban, 6 June 1967, *Israel's Foreign Relations: Selected Documents, 1947–1974,* vol. 2 (Jerusalem, 1976), 784–92.

63. See editorial note, *FRUS* 19: 293. The quotation is Secretary of State Dean Rusk's comment in a telephone conversation with President Johnson.

64. Jeremy Bowen, *Six Days: How the 1967 War Shaped the Middle East* (London: Simon and Schuster, 2003), 167.

65. Eban's comments in cabinet minutes, 11 June 1967, A/8164/6, ISA.

66. See, for example, Ya'acov Herzog's diary, 19 June 1967, A/4511/3, ISA.

67. Statement to the General Assembly by Foreign Minister Eban, 19 June 1967, *Israel's Foreign Relations,* 2: 802–17. In his autobiography, published a decade later—long after it had become clear that Israel initiated the hostilities—Eban astonishingly reiterates the lie about Egyptian planes advancing toward Israel on the morning of 5 June. Abba Eban, *An Autobiography* (London: Weidenfeld and Nicolson, 1978), 403.

68. John J. Mearsheimer, *Why Leaders Lie: The Truth about Lying in International Politics* (New York: Oxford University Press, 2011), 99, 86, 43, 86, 44, respectively.

69. Oren, *Six Days of War,* 100.

ONE The Two Options

1. Moshe Dayan, *Story of My Life* (London: Weidenfeld and Nicolson, 1976), 284.

2. *Davar,* 6 June 1967.

3. Eshkol's message to President Johnson, delivered in Barbour, Tel Aviv, 5 June 1967, *FRUS* 19: 302–3; Prime Minister Eshkol's Note to Premier Kosygin, 5 June 1967, *Israel's Foreign Relations,* 2: 780. A similar statement was included in Eshkol's radio address earlier that morning. See Broadcast to the Nation by Prime Minister Eshkol, 5 June 1967, ibid., 2: 778–79.

4. Sasson, *Without a Roundtable,* 52–54. For a fuller discussion of the refugees' delegation at the Lausanne Conference see Simha Flapan, *The Birth of Israel: Myths and Realities* (London: Croom Helm, 1987), 218–31.

5. In addition to primary records, the discussion of the Kimche-Bavly episode is based on the following complementary sources: Dan Bavly, *Halomot ve-Hizdamnuyot she-Huhmetsu 1967–1973* [Dreams and missed opportunities, 1967–1973] (Jerusalem: Carmel, 2002), 119–46; Dan Bavly, "An Experiment in Co-Existence," in Dan Bavly and David Farhi, *Israel and the Palestinians* (London: Anglo-Israel Association, Pamphlet no. 29, 1971), 4; David Kimche, *The Last Option: After Nasser, Arafat, and Saddam Hussein; The Quest for Peace in the Middle East* (London: Weidenfeld and Nicolson, 1991), 241–43; David Kimche, and Dan Bawly [sic], *The Sandstorm* (London: Secker and Warburg, 1968), 221–23, 311; Raja Shehadeh, *Strangers in the House* (South Royalton: Steerforth, 2002), 48–50; Gazit, *Carrot and the Stick,* 122–23; Dan Bavly, lecture delivered at the Truman Institute, Hebrew University of Jerusalem, 27 October 1999; interviews with David Kimche, 2 May 2004, Tel Aviv, and 4 October 1996, Ramat ha-Sharon, and with Dan Bavly, 29 August 1995, Tel Aviv.

6. Shehadeh's date is incorrect. He was referring to UN General Assembly Resolution 194, which was adopted on 11 December 1948 (see introduction).

7. Shehadeh's paper, untitled and undated, private papers, Israel (PPI). A summary of the document's main points, offered by Bavly—based on his recollection and contemporary notes (Bavly, *Dreams and Missed Opportunities,* 131, 133, n. 2)—is inaccurate.

8. David Kimche to Head of Military Intelligence, Summary of contacts with the political leadership in the West Bank, 13 June 1967, Moshe Sasson papers (MSP).

9. Shehadeh's paper, *Asma' al-Lajnah al-Tahdiriyyah* (The names of the Preparatory Committee), PPI.

10. Lieutenant General Tsur, a former chief of staff, was in fact Dayan's deputy. Under Israeli law, only a member of Knesset (MK) can serve as deputy minister. Tsur was thus given the title of assistant defense minister.

11. Interview with Hamdi Kan'an, *Al-Nahar* (Beirut), 1 December 1968; statement published by Hamdi Kan'an, *Al-Quds* (Jerusalem), 2 January 1969. See also interview with Kan'an, *Ma'ariv* (Tel Aviv), 13 June 1968. Defense Minister Dayan commented in the Knesset on Kan'an's disclosure: "I have never heard about this"; *Divrei ha-Knesset* [The Knesset proceedings], 22 January 1969, 1243.

12. Kimche to Head of Military Intelligence, Summary of contacts with the political leadership in the West Bank, 13 June 1967, MSP.

13. Kimche and Bawly [Bavly], *Sandstorm*, 222. The book does not give a reference for the *Economist* quotation.

14. Shlomo Hillel to Foreign Minister, 14 June 1967, FM/4088/10, ISA.

15. Ibid.

16. David Kimche, "The Political Leadership in the West Bank," 18 June 1967 [henceforth Political Leadership], MSP, rpt. in Bavly, *Dreams and Missed Opportunities,* appendix 2, 252–62.

17. Memorandum by Lt. Col. Yitzhak Oron, Lt. Col. Alouph Hareven, Capt. Dan Bavly, Lt. David Kimche: A Proposal for a Settlement of the Palestinian Problem, 14 June 1967, MSP, rpt. in Bavly, *Dreams and Missed Opportunities,* 137, appendix 1, 247–51. Apparently Kimche and Bavly gave the impression of having contacts with "many important leaders." See Hillel to Foreign Minister, 14 June 1967, FM/4088/10, ISA.

18. Kimche, Political Leadership. For some reason Kimche's final report omits two Palestinians mentioned in his first: Kimche to Head of Military Intelligence, Survey of the attitude of the West bank's political leadership—current report no. 1, 12 June 1967, MSP.

19. Memorandum by Oron et al., A proposal for a settlement of the Palestinian problem, 14 June 1967, MSP; Kimche to Head of Military Intelligence, 12 June 1967, MSP. See also Kimche to Head of Military Intelligence, 13 June 1967, MSP.

20. Rafi Sutton, *Ha-Hahmatsot ha-Gdolot: Hizdamnuyot Mediniyot ve-Yozmot le-Shalom she-Yisrael Hehmitsah* [The great missed opportunities: Political opportunities and peace initiatives that Israel missed] (Or Yehudah: Sifriyat Ma'ariv, 1994), 31–42; interview with Rafi Sutton, 15 October 1996, Jerusalem. For the Jericho Congress see Avi Shlaim, *Collusion across the Jordan: King Abdullah, the Zionist Movement, and the Partition of Palestine* (Oxford: Clarendon, 1988), 359–60; Shaul Mishal, *The PLO under 'Arafat* (New Haven: Yale University Press, 1986), 26–27, n. 6.

21. Barbour, Tel Aviv, 23 June 1967, POL 2 West Bank, RG84, Post Files: American Consulate-General, 1967, USNA. Barbour relied on what he heard from Harry

Ellis, a *Christian Science Monitor* correspondent, who had traveled unaccompanied in the West Bank 19–21 June and interviewed many notables. See also Ellis, "West Bank Seen Ready for Israel Accord," *Christian Science Monitor,* 24 June 1967.

22. Burns, Amman, 14 June 1967, POL 2 General—Jordan, RG84, Post Files: American Consulate-General, 1967, USNA; Burns, Amman, 18 June 1967, POL 27 ARAB-ISR, RG59, Central Files 1967–69, USNA.

23. Adams, Amman, to FO, 15 June 1967, FCO/17/212, UKNA. See also Adams, Amman, to FO, 21 June 1967, FCO/17/93, UKNA.

24. Pullar, Jerusalem, to FO, 16 June 1967, FCO/17/251, UKNA.

25. Wilson, Jerusalem, 17 June 1967 (telegram 1223), POL 27 ARAB-ISR, RG59, Central Files 1967–69, USNA. Wilson qualified his report by pointing out that the sampling of opinion was still "not very great."

26. Na'im Fourati [Gil'adi], "When Eshkol Proposed a Palestine Mini-State," *Ghorbah* (New York), 26 August 1987. According to Kimche's reports, Nimr argued for an autonomous West Bank as part of the State of Israel, and a Lebanese-style government system which would provide an agreed ratio of seats in government—for example, one Arab seat for every three Jewish seats.

27. *Haaretz* (Tel Aviv), 18 June 1967.

28. *Davar,* 18 June 1967; *Haaretz,* 21 June 1967; Kimche, Political Leadership. See also Moshe Ma'oz, *Palestinian Leadership on the West Bank* (London: Frank Cass, 1984), 95–96; Barbour, Tel Aviv, 24 June 1967, POL 27 ARAB-ISR, RG59 Central Files 1967–69, USNA.

29. Wilson, Jerusalem, 17 June 1967 (telegram 1222), POL 27 ARAB-ISR, RG59 Central Files 1967–69, USNA.

30. Raphael Levi to Director General's office, Foreign Ministry (FM), 12 June 1967, FM/4097/8, ISA. See also interview with Khatib, *Haaretz,* 19 June 1967.

31. Barbour, Tel Aviv, 13 June 1967, POL 27 ARAB-ISR, RG59 Central Files 1967–69, USNA. The official's name is not revealed. In his interview with *Haaretz,* 19 June 1967, Khatib rejected the idea of an independent Palestinian state and a separate peace between the West Bank Arabs and Israel: "We do not want to be considered traitors or quislings like the Arabs of the Galilee," he said.

32. Lt. Col. Raphael Efrat to C.G. of the Central Command, 15 June 1967, 67-117/1970, IDFA; Ruvik Rosenthal, "The First Hundred Days," *Panim,* 39 (June 2007), 43; interview with Uzi Narkiss, 10 December 1996, by telephone; interview with Raphael Vardi; Michael Shashar, *Milhemet ha-Yom ha-Shvi'i: Yoman ha-Mimshal ha-Tsva'i bi-Yehudah ve-Shomron* (Yuni–Detsember 1967) [The Seventh Day War: The diary of the Military Government in Judea and Samaria (June–December 1967)] (Tel Aviv: Sifriyat Po'alim, 1997), 30. See also Uzi Narkiss, *Soldier of Jerusalem* (London: Vallentine Mitchell, 1998), 218.

33. Memorandum by David Farhi, A visit to Salim al-Sharif, 31 July 1967, David Farhi papers (DFP); Kimche, Political Leadership; interview with Khatib, *Haaretz,* 19 June 1967.

34. David Farhi, "The West Bank: 1948–1971; Society and Politics in Judea and Samaria," *New Middle East,* November 1971, 35; Atallah Mansour, *Waiting for the Dawn* (London: Secker and Warburg, 1975), 106; Robert Slater, *Warrior Statesman: The Life of Moshe Dayan* (London: Robson, 1992), 297–98. Mansour argues that the order came from Eshkol, whereas Slater claims that this was Dayan's decision. See also Gazit, *Carrot and the Stick,* 133.

35. Wilson, Jerusalem, 17 June 1967 (telegram 1222), POL 27 ARAB-ISR, RG59, Central Files 1967–69, USNA; Pullar, Jerusalem, to FO, 22 June 1967, FCO/17/251, UKNA. Quotation from the latter.

36. Sari Nusseibeh, *Once upon a Country: A Palestinian Life* (London: Halban, 2007), 102–3. The author, a professor of philosophy and president of Al-Quds University in Jerusalem, is Anwar Nuseibeh's son. On All-Palestine Government see Avi Shlaim, "The Rise and Fall of the All-Palestine Government in Gaza," *Journal of Palestine Studies* 20, no. 1 (1990), 37–53.

37. Pullar, Jerusalem, to FO, 16 June 1967, FCO/17/251, UKNA.

38. The West Bank—prevailing moods (as of 24 June 67), 25 June 1967 (GSS report), DFP.

39. Kimche, Political Leadership; Barbour, Tel Aviv, 23 June 1967, POL 2 West Bank, RG84, Post Files: American Consulate-General, 1967, USNA.

40. P. J. Vatikiotis to David Farhi (personal letter), 30 July 1967, DFP.

41. Interview with Shmuel Albeq, 1 August 1997, Ramat ha-Sharon.

42. The account of the meeting at Nuseibeh's is based on Abdullah Schleifer, *The Fall of Jerusalem* (New York: Monthly Review Press, 1972), 213–14; Chaim Herzog, *Living History: A Memoir* (London: Weidenfeld and Nicolson, 1997), 177; Chaim Herzog, lecture delivered at the Dayan Center, Tel Aviv University, 26 March 1986; "A Bridge over an Abyss" (symposium), *Musaf Haaretz,* 6 February 1970; interview with Muhammad Nuseibeh (Anwar's younger brother, who was present at the meeting), 24 April 2004, Jerusalem. It should be noted that Herzog says in his autobiography that the meeting took place some time after the Khartoum Summit, that is, in September. This is clearly wrong even according to Herzog himself, as he mentions further the imminent removal of the barriers separating the two parts of Jerusalem: the barriers were removed on 29 June.

43. Schleifer, *Fall of Jerusalem,* 213–14.

44. David Kimche, "What Kind of a Nation? The Palestinian Dilemma," *New Middle East,* 1 October 1968, 30.

45. The idea of a binational state was broached at the meeting by City Councilor Dr. Rashid Nashashibi. See Hall, Jerusalem, 3 July 1967, POL 27 ARAB-ISR, RG59, Central Files 1967–69, USNA.

46. *Evening Standard* (London), 20 June 1967. See also Jon Kimche, *Palestine or Israel: The Untold Story of Why We Failed, 1917–1923, 1967–1973* (London: Secker and Warburg, 1973), 259–60.

47. Ya'acov Herzog's diary, 20 June 1967, A/4511/3, ISA.

48. Memorandum of conversation: Undersecretary of State Eugene Rostow and Counsellor Yuri Tcherniakov, USSR Embassy, 20 June 1967, *FRUS* 19: 522–24 (the Soviet diplomat told Rostow that he was not aware of the Palestinian-Israeli contacts); memorandum of conversation: Undersecretary of State Rostow et al. and Sir Patrick Dean, UK Ambassador, et al., 23 June 1967, *FRUS* 19: 562–63; Dean, Washington, to FO, 23 June 1967, FCO/17/503, UKNA.

49. Middle East Policy: Notes on relations with Israel and some Arab States in the short-medium term, undated (probably 21 June 1967), FCO/17/503, UKNA. The British paper recommended against a Palestinian state.

50. Memorandum from Acting Secretary of State Katzenbach to President Johnson, 27 June 1967, *FRUS* 19: 577–80. This memorandum, too, warned against the dangers involved in creating a Palestinian state.

51. Moshe Zak, *Hussein 'Oseh Shalom* [Hussein makes peace] (Ramat Gan: Bar Ilan University Press, 1996), 151, 171, n. 11; Prime Minister Sa'd Jum'ah's message to the people of the West Bank, 21 June 1967, *PAD 1967* (Beirut, 1969), 406.

52. Eliyahu Sasson to Prime Minister, 26 June 1967, A/7921/1, ISA.

53. Haim Hanegbi, "Peled, His Mouth and Heart," *Ma'ariv,* 7 April 1995. For Israeli censorship of Palestinian mail see, for example, Maj. Eliyahu Meron to chief of General Staff's office, [6] July 1967, 66–117/1970, IDFA; Michael Shashar's diary, 25 June 1969. Foreign diplomats in Jerusalem received numerous complaints from West Bankers regarding Israel's consistent postal censorship. See, for example, Campbell, Jerusalem, 7 December 1967, PO, RG84, Post Files: American Consulate-General, 1967, USNA. Nonetheless, "trusted" Israeli academics were given access to detained Palestinian mail for research purposes. See Rivkah Yadlin, *Attitudes and Viewpoints among the [West] Bank Arabs* (Jerusalem: Hebrew University, 1973), a 171-page Hebrew pamphlet, marked "Internal," based on 3,584 personal letters sent during 1970–71.

54. Lt. Col. Menachem Arkin to Commander of Brigade No. 5, 24 June 1967, 66–117/1970, IDFA. The report was forwarded to the chief of General Staff's office.

55. The West Bank—prevailing moods (as of 24 June 67), 25 June 1967, DFP; Hadow, Tel Aviv, to FO, 23 June 1967, FCO/17/93, UKNA.

56. Farhi to General Herzog, 24 June 1967, DFP. Farhi's source was Hilarion Capucci, the Greek Catholic bishop in Jerusalem, who, in the words of another Israeli document, "has been very active since we have entered the city and has made an effort to get close to us" (A summary [report] on the Jerusalem District, 19 June 1967, DFP). In 1974 Capucci was arrested and jailed for smuggling arms for the PLO from Lebanon to Israel. 'Aziz Shehadeh (who, incidentally, was Capucci's defense attorney) also told the Israelis that Khatib had been advising Palestinian notables not to negotiate with Israel. Kimche, Political Leadership.

57. Farhi to Chaim Herzog, 24 June 1967, DFP.

58. Evan M. Wilson, *Jerusalem, Key to Peace* (Washington, D.C.: Middle East Institute, 1970), 116.

59. Shashar, *Seventh Day War,* 161.

60. Schleifer, *Fall of Jerusalem*, 215.

61. The message was delivered by Gen. Odd Bull, the Norwegian commander of the Jerusalem-based UN Truce Supervisory Organization (UNTSO); through the American embassy in Tel Aviv; and by the Israeli representative to the Jordan-Israel Mixed Armistice Commission to his Jordanian opposite number. "Message from Prime Minister Eshkol to King Hussein, 5 June 1967," *Israel's Foreign Relations*, 2: 779; Yitzhak Rabin, *The Rabin Memoirs*, expanded ed. (Berkeley: University of California Press, 1996), 104–5; Oren, *Six Days of War*, 184, 186. For Hussein's reaction see Hussein de Jordanie, *Ma "guerre" avec Israël* (Paris: Albin Michel, 1968), 78–79.

62. Yitzhak Rabin, "Analogies as Regards the Present and the Future" [in Hebrew], *Ot* (Tel Aviv), 3 June 1971. See also Haber, *Today War Will Break Out*, 228.

63. Haber, *Today War Will Break Out*, 231; *Levi Eshkol: Rosh ha-Memshalah ha-Shlishi: Mivhar Te'udot mi-Pirkei Hayav (1895–1969)* [Levi Eshkol: The third prime minister: Selected documents from his lifetime, 1895–1969] (Jerusalem, 2002), 558.

64. Eshkol's comments in minutes, KFASC, 7 June 1967, A/8161/7, ISA. On 8 June he said at a party forum: "Until this very day I have feared to utter this word: *liberating* the West Bank completely." Remarks at a meeting of Mapai's Secretariat, 8 June 1967, *Levi Eshkol: Selected Documents*, 562–69 (quotation from 565).

65. Cabinet minutes, 11 June 1967, A/8164/6, ISA.

66. Morris, *1948*, 317–18.

67. Letter to the editor by Yehudith Shahar, a pilot's wife, *Haaretz*, 21 June 2004.

68. Barbour, Tel Aviv, 13 June 1967, POL 27 ARAB-ISR, RG59, Central Files 1967–69, USNA.

69. Remarks at a meeting of Mapai's Secretariat, 8 June 1967, *Levi Eshkol: Selected Documents*, 562–69 (quotation from 569).

70. Eshkol's comments in minutes, meeting of the Alignment's Political Committee, 7 July 1967, PPI.

71. Another example of Eshkol's bride-and-dowry metaphor: "Along with a dowry of real estate and perhaps water . . . —we also are getting a 'bride'—about one million and a quarter non-Jews—this is a heavy bride." Minutes, meeting of Mapai's Secretariat, 23 June 1967, 2-24-1967-90, Israeli Labor Party Archive, Beit Berl (ILPA).

72. A/6717, 13 June 1967, UNPR.

73. For the establishment of the committee see *FRUS* 19: 287–92, 346–48.

74. See Yigal Allon, oral history interview, third meeting (21 May 1979), A/5001/19, ISA.

75. *Davar*, 7 November 1956; Shlaim, *Iron Wall*, 179–82.

76. Summary of discussions at a meeting on 8.6.67 regarding proposals for "a political solution," 8 June 1967, FM/4097/3, ISA; interview with Yitzhak Navon, *Davar*, 7 March 1975.

77. Summary of Proposals, undated, FM/4088/10, ISA.

78. Gazit, *Trapped Fools*, 141–42. Almost six months before the war, Gazit broached the contingency that Israel might occupy the West Bank and later establish

a Palestinian state to be run by local collaborators. See his comments in a summary of discussion on Jordan which took place on 19 December 1966, dated 22 December 1966; see also his revised paper "Israel's Policy towards Jordan," undated (probably 23 December 1966), both in FM/4094/10, ISA.

79. Gazit, *Trapped Fools*, 142–43. In later years Ne'eman became the leader of *Ha-Tehiyah*, an extreme right-wing party, which advocated the annexation of the occupied territories to Israel.

80. Amnon Barzilai, "A Brief History of the Missed Opportunity," *Haaretz* (English edition), 5 June 2002. See also Chaim Herzog, "The Palestinians: Policy and Tactics," *Haaretz*, 21 June 1974.

81. Ya'acov Herzog's diary, 12 June 1967, A/4511/3, ISA.

82. Ibid.; Moshe Raviv, *Israel at Fifty: Five Decades of Struggle for Peace; A Diplomat's Narrative* (London: Weidenfeld and Nicolson, 1988), 116.

83. Shlomo Hillel to Foreign Minister et al., 12 June 1967, FM/4088/10, ISA.

84. Gen. Ze'evi to Chief of Staff et al., 15 June 1967, 67-117/1970, IDFA; Gazit, *Carrot and the Stick*, 123. Like Ne'eman, Ze'evi became the leader of an ultraextreme right-wing party, Moledet, which called for "transfer" of the Arab population out of *Eretz Yisrael*. In October 2001, at the height of Al-Aqsa Intifadah, and while serving as a cabinet minister in Ariel Sharon's government, he was assassinated by Palestinians.

85. See, for example, Gazit, *Trapped Fools*, 142, 143.

86. Moshe Dayan, *Avnei Derekh: Otobiyographyah* [Milestones: An autobiography] (Jerusalem: 'Edanim, 1976), 488.

87. Chaim Herzog, lecture delivered at the Dayan Center, Tel Aviv University, 26 March 1986; Herzog, *Living History*, 173–74. The misinterpretation of Khatib's proposal is immaterial while discussing the Israeli decision-making process because the misinterpreted idea was the one put forward before the policy makers. The English version of Herzog's autobiography refers to "an autonomous *Jordanian* area under Israeli sovereignty," while in the Hebrew version—*Derekh Hayim: Sipuro shel Lohem, Diplomat ve-Nasi* [A way of life: The story of a warrior, diplomat, and president] (Tel Aviv: Yediot Ahronot—Sifrei Hemed, 1997), 221—it is an *"Arab* autonomy" (emphases added).

88. Lt. Col. Efrat to Head of the General Staff Branch's aide de camp, 16 June 1967, 67-117/1970, IDFA; Gazit, *Carrot and the Stick*, 124.

89. *Washington Post*, 12 June 1967, citing Dayan's interviews on NBC's *Meet the Press; New York Times*, 12 June 1967, citing Dayan's interview's on CBS's *Face the Nation*; both interviews, prerecorded, were aired on 11 June. Quotation from the former.

90. See Gazit, *Carrot and the Stick*, 127; Arie Brown, *Hotam Ishi: Moshe Dayan be-Milhemet Sheshet ha-Yamim ve-Ahareha* [Personal imprint: Moshe Dayan during the Six Day War and afterward] (Tel Aviv: Yediot Ahronot, 1997), 99, 113, 150; "Ben-Gurion Diary, May–June 1967," *Israel Studies* 4, no. 2 (1999), 216 (entry for 11 June 1967); *Washington Post*, 16 June 1967. According to Gazit and Brown, in a discussion on 12 June, Dayan also mentioned the hypothetical possibility of returning the West Bank to

Jordan on condition that King Hussein agree to demilitarize the territory and to resettle the Gaza 1948 refugees in the East Bank.

91. Interview with Narkiss, quoted in Slater, *Warrior Statesman,* 298.

92. Yossi Beilin, *Mehiro shel Ihud: Mifleget ha-ʿAvodah ʿad Milhemet Yom ha-Kipurim* [The price of unity: The Labor Party up to the Yom Kippur War] (Ramat Gan: Revivim, 1985), 43; Pedatzur, *Triumph of Bewilderment,* 80.

93. Quoted in Amnon Kapeliouk, *Israël: La Fin des mythes* (Paris: Albin Michel, 1975), 282, n. 80; *Maʿariv,* 13 June 1967.

94. Sutton, *Great Missed Opportunities,* 39.

95. "To think too much of the [1949] Armistice Agreements would be like arguing that the peace in 1945 should have been based on the Treaty of Versailles," the British ambassador in Tel Aviv commented in a dispatch to London, and his foreign secretary agreed that indeed it would be unrealistic. Hadow, Tel Aviv, to FO, 8 June 1967, FCO/47/159, UKNA; SOSFA [Foreign Secretary] to Tel Aviv, 9 June 1967, FCO/47/160, UKNA.

96. *Levi Eshkol: Selected Documents,* 557, and Remarks at a meeting of Mapai's Secretariat, 8 June 1967, 562–69; Yossi Goldstein, *Eshkol: Biyographyah* [Eshkol: A biography] (Jerusalem: Keter, 2003), 573–74; Meir Avidan, "19 June 1967, the Government of Israel Hereby Resolves," part 1, *Davar,* 2 June 1987; *Knesset Proceedings,* 12 June 1967, 2330 (for official English translation see *Israel's Foreign Relations* 2: 794–801).

97. Gideon Rafael, *Destination Peace: Three Decades of Israeli Foreign Policy; A Personal Memoir* (London: Weidenfeld and Nicolson, 1981), 169–71.

98. *Levi Eshkol: Selected Documents,* 573–74; Dayan, *Milestones,* 490–91; Pedatzur, *Triumph of Bewilderment,* 44–47.

99. The discussion of the cabinet's deliberations is based on cabinet minutes, 18 June 1967 (morning), A/8164/6; 18 June 1967 (afternoon), A/8164/7; 19 June 1967 (morning and afternoon), A/8164/8; 19 June 1967 (3 p.m.), A/8164/9, all in ISA.

100. Cabinet Resolution 563, 19 June 1967, article 1(C), Israel Cabinet Secretariat, Jerusalem (ICS).

101. Begin's remark in cabinet on 10 September 1967; Pedatzur, *Triumph of Bewilderment,* 74.

102. Minutes, meeting of the Alignment's Political Committee, 8 June 1967, PPI.

103. See Brown, *Personal Imprint,* 113; "Ben-Gurion Diary, May–June 1967," 216 (entry for 11 June 1967).

104. Resolution 563, article 1(A).

105. Avidan, "19 June 1967," part 1, *Davar,* 2 June 1987.

106. Resolution 563, article 1(D) (2).

107. Rusk, New York, 22 June 1967, *FRUS* 19: 532–34.

108. Resolution 563, articles 1(A) and 1(B).

109. Cabinet Minutes, June 19, 1967 (3 p.m.).

110. In the course of the discussion Eshkol commented that some ministers ignored the fact that Israel was not free to do whatever it wished, and that it was necessary

to take into account the viewpoints of other countries, particularly the United States. "We are playing chess with ourselves," he warned his cabinet colleagues.

111. Rabin's comments in minutes, KFASC, 29 May 1968, A/8161/12, ISA. In his autobiography, which was first published in 1979, Rabin says that he learned "from American sources" about the 19 June resolution after he had taken up his ambassadorial post. Rabin, *Rabin Memoirs*, 135. It seems more likely, however, that Rabin's contemporary version is the correct one.

112. Abba Eban, *An Autobiography* (London: Weidenfeld and Nicolson, 1978), 436.

113. The long list includes, among others, Pedatzur, *Triumph of Bewilderment*, 57; Segev, *1967*, 500–501 (with an added caveat absent from the Hebrew original: "There is no confirmation of this account, however"); Gorenberg, *Accidental Empire*, 56; David A. Korn, *Stalemate: The War of Attrition and Great Power Diplomacy in the Middle East, 1967–1970* (Boulder, Colo.: Westview, 1992), 14–15; Benny Morris, *Righteous Victims: A History of the Zionist-Arab Conflict, 1881–1999* (London: John Murray, 2000), 330.

114. Rusk, New York, 22 June 1967, FRUS 19: 532–34. Avi Shlaim was the first to unearth the American record of the Rusk-Eban meeting and to call into question the accuracy of Eban's version. See Shlaim, *Iron Wall*, 253–54.

115. Eban to Eshkol, 22 June 1967, A/7938/10, ISA. Relying on interviews with former US and Israeli diplomats, David Korn says that Eban interpreted the Americans' silence as reflecting dumbfounded admiration for Israel's generosity. Korn, *Stalemate*, 14, 288, n. 13.

116. Shlaim, *Iron Wall*, 254.

117. Interview with Salah Bassiouny, 25 February 1997, for the BBC program *The Fifty Years War: Israel and the Arabs,* GB 165-0346, Middle East Centre Archive, St Antony's College, Oxford (MECA).

118. Interview with Isma'il Fahmi, conducted by Professor Avi Shlaim, 17 September 1982, Cairo.

119. Eban's comments in minutes, The meeting with Lt. Gen. Y. Rabin, 24 May 1968, A/7938/11, ISA.

120. Eban's comments in minutes, KFASC, 29 May 1968, A/8161/12, ISA. A day after the Rusk-Eban discussion on 21 June 1967, Arthur Goldberg, the US ambassador to the United Nations who had been present at the meeting, merely told Soviet Foreign Minister Andrei Gromyko, in passing, that "based on earlier conversation I had had with Eban," he did not think that Israel had "any particular interest in trying to retain Egyptian or Syrian territory." Goldberg, New York, 22 June 1967, FRUS 19: 535–36.

121. Abba Eban, *Personal Witness: Israel through My Eyes* (London: Jonathan Cape, 1993), 446.

122. For elaborate discussion of the 19 June resolution affair see Avi Raz, "The Generous Peace Offer That Was Never Offered: The Israeli Cabinet Resolution of 19 June 1967," *Diplomatic History* 37, no. 1 (January 2013, forthcoming).

123. Ya'acov Herzog's diary, 12 June 1967, A/4511/3, ISA. See also ibid., 22 June 1967; Dayan, *Milestones,* 493; Pedatzur, *Triumph of Bewilderment,* 31–32.

124. Barzilai, "Brief History." Abu Jildah (Arabic for "a man with an eye patch") was the sobriquet of a notorious Palestinian highwayman in the 1930s. Begin was the leader of the prestate underground Irgun, considered by the British as well as by the mainstream Jewish leadership to be a terrorist organization.

125. Avi'ad Yafeh to Defense Minister et al., 20 June 1967, A/7921/2, ISA; Goldstein, *Eshkol,* 585–86.

126. Dayan, *Milestones,* 493.

127. Rabin's comments in minutes, General Staff session, 19 June 1967, 206-117/1970, IDFA; Gazit, *Carrot and the Stick,* 76–77. See also Brown, *Personal Imprint,* 150–51; Herzog, *Living History,* 176.

128. Ya'acov Herzog to Director General of the Foreign Ministry, 26 June 1967, A/7921/2, ISA; memorandum: meeting of the Committee of Heads of the [intelligence] Services [*Varash*], 30 June 1967, MSP; Ya'acov Herzog's diary, 25 June 1967, A/4511/3, ISA. It is not clear when exactly the decision to establish the Committee of Four was taken. An untitled and unsigned document of 18 June (FM/4097/8, ISA) suggests that the decision had already been made on that date, if not earlier. Foreign Minister Eban wrote to Prime Minister Eshkol on 16 June, requesting that his men be allowed to take part in the contacts with Palestinian leaders; "It has been settled orally," scribbled the director general of the Foreign Ministry on the letter's copy on 19 June. Abba Eban to the Prime Minister, 16 June 1967, FM/4088/10, ISA.

129. It appears that the team was formally dissolved only on 30 July. See Gazit, *Carrot and the Stick,* 77–78.

130. Philip Gillon, *Israelis and Palestinians Co-Existence Or . . . : The Credo of Elie Eliachar* (London: Rex Collings, 1978), 35, 118–19. Facsimile of Eshkol's letter, in Hebrew, appears between 110 and 111.

131. Memorandum, meeting of the Committee of Heads of the Services, 30 June 1967, MSP.

132. See Ya'acov Herzog's diary, 16 July 1967, A/4511/3, ISA.

133. See Eban's comments in minutes, KFASC, 15 June 1967, A/8161/7, ISA; Ministers Hayyim Moshe Shapira and Menachem Begin's comments in cabinet minutes, 19 June 1967 (morning and afternoon), A/8164/8, ISA.

134. Middle East Policy: Notes on relations with Israel and some Arab States in the short-medium term, undated (apparently 21 June 1967), FCO/17/503, UKNA; Oren, *Six Days of War,* 242–44; Haber, *Today War Will Break Out,* 242–43, 268; Goldstein, *Eshkol,* 571 (the date indicated here as 6 June). Based on a report from a British statesman who had talked with Hussein's brother and concluded that there had been a good chance for a peace treaty with Jordan, the Israeli ambassador in London recommended agreeing to ceasefire on condition that Hussein would immediately enter into peace negotiations. Aharon Remez, London, to Foreign Minister et al., 7 June 1967, A/7920/4, ISA.

135. *Levi Eshkol: Selected Documents,* 575.

136. Meeting with Charles, 2 July 1967, YHP. As noted, "Charles" was the Israeli code name for Hussein. See also Ya'acov Herzog's diary, 25, 26, 27 June, 1, 2, 3 July 1967, A/4511/3, ISA.

137. In his diary, Herzog recorded a message from Harold Wilson, the British prime minister, suggesting a contact with Hussein. Ya'acov Herzog's diary, 15 June 1967, A/4511/3, ISA.

138. See introduction.

139. Meeting with Charles, 2 July 1967, YHP. On the Hussein-Herzog meeting see also Shlaim, *Lion of Jordan*, 259–63.

140. Meeting with Charles, 2 July 1967, YHP.

141. See Dean, Washington, to FO, 29 June 1967 (telegram 2209), PREM/13/1622, UKNA; Memorandum from Acting Secretary of State Katzenbach to President Johnson, 27 June 1967, *FRUS* 19: 577–80. Quotation is from the memorandum.

142. See Defense Minister Moshe Dayan's remarks at the General Commanding Staff meeting, 29 June 1967, 24-45/2008, IDFA.

TWO The Jerusalem Syndrome

1. Cabinet minutes, 11 June 1967, A/8164/6, ISA.

2. *Knesset Proceedings,* 27 June 1967, 2420–29, 2432–33; Meron Benvenisti, *Jerusalem: The Torn City* (Jerusalem: Isratypeset, 1976), 108–17; Uzi Benziman, *Yerushalayim: 'Ir le-lo Homah* [Jerusalem: A city without a wall] (Jerusalem: Schocken, 1973), 47–60; Usameh Halabi, *Al-Quds: Athar "Damm al-Quds ila Isra'il" 'ala Huquq wa-wad' al-Mawatin al-'Arab* [Jerusalem: The effects of "the annexation of Jerusalem by Israel" on the rights and condition of the Arab residents], 2nd ed. (Jerusalem: PASSIA, 1994), 7–9; Bernard Wasserstein, *Divided Jerusalem: The Struggle for the Holy City* (London: Profile, 2001), 211–15.

3. Gazit, *Carrot and the Stick,* 199.

4. See Halabi, *Jerusalem,* 14–17.

5. *Knesset Proceedings,* 3 July 1967, 2453; cabinet quotation from Pedatzur, *Triumph of Bewilderment,* 195. Shapira made this statement in the cabinet on 10 September 1967. He had already alerted his colleagues about breaching international law in the first cabinet discussion of the annexation of Jerusalem. See his comments in cabinet minutes, 11 June 1967, A/8164/6, ISA.

6. See cabinet minutes, 25 June, A/8164/10; 26 and 27 June 1967, A/8164/11, all in ISA.

7. Comay, FM, to Israel's diplomatic missions, 26 June 1967, A/7920/8, ISA.

8. Lord Caradon, New York, to FO, 21 June 1967, FCO/17/251, UKNA.

9. The Israeli attitude toward united Jerusalem emerged, however, only after the capture of the Old City; Wasserstein, *Divided Jerusalem,* 208.

10. Quoted in Benvenisti, *Jerusalem,* 84. A day or two later, in Sinai, when his daughter—then unmarried—told Dayan how eager she was to visit the Arab part of

Jerusalem, he responded: "What's the hurry? You'll be able to visit it even with your children." Yaël Dayan, *My Father, His Daughter* (London: Weidenfeld and Nicolson, 1985), 185.

11. Remarks at a meeting of Mapai's Secretariat, 8 June 1967, *Levi Eshkol: Selected Documents,* 562–69.

12. Bitan, FM, to Harman, Washington, et al., 23 June 1967, A/7938/10, ISA.

13. Memorandum for the President (draft), enclosed with Sisco to the Secretary, 26 April 1968, POL 27 ARAB-ISR, RG59, Central Files 1967–69, USNA.

14. Quoted in Halabi, *Jerusalem,* 13.

15. A/RES/2253 (ES-V), 4 July 1967, UNPR.

16. A/6753, S/8052, 10 July 1967, UNPR. On 14 July the General Assembly deplored the failure of Israel to implement the 4 July resolution, and reiterated it. A/RES/2254 (ES-V), 14 July 1967, UNPR.

17. Benziman, *Jerusalem,* 274.

18. Quotation from the first petition (in Arabic, with 465 signatories), dated 29 June 1967, DFP. See also Brig. Gen. Vardi's comments in minutes, KFASC, 13 February 1969, A/8162/4, ISA; Shashar, *Seventh Day War,* 71 (entry for 3 July).

19. Brown, *Personal Imprint,* 174.

20. See, for example, FM to Israel's diplomatic missions, 20 August 1967, FM/4088/7, ISA.

21. Official record, 1423rd meeting of the Security Council, S/PV.1423, 7 May 1968, UNPR.

22. Resolution 181 (II). Future Government of Palestine, 29 November 1947, A/RES/181 (II) (A+B), UNPR.

23. See Michael Brecher, "Jerusalem: Israel's Political Decisions, 1947–1977," *Middle East Journal* 32, no. 1 (1978), 13–23. See also Michael Brecher, *Decisions in Israel's Foreign Policy* (London: Oxford University Press, 1974), 9–55.

24. Ma'oz, *Palestinian Leadership on the West Bank,* 8–9.

25. Pullar, Jerusalem, to Foreign Secretary, 22 June 1967, FCO/17/206, UKNA.

26. See, for example: Shehadeh's plan (chapter 1); Kimche, Political Leadership; The West Bank—prevailing moods (as of 24 June 67), 25 June 1967, DFP.

27. Ruhi al-Khatib, *The Judaization of Jerusalem* (Beirut: PLO Research Center), 7–8.

28. Benziman, *Jerusalem,* 64.

29. Hall, Jerusalem, 3 July 1967, POL 27 ARAB-ISR, RG59, Central Files 1967–69, USNA.

30. Mansour, *Waiting for the Dawn,* 104–5.

31. Wilson, *Jerusalem, Key to Peace,* 116. See also Wilson, Jerusalem, 12 July 1967, POL 17 Status of Jerusalem, RG84, Post Files: American Consulate-General, 1967, USNA.

32. Eshkol to Ya'acov Herzog et al., 4 July 1967, A/7921/2, ISA.

33. Sasson, *Without a Roundtable,* 92–93. Sasson claims that each team held a series of talks with Palestinian leaders and eventually submitted a report summarizing

them. However, Bar-Haim said (in an interview, 25 March 1998, Jerusalem) that only Sasson and he met Palestinians. Indeed, no records of talks allegedly conducted by Herzog and Kimche have been found. Moreover, the Sasson-Bar-Haim report was adopted by the committee and appended verbatim to its letter of recommendations to the prime minister. See also Barbour, Tel Aviv, 14 July 1967, POL 27 ARAB-ISR, RG59, Central Files 1967–69, USNA.

34. "Organizational Proposal—M. Sasson," undated, MSP.

35. Preliminary Outline of the [West] Bank's Political Profile, undated, enclosed with A. Schreiber, Research Department, to Moshe Sasson, 4 July 1967, MSP. Emphasis in the original.

36. The statistical figures and the summary of political affiliations given here, and the discussion below of the meetings between Sasson and Bar-Haim and the Palestinian personalities, are based on the following twenty-three memoranda of conversation, all in MSP (note that all early-June dates appearing in the memoranda are in error and should be July): Ibrahim Bakr and Kamal Nasir, Ramallah, 4 June 1967; 'Aziz Shehadeh, Ramallah, 4 June 1967; Hikmat al-Masri, Nablus, 5 June 1967; Qadri Tukman [sic; should be Touqan], Nablus, 5 June 1967; Walid al-Shak'ah, Nablus, 5 June 1967; Musa Nasir, Ramallah, 6 July 1967; Nadim Salim Zaru, Ramallah, 6 June 1967; 'Abd al-Jawad Saleh, Ramallah, 6 June 1967; 'Isa 'Aql, Ramallah, 6 July 1967; Yusuf al-Takruri, Hebron, 7 July 1967; Muhammad 'Ali al-Ja'bari, Hebron, 7 July 1967; Hajj Fatin Tahbub, Hebron, 7 July 1967; Rashad al-Khatib and Sidqi al-Ja'bari, Hebron, 7 July 1967; Anwar Nuseibeh, Jerusalem, 9 July 1967; Anwar al-Khatib, Jerusalem, 9 July 1967; Ruhi al-Khatib, Jerusalem, 10 July 1967; Antoun 'Atallah, Jerusalem, 10 July 1967; Daud Bandali al-'Isa, Jerusalem, 10 July 1967; Jalil Harb, Jerusalem, 10 July 1967; Ibrahim Abu al-Rish, Jericho, 12 July 1967; Rashad 'Ariqat, Jericho, 12 July 1967; Dajani, Musa al-'Alami's Farm (near Jericho), 12 July 1967; Salah 'Abdu, Jericho, 12 July 1967.

37. The Military Government learned independently that Khatib "and his men" succeeded in influencing the West Bank's leaders to refrain from taking a stand until King Hussein revealed his intentions. Memorandum by Farhi, 13 July 1967, DFP.

38. Duncan, Amman, 16 July 1967, POL 27-14 ARAB-ISR/SANDSTORM, RG59, Central Files 1967–69, USNA. See also Burns, Amman, 12 July 1967, POL 27 ARAB-ISR, RG59, Central Files 1967–69, USNA; Barbour, Tel Aviv, 14 July 1967, POL 27 ARAB-ISR, RG59, Central Files 1967–69, USNA.

39. Two days earlier, on 7 July, Nuseibeh met US Senator Birch Bayh, told him that he had been approached by the Israelis regarding the establishment of a Palestinian entity in the West Bank, and said this would be possible only if based on a compromise between the area inside the demarcation line of 4 June 1967 and the area proposed in the UN Partition Resolution. In addition, Jerusalem must be the Palestinian capital under some sharing with Israel, and other Arab states must give their consent. Wilson, Jerusalem, 8 July 1967, POL 27 ARAB-ISR, RG59, Central Files 1967–69, USNA. As we saw in the previous chapter, Professor P. J. Vatikiotis, who met Nuseibeh in Jerusalem around that time, recorded: "Anwar is in the opinion that there should be an

autonomous Palestinian entity, in some form of economic union with Israel." Vatikiotis to Farhi, 30 July 1967, DFP.

40. Binyamin Landau, "A Day with the Governor of Ramallah," *Ba-Mahaneh,* 25
July 1967. In the course of a meeting with the mayors of Ramallah and al-Bireh and their
councilors in August 1968, Defense Minister Dayan said: "Don't I know that you pray
seven times a day that we [Israelis] will finally leave this area?" Mayor Saleh interjected:
"Not seven times a day, but seventy-seven." Gazit, "Consolidation of Policy," 296, n. 1.

41. 'Abd al-Jawad Saleh, "The Battle of the Entity and the Alternative Leadership" [in Arabic], *Al-Katib al-Filastini* 2 (1978), 54–56. Quotation from 56.

42. Shehadeh told an American diplomat a few days later that he felt that the
Palestinians had become disenchanted with the unification of Jerusalem, which signified to the West Bankers that they would be cut off from the city and later returned to
the Hashemite rule. Memorandum by D. T. Morrison, Notes on recent conversations
in Ramallah, 14 July 1967, POL 2 West Bank, RG84, Post Files: American Consulate-
General, 1967, USNA.

43. Palestinian resentment and anger following the annexation of Jerusalem were
recorded also by foreign diplomats. See, for example, Hall, Jerusalem, 3 July 1967, POL 27
ARAB-ISR, RG59, Central Files 1967–69, USNA; Wilson, Jerusalem, 12 July 1967 (telegram 109), POL 27 ARAB-ISR, RG59, Central Files 1967–69, USNA; Wilson, Jerusalem,
12 July 1967 (telegram 110), POL 17 Status of Jerusalem, RG84, Post Files: American
Consulate-General, 1967, USNA.

44. See Barbour, Tel Aviv, 14 July 1967, POL 27 ARAB-ISR, RG59, Central Files
1967–69, USNA. Ambassador Barbour relied on Assistant Director General Moshe
Bitan of the Foreign Ministry.

45. Memorandum of conversation: Daud Bandali al-'Isa, Jerusalem, 10 July 1967,
MSP.

46. Memorandum by Daud al-'Isa (Hebrew translation), 16 July 1967, MSP.

47. Dale, Tel Aviv, 19 July 1967, REF ARAB, RG59, Central Files 1967–69, USNA.

48. Memorandum by Moshe Sasson and Shaul Bar-Haim, Summary of impressions from talks with [West] Bank's notables, 6–18.7.67, undated, A/7921/2, ISA.

49. See Burns, Amman, 3 August 1967, POL 27-14 ARAB-ISR/SANDSTORM,
RG59, Central Files 1967–69, USNA. The names of the Foreign Ministry officials are not
mentioned, nor the dates of the conversations Khatib had with them, but clearly he was
referring to Sasson and Bar-Haim.

50. Kimche, *Palestine or Israel,* 260–61. Jon Kimche does not name the letter's
author, describing him only as "the Prime Minister's most senior adviser." David
Kimche confirmed (interview, 2004) that he had written the letter to his older brother.

51. In an attempt to explain his sudden change of heart, Kimche speculated
thirty-seven years later (interview, 2004) that he had been influenced by the older and
more senior members of the committee.

52. The Special Inter-Ministerial Committee for Political Contacts in the Occupied Areas, to the Prime Minister, 20 July 1967, A/7921/2, ISA. Five appendixes were

enclosed with the letter; Appendix A was Sasson and Bar-Haim's memorandum entitled Summary of impressions from talks with [West] Bank's notables, 6–18.7.67 (see
above). Though the committee reached its conclusions unanimously, General Herzog
(Defense Minister Dayan's representative) had two reservations. In a separate letter to
the prime minister, he said that the Jordan River should be Israel's eastern border, and
while he agreed that West Bankers should not be allowed to conduct any real estate
transactions within the State of Israel, Israeli citizens should be permitted to buy
properties in the West Bank. Gen. Chaim Herzog to the Prime Minister, 21 July 1967,
A/7921/2, ISA.

53. The Committee of Four's letter to the prime minister and its five appendixes
were copied almost entirely from a five-page document composed by Sasson and Bar-
Haim on 18 July, entitled "The West Bank[,] the Jordanian Kingdom[,] the Gaza Strip:
A Proposal for Resolution and Policy," A/7921/2, ISA.

54. Dr. Herzog raised these evaluations in an advisory committee's meeting
headed by Premier Eshkol. Ya'acov Herzog's diary, 16 July 1967, A/4511/3, ISA.

55. Interviews with Moshe Sasson (1996) and David Kimche (2004); Gazit,
Carrot and the Stick, 126; Brown, *Personal Imprint,* 154.

56. The Committee of Heads of the Services to the Prime Minister, 27 July 1967,
A/7921/2, ISA.

57. Ya'acov Herzog's diary, 28 July 1967, A/4511/3, ISA.

58. See George C. Denney, Jr., to Secretary of State, Israeli leaders unified
behind their basic demands, 11 July 1967, POL 27 ARAB-ISR, RG59, Central Files
1967–69, USNA.

59. Harry C. McPherson, Jr., to President Johnson, 11 June 1967, *FRUS* 19: 433–36.

60. *Le Monde,* 8 July 1967. Six months later, in an evasive response to two parliamentary questions about this statement, Eshkol said that "the [*Le Monde*] report is untrue. But it is obvious that the matter is not that simple, because otherwise I would have
contented myself with the answer 'no' "; *Knesset Proceedings,* 23 January 1968, 769–70.

61. Minutes, meeting of the Alignment's Political Committee, 7 July 1967, PPI.

62. Pedatzur, *Triumph of Bewilderment,* 77. As we shall see, Eshkol declared his
willingness to negotiate with Hussein in a meeting with US ambassador Barbour.

63. SOSFA [Foreign Secretary] to Embassy in Washington, 24 July 1967,
PREM/13/1622, UKNA.

64. Martin Van Creveld, *Moshe Dayan* (London: Weidenfeld and Nicolson,
2004), 139; Brown, *Personal Imprint,* 114, 129–30.

65. Yehiel Admoni, *'Asor shel Shikul Da'at: Ha-Hityashvut me-'ever la-Kav
ha-Yarok 1967–1977* [A decade of discretion: The settlement beyond the Green Line,
1967–1977] (Tel Aviv: Makhon Yisrael Galili le-Heker Ko'ah ha-Magen—Yad Tabenkin;
Ha-Kibbutz ha-Me'uhad, 1992), 44.

66. Cabinet Resolution 754, 20 August 1967, ICS.

67. Yigal Allon, A proposal for a [cabinet] resolution, 26 July 1967 (with
enclosed explanatory notes dated 13 July), A/7921/2, ISA. See also Van Creveld, *Moshe*

Dayan, 139; Avidan, "19 June 1967," part 2, *Davar,* 5 June 1987; Gazit, *Carrot and the Stick,* 156–59.

68. See Yaʻacov Herzog's diary, 30 July 1967, A/4511/3, ISA.

69. Memorandum of conversation: Abba Eban et al. and Dean Rusk et al., 15 July 1967, *FRUS* 19: 664–67.

70. Memorandum of conversation: Abba Eban et al. and Eugene Rostow et al., 15 July 1967, POL 27–14 ARAB-ISR/SANDSTORM, RG59, Central Files 1967–69, USNA.

71. Memorandum of conversation: Avraham Harman et al. and Henry Owen et al., 24 July 1967, POL 27 ARAB-ISR, RG59, Central Files 1967–69, USNA.

72. Rusk to US Mission to the UN, 13 July 1967, *FRUS* 19: 648–49; Adams, Amman, to FO, 17 July 1967, PREM/13/1622, UKNA; Dean, Washington, to FO, 17 July 1967, PREM/13/1622, UKNA. The British, apprehensive about Hussein's démarche, voiced concern that both the king and the Americans "show[ed] signs of being dangerously and unnecessarily precipitate"; SOSFA [Foreign Secretary] to Embassy in Washington, 14 July 1967, PREM/13/1622, UKNA. The British ambassador in Amman later told his American colleague that Britain's prime interest in the Middle East was to get the Suez Canal reopened, and this took precedence over all attempts to achieve a peace settlement. Burns, Amman, 4 August 1967, POL 27–14 ARAB-ISR/SANDSTORM, RG59, Central Files 1967–69, USNA.

73. Col. Carmon's remarks in minutes, General Staff session, 17 July 1967, 206-117/1970, IDFA. Col. David Carmon was the assistant head of Israel's Military Intelligence.

74. Memorandum of a meeting: Sandstorm, 15 July 1967, *FRUS* 19: 668–69. See also chapter 5.

75. Bitan, FM, to Eban, New York, 14 July 1967, A/7938/10, ISA; Yaʻacov Herzog's diary, 14 July 1967, A/4511/3, ISA; Barbour, Tel Aviv, 14 July 1967, *FRUS* 19: 662–64.

76. Goldberg, New York, 14 July 1967, *FRUS* 19: 657–58. A day later Eban told Rusk that it was inconceivable that Jordan could return to Jerusalem. Memorandum of conversation: Abba Eban et al. and Dean Rusk et al., 15 July 1967, *FRUS* 19: 664–67.

77. Duncan, Amman, 17 and 19 July 1967, POL 27–14 ARAB-ISR/SANDSTORM, RG59, Central Files 1967–69, USNA; Harman, Washington, to ForMin Eban, 25 July 1967, A/7938/10, ISA.

78. Dean, Washington, to FO, 17 July 1967, PREM/13/1622, UKNA.

79. Telegram 534, London to Kuwait, 20 July 1967, FO/960/10, UKNA, citing telegram 887, Amman to FO, 20 July 1967.

80. Adams, Amman, to FO, 17 July 1967, PREM/13/1622, UKNA.

81. Bahjat Abu Gharbiyyah, *Min Mudhakkirat al-Munadil Bahjat Abu Gharbiyyah: Min al-Nakbah ila al-Intifadah, 1949–2000* [From the memoirs of the Fighter Bahjat Abu Gharbiyyah: From the *Nakbah* to the Intifadah, 1949–2000] (Beirut: Muʾassasah al-ʿArabiyyah lil-Dirasat wa-al-Nashr, 2004), 324–25.

82. Adams, Amman, to FO, 17 July 1967, PREM/13/1622, UKNA; Duncan, Amman, 22 July 1967, POL 27–14 ARAB-ISR/SANDSTORM, RG59, Central Files 1967–69, USNA.

83. Adams, Amman, to FO, 15 July 1967, PREM/13/1622, UKNA.

84. Dean, Washington, to FO, 21 July 1967, PREM/13/1622, UKNA.

85. Burns, Amman, 4 August 1967, POL 27-14 ARAB-ISR/SANDSTORM, RG59, Central Files 1967–69, USNA. Foreign Secretary George Brown's private reaction was blunt: "If British interests require the Israelis to yield on Jerusalem, I will bloody hell make them do it"; ibid.

86. CIA intelligence information cable, 14 July 1967, http://www.foia.cia.gov /docs/DOC_0000096584/DOC_0000096584.pdf (accessed on 15 May 2011).

87. Secretary of State Dean Rusk to Foreign Secretary George Brown, 25 July 1967, PREM/13/1622, UKNA.

88. Memorandum of a meeting: Sandstorm, 16 July 1967, FRUS 19: 671–72; Harman, Washington, to Bitan, FM, 20 July 1967, A/7938/10, ISA; SOSFA [Foreign Secretary] to Embassy in Washington, 24 July 1967, PREM/13/1622, UKNA; Memorandum of conversation: Walt Rostow and Ephraim Evron, 31 July 1967, POL 27-14 ARAB-ISR/ SANDSTORM, RG59, Central Files 1967–69, USNA; Rusk to Embassy in London, 19 July 1967, POL 27-14 ARAB-ISR/SANDSTORM, RG59, Central Files 1967–69, USNA; Dean, Washington, to FO, 21 July 1967, PREM/13/1622, UKNA; SOSFA [Foreign Secretary] to Embassy in Washington, 28 July 1967, PREM/13/1622, UKNA.

89. Barbour, Tel Aviv, 7 August 1967, POL 27-14 ARAB-ISR/SANDSTORM, RG59, Central Files 1967–69, USNA.

90. Memorandum of conversation: Abba Eban et al. and Dean Rusk et al., 15 July 1967, FRUS 19: 664–67.

91. SOSFA [Foreign Secretary] to Embassy in Washington, 24 July 1967, PREM/13/1622, UKNA.

92. Memorandum of conversation: Walt Rostow and Ephraim Evron, 18 July 1967, FRUS 19: 686–87.

93. Ya'acov Herzog's diary, 19 July 1967, A/4511/3, ISA; Ya'acov Herzog's diary, Special chapter on Charles, dictated on 3.11.67, YHP; Memorandum from Director of Central Intelligence Helms to President Johnson, 28 October 1968, FRUS 20: 579–80; Mossad representative in Washington to Mossad, 26 July 1967, A/7938/10, ISA. Quotation from Herzog's diary, 19 July. Surprisingly, there is no mention of the CIA involvement in this episode in the myriad contemporary State Department records. Hussein's biographer Nigel Ashton argues that Dayan initiated the CIA-brokered meeting in Switzerland. In Ashton's telling, Dayan contacted CIA's Angleton privately, saying that he was concerned that General Ariel Sharon, among others, wanted formally to annex the West Bank, thereby preventing future resolution of the Arab-Israeli conflict. Dayan thus proposed that a meeting with Hussein should be arranged without delay, to bring about a covert peace process which might provide a way out of the situation. The meeting, scheduled to take place in Geneva, was canceled at the last minute because the State Department at the highest level had got wind of the rendezvous and vetoed it. Ashton, King Hussein of Jordan, 125–26. However, neither Ashton's sources nor the available Israeli records corroborate the claim that Dayan initiated the meet-

ing. Furthermore, Sharon, a junior general in 1967, was in no position to bring about the annexation of the West Bank.

94. Dean, Washington, to FO, 21 July 1967, PREM/13/1622, UKNA.

95. Duncan, Amman, 22 July 1967, POL 27-14 ARAB-ISR/SANDSTORM, RG59, Central Files 1967–69, USNA; Dean, Washington, to FO, 22 July 1967, PREM/13/1622, UKNA.

96. Memorandum, Bundy to President Johnson, 21 July 1967, *FRUS*, 19: 707–9; Paper Prepared by the President's Consultant (Bundy), 18 July 1967, *FRUS* 19: 682–84; Bundy's memorandum to the President, 17 July 1967, cited ibid., n. 2. Quotation from the 21 July memorandum.

97. Rusk to Embassy in Amman, 21 and 25 July 1967, *FRUS* 19: 709–11, 718–19; Burns, Amman, 25, 27 and 29 July 1967, all in POL 27-14 ARAB-ISR/SANDSTORM, RG59, Central Files 1967–69, USNA; Burns, Amman, 28 July 1967, *FRUS* 19: 723–27.

98. Nigel Ashton, "Cold War, Hot War and Civil War: King Hussein and Jordan's Regional Role, 1967–73," in *The Cold War in the Middle East: Regional Conflict and the Superpowers, 1967–73,* ed. Nigel Ashton (London: Routledge, 2007), 195.

99. Transcript, Press conference with Foreign Minister Abba Eban, 14 August 1967, FCO/17/506, UKNA.

100. See "A Tour in the West Bank," *Hadha al-'Alem* 41 (August 1967), 4–5; Amnon Kapeliuk, "Talking on the West Bank," *New Outlook* 10, no. 6 (1967), 38–41, 46; Rene Eijbersen, "A Living with Justice and Honor," *New Outlook* 10, no. 7 (1967), 36–39.

101. Narkiss, *Soldier of Jerusalem,* 222–24; Zvi Lavie, "When the Notables of Judea and Samaria Requested Self Rule and Were Rejected by Dayan," *Ma'ariv,* 10 November 1978. Quotation from Slater, *Warrior Statesman,* 298. In addition to She-hadeh and Janho, Narkiss remembered (in an interview, 1996) only one other name: 'Izzat Karman from Ramallah. In his talk with Kimche and Bavly, Karman expressed similar views to those of Shehadeh. See Kimche, Political Leadership. According to the military commander of the Ramallah District, Karman was regarded as a traitor because "he had always been for Israel." See Shashar, *Seventh Day War,* 65 (entry for 3 July).

102. Vardi to Chief of Staff's aide de camp, 10 July 1967, 65–32/1984, IDFA. The list of eighty-three names is enclosed with Vardi's letter.

103. Memorandum by Farhi, 13 July 1967, DFP.

104. Shashar, *Seventh Day War,* 89 (entry for 11 July).

105. Interview with Raphael Vardi.

106. Raphael Vardi, "The Beginning of Israeli Rule in Judea and Samaria," an article based on a presentation delivered at the Jerusalem Center for Public Affairs, March 1989, http://www.jcpa.org/jl/hito8.htm (accessed: 21 October 2010).

107. Unsigned letter to the Defense Minister, 23 June 1967, HZ/4088/10, ISA. Moshe Sasson confirmed (interview, December 2001) that he had written the letter.

108. Mordekhai Bentov, *Yamim Mesaprim: Zikhronot meha-Me'ah ha-Makhra'at* [Days tell: Reminiscences from the overwhelming century] (Tel Aviv: Sifriyat Po'alim, 1984), 158–59, quotation from 159.

109. See Meron Benvenisti, "Reunion without Reconciliation: Jews and Arabs in Jerusalem," *New Middle East,* March 1973, 19.

110. Interview with Raphael Vardi.

111. Shlomo Gazit, "Policies in the Administered Territories," in *The Impact of the Six-Day War: A Twenty-Year Assessment,* ed. Stephen J. Roth (Basingstoke: Macmillan, 1988), 56.

112. Haim Holzman, *Tehikat ha-Bitahon ba-Shtahim ha-Muhzakim* [The security legislation in the administered territories] (Giv'at Havivah: Center for Arabic and Afro-Asian Studies, 1968), 81–82; Ann Mosely Lesch, *Political Perceptions of the Palestinians on the West Bank and the Gaza Strip* (Washington, D.C.: Middle East Institute, 1980), 27, n. 35. Propaganda pamphlet: *Dapei Meida'* [Information leaves] (Jerusalem: Publication Service, Prime Minister's Office, 1969), Current Topics, English Summary, xv. The Hebrew version goes even farther (22): "In Judea and Samaria, the inhabitants enjoy *absolute* freedom of political-partisan organization. *Assemblies of Arab activists, of all parties, are taking place openly,* and their resolutions are being published in the press." Emphases added.

113. Telegram: Col. Vardi to Brigades 4, 5, 9, 16 and HQ of the City of [Arab] Jerusalem, 20 June 1967, DFP.

114. Rabin's comments in minutes, General Staff session, 19 June 1967, 206-117/1970, IDFA.

115. Ben-Horin to Avnon et al., 21 June 1967, FM/4097/8, ISA.

116. Dayan's comments in cabinet minutes, 25 June 1967, A/8164/10, ISA; Levavi, FM, to Israel Mission, New York, 28 June 1967, FM/4088/10, ISA.

117. Memorandum, Committee of Four's meeting, 5 July 1967, A/7921/2, ISA. See also Ya'acov Herzog's diary, 16 July 1967, A/4511/3, ISA.

118. Gazit, *Carrot and the Stick,* appendix C, 304–5.

119. Tat-Aluf [Brig. Gen.] Sh. Gazit, *"Ha-Shtahim ha-Muhzakim—Mediniyut u-Ma'as* [The administered territories—Policy and practice]" [in Hebrew], *Ma'arakhot* 204 (January 1970), 29–30.

120. Gazit, *Carrot and the Stick,* 92.

121. Shlomo Hillel to Foreign Minister Eban, 10 July 1967, FM/4088/9, ISA.

122. Unsigned letter (written by Moshe Sasson) to the Defense Minister, 23 June 1967, FM/4088/10, ISA. The subject of the "new refugees," including the destruction of Palestinian villages, is discussed in chapter 4.

123. "Jerusalem syndrome" is a psychotic condition which afflicts fervent religious believers who visit Jerusalem. See Yair Bar-El et al., "Jerusalem Syndrome," *British Journal of Psychiatry* 176, no. 1 (2000), 86–90. Obviously, I am using this term in a metaphorical sense.

124. *Knesset Proceedings,* 1 August 1967, 2825–27.

THREE In Search of Docile Leadership

1. Michael Bar-Zohar, *Facing a Cruel Mirror: Israel's Moment of Truth* (New York: Scribner's, 1990), 8.

2. For Dayan's policy see Nimrod Raphaeli, "Military Government in the Occupied Territories: An Israeli View," *Middle East Journal* 23, no. 2 (1969), 179–83; Gazit, *Trapped Fools,* 47–49, 56–58; Gazit, *Carrot and the Stick,* 27–30. Dayan's quotation from Slater, *Warrior Statesman,* 293. See also 'Isa 'Abd al-Hamid, *Sitt Sanawat min Siyasat al-Jusur al-Maftuhah* [Six years of open bridges policy] (Beirut: Markaz al-Abhath, Munazzamat al-Tahrir al-Filastiniyyah, 1973). This study uses Israeli sources extensively and on the whole subscribes to the official Israeli account. Yet its author argues that the real motive behind the "open bridges" was Israel's desire to open Arab markets to its products, whereas Jordan cooperated with Israel because it saw in that policy a means to maintain political influence in the West Bank.

3. Gazit, *Carrot and the Stick,* 175; Gazit, "Policies in the Administered Territories," 57. Amnon Cohen, a scholar at the Hebrew University of Jerusalem who served several stints as an adviser on Arab affairs in the West Bank Military Government between the late 1960s and mid-1970s, insisted in 1979: "[N]o attempt was made to promote Quisling-type collaborators"; Amnon Cohen, "Thoughts on Israel's Palestinian Policies," *Middle East Focus* 2, no. 1 (May 1979), 12. Yet Gazit, who handled the occupied territories between 1967 and 1974, admits that there were "a few exceptions to this principle"; Gazit, "Policies in the Administered Territories," 57.

4. Gazit, "Consolidation of Policy," 135, n. 1. For an extensive discussion on the co-optation of Arab leaders within Israel by granting them personal gains see Ian Lustick, *Arabs in the Jewish State: Israel's Control of a National Minority* (Austin: University of Texas Press, 1980), 198–231. See also Alina Korn, "Military Government, Political Control, and Crime: The Case of Israeli Arabs," *Crime, Law, and Social Change* 34 (2000), 159–82, esp. 167–70.

5. See Chief of Staff Rabin's comments in minutes of General Staff session, 31 July 1967, 206-117/1970, IDFA.

6. Gazit, *Trapped Fools,* 144; Gazit, *Carrot and the Stick,* 123.

7. Memorandum, Committee of Four's meeting, 5 July 1967, A/7921/2, ISA. The memorandum states that the Mossad expressed readiness to carry out this assignment.

8. The Special Inter-Ministerial Committee for Political Contacts in the Occupied Areas to the Prime Minister, 20 July 1967, appendix C, A/7921/2, ISA. The recommendation was copied from Sasson and Bar-Haim's "The West Bank[,] the Jordanian Kingdom[,] the Gaza Strip: A Proposal for Resolution and Policy," 18 July 1967, A/7921/2, ISA.

9. Summary of a meeting, the West Bank Committee, 11 July 1967, FM/4088/9, ISA. A handwritten marginal note next to this paragraph reads: "cancelled."

10. Ya'acov Herzog's diary, 16 July 1967, A/4511/3, ISA.

11. Summary of a meeting, the West Bank Committee, 19 July 1967, A/7921/2, ISA.

12. Moshe Sasson to Foreign Minister, undated (apparently 23, 24, or 25 July 1967), A/7921/4, ISA.

13. Gazit, *Carrot and the Stick*, 188, 192.

14. Kimche, Political Leadership.

15. Hillel, FM, to Ambassador, London, 21 July 1967, FM/4088/6, ISA. The Israeli embassy in London acted on Mayor Kollek's request and contacted Nuseibeh's sons in London. A visa was issued to one of them, Sari, in August (the other, Zaki, flew to Jordan and crossed over to the West Bank "illegally"). See Ambassador, London, to Hillel, FM, 31 July 1967, and Hillel to Kollek, 2 August 1967, both in FM/4088/6, ISA; Levi, London, to FM, 16 August 1967, FM/4088/7, ISA; Nusseibeh, *Once upon a Country*, 95–96.

16. Bar-Haim to Commanding General of the Central Command [Gen. Narkiss], 18 July 1967, FM/4097/3, ISA. The word "lend" appears in quotation marks in the original document. In August an Israeli interdepartmental panel recommended the allocation of 1 million Israeli pounds ($333,333) for loans to bodies and individuals in Arab Jerusalem in order "to increase the cooperation with Israeli institutions" and to convince the inhabitants that Israeli rule was permanent. Col. Gazit to Ahituv et al., Summary of discussion at the Coordinating Committee on 24 August 1967, 65-117/1970, IDFA.

17. Quotations of Victor Cohen, and the entire discussion on Operation Saddu-cees, are based on Cohen's recorded account, 3 February 1987. David Ronen, himself a former senior GSS officer, interviewed Cohen for his book *The Year of the Shabak*. The version offered in Ronen's book (31–32), however, does not conform at all to his inter-viewee's account.

18. The Palestinian idiom is quoted, although in a distorted context, in Ronen, *Year of the Shabak*, 32.

19. Indeed, Police Minister Eliyahu Sasson, who had known Ja'bari from the days before the foundation of Israel, warned that the Israelis should be careful not to get involved with the mayor, "who is corrupt." See Summary of the Political Contacts Committee's Discussion Headed by the PM, 3 July 1968, A/7921/5, ISA.

20. "Quislings": interview with Raphael Vardi.

21. See Avi Raz, "The Shabak Man," *Sofshavu'a* (*Ma'ariv* weekend magazine), 13 April 1990.

22. Col. Gazit to Ahituv et al.; "Operational Principles for the Administered Territories," both 13 October 1967, in Shlomo Gazit, *Ha-Makel ve-ha-Gezer: Ha-Mimshal ha-Yisre'eli bi-Yehudah ve-Shomron* [The stick and the carrot: The Israeli administration in Judea and Samaria] (Tel Aviv: Zmora, Bitan, 1985), 355–59. The English version of Gazit's book, *The Carrot and the Stick*, does not include his letter to Ahituv and, more important, provides an inaccurate translation of the clause cited here.

23. Moshe Sasson to Foreign Minister, undated (apparently 23, 24, or 25 July 1967), A/7921/4, ISA.

24. Memorandum by D. T. Morrison, Notes on recent conversations in Ramallah, 14 July 1967, POL 2 West Bank, RG84, Post Files: American Consulate-General, 1967, USNA.

25. "The second leaflet of the Popular Struggle movement, Jerusalem," Hebrew translation, 10 July 1967, GL/17035/1, ISA. The leaflet, dated 29 June, was brought to the Israelis' attention only eleven days later. See also Shashar, *Seventh Day War*, 89.

26. Memorandum by Farhi, "A Communist leaflet, July 1967," undated, DFP; summary of leaflet signed "The Free Sons of Jerusalem" (in Hebrew, with quotes in Arabic) by Farhi, 22 July 1967, DFP.

27. Bassam al-Salihi, *Al-Za'amah al-Siyasiyyah wa-al-Diniyyah fi al-Ard al-Muhtallah: Waqi'uha wa-Tatawwuruha, 1967–1993* [The political and religious leadership in the occupied land: Its reality and development, 1967–1993] (Jerusalem: Dar al-Quds lil-Nashr wa-al-Tawzi', 1993), 39–40. For a discussion of the JCP in the West Bank before the Israeli occupation, and of its activity and ideology, see Amnon Cohen, *Political Parties in the West Bank under the Jordanian Regime, 1949–1967* (Ithaca, N.Y.: Cornell University Press, 1982), 27–93.

28. Na'im al-Ashhab, *Durub al-Alam . . . Durub al-Amal* [Ways of pain . . . ways of hope] (Ramallah: Dar al-Tanwir lil-Nashr wa-al-Tarjamah wa-al-Tawzi', 2009), 182–87.

29. Jerusalem-East—a platform for discussion, unsigned, 11 September 1967, enclosed with Col. Vardi to Chief of Staff's office, 11 September 1967, 70-117/1970, IDFA.

30. Benvenisti, *Jerusalem*, 104–6; Rouhi El-Khatib [*sic*], Address delivered at a meeting held in the House of Commons Members Dining Room, during the Jordan Refugee Week in London, June 13th, 1968, 8.

31. Memorandum, Ruhi al-Khatib (a meeting at his home with Meron Benvenisti), 20 July 1967, DFP.

32. Dr. Ibrahim Talil et al. to Raphael Levi, 22 July 1967: facsimile of the Arabic original in Benziman, *Jerusalem*, 73; English and Hebrew translations in S/8107, A/6780, 3 August 1967, UNPR; and A/7921/4, ISA (respectively). The remaining four councilors who did not sign the letter had fled the West Bank during or shortly after the hostilities.

33. Wilson, Jerusalem, 26 July 1967, POL ARAB-ISR, RG59, Central Files 1967–69, USNA.

34. Col. Vardi to Chief of Staff's aide de camp, 24 July 1967, 64-32/1984, IDFA; a Hebrew translation of the statement is enclosed with Vardi's letter. Vardi also enclosed a memorandum (by Farhi, Details on the petition's signatories . . . , 24 July 1967, FM/4088/7, ISA) giving the basic available information about each of the twenty signatories. In the discussion of the 24 July assembly, its background, and the creation of the Islamic Council, I have relied on 'Abd al-Hamid al-Sa'ih, *Filastin, La Salah tahta al-Hirab: Mudhakkirat al-Shaykh 'Abd al-Hamid al-Sa'ih* [Palestine, no prayer under bayonets: The memoirs of Sheikh 'Abd al-Hamid al-Sa'ih] (Beirut: Mu'assasat al-Dirasat al-Filastiniyyah, 1994), 82–86; Anwar al-Khatib al-Tamimi, *Ma'a Salah*

al-Din fi al-Quds: Ta'ammulat wa-Dhikrayat [With Salah al-Din in Jerusalem: Reflections and reminiscences] (Jerusalem: 1989), 179–86 (the statement's Arabic original is reprinted on 180–83; Khatib says that upon his arrest and exile, the original letter was returned to him); 'Abd al-Muhsin Abu Mayzar, "The West Bank: Occupation, Resistance, and View of the Future (symposium)" [in Arabic], *Shu'un Filastiniyyah* 32 (1974), 44; Benvenisti, *Jerusalem*, 284–86; David Farhi, "The Muslim Council in East Jerusalem and Judea and Samaria since the Six Day War" [in Hebrew], *Ha-Mizrah he-Hadash* 28, nos. 1–2 (1979), 3–21; Yehoshua Porath, *The Emergence of the Palestinian-Arab National Movement, 1918–1929* (London: Frank Cass, 1974), 194–207; Ibrahim Dakkak, "Back to Square One: A Study in the Re-emergence of the Palestinian Identity in the West Bank, 1967–1980," in *Palestinians over the Green Line*, ed. Alexander Schölch (London: Ithaca, 1983), 70; Wasserstein, *Divided Jerusalem*, 222–25.

35. Nusseibeh, *Once upon a Country*, 99.

36. Wilson, Jerusalem, 27 July 1967, POL 27 ARAB-ISR, RG59, Central Files 1967–69, USNA; memorandum by Farhi, Meeting with Anwar Nuseibeh, 27 July 1967, DFP. According to Benziman (*Jerusalem,* 71), not all of the invitees to the notables' gathering showed up, and Nuseibeh's absence was interpreted by some of the participants as cowardliness. Both Sheikh Sa'ih (*Palestine*, 82–83) and Consul General Wilson (Jerusalem, 26 July 1967, POL ARAB-ISR, RG59, Central Files 1967–69, USNA) mistakenly maintained that Nuseibeh had been one of the signatories of the 24 July statement. In fact, Nuseibeh's name, along with the name of another person, were added after the fact in August, when a copy of the statement was delivered to the UN secretary general's personal representative. See doc. C in Annex I, Report of the Secretary-General under General Assembly Resolution 2254 (ES-V) Relating to Jerusalem [henceforth: Thalmann Report], S/8146, A/6793, 12 September 1967, UNPR.

37. Ya'acov Herzog's diary, 25 July 1967, A/4511/3, ISA.

38. James Feron, "Arabs Cautioned Not to Cooperate," *New York Times,* 26 July 1967; Wilson, Jerusalem, 27 July 1967, POL 27 ARAB-ISR, RG59, Central Files 1967–69, USNA.

39. See Moshe Sasson to Foreign Minister, undated (apparently 23, 24, or 25 July 1967), A/7921/4, ISA; Ya'acov Herzog's diary, 25 July 1967, A/4511/3, ISA; letter by Major Shimron, "Judges from Nablus District," 24 July 1967, DFP.

40. Summary of a meeting on signs of disobedience among Arab notables in Jerusalem and the [West] Bank—25 July 1967, MSP; Zerah Warhaftig, *Hamishim Shanah ve-Shanah: Pirkei Zikhronot* [Fifty years from year to year: Memoirs] (Jerusalem: Yad Shapira, 1998), 216.

41. Minutes, Political Committee report—28.7.67, A/7921/2, ISA.

42. *Yitzhak Rabin: Rosh Memshelet Yisrael 1974–1977, 1992–1995: Mivhar Te'udot mi-Pirkei Hayav* [Yitzhak Rabin: Prime minister of Israel, 1974–1977, 1992–1995: Selected documents from his lifetime], vol. 1, *1922–1967* (Jerusalem, 2005), 533. The cabinet sessions took place on 27 and 30 July. See also The Interdepartmental Political Committee—summary of discussion, 26.7.67, MSP; Ya'acov Herzog's diary, 25, 26 July

1967, A/4511/3, ISA; Ben-Horin to Foreign Minister and Director General, 29 July 1967, FM/4088/6, ISA; minutes, Ministerial Committee, 29 July 1967, File: "The Policy in the Occupied Territories—A," Eshkol Memorial Archive, Jerusalem (EMA).

43. Rabin's comments in minutes of General Staff session, 31 July 1967, 206-117/1970, IDFA.

44. Ibid.

45. Note by Farhi, Agreement with Yoskeh, 25 July 1967, DFP. See also Bar-Haim to Raphael Levi, 24 July 1967, FM/4097/3, ISA; Moshe Sasson to Foreign Minister, undated (apparently 23, 24, or 25 July 1967), A/7921/4, ISA.

46. Memorandum by Farhi, Arrests, 31 July 1967, DFP. According to the Communist leader Na'im al-Ashhab, Dazdar managed to cross over to the East Bank. Interview with Na'im al-Ashhab, 23 January 2006, Jerusalem.

47. Memorandum by Farhi, Proposed draft of General U. Narkiss's announcement . . . ," 1 August 1967, DFP.

48. Memoranda by Farhi, A visit to Salim al-Sharif, 31 July 1967, and Meeting with Hazem al-Khalidi 3/8/67, DFP; GSS report, The West Bank, 6 August 1967, FM/4088/6, ISA.

49. Wilson, Jerusalem, 5 August 1967, POL 27 ARAB-ISR, RG59, Central Files 1967–69, USNA; Hall, Jerusalem, 5 September 1967, POL 23-8 Demonstrations, Riots, Protests, RG84, Post Files: American Consulate-General, 1967, USNA.

50. *Jerusalem Post,* 4 August 1967.

51. Wilson, Jerusalem, 29 July 1967, POL 2 West Bank, RG84, Post Files: American Consulate-General, 1967, USNA; memorandum by Farhi, Yoskeh, 2 August 1967, DFP; petitions and statements in various files in IDFA, USNA and DFP.

52. Rafik Halabi, *The West Bank Story* (San Diego: Harcourt Brace Jovanovich, 1985), 38.

53. Review by the GSS's Kedem in memorandum by Farhi, "Meeting with Col. Vardi," 7 August 1967, DFP.

54. See *PAD, 1967,* 520–28, 534, 547–48, 556, 558–62, 573–79, 581–83, 587–91, 594–95, 619; *The Resistance of the Western Bank of Jordan to Israeli Occupation, 1967* (Beirut, 1967), 17–34, 38–49, 57–64, 67. A list of some twenty organizations that expressed their support for the Islamic Council is recorded in Thalmann Report (article 123).

55. Shashar, *Seventh Day War,* 144 (entry for 11 August).

56. Ashhab, *Ways of Pain . . . Ways of Hope,* 188–91, 333–37; memorandum by Farhi, The source: Sheikh Mustafa al-Ansar, 8 August 1967, DFP; Hall, Jerusalem, 16 August 1967, POL 23-8 Demonstrations, Riots, Protests, RG84, Post Files: American Consulate-General, 1967, USNA; Shashar, *Seventh Day War,* 136–37. See also Benvenisti, *Jerusalem,* 208.

57. Ashhab, *Ways of Pain . . . Ways of Hope,* 191–92. Ashhab relates that the National Guidance Committee was preceded by another committee whose activity was limited to exchanges of views. Ruhi al-Khatib, Anwar Nuseibeh, and some other members of the National Guidance Committee were members of the previous committee.

58. 'Abd al-Muhsin Abu Mayzar in "West Bank," 45 (see also 'Arabi, 'Awad, ibid, 53–54); Dakkak, "Back to Square One," 71.

59. Ashhab, *Ways of Pain . . . Ways of Hope,* 192; interview with Na'im al-Ashhab.

60. Farhi to Gen. Narkiss, [24] August 1967, 65-117/1970, IDFA. Farhi's Palestinian source mentioned the names of only five members of the NGC: Sheikh Sa'ih, Ruhi al-Khatib, Sa'id 'Ala' al-Din, and Tiyasir Kan'an, plus Anwar Nuseibeh with a question mark.

61. Sahliyeh, *In Search of Leadership,* 24.

62. Proposals for action following the shutdown of shops and public transportation in East Jerusalem (summary of a meeting with Col. R. Vardi), 7 August 1967, DFP; Proposals for reaction following the strike in Jerusalem on 7.8.1967, A/4510/16, ISA (a handwritten marginal note reads: "Submitted by the defense minister during the ministerial committee [session]"); Brown, *Personal Imprint,* 194.

63. Memorandum by Farhi, Reactions on the closing of shops, the arrests and the shutdown of the bus service, in the wake of the strike, 8 September (*sic;* should be August) 1967, DFP.

64. Hall, Jerusalem, 21 August 1967 (telegram 371), POL 27 ARAB-ISR, RG59, Central Files 1967–69, USNA.

65. Hall, Jerusalem, 16 August 1967, POL 27 ARAB-ISR, RG59, Central Files 1967–69, USNA. For the appeal's text see *PAD, 1967,* 558, 581 (mistakenly, it appears twice: the first carries the date it was sent, 7 August, the second the date of its broadcast on Amman Radio, 13 August).

66. Farhi to Gen. Narkiss, 21 August 1967, 65-117/1970, IDFA (a Hebrew translation of the petition is enclosed with Farhi's letter); Hall, Jerusalem, 21 August 1967, POL 27 ARAB-ISR, RG59, Central Files 1967–69, USNA.

67. Moshe Dayan, *Story of My Life,* 326. See also Dayan's similar comments in minutes, KFASC, 26 September 1967, A/8161/8, ISA.

68. *PAD, 1967,* 587–89. According to Secretary of State Rusk, the statement was drafted in a meeting attended by more than 100 Palestinians. Rusk to Embassy in Tel Aviv, 16 August 1967, REF ARAB, RG59, Central Files 1967–69, USNA.

69. Farhi to Gen. Narkiss, 10 August 1967, DFP.

70. Farhi to Gen. Narkiss, 11 August 1967, DFP.

71. See Lt. Col. Vered to Central Command HQ, Weekly activity report for the liberated [*sic*] territories, 19 September 1967, FM/4095/4, ISA.

72. Memorandum by Farhi, 11 August 1967, DFP; Ben-Horin to Foreign Minister and Director General, 14 August 1967, FM/4088/6, ISA.

73. For petitions, letters, and statements see *PAD, 1967,* 575, 580, 613, 670; *Resistance of the Western Bank of Jordan to Israeli Occupation 1967,* 50–52, 65–66, 91; various files in ISA (in particular FM/4097/3, FM/4088/7), USNA and DFP. Two teachers in Jenin were fired for signing a petition. Shashar, *Seventh Day War,* 129 (entry for 3 August).

74. For an illuminating account of the crude Israeli intervention in the Palestinian educational system during the period under discussion see Ann Mosely Lesch, *Israel's Occupation of the West Bank: The First Two Years* (Santa Monica, Calif.: Rand, 1970), 47–54.

75. A comprehensive list of such deletions and changes is offered in Najla Nasir Bashur, "The Alteration of the School Curricula in the West Bank of Jordan after 1967" [in Arabic], *Shu'un Filastiniyyah* 3 (1971), 229–41.

76. Maj. Farhi to Gen. Narkiss, 16 October 1967, 72-117/1970, IDFA; Shlomo 'Azaryah to chief of staff [presumably of the Central Command], 17 October 1967, 71-117/1970, IDFA. Quotations from the 'Azaryah communiqué.

77. Joseph Alsop, "Moshe Dayan Faces Issue of Israel's Million Arabs," *Washington Post,* 11 September 1967.

78. Col. Shlomo Gazit to the office of Head of the General Staff Brunch, 13 September 1967, 69-117/1970, IDFA; Lt. Col. Reuven Davidi to the Office of the C.G. of the Central Command, 19 September 1967, 70-117/1970, IDFA.

79. Memorandum, Summaries [taken] from the weekly meeting, Defense Minister's office[,] Ha-Kiryah, 18.8.67, 118-117/1970, IDFA; Col. Gazit to Agam/Batmar [Hebrew acronyms for General Staff Brunch / Spatial Security Department], 2 October 1967, 72-117/1970, IDFA.

80. For a detailed list of the sanctions see Gazit, *Carrot and the Stick,* 279–80 (quotation from 279); see also Col. Gazit to Acting C.G. of the Central Command, and to Chief of Staff's aide-de-camp (#GM/32)—both 21 September 1967, 70-117/1970, IDFA; memorandum by Key, Jerusalem, Situation in Nablus since September 19, 30 September 1967, FCO/17/212, UKNA. The school strike ended after two months, following ostensible mutual concessions; in fact, Israel backed down. For an extensive discussion of the whole affair from the Israeli perspective, with special focus on Nablus, see Gazit, *Carrot and the Stick,* 273–87. See also Brown, *Personal Imprint,* 195–97.

81. Vardi, "The Beginning of Israeli Rule in Judea and Samaria."

82. Interview with Raphael Vardi; Amos Elon, "The Israeli Occupation," *Commentary* 45, no. 3 (1968), 45.

83. See Notes on meeting [of U Thant and Ralph Bunch of the United Nations and Ambassadors Gideon Rafael and Shabtai Rosenne of Israel] in the Secretary-General's Office on 14 August 1967, 370-43-5, United Nations Archives, New York (UNA); Dayan's comments in minutes, KFASC, 17 August 1967, A/8161/8, ISA; memorandum by Farhi, A meeting at Col. Vardi's office on 17.8.67, 21 August 1967, 70-117/1970, IDFA; Hall, Jerusalem, 25 August 1967, POL 17 Status of Jerusalem, RG84, Post Files: American Consulate-General, 1967, USNA.

84. *Resistance of the Western Bank of Jordan to Israeli Occupation 1967,* 76–81.

85. See Hall, Jerusalem, 16 September 1967, POL 2 SITREP, RG84, Post Files: American Consulate-General, 1967, USNA; Lewen, Jerusalem, to Moberly, FO, 28 September 1967, FCO/17/202, UKNA.

86. GSS report, Digest of events in the West Bank, 15 September 1967, FM/4088/8, ISA.

87. Hebrew translation of the appeal, signed by the mayors of Nablus, Jenin, Tulkarm, Salfit, Tubas, Ya'bad, and 'Arabeh, undated (apparently late September 1967), 72-117/1970, IDFA. Quotation from Maj. Tzadok Ophir to Chief of Staff's office, 15 October 1967, 72-117/1970, IDFA. The letter includes a Hebrew translation of the leaflet.

88. Sayigh, *Armed Struggle and the Search for State*, 147. Sayigh's authoritative volume offers a thorough discussion of the guerrilla activity and its failure during these months, 153–77.

89. Burns, Amman, 31 July 1967, POL 27-14 ARAB-ISR/SANDSTORM, RG59, Central Files 1967–69, USNA.

90. See examples presented by Israel to the State Department in Rusk to Embassy in Tel Aviv, 16 August 1967, REF ARAB, RG59, Central Files 1967–69, USNA; and in an Israeli five-page report, Jordanian incitements to the West Bank population as at 16.8.67, enclosed with Goring-Morris, Tel Aviv, to MoD, 5 September 1967, FCO/17/93, UKNA. For example, an assortment of Arab broadcasts and publications, gleaned by the Research Department of Israel's Foreign Ministry (Arab threats of war and annihilation and incitement against Israel since the Six Days War, 1 October 1967, G/6303/1059, ISA), cited under the heading "Incitement for civil disobedience in the West Bank" the following Amman Radio broadcast of 27 July, calling upon the West Bankers: "Be steadfast and do not give up your rights. Remember that the enemy cannot make you accept anything that you do not agree to."

91. Hall, Jerusalem, 23 August 1967, POL 23-8 Demonstrations, Riots, Protests, RG84, Post Files: American Consulate-General, 1967, USNA; Hall, Jerusalem, 21 August 1967 (telegram 377), POL 27 ARAB-ISR, RG59, Central Files 1967–69, USNA. See also Ben-Horin to Foreign Minister and Director General, 10 August 1967, FM/4088/6, ISA.

92. Hall's telegram of 23 August, ibid.

93. Hall, Jerusalem, 23 September 1967, POL 2 SITREP, RG84, Post Files: American Consulate-General, 1967, USNA; Lewen, Jerusalem, to Moberly, FO, 21 September 1967, FCO/17/202, UKNA. For the text of the leaflets see *PAD, 1967,* 730–31. The call for a strike was publicized several times through Amman Radio; Shabtai Teveth, *The Cursed Blessing: The Story of Israel's Occupation of the West Bank* (London: Weidenfeld and Nicolson, 1970), 199.

94. See Hall, Jerusalem, 26 August 1967, POL 2 SITREP, RG84, Post Files: American Consulate-General, 1967, USNA; Benvenisti, *Jerusalem,* 208–9.

95. Col. Gazit to Chief of Staff's aide de camp (#GM/31), 21 September 1967, 70-117/1970, IDFA. One day after Sheikh Sa'ih's deportation, the Israeli authorities were told by Bishop Capucci that he had convened a few dignitaries at his home on 21 September, to discuss the "aggravation of the struggle against Israel." Farhi to Gen. Narkiss, 24 September 1967, FM/4095/4, ISA.

96. Raphael Levi, a high-ranking Israeli official, who was resentful of the "pilgrimage" to the places of exile of the four, had already suggested cynically on 30 August: "The notables claim that they are Jordanians, so why don't we expel them to their 'homeland'"; Shashar, *Seventh Day War,* 124–25 (entry for 30 July).

97. When written without the diacritical signs for vowels (*niqqud*), the Hebrew word *p-r-sh* can be read *peresh* (excrement) or *parash* (horseman). I was assured by a senior Israeli official from the time, speaking on condition of anonymity, that the code name used for the expulsion operations was the former.

98. Superintendent Nahum Bosmi to Chief of Police's Southern District, 25 September 1967, 70-117/1970, IDFA. Sheikh Sa'ih's retrospective version of his expulsion fails to mention the National Guidance Committee and gives the wrong date, 25 September instead of 23; Sa'ih, *Palestine, No Prayer under Bayonets,* 89–93.

99. Gazit, *Carrot and the Stick,* 238.

100. Vardi, "Beginning of Israeli Rule in Judea and Samaria." Vardi erroneously states that the number of notables who requested permission to assemble was 200. For the affair of the 83 notables see chapter 2.

101. Eliyahu Sasson to Prime Minister, 16 August 1967, A/7921/2, ISA. The call for the Palestinians under occupation to become a thorn in Israel's flesh will be discussed in chapter 4.

102. Cabinet Resolution 692, 27 July 1967, ICS.

103. Minutes of General Staff session, 31 July 1967, 206-117/1970, IDFA.

104. Ahituv's comments in minutes, KFASC, 17 August 1967, A/8161/8, ISA.

105. Dayan's comments ibid.

106. Barbour, Tel Aviv, 23 August 1967, POL 27 ARAB-ISR, RG59, Central Files 1967–69, USNA.

107. Dayan, *My Father, His Daughter,* 195.

108. Moshe Dayan, "Hopeful Truth of the New Reality," *Life* (New York), 29 September 1967.

109. Dayan's comments in minutes, KFASC, 26 September 1967, A/8161/8, ISA.

110. Farhi to Gen. Narkiss et al., 24 September 1967, FM/4095/4, ISA.

111. Benziman, *Jerusalem,* 77. Benziman argues that the natural candidates to head the National Guidance Committee, Anwar al-Khatib and Anwar Nuseibeh, shirked this incumbency.

112. Telegram (Hebrew translation), 25 September 1967, FM/4088/8, ISA. An attached letter (Tokatli to GSS' Unit 249[2] et al., 26 September), states: "So far we have not responded to the telegram's content, and did not acknowledge it." Copies of the telegram, signed by thirty-one prominent dignitaries, were sent to the UN secretary general and to Israel's defense minister. The number of signatories is confirmed by an American record (Campbell, Jerusalem, 28 September 1967, POL 27 ARAB-ISR, RG59, Central Files 1967–69, USNA), whereas two Palestinian sources give smaller numbers (*PAD, 1967,* 759: eighteen names; *Resistance of the Western Bank of Jordan to Israeli Occupation 1967,* 92–93: twenty names).

113. Ahmad Khalifah, "Israel's Policy in the Occupied Territories" [in Arabic], *Shu'un Filastiniyyah* 1 (1971), 38.

114. Salihi, *Political and Religious Leadership in the Occupied Land,* 152. Salihi offers a fuller discussion and analysis of the civil disobedience and its failure on 39–47, esp. 45–46.

115. Lesch, *Political Perceptions of the Palestinians on the West Bank and the Gaza Strip,* 103–4.

FOUR The Right of No Return

1. For legal definitions see Usama Halabi, "The Legal Status and Rights of the Palestinians Displaced as a Result of the June 1967 War," *Palestine-Israel Journal* 15, no. 4–16, no. 1 (2009), 54–56.

2. Report of the Secretary-General under General Assembly Resolution 2252 (ES-V) and Security Council Resolution 237 (1967) [henceforth: Gussing Report] (article 159), S/8158, 2 October 1967, A/6797, 15 September 1967, UNPR. Precise statistics are nonexistent, and the figures offered by Israel on the one hand and by the Arabs on the other, as well as by a number of studies and other sources, are conflicting. The issue of the captured Syrian territory and its residents is not within the compass of this book and thus will not be discussed here.

3. Yosef Argaman, *Zeh Hayah Sodi Be-Yoter: 30 Parshiyot Modi'in u-Vitahon be-Yisrael; Ha-Sipur ha-Male* [This was top secret: Thirty intelligence and security affairs in Israel; The full story] (Tel Aviv: Ba-Mahaneh, 1990), 245.

4. Brown, *Personal Imprint,* 66; Golan, *War on Three Fronts,* 237.

5. Brown, *Personal Imprint,* 68.

6. Golan, *War on Three Fronts,* 258.

7. Gen. Narkiss's HQ diary, cited in Bondy et al., *Not By the Sword Alone,* 190. This entry was not included in the English version of the book, *Mission Survival: The People of Israel's Story in Their Own Words: From the Threat of Annihilation to Miraculous Victory* (London: W. H. Allen, 1968), 227. According to Golan (*War on Three Fronts,* 269), Rabin did not order that the Arabs should be expelled, only that they should be allowed to depart from the West Bank.

8. "The Six Day War: The Campaign in the Jordanian Arena," a comprehensive study prepared by the army's History Department, June 1972, 386. See also *Yitzhak Rabin: Selected Documents,* 501. The Allenby Bridge and two other bridges were dynamited the next day, 8 June. See Central Command, The Six Day War: Concluding Report, September 1967, 1-901/1967 and 3-901/1967, IDFA.

9. Sasson's comments in cabinet minutes, 18 June 1967 (afternoon), A/8164/7, ISA.

10. Segev, *1967,* 407, quoting from the cabinet minutes of 25 June 1967 obtained by Segev privately. This passage does not appear in the minutes as available at ISA (A/8164/10), but parts are still classified.

11. Pryce-Jones, *Face of Defeat,* 6.

12. "La guerre à Jérusalem" [the diary of Sister Marie-Thérèse], *Témoignage Chrétien* (Paris), 27 July 1967 (entry for 9 June). For more evidence see Frank H. Epp, *The Palestinians: Portrait of a People in Conflict* (Toronto: McClelland and Stewart, 1976), 114.

13. Dana Adams Schmidt, "100,000 in Jordan Said to Have Fled across River," *New York Times*, 12 June 1967. See also Ian Gilmour, M.P., and Dennis Walters, M.P., "'There Is a Great Deal of Talk about Peace, but None about Justice,'" *The Times* (London), 27 July 1967; S/7974 and S/7975, 12 June 1967, UNPR.

14. Interview with Col. (ret.) Eliezer Amitai, 17 December 2007, Ramat Ha-Sharon.

15. Col. Shaham's account in "Central Command, The Six Day War: Concluding Report," part 1, section 2, appendix C, September 1967, 1-901/1967, IDFA.

16. Wilson, Jerusalem, 28 June 1967, POL 27-9 ARAB-ISR, RG59, Central Files 1967–69, USNA; Wilson, *Jerusalem*, 112. No air raid, Iraqi or otherwise, occurred.

17. "La guerre à Jérusalem," entry for 1 July; Bowen, *Six Days*, 212.

18. Quoted in Raymonda Hawa Tawil, *My Home, My Prison* (London: Zed, 1983), 95. See also *Ha-'Olam ha-Zeh* (Tel Aviv), 23 August 1967.

19. Amos Ettinger, *My Land of Tears and Laughter: The Story of "Zonik" (Col. Ze'ev Shaham); A Man of Many Friends* (New York: Cornwall, 1994), 228; Ehud Maltz and Michal Sela, "And Perhaps These Villages Never Existed," *Kol ha-'Ir* (Jerusalem), 31 August 1984. Quotation from Ettinger.

20. Golan, *War on Three Fronts*, 291.

21. Gussing Report (article 54). See also Lewen, Jerusalem, to Moberley, FO, 24 August 1967, FCO/17/212, UKNA; Dayan, *Story of My Life*, 320.

22. Resolution 565, cabinet minutes, 25 June 1967, A/8164/10, ISA.

23. S/8004, A/6725, 22 June 1967, UNPR.

24. Wilson, Jerusalem, 30 June 1967, POL 27-9 ARAB-ISR, RG59, Central Files 1967–69, USNA. For eyewitness account see "La guerre à Jérusalem," entry for 12–14 June.

25. Dayan's comments (based on what the mayor of Qalqilyah had allegedly told him) in cabinet minutes, 29 June 1967, A/8164/11, ISA.

26. For Israel's false official explanations see, for example, S/8013, A/6729, 23 June 1967, UNPR; FM to all Israel's diplomatic missions, 22 June 1967, FM/4088/10, ISA; Gussing Report (article 55).

27. Golan, *War on Three Fronts*, 232–33.

28. Hasan Ahmad Hasan Abu Ghosh's account, enclosed with Campbell, Jerusalem, 29 November 1967, POL 27 Military Operation, RG84, Post Files: American Consulate-General, 1967, USNA; petition sent by the 'Imwas, Yalu, and Bayt Nuba villagers to UN Secretary General, 25 August 1968, *PAD, 1968* (Beirut, 1970), 641–43; Wilson, Jerusalem, 29 June and 6 July 1967 (telegrams 1395 and 34, respectively), both in POL 27-9 ARAB-ISR, RG59, Central Files 1967–69, USNA. Dayan's quotation from Uzi Narkiss, *The Liberation of Jerusalem: The Battle of 1967* (London: Vallentine, Mitchell, 1983), 221. Figures from Epp, *Palestinians*, 81–82 (quoting the Palestinian

historian 'Arif al-'Arif); Husam Izzeddin, "A Tale of Three Villages," *Jerusalem Times,*
14 June 1996.

29. Narkiss, *Liberation of Jerusalem,* 199. See also interview with Narkiss, *Musaf
Haaretz,* 21 October 1988. The Israeli military historian and retired army colonel Meir
Pa'il revealed that the Central Command had had a "minimal" contingency plan to
seize the Latrun Salient and destroy the three villages long before the June War. See
Maltz and Sela, "And Perhaps These Villages Never Existed."

30. Yosef Algazy, "Three That Were Wiped Out," *Musaf Haaretz,* 11 July 1997.
See also David Erlich, "Occupational Therapy," *Musaf Haaretz,* 4 December 1987.

31. Brown, *Personal Imprint,* 153; quotations from, respectively, Eshkol's comments in minutes, Expanded Political Committee, 3 June 1968, A/7921/13, ISA; Eshkol's speech at the Kibbutzim Union's conference, 22 November 1967, A/7920/7, ISA.

32. Saleh, *Israel's Policy of De-Institutionalization,* 57, 127.

33. Wilson, Jerusalem, 26 June 1967 (telegram 1357), POL 27-9 ARAB-ISR, RG59,
Central Files 1967–69, USNA.

34. Hall, Jerusalem, 30 August 1967, REF ARAB, RG59, Central Files 1967–69,
USNA.

35. Orders no. 97 of 10 September 1967, no. 146 of 23 October 1967, both in 60-
632/1977, IDFA. For the refusal to allow foreign diplomats and journalists access to Latrun see Wilson, Jerusalem, 14 August 1967, POL 27-9 ARAB-ISR, RG59, Central Files
1967–69, USNA; Hall, Jerusalem, 19 August 1967, POL 2 SITREP, RG84, Post Files:
American Consulate-General, 1967, USNA; Campbell, Jerusalem, 7 November 1967,
REF 3 UNRWA, RG84, Post Files: American Consulate-General, 1967, USNA.

36. The journalist and author Amos Kenan, who served in a reserve unit that
was ordered to supervise the demolition of Bayt Nuba and to drive away the returning villagers, wrote a heartrending eyewitness account of his experience. Kenan
wished his report to be sent only to Premier Eshkol, Defense Minister Dayan, and
two left-wing politicians. However, to his fury a mimeographed English translation
of the report was circulated by an unknown movement called "The Third Force"
among foreign diplomats and foreign correspondents during the following weeks.
See Amos Kenan, *Israel—A Wasted Victory* (Tel Aviv: Amikam, 1970), 17–23; Wilson, Jerusalem, 17 July 1967, POL 27 ARAB-ISR, RG59, Central Files 1967–69, USNA;
Fouzi el-Asmar, *To Be an Arab in Israel* (London: Frances Pinter, 1975), 123–27 (all
these sources include Kenan's account); letter to the editor by Amos Kenan, *Ma'ariv,*
25 June 1967.

37. Israeli officials claimed that the Latrun peasants had billeted Egyptian commandos, or had actually sniped at Israeli troops during and after the fighting, and
denied the deliberate destruction of the villages. See *Newsweek* interview with General Narkiss, conducted on 3 August 1967 and reported in Shashar, *Seventh Day War,*
131–32 (Shashar was present at the interview); Wilson, Jerusalem, 20 July 1967, POL
27-9 ARAB-ISR, RG59, Central Files 1967–69, USNA; Vered, FM, to Aranne, Paris, 6
August 1967, FM/4088/6, ISA; Gussing Report (article 59); statement by Israel's em-

bassy in London in George Mikes, *The Prophet Motive: Israel Today and Tomorrow* (Harmondsworth: Penguin, 1971), 102.

38. Resolution 565, cabinet minutes, 25 June 1967, A/8164/10, ISA.

39. Minister of Agriculture Haim Gvati's comments, *Knesset Proceedings,* 4 March 1968, 1258–59; Shashar, *Seventh Day War,* 158.

40. Haggai Huberman, *Ke-Neged Kol ha-Sikuyim: 40 Shnot Hityashvut bi-Yehudah ve-Shomron, Binyamin ve-ha-Bik'ah, 5727–5767* [Against all odds: Forty years of settlement in Judea and Samaria, Binyamin, and the {Jordan} Valley, 1967–2007] (Jerusalem[?]: Sifriyat Netsarim, 2008), vol. 1, 65–66.

41. Hall, Jerusalem, 23 August 1967, POL 27 ARAB-ISR, RG59, Central Files 1967–69, USNA. See also Michael Adams, "Zeita . . . Beit Nuba . . . Yalu . . . and How the Israelis Have Erased Them from the Holy Land," *Sunday Times* (London), 16 June 1968; Harold Jackson, "Vanished Villages," *Guardian* (London), 5 June 1968.

42. Gussing Report (article 67); Wilson, Jerusalem, 26 June 1967 (telegram 1358), POL 27-9 ARAB-ISR, RG59, Central Files 1967–69, USNA. In September Defense Minister Dayan granted the men of Bayt 'Awa and Bayt Mirsim, whose representatives complained to him about their economic difficulties, permission to go to the East Bank for work purposes. Dayan hoped that at least some of the departed workers would choose to settle in an Arab state. Gazit, *Carrot and the Stick,* 187; Brown, *Personal Imprint,* 177.

43. Shashar, *Seventh Day War,* 122–23 (emphasis in the original).

44. See George Dib and Fuad Jabber, *Israel's Violation of Human Rights in the Occupied Territories: A Documented Report,* 3rd ed. (Beirut: Institute for Palestine Studies, 1970), 234 ff. and passim (it should be noted, however, that the details offered by this source—dates, for example—are not always accurate); Peter Dodd and Halim Barakat, "Palestinian Refugees of 1967: A Sociological Study," *Muslim World* 60, no. 2 (1970), 60; Gussing Report (article 71).

45. Interviews with Colonel Amitai, 2007; and by phone, 3 July 2006.

46. Colonel Amitai's account in Central Command, The Six Day War: Concluding Report, part 2, section 3, September 1967, 3-901/1967, IDFA. See also The Six Day War: The Campaign in the Jordanian Arena, 384.

47. "La guerre à Jérusalem," entry for 4 July.

48. See Esther Rosalind Cohen, *Human Rights in the Israeli-Occupied Territories, 1967–1982* (Manchester: Manchester University Press, 1985), 100. Israel ratified the Fourth Geneva Convention in July 1951. See also Col. Meir Shamgar, Military Advocate General, to Chief of Staff, 10 August 1967, 11-218/1974, IDFA.

49. Brown, *Personal Imprint,* 153–54.

50. Dayan, *Milestones,* 496. The English version of Dayan's autobiography omits the segment about the intention to drive away the Arab villagers (Dayan, *Story of My Life,* 320–21).

51. Interview with Gen. (ret.) Uzi Narkiss, 10, 15, and 24 July 1997, Oral History Project, Yitzhak Rabin Center for Israel Studies. For Rabin's order and threat see also

Dayan's letter to Health Minister Yisrael Barzilai, quoted by the former in minutes, KFASC, 13 June 1967, A/8161/7, ISA. Narkiss revealed his responsibility for the destruction in a somewhat more "modest" way in Pedatzur, *Triumph of Bewilderment*, 106, 265, n. 5; Hadar Horesh, "An Agency's Death," *Kol ha-'Ir*, 6 June 1986; Aryeh Bender, "I Alone Decided to Expel the Inhabitants of the Latrun Area," *Ma'ariv*, 8 May 1994; "Uzi Narkiss: A Local Initiative" (transcript of a telephone conversation between Ra'anan Lurie and Narkiss, 21 June 1997), *Musaf Haaretz*, 5 June 1998. For the involvement of Col. Baruch Bar-Lev, the chief of staff of the Central Command, see Gazit, "Consolidation of Policy," 47; and interview with Amitai (2007).

52. Gazit, *Carrot and the Stick*, 171–72.

53. Dayan's letter to Health Minister Yisrael Barzilai, quoted by the former in minutes, KFASC, 13 June 1967, A/8161/7, ISA; Dayan's comments in minutes, KFASC, 28 June 1967, A/8161/7, ISA.

54. Gussing Report (article 60).

55. Dayan, *Milestones*, 456. The English translation offers only the first part of the quote (*Story of My Life*, 300). Dayan, characteristically contradictory, stated in the Knesset at the time, in response to a question concerning the Latrun villages, that the West Bankers had not been "an objective neutral populace in this war. . . . They had constituted a part of [Jordan's] disposition of fortifications." *Knesset Proceedings*, 21 June 1967, 2386.

56. See Brown, *Personal Imprint*, 114, 129.

57. Bentov, *Days Tell*, 161.

58. Eshkol's comments in KFASC, 27 June 1967, A/8161/7, ISA.

59. Ya'acov Herzog's diary, 14 June 1967, A/4511/3, ISA; Haber, *Today War Will Break Out*, 275–76. Notwithstanding, some 3,000 people were evicted from the Jewish Quarter in the following days, and land in this area was expropriated. Wilson, *Jerusalem*, 130; Gussing Report (article 114).

60. See Rashid Khalidi, "Future of Arab Jerusalem," 139–40.

61. Benziman, *Jerusalem*, 37–43 (Shapira quotation on 40); Narkiss, *Soldier of Jerusalem*, 213–15; Herzog, *Living History*, 175; Gorenberg, *Accidental Empire*, 42–45; Thalmann Report (article 113). In his autobiography Kollek states that Dayan gave him the go-ahead to level the Moroccan quarter; Teddy Kollek, with Amos Kollek, *For Jerusalem: A Life* (London: Weidenfeld and Nicolson, 1978), 197.

62. Cabinet minutes, 11 June 1967, A/8164/6, ISA. For the Jewish attempts to purchase the area of Harat al-Magharibah see Porath, *Emergence of the Palestinian-Arab National Movement*, 258–59.

63. Herzog, *Living History*, 175; Gazit, *Carrot and the Stick*, 41–42.

64. Benvenisti, *Jerusalem*, 306; Halabi, *West Bank Story*, 35.

65. Interview with Gen. (ret.) Shlomo Lahat, 22 February 2001, Oral History Project, Yitzhak Rabin Center for Israel Studies.

66. Gavin Young, "Jordan's Tragic Nightmare," *Observer* (London), 25 June 1967; Bowen, *Six Days*, 280. Quotation from Young.

67. Campbell, Jerusalem, 29 February 1968, POL 27 ARAB-ISR, RG59, Central Files 1967–69, USNA.

68. Gideon Levy, "Shaham Ordered to Expel. I Refused to Obey the Order," *Musaf Haaretz*, 5 June 1998. In later years Lurie has become a famous political cartoonist and journalist in the United States.

69. Ibid.

70. Zvi Shiloah, *Ashmat Yerushalayim* [The guilt of Jerusalem] (Tel Aviv: Karni, 1989), 53. Allon's proposal: Brown, *Personal Imprint*, 53–54. Dayan rejected the proposal, saying that the action "might turn into a barbaric and inhuman operation like no other."

71. Burns, Amman, 10 June 1967, POL 27 ARAB-ISR, RG59, Central Files 1967–69, USNA.

72. Peter Dodd and Halim Barakat, *River without Bridges: A Study of the Exodus of the 1967 Palestinian Arab Refugees* (Beirut: Institute for Palestine Studies, 1968), 40.

73. Burns, Amman, 10 June 1967, POL 27 ARAB-ISR, RG59, Central Files 1967–69, USNA; Dana Adams Schmidt, "100,000 in Jordan Said to Have Fled across River," *New York Times*, 12 June 1967; Dodd and Barakat, *River without Bridges*, 40–42; Middleton, Beirut, 25 June 1967, REF ARAB, RG59, Central Files 1967–69, USNA.

74. For the causes of the West Bankers' flight see Dodd and Barakat, *River without Bridges,* particularly chapter 5 (p. 54 offers a concise summary). The authors, a sociologist and a social psychologist at the American University of Beirut, based their study on a survey conducted among refugee families in Jordan shortly after the war. See also Don Peretz, "Israel's New Arab Dilemma," *Middle East Journal* 22, no. 1 (1968), 46–47; Gussing Report (articles 48–50).

75. See Barbour, Tel Aviv, 10 June 1967, POL 27 ARAB-ISR, RG59, Central Files 1967–69, USNA.

76. Barbour, Tel Aviv, 13 June 1967 (telegram 4110), POL 27 ARAB-ISR, RG59, Central Files 1967–69, USNA.

77. SOSFA [Foreign Secretary] to UK Embassy in Tel Aviv, 13 June 1967, PREM/13/1621, UKNA.

78. Barbour, Tel Aviv, 13 June 1967 (telegram 4115), POL 27 ARAB-ISR, RG59, Central Files 1967–69, USNA. The official, whose name is not mentioned in the cable, was almost certainly Shaul Bar-Haim, the director of the Middle East Department.

79. Anwar al-Khatib to Gen. Herzog, 23 June 1967, facsimile of the Arabic original in Benziman, *Jerusalem,* 31. Khatib's letter gives a wrong date for the meeting (7 instead of 9 June).

80. For Herzog's version see his *Living History,* 174, and a statement on his behalf quoted in Shmuel Me'iri, "Herzog's Transfer," *Kol ha-'Ir,* 8 November 1991. For Anwar al-Khatib's account see Hillel Cohen, "I Was Not a Partner," *Kol ha-'Ir,* 15 November 1991.

81. Benziman, *Jerusalem*, 29–30.

82. Wilson, Jerusalem, 15 June 1967, POL 27 ARAB-ISR, RG59, Central Files 1967–69, USNA.

83. Interview with General Narkiss, *Musaf Haaretz*, 21 October 1988.

84. Address to the State Department's Foreign Policy Conference for Educators, June 19, 1967, *Public Papers of the Presidents of the United States: Lyndon B. Johnson, 1967*, book I (Washington, D.C., 1968), 630–34.

85. S/RES/237 (1967), 14 June 1967, UNPR. The resolution was endorsed by the General Assembly on 4 July. A/RES/2252 (ES-V), 4 July 1967, UNPR.

86. Dayan's comments in KFASC, 13 June 1967, A/8161/7, ISA.

87. Peretz, "Israel's New Arab Dilemma," 46.

88. President Johnson to Senator Gore, 12 July 1967; Rusk to Embassy in Tel Aviv, 1 July 1967, both in REF ARAB, RG59, Central Files 1967–69, USNA. Quotation from Rusk's cable.

89. Middleton, Beirut, 25 June 1967, REF ARAB; Wilson, Jerusalem, 28 June 1967, POL 27 ARAB-ISR, both in RG59, Central Files 1967–69, USNA. See also Summary—Informal Staff Report . . . , Senate Judiciary Subcommittee on Refugees, 10 August 1967, REF ARAB, RG59, Central Files 1967–69, USNA.

90. Hadow, Tel Aviv, to FO, 26 June 1967, FCO/17/214, UKNA; James Feron, "Israelis to Allow Refugees to Go Back to West Bank," *New York Times*, 3 July 1967. Quotation from the *Times* story.

91. See Eshkol's comments and Resolution 565 in cabinet minutes, 25 June 1967, A/8164/10, ISA.

92. Ibid.

93. See, for instance, Ambassador Hadow's report to FO on his talk with General Herzog, 21 June 1967, FCO/17/212, UKNA.

94. Statement by General Chaim Herzog, Commander of the Forces in the West Bank, 14 June 1967, FM/4097/8, ISA.

95. Hadow, Tel Aviv, to FO, 19 June 1967, FCO/17/212, UKNA.

96. Herzog, *Living History*, 174. In a statement issued on Herzog's behalf in 1991, when he was the president of Israel (quoted in Me'iri, "Herzog's Transfer," *Kol ha-'Ir*, 8 November 1991), the number given for those who had left the West Bank was "about 200,000."

97. Statement by General Chaim Herzog, 16 June 1967, FM/4097/8, ISA.

98. Arazi to director of Middle East Dept., 27 June 1967, FM/4097/3, ISA.

99. Rusk, New York, 22 June 1967, *FRUS* 19: 532–34.

100. Katzenbach to US Embassy in Tel Aviv et al., 21 June 1967; more detailed instructions to this effect in Katzenbach to US Embassy in Tel Aviv et al., 26 June 1967, both in REF ARAB, RG59, Central Files 1967–69, USNA.

101. Ben-Horin to Levavi, 23 June 1967, FM/4097/8, ISA.

102. Rafael, *Destination Peace*, 177, 170 (quotation from 170).

103. See, for example, Harman, Washington, to Prime Minister et al., 22 June 1967, A/7936/3, ISA; Rafael, New York, to Levavi, FM, 24 June 1967, A/7921/2, ISA.

104. Sapir, London, to Eshkol, 27 June 1967, A/7921/2, ISA. Literally the Hebrew word *hasbarah* means "explanation" or "information," but in political terms it essentially refers to propaganda. Sapir's phone calls: interview with General Narkiss, *Musaf Haaretz*, 21 October 1988.

105. Eban, New York, to Eshkol, 24 June 1967, A/7936/3, ISA.

106. Resolution 565, cabinet minutes, 25 June 1967, A/8164/10, ISA; Levavi, FM, to Eban, New York, 25 June 1967, A7936/3, ISA.

107. Yafeh to Levavi, 28 June 1967, A/7921/2, ISA. Premier Eshkol made a similar statement at the Knesset Foreign Affairs and Security Committee: the free buses, he said, were merely intended to facilitate the departure of those wishing to leave. Eshkol's comments in KFASC, 27 June 1967, A/8161/7, ISA.

108. Comay, FM, to Eban, New York, 25 June 1967, A/7936/3, ISA.

109. Stephen Jessel, "Israeli General Has Faith in Coexistence with the Arabs," *The Times* (London), 13 July 1967.

110. Hadow, Tel Aviv, to FO, 26 June 1967, FCO/17/214, UKNA.

111. For the conditions of the new refugees in Jordan see Report of the Commissioner-General of the United Nations Relief and Works Agency for Palestine Refugees in the Near East[,] 1 July 1966–30 June 1967, supplement no. 13 (article 32), A/6713, 30 June 1967 (submitted on 15 September 1967) [henceforth: UNRWA Report], UNPR; Gussing Report, annex II: Aide-memoire submitted . . . by the Jordanian authorities. See also Gilmour and Walters, "'There Is a Great Deal of Talk about Peace . . . ,'" *The Times* (London), 27 July 1967.

112. Muhammad El-Farra, *Years of No Decision* (London: KPI, 1987), 72. Ambassador Farra claims that he cabled his advice to Amman, but mysteriously the dispatch never reached its destination.

113. SOSFA [Foreign Secretary] to UK Embassy in Amman, 29 June 1967, FCO/17/214, UKNA; Katzenbach to Embassy in Tel Aviv et al., 26 June 1967; Adams, Amman, 27 June 1967, both in REF ARAB, RG59, Central Files 1967–69, USNA.

114. See, for example, Talking points for use with King Hussein, [27 June 1967], POL 7 Jordan, RG59, Central Files 1967–69, USNA.

115. Eban, New York, to Prime Minister, 29 June 1967, A/7938/10, ISA.

116. Embassy of Israel, Washington, Statement Following the Meeting of the Government of Israel, 29 June, 1967, POL 27 ARAB-ISR, RG59, Central Files 1967–69, USNA.

117. Adams, Amman, 30 June and 3 July 1967, both in POL 27-9 ARAB-ISR, RG59, Central Files 1967–69, USNA.

118. Bentov's comments in cabinet minutes, 29 June 1967, A/8164/11, ISA.

119. Note by Ya'acov Herzog, quoted in Segev, *1967*, 407. The translation here is my own, relying on the Hebrew original (*1967*, 428).

120. Wilson, Jerusalem, 24 June 1967, POL 2 SITREP, RG84, Post Files: American Consulate-General, 1967, USNA; Adams, Amman, 30 June 1967, POL 27-9 ARAB-ISR, RG59, Central Files 1967–69, USNA; Adams, Amman, 22 June 1967, REF ARAB, USNA; Sharon, London, to FM, 25 June 1967, FM/4088/10, ISA; Bruce, London, 27 June 1967, POL 27-9 ARAB-ISR, RG59, Central Files 1967–69, USNA.

121. Memorandum by Paul K. Lapp to Herbert J. Chase, 8 July 1967, Jerusalem East Mission, GB165-0161, Box 73/2, MECA; Wilson, Jerusalem, 14 July 1967, REF ARAB, RG59, Central Files 1967–69, USNA.

122. Foreign Minister to Prime Minister, 7 August 1967, G/6692/16, ISA.

123. Lewen, Jerusalem, to Moberly, FO, 12 September 1967, FCO/17/212, UKNA.

124. Pethybridge, Jerusalem, to Moberly, FO, 11 October 1967, FCO/17/212, UKNA.

125. Interview with Uzi Narkiss, *Musaf Haaretz*, 21 October 1988.

126. Interview with Amitai (2007).

127. Memorandum, Infiltration from the East Bank to the West, [17 September 1967], 70-117/1970, IDFA. The historian Michael Oren argues (*Six Days of War*, 306) that Dayan deemed the ambushes inhuman and ended them a week after the war, but this military document states unequivocally, and in the present tense: "In order to stop the infiltration, the Central Command lays about 50 ambushes along the Jordan every night."

128. A testimony of a soldier, recorded by MK Uri Avnery, 10 September 1967. Five days earlier, Avnery sent a letter to Chief of Staff Rabin in which he listed a number of similar lethal incidents. Avnery to Lt. Gen. Rabin, 5 September 1967. I am grateful to Mr. Avnery for providing me with copies of these records. For an English translation (not entirely accurate) of the soldier's statement see Schleifer, *Fall of Jerusalem*, 221–22. Other soldiers also testified to the explicit order to shoot to kill anyone crossing the Jordan River, regardless of who he or she was. See Alon Gan, "Ha-Si'ah she-Gava'? 'Tarbut ha-Sihim' ke-Nisayon le-Gabesh Zehut Meyahedet la-Dor ha-Sheni ba-Kibbutzim" [The discourse that faded away? The 'discourses' culture' as an attempt to form a distinctive identity to the kibbutzim's second generation], Ph.D. diss., Tel Aviv University, 2002, 117–18.

129. Segev, *1967*, 540.

130. Haber, *Today War Will Break Out*, 291; Segev, *1967*, 540.

131. Lewen, Jerusalem, to FO, 11 October 1967; Pethybridge, Jerusalem, to Moberly, FO, 11 October 1967, both in FCO/17/212, UKNA. According to the latter, the Israeli Army Command said in the press that "anything that moves" at night would be shot; those caught crossing by day would be turned back.

132. Shashar, *Seventh Day War*, 269 (entry for 27 December).

133. Teveth, *Cursed Blessing*, 321.

134. Interview with Gen. (ret.) Gazit, 28 April 2004, Tel Aviv.

135. Middleton, Beirut, 27 July 1967, REF ARAB, RG59, Central Files 1967–69, USNA; see also *PAD, 1968*, 245–49; UNRWA Report (article 40).

136. Ruvik Rosentahl, "The First Hundred Days" [in Hebrew], *Panim* 39 (2007), 42.

137. Wilson, Jerusalem, 8 August 1967, REF 11 West Bank Refugees, RG84, Post Files: American Consulate-General, 1967, USNA; interview with Col. (ret.) Beni Meitiv, the military commander of the southern district of the Gaza Strip in 1967–1969, 19 November 2003, Ashkelon.

138. Ruhi al-Khatib, *Judaization of Jerusalem*, 9.

139. Thalmann Report (articles 17–18).

140. Cabinet resolution 591, 2 July 1967, G/6304/1074, ISA; *Levi Eshkol: Selected Documents*, 577. See also Embassy of Israel, Washington, Actions of the Government of Israel on the West Bank and the Gaza Strip, 3 July 1967, POL 27 ARAB-ISR, RG59, Central Files 1967–69, USNA; Gvati's diary, 29 June and 2 July 1967, File 2, Box 12, Record Group 15 (Gvati), TMA.

141. Unsigned telegram from UK Embassy in Tel Aviv, 3 July 1967, FCO/17/93, UKNA.

142. Memorandum by Dr. Herzog, Meeting with Charles, 2 July 1967, YHP.

143. Burns, Amman, 9 July 1967, REF ARAB, RG59, Central Files 1967–69, USNA.

144. Barbour, Tel Aviv, 9 July 1967, POL 27-9 ARAB-ISR, RG59, Central Files 1967–69, USNA.

145. Minutes, meeting of the Alignment's Political Committee, 7 July 1967, PPI.

146. Yigal Allon, Explanatory Notes to a Proposal for a Resolution [later dubbed the Allon Plan], 26 July 1967 (the Explanatory Notes are dated 13 July), A/7921/2, ISA.

147. SOSFA [Foreign Secretary] to UK Embassy in Tel Aviv, 20 July 1967, PREM/13/1622, UKNA.

148. Harold Jackson, "King Hussein Facing Threat of Overthrow," *Guardian* (London), 17 July 1967.

149. Battle to Secretary, 14 July 1967, POL ISR-US, RG59, Central Files 1967–69, USNA.

150. Rusk to Embassies in Amman, Geneva, and Tel Aviv, 12 July 1967, REF ARAB, RG59, Central Files 1967–69, USNA.

151. Eban, New York, to Prime Minister, 12 July 1967, A/7921/2, ISA.

152. Gussing Report (articles 186–87); Dale, Tel Aviv, and Duncan, Amman, both 20 July 1967, REF ARAB, RG59, Central Files 1967–69, USNA; Memorandum of Conversation [Evron-Rostow], 30 July 1967, *FRUS* 19: 737–38; News from the Arabs under Israeli Control, 20 July 1967, FM/4088/6, ISA; Ya'ish, Washington, to Tekoah, FM, 26 July 1967, A/7938/10, ISA. Copy of the disputed application form in FM/4088/8, ISA. See also Gilmour and Walters, "'There Is a Great Deal of Talk . . . ,'" *The Times* (London), 27 July 1967.

153. Burns, Amman, 29 July 1967, POL 27-14 ARAB-ISR/ SANDSTORM, and Burns, 3 August 1967, REF ARAB; Barbour, Tel Aviv, 3 August 1967, REF ARAB, all in RG59, Central Files 1967–69, USNA.

154. Memorandum by Tekoah, The return of the Arabs to the West Bank[,] a meeting with Jordan's representative, 4 August 1967, FM/4097/3, ISA; Burns, Amman, 5, 7 and 10 August 1967, all in REF ARAB, RG59, Central Files 1967–69, USNA.

155. Transcript, Press conference with Foreign Minister Abba Eban, 14 August 1967, FCO/17/506, UKNA.

156. Gussing Report (article 189).

157. Cabinet Resolution 718, 6 August 1967, G/6304/1074, ISA.

158. Comay to Foreign Minister, 11 August 1967, FM/4088/7, ISA.

159. Transcript, Press conference with Foreign Minister Abba Eban, 14 August 1967, FCO/17/506, UKNA.

160. PM Jum'ah in a press conference, 10 September 1967, *PAD, 1967,* 693–97.

161. Israeli estimate: *Knesset Proceedings,* 13 May 1968, 1835.

162. See, for example, Israel's letter of 11 September to the UN Secretary-General in S/8153, A/6795, 12 September 1967, UNPR; Eshkol to Bordier (Vice President of ICRC, Geneva), 22 October 1967, A/7231/2, ISA.

163. Minutes, meeting of the Alignment's Political Committee, 18 July 1967, PPI.

164. Barbour, Tel Aviv, 3 November 1967, POL 27 ARAB-ISR, RG59, Central Files 1967–69, USNA. See also *Levi Eshkol: Selected Documents,* 577.

165. Burns, Amman, 21 August 1967, and Jordan's Foreign Ministry note, enclosed with Burns, Amman, 28 August 1967, both in REF ARAB, RG59, Central Files 1967–69, USNA; Gussing Report (articles 192–93); PM Jum'ah in a press conference, 10 September 1967, *PAD, 1967,* 693–97.

166. UNRWA Report (article 36); Burns, Amman, 21, 24 (enclosure: Jordan's Foreign Ministry note), 28, 29, 31 August 1967, all in REF ARAB, RG59, Central Files 1967–69, USNA; Campbell, 26 October 1967, REF 3 UNRWA, RG84, Post Files: American Consulate-General, 1967, USNA.

167. Copy: [Rusk?] to Embassy in Tel Aviv, undated (probably 23 August 1967), FCO/17/505, UKNA.

168. See Chief of Staff Rabin's comments in minutes of General Staff session, 19 June 1967, 206-117/1970, IDFA; a military prosecutor's statement, quoted in Felicia Langer, *With My Own Eyes: Israel and the Occupied Territories, 1967–1973* (London: Ithaca, 1975), 68.

169. Schleifer, *Fall of Jerusalem,* 220 (Schleifer does not name the official); Lt. Gen. Rabin's comment in minutes of General Staff session, 14 August 1967, 206-117/1970, IDFA.

170. "Refugees Urged to Go Home," *New York Times,* 8 August 1967.

171. Pryce-Jones, *Face of Defeat,* 31.

172. FM to Israel's diplomatic missions, 14 August 1967, FM/4088/6, ISA.

173. Transcript, Press conference with Foreign Minister Abba Eban, 14 August 1967, FCO/17/506, UKNA.

174. Ya'acov Herzog's diary, 13 July 1967, A/4511/3, ISA.

175. SOSFA [Foreign Secretary] to UK Embassy in Tel Aviv, 17 August 1967, PREM/13/1623, UKNA; Hall, Jerusalem, 19 August 1967, POL 27 ARAB-ISR, RG59, Central Files 1967–69, USNA.

176. Burns, Amman, 10 August 1967 (telegram 800), POL 27-9 ARAB-ISR, RG59, Central Files 1967–69, USNA. Burns's argument that certain Israelis wished to keep the West Bank for *Lebensraum* was vindicated within a few days, when Defense Minister Dayan stated in a party rally that Israel needed "living space." See chapter 5.

177. Rusk to Embassy in Tel Aviv, 26 August 1967, REF ARAB, RG59, Central Files 1967–69, USNA. The phrase "violent campaign of incitement" appears in Israel's letter of 11 September to the UN Secretary-General in S/8153, A/6795, 12 September 1967, UNPR.

178. Ya'acov Herzog's diary, 16 August 1967, A/4511/3, ISA.

179. Draft record of a meeting between the Foreign Secretary and the Israel Ambassador, 30 August, 1967, PREM/13/1623, UKNA.

180. Rusk to Embassy in Tel Aviv, 26 August 1967, REF ARAB, RG59, Central Files 1967–69, USNA.

181. Hall, Jerusalem, 6 September 1967, REF ARAB, RG59, Central Files 1967–69, USNA.

182. Campbell, Jerusalem, 8 November 1967, POL 2 West Bank, RG84, Post Files: American Consulate-General, 1967, USNA. Coming from an expert on Arab affairs, Farhi's last remark was exceptionally odd. PLO Chairman Ahmad al-Shuqayri was the only Arab leader to whom the verbal threat of throwing the Jews into the sea was attributed, and even his remark had been allegedly made before the war. See Moshe Shemesh, "Did Shuqayri Call for 'Throwing the Jews into the Sea'?" *Israel Studies* 8, no. 2 (2003), 70–81.

183. Cabinet resolution 763, 27 August 1967, ICS; Barbour, Tel Aviv, 28 August 1967, REF ARAB, RG59, Central Files 1967–69, USNA. According to Jordan, there were 3,722 "no-shows"; PM Jum'ah in a press conference, 10 September 1967, *PAD, 1967*, 693–97. In fact, they amounted to about 7,000: two or three days before the deadline Israel stopped transmitting processed forms to the Jordanian authorities, so there were additional approved applicants of whom Jordan did not know; Barbour, Tel Aviv, and Rusk to Embassy in Tel Aviv, both 29 August 1967, REF ARAB, RG59, Central Files 1967–69, USNA.

184. Cabinet resolution 785, cabinet session (summary), 3 September 1967, G/10136/4, ISA.

185. Rusk to Eban, 2 September 1967, A/7921/2, ISA.

186. Ya'acov Herzog's diary, 4, 5, 9, 10 September 1967, A/4511/3, ISA; Eban, New York, to Eshkol, 4 October 1967, A/7936/3, ISA; Uzai to Finance and Foreign Ministers, 9 October 1967, G/6405/4220, ISA; U Thant, *View from the UN* (London: David and Charles; Newton Abbot, 1978), 288.

187. Handley to Under Secretary, 8 September 1967, POL 27 ARAB-ISR, RG59, Central Files 1967–69, USNA.

188. According to Jordan, 14,150; according to Israel, 14,056; Gussing Report (article 190).

189. PM Jum'ah in a press conference, 10 September 1967, *PAD, 1967*, 693–97.

190. See Alexander Dotan, Those who leave for Jordan—their make-up and the motives for their departure (summary), 22 August 1967, FM/4097/3, ISA; Burns, Amman, 10 June 1967, POL 27 ARAB-ISR, RG59, Central Files 1967–69, USNA.

191. Eban, New York, to Eshkol, 20 September 1967, A/7936/3, ISA.

192. Minutes, meeting of Mapai's Secretariat, 14 September 1967, 2-24-1967-91, ILPA.

193. Family reunion program: Cabinet Resolution 777, 27 August 1967, ICS; Galili to Members of the Cabinet, 22 August 1967, G/6304/1074, ISA; Ya'acov Herzog's diary, 22 August 1967, A/4511/3, ISA.

194. Hadow, Tel Aviv, to FO, 16 October 1967, PREM/13/1623, UKNA.

195. Memorandum by Jarring, undated (probably mid-1969), 370-26-1, UNA. Ambassador Jarring recorded what Eban had told him. Dr. Herzog's report on the secret Hussein-Eban meeting on 25 May 1969 (Main points in meeting of May 25 1969, YHP) does not mention this issue.

196. Cited in "Palestinian Emigration and Israeli Land Expropriation in the Occupied Territories, *Journal of Palestine Studies* 3, no. 1 (1973), 111.

197. Hadow, Israel: Annual Review for 1967, FCO/17/468, UKNA.

198. Peretz, "Israel's New Arab Dilemma," 46.

199. See Yosef Weitz, *Yomani ve-Igrotai la-Banim* [My diary and letters to my sons], vol. 3, *Mishmar Homot (1945–1948)* [Walls' guard, 1945–1948] (Tel Aviv: Masadah, 1965), 293 (entry for 28 May 1948).

200. Gabriel Piterberg, "Erasures," *New Left Review* 10 (2001), 33–36 (quotation from 36).

201. *PAD, 1967,* 587–89.

202. Hall, Jerusalem, 1 September 1967, POL 2 SITREP Jerusalem, RG84, Post Files: American Consulate-General, 1967, USNA.

FIVE   An Entity versus a King

1. Minutes, Political Committee report—28.7.67, A/7921/2, ISA.

2. For text of the Khartoum summit's resolutions see *International Documents on Palestine (IDP), 1967* (Beirut, 1970), 656–57. The Arabic term *sulh* means peace in its deepest sense; reconciliation.

3. Moshe Shemesh, *Arab Politics, Palestinian Nationalism, and the Six Day War: The Crystallization of Arab Strategy and Nasir's Descent to War, 1957–1967* (Brighton: Sussex Academic Press, 2008), 242.

4. Mohamed Heikal, *Secret Channels: The Inside Story of Arab-Israeli Peace Negotiations* (London: HarperCollins, 1996), 131.

5. Laura M. James, *Nasser at War: Arab Images of the Enemy* (Basingstoke: Palgrave Macmillan, 2006), 133.

6. See Haytham al-Kilani, *Al-Istiratijiyat al-'Askariyyah lil-Hurub al-'Arabiyyah-al-Isra'iliyyah, 1948–1988* [The military strategies of the Arab-Israeli wars, 1948–1988] (Beirut: Markaz Dirasat al-Wahdah al-'Arabiyyah, 1991), 260.

7. Dean, Washington, to FO, 27 September 1967, PREM/13/1623, UKNA.

8. Briefing paper, Visit of Belgian Prime Minister to London, 10 November 1967, FCO/17/508, UKNA.

9. Mohamed Ahmed Mahgoub, *Democracy on Trial: Reflections on Arab and African Politics* (London: Andre Deutsch, 1974), 145. There are a number of works on the Khartoum Summit written by participants and scholars. Most prominent among the firsthand accounts: ibid., 136–46; Shafiq al-Hut, *'Ishrun 'Aman fi Munazzamat al-Tahrir al-Filastiniyah (1964–1984): Ahadith al-Dhikrayat* [Twenty years with the Palestinian Liberation Organization, 1964–1984: Memoir tales] (Beirut: Dar al-Istiqlal, 1986), 109–77; Abdel Magid Farid, *Nasser: The Final Years* (Reading: Ithaca, 1994), 51–67; Ahmad al-Shuqayri, "Memories of the Khartoum Summit Conference" [in Arabic], *Shu'un Filastiniyyah* 4 (1971), 90–99.

10. Rafi Sutton and Yitzhak Shoshan, *Anshei ha-Sod ve-ha-Seter: Me-'Alilot ha-Modi'in ha-Yisre'eli me-'Ever la-Gvulot* [Men of secret and stealth: Tales of Israeli intelligence ventures beyond the borders] (Tel Aviv: 'Edanim; Yediot Ahronot, 1990), 318–25; Kimche, *Palestine or Israel,* 262. From the Knesset podium Premier Eshkol quoted an extract of Nasser's keynote speech at Khartoum, and later read a much longer chunk of that speech before the KFASC; *Knesset Proceedings,* 13 November 1967, 122; minutes, KFASC, 14 November 1967, A/8161/9, ISA. The CIA allegedly bugged the Khartoum Summit and thus also obtained a full record of its proceedings; Ashton, *King Hussein of Jordan,* 394, n. 35.

11. Minutes, KFASC, 26 September 1967, A/8161/8, ISA.

12. Ya'acov Herzog's diary, 4 September 1967, A/4511/3, ISA. Eshkol, too, alluded in a press interview to "some limited progress" at Khartoum; *Ma'ariv,* 4 October 1967.

13. Ya'acov Herzog's diary, 3 September 1967, A/4511/3, ISA; minutes, KFASC, 5 September 1967, A/8161/8, ISA. Eban's quotation from the latter.

14. Minutes, KFASC, 20 October 1967, A/8161/8, ISA.

15. Ya'acov Herzog's diary, 3 September 1967, A/4511/3, ISA.

16. Cabinet Statement, 17 October 1967, G/10136/5, ISA; *Knesset Proceedings,* 13 November 1967, 123–24.

17. Cabinet Resolutions 46 (draft), 7 November 1967, and 49, 8 November 1967, ICS; Goldberg, New York, to President and Secretary of State, 12 November 1967, POL 27-14 ARAB-ISR, RG59, Central Files 1967–69, USNA. Emphasis added.

18. *Levi Eshkol: Selected Documents,* 589.

19. Resolutions B/9 of 18 October 1967 and B/21 of 12 November 1967 of the Ministerial Committee for Security Affairs, ICS. The initiative to erase the Green Line from Israel's maps came from Labor Minister Yigal Allon. *Levi Eshkol: Selected Documents,* 589.

20. Yigal Allon, oral history interviews, fourth and sixth meetings (28 May and 26 June 1979, respectively), A/5001/19, ISA; Gorenberg, *Accidental Empire,* 72–78.

21. Haim Gvati, *100 Shnot Hityashvut: Toldot ha-Hityashvut ha-Yehudit be-Eretz-Yisrael* [One hundred years of settlement: The history of Jewish settlement in the Land of Israel], vol. 2 (Tel Aviv: Ha-Kibbutz ha-Me'uhad, 1981), 211.

22. Pedatzur, *Triumph of Bewilderment,* 194–95.

23. Meron to Foreign Minister, 14 September 1967; Meron to Yafeh, 18 September 1967, both in FM/4088/8, ISA.

24. Gvati's diary, 10 September 1967, File 3, Box 12, Record Group 15 (Gvati), TMA.

25. For a thorough discussion see Gorenberg, *Accidental Empire,* 69–70, 102–18.

26. See Morris, *1948,* 167–71.

27. See cabinet session (summary), 24 September 1967, a.m., G/10136/4, ISA.

28. See, for example, Harman, New York, to Levavi and Bitan, FM, 25 September 1967 (telegrams 466, 467), A/7938/10, ISA; Rafael, New York, to Lurie, FM, 26 September 1967, FM/4088/8, ISA.

29. Eban, New York, to Levavi, FM, 24 September 1967, FM/4088/8, ISA.

30. Cabinet resolution 866, 1 October 1967, ICS.

31. Col. Gazit to Chief of Staff's Office, 27 September 1967, 46-2845/1997, IDFA.

32. Gorenberg, *Accidental Empire,* 121.

33. See FM to Embassy, Canberra, 27 September 1967, FM/4088/8, ISA; Rusk to US Embassy in Tel Aviv, 7 October 1967, *FRUS* 19: 874–76.

34. See Huberman, *Against All Odds,* 1: 32–36.

35. Gorenberg, *Accidental Empire,* 120–21.

36. Israeli Settlements in Occupied Territories, undated, NSF/Country File/Israel, Memos, Vol. VII, 8/67–12/67, Box 140, Lyndon B. Johnson Library, Austin, Texas (LBJL). The paper was part of a brief prepared for Eban's visit on 23–24 October.

37. See, for example, Moshe Dayan, *Mapah Hadashah Yahasim Aherim* [A new map, different relations] (Tel Aviv: Sifriyat Ma'ariv; Shikmonah, 1969), 179–80.

38. Memorandum, Battle to Secretary of State, 17 November 1967, *FRUS* 19: 1043–45. Already in September, the United States expressed its growing concern regarding Israel's shift toward "territorial expansionism." See memorandum, W.W.R. [Rostow] to President, 15 September 1967, and attached draft cable addressed to US Ambassador in Tel Aviv of 14 September 1967; and Goldberg, New York, 23 September 1967 (telegram 950), all in NSF/Country File/Israel, Memos, Vol. VII, 8/67–12/67, Box 140, LBJL. See also Donald Neff, *Warriors for Jerusalem: The Six Days that Changed the Middle East* (New York: Linden / Simon and Schuster, 1984), 322, 403 n.

39. Eshkol's comments in minutes, KFASC, 14 November 1967, A/8161/9; 4 October 1968, A/8162/2, both in ISA.

40. Minutes, Alignment's Political Committee, 18 August 1967, PPI. The verse invoked by Eshkol appears several times in Genesis 1 ("and God saw that it was good").

41. "M. Dayan: 'We Must Not Return to the Borders Determined in 1948,' " *Davar,* 10 August 1967. Dayan distinguished the West Bank from the other occupied territories by citing its historical significance for Jews.

42. Dean Rusk, *As I Saw It: A Secretary of State's Memoirs* (London: I. B. Tauris, 1991), 332. A secret State Department research paper offers a slightly different version:

when Rusk mentioned Israel's June assurance that it had no territorial ambitions, Eban replied, "That was before Syria and Jordan entered the war"; quoted in Neff, *Warriors for Jerusalem,* 336–37. See also Moshe Bitan's account of the Rusk-Eban meeting on 22 October in minutes, KFASC, 31 October 1967, A/8161/9, ISA.

43. Hut, *Twenty Years with the Palestinian Liberation Organization,* 139, 158, 160–61, 169. See also ʿAbd al-Majid Farid's article in *Al-Rai* (Amman), 9 May 1983. Anwar al-Khatib, still in exile in the Israeli town of Safed, denied sending a letter or a cable to Hussein. See "The Solution Is—a Federation," *Ha-ʿOlam ha-Zeh,* 6 September 1967; Katz to Adviser on Arab Affairs, 12 September 1967, GL/17035/1, ISA.

44. Mahmoud Riad, *The Struggle for Peace in the Middle East* (London: Quartet, 1981), 46–48; Mutawi, *Jordan in the 1967 War,* 174. See also Avi Shlaim's interview with King Hussein, 3 December 1996, Ascot; Memorandum of a meeting: Sandstorm, 15 July 1967, *FRUS* 19: 668–69.

45. Col. Carmon's remarks in minutes, General Staff session, 17 July 1967, 206-117/1970, IDFA.

46. Farid, *Nasser,* 48.

47. Wilson, Jerusalem, 5 August 1967, POL 2 SITREP, RG84, Post Files: American Consulate-General, 1967, USNA. On Israel's rejection of the West Bank elite's request for representation see Chaim Herzog, "The Palestinians: Policy and Tactics," *Haaretz,* 21 June 1974. According to Benziman (*Jerusalem,* 289), the request to send a West Bank deputation to Khartoum was submitted by Anwar al-Khatib.

48. Hall, Jerusalem, 16 September 1967, POL 27 ARAB-ISR, RG59, Central Files 1967–69, USNA.

49. Weekly activity report for the liberated [*sic*] areas 7/67, [6] September 1967, 69-117/1970, IDFA; Weekly report of the [Military] Government in the West Bank, 5–12 September 1967, 70-117/1970, IDFA; Digest of events in the West Bank (GSS report), 7 September 1967, FM/4088/8, ISA. Quotation from Arie Hauslich, "Palestinians Reject Khartoum," *Jewish Observer and Middle East Review,* 15 September 1967.

50. Shashar, *Seventh Day War,* 170–71; *Ha-ʿOlam ha-Zeh,* 13 September 1967; *Jerusalem Post,* 7 September 1967; Hauslich, "Palestinians Reject Khartoum" *Jewish Observer and Middle East Review,* 15 September 1967; FM to Israel's diplomatic missions, 7 September 1967, FM/4088/7, ISA. Some press reports described Shehadeh as "Acting President of the West Bank High Court of Appeal."

51. A survey exploring the Palestinian attitudes toward the future of the West Bank, conducted with 500 respondents between September 1967 and January 1968, showed that 58 percent desired the return of the Hashemite regime, while 40 percent favored an independent Palestinian state; Yohanan Peres, "Attitudes and Values in the West Bank: A Research Report, Submitted to the [Cabinet] Committee of the Administered Territories' Affairs," undated, 14, Library of the Hebrew University of Jerusalem, Mount Scopus.

52. Memorandum by Farhi, Yoskeh, 15 September 1967, DFP. For Jaʿbari's public statements see, for example, *Haaretz,* 26 July 1967; Burns, Amman, 12 September 1967, POL 27 ARAB-ISR, RG59, Central Files 1967–69, USNA.

53. Farhi to Gen. Narkiss, 7 September 1967 (Hebrew translation of the manifesto attached to Farhi's letter), 69-117/1970, IDFA. Six weeks later Darwish proposed the creation of a "United States of Israel," with local parliaments and a supreme legislator. See Shashar, *Seventh Day War*, 216 (entry for 23 October); *Ha-'Olam ha-Zeh*, 1 November 1967.

54. Shashar, *Seventh Day War*, 172; *Ha-'Olam ha-Zeh*, 13 September 1967.

55. As a contemporary leading Communist leader put it: "We considered that they [Shehadeh and his followers] were persuaded by the Israelis"; Interview with Na'im al-Ashhab.

56. Col. Gazit to Ahituv et al., Summary of discussion at the Coordinating Committee, 15 September 1967, 70-117/1970, IDFA. Comprising high-level representatives of the military and security apparatuses, the police, and the Foreign Ministry, this committee was entrusted with the task of coordinating political and security activities in the occupied territories. See Gazit, *Carrot and the Stick*, 83–85.

57. Rusk, New York, 26 September 1967, *FRUS* 19: 851–54.

58. Digest of events in the West Bank (GSS report), 17 September 1967, FM/4088/8, ISA. One of the dignitaries was tasked to consult Sheikh Ja'bari of Hebron, as well as the representative of Israel's Foreign Ministry in the West Bank.

59. Quoted in 'Atallah Mansour, "The Revival of the Palestinian Entity," *Haaretz*, 15 September 1967.

60. Weekly activity report for the liberated [*sic*] areas 9/67, 22 September 1967; Weekly report of the [Military] Government in the West Bank, 12–19 September 1967, both in 70-117/1970, IDFA.

61. Statement by a "responsible Jordanian source," 8 September 1967; PM Jum'ah in a press conference, 10 September 1967, both in *PAD, 1967*, 690, 693–97; Burns, Amman, 12 September 1967, POL 27 ARAB-ISR, and 25 September 1967, REF-ARAB, both in RG59, Central Files 1967–69, USNA.

62. Yasin, *Experience of the National Front in the Gaza Strip*, 93, 109, 112–14. Quotation from 93 (article 4 of the Front's charter).

63. Digest of events in the West Bank (GSS report), 15 September 1967, FM/4088/8, ISA. According to this report, among the members who took the decision were the committee's head Sheikh Sa'ih, Ruhi al-Khatib, and—oddly enough—Anwar Nuseibeh. See also the committee's announcement, *PAD, 1967*, 730–31.

64. Hall, Jerusalem, 21 September 1967, POL 27 ARAB-ISR, RG59, Central Files 1967–69, USNA.

65. Information and [Military] Government's contacts from August to 13.11.67 (register prepared by Moshe Sasson), entry for 29 September 1967, MSP.

66. Shashar, *Seventh Day War*, 206 (entry for 6 October).

67. See Ja'bari's remarks in Gideon Weigert, "Going Down to Details," *Jewish Observer and Middle East Review*, 6 October 1967.

68. The Interim National Covenant . . . , 4 October 1967, *PAD, 1967*, 782–91; *Al-Nahar* (Beirut), 4 October 1967; *Al-Hayat* (Beirut), 6 October 1967; interview with

Na'im al-Ashhab; Digest of events in the West Bank (GSS report), 17 October 1967, FM/4088/8, ISA. See also Farhi, "West Bank," 35.

69. In mid-September the Coordinating Committee recommended reducing Khatib's three-month exile by one month, in consequence of the moderation of his declared views. Col. Gazit to Ahituv et al., Summary of discussion at the Coordinating Committee, 15 September 1967, 70-117/1970, IDFA.

70. "The Solution Is—a Federation," *Ha-'Olam ha-Zeh,* 6 September 1967. The interview was published also in the Arabic offshoot of the Hebrew magazine: "Now, Now, Not Tomorrow," *Hadha al-'Alem* 43 (October 1967). See also Farhi to Gen. Narkiss and Col. Vardi, 22 August 1967, FM/4095/5, ISA.

71. Katz to Adviser on Arab Affairs, 12 September 1967, GL/17035/1, ISA.

72. Farhi to Gen. Narkiss et al., 1 October 1967, 72-117/1970, IDFA.

73. Maj. Farhi to Gen. Narkiss et al., 12 October 1967, 72-117/1970, IDFA.

74. Campbell, Jerusalem, 12 October 1967 (A-48); Hall, Jerusalem, 5 September 1967; Hall, Jerusalem, 30 August 1967 and 5 September 1967, all in POL 27 ARAB-ISR, RG59, Central Files 1967–69, USNA.

75. Hall, Jerusalem, 12 September 1967, POL 27 ARAB-ISR, RG59, Central Files 1967–69, USNA.

76. Maj. Farhi to Gen. Narkiss et al., 16 October 1967, 72-117/1970, IDFA.

77. Arie Hauslich, "Nablus Co-operates," *Jewish Observer and Middle East Review,* 1 December 1967.

78. Pethybridge, Jerusalem, to Moberley, FO, 25 October 1967, FCO/17/212, UKNA.

79. Program's text (described as a *manshur,* or leaflet, prepared by Shehadeh as a personal venture), undated, in Mahdi 'Abd al-Hadi, *Al-Mas'alah al-Filastinyyah wa-Mashari' al-Hulul al-Siyasiyyah 1934–1974* [The Palestinian question and proposals for political solutions, 1934–1974] (Beirut-Saida: al-Maktabah al-'Asariyyah, 1975), 333–35; discussion ibid., 324–26; Maj. Farhi to Gen. Narkiss et al., 27 October 1967, 71-117/1970, IDFA (Hebrew translation of the program enclosed with Farhi's letter); 'Anan Safadi, "West Bank Group Aims at 'Palestine Entity,'" *Jerusalem Post,* 29 October 1967; "Jordan or Arab Palestine?" *Jewish Observer and Middle East Review,* 3 November 1967.

80. The two Israeli troopers were tried for murder in the first degree. At the end of the legal process one was found guilty and sentenced to life imprisonment; the other was convicted of aiding in homicide and sentenced to five years in jail. See Dov Shefi, "The Reports of the U.N. Special Committees on Israeli Practices in the Territories: A Survey and Evaluation," in *Military Government in the Territories Administered by Israel, 1967–1980,* vol. 1, *The Legal Aspects,* ed. Meir Shamgar (Jerusalem: Hebrew University, 1982), 324–25, n. 79.

81. 'Abd al-Jawad Saleh, "Battle of the Entity," 57–59. Saleh writes further that in the wake of the dignitaries' gathering he was summoned by Major Farhi, who attempted to persuade him to agree to Palestinian self-rule; he rejected the idea (ibid., 59–62). The

Israeli documentation does not corroborate Saleh's account about such a meeting with Farhi.

82. Quotation from the traveler Alexander William Kinglake in 1834, in his *Eothen* (London: Century, 1982), 196.

83. CAS #NJJ 919 of 28 October 1967, summarized in Campbell, Jerusalem, 14 November 1967, POL 3 PAL Entity, RG59, Central Files 1967–69, USNA.

84. Digest of events in the West Bank (GSS intelligence review), 8 November 1967, FM/4088/8, ISA; Information and [Military] Government's contacts from August to 13.11.67 (register prepared by Moshe Sasson), entries for 29–30 October 1967, MSP; 'Abd al-Hadi, *Palestinian Question*, 325.

85. Farouqi's plan and covering letter in 'Abd al-Hadi, *Palestinian Question*, 327–32; Maj. Farhi to Gen. Narkiss et al., 11 November 1967, 73-117/1970, IDFA (Hebrew translation of the plan enclosed with Farhi's letter). For Farouqi's appeals for approval from outside the occupied territories see Digest of events in the West Bank (GSS reports), 26 November and 6 December 1967, both in FM/4088/5, ISA.

86. The Military Government's practical policy was to take no steps against "small gatherings for 'a discussion of the situation.'" See Michael Shashar, Main points for a lecture on the subject: The policy of the [Military] Government in Judea and Samaria, 4 December 1968, 48-52/85, IDFA.

87. Burns, Amman, 4 November 1967, POL 27 ARAB-ISR, RG59, Central Files 1967–69, USNA. A contemporary Palestinian journalist claimed that Shehadeh's entity initiative appealed to a large segment of the West Bank population, but "many" of his collaborators, who pretended to work for that cause, sent distorted reports behind his back to King Hussein in which they denounced it as a plot contrived by Israel; Jamil Hamad, "Palestinian Future—New Directions," *New Middle East,* August 1971, 18.

88. Burns, Amman, 4 November 1967, POL 27 ARAB-ISR, RG59, Central Files 1967–69, USNA.

89. Burns, Amman, 13 October 1967, POL 2 General-Jordan, RG84, Post Files: American Consulate-General, 1967, USNA; Talhuni's cable, quoted verbatim in *Al-Quds,* 27 September 1970.

90. Ya'acov Herzog's diary, 10 September 1967, A/4511/3, ISA.

91. Neff, *Warriors for Jerusalem,* 337; Eban's comments in minutes, KFASC, 20 October 1967, A/8161/8, ISA.

92. See, for example, memorandum of conversation: Abba Eban et al. and Walt Rostow and Harold Saunders, 23 October 1967, *FRUS* 19: 928–33.

93. Memorandum, Walt Rostow to President Johnson, 24 October 1967, *FRUS* 19: 941–43.

94. Katzenbach to Ambassador, Tel Aviv, 24 October 1967, NSF/Country File/ Israel, Cables, Vol. VII, 8/67–12/67, Box 140, LBJL.

95. Abba Eban, Live or Perish, unpublished manuscript (1969), 447–48. Emphasis added.

96. Galili to Eshkol, 30 October 1967, A/7231/1, ISA.

97. Ya'acov Herzog, Special chapter on Charles, dictated on 3 November 1967, YHP.

98. See Neff, *Warriors for Jerusalem*, 342 (Neff relies on his 1983 interview with Hussein); Shlaim's interview with King Hussein, 3 December 1996, Ascot.

99. Goldberg, New York, 4 November 1967, *FRUS* 19: 981–87. On the Hussein-Nasser understanding see also Samir Mutawi, *Jordan in the 1967 War*, 177–78; Heikal, *Secret Channels*, 132. In his published account Hussein argues that he and Nasser forged their position on 30 September. Hussein de Jordanie, *Ma "guerre" avec Israël*, 146–48.

100. Telegram to the White House, 3 November 1967, *FRUS* 19: 973–81. Anderson, an investment specialist and former secretary of the treasury, was a longtime acquaintance of Nasser's.

101. Goldberg, New York, 5 November 1967, *FRUS* 19: 988–91; Rafael, Report on Goldberg-ForMin conversation on 4 November 1967, A/4510/16, ISA (the Israeli document does not include Eban's response).

102. Information received from a high-ranking Foreign Ministry official in Bonn and a British diplomat in Washington in FM to Israel's missions in Washington, New York, London, 1 November 1967, FM/3835/5; Ya'ish to FM, 3 November 1967, A/7936/6, both in ISA. British politician Julian Amery related in detail Hussein's ideas to Dr. Herzog on 2 November. See Ya'acov Herzog, Special chapter on Charles, dictated on 3.11.67, YHP.

103. Eshkol to Eban, 12 November 1967, A/7936/3, ISA; Ya'acov Herzog, Special chapter on Charles, dictated on 3.11.67, YHP (Herzog's accounts here refer to 5 November; obviously, the final part of this twenty-page paper was dictated after 3 November). Eshkol also alluded to the feelers that he had had from Hussein in an interview with *Ma'ariv*, 4 October 1967, and later at KFASC, 7 November 1967, A/8161/9, ISA. These careless pronouncements angered the Jordanians. Campbell, Jerusalem, 26 December 1967, POL 22 Israel/Arab Nov–Dec 1967, RG84, Post Files: American Consulate-General, 1967, USNA.

104. Yosef Nevo, Minister Yisrael Galili's Office, to members of the Committee of Directors General for *Hasbarah*, 2 October 1967, G/6692/19, ISA.

105. Netanel Lorch, FM, to Israel's missions in London, New York, Bonn, Paris, Rome, 12 November 1967, G/6692/19, ISA.

106. See memorandum of Conversation: Ephraim Evron and Rodger P. Davis, 21 December 1967, POL ISR-US, RG59, Central Files 1967–69, USNA.

107. Eban to FM (for the PM), 14 November 1967, A/7936/3, ISA; Duncan, Amman, 18 November 1967, POL 27 ARAB-ISR, RG59, Central Files 1967–69, USNA.

108. Katzenbach to Ambassador, Tel Aviv, 24 October 1967, NSF/Country File/Israel, Cables, Vol. VII, 8/67–12/67, Box 140, LBJL.

109. Meeting of Foreign Minister Eban with President L. B. Johnson, 24 October 1967, A/4510/16, ISA; Memorandum of Conversation: President Johnson et al. and Abba Eban et al., 24 October 1967, *FRUS* 19: 944–48. Quotation from the Israeli minutes, which are literal. The slightly different and more succinct American version recorded Eban as saying that "*some* [not *many*] Arabs in the West Bank are telling the

Israelis that they wish Israel would forget Hussein" (emphasis added). See also Harman's analysis in his telegram to Bitan, FM, 25 October 1967, A/4510/16, ISA. Ambassador Harman was present at the meeting.

110. Eban's comments in minutes, KFASC, 20 October 1967, A/8161/8, ISA.

111. Two months later Eban announced in the Knesset that certainly Israel *would* form its stance before any bilateral negotiations with an Arab state were to commence. *Knesset Proceedings,* 1 December 1967, 369.

112. Memorandum of Conversation: Evron and Davis, 21 December 1967, POL ISR-US, RG59, Central Files 1967–69, USNA. Davis referred to a meeting with Herzog which took place in Washington on 21 November 1967. See also *FRUS* 19: 1056, n. 1.

113. Eban's comments in minutes, KFASC, 20 October 1967, A/8161/8, ISA.

114. Yigal Allon, *Masakh shel Hol: (Yisrael ve-Arav bein Milhamah le-Shalom)* [A curtain of sand: Israel and the Arabs between war and peace], expanded ed. (Tel Aviv: Ha-Kibbutz ha-Me'uhad, 1968), 412–13.

115. Shiloah, *Guilt of Jerusalem,* 54–55. On the Movement for the Whole Land of Israel, also known as the Movement for Greater Israel, see Rael Jean Isaac, *Israel Divided: Ideological Politics in the Jewish State* (Baltimore: Johns Hopkins University Press, 1976), particularly chapter 4.

116. Ya'acov Herzog, Special chapter on Charles, YHP.

117. Col. Gazit to Gen. Narkiss et al., 12 November 1967, 71-117/1970, IDFA; Brown, *Personal Imprint,* 163–66. All mentions of the emigration issue have been systematically sanitized by the IDFA, including in Gazit's record.

118. Col. Gazit to Ahituv et al., Summary of discussion of the Coordinating Committee, 17 November 1967, 73-117/1970, IDFA; Hillel to Foreign Minister's office et al., 3 December 1967, FM/4088/5, ISA; Brown, *Personal Imprint,* 166–68. See also Shlomo Gazit, "Early Attempts at Establishing West Bank Autonomy (The 1968 Case Study)," *Harvard Journal of Law and Public Policy* 3, no. 1 (1980), 139–41.

119. Eban's comments in minutes, KFASC, 8 December 1967, A/8161/9, ISA.

120. Minutes, Arab contacts, 12 November 1967, A/7921/3, ISA. The other participants in the consultation were Police Minister Eliyahu Sasson, Dr. Herzog, and Avi'ad Yafeh, Eshkol's private secretary.

121. Yafeh to Dr. Herzog (handwritten note), 12 November 1967, A/7921/3, ISA.

122. Ya'acov Herzog's diary, 18 October 1967, A/4511/3, ISA. Moshe Sasson was the son of Minister Eliyahu Sasson, one of the committee's members. Avi'ad Yafeh, Eshkol's private secretary, was his brother-in-law.

123. PM Eshkol to Moshe Sasson, 12 November 1967, A/7921/3, ISA.

124. Dr. Herzog's comments in minutes, A meeting at the Prime Minister's office in Jerusalem, 7 November 1967, A/7936/3, ISA. See also Eban, New York, to Lurie, FM, 11 November 1967, A/7936/3, ISA; Rusk to Embassy in Tel Aviv, 5 November 1967, *FRUS* 19: 994–97.

125. Ya'acov Herzog's diary, 27–28 September 1967, A/4511/3, ISA; Ya'acov Herzog, Special chapter on Charles, YHP. Quotation from the latter.

126. Report by Ya'acov Herzog, Two Meetings with Charles (On the morning of November 19th and on the morning of November 20th respectively); Herzog to PM, 21 November 1967, both in YHP. All quotations from the former. These two records are the only available primary sources for this meeting. Years later, Hussein's recollection of the meeting was rather vague: "We were talking about our hopes that we would see this resolution [Resolution 242, adopted by the Security Council three days later] implemented"; Shlaim's interview with King Hussein, 3 December 1996, Ascot. Julian Amery and Air Vice Marshall Sir Erik Bennet, a former adviser to Hussein, were also present at the first meeting.

127. Memorandum, Political moods in the West Bank (according to governors' reporting), undated, MSP; Moshe Sasson to PM, The political contacts with Arab leaders in Jerusalem and the [West] Bank (first summary for the period 14.11.67–14.12.67), 15 December 1967, A/7921/3, ISA.

128. Political contacts with Palestinian leaders—summary of a discussion chaired by the PM on 21.11.67, A/7921/3, ISA. Col. Gazit, Avi'ad Yafeh and Moshe Sasson were also present (Sasson drafted the summary).

129. Eshkol's speech at the Kibbutzim Union's conference, 22 November 1967, A/7920/7, ISA. Eshkol delivered the same message, including the bride-and-dowry metaphor, at KFASC, 7 November 1967, A/8161/9, ISA. His figures were wrong: in 1967 the Arab citizens of Israel constituted 14.2 percent of the population (see introduction).

130. S/RES/242 (1967), 22 November 1967, UNPR. Regarding "withdrawal," the French version reads: "Retrait des forces armées israéliennes *des* territoires occupés lors du récent conflit" (emphasis added). For an elaborate discussion of the tussle over the resolution's wording see Neff, *Warriors for Jerusalem,* 334–47.

131. Rusk in a letter to Neff, 23 August 1983, cited in Neff, *Warriors for Jerusalem,* 405, note referring to p. 335.

132. Lord Caradon, "Security Council Resolution 242," in *U.N. Security Council Resolution 242: A Case Study in Diplomatic Ambiguity* (Washington, D.C.: Institute for the Study of Diplomacy, 1981), 13.

133. Adams, Amman, to Moore, FO, 1 December 1967, FCO/17/533, UKNA.

134. Campbell, Jerusalem, 25 November 1967, POL 3 United Nations—Arab Israeli Dispute, RG84, Post Files: American Consulate-General, 1967, USNA.

135. Digest of events in the West Bank (GSS report), 23 November 1967, FM/4088/5, ISA.

136. Barbour, Tel Aviv, 21 November 1967, POL 15-1 ISR, RG59, Central Files 1967–69, USNA.

SIX A One-Way Dialogue

1. Sasson's comments in minutes, KFASC, 9 February 1968, A/8161/10, ISA. Emphasis added.

2. Interview with Moshe Sasson (October 1996).

3. Brown, *Personal Imprint,* 167.

4. Barbour, Tel Aviv, 21 November 1967, POL 15-1 ISR, RG59, Central Files 1967–69, USNA.

5. For example, 'Amer, a manager of a bus company; memorandum of conversation by Sasson: 'Amer, 8 November 1967, MSP.

6. See, for instance, memorandum of conversation by Sasson: Antoun 'Atallah, 9 November 1967, MSP; Campbell, Jerusalem, 14 November 1967, POL 3 PAL Entity, RG59, Central Files 1967–69, USNA.

7. Memorandum of conversation by Sasson: 'Aziz Shehadeh, 15 November 1967, MSP. See also memorandum of conversation by Sasson: 'Ismat al-Dajani, 16 November 1967, MSP.

8. Maj. Farhi to Gen. Narkiss et al., 22 November 1967, 73-117/1970, IDFA. The identity of Farhi's source was concealed by IDFA.

9. Memorandum of conversation by Sasson: Janho and Shehadeh, 27 November 1967, MSP; Sasson to PM, The political contacts with Arab leaders in Jerusalem and the [West] Bank (first summary for the period 14.11.67–14.12.67), 15 December 1967, A/7921/3, ISA. The records do not give the exact date of Janho's meeting with the king. Hussein arrived in Paris on 23 October and left on the 29th.

10. Memorandum of conversation by Sasson: Janho and Shehadeh, 27 November 1967, MSP.

11. Memoranda of conversation by Sasson: Janho, Shehadeh, and 'Aql; Anwar Nuseibeh, both on 30 November 1967, MSP.

12. Memorandum of conversation by Sasson: Janho, Shehadeh, and 'Aql, 30 November 1967, MSP.

13. Memorandum, Meeting with the PM, 30 November 1967, A/7921/3, ISA.

14. Memorandum of conversation by Sasson: 'Aziz Shehadeh, 5 December 1967, MSP. In fact, Shehadeh had already given Sasson a list of twenty people whom he claimed to be supportive of his movement. However, most of them were not prominent leaders. Memorandum of conversation by Sasson: 'Aziz Shehadeh, 15 November 1967, MSP.

15. Maj. Farhi to Gen. Narkiss et al., 10 and 14 December 1967, both in 74-117/1970, IDFA; Sasson to PM, The political contacts with Arab leaders in Jerusalem and the [West] Bank (first summary for the period 14.11.67–14.12.67), 15 December 1967, A/7921/3, ISA.

16. The figures are based on the memoranda of these meetings, MSP.

17. Memorandum of conversation by Sasson: Anwar al-Khatib, 23 November 1967, MSP.

18. Memorandum of conversation by Sasson: Hamdi Kan'an, 29 November 1967, MSP.

19. Memoranda of conversation by Sasson: Hikmat al-Masri and Walid al-Shak'ah, both on 29 November 1967, MSP. The records do not disclose the names of the other four notables. For Nasser's speech, delivered at Egypt's National Assembly on 23 November 1967, see *IDP, 1967,* 701–15 (quotation from 712).

20. Col. Gazit to Ahituv et al., Summary of discussion of the Coordinating Committee, 17 November 1967, 73-17/1970, IDFA; Hillel to Foreign Minister's office et al., 3 December 1967, FM/4088/5, ISA (quotation appears in both documents); Brown, *Personal Imprint,* 148; Raphaeli, "Military Government in the Occupied Territories," 188.

21. Col. Gazit, Summary of discussion of the Core Coordinating Committee, 8 December 1967; Col. Gazit, Summary of discussion of the Expanded Coordinating Committee, 8 December 1967, both in 74-17/1970, IDFA.

22. Sasson to PM, The Political contacts with Arab leaders in Jerusalem and the [West] Bank (first summary for the period 14.11.67–14.12.67), 15 December 1967, A/7921/3, ISA. The memoranda of conversation with Shehadeh and his associates do not reflect their alleged support of the Nablus scheme.

23. Sasson to PM (covering letter), 15 December 1967, A/7921/3, ISA.

24. See Edouard H. Saab, "Avec ceux qui viennent de partir," *Le Monde,* 10 February 1968.

25. *Knesset Proceedings,* 20 February 1968, 1109.

26. Col. Gazit., Summary of discussion of the Core Coordinating Committee, 8 December 1967 and 15 December 1967, both in 74-117/1970, IDFA.

27. Lt. Col. Vered to C.G. of the Central Command et al., Operation Excrement 3 Execution Report, [?] December 1967, 74-117/1970, IDFA.

28. Campbell, Jerusalem, 21 December 1967, POL 30 Defectors and Expellees, RG84, Post Files: American Consulate-General, 1967, USNA.

29. Memorandum of conversation by Sasson: 'Izzat Karman, 7 December 1967, MSP.

30. Memorandum of conversation by Sasson: Shehadeh and Janho, 10 December 1967, MSP.

31. Digest of events in the West Bank (GSS report), 26 December 1967, FM/4088/5, ISA.

32. Sayigh, *Armed Struggle and the Search for State,* 173; Shuaibi, "Development of Palestinian Entity-Consciousness," part II, 60; Campbell, Jerusalem, 23 December 1967, POL 2 SITREP, RG84, Post Files: American Consulate-General, 1967, USNA; Ehud Yaari, *Strike Terror: The Story of Fatah* (New York: Sabra, 1970), 147–48. See also Shemesh, *Palestinian Entity,* 177.

33. Memorandum of conversation by Sasson: 'Aziz Shehadeh, 30 December 1967, A/7045/12, ISA.

34. Memorandum of conversation by Sasson: Muhammad Darwish, 7 November 1967, MSP.

35. Digest of events in the West Bank (GSS report), 26 December 1967, FM/4088/5, ISA.

36. Maj. Farhi to Gen. Narkiss et al., 22 November 1967, 73-117/1970, IDFA.

37. Rabin's comments in minutes, General Staff session, 31 July 1967, 206-117/1970, IDFA.

38. For Zaru see Lt. Col. Efrat to Defense Minister's military aide de camp, [7?] August 1967; Col. Gazit to C.G. of the Central Command et al., Summary of a meeting with the C.G. of the Central Command and the chief of staff of the West Bank's Government, 23 August 1967, both in 65-117/1970, IDFA; Maj. Rabinovich to Ahituv et al. (summary of the Coordinating Committee's discussion on 12 September 1967), 13 September 1967, 69-117/1970, IDFA. For Saleh see A proposal for operations in the Ramallah-Al-Bireh area, [?] October 1967; Col. Gazit to head of Batmar (Hebrew acronym for Spatial Security), 9 October 1967; Lt. Col. Davidi to chief of staff of the [West Bank's Military] Government, 10 October 1967; Col. Gazit., Summary of discussion of the Core Coordinating Committee, 10 October 1967, all in 72-117/1970, IDFA. In mid-October it was decided to postpone the removal of Mayor Saleh "for the time being;" Lt. Col. Vered to Batmar, 15 October 1967, 72-117/1970, IDFA. Both mayors were later expelled to Jordan—Zaru on 6 October 1969 and Saleh on 10 December 1973. See Ann Mosely Lesch, "Israeli Deportation of Palestinians from the West Bank and the Gaza Strip, 1967-1978," part I, *Journal of Palestine Studies* 8, no. 2 (1979), 123, and part II, *Journal of Palestine Studies* 8, no. 3 (1979), 109.

39. Gideon Weigert, "Palestinian Backs Peace Treaty," *Jewish Observer and Middle East Review,* 1 December 1967.

40. Symmes, Amman; Campbell, Jerusalem, both 27 December 1967, POL 27 ARAB-ISR, RG59, Central Files 1967-69, USNA.

41. Barbour, Tel Aviv, 29 December 1967, POL 30 Defectors and Expellees, RG84, Post Files: American Consulate-General, 1967, USNA.

42. Campbell, Jerusalem, 10 January 1968, POL 27 ARAB-ISR, RG59, Central Files 1967-69, USNA.

43. Argov, FM, to Embassy in Washington, 29 December 1967, FM/4088/5, ISA.

44. *Knesset Proceedings,* 13 February 1968, 1027. Four months later Dayan offered a different reason: the ban on 'Atallah's return, he told the Knesset, was meant to express objection to King Hussein's influence in the West Bank; *Knesset Proceedings,* 12 June 1968, 2230.

45. Digest of events in the West Bank (GSS report), 14 December 1967, FM/4088/5, ISA.

46. Lewen, Jerusalem, to FO, 28 December 1967, FCO/17/98, UKNA.

47. Shlomo Gazit, who worked very closely with Dayan and was privy to Israel's inner thinking, argued that all the talks with the Palestinians aimed at putting pressure on Hussein; interview with Gen. (ret.) Gazit (April 2004).

48. For example: Ruhi al-Khatib, *Judaization of Jerusalem,* 43-45; Saleh, *Israel's Policy of De-Institutionalization,* 10, 77-78; Sahliyeh, *In Search of Leadership,* 33, 46; Rami Khouri, *Jordan Times,* 8 November 1977, quoted in Lesch, "Israeli Deportation of Palestinians . . . ," part I, 108; Meir Litvak, "Inside versus Outside," in *The PLO and Israel: From Armed Conflict to Political Solution, 1964-1994,* ed. Avraham Sela and Moshe Ma'oz (Basingstoke: Macmillan, 1997), 187; Zeev Schiff, "The Year of the Bludgeon," *Haaretz,* special supplement, Passover Eve 1988 [1 April 1988].

49. Dayan's comments in minutes, KFASC, 26 September 1967, A/8161/8, ISA.

50. Digest of events in the West Bank (GSS reports), 21 and 24 December 1967, both in FM/4088/5, ISA; memorandum of conversation by Sasson: Anwar al-Khatib, 22 December 1967, A/7045/12, ISA; Ya'acov Herzog's diary, The Dayan incident—the danger of disintegration of the Unity Government, December 1967, A/4511/3, ISA; Sasson to PM, 24 December 1967, A/7921/3, ISA. Anwar al-Khatib's reference to Shuqayri was made two days before the latter was forced to resign the chairmanship of the PLO. When the Israeli French language newspaper *L'Information* reported on 29 December 1967 Kan'an's plea to the Israeli authorities regarding the summit delegation, the Nablus mayor hastened to send a written denial to the Israeli English daily, *Jerusalem Post,* which was published on 5 January 1968 ("West Bank Leaders Awaiting Arab Summit"). See also Pethybridge, Jerusalem, to Moberly, FO, 30 December 1967, FCO/17/41, UKNA.

51. Minutes, Ministerial Committee for West Bank Affairs, 24 December 1967; Political contacts with Palestinian leaders—summary of a discussion chaired by the PM (drafted by Sasson), 24 December 1967, both in A/7921/3, ISA.

52. Memoranda of conversation by Sasson: Anwar al-Khatib, 27 December 1967, and 'Aziz Shehadeh, 30 December 1967, both in A/7045/12, ISA; Digest of events in the West Bank (GSS reports), 24 and 26 December 1967, both in FM/4088/5, ISA.

53. Memorandum of conversation by Sasson: Anwar al-Khatib, 27 December 1967, A/7045/12, ISA.

54. Digest of events in the West Bank (GSS report), 26 December 1967, FM/4088/5, ISA; memorandum of conversation by Sasson: Fa'iq Barakat, 10 January 1968, A/7045/12, ISA.

55. Memorandum of conversation by Sasson: 'Aziz Shehadeh, 31 December 1967, A/7045/12, ISA.

56. Dayan's comments in minutes, KFASC, 9 January 1968, A/8161/10, ISA.

57. Sasson, First attempt at political initiative and its lesson, 22 January 1968, A/7921/4, ISA.

58. See Eban's testimony in Avi Shlaim, "Interview with Abba Eban, 11 March 1976," *Israel Studies* 8, no. 1 (2003), 162–63, 170–72. For scathing analysis of the government's decision-making process over the years see Israel's State Comptroller's Annual Report 53B (2003), 5–109, and a follow-up review in Annual Report 55B (2005), 191–203.

59. Given the government's disingenuous intention to reach an accommodation with the Palestinians, one can argue with cogency that this state of affairs was of no real significance. Still, throughout Israel's history there have been recurrent instances of disorderly policy making.

60. Ahituv's comments in minutes, KFASC, 20 February 1968, A/8161/10, ISA.

61. Symmes, Amman, 19, 23, and 25 January 1968, all in POL 27 ARAB-ISR, RG59, Central Files 1967–69, USNA; Tripp, Amman, to Moore, FO, 20 January 1968, FCO/17/248, UKNA.

62. After making a series of formulations of qualified acceptance during the early months of 1968, Ambassador Yosef Tekoah delivered a seeming full acceptance before the Security Council on 1 May 1968. See Eban's comments, *Knesset Proceedings,* 29 May 1968, 2073–74; Saadia Touval, *The Peace Brokers: Mediators in the Arab-Israeli Conflict, 1948–1979* (Princeton: Princeton University Press, 1982), 144–45; Korn, *Stalemate,* 41–45; Rafael, *Destination Peace,* 195–99.

63. Eban's comments in minutes, KFASC, 19 January 1968, A/8161/10, ISA; and also 8 and 13 December 1967, both in A/8161/9, ISA; 27 February 1968, A/8161/11, ISA.

64. Shlaim, "Interview with Abba Eban, 11 March 1976," 159.

65. Rabin, *Rabin Memoirs,* 123–24.

66. See Eban's comments in minutes, KFASC, 2 January 1968, A/8161/10, ISA; Stephen Green, *Living by the Sword: America and Israel in the Middle East, 1967–87* (London: Faber and Faber, 1988), 11.

67. Gen. Hod's comments in minutes, General Staff session, 19 June 1967, 206-117/1970, IDFA.

68. Korn, *Stalemate,* 63–64.

69. Eshkol's comments in minutes, A meeting with the Prime Minister, 5 December 1967, A/7921/3, ISA.

70. Minutes, Alignment's Political Committee, 18 August 1967, PPI.

71. Minutes, Political Committee report—28.7.67, A/7921/2, ISA.

72. Meir's comments in minutes, KFASC, 8 September 1967, A/8161/8, ISA.

73. Minutes, Political Committee report—28.7.67, A/7921/2, ISA.

74. Hadow, Tel Aviv, to FO, 1 August 1967, PREM/13/1623, UKNA.

75. Rusk to Embassy in Tel Aviv, 9 August 1967, *FRUS* 19: 764–66.

76. PM Eshkol to ForMin Eban, 17 November 1967, A/7938/11, ISA.

77. Barbour, Tel Aviv, 15 August 1967, POL ARAB-ISR, RG59, Central Files 1967–69, USNA.

78. Isaac, *Israel Divided,* 17–18.

79. Yafeh to Harman, 4 December 1967, A/7921/3, ISA.

80. See Dayan's letter, cited in minutes, KFASC, 20 February 1968, A/8161/10, ISA; Eshkol's comments, *Knesset Proceedings,* 5 February 1968, 914–15; Gazit, *Carrot and the Stick,* 2.

81. Col. Li'or to Ra'anan Weitz, 31 December 1967, A/7920/7, ISA. The decision to establish these settlements was taken by Eshkol, Dayan, Allon, and Haim Gvati, the agriculture minister.

82. Cabinet Resolution 217, 28 January 1968, ICS.

83. Lt. Col. Efrat to Defense Minister et al., 10 March 1968, 1114-953/1985, IDFA.

84. See Moshe Netzer, *Netzer mi-Shorashav: Sipur Hayim* [A branch from his roots: A life story] (Tel Aviv: Misrad ha-Bitahon—ha-Hotsa'ah la-Or, 2002), 253–55, 262.

85. Gen. Bar-Lev's comments in minutes, KFASC, 20 February 1968, A/8161/10, ISA.

86. Netzer, *Branch from His Roots*, 249–50.

87. Eshkol's comments, *Knesset Proceedings*, 26 February 1968, 1169.

88. Ibn Asad's account, quoted in Frank H. Epp, *The Israelis: Portrait of a People in Conflict* (Scottsdale, Ariz.: Herald, 1980), 65–66; Jan Metzger et al., *This Land Is Our Land: The West Bank under Israeli Occupation* (London: Zed, 1983), 109–10. Mekorot, Israel's national water company, agreed to substitute local water losses with limited quantities of water from the new well. Consequently, the Palestinian villagers became completely dependent on Israel for their water needs. See Ibrahim Matar, "Exploitation of Land and Water Resources for Jewish Colonies in the Occupied Territories," in *International Law and the Administration of Occupied Territories: Two Decades of Israeli Occupation of the West Bank and Gaza Strip*, ed. Emma Playfair (Oxford: Clarendon, 1992), 453.

89. Lewen, Jerusalem, to Moberly, FO, 14 December 1967, FCO/17/630, UKNA; Campbell, Jerusalem, 20 December 1967, POL 13 ISR, RG59, Central Files 1967–69, USNA.

90. Terence Smith, "Israeli Army Razes West Bank Village Called Terrorist Base," *New York Times*, 30 November 1967; Campbell, Jerusalem, 16 and 29 November 1967; Rusk to Embassy in Tel Aviv, 28 November 1967, all in POL 27 ARAB-ISR, RG59, Central Files 1967–69, USNA; Dayan's comments, *Knesset Proceedings*, 20 December 1967, 488.

91. Ra'anan Weitz, Settlement Department, to PM, 18 September 1967, G/6303/1059, ISA.

92. Herzog's comments in minutes, KFASC, 9 February 1968, A/8161/10, ISA.

93. The following discussion of Eshkol's meeting with the general is based on minutes, A meeting with the Prime Minister, 5 December 1967, A/7921/3, ISA.

94. Harry C. McPherson, Jr., to President Johnson, 11 June 1967, *FRUS* 19: 433–36; Haber, *Today War Will Break Out*, 292–93.

95. Minutes, The Prime Minister's meeting with Prof. Raymond Aron, 17 August 1967, A/7921/2, ISA.

96. Eshkol to Defense Minister, 24 December 1967, A/7231/2, ISA.

97. Tom Segev, *1967: Ve-ha-Aretz Shintah et Paneha* [1967: And the land changed its face] (Jerusalem: Keter, 2005), 616 (this part of Dayan's comments is not included in the English translation of Segev's *1967*); Pedatzur, *Triumph of Bewilderment*, 81.

98. Chaim Nadel, *Bein Shtei ha-Milhamot: ha-Pe'ilut ha-Bithonit ve-ha-Tsva'it la-Konenut ve-ha-Hitkonenut shel Tsahal, mi-Tom Milhemet Sheshet ha-Yamim ve-'ad Milhemet Yom ha-Kipurim* [Between the two wars: IDF security and military action to achieve alertness and readiness, from the end of the Six Day War to the Yom Kippur War] (Tel Aviv: Ma'arakhot, 2006), 96–100, 39, n. 15; *Yitzhak Rabin: Selected Documents*, 561–65.

99. *Yitzhak Rabin: Selected Documents*, 561–62; Eban's comments in minutes, KFASC, 2 January 1968, A/8161/10, ISA. For the 19 June Resolution see chapter 1; for

the August deliberations see Ya'acov Herzog's diary, 31 July and 21 August 1967, A/4511/3, ISA.

100. Eban's comments in minutes, Mapai's Secretariat meeting, 2 January 1968, 2-24-1968-92, ILPA.

101. Eban's comments in minutes, KFASC, 2 January 1968, A/8161/10, ISA.

102. *Yitzhak Rabin: Selected Documents,* 562; Ya'acov Herzog's diary, 22 September 1968, A/4511/4, ISA; Dayan's comments in minutes, Labor Party's Political Committee, 30 October 1968, A/7921/13, ISA; Begin's comments in cabinet minutes, 31 October 1968 (morning), PPI.

103. Memoranda of conversation: President Johnson et al. and PM Eshkol et al., 7–8 January 1968 (sessions I–III), *FRUS* 20: 79–99; Eshkol and Herzog's comments in minutes, KFASC, 23 January 1968 and 9 February 1968, both in A/8161/10, ISA. Johnson's quotations from the American record of Session II. Johnson's pun as cited by Eshkol in Minutes—the meeting with Lt. Gen. Y. Rabin, 24 May 1968, A/7938/11, ISA. For Katzenbach's advice see Memorandum from Acting Secretary of State Katzenbach to President Johnson, 11 December 1967, *FRUS* 20: 29–30. For Rusk's warning see Herzog's comments at KFASC, 9 February.

104. Campbell, Jerusalem, 13 January 1968, POL 27 ARAB-ISR, RG59, Central Files 1967–69, USNA. The joint communiqué merely said: "The President agreed to keep Israel's military defense capability under active sympathetic examination and review in the light of all relevant factors, including the shipment of military equipment by others to the area." See "Joint Statement Following Discussions with Prime Minister Eshkol of Israel," 8 January 1968, *Public Papers of the Presidents of the United States: Lyndon B. Johnson, 1968–1969,* book I (Washington, D.C. 1970), 20–21.

105. Maj. Farhi to Gen. Narkiss et al., 10 December 1967, 74-117/1970, IDFA; Digest of events in the West Bank (GSS report), 26 December 1967, FM/4088/5, ISA; memoranda of conversation by Sasson: Shehadeh and Janho, 10 December 1967, MSP; Fa'iq Barakat, 10 January 1968; Sa'id 'Ala al-Din, 22 January 1968, both in A/7045/12, ISA.

106. Memorandum of conversation by Sasson: Anwar Nuseibeh, 22 January 1968, A/7045/12, ISA.

107. Symmes, Amman, 26 January 1968, POL 27 ARAB-ISR, RG59, Central Files 1967–69, USNA. The British chargé d'affaires in Jordan shared with his American colleagues Ambassador Hadow's report on his meeting with Eban.

108. Yigal Allon, oral history interviews, 17th meeting (28 August 1979), A/5001/21, ISA. According to the available cabinet records, Allon's first trip abroad after the war took place in late January 1968.

109. Interview with Dayan, *Musaf Haaretz,* 19 January 1968.

110. See, for example, *Haaretz,* 1 December 1967.

111. Barbour, Tel Aviv, 20 February 1968, POL 15-1 ISR, RG59, Central Files 1967–69, USNA.

112. Sasson to PM, The views and political assessments of Arab leaders and notables in the West Bank and Jerusalem (report on the period 14.12.67–25.1.68), 28 January 1968, A/7921/4, ISA.

113. All memoranda of conversations of these meetings are in A/7045/12, ISA, and MSP.

114. For the inter-Palestinian wrangle leading to the overthrow of Shuqayri see Moshe Shemesh, *Me-ha-Nakbah la-Naksah: Ha-Sikhsukh ha-'Arvi-Yisre'eli ve-ha-Be'ayah ha-Le'umit ha-Falastinit 1957–1967; Darko shel Nasser le-Milhemet Sheshet ha-Yamim* [From the *Nakbah* to the *Naksah*: The Arab-Israeli conflict and the palestinian national problem, 1957–1967; Nasser's Road to the Six Day War] (Sede Boqer: Ben-Gurion Institute and Ben-Gurion University Press, 2004), 674–88.

115. Sasson to PM, The views and political assessments of Arab leaders and notables in the West Bank and Jerusalem (report on the period 14.12.67–25.1.68), 28 January 1968, A/7921/4, ISA.

116. See, for example, Maj. Farhi to Gen. Narkiss et al., 29 December 1967, 75-117/1970, IDFA.

117. Memoranda of conversation by Sasson: 'Aziz Shehadeh, 30 December 1967; Nadim al-Zaru, 14 January 1968; Sa'id 'Ala al-Din, 22 January 1968, all in A/7045/12, ISA.

118. Memorandum of conversation by Sasson: Anwar Nuseibeh, 22 January 1968, A/7045/12, ISA.

SEVEN Go-Betweens

1. Memorandum by Kaye, 14 February 1968, FCO/17/620, UKNA.

2. Interview with Sasson (October 1996). See also Sasson, *Without a Roundtable,* 101. Foreign Minister Eban, who also received a handful of West Bank politicians in 1968, indicated that the initiative was Sasson's. Eban, *Personal Witness,* 494.

3. See, for example, memorandum of conversation by Sasson: 'Aziz Shehadeh, 31 December 1967, A/7045/12, ISA. On the less-willing participants see Campbell, Jerusalem, 15 February 1968 (airgram A-153), POL 27 ARAB-ISR, RG59, Central Files 1967–69, USNA; memorandum of conversation by Sasson: Hikmat al-Masri and Walid al-Shak'ah, 22 February 1968, A/7045/12, ISA; memorandum of conversation: Consul-General Campbell and Anwar al-Khatib, 30 May 1968, enclosed with Campbell, Jerusalem, 12 June 1968, POL 3 PAL ENTITY, RG59, Central Files 1967–69, USNA.

4. Memoranda, PM's talk with Ayub Musallam and PM's talk with 'Aziz Shehadeh, both 5 February 1968, MSP.

5. Sayigh, *Armed Struggle and the Search for State,* 176–77.

6. Memorandum, PM's talk with Anwar Nuseibeh, 6 February 1968, MSP; Campbell, Jerusalem, 15 February 1968: telegram 980, NSF/Country File/Israel, Cables, Vol. VIII, 12/67–2/68, Box 141, LBJL; airgrams A-152, A-153, POL 27 ARAB-ISR,

RG59, Central Files 1967–69, USNA. Campbell's meeting with Nuseibeh took place on 9 February.

7. *FRUS* 20: 173, n. 4; Michael Hadow, Tel Aviv, Israel: Annual Review for 1968, 21 January 1969, FCO/17/897, UKNA; "6 Killed as Israelis Battle Terrorists," *Washington Post,* 10 February 1968.

8. Col. Carmon's comments in minutes, KFASC, 9 February 1968, A/8161/10, ISA; Sayigh, *Armed Struggle and the Search for State,* 177. In January, Jordan requested American assistance in "controlling terrorist activity," including a supply of anti-infiltration equipment. See Symmes, Amman, 16 February 1968, *FRUS* 20: 173–74.

9. Israel's message to the king, 9 February 1968, enclosed with memorandum by Sasson: Anwar Nuseibeh's mission to King Hussein, an oral report . . . , 11 February 1968, MSP; Barbour, Tel Aviv, 11 February 1968 (telegram 2481), NSF/Country File/ Israel, Cables, Vol. VIII, 12/67–2/68, Box 141, LBJL. Available records do not relate how Nuseibeh's assignment was arranged.

10. Barbour, Tel Aviv, 12 February 1968, POL ISR-Jordan, RG59, Central Files 1967–69, USNA.

11. Symmes, Amman, 12 and 14 February 1968, both in POL ISR-Jordan, RG59, Central Files 1967–69, USNA.

12. Barbour, Tel Aviv, 14 and 15 February 1968, both in NSF/Country File/Israel, Cables, Vol. VIII, 12/67–2/68, Box 141, LBJL; Rusk to Embassies in Amman and Tel Aviv, 15 February 1968, POL 27 ARAB-ISR, RG59, Central Files 1967–69, USNA. Quotation from the last.

13. "Israelis Use Jets in Daylong Clash with Jordanians," *New York Times,* 16 February 1968. According to a Jordanian communiqué, twenty-three were killed, including sixteen civilians, and fifty-nine were injured, including thirty-two civilians; "Hussein Cautions Arab Terrorists," *New York Times,* 17 February 1968.

14. Symmes, Amman, 20 February 1968, POL 27-9 ARAB-ISR, and 23 February 1968, POL 27 ARAB-ISR, both in RG59, Central Files 1967–69, USNA.

15. Barbour, Tel Aviv, 4 March 1968, POL 27 ARAB-ISR, RG59, Central Files 1967–69, USNA.

16. Barbour, Tel Aviv, 21 February 1968, POL 27 ARAB-ISR, RG59, Central Files 1967–69, USNA.

17. "Hussein Cautions Arab Terrorists," *New York Times,* 17 February 1968; Sayigh, *Armed Struggle and the Search for State,* 177.

18. Symmes, Amman, 17 February 1968, POL ISR-Jordan, RG59, Central Files 1967–69, USNA.

19. Rusk to Embassy in Amman, 17 February 1968, *FRUS* 20: 175–76; Barbour, Tel Aviv, 17 February 1968, NSF/Country File/Israel, Cables, Vol. VIII, 12/67–2/68, Box 141, LBJL.

20. Memorandum of conversation: PM Talhuni and Ambassador Symmes, 15 February 1968, enclosed with Symmes, Amman, 20 February 1968, NSF/Country File/ Jordan, Cables, Vol. V, 3/68–1/69, Box 147, LBJL.

21. Ibid.; Barbour, Tel Aviv, 20 February 1968, POL 27-14 ARAB-ISR, RG59, Central Files 1967–69, USNA (the latter record does not give the name of the other Palestinian suggested by Talhuni, but taking it together with the former, we can quite safely conclude that it was Hikmat al-Masri); memorandum by Sasson: Anwar Nuseibeh's mission to King Hussein, an oral report . . . , 11 February 1968, MSP.

22. Eban, *Personal Witness,* 494–95.

23. Memorandum, ForMin—Anwar Nuseibeh's meeting, 20 February 1968, C-1/F-7, Abba Eban Center for Israeli Diplomacy, Truman Institute, Hebrew University of Jerusalem, (AEA); Campbell, Jerusalem, 20 March 1968, POL Jordan, RG59, Central Files 1967–69, USNA. Quotations from the latter.

24. Memorandum by Sasson: Anwar Nuseibeh's mission to King Hussein, an oral report . . . ," 11 February 1968, MSP; Memorandum by Sasson: Anwar Nuseibeh's meeting with King Hussein on Saturday 24.2.1968 at 12.30, undated, A/7921/4, ISA.

25. Minutes, Labor Party's Political Committee, 27 February 1968, PPI.

26. Hadow, Tel Aviv, to FO, 28 February 1968, FCO/17/221, UKNA.

27. Memorandum of conversation: Consul-General Campbell et al. and Shlomo Argov et al., 5 March 1968, enclosed with Campbell, Jerusalem, 20 March 1968, POL 27 ARAB-ISR, RG59, Central Files 1967–69, USNA. The cited comment was attributed to Shaul Bar-Haim.

28. Campbell, Jerusalem, 21 February 1968, POL 27 ARAB-ISR, RG59, Central Files 1967–69, USNA.

29. Minutes, KFASC, 8 December 1967, A/8161/9, ISA.

30. Memorandum, PM's talk with Hikmat al[-]Masri and Walid al[-]Shak'ah, 26 February 1968, MSP; Symmes, Amman, 23 May 1968, POL 27 ARAB-ISR, RG59, Central Files 1967–69, USNA. A detailed and indeed stormy account of Eshkol's meeting with the two Nablus notables, whose source was Hikmat al-Masri, was published two decades later in Na'im Fourati [Gil'adi], "When Eshkol Proposed a Palestine Mini-State," *Ghorbah,* 26 June 1987.

31. Memorandum by Sasson: A conversation at Abu Bandali's home . . . , 28 February 1968, A/7045/12, ISA; An oral message from PM Bahjat al-Talhuni to GoI [Government of Israel] through Raja al-'Isa and Salim [al-]Sharif (3.3.68), A/7921/4, ISA.

32. Adams, Amman, to FO, 7 March 1968, FCO/17/247, UKNA.

33. Memoranda of conversation by Sasson: Anwar Nuseibeh, 9 and 15 March 1968; Monsignor Capucci, 27 March 1968; 'Aziz Shehadeh, 28 March 1968; Hikmat al-Masri, 31 March 1968, all in A/7045/12; Symmes, Amman, 11 March 1968, POL 27-14 ARAB-ISR, RG59, Central Files 1967–69, USNA; Adams, Amman, to FO, 13 March 1968, FCO/17/54 and 16 March 1968, FCO/17/207, UKNA.

34. Inspector A. Ben Shmuel, Police's Judea Subdistrict, to Headquarters of the Police's Southern District et al., 17 June 1968, 17/451/RG79, ISA. According to this summary of investigation, the assassin, twenty-seven-year-old Ahmad al-Tarifi of al-Bireh, told his Israeli interrogators that the task had been assigned to him by one Abu 'Amar, also known as "the old man" (*al-Khityar* in Arabic). Abu 'Amar was the nom de guerre

of Yasir 'Arafat, who was also affectionately nicknamed al-Khityar (he was then thirty-eight).

35. Bar-Lev's comments in minutes, KFASC, 26 March 1968, a.m., A/8161/11, ISA.

36. James Feron, "Israelis Hint Use of Terror Tactics," *New York Times,* 10 April 1968.

37. See Katzenbach to US Embassy in Tel Aviv, 6 April 1968; Saunders to Walt Rostow, 27 May 1968, both in *FRUS* 20: 261–62, 358.

38. Karmit Gai, *Bar-Lev* [Hebrew] (Tel Aviv: 'Am 'Oved; Sifriyat Po'alim, 1998), 167.

39. Ya'acov Herzog, Special chapter on Jordan: The IDF raid on al-Fateh's bases in the East Bank on Thursday 21.3.68, YHP. Unless otherwise indicated, the following discussion of the developments leading to, and resulting from, the Karameh raid is based on Herzog's twenty-six-page paper and Haber, *Today War Will Break Out,* 337–40.

40. Symmes, Amman, 19 March 1968, *FRUS* 20: 237–39.

41. Begin's comments in minutes, KFASC, 22 March 1968 a.m., A/8161/11, ISA. Iraqi expeditionary forces had been stationed in Jordan since the June War, and their withdrawal was desired by Hussein.

42. Herzog's paper does not mention any decision taken in this meeting, so it is unlikely that the committee reversed the previous day's ruling.

43. For the American pressure see also Rusk to Embassy in Tel Aviv, 20 March 1968, *FRUS* 20: 239–40; Barbour, Tel Aviv, to Secretary, 20 March 1968, NSF/Country File/Israel, Cables, Vol. IX, 3/68–5/68, Box 141, LBJL; Rostow to President, 20 March 1968, *FRUS* 20: 240–41; Begin, Eshkol, Rafael and Eban's comments in minutes, KFASC, 22 March 1968, a.m.; 22 March 1968, p.m.; 26 March 1968, a.m.; 9 April 1968, all in A/8161/11, ISA.

44. See Jarring to Secretary-General, 20 March 1968, 370-32-13, UNA; Eban's comments in minutes, KFASC, 9 April 1968, A/8161/11, ISA.

45. Gideon Rafael, the then director general of the Foreign Ministry, quotes Eshkol as saying: "Do you want the Arabs to believe that there is no action when Dayan is ill?" Rafael, *Destination Peace,* 202–3.

46. Memorandum for the Record of a conversation with Ephraim Evron, 19 March 1968, NSF/Country File/Israel, Memos, Vol. IX, 3/68–5/68, Box 141, LBJL.

47. For Eshkol's suggestion of calling the raid off if Hussein announced publicly his wish to negotiate peace see also Gai, *Bar-Lev,* 162–63.

48. See minutes, Talks with U.S. Ambassador to the United Nations (meeting with Eshkol), 15 July 1968, A/7043/12, ISA; Rafael to ForMin, 16 July 1968, A/7044/5, ISA.

49. For Johnson's message and its delivery see Rusk to Embassy in Tel Aviv, 21 March 1968, *FRUS* 20: 241–42.

50. Lt. Gen. Bar-Lev's detailed account in minutes, KFASC, 26 March 1968, a.m., A/8161/11, ISA.

51. On al-Fateh numbers: Lt. Gen. Bar-Lev and Maj. Landsberg's comments in minutes, KFASC, 22 March 1968 p.m., A/8161/11, ISA; Helena Cobban, *The Palestinian Liberation Organisation: People, Power and Politics* (Cambridge: Cambridge University Press, 1984), 42.

52. In addition to Karameh, the Israelis simultaneously raided another, much smaller al-Fateh target, in the village of al-Safi, south of the Dead Sea. In this foray, Operation *Asuta* (Hebrew for remedy), they suffered no casualties.

53. Zeev Schiff and Raphael Rothstein, *Fedayeen: The Story of the Palestinian Guerrillas* (London: Vallentine, Mitchell, 1972), 83.

54. Quotation in *Knesset Proceedings*, 21 March 1968, 1577.

55. Thomas F. Brady, "Guerrillas Back at Jordan Camp," *New York Times*, 23 March 1968; Rafael's comments in minutes, KFASC, 26 March 1968, p.m., A/8161/11, ISA; Barbour, Tel Aviv, 2 April 1968, POL 27 ARAB-ISR, RG59, Central Files 1967–69, USNA. The fatal incident occurred on 29 March.

56. See Hadow, Israel: Annual Review for 1968, FCO/17/897, UKNA.

57. Rashid Khalidi, *Palestinian Identity: The Construction of Modern National Consciousness* (New York: Columbia University Press, 1997), 196–97.

58. Sayigh, *Armed Struggle and the Search for State*, 179.

59. Nusseibeh, *Once upon a Country*, 136.

60. Quoted in Epp, *Palestinians*, 144. See also Munir Shafiq, "The Battle of Karameh" [in Arabic], *Shu'un Filastiniyyah*, 19 (1973), 103–4, 109–10.

61. Shashar's diary, 27 March 1968.

62. For the huge inrush of volunteers to join the guerrilla groups see Abu Iyad, *My Home, My Land*, 60; Sayigh, *Armed Struggle and the Search for State*, 181.

63. Roger Owen, *State, Power, and Politics in the Making of the Modern Middle East*, 2nd ed. (London: Routledge, 2000), 75. Owen's definition of Israel as a "warfare state," ibid., 199.

64. S/RES/248 (1968), 24 March 1968, UNPR.

65. Eban's comments in minutes, KFASC, 9 April 1968, A/8161/11, ISA.

66. Ada Sereni's comments in minutes, Meeting with Mrs. Ada Sereni, 27 March 1968, ISA; Col. Mordechai Gur's comments in minutes, KFASC, 16 July 1968, A/8162/1, ISA.

67. See Eshkol's comments, meeting of the Labor Party's Secretariat, 21 March 1968, 2-24-1968-92, ILPA; Herzog's comments in minutes, Ministerial Committee for Security Affairs session, 8 May 1968, YHP.

68. After consulting Secretary General U Thant, Jarring declined the Israeli request. See Jarring to Secretary-General, 22 March ("unnumbered 'B'" and "unnumbered CCC"); and 23 March 1968, all in 370-32-13, UNA; Secretary General to Jarring, 22 March 1968, 370-32-14, UNA. Quotation from telegram "unnumbered CCC," 22 March.

69. See, for example, Eshkol's comments in minutes, KFASC, 22 March 1968, p.m., A/8161/11, ISA.

70. Rusk to Embassy in Tel Aviv, 27 March 1968, POL 27 ARAB-ISR, RG59, Central Files 1967–69, USNA.

71. Eban's comments in minutes, KFASC, 9 April 1968, A/8161/11, ISA.

72. *Al-Dustur* (Amman), 24 March 1968.

73. See, for example, Gen. Yariv's comments in minutes, KFASC, 26 March 1968, a.m., A/8161/11, ISA.

74. See, for example, Barbour, Tel Aviv, 2 April 1968, NSF/Country File/Israel, Cables, Vol. IX, 3/68–5/68, Box 141, LBJL (quoting Bar-Haim of the FM); memorandum by Alston, FO, 2 April 1968. FCO/17/95, UKNA (quoting Anug of the Israeli embassy in London). The British ambassador in Amman reported: "We have every indication that the Israelis do not care twopence for King Hussein"; Adams, Amman, to Allen, FO, 2 April 1968, FCO/17/550, UKNA.

75. Rusk to Embassy in Tel Aviv, 8 April 1968, *FRUS* 20: 270–71.

76. Memorandum for the Record by Saunders, 1 April 1968, *FRUS* 20: 252–54. Evron claimed that he was expressing his personal view.

77. Memorandum by Sasson, Sheikh Muhammad 'Ali al-Ja'bari, 15 March 1968, A/7045/12, ISA; Peter Nichols, "Hebron Finds Accord with Israel," *The Times* (London), 15 March 1968; Hezi Carmel, "The Disagreement between Nablus, Hebron, and Jerusalem," *Ma'ariv*, 15 March 1968; Shashar's diary, 27 March 1968; Campbell, Jerusalem, 15 March 1968, POL 3 PAL ENTITY, RG59, Central Files 1967–69, USNA. Imparting his suspicions regarding Israel's aims to Consul General Campbell, Shehadeh urged US influence on Hussein to stop sending funds to his followers in the West Bank, in order to give the advocates of the entity scheme the chance to rally supporters.

78. Memorandum of conversation by Sasson: Bishop Capucci, 27 March 1968, A/7045/12, ISA. Capucci recounted a conversation he and Tiyasir Kan'an had had with Hikmat al-Masri.

79. Memorandum of conversation by Sasson: 'Aziz Shehadeh, 28 March 1968, A/7045/12, ISA. Shehadeh had represented the Palestinian refugees at Lausanne (see chapter 1).

80. Memoranda of conversation by Sasson: Walid al-Shak'ah, 31 March 1968; 'Aziz Shehadeh, 3 April 1968, both in A/7045/12, ISA.

81. Memoranda of conversation by Sasson: 'Ali al-Sharif, 27 February 1968; 'Aziz Shehadeh, 30 December 1967; Nadim al-Zaru, 14 January 1968; Sa'id 'Ala al-Din, 22 January 1968, all in A/7045/12, ISA.

82. Memorandum of conversation by Sasson: 'Aziz Shehadeh, 18 March 1968, A/7045/12, ISA.

83. Memoranda by Sasson: Discussion with the Defense Minister, 6 April 1968; Reporting and PM's instructions, 9 April 1968, both in A/7921/4, ISA.

84. Minutes (recorded by Col. Gazit), The Defense Minister's meeting with Hamdi Kan'an, 31.3.1968, 1 April 1968, MSP; memorandum by Sasson: Discussion

with the Defense Minister, 6 April 1968, A/7921/4, ISA. The journalist Shabtai Teveth argues that in his meeting with Kan'an, Dayan advocated the establishment of a Palestinian entity. Teveth, *Cursed Blessing,* 264–65.

85. Memorandum by Sasson: Discussion with the Defense Minister, 1 April 1968, A/7921/4, ISA.

86. Memorandum by Sasson: Reporting to the PM, 2 April 1968, A/7921/4, ISA.

87. Eban's comments in minutes, KFASC, 27 February 1968, A/8161/11, ISA.

88. Eban's comments in minutes, KFASC, 19 March 1968, A/8161/11, ISA.

89. Foreign Minister to Ambassador, Washington, 18 April 1968, C-1/F-7, AEA.

90. Minutes, Eban's political review, meeting of the Labor Party's Secretariat, 4 April 1968, 2-24-1968-93, ILPA.

91. Memorandum of conversation by Sasson: Hikmat al-Masri, 31 March 1968, A/7045/12, ISA.

92. Saul Bellow, *To Jerusalem and Back: A Personal Account* (New York: Penguin, 1985), 40.

93. Memorandum, ForMin's conversation with Hikmat al-Masri, 4 April 1968, MSP; Symmes, Amman, 8 April 1968, POL 27-14 ARAB-ISR/SANDSTORM, RG59, Central Files 1967–69, USNA; memorandum, Saunders and Foster to Walt Rostow, 9 April 1968, *FRUS* 20: 271–72. Eban's threat is not recorded in the Israeli document. In his autobiography Eban again offers a false version, according to which he met "members of the Masri family," who at the end of the conversation volunteered to communicate its content to Nasser. Eban, *Personal Witness,* 495.

94. 'Abd al-Majid Farid, the secretary general of the Egyptian presidency, says that during the Nasser-Hussein meeting on 6 April, Premier Talhuni related an Israeli message received through Hikmat al-Masri. In his telling, however, Israel contemplated a new military operation in the East Bank in order to force Hussein to form a new cabinet constituted of West Bankers who cooperated with the occupation authorities. Farid, *Nasser,* 117. Farid's version is incompatible with the available primary sources, and seems to be distorted.

95. Eban's comments in minutes, KFASC, 9 April 1968, A/8161/11, ISA.

96. Eban's comments in minutes, KFASC, 26 April 1968, A/8161/11, ISA.

97. Eban's political review, meeting of the Labor Party's Secretariat, 4 April 1968, 2-24-1968-93, ILPA.

98. Memorandum by Saunders for Walt Rostow, 9 April 1968, *FRUS* 20: 274–76. Ambassador Barbour, relying on conversations with Eban's adviser Mordechai Gazit and the director of the Research Department Michael Michael, also reported that the Foreign Ministry favored a "Palestinian solution." Barbour, Tel Aviv, 17 April 1968, POL 27 ARAB-ISR, RG59, Central Files 1967–69, USNA.

99. Memorandum by Sasson: Reporting and PM's instructions, 9 April 1968, A/7921/4, ISA.

100. Maj. Farhi to Defense Minister, Summary of a meeting with Hamdi Kan'an and 'Aziz Shehadeh, 16 April 1968, MSP. A Palestinian volume of selected documents offers the meeting's minutes, which are in fact an Arabic translation of the Israeli record, obtained from Shehadeh—excluding its last part and Farhi's comments. See 'Abd al-Hadi, *Palestinian Question,* 338–43.

101. Maj. Farhi to Defense Minister, A conversation with 'Aziz Shehadeh, 21 April 1968, MSP. Among the delegates who conveyed Nablus's response were Hamdi Kan'an, Walid al-Shak'ah, an unnamed representative of Hikmat al-Masri, and the Jerusalemite Tiyasir Kan'an, who acted as liaison with Nablus.

102. Dayan suggested taking Amman only if Hussein was assassinated and the United States gave its approval, or in case of a developing incident which would require the seizure of Jordan's capital. Political evaluation of the situation (M. D. 18.4.68), A/7921/4, ISA. The record does not disclose where this stocktaking took place.

103. Defense Minister to Prime Minister, 21 January 1968, MSP. See also Dayan's comments in minutes, A meeting with Ministers Eban, Allon and Dayan, 29 May 1968, A/7921/4, ISA. For a comprehensive summary of the whole affair see Sasson to Foreign Minister et al., 23 April 1968, A/7921/4, ISA.

104. Unless indicated otherwise, the discussion of Eshkol's meetings with Kan'an and Khatib is based on memoranda by Sasson: PM's talk with Tiyasir Kan'an, 24 April 1968, MSP; PM's talk with Anwar al-Khatib, 25 April 1968, MSP; Anwar al-Khatib's proposal, undated, A/7921/4, ISA; Maj. Farhi to C.G. of the [Central] Command et al., 5 May 1968, A/7921/4, ISA.

105. Memorandum of conversation: Consul-General Campbell and Anwar al-Khatib, 30 May 1968, enclosed with Campbell, Jerusalem, 12 June 1968, POL 3 PAL ENTITY, RG59, Central Files 1967–69, USNA.

106. Anwar al-Khatib al-Tamimi, *With Salah al-Din in Jerusalem,* 21–22. A third version lacks any reference to the discussion of political contacts regarding a settlement. J. Robert Moskin, *Among Lions: The Battle for Jerusalem June 5–7, 1967* (New York: Arbor, 1982), 30–31.

107. Memorandum of conversation by Sasson: Tiyasir Kan'an, 30 April 1968, A/7045/12, ISA.

108. Campbell, Jerusalem, 3 June 1968, POL 27 ARAB-ISR, RG59, Central Files 1967–69, USNA.

109. Maj. Farhi to C.G. of the [Central] Command et al., 5 May 1968, A/7921/4, ISA. It is doubtful whether Wasfi al-Tall would have agreed to negotiate with Israel. The British ambassador in Amman reported that Tall firmly opposed any action to seek political solution. Adams, Amman, to Moore, FO, 23 May 1968, FCO/17/219, UKNA.

110. Memorandum of conversation by Sasson: Tiyasir Kan'an, 30 April 1968, A/7045/12, ISA.

111. Summary of A.E. [Abba Eban] and G.M. [Golda Meir]'s talk, 16 April 1968, A/7936/4, ISA.

112. Untitled memorandum beginning "The purpose of the meeting . . . ," 25 April 1968, A/7936/4, ISA. See also Report of a discussion about the forthcoming journey of the Foreign Minister (participants: Eshkol, Eban, Dr. Herzog, and Avi'ad Yafeh), 1 May 1968, A/7936/4, ISA.

113. See Eshkol's comments in minutes, the Expanded Political Committee, 3 June 1968, A/7921/13, ISA. According to Eshkol, the representatives of the right-wing Gahal faction (Ministers Begin and Yosef Sapir) voted against, then tried to tie Eban's hands.

114. Eban's comments in minutes, the Labor Party's Political Committee, 19 May 1968, A/7936/4, ISA.

115. Ya'acov Herzog's seven-page memorandum, Record of meeting held on 3.5.68, YHP, is the main source for the discussion here. I also relied on Herzog's detailed account in minutes, the Ministerial Committee for Security Affairs, 8 May 1968, YHP; and Eban's accounts in: minutes, the Labor Party's Political Committee, 19 May 1968, A/7936/4; minutes, A meeting with Ministers Eban, Allon and Dayan, 29 May 1968, A/7921/4 (which also include Herzog's comments); and minutes, the Expanded Political Committee, 3 June 1968, A/7921/13, all in ISA. The memories of both King Hussein and Zayd al-Rifa'i regarding the May 1968 exchanges were vague when they were interviewed by Professor Avi Shlaim (Hussein on 3 December 1996, Ascot; Rifa'i on 19 September and 20 December 2002, Amman).

116. See Daniel Dishon, ed., *Middle East Record,* vol. 4, *1968* (Jerusalem: Israeli Universities Press, 1973), 411. The decrees were issued by the interior minister without consulting his cabinet colleagues about the move beforehand. See MK Yizhar Harari's comments in minutes, KFASC, 5 March 1968, A/8161/11, ISA; Eban's answer to a question, *Knesset Proceedings,* 19 June 1968, 2330. For the hardening position of Egypt resulting from the decrees see Eban's comments in minutes, KFASC, 19 March and 26 April 1968, A/8161/11, ISA. Bishop Capucci informed Sasson that both Premier Talhuni and Hikmat al-Masri had told him about Nasser's decision to renege on the green light which he had given Hussein. Memoranda of conversation by Sasson: Capucci, 12 and 27 March 1968, both in A/7045/12, ISA.

117. Farid, *Nasser,* 129.

118. See Eban's comments in minutes, KFASC, 29 May 1968, A/8161/12, ISA.

119. Memorandum by Ya'acov Herzog: Two talks with S.R.—on 5–6/5/68, YHP; Herzog's account in minutes, the Ministerial Committee for Security Affairs, 8 May 1968, YHP.

120. Minutes, the Ministerial Committee for Security Affairs, 8 May 1968, YHP (this session was in fact a cabinet meeting, sitting as the Ministerial Committee for Security Affairs); Record of conversation between the Foreign Secretary and His Majesty, King Hussein of Jordan . . . , 6 May 1968, FCO/17/247, UKNA.

121. See Yafeh to Levi et al., 29 February 1968, A/7234/7, ISA.

122. Cabinet session (summary), 12 May 1968, G/10136/8, ISA; Cabinet Resolution 453, 12 May 1968, ICS. In early May the Security Council unanimously "deeply

deplore[d]" the holding on 2 May, Israel's Independence Day, of a large-scale military parade in Jerusalem—including the Arab sector of the city—in defiance of a previous Council resolution and strong international pressure. S/RES/250 (1968), 27 April 1968, and S/RES/251 (1968), 2 May 1968, UNPR.

123. See Campbell, Jerusalem, 14 March 1968, POL 27 ARAB-ISR, RG59, Central Files 1967–69, USNA; Shashar's diary, 7 March 1968. The historian Bernard Wasserstein says that another probable reason for the deportation was that Khatib supplied foreign diplomats with information considered damaging to Israeli interests. Wasserstein, *Divided Jerusalem,* 228.

124. Dayan's comments, *Knesset Proceedings,* 13 May 1968, 1822.

125. See, for example, Eshkol's comments in minutes, KFASC, 2 July 1968, A/8162/1, ISA.

126. Eshkol's comments in minutes, KFASC, 2 July 1968, A/8162/1, ISA (emphasis added); Eban's comments in minutes, KFASC, 26 April 1968, A/8161/11, and 5 July 1968, A/8162/1, ISA. For an elaborate discussion of the Hebron affair see Gorenberg, *Accidental Empire,* 143 ff.

127. Harold Jackson, "Israelis Oblivious of Their Own Isolation," *Guardian,* 12 June 1967.

128. Barbour, Tel Aviv, 6 May 1968, POL 27 ARAB-ISR, RG59, Central Files 1967–69, USNA; Barbour, Tel Aviv, 24 April 1968, NSF/Country File/Israel, Memos, Vol. IX, 3/68–5/68, Box 141, LBJL. The first quotation from the former; the second from the latter.

129. Quoted by Professor Israel Shahak in Epp, *Israelis,* 147.

EIGHT   The Double Game Redoubled

1. Eban's comments in minutes, A meeting with Ministers Eban, Allon and Dayan, 29 May 1968, A/7921/4, ISA.

2. Eban's comments in minutes, Expanded Political Committee, 3 June 1968, A/7921/13, ISA.

3. See, for example, Barbour, Tel Aviv, 17 August 1968, POL 15-1 ISR, RG59, Central Files 1967–69, RG59, Central Files 1967–69, USNA; Ya'acov Herzog's diary, Political contacts and clarifications—Israel-US, A/4511/4, ISA.

4. A handwritten note on a memorandum from Walt Rostow to President Johnson, 29 February 1968, *FRUS* 20: 194–95. Apparently Rostow recorded the president's comment.

5. On 31 March 1968 President Johnson, battered by the Vietnam War, announced that he would not run for another term in office.

6. Eban's comments in minutes, The meeting with Lt. Gen. Y. Rabin, 24 May 1968, A/7938/11, ISA.

7. "Plan to Recreate a Palestinian Arab Community," *The Times* (London), 17 May 1968.

8. Cecil Hourani, *An Unfinished Odyssey: Lebanon and Beyond* (London: Weidenfeld and Nicolson, 1984), 92–96; interview with Dr. Cecil Hourani, 24 February 2005, London; Bruce, London, 13 July 1967, PS 7 Musa Alami Farm (ADS), RG84, Post Files: American Consulate-General, 1967, USNA; Emmet Holt, Report: A Middle East Trip—July 23–28, 1967, FM/4088/7, ISA; Nasser al-Din al-Nashashibi, *Akhir al-'Amaliqah Ja'a min al-Quds: Qissat al-Za'im al-Filastini Musa al-'Alami* [The last giant came from Jerusalem: The story of the Palestinian leader Musa al-'Alami (Madrid?: Novograph? 1986), 165; 'Alami's ten-page plan, entitled "The Arabs of Palestine," enclosed with Lord Caradon, New York, to Arthur, FO, 21 April 1969, FCO/17/687, UKNA. 'Alami and Hourani's diplomatic efforts are recorded in numerous dispatches. See, for instance, Moore, FO, to Killick, Washington, 6 October 1967, FCO/17/95, UKNA; Kaiser, London, 23 April 1968, POL 27 ARAB-ISR, RG59, Central Files 1967–69, USNA. Following the Arab defeat in June, Hourani wrote a penetrating essay which scathingly criticized the Arab rulers and regimes for their misjudgment, incompetence, and demagoguery. A censored version of the article was published in the Beirut daily *Al-Nahar* in October; the full version appeared in the November issue of the British highbrow monthly *Encounter* under the heading "The Moment of Truth" (3–14), and earned Hourani much international acclaim.

9. Benziman, *Jerusalem,* 213; Brenchley, FO, to Glass, New York, 1 May 1968; Lewen, Jerusalem, to Moore, FO, 15 May 1968, both in FCO/17/95, UKNA; memorandum of conversation by Sasson: Bishop Capucci, 28 February 1968, MSP.

10. Memoranda of conversation by Sasson: 'Aziz Shehadeh, 9 May 1968; Bishop Capucci, 13 May 1968, both in A/7045/12, ISA; unsigned telegram (no. 4883), Amman; and Bruce, London, both 17 May 1968, POL 27 ARAB-ISR, RG59, Central Files 1967–69, USNA; memorandum by Adams, Amman, 21 May 1968, FCO/17/219, UKNA; Key, Jerusalem, to Evans, FO, 4 July 1968, FCO/17/95, UKNA. See also news reports in *Haaretz,* 1, 2, 3, 7 July 1968.

11. Memorandum, ForMin's talk with Anwar Nuseibeh, 4 June 1968, MSP. In November, Eban claimed from the podium of the Knesset that the Foreign Ministry was never informed about the 'Alami-Hourani plan. *Knesset Proceedings,* 20 November 1968, 381–82.

12. Prime Minister to Defense Minister, 13 June 1968; Defense Minister to Prime Minister, 17 June 68, both in 216-953/1985, IDFA.

13. Gazit, "Consolidation of Policy," 346; Maj. Farhi to C.G. of the Central Command et al., 5 May 1968, A/7921/4, ISA. See also memorandum of conversation by Sasson: Nasser al-Din al-Nashashibi, 5 May 1968, A/7045/12, ISA.

14. Yafeh to Cabinet Secretary, 14 May 1968, A/7921/4, ISA.

15. Sasson's comments in minutes, Consultation on the issue of Arabs in the administered territories, 21 May 1968, A/7921/4, ISA.

16. See memorandum of conversation by Sasson: *Mutran* Capucci, 13 May 1968, A/7045/12, ISA; *'Amman al-Masa'* (Amman), 13 and 20 May 1968; *Akhbar al-Usbu'* (Amman), 17 May 1968; *Jerusalem Post,* 15 and 16 May 1968; *Haaretz,* 19 May 1968. For

the statement see *PAD, 1968,* 329–30. See also Symmes, Amman, 23 May 1968, POL 27 ARAB-ISR, RG59, Central Files 1967–69, USNA.

17. *Ma'ariv,* 21 May 1968.

18. For Ja'bari's statements in May 1968 see Philip Kleinman, "An Arab Case for Palestine," *Daily Telegraph* (London), 7 May 1968; William Frankel, "Arab Leader Ready to Negotiate," *Jewish Chronicle* (London), 24 May 1968.

19. According to the prime minister's meeting calendar (A/7089/6, ISA), Eshkol was scheduled to see Moshe Sasson and "a guest" at his residence on 28 April. Sasson was always present at Eshkol's talks with Palestinian personalities.

20. Eshkol's comments in: minutes, Consultation on the issue of Arabs in the administered territories, 21 May 1968, A/7921/4, ISA; minutes, Expanded Political Committee, 3 June 1968, A/7921/13, ISA; minutes, KFASC, 25 June 1968, A/8161/12, ISA; *Knesset Proceedings,* 22 July 1968, 2773. Memorandum by Sasson: Reporting to the PM, 20 June 1968, A/7921/5, ISA; memorandum of conversation by Sasson: Ja'bari, 23 June 1968, A/7045/12, ISA; *'Amman al-Masa',* 13 May 1968; *Haaretz,* 13 June 1968.

21. Eshkol to Ja'bari, 19 May 1968, 47-2845/1997, IDFA.

22. Minutes, Consultation on the issue of Arabs in the administered territories, 21 May 1968; Summary of the discussion at the Political Contacts Committee presided over by the PM, 21 May 1968, both in A/7921/4, ISA. Quotations from the latter. The members of the Contacts Committee, headed by Eshkol, were Ministers Dayan, Eban, Allon, and Eliyahu Sasson, and a number of senior officials also attended its sessions. Allon was not present at the 21 May discussion.

23. Minutes, A meeting with Ministers Eban, Allon and Dayan, 29 May 1968, A/7921/4, ISA.

24. Minutes, PM—Nasser al-Din [al-]Nashashibi's conversation, 27 May 1968, MSP. Two decades later Nashashibi offered a quite different version of the discussion. See Nasser Eddin [*sic*] Nashashibi, *Jerusalem's Other Voice: Ragheb Nashashibi and Moderation in Palestinian Politics, 1920–1948* (Exeter: Ithaca, 1990), 230–32. However, when I read the Israeli record to Nashashibi (during an interview, 3 March 1998, Jerusalem), he confirmed its accuracy.

25. Memorandum of conversation by Sasson: Wadi' Di'mas, 28 May 1968, A/7045/12, ISA.

26. Sasson, *Without a Roundtable,* 102–3.

27. Minutes, Expanded Political Committee, 3 June 1968, A/7921/13, ISA; memoranda, Summary of discussion with the Defense Minister, 7 June 1968, MSP; Instructions for the continuation of contacts and laying the foundations for negotiations with the Palestinians, 9 June 1968, A/7921/5, ISA. See also Gazit, *Carrot and the Stick,* 143–45; Brown, *Personal Imprint,* 183–84.

28. Memoranda by Sasson: conversations with 'Aziz Shehadeh, 17 and 19 June 1968, both in A/7045/12, ISA; Anwar Nuseibeh—King Hussein's talk, undated [12 June 1968], MSP; Reporting to the PM, 20 June 1968, A/7921/5, ISA. Sasson, *Without*

NOTES TO PAGES 235–39

a Roundtable, 103. According to Sasson's log—The development of handling the subject of civil administration (a personal diary), MSP—he started the field work on 15 June.

29. See The Palestinians' political activity (main points)—a briefing paper prepared for Premier Eshkol's appearance before KFASC on 25 June 1968, undated, A/7921/5, ISA.

30. Memoranda of conversation by Sasson: Muhammad ʿAli al-Jaʿbari, 23 and 28 June 1968; Wadiʿ Diʿmas, 25 and 26 June 1968; Ayub Musallam, 26 June 1968; Elias al-Bandak, 26 June 1968; ʿAziz Shehadeh, 26 June 1968, all in A/7045/12, ISA; Sasson's log, MSP. Maj. Farhi was present at some of the meetings.

31. Memorandum of conversation by Sasson: Diʿmas and Musallam, 1 July 1968, and a Hebrew translation of the draft petition, A/7045/12, ISA; Arabic original of the draft, MSP.

32. Minutes, Consultation on the Arabs' problems in the administered territories; Summary of the Contacts Committee's discussion, headed by the PM, both 3 July 1968, A/7921/5, ISA. Quotations from the former. For Diʿmas's opinion on Jaʿbari see memoranda of his conversations with Sasson, 25 and 26 June 1968, A/7045/12, ISA.

33. Memoranda by Sasson: conversations with Jaʿbari; Musallam and Diʿmas; Bandak, all on 7 July 1968, A/7045/12, ISA; Reporting to the PM, DefMin, PolMin, 7 and 8 July 1968, MSP.

34. Memorandum of conversation by Sasson: Jaʿbari, 10 July 1968, A/7045/12, ISA (the document was mistakenly dated 7 July); Sasson's log, MSP. For the draft petition— the original Arabic and its Hebrew translation—see Sasson, *Without a Roundtable,* 106–7.

35. Minutes, The discussion about the continuation of contacts with the Arabs, 12 July 1968; summary by Col. Gazit: Contacts Committee's discussion of 12.7.68; Corrected draft of Jaʿbari's letter—all in A/7921/5, ISA; Sasson's log, MSP. The civil administration affair was wrongly presented in a number of works as a Palestinian initiative. For example: Pedatzur, *Triumph of Bewilderment,* 86–87; Gorenberg, *Accidental Empire,* 155; Pryce-Jones, *Face of Defeat,* 92.

36. "A New Israeli Plan for the West Bank," *Al-Ittihad* (Haifa), 16 July 1968.

37. Head of Arab Affairs Branch [Ahituv], GSS, to Col. Gazit et al., 17, 21 and 22 July 1968, all in MSP; Military Intelligence (Unit 154)'s report, Prevailing moods regarding Moshe Sasson's talks in the Bethlehem-Hebron areas, 17 July 1968, MSP; memoranda of conversation by Sasson: Musallam, 14 July 1968; Khamis, 21 July 1968, both in A/7045/12, ISA; Sasson's log, MSP.

38. Dayan's comments in minutes, The consultation in preparation for the Americans' visit, 14 July 1968, A/7921/8, ISA. The American envoys, due to arrive the next day, were George Ball, the new ambassador to the United Nations, and Joseph Sisco of the State Department.

39. Yaʿacov Herzog's diary, 19 July 1968, A/4511/4, ISA; Reporting to the PM, DefMin, PolMin, 7 and 8 July 1968, MSP.

40. A proposal for regional Arab self-administration in the Judea and Samaria area, signed by Col. Vardi, 14 July 1968, in Gazit, The Consolidation of Policy . . . , appendix 7, 381–88.

41. Minutes, A discussion at the Political Contacts Committee on 17.7.68 at the PM's office, A/7921/5, ISA.

42. Memoranda of conversation by Sasson: Khamis; Abu 'Itah; Bandak, all 21 July 1968, A/7045/12, ISA.

43. Memoranda of conversation by Sasson: Ja'bari, 22 July 1968; Di'mas and Musallam, 23 July 1968, both in A/7045/12, ISA; Head of Arab Affairs Branch, GSS, to Col. Gazit et al., 26 July 1968, MSP (enclosed with Ja'bari's draft letter).

44. Memorandum of conversation by Sasson: Di'mas and Musallam, 24 July 1968, A/7045/12, ISA.

45. Minutes, The consultation on our conduct in the administered territories, 23 July 1968, A/7921/5, ISA; Sasson's log, MSP.

46. Text of the broadcast, MSP. Sasson argues (Without a Roundtable, 108) that Talhuni made the statement on King Hussein's order.

47. "The Secrets of the Meeting between Wadi' Di'mas, Musallam and Sasson," Akhbar al-Usbu', 26 July 1968.

48. "The Adon [Hebrew for Mister]: Ayub Musallam," ibid.

49. Memoranda of conversation by Sasson: Musallam, 5 August 1968; Darwish, 15 August 1968, both in A/7045/12, ISA; Sasson's log, MSP. For Ribhi Mustafa's version see his letter to Al-Ittihad, 2 August 1968, published verbatim under the heading "Reverberations of a Plan to Establish an Arab Civil Administration in the Occupied Territories."

50. Memoranda of conversation by Sasson: Khamis, 26 July 1968; Di'mas and Musallam, 29 July 1968, both in A/7045/12, ISA. The three men advised unilateral Israeli imposition of the plan.

51. "On ice": Brig. Gen. Gazit to Justice Minister's office et al., 29 July 1968, MSP (enclosed with this covering letter was a draft of the Arab governor's powers, couched in palatable language, dated 24 July 1968, 1406-953/1985, IDFA). Dayan's comments in minutes, KFASC, 29 July 1968, A/8162/1, ISA.

52. Sasson's log (entries for 7 August), MSP; draft brief, Interim report on the negotiations with the Palestinians, 1 August 1968, A/7921/5, ISA. Quotation from the latter. The brief was prepared for Eshkol's presentation at KFASC. His appearance was postponed, and the discussion of the subject never took place.

53. Minutes, PM—al-Ja'bari's conversation, 12 August 1968, A/7045/12, ISA; Sasson's log, MSP.

54. Memoranda of conversation by Sasson: Shak'ah, 3 August 1968; Kan'an and Shak'ah, 7 and 11 August 1968; Masri, 11 August 1968, all in A/7045/12, ISA; Sasson's log, MSP; memorandum of conversation with Walid al-Shak'ah, 19 March 1969, enclosed with Campbell, Jerusalem, 26 March 1969, POL 27 ARAB-ISR, RG59, Central Files 1967–69, USNA. Quotation from the last.

55. Memorandum of conversation by Sasson: Ja'bari, 6 August 1968, A/7045/12, ISA. Bethlehem was represented by the mayor's deputy because Mayor Bandak was abroad.

56. Discussion about the civil administration at mayors' assembly in Nablus (GSS report), 11 August 1968, MSP; See also *Ma'ariv*, 15 August 1968.

57. Mayor of Jerusalem et al., to the Minister of Defence, 26 August 1968, A/7921/5, ISA. Symbolically, first on the list of signatories was the deported mayor of Arab Jerusalem, whose office ceased to exist following the Israeli annexation of the Arab sector of the city. The petition sent to the Israelis was an English translation of the Arabic original, typed on Nablus municipality stationery. For the Arabic version see *PAD, 1968*, 671–72.

58. Brig. Gen. Vardi to Brig. Gen. Gazit, 29 August 1968, A/7921/5, ISA.

59. Dayan to PM, 30 August 1968, A/7921/5, ISA; Yafeh to Cabinet Secretary, 3 September 1968, file: Security—Six Day War, Administered Territories / Settlements, EMA.

60. Key, Jerusalem, to Evans, FO, 12 September 1968, FCO/17/621, UKNA; Teveth, *Cursed Blessing*, 311–12 (Teveth's one-sided account is quite inaccurate).

61. Draft brief, Interim report on the negotiations with the Palestinians, 1 August 1968, A/7921/5, ISA.

62. Maj. Farhi to C.G. of the Central Command et al., 9 June 1968, 42-2845/1997, IDFA.

63. Memorandum of conversation by Sasson: Ja'bari, 23 June 1968, A/7045/12, ISA.

64. Memorandum of conversation by Sasson: Ja'bari, 26 November 1967, MSP.

65. Ronen, *Year of the Shabak*, 197–98.

66. See, for example, Eban to Rabin, Washington, 4 July 1968 [the letter's content indicates that it was actually written in late July], C-1/F-7, AEA.

67. The civil administration (summary of the handling [of] phase A): analysis and lessons (handwritten draft by Sasson), undated, MSP; Dayan's comments in minutes, KFASC, 29 July 1968, A/8162/1, ISA; Shlomo Gazit, "Policies in the Administered Territories," in Roth, *Impact of the Six-Day War*, 65; Zurhellen, Tel Aviv, 21 September 1968, POL 27 ARAB-ISR, RG59, Central Files 1967–69, USNA.

68. See Cobban, *Palestinian Liberation Organisation*, 43–44; for the text of the 1968 charter see *PAD, 1968*, 520–23; the PNC resolutions ibid., 523–33 (the cited clause on 525–26). For a detailed but one-sided discussion of the power struggle between the PLO and the resistance organizations, leading to the fourth session of the PNC (10–17 July), see Bahjat Abu Gharbiyyah, *From the Memoirs of the Fighter Bahjat Abu Gharbiyyah*, 344–59. According to Abu Gharbiyyah, the stricter version of the PLO charter was drafted by Ibrahim Bakr, whom the Israelis had deported in December 1967 (see chapter 6); ibid., 356.

69. Report by Ya'acov Herzog, Conversations with Charles and His Adviser on August 22nd and August 24th [1968], YHP.

70. Unless otherwise indicated, the discussion of the policy makers' attitude is based on minutes, A meeting with Ministers Eban, Allon and Dayan, 29 May 1968, A/7921/4, ISA; minutes, Expanded Political Committee, 3 June 1968, A/7921/13, ISA; minutes, Consultation on the Arabs' problems in the administered territories, 3 July 1968, A/7921/5, ISA; Ya'acov Herzog's diary, From 12 June to 20 July 1968, A/4511/4, ISA.

71. Eshkol's comments on 3 July, ibid; "Heir Apparent," *Time* (New York), 28 June 1968.

72. Ya'acov Herzog's diary, From 12 June to 20 July 1968 (8 July), A/4511/4, ISA.

73. Bitan, FM, to Rabin, Washington, 10 December 1968, File 7, Box 85, Record Group 15 (Galili), TMA.

74. Barbour, Tel Aviv, 11 December 1968 (telegram 6447), NSF/Country File/Israel, Cables, Vol. XI, 12/68–1/69, Box 143, LBJL; Dean, Washington, to FO, 12 December 1968, FCO/17/748, UKNA.

75. Eshkol and Dayan's comments at the Expanded Political Committee, 3 July.

76. Quoted by Gen. (ret.) Ze'evi in Michael Shashar (Shershevski), *Sihot 'im Rehav'am-Gandi-Ze'evi* [Conversations with Rehav'am-Gandi-Ze'evi] (Tel Aviv: Yediot Ahronot; Sifrei Hemed, 1992), 208.

77. Quoted in Thomas Friedman, *From Beirut to Jerusalem* (London: Collins, 1990), 261.

78. See Allon's comments in minutes, meeting of the Labor Party's Secretariat, 19 December 1968, 2-24-1968-95, ILPA; Allon's letter (marked "personal—not for publication") to Hal-Or, 1 April 1969, G/6721/17, ISA. Quotation from the latter.

79. Memorandum of conversation: Eugene Rostow et al. and Yitzhak Rabin et al., 4 June 1968, *FRUS* 20: 367–68. Gideon Rafael, the director general of the Foreign Ministry, revealed that during Hussein's recent meeting with Premier Harold Wilson, the king had stated that he had obtained Nasser's consent to negotiate a settlement with Israel. Rafael's comments in minutes, A meeting with Ministers Eban, Allon and Dayan, 29 May 1968, A/7921/4, ISA.

80. Memorandum by Sasson, ForMin's talk with Anwar Nuseibeh, 4 June 1968, MSP. For Eban's awareness of the green light Nasser had given Hussein see also his comments in minutes, KFASC, 29 May 1968, A/8161/12, ISA.

81. Eban's comments in minutes, A meeting with Ministers Eban, Allon and Dayan, 29 May 1968, A/7921/4, ISA.

82. Memorandum by Sasson: Anwar Nuseibeh—King Hussein's talk, undated, MSP. Nuseibeh's audience with the king took place on 11 June. The memorandum was sent promptly to Eshkol; Sasson to PM, 13 June 1968, MSP.

83. Herzog to ForMin et al., 19 June 1968, YHP; Herzog's comments in minutes, Consultation on the Arabs' problems in the administered territories, 3 July 1968, A/7921/5, ISA.

84. Yaʻacov Herzog's diary, From 12 June to 20 July 1968 (29–30 June), A/4511/4, ISA; Eshkol's comments on 3 July, ibid.

85. See, for example, Gvati's diary, 3 June 1968, File 3, Box 12, Record Group 15 (Gvati), TMA.

86. Yigal Allon, oral history interviews, second, fourth and fifth meetings (26 March, 28 May, 4 June 1979, respectively), all in A/5001/19, ISA.

87. Korn, *Stalemate*, 72, and 293, n. 27. There is nothing in the American documentation to corroborate Allon's version. See, for example, Symmes, Amman, 17 July 1968, *FRUS* 20: 424–26.

88. Symmes, Amman, 17 July 1968, ibid.

89. Minutes, Talks with U.S. Ambassador to the United Nations (meeting with Eshkol), 15 July 1968, A/7043/12, ISA; Barbour, Tel Aviv, 17 July 1968, *FRUS* 20: 418–21; George W. Ball, *The Past Has Another Pattern: Memoirs* (New York: W. W. Norton, 1982), 439.

90. Foreign Minister to Prime Minister, 19 June 1968, C-21/F-188, AEA.

91. Minutes, meeting between Ball et al. and Dayan et al., 16 July 1968, A/7044/5, ISA.

92. Porter, Beirut, 18 July 1968, *FRUS* 20: 426–29; Dean, Washington, to FO, 19 July 1968, FCO/17/54, UKNA; Symmes, Amman, 3 August 1968, *FRUS* 20: 443–45; Yaʻacov Herzog's diary, Political contacts and clarifications—Israel-US, A/4511/4, ISA; Symmes, Amman, 5 August 1968, *FRUS* 20: 450–51. Quotation from the last.

93. Barbour, Tel Aviv, 9 August 1968, POL 27-14 ARAB-ISR/SANDSTORM, RG59, Central Files 1967–69, USNA.

94. Symmes, Amman, 3 August 1968 (telegram 6013), NSF/Country File/Jordan, Cables, Vol. V, 3/8–1/69, Box 147, LBJL.

95. Memorandum by Saunders to President, 8 August 1968, *FRUS* 20: 454–56.

96. Memorandum by Sisco to Rusk, 28 June 1968, *FRUS* 20: 393–94; Yaʻacov Herzog's diary, From 12 June to 20 July 1968, A/4511/4, ISA. For Eshkol's reference to Goldberg see his speech at the Kibbutzim Union's conference, 22 November 1967, A/7920/7, ISA.

97. Barbour, Tel Aviv, 9 August 1968, *FRUS* 20: 456–58; memorandum by Saunders to Walt Rostow, 14 August 1968, *FRUS* 20: 462–63.

98. Rusk to Barbour, Tel Aviv, 17 August 1968, *FRUS* 20: 468–69.

99. Yaʻacov Herzog's diary, Jarring mission—summary of telegrams 26.7–22.8.68; Political contacts and clarifications—Israel-US, both in A/4511/4, ISA; Rusk to Embassy in Tel Aviv, 21 August 1968, *FRUS* 20: 472–73.

100. Gideon Rafael to ForMin, 29 June 1968, C-1/F-7, AEA.

101. Eban to Rabin, Washington, 4 July 1968 [the letter's content indicates that it was actually written in late July], C-1/F-7, AEA.

102. Herzog met Rifaʻi on 19 and 20 June, 20 July and 22 August, and Hussein on 24 August. See Herzog to ForMin et al., 19 June 1968 and 20 June 1968, both in YHP; Yaʻacov

Herzog's diary, From 12 June to 20 July 1968 (20 July), A/4511/4, ISA; Herzog's report, Conversations with Charles and his adviser on August 22nd and August 24th, YHP.

103. For the king's argument see, for example, Symmes, Amman, 4 September 1968, *FRUS* 20: 475–78.

104. For Israel's awareness see, for example, Gen. Yariv's comments in minutes, KFASC, 18 October 1968, A/8162/2, ISA.

105. See Hadow, Israel: Annual Review for 1968, FCO/17/897, UKNA; Philip Adams, Amman, Jordan: Annual Review for 1968, 31 January 1968, obtained from the Foreign and Commonwealth Office, London; Terence Smith, "Israel and Jordan Clash; Artillery and Planes Used," *New York Times,* 5 June 1968.

106. Memorandum, ForMin's talk with Anwar Nuseibeh, 4 June 1968, MSP.

107. Terence Smith, "Israeli Jets Raid Site Near Amman," *New York Times,* 5 August 1968; Terence Smith, "Israeli Raid Seen as Warning to Amman Regime," *New York Times,* 6 August 1968 (quotation from the latter); Hussein and Rifaʻi's comments in Herzog's report, Conversations with Charles and His Adviser on August 22nd and August 24th [1968], YHP; Gen. Yariv's comments in minutes, KFASC, 25 February 1969, A/8162/4, ISA.

108. Quoted in Yaʻacov Herzog's diary (19 August 1968), A/4511/4, ISA.

109. S/RES/256 (1968), 16 August 1968, UNPR.

110. Yaʻacov Herzog's diary (18 August 1968), A/4511/4, ISA.

111. Minutes, KFASC, 20 May 1969, A/8162/4, ISA.

112. Shlaim, *Lion of Jordan,* 284–85; Hussein's shock: Elitsur, Jerusalem, to Rabin, Washington, et al., 22 August 1968, A/7040/3, ISA.

113. Herzog's report, Conversations with Charles and his adviser on August 22nd and August 24th, YHP.

114. Yaʻacov Herzog's diary (25, 29, 26 August 1968), A/4511/4, ISA.

115. Memorandum, ForMin's talk with Anwar Nuseibeh, 8 September 1968, A/7045/12, ISA.

116. Yaʻacov Herzog's diary (16 September 1968), A/4511/4, ISA.

117. Minutes, Political Committee, 20 September 1968, A/7921/13, ISA.

118. Yaʻacov Herzog's diary (24 September 1968), A/4511/4, ISA.

119. Memorandum of conversation: Rusk et al. and Rabin et al., 18 September 1968, *FRUS* 20: 504–8; memorandum, Walt Rostow to President, 19 September 1968, *FRUS* 20: 508–9. Quotation from the former.

120. Memorandum of conversation: Rostow et al. and Rabin et al., 25 September 1968, *FRUS* 20: 517–20.

121. Minutes, Meeting with Charles, on September 27th, 1968, in London (15.30–17.0 p.m.), YHP.

122. Ibid.

123. See Herzog's papers, untitled summary of cables, 11–30 September 1968, A/4511/4, ISA.

124. Eban, London, to Eshkol, 29 September 1968, PPI.

125. Rusk, New York, to State Department, 1 October 1968, *FRUS* 20: 529–34; Eban, New York, to FM, 1 October 1968, A/7936/4, ISA.

126. Walt Rostow to President, 30 September 1968, NSF/ Files of Walt W. Rostow/ Arab-Israeli Private Talks, Box 12, LBJL.

127. PM Eshkol to President Johnson, 29 September 1968, A/7231/4, ISA; memorandum, Walt Rostow to President, 5 October 1968, *FRUS* 20: 543.

128. See Neil Sheehan, "President Orders Talks with Israel on Phantom Jets," *New York Times,* 10 October 1968; memorandum of conversation: Johnson and Eban, 22 October 1968, *FRUS* 20: 563; Eban, *An Autobiography,* 458–59.

129. President Johnson to PM Eshkol, 23 October 1968, *FRUS* 20: 564.

130. Rusk to Embassy in Amman, 9 November 1968, *FRUS* 20: 619–21; Symmes, Amman, 11 November 1968, NSF/Country File/Jordan, Memos, Vol. V, Box 148, LBJL; Symmes, Amman, 20 November 1968, *FRUS* 20: 653–55.

131. Katzenbach to Embassy in Tel Aviv, 13 November 1968, *FRUS* 20: 633–37.

132. Memorandum of conversation: Saunders and Shlomo Argov, 14 November 1968, *FRUS* 20: 638–40.

133. Memorandum, Walt Rostow to President, 15 November 1968, *FRUS* 20: 640–41.

134. See Rabin's comments in minutes, KFASC, 20 May 1969, A/8162/5, ISA.

135. Cabinet session (summary), 31 October 1968, G/10137/2, ISA; Cabinet Resolution 95, 31 October 1968, ICS.

136. Walt Rostow to President, 4 November 1968, *FRUS* 20: 601–2.

137. Memorandum of conversation: Walt Rostow et al. and Yitzhak Rabin et al., 18 November 1968, POL ISR-US, RG59, Central Files 1967–69, USNA. The Polish Corridor was a strip of German territory which gave Poland access to the Baltic Sea between the two world wars, thereby separating East Prussia from the rest of Germany. It was a source of chronic friction between the two countries.

138. On 16 October Israel and Jordan's chiefs of staff met in London, with Herzog and Rifaʿi in attendance. Two days later King Hussein joined the four when they convened for a second discussion. A third summit took place aboard an Israeli navy vessel in the Aqaba Bay near Eilat on 19 November, with Allon, Eban, and Herzog representing Israel. See Shlaim, *Lion of Jordan,* 292–95. There were many more meetings, including summits, in the following months.

139. Yaʿacov Herzog's diary, undated paper marked "Introduction" (printed) and "October 1968" (handwritten), YHP.

140. See memorandum of conversation with Khatib, 21 October 1968, enclosed with Campbell, Jerusalem, 29 October 1968, POL 27 ARAB-ISR, RG59, Central Files 1967–69, USNA. See also memorandum of conversation by Sasson: Hikmat al-Masri, 21 October 1968, A/7045/12, ISA.

141. See Eban's self-congratulatory version in his *An Autobiography,* 456–58; cf. Ambassador Hadow's review paper, Israel and the Jarring Mission, 14 January 1969 (paragraph 8), FCO/17/767, UKNA.

142. Meir's comments in minutes, KFASC, 11 October 1968, A/8162/2, ISA.

143. Memorandum of conversation: U Thant et al. and Eban et al., 5 October 1968, 370-26-1, UNA. Eban made the statement using present tense. Anwar Nuseibeh, who previously had accepted Eban's futile requests to serve as a courier to Hussein, had retired his last ministerial position in 1955.

144. Eshkol said this in a cable to Eban in which he rebuked the foreign minister for telling Hussein and the Americans that the Allon Plan enjoyed the prime minister's support. See Ya'acov Herzog's diary, Additional comments regarding the conversation with Charles on 27.9, YHP.

NINE "The Whole World Is Against Us"

1. Cabinet Resolution 727 (ST/35), 1 September 1968, ICS.

2. Goldstein, *Eshkol*, 597, 599–600; Meron Medzini, *Ha-Yehudiyah ha-Ge'ah: Golda Meir ve-Hazon Yisrael: Biyographyah Politit* [The proud Jewess: Golda Meir and Israel's vision, a political biography] (Jerusalem: 'Edanim, Yediot Ahronot, 1990), 351. For security reasons Eshkol eventually was buried in Jerusalem's Har Herzl National Cemetery. See Gvati's diary, 26 February 1969, File 3, Box 12, Record Group 15 (Gvati), TMA.

3. "Golda Meir: Who Can Blame Israel?" *Sunday Times* (London), 15 June 1969. Meir made a similar statement at a meeting of the Labor Party's Secretariat on 30 January 1969; minutes, 2-24-1969-96, ILPA.

4. Meir's comments in minutes, KFASC, 3 June 1969, A/8162/5, ISA. For the origins of the "Palestinian entity" idea see Shemesh, *Palestinian Entity, 1959–1974*, xi–xiii.

5. Quoted in Terence Prittie, *Eshkol of Israel: The Man and the Nation* (London: Museum Press, 1969), 309.

6. Memorandum of conversation: PM Eshkol et al. and Senator Mark Hatfield et al., 8 December 1968, enclosed with Barbour, Tel Aviv, 18 December 1968, POL 27 ARAB-ISR, RG59, Central Files 1967–69, USNA.

7. "Eshkol: A Reply to Nasser," *Newsweek* (New York), 17 February 1969 (published on 10 February).

8. Population in 1914: Janet L. Abu-Lughod, "The Demographic Transformation of Palestine," in *The Transformation of Palestine: Essays on the Origin and Development of the Arab-Israeli Conflict*, ed. Ibrahim Abu-Lughod (Evanston: Northwestern University Press, 1971), 141; population in the 1880s: Alexander Schölch, *Palestine in Transformation: Studies in Social, Economic and Political Development* (Washington, D.C.: Institute for Palestine Studies, 1993), 42.

9. See Walid Kamhawi [Qamhawi], *The Concise Life Story of an Uprooted Citizen from Palestine*, chapter 4, "War and No Peace (Under Israeli Occupation, 1967–1973)," http://www.jerusalemites.org/memoirs/men/1.htm (accessed on 4 April 2011); Ma'mun al-Qutub, "Hikmat al-Masri, Qadri Touqan and Walid Qamhawi," *Al-Quds*,

20 February 1969. For the Zionist claim of "a land without a people for a people without a land" see Anita Shapira, *Land and Power: The Zionist Resort to Force, 1881-1948* (Stanford: Stanford University Press, 1999), 41-42.

10. Bernard Lewis, "The Palestinians and the PLO: A Historical Approach," *Commentary* 59, no. 1 (January 1975), 38.

11. Nusseibeh, *Once upon a Country,* 136.

12. Memoranda of conversations by Sasson: Shak'ah, 8 September, 20 and 23 October, 17 December 1968, all in A/7045/12, ISA; Memorandum of conversation by Sasson: Shak'ah, 13 January 1969, A/7921/5, ISA; Sasson to PM, 10 September, 3, 22, 24 October, 6, 25, 27 November, 9 December 1968, all in A/7045/12, ISA; Sasson, *Without a Roundtable,* 108-9. For Shak'ah's March 1968 proposal see chapter 7.

13. See interview with Eban, *Washington Post,* 6 March 1969.

14. Hadow, Tel Aviv, to Arthur, FO, 13 January 1969, FCO/17/767, UKNA.

15. Dayan's comments in minutes, KFASC, 24 December 1968, A/8162/3, ISA; Dayan, *Story of My Life,* 333-34; Fadwa Touqan, *Al-Rihlah al-As'ab* [The harder journey] (Amman: Dar al-Shuruq, 1993), 59-60.

16. Benvenisti, *Jerusalem,* 233-41.

17. Minister Gvati's comments, *Knesset Proceedings,* 21 January 1969, 1194-95.

18. Cabinet Resolution 324, 26 January 1969, ICS.

19. Eban, *New Diplomacy,* 224.

20. For Israel's security perceptions see Dan Horowitz, "The Israeli Concept of National Security," in *National Security and Democracy in Israel,* ed. Avner Yaniv (Boulder, Colo.: Lynne Rienner, 1993), 11-53.

21. Eban's comments in minutes, Mapai's Secretariat meeting, 2 January 1968, 2-24-1968-92, ILPA.

22. Eshkol's comments, *Knesset Proceedings,* 7 August 1968, 3125.

23. Cabinet Resolution 563, 19 June 1967, article 1(A), ICS.

24. Transcript, Meeting held on November 19, 1968, YHP.

25. In July 1968 Col. Mordechai Gur, the military commander of the Gaza Strip and Northern Sinai, estimated the number of 1948 refugees living in the area at 180,000-210,000 and the number of native Gazans at 130,000-140,000. Gur's comments in minutes, KFASC, 16 July 1968, A/8162/1, ISA.

26. Goldberg, New York, 23 September 1967, *FRUS* 19: 834-38.

27. See Eshkol's comments in minutes, The meeting with Lt. Gen. Y. Rabin, 24 May 1968, A/7938/11, ISA.

28. This subject is still considered highly sensitive by the Israeli government, and consequently many of the relevant records are still classified. But there is enough in the available material in Israeli official archives to allow a comprehensive study. Alas, the scope of this book does not permit a fuller discussion. In the succinct account here I have relied on, among other sources, Gur's comments in minutes, KFASC, 19 January 1968, A/8161/10, ISA, and 16 July 1968, A/8162/1, ISA; interviews with Col. (ret.) Beni Meitiv, the military commander of the southern district of the Gaza Strip in 1967-69, and

Gen. (ret.) Shlomo Gazit, 6 October 2002; 28 April 2004, Tel Aviv. The little which has been written on this subject thus far is either inaccurate or incomplete. Good examples of the former are Nur Masalhah, *A Land without a People: Israel, Transfer, and the Palestinians, 1949–1996* (London: Faber and Faber, 1996), 91–95, and Nur Masalhah, *The Politics of Denial: Israel and the Palestinian Refugee Problem* (London: Pluto, 2003), 103–11. Partial discussions are offered in Michael Palumbo, *Imperial Israel: The History of the Occupation of the West Bank and Gaza* (London: Bloomsbury, 1990), 83–100; Segev, *1967*, 523–42; Gorenberg, *Accidental Empire*, 141–42, 152.

29. Dayan's comments in minutes, KFASC, 29 July 1968, A/8162/1, ISA.

30. See Adams, Amman, to FO, 30 July 1968, FCO/17/623, UKNA.

31. Interviews with Maj. Gen. (ret.) Meir Amit, 14 April 2002, Ramat Gan.

32. Eshkol's comments in Minutes, [Labor Party's] Political Committee, 30 October 1968, A/7921/13, ISA.

33. Cabinet Resolution 797, 10 September 1967, ICS; Procedure for family reunion in the West Bank—a draft for comments, FM/4092/5, ISA; Dayan's comments in minutes, KFASC, 23 July 1968, A/8162/1, ISA; Shashar's diary, 12 January 1969; 11 January 1970.

34. Meir's address, *Knesset Proceedings*, 17 March 1969, 1953–57 (quotation from 1956).

35. Beilin, *Price of Unity*, 11–162, 213–16 (particularly 155–58). For similar argument see Medzini, *Proud Jewess*, 348–49.

36. Allon, *Curtain of Sand*, 407–8.

37. Herzog's report, Conversations with Charles and his adviser on August 22nd and August 24th, YHP.

38. *Knesset Proceedings*, 7 August 1968, 3125. Eshkol was using a pun on the Hebrew phrase *la-vo el ha-menuhah ve-el ha-nahalah* (based on Deuteronomy 12:9: "For ye are not as yet come to the rest and to the inheritance, which the Lord your God giveth you"), which means to end one's travails and reach a state of tranquillity. Literally, however, it means to achieve rest and arrive at an estate or land.

39. Pedatzur, *Triumph of Bewilderment*. For a concise English version of Pedatzur's argument see Reuven Pedatzur, "Coming Back Full Circle: The Palestinian Option in 1967," *Middle East Journal* 49, no. 2 (1995), 269–91. These works are based on the author's doctoral dissertation, submitted in 1992, long before many of the relevant records became available in Israeli archives. Furthermore, despite the foreign policy aspects of its subject, the study relies almost exclusively on Israeli sources. Without consulting the abundance of primary sources which have been declassified in later years, Pedatzur repeats the same argument in a recently published article while drawing on his 1990s writings. Reuven Pedatzur, "The Rescue of King Hussein's Regime," *Civil Wars* 10, no. 3 (2008), 294–98.

40. 'Ali al-Din Hilal, *Mashru'at al-Dawlah al-Filastiniyyah* [The plans for a Palestinian state] (Cairo: Markaz al-Dirasat al-Siyasiyyah wa-al-Istiratijiyah bi-al-Ahram, 1978), 76.

41. See King Hussein's open letter to PM Talhuni, *Al-Dustur,* 14 September 1968. Cf. his comments in the meeting with Ball and Sisco, reported in Porter, Beirut, 18 July 1968, *FRUS* 20: 426–29.

42. This passage, including the quotations, is largely based on chapter 8.

43. Ashton, *King Hussein of Jordan,* 132.

44. Quoted in Symmes, Amman, 9 December 1968, NSF/Country File/Jordan, Memos, Vol. V, Box 148, LBJL.

45. Rusk to Embassy in Amman, 24 December 1968, *FRUS* 20: 714–15.

46. Ya'acov Herzog's diary, Charles—from December 1968 to the end of August 1969, YHP.

47. Mearsheimer, *Why Leaders Lie,* 86–90.

48. Hadow, Tel Aviv, to Arthur, FO, 13 January 1969, FCO/17/767, UKNA. Less than three weeks after the war Dayan told the General Command Staff that sooner or later the army might need to take Cairo, Amman, Damascus, and Beirut in order to achieve a final and decisive victory. Defense Minister Moshe Dayan's remarks at the General Command Staff conference, 29 June 1967, 24-45/2008, IDFA.

49. Quoted in Gazit, *Trapped Fools,* 242.

50. Yeshayahu Leibowitz, *Judaism, Human Values, and the Jewish State* (Cambridge: Harvard University Press, 1992), 233.

51. Meir Amit, *Rosh be-Rosh: Mabat Ishi 'al Eiru'im Gdolim u-Farshiyot 'Alumot* [Head-on: A personal view of great events and secret affairs] (Or Yehudah: Hed Aartsi, 1999), 246.

52. Harold Saunders, *The Other Walls: The Politics of the Arab-Israeli Peace Process* (Washington, D.C.: American Enterprise Institute for Public Policy Research, 1985), 10; W. W. Rostow, *The Diffusion of Power: An Essay in Recent History* (New York: Macmillan, 1972), 419. Quotation from the former. See also Steven L. Spiegel, *The Other Arab-Israeli Conflict: Making America's Middle East Policy, from Truman to Reagan* (Chicago: University of Chicago Press, 1985), 164–65.

53. Meir's comments in minutes, KFASC, 27 May 1969, A/8162/5, ISA.

54. Quoted in I. L. Kenen, *Israel's Defense Line: Her Friends and Foes in Washington* (Buffalo, N.Y.: Prometheus, 1981), 173.

55. Spiegel, *Other Arab-Israeli Conflict,* 128–29, quotation from 123; Edward Tivnan, *The Lobby: Jewish Political Power and American Foreign Policy* (New York: Simon and Schuster, 1987), 59–60.

56. Shashar's diary, 14 February 1969. Califano, the son of a first generation Italian-American, said that Johnson felt the same way about Italians.

57. Lyndon Baines Johnson, *The Vantage Point: Perspectives of the Presidency, 1963-1969* (London: Weidenfeld and Nicolson, 1972), 287–304, quotations from 297 and 304; Arab refugees: 303.

58. Muhammad Hasanayn Heikal, *1967 al-Infijar* [1967, the Explosion] (Cairo: Markaz al-Ahram lil-Tarjamah wa-al-Nashr, Mu'assasat al-Ahram, 1990), 868–69.

59. Johnson, *Vantage Point,* 304.

60. "2 Arab Terrorists Attack Israeli Jetliner in Athens," *New York Times,* 27 December 1968.

61. Gvati's diary, 20 January 1969, File 3, Box 12, Record Group 15 (Gvati), TMA; Dishon, *Middle East Record,* vol. 4, *1968,* 380–81.

62. Gai, *Bar-Lev,* 202.

63. Interview with Eshkol, *Davar ha-Shavu'a* (*Davar* weekend magazine), 24 January 1969.

64. S/RES/262 (1968), 31 December 1968, UNPR; Eban's comments in minutes, KFASC, 7 January 1969; Ambassador Tekoah's comments in minutes, KFASC, 24 January 1969, both in A/8162/3, ISA; Dishon, *Middle East Record,* vol. 4, *1968,* 381.

65. MK Aryeh Ben-Eliezer's comments, *Knesset Proceedings,* 20 February 1969, 1700–1702 (quotation from 1701). Ben-Eliezer blamed Abba Eban for this prevailing "ugly image," claiming that the foreign minister was presenting Israel as holding the occupied territories while seeking security rather than liberating the Jewish homeland.

66. Nixon's comments, scribbled at the end of a memorandum from National Security Adviser Dr. Henry Kissinger, as quoted in Henry Kissinger, *Years of Upheaval* (London: Weidenfeld and Nicolson and Michael Joseph, 1982), 212. Emphases in the original.

67. Shlaim, *Iron Wall,* 317.

68. "Two-legged beasts": see MK Ariel Sharon's comments, citing former Prime Minister Menachem Begin, *Knesset Proceedings,* 21 December 1992, 1270.

69. Eshkol's comments in minutes, KFASC, 25 June 1968, A/8161/12, ISA.

70. Ehud Olmert, "Israel's Dilemmas: No Simple Short Cuts," in Roth, *Impact of the Six-Day War,* 37.

71. See Ehud Olmert, "How I Almost Brought About Peace," extracts from Olmert's forthcoming autobiography, *7 Yamim* (*Yedioth Ahronot* weekend magazine), 28 January 2011.

72. "Statement to the Security Council by Foreign Minister Eban, 6 June 1967," *Israel's Foreign Relations,* 2: 784–92 (quotation from 790).

73. Quoted in Gad Ya'acobi, *Pgishot be-Maslul Hayai* [Encounters in the course of my life] (Jerusalem: Carmel, 2009), 194.

74. Interview with Dov Weisglass, Sharon's closest adviser: "In His Client's Name," *Musaf Haaretz,* 8 October 2004.

75. For the full text of the Arab peace initiative see "Arab Heads of State, Declaration on the Saudi Peace Initiative, Beirut 28 March 2002," *Journal of Palestine Studies* 31, no. 4 (2002), 182.

76. Aziz Shihadeh [*sic*], "Remember Sparta! The Cost of Indecision in Jerusalem," *New Middle East,* October 1969, 5, 7.

77. Quoted in Amos Shifris, *Yisrael Galili: Shomer ha-Masad ve-Noteh ha-Kav* [Yisrael Galili: The guardian of the foundations and establisher of the line] (Ramat Ef'al: Yad Tabenkin, 2010), 401.

78. See, for example, Bentov, *Days Tell,* 161; Chaim Herzog, *Living History,* 178; David Kimche, "Dawafi' Isra'il lil-Harb wa-Ta'thiruha 'Alayha" [Israel's motives for war and the war's effect on Israel], in *Harb Yuniyu 1967: Ba'da 30 Sanah* [The June 1967 War: Thirty years later], ed. Lutfi al-Khuli (Cairo: Mu'assasat al-Ahram, Markaz al-Ahram lil-Tarjamah wa-al-Nashr, 1997), 218; Shimon Shamir, "The Palestinians Are a Nation," *New Outlook* 12, nos. 5–6 (1969), 196.

79. Eban, *Personal Witness,* 498.

80. "*Ha-'Olam Kulo Negdenu*" ["The whole world is against us"], lyrics by Yoram Taharlev (for the full text of the song in the Hebrew original see http://www.taharlev .com/songs_selection_song.asp?id=79; accessed on 4 May 2011); Korn, *Stalemate,* 215.

Sources and Bibliography

Primary Sources

ARCHIVES AND LIBRARIES

Abba Eban Archive, Abba Eban Center for Israeli Diplomacy, Truman Institute, Hebrew University of Jerusalem (AEA).

Bodleian Library, University of Oxford (BOD), Special Collections: Harold Wilson's papers.

Central Intelligence Agency, Electronic Reading Room, http://www.foia.cia.gov/.

Eshkol Memorial Archive, Jerusalem (EMA).

Israel Cabinet Secretariat, Jerusalem (ICS), records obtained under the Freedom of Information Law.

Israel Defense Forces and Defense Establishment Archive, Tel ha-Shomer (IDFA).

Israel State Archives, Jerusalem (ISA).

Israeli Labor Party Archive, Beit Berl (ILPA).

Lavon Institute for Labor Movement Research Archive, Tel Aviv (LIA).

Lyndon B. Johnson Library, Austin, Texas (LBJL).

Middle East Centre Archive, St Antony's College, University of Oxford (MECA).

Tabenkin Memorial Archive, Ef'al, Israel (TMA).

United Kingdom National Archives (formerly Public Record Office), Kew, London (UKNA).

United Nations Archives, New York (UNA).

United Nations public records (UNPR), mostly available online, http://domino
.un.org/unispal.nsf.

United States National Archives, College Park, Maryland (USNA).

PRIVATE PAPERS

David Farhi papers (DFP).

Dr. Ya'acov Herzog papers (YHP).

Moshe Sasson papers (MSP).

Other sources, anonymous (PPI).

UNPUBLISHED DIARIES

Haim Gvati, Box 12, Record Group 15 Gvati Haim, TMA.

Ya'acov Herzog Dr. *1967:* A/4511/3, ISA; *1968–69:* A/4511/4, ISA.

Michael Shashar, *1968–1971:* obtained privately from Mr. Shashar.

PUBLISHED DOCUMENTS
English

The Arab-Israeli Conflict. Vol. 3, *Documents.* Ed. John Norton Moore. Princeton: Princeton University Press, 1974.

The Arab-Israel Conflict and Its Resolutions: Selected Documents. Ed. Ruth
Lapidoth and Moshe Hirsch. Dordrecht: Martinus Nijhoff, 1992.

Foreign Relations of the United States, 1964–1968. Vol. 14, *The Soviet Union.* Ed.
David C. Humphrey, Charles S. Sampson; gen. ed. David S. Patterson. Washington, D.C.: United States Printing Office, 2001.

———. Vol. 19, *Arab-Israeli Crisis and War, 1967.* Ed. Harriet Dashiell Schwar;
gen. ed. Edward C. Keefer. Washington, D.C.: United States Printing Office,
2004.

———. Vol. 20, *Arab-Israeli Dispute, 1967–1968.* Ed. Louis J. Smith; gen. ed.
David S. Patterson. Washington, D.C.: United States Printing Office, 2001.

International Documents on Palestine, 1967. Ed. Fuad A. Jabber. Beirut: Institute for Palestine Studies, 1970.

International Documents on Palestine, 1968. Ed. Zuhair Diab. Beirut: Institute
for Palestine Studies; Kuwait: University of Kuwait, 1971.

International Documents on Palestine, 1969. Ed. Walid Khadduri. Beirut: Institute for Palestine Studies; Kuwait: University of Kuwait, 1972.

Israel's Foreign Relations: Selected Documents, 1947–1974. Vol. 2. Ed. and historical notes, Meron Medzini. Jerusalem: Ministry for Foreign Affairs, 1976.

Public Papers of the Presidents of the United States: Lyndon B. Johnson, 1967. Washington, D.C.: United States Government Printing Office, 1968.

Public Papers of the Presidents of the United States: Lyndon B. Johnson, 1968–1969. Washington, D.C.: United States Government Printing Office, 1970.

The Resistance of the Western Bank of Jordan to Israeli Occupation 1967. Beirut: Institute of Palestine Studies, 1967.

The State Papers of Levi Eshkol. Ed. Henry M. Christman. New York: Funk and Wagnalls, 1969.

Arabic

Al-Watha'iq al-Filastiniyyah al-'Arabiyyah li-'Am 1967 [Palestinian Arab documents, 1967]. Compiled and sorted, George Khouri Nasrallah. Beirut: Mu'assasat al-Dirasat al-Filastiniyyah, 1969.

Al-Watha'iq al-Filastiniyyah al-'Arabiyyah li-'Am 1968 [Palestinian Arab documents, 1968]. Compiled and sorted, George Khouri Nasrallah. Beirut: Mu'assasat al-Dirasat al-Filastiniyyah, 1970.

Al-Watha'iq al-Filastiniyyah al-'Arabiyyah li-'Am 1969 [Palestinian Arab documents, 1969]. Compiled and sorted, George Khouri Nasrallah. Beirut: Mu'assasat al-Dirasat al-Filastiniyyah, 1971.

Hebrew

Divrei ha-Knesset [The Knesset proceedings].

Levi Eshkol: Rosh ha-Memshalah ha-Shlishi: Mivhar Te'udot mi-Pirkei Hayav (1895–1969) [Levi Eshkol: The third prime minister, selected documents from his lifetime, 1895–1969]. Ed. and historical notes, Arnon Lammfromm and Haggai Tsoref. Jerusalem: Israel State Archives, 2002.

Mevaker ha-Medinah: Du'ah Shnati 53 Bet li-Shnat 2002 u-le-Heshbonot Shnat ha-Ksafim 2001 [State comptroller's annual report 53B for 2002 and audit of the fiscal year 2001]. Jerusalem: Mevaker ha-Medinah, 2003.

Mevaker ha-Medinah: Du'ah Shnati 55 Bet li-Shnat 2004 u-le-Heshbonot Shnat ha-Ksafim 2003 [State comptroller's annual report 55B for 2004 and audit of the fiscal year 2003]. Jerusalem: Mevaker ha-Medinah, 2005.

Yitzhak Rabin: Rosh Memshelet Yisrael 1974–1977, 1992–1995: Mivhar Te'udot mi-Pirkei Hayav [Yitzhak Rabin: Prime minister of Israel, 1974–1977, 1992–1995, selected documents from his lifetime]. Vol. 1, 1922–67. Ed. and historical notes, Yemima Rosenthal. Jerusalem: Israel State Archives, 2005.

PERIODICALS

English-language dailies: *Christian Science Monitor* (Boston); *Guardian* (London); *Jerusalem Post; New York Times; Telegraph* (London); *The Times* and *The Sunday Times* (London); *Washington Post.*

English-language weeklies: *Jewish Observer and Middle East Review* (London); *Newsweek* (New York); *Time* (New York).

Arabic dailies: *Al-Anba'* (Jerusalem); *Al-Difaʻ* (Amman); *Al-Dustur* (Amman); *Al-Ittihad* (Haifa); *Al-Nahar* (Beirut); *Al-Quds* (Jerusalem); *Al-Rai* (Amman).

Arabic weeklies: *'Amman al-Masa'* (Amman); *Ghorbah* (New York); *Hadha al-'Alem* (Tel Aviv).

Hebrew dailies: *'Al ha-Mishmar* (Tel Aviv); *Davar* and *Davar ha-Shavuʻa* (Tel Aviv); *Haaretz* and *Musaf Haaretz* (Tel Aviv); *La-Merhav* (Tel Aviv); *Maʻariv* (Tel Aviv); *Yediot Ahronot* (Tel Aviv).

Hebrew weeklies: *Ba-Mahaneh* (Tel Aviv); *Ha-'Olam ha-Zeh* (Tel Aviv); *Kol ha- 'Ir* (Jerusalem).

ORAL HISTORY
Sources

AR   Interviews and conversations conducted by the author
AS   Interviews and conversations conducted by Professor Avi Shlaim
BBC   Transcripts of interviews for the BBC 1998 six-part program *The Fifty Year War: Israel and the Arabs* (GB 165-0346, MECA)
DR   Interview with Victor Cohen, conducted by David Ronen
ISA   Series of interviews with Yigal Allon, conducted by Re'udor Manor, Oral History Department, Leonard Davis Institute for International Relations, the Hebrew University of Jerusalem: files 19–22, Box A/5001
LBJL   Oral history collection, also available online: http://www.lbjlib.utexas.edu/johnson/archives.hom/biopage.asp#anchor24993.
MECA   Interview with Uzi Narkiss, conducted by Tad Szulc: GB 165-0368
YRC   Oral history project, Yitzhak Rabin Center for Israel Studies

Name	Position in 1967–69	Interview Details
Israelis		
Col. (ret.) Shmuel Albeq	deputy military governor of Arab Jerusalem in June 1967	1 August 1997, Ramat ha-Sharon (AR)
Yigal Allon	member of cabinet	1979 (ISA)

Name	Position in 1967–69	Interview Details
Maj. Gen. (ret.) Meir Amit	Mossad chief until mid-1968	2003 (YRC); 21 March 2003, Tel Aviv (AS); 14 April 2002, Ramat Gan (AR)
Col. (ret.) Eliezer Amitai	commander of Brigade No. 16	3 July 2006, by telephone (AR); 17 December 2007, Ramat ha-Sharon (AR)
Shaul Bar-Haim	Foreign Ministry official	25 March 1998, Jerusalem (AR)
Dan Bavly	reserve officer, West Bank Military Government	29 August 1995, Tel Aviv (AR)
Col. (ret.) David Brin	military governor of Ramallah	23 June 2006, Tel Aviv (AR)
Victor Cohen	GSS (*Shabak*) official	3 February 1987 (DR)
Abba Eban	foreign minister	29 January 1997 (BBC)
Miryam Eshkol	wife of Prime Minister Levi Eshkol	17 November 2003, Jerusalem (AR)
Mordechai Gazit	Foreign Ministry official	22 June 2004, Jerusalem (AS)
Maj. Gen. (ret.) Shlomo Gazit	chief of the Military Intelligence's Research Division until mid-August 1967; thereafter in charge of handling the occupied territories on behalf of Defense Minister Dayan	6 October 2002, Tel Aviv (AR); 28 April 2004, Tel Aviv (AR); 23 June 2004, Tel Aviv (AS)
Col. (ret.) Yoel Herzel	adjutant to Maj. Gen. Uzi Narkiss	25 June 2006, Netanya (AR)
Dr. David Kimche	reserve Military Intelligence officer; Mossad official	4 October 1996, Ramat ha-Sharon (AR); 2 May 2004, Tel Aviv (AR)
Maj. Gen. (ret.) Shlomo Lahat	military governor of Arab Jerusalem in June 1967; thereafter chief of staff of Central Command	2000–2001 (YRC)
Col. (ret.) Beni Meitiv	military commander of the southern district of the Gaza Strip	19 November 2003, Ashkelon (AR)

Name	Position in 1967–69	Interview Details
Maj. Gen. (ret.) Uzi Narkiss	commanding general of the Central Command until mid-1968	1989, Jerusalem (MECA); 10 December 1996, by telephone (AR); 21 January 1997 (BBC); 1997 (YRC)
Gideon Rafael	ambassador to the United Nations until late 1967; thereafter director general of the Foreign Ministry	19, 29 January 1997 (BBC)
David Ronen	junior GSS (*Shabak*) operative in the West Bank	2 October 1996, Bat Yam (AR)
Moshe Sasson	Foreign Ministry official; from November 1967 Prime Minister Eshkol's representative for political contacts with the West Bank leadership	15 October 1996, Jerusalem (AR); 20 November 1996, Jerusalem (AR); 9 August 2001, Jerusalem (AR); 24 December 2001, Jerusalem (AR); 21 March 2002 (AS)
Lt. Col. (ret.) Rafi Sutton	commander of intelligence-collection unit, based in Jerusalem	15 October 1996, Jerusalem (AR)
Eliezer Tsafrir	adviser on Arab affairs at the West Bank Military Government between late 1967 and late 1968; thereafter assistant to Moshe Sasson	6 October 1996, Ramat ha-Sharon (AR)
Lt. Gen. (ret.) Zvi Tsur	assistant defense minister	2000–2001 (YRC)
Maj. Gen. (ret.) Raphael Vardi	military governor of the West Bank	9 December 2002, Tel Aviv (AR)

Jordanians and Palestinians

Na'im al-Ashhab	leader of the Communist Party in the West Bank	23 January 2006, Jerusalem (AR)
Hussein bin Talal	king of Jordan	3 December 1996, Ascot (AS)

Name	Position in 1967–69	Interview Details
Nasser al-Din Nashashibi	prominent journalist in Egypt, son of a notable Jerusalem family	3 March 1998, Jerusalem (AR)
Dr. Hazem Nuseibeh	minister of reconstruction and development	18 September 2002, Amman (AS)
Muhammad Nuseibeh	brother of Anwar Nuseibeh	24 April 2004, Jerusalem (AR)
Zayd al-Rifa'i	private secretary to King Hussein	19 September 2002, Amman (AS); 20 December 2002, Amman (AS)

Americans

McGeorge Bundy	special consultant to President Johnson	interview 3 by Paige E. Mulhollan, 19 March 1969 (LBJL)
Arthur J. Goldberg	ambassador to the United Nations until mid-1968	interview 1 by Ted Gittinger, 23 March 1983 (LBJL)
Nicholas D. Katzenbach	undersecretary of state	interview 3 by Paige E. Mulhollan, 11 December 1968 (LBJL)
Robert McNamara	secretary of defense	interview 1 by Walt W. Rostow, 8 January 1975 (LBJL); special interview 1 by Robert Dallek, 26 March 1993 (LBJL)
Harry C. McPherson	special counsel to President Johnson	interview 3 by T. H. Baker, 8 January 1975 (LBJL); interview 7 by Michael L. Gillette, 19 September 1985 (LBJL)
Dean Rusk	secretary of state	interview 4 by Paige E. Mulhollan, 8 March 1970 (LBJL)

Others

Salah Bassiouny	Egyptian Foreign Ministry official	25 February 1997 (BBC)

Name	Position in 1967–69	Interview Details
Anatoly Dobrynin	USSR ambassador to the United States	March 1997 (BBC)
Ismaʻil Fahmy	Egyptian diplomat at the United Nations until 1968	17 September 1982, Cairo (AS)
Dr. Cecil Hourani	Arab-British intellectual	24 February 2005, London (AR)

LECTURES

Dan Bavly, 27 October 1999, Truman Institute, Hebrew University of Jerusalem.

Abba Eban, 19 March 1986, Dayan Center, Tel Aviv University.

Shlomo Gazit, 5 March 1986, Dayan Center, Tel Aviv University; 25 March 1969, Jerusalem (1577-922/1975, IDFA).

Chaim Herzog, 26 March 1986, Dayan Center, Tel Aviv University.

Moshe Sasson, 28 November 1999, Truman Institute, Hebrew University of Jerusalem.

Secondary Sources
BOOKS AND ARTICLES IN ENGLISH AND FRENCH

Abdul ['Abd al-]Hadi, Mahdi F. *Notes on Palestinian-Israeli Meetings in the Occupied Territories, 1967–1987.* East Jerusalem: PASSIA, 1987.

al-Abid, Ibrahim. *Israel and Human Rights.* Beirut: Palestine Liberation Organization, Research Center, 1969.

Abowd, Tom. "The Moroccan Quarter: A History of the Present." *Jerusalem Quarterly File,* Winter 2000, 6–16.

Abu Iyad, with Eric Rouleau. *My Home, My Land: A Narrative of the Palestinian Struggle.* New York: Times Books, 1981.

Abu-Lughod, Janet L. "The Demographic Transformation of Palestine." In *The Transformation of Palestine: Essays on the Origin and Development of the Arab-Israeli Conflict,* ed. Ibrahim Abu-Lughod, 139–63. Evanston: Northwestern University Press, 1971.

Aburish, Said K. *Children of Bethany: The Story of a Palestinian Family.* London: I. B. Tauris, 1988.

Abu Sharif, Bassam. *Arafat and the Dream of Palestine: An Insider's Account.* New York: Palgrave Macmillan, 2009.

Abu Shelbaya [Shalbayah], Muhammad. "New Palestinians Challenge the Old." *New Middle East,* September 1969, 8–9.

———. "Jerusalem before and after June 1967: An Arab View." *New Middle East,* March–April 1972, 43–45.

Adams, Michael. *Chaos or Rebirth: The Arab Outlook.* London: British Broadcasting Corporation, 1968.

———. *Signposts to Destruction: Israeli Settlements in the Occupied Territories.* London: Council for the Advancement of Arab-British Understanding, [1977?].

Adams, Michael, and Christopher Mayhew. *Publish It Not . . . : The Middle East Cover-Up.* London: Longman, 1975.

Ajami, Fuad. *The Arab Predicament: Arab Political Thought and Practice since 1967.* Updated ed. Cambridge: Cambridge University Press, 1992.

———. *The Dream Palace of the Arabs: A Generation's Odyssey.* New York: Pantheon, 1998.

Alami, Musa. Preface to *The Future of Palestine,* vii–xviii. Beirut: Hermon, 1970.

Amad, Adnan, comp. and ed. *Israeli League for Human and Civil Rights (The Shahak Papers).* Beirut: Palestine Research Center, 1973.

Antonius, George. *The Arab Awakening: The History of the Arab National Movement.* London: Hamish Hamilton, 1938.

Arian, Asher. *The Second Republic: Politics in Israel.* Chatham, N.J.: Chatham House, 1998.

Aronson, Geoffrey. *Israel, Palestinians, and the Intifada: Creating Facts on the West Bank.* London: Kegan Paul International in association with the Institute for Palestine Studies, 1990.

Aronson, Shlomo. *Conflict and Bargaining in the Middle East: An Israeli Perspective.* Baltimore: Johns Hopkins University Press, 1978.

———. *Levi Eshkol: From Pioneering Operator to Tragic Hero—A Doer.* London: Vallentine Mitchell, 2011.

Ashton, Nigel. "Cold War, Hot War, and Civil War: King Hussein and Jordan's Regional Role, 1967–73." In *The Cold War in the Middle East: Regional Conflict and the Superpowers 1967–73,* ed. Nigel Ashton, 188–209. London: Routledge, 2007.

———. *King Hussein of Jordan: A Political Life.* New Haven: Yale University Press, 2008.

el-Asmar, Fouzi. *To Be an Arab in Israel.* London: Frances Pinter, 1975.

Avineri, Shlomo, ed. *Israel and the Palestinians.* New York: St. Martin's, 1971.

Azoury, Nagib. *Le Réveil de la Nation Arabe.* Paris: Plon-Nourrit, 1905.

Baha ed-Dine, Ahmed [Baha' al-Din, Ahmad]. "Returning to Palestine." *New Outlook* 11, no. 5 (June 1968), 31–35, 42.

Bailey, Clinton. "Changing Attitudes toward Jordan in the West Bank." *Middle East Journal* 32, no. 2 (Spring 1978), 155–66.

Bailey, Sydney D. *Four Arab-Israeli Wars and the Peace Process.* Basingstoke: Macmillan, 1990.

Ball, George W. *The Past Has Another Pattern: Memoirs.* New York: Norton, 1982.

Bar-El, Yair, Rimona Durst, Gregory Katz, Josef Zislin, Ziva Strauss, and Haim Y. Knobler. "Jerusalem Syndrome." *British Journal of Psychiatry* 176, no. 1 (2000), 86–90.

Baroud, Ramzy. *My Father Was a Freedom Fighter: Gaza's Untold Story.* London: Pluto, 2010.

Bar-Zohar, Michael. *Facing a Cruel Mirror: Israel's Moment of Truth.* New York: Scribner's, 1990.

———. *Yaacov Herzog: A Biography.* London: Halban, 2005.

Baumgarten, Helga. "The Three Faces/Phases of Palestinian Nationalism, 1948–2005." *Journal of Palestine Studies* 34, no. 4 (Summer 2005), 25–48.

Bavly, Dan, and David Farhi. *Israel and the Palestinians.* London: Anglo-Israel Association, pamphlet no. 29, January 1971.

Becker, Abraham S. *Israel and the Palestinian Occupied Territories: Military-Political Issues in the Debate.* Santa Monica, Calif.: Rand, 1971.

Bellow, Saul. *To Jerusalem and Back: A Personal Account.* New York: Penguin, 1985.

Ben-Ami, Shlomo. *Scars of War, Wounds of peace: The Israeli-Arab Tragedy.* Oxford: Oxford University Press.

Ben-Gurion, David. "Ben-Gurion Diary May–June 1967." *Israel Studies* 4, no. 2 (Fall 1999), 199–220.

Bentwich, Norman. *Israel: Two Fateful Years, 1967–1969.* London: Elek, 1970.

———. "Musa Alami's Old-New Outlook: A Personal Sketch." *New Outlook* 14, no. 3 (April 1971), 24–27.

Benvenisti, Meron. "Dialogue of Action in Jerusalem." *Jerusalem Quarterly 19* (Spring 1981), 10–22.

———. *Jerusalem: The Torn City.* Jerusalem: Isratypeset, 1976.

———. "Reunion without Reconciliation: Jews and Arabs in Jerusalem." *New Middle East,* March 1973, 15–19.

Benziman, Uzi. "Israeli Policy in East Jerusalem after Reunification." In *Jerusalem: Problems and Prospects,* ed. Joel L. Kraemer, 100–130. New York: Praeger, 1980.

Ben-Zvi, Abraham. *Lyndon B. Johnson and the Politics of Arms Sales: Israel in the Shadow of the Hawk.* London: Frank Cass, 2004.

Black, Ian, and Benny Morris. *Israel's Secret Wars: The Untold History of Israeli Intelligence.* London: Hamish Hamilton, 1991.

Bondy, Ruth, Ohad Zmora, and Rapahel Bashan, eds. *Mission Survival: The People of Israel's Story in Their Own Words: From the Threat of Annihilation to Miraculous Victory.* London: W. H. Allen, 1968.

Bowen, Jeremy. *Six Days: How the 1967 War Shaped the Middle East.* London: Simon and Schuster, 2003.

Braizat, Musa S. *The Jordanian-Palestinian Relationship: The Bankruptcy of the Confederal Idea.* London: British Academic Press, 1998.

Brecher, Michael. *Decisions in Israel's Foreign Policy.* London: Oxford University Press, 1974.

———. *The Foreign Policy System of Israel: Setting, Images, Process.* London: Oxford University Press, 1972.

———. "Jerusalem: Israel's Political Decisions, 1947–1977." *Middle East Journal* 32, no. 1 (Winter 1978), 13–34.

Brecher, Michael, with Benjamin Geist. *Decisions in Crisis: Israel, 1967 and 1973.* Berkeley: University of California Press, 1980.

Brenchley, Frank. *Britain, the Six-Day War, and Its Aftermath.* London: I. B. Tauris, 2005.

Brown, George. *In My Way: The Political Memoirs of Lord George-Brown.* Harmondsworth: Penguin, 1972.

Brynen, Rex. "The Dynamics of Palestinian Elite Formation." *Journal of Palestine Studies* 24, no. 3 (Spring 1995), 31–43.

Bull, Odd. *War and Peace in the Middle East: The Experience and Views of a U.N. Observer.* London: Leo Cooper, 1976.

Bunch, Clea Lutz. "Strike at Samu: Jordan, Israel, the United States, and the Origins of the Six-Day War." *Diplomatic History* 32, no. 1 (January 2008), 55–76.

Burdett, Winston. *Encounter with the Middle East: An Intimate Report on What Lies behind the Arab-Israeli Conflict.* London: Andre Deutsch, 1970.

Caplan, Neil. *The Lausanne Conference, 1949: A Case Study in Middle East Peacemaking.* Tel Aviv: Tel Aviv University, Moshe Dayan Center for Middle Eastern and African Studies, 1993.

Caradon, Lord [Hugh Foot], Arthur J. Goldberg, Mohamed H. El-Zayyat, and Abba Eban. *U.N. Security Council Resolution 242: A Case Study in Diplomatic Ambiguity.* Washington, D.C.: Institute for the Study of Diplomacy, Edmund A. Walsh School of Foreign Service, Georgetown University, 1981.

Cheshin, Amir, Bill Hutman, and Avi Melamed. *Separate and Unequal: The Inside Story of Israeli Rule in East Jerusalem*. Cambridge: Harvard University Press, 1999.

Christison, Kathleen, "Bound by a Frame of Reference, Part II: U.S. Policy and the Palestinians, 1948–88." *Journal of Palestine Studies* 27, no. 3 (Spring 1998), 20–34.

Cobban, Helena. *The Palestinian Liberation Organisation: People, Power, and Politics*. Cambridge: Cambridge University Press, 1984.

Cockburn, Andrew, and Leslie Cockburn. *Dangerous Liaison: The Inside Story of the U.S.-Israeli Covert Relationship*. London: Bodley Head, 1992.

Cohen, Amnon. "The Changing Patterns of West Bank Politics." *Jerusalem Quarterly* 5 (Fall 1977), 105–13.

——. "Does a 'Jordanian Option' Still Exist?" *Jerusalem Quarterly* 16 (Summer 1980), 111–20.

——. *Political Parties in the West Bank under the Jordanian Regime, 1949–1967*. Ithaca, N.Y.: Cornell University Press, 1982.

——. "Thoughts on Israel's Palestinian Policies." *Middle East Focus* 2, no. 1 (May 1979), 10–13.

——. "West Bank Sentiments 1967–1973." In *The Palestinians: People, History, Politics*, ed. Michael Curtis, Joseph Neyer, Chaim I. Waxman, and Allen Pollack, 88–93. New Brunswick, N.J.: Transaction, 1975.

Cohen, Esther Rosalind. *Human Rights in the Israeli-Occupied Territories, 1967–1982*. Manchester: Manchester University Press, 1985.

Cohen, Gerda L. "A Visit to Bethlehem." *Midstream* 14, no. 10 (December 1968), 52–57.

Cohen, Hillel. *Army of Shadows: Palestinian Collaboration with Zionism, 1917–1948*. Berkeley: University of California Press, 2008.

Cossali, Paul, and Clive Robson. *Stateless in Gaza*. London: Zed, 1986.

Dayan, Moshe. *Breakthrough: A Personal Account of the Egypt-Israel Peace Negotiations*. London: Weidenfeld and Nicolson, 1981.

——. *Story of My Life*. London: Weidenfeld and Nicolson, 1976.

Dayan, Yaël. *My Father, His Daughter*. London: Weidenfeld and Nicolson, 1985.

Dib, George, and Fuad Jabber. *Israel's Violation of Human Rights in the Occupied Territories: A Documented Report*. 3rd ed. Beirut: Institute for Palestine Studies, 1970.

Dishon, Daniel, ed. *Middle East Record*. Vol. 3, *1967*. Jerusalem: Israeli Universities Press, 1971.

——. *Middle East Record*. Vol. 4, *1968*. Jerusalem: Israeli Universities Press, 1973.

——. *Middle East Record.* Vol. 5, *1969–1970.* Jerusalem: Israeli Universities Press, 1977.

Dodd, Peter, and Halim Barakat. "Palestinian Refugees of 1967: A Sociological Study." *Muslim World* 60, no. 2 (April 1970), 123–42.

——. *River without Bridges: A Study of the Exodus of the 1967 Palestinian Arab Refugees.* Beirut: Institute for Palestine Studies, 1968.

Douglas-Home, Charles. *The Arabs and Israel.* London: Bodley Head, 1968.

Eban, Abba. *An Autobiography.* London: Weidenfeld and Nicolson, 1978.

——. [Live or Perish.] Unpublished manuscript, 1969.

——. *My Country: The Story of Modern Israel.* London: Weidenfeld and Nicolson, 1972.

——. *The New Diplomacy: International Affairs in the Modern Age.* London: Weidenfeld and Nicolson, 1983.

——. *Personal Witness: Israel through My Eyes.* London: Jonathan Cape, 1993.

Eban, Suzy. *A Sense of Purpose: Recollections.* London: Halban, 2008.

el-Edroos, Sayed Ali. *The Hashemite Arab Army, 1908–1979: An Appreciation and Analysis of Military Operations.* Amman: Publishing Committee, 1980.

Eijbersen, Rene. "A Living with Justice and Honor." *New Outlook* 10, no. 7 (September–October 1967), 36–39.

Elath, Eliahu. "Conversations with Musa al-'Alami." *Jerusalem Quarterly* 41 (Winter 1987), 31–75.

Elazar, Daniel J., ed. *Judea, Samaria, and Gaza: Views on the Present and Future.* Washington, D.C.: American Enterprise Institute, 1982.

Elon, Amos. "The Israeli Occupation." *Commentary* 45, no. 3 (March 1968), 41–47.

Enderlin, Charles. *Paix ou guerres: Les secrets des négociations israélo-arabes, 1917–1995.* New ed. Paris: Fayard, 2004.

Epp, Frank H. *The Israelis: Portrait of a People in Conflict.* Scottdale, Pa.: Herald, 1980.

——. *The Palestinians: Portrait of a People in Conflict.* Toronto: McClelland and Stewart, 1976.

Ettinger, Amos. *My Land of Tears and Laughter: The Story of "Zonik" (Col. Ze'ev Shaham); A Man of Many Friends.* New York: Cornwall, 1994.

Farhi, David. "The West Bank, 1948–1971: Society and Politics in Judea and Samaria." *New Middle East,* November 1971, 33–36.

Farid, Abdel Magid ['Abd al-Majid]. *Nasser: The Final Years.* Reading: Ithaca, 1994.

[al-]Farouqi, Hamdi [al-]Taji. "What Palestinians Want." *New Middle East,* July 1969, 13–15.

el-Farra, Muhammad. *Years of No Decision.* London: KPI, 1987.

Farsoun, Samih K., with Christina E. Zacharia. *Palestine and the Palestinians.* Boulder, Colo.: Westview, 1997.

Fawcett, Louise, ed. *International Relations of the Middle East.* Oxford: Oxford University Press, 2005.

Finkelstein, Norman G. *Image and Reality of the Arab-Israeli Conflict.* 2nd ed. London: Verso, 2003.

Flapan, Simha. *The Birth of Israel: Myths and Realities.* London: Croom Helm, 1987.

——, ed. *When Enemies Dare to Talk: An Israeli-Palestinian Debate (5/6 September 1978).* London: Croom Helm, 1979.

Friedlander, Dov, and Calvin Goldscheider. *The Population of Israel.* New York: Columbia University Press, 1979.

Friedman, Thomas. *From Beirut to Jerusalem.* London: Collins, 1990.

Furlonge, Geoffrey. *Palestine Is My Country: The Story of Musa Alami.* London: John Murray, 1969.

Garfinkle, Adam. *Politics and Society in Modern Israel: Myths and Realities.* Armonk: M. E. Sharpe, 1997.

Gat, Moshe. "Britain and Israel before and after the Six Day War, June 1967: From Support to Hostility." *Contemporary British History* 18, no. 1 (Spring 2004), 54–77.

Gazit, Shlomo. *The Carrot and the Stick: Israel's Policy in Judaea and Samaria, 1967–68.* Washington, D.C.: B'nai Brith Books, 1995.

——. "Early Attempts at Establishing West Bank Autonomy (the 1968 Case Study)." *Harvard Journal of Law and Public Policy* 3, no. 1 (1980), 129–53.

——. "Policy in the Administered Territories." *Israel Yearbook on Human Rights* 1 (1971), 278–82.

——. *Trapped Fools: Thirty Years of Israeli Policy in the Territories.* London: Frank Cass, 2003.

Gelvin, James L. *The Israel-Palestinian Conflict: One Hundred Years of War.* Cambridge: Cambridge University Press, 2005.

Gera, Gideon. "Israel and the June 1967 War: 25 Years Later." *Middle East Journal* 46, no. 2 (Spring 1992), 229–43.

Gilbar, Gad G. *Population Dilemmas in the Middle East: Essays in Political Demography and Economy.* London: Frank Cass, 1997.

Gillon, Philip. *Israelis and Palestinians, Co-Existence or . . . : The Credo of Elie Eliachar.* London: Rex Collings, 1978.

Gluska, Ami. *The Israeli Military and the Origins of the 1967 War: Government, Armed Forces, and Defence Policy, 1963–1967.* London: Routledge, 2007.

Golan, Galia. "The Soviet Union and the Outbreak of the June 1967 Six-Day War." *Journal of Cold War Studies* 8, no. 1 (Winter 2006), 3–19.

Goldberg, Arthur J. Resolution 242 after Twenty Years. National Committee on American Foreign Policy Website, April 2002, http://www.mefacts.com /cached.asp?x_id=10159 (last accessed: 14 November 2011).

Goldstein, Yossi. "Israel's Prime Ministers and the Arabs: Levi Eshkol, Golda Meir and Yitzhak Rabin." *Israel Affairs* 17, no. 2 (April 2011), 177–93.

Gorenberg, Gershom. *The Accidental Empire: Israel and the Birth of the Settlements, 1967–1977.* New York: Times Books, 2006. The same book was published in the United Kingdom as *Occupied Territories: The Untold Story of Israel's Settlements.* London: I. B. Tauris, 2007.

Gowers, Andrew, and Tony Walker. *Behind the Myth: Yasser Arafat and the Palestinian Revolution.* London: W. H. Allen, 1990.

Green, Stephen. *Living by the Sword: America and Israel in the Middle East, 1967–87.* London: Faber and Faber, 1988.

———. *Taking Sides: America's Secret Relations with a Militant Israel.* New York: William Morrow, 1984.

Gresh, Alain. *The PLO: The Struggle Within: Toward an Independent Palestinian State.* Rev. and updated ed. London: Zed, 1988.

Haddadin, Munther J. *Diplomacy on the Jordan: International Conflict and Negotiated Resolution.* Boston: Kluwer Academic, 2002.

Halabi, Rafik. *The West Bank Story.* San Diego: Harcourt Brace Jovanovich, 1985.

Halabi, Usama. "The Legal Status and Rights of the Palestinians Displaced as a Result of the June 1967 War." *Palestine-Israel Journal* 15, no. 4 (2008)–16, no. 1 (2009), 54–64.

Hamad, Jamil. "Palestinian Future—New Directions." *New Middle East,* August 1971, 16–19.

Harkabi, Yehoshafat. *Arab Strategies and Israel's Response.* New York: Free Press, 1977.

———. "We Must Learn to Understand the Substance of the Arab Case . . ." *New Middle East,* November 1968, 26–30.

Harris, William Wilson. *Taking Root: Israeli Settlement in the West Bank, the Golan, and Gaza-Sinai, 1967–1980.* Chichester: Research Studies Press, 1980.

Hassouna, Hussein A. *The League of Arab States and Regional Disputes: A Study of Middle East Conflicts.* Dobbs Ferry, N.Y.: Oceana, 1975.

Hawary, Mohamed. "Between the Right of Return and Attempts of Resettlement." In *The Palestinian Refugees: Old Problems—New Solutions,* ed. Joseph Ginat and Edward J. Perkins, 34–45. Brighton: Sussex Academic Press, 2001.

Heikal, Mohamed. *The Road to Ramadan.* London: Collins, 1975.

———. *Secret Channels: The Inside Story of Arab-Israeli Peace Negotiations.* London: HarperCollins, 1996.

Helms, Richard, with William Hood. *A Look over My Shoulder: A Life in the Central Intelligence Agency.* New York: Random House, 2003.

Herzog, Chaim. *Living History: A Memoir.* London: Weidenfeld and Nicolson, 1997.

Hirst, David. *The Gun and the Olive Branch: The Roots of Violence in the Middle East.* 3rd ed. London: Faber and Faber, 2003.

———. "Rush to Annexation: Israel in Jerusalem." *Journal of Palestine Studies* 3, no. 4 (Summer 1974), 3–31.

Hofnung, Menachem. *Democracy, Law, and National Security in Israel.* Aldershot: Dartmouth, 1996.

Horowitz, Dan. "The Israeli Concept of National Security." In *National Security and Democracy in Israel,* ed. Avner Yaniv, 11–53. Boulder, Colo.: Lynne Rienner, 1993.

Hourani, Albert. "Ottoman Reform and the Politics of Notables." In *Beginnings of Modernization in the Middle East,* ed. William R. Polk and Richard L. Chambers, 41–68. Chicago: University of Chicago Press, 1968.

Hourani, Cecil [unsigned]. "The Moment of Truth: Towards a Middle East Dialogue." *Encounter* (London) 29, no. 5 (November 1967), 3–14.

———. *An Unfinished Odyssey: Lebanon and Beyond.* London: Weidenfeld and Nicolson, 1984.

Hudson, Michael C. "Jerusalem: A City Still Divided." *Mid East* 8, no. 4 (special issue, September 1968), 20–25.

Hussein de Jordanie. *Ma "guerre" avec Israël.* Paris: Albin Michel, 1968.

Isaac, Rael Jean. *Israel Divided: Ideological Politics in the Jewish State.* Baltimore: Johns Hopkins University Press, 1976.

"Israel and the Palestinians: A Discussion," *Midstream* 16, no. 4 (April 1970), 42–57. This is an English translation of a roundtable discussion which appeared in *Musaf Haaretz* on 6 February 1970.

"Israel's Occupation Policies" [translated transcript of a call-in radio program whose guest was Brig. Gen. Shlomo Gazit]. *New Outlook* 11, no. 6 (July–August 1968), 47–55.

Jamal, Amal. *The Palestinian National Movement: Politics of Contention, 1967–2005.* Bloomington: Indiana University Press, 2005.

James, Laura M. *Nasser at War: Arab Images of the Enemy.* Basingstoke: Palgrave Macmillan, 2006.

Johnson, Lyndon Baines. *The Vantage Point: Perspectives of the Presidency, 1963–1969.* London: Weidenfeld and Nicolson, 1972.

Kamhawi [Qamhawi], Walid. The Concise Life Story of an Uprooted Citizen from Palestine. http://www.jerusalemites.org/memoirs/men/1.htm (last accessed: 28 January 2011).

Kanovsky, Eliyahu. The Economic Impact of the Six-Day War: Israel, the Occupied Territories, Egypt, Jordan. New York: Praeger, 1970.

Kapeliouk [Kapeliuk], Amnon. "'First of All Evacuate the Occupied Territories.'" New Outlook 10, no. 7 (September–October 1967), 39–44.

———. Israël: La fin des mythes. Paris: Albin Michel, 1975.

——— [Kapeliuk]. "Talking on the West Bank." New Outlook 10, no. 6 (July–August 1967), 38–41, 46.

Kelman, Herbert C. "The Palestinianization of the Arab-Israeli Conflict." Jerusalem Quarterly 46 (Spring 1988), 3–15.

Kenan, Amos. Israel—A Wasted Victory. Tel Aviv: Amikam, 1970.

———. "A Letter to All Good People (To Fidel Castro, Sartre, Russell, and All the Rest)." New Outlook 11, no. 4 (May 1968), 47–53. Published also in New Statesman, 12 July 1968, 41–42.

Kenen, I. L. Israel's Defense Line: Her Friends and Foes in Washington. Buffalo: Prometheus, 1981.

Kerr, Malcolm H. The Arab Cold War: Gamal 'Abd al-Nasir and His Rivals. 3rd ed. Oxford: Oxford University Press for the Royal Institute of International Affairs, 1971.

Khalidi, Rashid. "The Future of Arab Jerusalem." British Journal of Middle Eastern Studies 19, no. 2 (1992), 133–43.

———. The Iron Cage: The Story of the Palestinian Struggle for Statehood. Boston: Beacon, 2006.

———. Palestinian Identity: The Construction of Modern National Consciousness. New York: Columbia University Press, 1997.

Khalidi, Walid. Before the Diaspora: A Photographic History of the Palestinians. Washington, D.C.: Institute for Palestine Studies, 1984.

el-Khatib, Rouhi [al-Khatib, Ruhi]. Address Delivered at a Meeting Held in the House of Commons Members Dining Room, during the Jordan Refugee Week in London, June 13th, 1968.

———. The Judaization of Jerusalem. Beirut: PLO Research Center, 1970.

Khouri, Fred J. The Arab-Israeli Dilemma. 2nd ed. Syracuse, N.Y.: Syracuse University Press, 1976.

Kimche, David. The Last Option: After Nasser, Arafat, and Saddam Hussein; The Quest for Peace in the Middle East. London: Weidenfeld and Nicolson, 1991.

———. "What Kind of a Nation? The Palestinian Dilemma." New Middle East, October 1968, 26–30.

Kimche, David, and Dan Bawly [Bavly]. *The Sandstorm*. London: Secker and Warburg, 1968.

Kimche, Jon. *Palestine or Israel: The Untold Story of Why We Failed, 1917–1923, 1967–1973*. London: Secker and Warburg, 1973. The US edition of this book was published as *There Could Have Been Peace*. New York: Dial, 1973.

Kimmerling, Baruch, and Joel S. Migdal. *The Palestinian People: A History*. Cambridge: Harvard University Press, 2003.

Kinglake, William. *Eothen*. London: Century, 1982.

Kissinger, Henry. *Years of Upheaval*. London: Weidenfeld and Nicolson, and Michael Joseph, 1982.

Kollek, Teddy, with Amos Kollek. *For Jerusalem: A Life*. London: Weidenfeld and Nicolson, 1978.

Korn, Alina. "Military Government, Political Control, and Crime: The Case of Israeli Arabs." *Crime, Law and Social Change* 34 (2000), 159–82.

Korn, David A. *Stalemate: The War of Attrition and Great Power Diplomacy in the Middle East, 1967–1970*. Boulder, Colo.: Westview, 1992.

Lall, Arthur. *The UN and the Middle East Crisis, 1967*. Rev. ed. New York: Columbia University Press, 1970.

Langer, Felicia. *With My Own Eyes: Israel and the Occupied Territories, 1967–1973*. London: Ithaca, 1975.

Leibowitz, Yeshayahu. *Judaism, Human Values, and the Jewish State*. Cambridge: Harvard University Press, 1992.

Lesch, Ann Mosely. "Israeli Deportation of Palestinians from the West Bank and the Gaza Strip, 1967–1978." Part I, *Journal of Palestine Studies* 8, no. 2 (Winter 1979), 101–31; part II, 8, no. 3 (Spring 1979), 81–112.

———. "Israeli Settlements in the Occupied Territories, 1967–1977." Part I, *Journal of Palestine Studies* 7, no. 1 (Autumn 1977), 26–47; part II, 8, no. 1, (Autumn 1978), 100–119.

———. *Israel's Occupation of the West Bank: The First Two Years*. Santa Monica, Calif.: Rand, 1970.

———. *Political Perceptions of the Palestinians on the West Bank and the Gaza Strip*. Washington, D.C.: Middle East Institute, special study no. 3, 1980.

Lewis, Bernard. "The Consequences of Defeat." *Foreign Affairs* 46, no. 2 (January 1968), 321–35.

———. "The Palestinians and the PLO: A Historical Approach." *Commentary* 59, no. 1 (January 1975), 32–48.

Litani, Yehuda. "Leadership in the West Bank and Gaza." *Jerusalem Quarterly* 14 (Winter 1980), 99–109.

Litvak, Meir. "Inside versus Outside: The Challenge of the Local Leadership, 1967–1994." In *The PLO and Israel: From Armed Conflict to Political Solu-*

tion, 1964–1994, ed. Avraham Sela and Moshe Ma'oz, 171–95. Basingstoke: Macmillan, 1997.

Lustick, Ian. *Arabs in the Jewish State: Israel's Control of a National Minority.* Austin: University of Texas Press, 1980.

Mahgoub, Mohamed Ahmed. *Democracy on Trial: Reflections on Arab and African Politics.* London: Andre Deutsch, 1974.

Mansour, Atallah. *Waiting for the Dawn.* London: Secker and Warburg, 1975.

Ma'oz, Moshe. *Palestinian Leadership on the West Bank.* London: Frank Cass, 1984.

———. *Syria and Israel: From War to Peacemaking.* Oxford: Clarendon, 1995.

Marie-Thérèse. "La guerre à Jérusalem." *Témoignage Chrétien* (Paris), 27 July 1967.

Masalha, Nur. *A Land without a People: Israel, Transfer, and the Palestinians, 1949–1996.* London: Faber and Faber, 1996.

———. *The Politics of Denial: Israel and the Palestinian Refugee Problem.* London: Pluto, 2003.

Matar, Ibrahim. "Exploitation of Land and Water Resources for Jewish Colonies in the Occupied Territories." In *International Law and the Administration of Occupied Territories: Two Decades of Israeli Occupation of the West Bank and Gaza Strip*, ed. Emma Playfair, 443–56. Oxford: Clarendon, 1992.

McDowall, David. *Palestine and Israel: The Uprising and Beyond.* London: I. B. Tauris, 1989.

Mearsheimer, John J. *Why Leaders Lie: The Truth about Lying in International Politics.* New York: Oxford University Press, 2011.

Meital, Yoram. "The Khartoum Conference and Egyptian Policy after the 1967 War: A Reexamination." *Middle East Journal* 54, no. 1 (Winter 2000), 64–82.

Merlin, Samuel, ed. *The Big Powers and the Present Crisis in the Middle East: A Colloquium.* Rutherford, N.J.: Fairleigh Dickinson University Press, 1968.

Metzger, Jan, Martin Orth, and Christian Sterzing. *This Land Is Our Land: The West Bank under Israeli Occupation.* London: Zed, 1983.

"The Middle East Activities of the International Committee of the Red Cross, June 1967–June 1970." Part I, *International Review of the Red Cross* 113 (August 1970), 424–59; part II, 114 (September 1970), 485–511.

Migdal, Joel S., with contributions by Gabriel Baer, Donna Robinson Divine, Mark Heller, Ylana N. Miller, Shaul Mishal, Shimon Shamir, Kenneth W. Stein, and Rachelle Taqqu. *Palestinian Society and Politics.* Princeton: Princeton University Press, 1980.

Mikes, George. *The Prophet Motive: Israel Today and Tomorrow.* Harmondsworth: Penguin, 1971.

Mishal, Shaul. "Nationalism through Localism: Some Observations on the West Bank Political Elite." *Middle Eastern Studies* 17, no. 4 (October 1981), 477–91.

———. *The PLO under 'Arafat.* New Haven: Yale University Press, 1986.

———. *West Bank / East Bank.* New Haven: Yale University Press, 1978.

Morris, Benny. *The Birth of the Palestinian Refugee Problem Revisited.* 2nd ed. Cambridge: Cambridge University Press, 2004.

———. *1948: A History of the First Arab-Israeli War.* New Haven: Yale University Press, 2008.

———. *Righteous Victims: A History of the Zionist-Arab Conflict, 1881–1999.* London: John Murray, 2000.

"Moshe Dayan on Peace and War: An Interview." *Midstream* 14, no. 10 (December 1968), 46–51. This is an English translation of an interview by journalist Ge'ulah Cohen, published in *Ma'ariv,* 22 September 1968.

Moskin, J. Robert. *Among Lions: The Battle for Jerusalem, June 5–7, 1967.* New York: Arbor House, 1982.

Musallam, Ayoub. "Peace Depends upon Israel." *New Outlook* 11, no. 6 (July–August 1968), 28–32.

Mutawi, Samir A. *Jordan in the 1967 War.* Cambridge: Cambridge University Press, 1987.

Nahumi, Mordechai. "Israel as an Occupying Power." *New Outlook* 15, no. 5 (June 1972), 16–34.

———. "Policies and Practice of Occupation." *New Outlook* 11, no. 4 (May 1968), 26–42.

Narkiss, Uzi. *The Liberation of Jerusalem: The Battle of 1967.* London: Vallentine, Mitchell, 1983.

———. *Soldier of Jerusalem.* London: Vallentine Mitchell, 1998.

Nashashibi, Nasser Eddin [al-Din]. *Jerusalem's Other Voice: Ragheb Nashashibi and Moderation in Palestinian Politics, 1920–1948.* Exeter: Ithaca, 1990.

Neff, Donald. *Warriors for Jerusalem: The Six Days That Changed the Middle East.* New York: Linden / Simon and Schuster, 1984.

Nevo, Joseph. *King Hussein and the Evolution of Jordan's Perception of a Political Settlement with Israel, 1967–1988.* Brighton: Sussex Academic Press, 2006.

Nuseibeh, Anwar. "Can We Meet the Challenge?" *New Outlook* 11, no. 2 (February 1968), 3–5, 23.

———. "Jerusalem the Holy: Images and Reality." *New Middle East,* March 1973, 11–14.

———. "On Jerusalem." *New Outlook* 11, no. 7 (September 1968), 50–53.

Nusseibeh, Sari, with Anthony David. *Once upon a Country: A Palestinian Life.* London: Halban, 2007.

O'Balance, Edgar. *Arab Guerrilla Power, 1967–1972.* London: Faber and Faber, 1974.

Oren, Michael B. "The Revelations of 1967: New Research on the Six Day War and Its Lessons for the Contemporary Middle East." *Israel Studies* 10, no. 2 (Summer 2005), 1–14.

———. *Six Days of War: June 1967 and the Making of the Modern Middle East.* New York: Oxford University Press, 2002.

Owen, Roger. *State, Power, and Politics in the Making of the Modern Middle East.* 2nd ed. London: Routledge, 2000.

"Palestinian Emigration and Israeli Land Expropriation in the Occupied Territories." *Journal of Palestine Studies* 3, no. 1 (Autumn 1973), 106–18.

Palumbo, Michael. *Imperial Israel: The History of the Occupation of the West Bank and Gaza.* London: Bloomsbury, 1990.

Parker, Richard, B. *The Politics of Miscalculation in the Middle East.* Bloomington: Indiana University Press, 1993.

———. *The Six-Day War: A Retrospective.* Gainesville: University Press of Florida, 1996.

Pedatzur, Reuven. "Coming Back Full Circle: The Palestinian Option in 1967." *Middle East Journal* 49, no. 2 (Spring 1995), 269–91.

———. "The Rescue of King Hussein's Regime." *Civil Wars* 10, no. 3 (September 2008), 294–318.

Peretz, Don. "Israel's Administration and Arab Refugees." *Foreign Affairs* 46, no. 2 (January 1968), 336–46.

———. "Israel's New Arab Dilemma." *Middle East Journal* 22, no. 1 (Winter 1968), 45–57.

———. "Peace Is Not around the Corner." *New Middle East,* November 1968, 15–20.

———. *The West Bank: History, Politics, Society, and Economy.* Boulder, Colo.: Westview, 1986.

Perlmutter, Amos. "Israel's Dilemma." *Foreign Affairs* 68, no. 5 (Winter 1989–90), 119–32.

Piterberg, Gabriel. "Erasures." *New Left Review,* July–August 2001, 31–46.

Podeh, Elie. "The 'Big Lie': Inventing the Myth of British-US Involvement in the 1967 War." *Review of International Affairs* 2, no. 1 (Autumn 2002), 1–23.

Porath, Yehoshua. *The Emergence of the Palestinian-Arab National Movement, 1918–1929.* London: Frank Cass, 1974.

———. "On the Writing of Arab History by Israeli Scholars." *Jerusalem Quarterly* 32 (Summer 1984), 28–35.

——. *The Palestinian Arab National Movement: From Riots to Rebellion.* Vol. 2, *1929–1939.* London: Frank Cass, 1977.

——. "Palestinian Historiography." *Jerusalem Quarterly* 5 (Fall 1977), 95–104.

Prittie, Terence. *Eshkol of Israel: The Man and the Nation.* London: Museum Press, 1969.

Pryce-Jones, David. *The Face of Defeat: Palestinian Refugees and Guerrillas.* London: Quartet, 1974.

——. "Personal Glimpses: A View of Life on the West Bank." *New Middle East,* August 1972, 20–24.

Quandt, William B. "Lyndon Johnson and the June 1967 War: What Color Was the Light?" *Middle East Journal* 46, no. 2 (Spring 1992), 198–228.

——. *Peace Process: American Diplomacy and the Arab-Israeli Conflict since 1967.* Washington, D.C.: Brookings Institution; Berkeley: University of California Press, 1993.

Quandt, William B., Fuad Jabber, and Ann Mosely Lesch. *The Politics of Palestinian Nationalism.* Berkeley: University of California Press, 1973.

Rabin, Yitzhak. *The Rabin Memoirs.* Expanded ed. Berkeley: University of California Press, 1996.

Rafael, Gideon. *Destination Peace: Three Decades of Israeli Foreign Policy; A Personal Memoir.* London: Weidenfeld and Nicolson, 1981.

Raphaeli, Nimrod. "Military Government in the Occupied Territories: An Israeli View." *Middle East Journal* 23, no. 2 (Spring 1969), 177–90.

——. "Problems of Military Administration in the Controlled Territories." *Public Administration in Israel and Abroad* 8 (1968), 48–51.

Raviv, Moshe. *Israel at Fifty: Five Decades of Struggle for Peace; A Diplomat's Narrative.* London: Weidenfeld and Nicolson, 1988.

Raz, Avi. "The Generous Peace Offer That Was Never Offered: The Israeli Cabinet Resolution of 19 June 1967." *Diplomatic History* 37, no. 1 (January 2013, forthcoming).

Reinhart, Tanya. *Israel / Palestine: How to End the War of 1948.* New York: Seven Stories, 2002.

Rekhess, Elie, and Asher Susser. "Political Factors and Trends in the Israeli-Administered Territories." In *From June to October: The Middle East between 1967 and 1973,* ed. Itamar Rabinovich and Haim Shaked, 269–91. New Brunswick, N.J.: Transaction, 1978.

Riad, Mahmoud. *The Struggle for Peace in the Middle East.* London: Quartet, 1981.

Ricks, Thomas M. "Memoirs of Palestine: Uses of Oral History and Archaeology in Recovering the Palestinian Past." In *Archaeology, History and Cul-*

ture in Palestine and the Near East: Essays in Memory of Albert E. Glock, ed. Tomis Kapitan, 23–46. Atlanta: Scholars, 1999.

Rostow, Eugene V. "Legal Aspects of the Search for Peace in the Middle East." *American Journal of International Law* 64, no. 4 (September 1970), 64–71.

———. *Peace in the Balance: The Future of American Foreign Policy.* New York: Simon and Schuster, 1972.

Rostow, W. W. *The Diffusion of Power: An Essay in Recent History.* New York: Macmillan, 1972.

Roth, Stephen J., ed. *The Impact of the Six-Day War: A Twenty-Year Assessment.* Basingstoke: Macmillan, 1988.

Rouleau, Eric. "The Palestinian Quest." *Foreign Affairs* 53, no. 2 (January 1975), 264–83.

Roy, Sara. "The Gaza Strip: Critical Effects of the Occupation." *Arab Studies Quarterly* 10, no. 1 (Winter 1988), 59–103.

Rubin, Barry, Joseph Ginat, and Moshe Ma'oz, eds. *From War to Peace: Arab-Israeli Relations, 1973–1993.* Brighton: Sussex Academic Press, 1994.

Rusk, Dean. *As I Saw It: A Secretary of State's Memoirs.* London: I. B. Tauris, 1991.

Sahliyeh, Emile. *In Search of Leadership: West Bank Politics since 1967.* Washington, D.C.: Brookings Institution, 1988.

———. "The PLO and the Politics of Ethnonational Mobilization." In *The PLO and Israel: From Armed Conflict to Political Solution, 1964–1994,* ed. Avraham Sela and Moshe Ma'oz, 3–22. Basingstoke: Macmillan, 1997.

———. "The West Bank Pragmatic Elite: The Uncertain Future." *Journal of Palestine Studies* 15, no. 4 (Summer 1986), 34–45.

Saleh, Abdul ['Abd al-]Jawad. *Israel's Policy of De-Institutionalization: A Case Study of Palestinian Local Government.* Amman: Jerusalem Center for Development Studies, 1987.

———. The Palestinian Non-Violent Resistance Movement. Alternative Palestinian Agenda, 3 September 2002, http://www.ap-agenda.org/11-02/asaleh.htm (last accessed: 14 November 2011).

Salibi, Kamal. *The Modern History of Jordan.* London: I. B. Tauris, 1993.

Saunders, Harold. *The Other Walls: The Politics of the Arab-Israeli Peace Process.* Washington, D.C.: American Enterprise Institute for Public Policy Research, 1985.

Sayigh, Yezid. "The Armed Struggle and Palestinian Nationalism." In *The PLO and Israel: From Armed Conflict to Political Solution, 1964–1994,* ed. Avraham Sela and Moshe Ma'oz, 23–35. Basingstoke: Macmillan, 1997.

———. *Armed Struggle and the Search for State: The Palestinian National Movement, 1949–1993.* Oxford: Clarendon, 1997.

———. "Turning Defeat into Opportunity: The Palestinian Guerrillas after the June 1967 War." *Middle East Journal* 46, no. 2 (Spring 1992), 244–65.

Schiff, Zeev, and Raphael Rothstein. *Fedayeen: The Story of the Palestinian Guerrillas.* London: Vallentine, Mitchell, 1972.

Schleifer, Abdullah. "The Fall of Jerusalem." *Evergreen Review,* December 1967, 26–29, 82–90.

———. *The Fall of Jerusalem.* New York: Monthly Review Press, 1972.

Schoenbaum, Thomas J. *Waging Peace and War: Dean Rusk in the Truman, Kennedy, and Johnson Years.* New York: Simon and Schuster, 1988.

Schölch, Alexander. *Palestine in Transformation: Studies in Social, Economic, and Political Development.* Washington, D.C.: Institute for Palestine Studies, 1993.

———, ed. *Palestinians over the Green Line.* London: Ithaca, 1983.

Segev, Tom. "The June 1967 War and the Palestinian Refugee Problem." *Journal of Palestine Studies* 36, no. 3 (Spring 2007), 6–22.

———. *1967: Israel, the War, and the Year That Transformed the Middle East.* London: Little, Brown, 2007.

Sela, Avraham. *The Decline of the Arab-Israeli Conflict: Middle East Politics and the Quest for Regional Order.* Albany: State University of New York Press, 1998.

Sella, Amnon. "Custodians and Redeemers: Israeli Leaders' Perceptions of Peace, 1967–79." *Middle Eastern Studies* 22, no. 2 (April 1986), 236–51.

Shai, Aron. "The Fate of Abandoned Arab Villages in Israel, 1965–1969." *History and Memory* 18, no. 2 (Fall–Winter 2006), 86–106.

Shamgar, Meir, ed. *Military Government in the Territories Administered by Israel, 1967–1980: The Legal Aspects.* Vol. 1. Jerusalem: Hebrew University Jerusalem, Faculty of Law, Harry Sacher Institute for Legislature Research and Comparative Law, 1982.

Shamir, Shimon. "Arab Intellectuals and the War." *New Outlook* 12, nos. 5–6 (June–August 1969), 109–14.

———. "The Palestine Challenge." *New Outlook* 12, no. 3 (March–April 1969), 12–19, 49.

———. "The Palestinians Are a Nation," *New Outlook* 12, nos. 5–6 (June–August 1969), 191–97.

Shapira, Anita. *Land and Power: The Zionist Resort to Force, 1881–1948.* Stanford: Stanford University Press, 1999.

Sharabi, Hisham. "Liberation or Settlement: The Dialectics of Palestinian Struggle." *Journal of Palestine Studies* 2, no. 2 (Winter 1973), 33–48.

Sharkansky, Ira. *Policy Making in Israel: Routines for Simple Problems and Coping with the Complex.* Pittsburgh: University of Pittsburgh Press, 1997.

Sharon, Ariel, with David Chanoff. *Warrior: The Autobiography of Ariel Sharon.* London: Mcdonald, 1989.

Shehadeh, Raja. *Strangers in the House.* South Royalton: Steerforth, 2002.

Shemesh, Moshe. *Arab Politics, Palestinian Nationalism and the Six Day War: The Crystallization of Arab Strategy and Nasir's Descent to War, 1957–1967.* Brighton: Sussex Academic Press, 2008.

———. "Did Shuqayri Call for 'Throwing the Jews into the Sea'?" *Israel Studies* 8, no. 2 (Summer 2003), 70–81.

———. "On Two Parallel Tracks—The Secret Jordanian-Israeli Talks (July 1967–September 1973)." *Israel Studies* 15, no. 3 (Fall 2010), 87–120.

———. *The Palestinian Entity, 1959–1974.* 2nd rev. ed. London: Frank Cass, 1996.

———. "The West Bank: Rise and Decline of Traditional Leadership, June 1967 to October 1973." *Middle Eastern Studies* 20, no. 3 (July 1984), 290–323.

Shihadeh [Shehadeh], Aziz. "Freedom from Outside Influences." *New Outlook* 12, no. 9 (November–December 1969), 41–43.

———. "Must History Repeat Itself? The Palestinian Entity and Its Enemies." *New Middle East,* January 1971, 36–37.

———. "'The Palestinians Demand Is for Peace, Justice and an End to Bitterness—the Initiative Is with Israel—the Time to Negotiate Is Now.'" *New Middle East,* August 1971, 20–22.

———. "The Problem That Only the Palestinians Can Solve." *New Middle East,* June 1971, 29.

———. "Remember Sparta! The Cost of Indecision in Jerusalem." *New Middle East,* October 1969, 5–7.

———. "The Voice of the Forgotten Palestinian." *New Middle East,* December 1968, 14–15.

———. "Why Fatah Does Not Speak for Democratic Palestine." *New Middle East,* March 1969, 14–15.

Shindler, Colin. *A History of Modern Israel.* Cambridge: Cambridge University Press, 2008.

Shlaim, Avi. *Collusion across the Jordan: King Abdullah, the Zionist Movement, and the Partition of Palestine.* Oxford: Clarendon, 1988.

———. "His Royal Shyness: King Hussein and Israel." *New York Review of Books,* 15 July 1999, 14–19.

———. "Interview with Abba Eban, 11 March 1976." *Israel Studies* 8, no. 1 (Spring 2003), 153–77.

———. *The Iron Wall: Israel and the Arab World*. London: Allen Lane, Penguin, 2000.

———. *Lion of Jordan: The Life of King Hussein in War and Peace*. London: Allen Lane, 2007.

———. "The Middle East: The Origins of Arab-Israeli Wars." In *Explaining International Relations since 1945*, ed. Ngaire Woods, 219–40. Oxford: Oxford University Press, 1996.

———. "The Rise and Fall of the All-Palestine Government in Gaza." *Journal of Palestine Studies* 20, no. 1 (Autumn 1990), 37–53.

al-Shuaibi, Issa. "The Development of Palestinian Entity-Consciousness." Part I, *Journal of Palestine Studies* 9, no. 1 (Autumn 1979), 67–84; part II, no. 2 (Winter 1980), 50–70.

Slater, Robert. *Warrior Statesman: The Life of Moshe Dayan*. London: Robson, 1992.

Smith, Charles D. *Palestine and the Arab-Israeli Conflict*. 3rd ed. New York: St. Martin's, 1996.

Smith, Pamela Ann. *Palestine and the Palestinian, 1876–1983*. London: Croom Helm, 1984.

Spiegel, Steven L. *The Other Arab-Israeli Conflict: Making America's Middle East Policy, from Truman to Reagan*. Chicago: University of Chicago Press, 1985.

St. John, Robert. *Eban*. London: W. H. Allen, 1973.

Susser, Asher. "Jordanian Influence in the West Bank." *Jerusalem Quarterly 8* (Summer 1978), 53–65.

Taraki, Lisa. "Mass Organizations in the West Bank." In *Occupation: Israel over Palestine*, ed. Nasser H. Aruri, 431–63. Belmont, Mass.: Association of Arab-American University Graduates, 1989.

Tawil, Raymonda Hawa [signed R.T.]. "June Days in Nablus." *New Outlook* 15, no. 6 (July–August 1972), 22–34.

———. *My Home, My Prison*. London: Zed, 1983.

Terrill, W. Andrew. "The Political Mythology of the Battle of Karameh." *Middle East Journal* 55, no. 1 (Winter 2001), 91–111.

Tessler, Mark. *A History of the Israeli-Palestinian Conflict*. Bloomington: Indiana University Press, 1994.

Teveth, Shabtai. *The Cursed Blessing: The Story of Israel's Occupation of the West Bank*. London: Weidenfeld and Nicolson, 1970.

———. *Moshe Dayan*. London: Weidenfeld and Nicolson, 1972.

Thant, U. *View from the UN*. London: David and Charles; Newton Abbot, 1978.

Tibawi, A. L. "Special Report: The Destruction of an Islamic Heritage in Jerusalem." *Arab Studies Quarterly* 2, no. 2 (Spring 1980), 180–89.

Tivnan, Edward. *The Lobby: Jewish Political Power and American Foreign Policy.* New York: Simon and Schuster, 1987.

Tolan, Sandy. *The Lemon Tree: The True Story of a Friendship Spanning Four Decades of Israeli-Palestinian Conflict.* London: Bantam, 2006.

Touval, Saadia. *The Peace Brokers: Mediators in the Arab-Israeli Conflict, 1948–1979.* Princeton: Princeton University Press, 1982.

Turki, Fawaz. *The Disinherited: Journal of a Palestinian Exile.* New York: Monthly Review Press, 1972.

Van Creveld, Martin. *Moshe Dayan.* London: Weidenfeld and Nicolson, 2004.

———. *The Sword and the Olive: A Critical History of the Israeli Defense Force.* New York: Public Affairs, 1998.

Vardi, Raphael. The Beginning of Israeli Rule in Judea and Samaria. Jerusalem Center for Public Affairs, 16 April 1989, http://www.jcpa.org/jl/hit08 .htm (last accessed: 14 November 2011).

Wasserstein, Bernard. *Divided Jerusalem: The Struggle for the Holy City.* London: Profile, 2001.

Weber, Max. *Economy and Society: An Outline of Interpretive Sociology.* Berkeley: University of California Press, 1978.

Wilson, Evan M. "The Internationalization of Jerusalem." *Middle East Journal* 23, no. 1 (Winter 1969), 1–13.

———. *Jerusalem, Key to Peace.* Washington, D.C.: Middle East Institute, 1970.

Wilson, Harold. *The Chariot of Israel: Britain, America, and the State of Israel.* London: Weidenfeld and Nicolson; Michael Joseph, 1981.

Yaari, Ehud. "Al-Fath's Political Thinking." *New Outlook* 11, no. 9 (November–December 1968), 20–33.

———. *Strike Terror: The Story of Fatah.* New York: Sabra, 1970.

Yehoshua, A. B. *The Liberated Bride.* Trans. Hillel Halkin. London: Peter Halban, 2003.

Zak, Moshe. "Israeli-Jordanian Negotiations." *Washington Quarterly* 8, no. 1 (Winter 1985), 167–76.

BOOKS AND ARTICLES IN ARABIC

'Abd al-Hadi, Mahdi. *Al-Mas'alah al-Filastinyyah wa-Mashari' al-Hulul al-Siyasiyyah 1934–1974* [The Palestinian question and proposals for political solutions, 1934–1974]. Beirut: al-Maktabah al-'Asariyyah, 1975.

'Abd al-Hamid, 'Isa. *Sitt Sanawat min Siyasat al-Jusur al-Maftuhah* [Six years of the open bridges policy]. Beirut: Markaz al-Abhath, Munazzamat al-Tahrir al-Filastiniyyah, 1973.

'Abd al-Jawad, Saleh. "Limadha La Nastati' Kitabat Ta'rikhina al-Mu'asir min dun Istikhdam al-Ta'rikh al-Shafawi? Harb 1948 ka-Halah Dirasiyya" [Why cannot we write our contemporary history without using oral history? The 1948 War as a case study]. *Majallat al-Dirasat al-Filastiniyyah* 64 (2005), 42–63.

Abu Gharbiyyah, Bahjat. *Min Mudhakkirat al-Munadil Bahjat Abu Gharbiyyah: Min al-Nakbah ila al-Intifadah, 1949–2000* [From the memoirs of the fighter Bahjat Abu Gharbiyyah: From the Nakbah to the Intifadah, 1949–2000]. Beirut: Mu'assasah al-'Arabiyyah lil-Dirasat wa-al-Nashr, 2004.

Abu Shalbayah, Muhammad. *La Salam bi-Ghayr Dawlah Filastiniyyah Hurrah* [No peace without an independent Palestinian state]. Jerusalem: Matabi' al-Quds al-'Arabiyyah, 1971.

al-'Arif, 'Arif. *Awraq 'Arif al-'Arif* ['Arif al-'Arif's papers]. Beirut: Markaz al-Abhath, Munazzamat al-Tahrir al-Filastiniyyah, 1973.

al-Ashhab, Na'im. *Durub al-Alam . . . Durub al-Amal* [Ways of pain . . . ways of hope]. Ramallah: Dar al-Tanwir lil-Nashr wa-al-Tarjamah wa-al-Tawzi', 2009.

Baha al-Din, Ahmad. *Iqtirah Dawlat Filastin wa-Ma Dara Hawlahu min Munaqashat* [The proposal for a Palestinian state and the debates about it]. Beirut: Dar al-Adab, 1968.

al-Baquri, 'Abd al-'Al. "Al-Di'ayah al-Sihyuniyyah—al-Isra'iliyyah wa-al-Qawl bi-an 'al-'Arab Yuridun Ilqa' al-Yahud fi al-Bahr'" [The Zionist-Israeli propaganda and the allegation that "the Arabs want to throw the Jews into the sea"]. *Shu'un Filastiniyyah* 27 (November 1973), 167–96.

al-Bashtawi, 'Imad Rif'at. *Al-Shaykh Muhammad 'Ali al-Ja'bari wa-Dawruhu fi al-Hayat al-'Ammah, 1900–1980* [Sheikh Muhammad 'Ali al-Ja'bari and his role in public life, 1900–1980]. Amman: Dar al-Shuruq lil-Nashr wa-al-Tawzi', 2005.

Bashur, Najla Nasir. "Taghyir al-Manahij al-Madrasiyyah fi al-Daffah al-Gharbiyyah lil-Urdun ba'da 1967" [The alteration of the school curricula in the West Bank of Jordan after 1967]. *Shu'un Filastiniyyah* 3 (July 1971), 229–41.

Baumgarten, Helga. *Min al-Tahrir ila al-Dawlah: Ta'rikh al-Harakah al-Wataniyyah al-Filastiniyyah 1948–1988* [From the liberation to the state: The history of the Palestinian national movement, 1948–1988]. Ramallah: Muwatin, 2006.

al-Bustani, Muhammad Farid. "Al-Sukan fi al-Aradi al-Muhtallah ba'da Harb 1967: Tahlil Ihsa'i wa-Taqdirat" [The population in the occupied territories after the 1967 War: Statistical analysis and estimates]. *Shu'un Filastiniyyah* 23 (July 1973), 189–96.

"Al-Daffah al-Gharbiyyah: Ihtilal, Muqawamah, wa-Nazrah ila al-Mustaqbal (Nadwah)" [The West Bank: Occupation, resistance, and view of the future (symposium)]. *Shu'un Filastiniyyah* 32 (April 1974), 30–55.

Farid, 'Abd al-Majid. "Watha'iq wa-Asrar wa-Waqa'i': Liqa'at al-Husayn wa-'Abd al-Nasir" [Records, secrets, and minutes: The meetings of Hussein and 'Abd al-Nasser]. *Al-Rai* (Amman), 6, 9, 11, 15, 19, 23, 27, 30 April, 5, 9, 14, 17, 21 May 1983.

Hajawi, Sulafa. "Dawlat Filastin al-Mujhadah al-Murtaqabah: Qira'ah fi al-'Aql al-Siyasi al-Filastini 1953–1993" [The aborted-anticipated State of Palestine: A reading of the Palestinian political mind, 1953–1993]. *Majallat al-Dirasat al-Filastiniyyah* 53 (Winter 2003), 39–53.

Halabi, Usameh. *Al-Quds: Athar "Damm al-Quds ila Isra'il" 'ala Huquq wa-wad' al-Mawatin al-'Arab* [Jerusalem: The effects of "the annexation of Jerusalem by Israel" on the rights and condition of the Arab residents]. 2nd ed. Jerusalem: PASSIA, 1994.

Hamud, Sa'id. "Al-Dughut al-Iqtisadiyyah al-Isra'iliyyah fi al-Daffah al-Gharbiyyah wa-Qita' Ghazah" [The Israeli economic pressures in the West Bank and the Gaza Strip]. *Shu'un Filastiniyyah* 3 (July 1971), 72–83.

——. "Intikhabat al-Majalis al-Baladiyyah fi al-Daffah al-Gharbiyyah al-Muhtallah" [The municipal elections in the occupied West Bank]. *Shu'un Filastiniyyah* 8 (April 1972), 8–14.

Haykal [Heikal], Muhammad Hasanayn. *1967 al-Infijar* [1967, the explosion]. Cairo: Markaz al-Ahram lil-Tarjamah wa-al-Nashr, Mu'assasat al-Ahram, 1990.

Hilal, 'Ali al-Din. *Mashru'at al-Dawlah al-Filastiniyyah* [The plans for a Palestinian state]. Cairo: Markaz al-Dirasat al-Siyasiyyah wa-al-Istiratijiyah bi-al-Ahram, 1978.

Hilal, Jamil. *Takwin al-Nukhbah al-Filasiniyyah: Mundh Nushu' al-Harakah al-Wataniyyah al-Filastiniyyah ila ma ba'da al-Qiyam al-Sultah al-Wataniyyah* [The formation of the Palestinian elite: From the rise of the Palestinian national movement until after the foundation of the national authority]. Ramallah: Muwatin, al-Mu'assasah al-Filastiniyyah li-Dirassat al-Dimmuqratiyyah, 2002.

Hindi, Khalil. "Al-Ta'bi'a al-Urduniyyah dida al-Muqawamah al-Filastiniyyah qabl Hajmat Sabtambar 1970" [The Jordanian mobilization against the Palestinian resistance before the September 1970 onslaught]. *Shu'un Filastiniyyah* 4 (September 1971), 31–54.

Hurani, Faysal. *Al-Fikr al-Siyasi al-Filastini, 1964–1974: Dirasah lil-Mawathiq al-Ra'isiyyah li-Munazzamat al-Tahrir al-Filsatiniyyah* [Palestinian political thought, 1964–1974: A study of the main charters of the Palestine Liberation Organization]. Beirut: Munazzamat al-Tahrir al-Filsatiniyyah, Markaz al-Abhath, 1980.

al-Husayni, 'Ali Zayn al-'Abidin. "Malamih min al-Tajribah al-Nidaliyyah al-Filastiniyyah: Harb al-'Isabat fi Mudun wa-Mukhayyamat Qita' Ghazah" [Features of the Palestinian experience of struggle: The guerrilla war in the towns and camps of the Gaza Strip]. *Shu'un Filastiniyyah* 35 (July 1974), 62–75.

al-Hut, Shafiq. *'Ishrun 'Aman fi Munazzamat al-Tahrir al-Filastiniyyah: (1964–1984); Ahadith al-Dhikrayat* [Twenty years with the Palestinian Liberation Organisation, 1964–1984, memoirs]. Beirut: Dar al-Istiqlal, 1986.

Izzat, Muna. "Al-Muhawalat al-Mubakirah li-Zuhur al-Kiyan al-Filastini" [The early attempts to create a Palestinian entity]. *Al-Samid al-Iqtisadi* 136 (April–June 2004), 98–111.

"al-Jabarti al-Saghir" [pseud. Young Jabarti]. "Risalah Khasah min al-Ard al-Muhtallah: Ma'sat Qura al-Latrun al-Thulath fi Dhikraha al-Sadisah" [A special article from the occupied land: The tragedy of the three villages of Latrun on its sixth anniversary]. *Shu'un Filastiniyyah* 22 (June 1973), 178–82.

al-Ju'abah, Nazmi. "Ta'rih al-Istitan al-Yahudi fi al-Baldah al-Qadimah [The history of Jewish settlement in the Old City]. *Jerusalem Quarterly File* 13 (Summer 2001), 64–58; English summary 56–57.

Jum'ah, Sa'd. *Al-Mu'amarah wa-Ma'rakat al-Masir* [The conspiracy and the fateful battle]. Beirut: Dar al-Katib al-'Arabi, 1969.

Khalifah, Ahmad. "Siyasat Isra'il fi al-Manatiq al-Muhtallah" [Israel's policy in the occupied territories]. *Shu'un Filastiniyyah* 1 (March 1971), 77–94.

al-Khatib, 'Ali. "Al-Itijahat al-Siyasiyyah fi al-Ard al-Muhtallah wa-al-Mawaqif al-Mukhtalifah min Mu'amarat al-'Aduw al-Sihyuni li-Insha' Idarah Madani-yyah fi al-Daffah wa-al-Qita'" [The political orientations in the occupied land and the different positions regarding the Zionist enemy's plot to establish civil administration in the {West} Bank and the {Gaza} Strip]. *Shu'un Filas-tiniyyah* 55 (March 1976), 61–68.

al-Khatib al-Tamimi, Anwar. *Ma'a Salah al-Din fi al-Quds: Ta'ammulat wa-Dhikrayat* [With Salah al-Din in Jerusalem: Reflections and reminiscences]. Jerusalem, 1989.

Khayri, Bashir. *Khafaqat Dhakirah: Qissah* [Memory throbs: A story]. Jerusalem: Markaz al-Ma'lumat al-Badilah, 1993.

al-Kilani, Haytham. *Al-Istiratijiyat al-'Askariyyah lil-Hurub al-'Arabiyyah—al-Isra'iliyyah, 1948–1988* [The military strategies of the Arab-Israeli wars, 1948–1988]. Beirut: Markaz Dirasat al-Wahdah al-'Arabiyyah, 1991.

Kimche, David. "Dawafi' Isra'il lil-Harb wa-Ta'thiruha 'Alayha" [Israel's motives for the war and the war's effect on Israel]. In *Harb Yuniyu 1967: Ba'da 30 Sanah* [The June 1967 War: Thirty years later], ed. Lutfi al-Khuli, 209–19. Cairo: Mu'assasat al-Ahram, Markaz al-Ahram lil-Tarjamah wa-al-Nashr, 1997.

Masalhah, Nur al-Din. "'Al-Tasawwur al-Sihyuni li-'al-Tarhil': Nazrah Ta'rikhiyyah 'Amma" [The Zionist concept of the "transfer": A historical view]. *Majallat al-Dirasat al-Filastiniyyah* 7 (Summer 1991), 19–45.

Muharib, 'Abd al-Hafiz. "Al-Istitan al-Isra'ili fi al-Manatiq al-Muhtallah fi Harb Haziran" [The Israeli settlement in the territories occupied in the June war]. *Shu'un Filastiniyyah* 3 (July 1971), 84–112.

al-Nashashibi, Nasser al-Din. *Akhir al-'Amaliqah Ja'a min al-Quds: Qissat al-Za'im al-Filastini Musa al-'Alami* [The last giant came from Jerusalem: The story of the Palestinian leader Musa al-'Alami]. [Madrid?]: [Novograph?], 1986.

———. *Qissati Ma'a al-Sihafah* [My story with the press]. [Madrid?]: [Sharikat Nufughraf?], 1983.

———. *Tadhkirat 'Awdah* [A return ticket]. Beirut: al-Maktab al-Tijari, 1962.

al-Qadi, Layla Salim. "Taqrir hawl Mashari' al-Taswiyat al-Silmiyyah lil-Niza' al-'Arabi al-Isra'ili 1948–1972" [A report on proposals for a peaceful settlement of the Arab-Israeli conflict, 1948–1972]. *Shu'un Filastiniyyah* 22 (June 1973), 84–123.

al-Sa'ih, 'Abd al-Hamid. *Filastin, La Salah tahta al-Hirab: Mudhakkirat al-Shaykh 'Abd al-Hamid al-Sa'ih* [Palestine, no prayer under bayonets: The memoirs of Sheikh 'Abd al-Hamid al-Sa'ih]. Beirut: Mu'assasat al-Dirasat al-Filastiniyyah, 1994.

Sakhnini, 'Isam. "*Al-Kiyan al-Filastini* 1964–1974" [The Palestinian entity, 1964–1974]. *Shu'un Filastiniyyah* 41–42 (January–February 1975), 46–74.

Saleh, 'Abd al-Jawad. "Ma'rakat al-Kiyan wa-al-Qiyadah al-Badilah" [The battle of the entity and the alternative leadership]. *Al-Katib Al-Filastini* 2 (April 1978), 52–74.

al-Salihi, Bassam. *Al-Za'amah al-Siyasiyyah wa-al-Diniyyah fi al-Ard al-Muhtallah: Waqi'uha wa-Tatawwuruha, 1967–1993* [The political and religious leadership in the occupied land: Its reality and development, 1967–1993]. Jerusalem: Dar al-Quds lil-Nashr wa-al-Tawzi', 1993.

Sayigh, Yezid. "Mawqi' al-Kifah al-Musallah wa-al-Intifidah fi Itar al-Nidal al-Watani al-Filastini" [The role of the armed struggle and the uprising in the Palestinian national struggle]. *Shu'un 'Arabiyyah* 67 (September 1991), 65–79.

Shafiq, Munir. "Limadha Yarfud al-Filastiniyyun Mashru' al-Dawlah al-Filastiniyyah fi al-Daffah al-Gharbiyyah wa-Qita' Ghazzah" [Why do the Palestinians reject the proposal for a Palestinian state in the West Bank and the Gaza Strip]. *Shu'un Filastiniyyah* 7 (March 1972), 65–73.

———. "Ma'rakat al-Karamah" [The battle of Karameh]. *Shu'un Filastiniyyah* 19 (March 1973), 103–10.

al-Sharif, Maher. "Al-Qadiyah al-Filastiniyyah fi al-Kitabah al-Ta'rikhiyyah al-'Arabiyyah: Hal hunak Hajah ila Ta'rikh Jadid?" [The Palestinian problem in Arab historiography: Is there a need for new history?]. *Majallat al-Dirasat al-Filastiniyyah* 55 (Summer 2003), 29–41.

al-Shu'aybi, 'Isa. *Al-Kiyaniyyah al-Filastiniyyah: al-Wa'y al-Dhati wa-al-Tatawwur al-Mu'assasati, 1947–1977* [Palestinian entitism: Self-consciousness and institutional development, 1947–1977]. Beirut: Markaz al-Abhath, Munazzamat al-Tahrir al-Filastiniyyah, 1979.

al-Shuqayri, Ahmad. "*Dhikrayat 'an Mu'tamar al-Qimmah fi al-Khartum*" [Memories of the Khartoum summit conference]. *Shu'un Filastiniyyah* 4 (September 1971), 90–99.

"Taqriran 'an al-Awda' al-Daffah al-Gharbiyyah al-Muhtallah fi al-Sanatayn al-Awalayn lil-Ihtilal" [Two reports on the situation in the occupied West Bank during the first two years of the occupation]. *Shu'un Filastiniyyah* 10 (June 1972), 140–59.

Touqan, Fadwa. *Al-Rihlah al-As'ab* [The harder journey]. Amman: Dar al-Shuruq, 1993.

———. *Rihlah Jabaliyah, Rihlah Sa'bah* [Mountainous journey, hard journey]. Amman: Dar al-Shuruq, 1988.

Yahya, 'Abd al-Razzak. *'Abd al-Razzak Yahya Bayna al-'Askariyah wa-al-Siyasah: (Dhikrayat)* ['Abd al-Razzak Yahya between the military and politics: Memoirs]. Ramallah: Markaz al-Laji'in wa-al-Shatat al-Filastini, 2006.

Yasin, 'Abd al-Qadir. "Al-Qissah al-Kamilah li-Insha' al-Jabhah al-Wataniyyah al-Muttahidah fi Qita' Ghazzah" [The full story of the establishment of the United National Front in the Gaza Strip]." *Shu'un Filastiniyyah* 101 (April 1980), 34–44.

———. *Tajribat al-Jabhah al-Wataniyyah fi Qita' Ghazzah* [The experience of the National Front in the Gaza Strip]. Beirut: Dar Ibn Khaldun, 1980.

BOOKS AND ARTICLES IN HEBREW

Adam, Ron, ed. *Abba Eban, Medinai ve-Diplomat: Sefer le-Zikhro shel Sar ha-Huts le-She'avar* [Abba Eban, statesman and diplomat: In memory of the former foreign minister]. Jerusalem: Ministry of Foreign Affairs, 2003.

Admoni, Yehiel. *'Asor shel Shikul Da'at: Ha-Hityashvut me-'ever la-Kav ha-Yarok 1967–1977* [A decade of discretion: The settlement beyond the Green Line, 1967–1977]. Tel Aviv: Makhon Yisrael Galili le-Heker Ko'ah ha-Magen—Yad Tabenkin; Ha-Kibbutz ha-Me'uhad, 1992.

Algazy (Galili), Yosef. *Aba, Ma 'Asita kshe-Harsu et Beito shel Nader?: 1967–1974; Ra'iti, Shama'ti ba-Shtahim ha-Kvushim—Leket Reportajot* [Daddy, what did you do when they destroyed Nader's house? 1967–1974; I saw, I heard in the occupied territories—A collection of reportages]. Tel Aviv: 1974.

Allon, Yigal. *Masakh shel Hol: (Yisrael ve-'Arav bein Milhamah le-Shalom)* [A curtain of sand: Israel and the Arabs between war and peace]. Expanded ed. Tel Aviv: Ha-Kibbutz ha-Me'uhad, 1968.

Amit, Meir. *Rosh be-Rosh: Mabat Ishi 'al Eiru'im Gdolim u-Farashiyot 'Alumot* [Head-on: A personal view of great events and secret affairs]. Or Yehudah: Hed Aartsi, 1999.

Arba' Shnot Mimshal Ttsva'i, 1967–1971: Netunim 'al ha-Pe'ilut ha-Ezrahit bi-Yehudah ve-Shomron, Retsu'at 'Azah u-Tsfon Sinai [Four years of military government, 1967–1971: Data on the civil activities in Judea and Samaria, the Gaza Strip and Northern Sinai]. Tel Aviv: Ha-Yehidah le-Te'um Pe'ulah ba-Shtahim, Misrad ha-Bitahon, [1971?].

Argaman, Yosef. *Zeh Hayah Sodi Be-Yoter: 30 Parshiyot Modi'in u-Vitahon be-Yisrael; Ha-Sipur ha-Male* [This was top secret: Thirty intelligence and security affairs in Israel; The full story]. Tel Aviv: Ba-Mahaneh, 1990.

Barnoah-Matalon, Neorah. *Makom Tov ba-Tsad* [A good place on the side]. Ra'ananah: Kotarim, 2009.

Bavly, Dan. *Halomot ve-Hizdamnuyot she-Huhmetsu 1967–1973* [Dreams and missed opportunities, 1967–1973]. Jerusalem: Carmel, 2002.

Beilin, Yossi. *Mehiro shel Ihud: Mifleget ha-'Avodah 'ad Milhemet Yom ha-Kipurim* [The price of unity: The Labor Party up to the Yom Kippur War]. Ramat Gan: Revivim, 1985.

Ben-'Amram, Eliyahu. "Mifkad ha-Ukhlusin be-Shit'hei ha-Mimshal (September 1967)" [The census in the territories under the {Military} Government (September 1967)], *Ha-Mizrah he-Hadash* 17, nos. 3–4 (1967), 290–97.

Bentov, Mordekhai. *Yamim Mesaprim: Zikhronot me-ha-Me'ah ha-Makhra'at* [Days tell: Reminiscences from the overwhelming century]. Tel Aviv: Sifriyat Po'alim, 1984.

Benvenisti, Meron. *Ha-Kela' ve-ha-Alah: Shtahim, Yehudim ve-'Arvim* [The sling and the club: Territories, Jews, and Arabs]. Jerusalem: Keter, 1989.

———. *Mul ha-Homah ha-Sgurah: Yerushalayim ha-Hatsuyah ve-ha-Me'uhedet* [Against the closed wall: Divided and unified Jerusalem]. Jerusalem: Weidenfeld and Nicolson, 1973.

———. *Yerushalayim 'Ir u-ve-Libah Homah* [Jerusalem a city and a wall in its midst]. Tel-Aviv: Ha-Kibbutz ha-Me'uhad, 1981.

Benziman, Uzi. *Yerushalayim: 'Ir le-lo Homah* [Jerusalem: A city without a wall]. Jerusalem-Tel Aviv: Schocken, 1973.

Boaz, Aryeh. Biyografyah Politit shel Ahmad al-Shuqayri [A political biography of Ahmad al-Shuqayri]. M.A. diss., Tel Aviv University, 1987.

Bondy, Ruth, Ohad Zmora, and Raphael Bashan, eds. *Lo 'al ha-Herev Levadah: Ha-Sipur ha-Mufla 'al Gvurat 'Am Yisrael ve-Nitshono be-Milhemet Sheshet ha-Yamim* [Not by the sword alone: The miraculous story of the heroism of the Israeli people and its victory in the Six Day War]. Tel Aviv: A. Levin Epstein, 1968.

Brecher, Michael. "Ha-Ma'avak ha-Medini 'al Yerushalayim" [The political struggle for Jerusalem]. In *Prakim be-Toldot Yerushalayim ba-Zman he-Hadash: Sefer Zikaron le-Ya'acov Herzog* [Chapters in the history of Jerusalem in the modern age: In memory of Ya'acov Herzog], ed. Eli Shaltiel, 384–417. Jerusalem: Yad Itzhak Ben-Zvi; Misrad ha-Bitahon—ha-Hotsa'ah la-Or, 1981.

Brown, Arie. *Hotam Ishi: Moshe Dayan be-Milhemet Sheshet ha-Yamim ve-Ahareha* [Personal imprint: Moshe Dayan during the Six Day War and afterward]. Tel Aviv: Yediot Ahronot, 1997.

Cohen, Hillel. *Kikar ha-Shuk Reikah: 'Aliyatah u-Nefilatah shel Yerushalayim ha-'Arvit 1967–2007* [The marketplace is empty: The rise and fall of Arab Jerusalem, 1967–2007]. Jerusalem: 'Ivrit; Jerusalem Institute for Israel Studies, 2007.

Cohen, Yeroham. *Tokhnit Allon* [The Allon plan]. Tel Aviv: Ha-Kibbutz ha-Me'uhad, 1972.

Dayan, Moshe. *Avnei Derekh: Otobiyographyah* [Milestones: An autobiography]. Jerusalem: 'Edanim, 1976.

———. *Mapah Hadashah Yahasim Aherim* [A new map, different relations]. Tel Aviv: Sifriyat Ma'ariv; Shikmonah, 1969.

Drori, Moshe. *Ha-Hakikah be-Ezor Yehudah ve-Shomron* [The legislation in the area of Judea and Samaria]. Jerusalem: The Harry Sacher Institute for Legislative Research and Comparative Law, Faculty of Law, Hebrew University of Jerusalem, 1975.

Eli'av, Lovah Aryeh. *Taba'ot 'Edut* [Rings of testimony]. Tel Aviv: 'Am 'Oved, 1983.

Farhi, David. "'Amadot Politiyot bi-Yehudah ve-Shomron 1972–1973" [Political views in Judea and Samaria, 1972–1973]. *Ma'arakhot* 231 (July 1973), 9–14.

———. "Hevrah u-Politikah bi-Yehudah ve-Shomron" [Society and politics in Judea and Samaria]. *Ma'arakhot* 215 (June 1971), 12–19.

———. "Ha-Mo'atsah ha-Muslemit be-Mizrah Yerushalayim u-vi-Yehudah ve-Shomron me-az Milhemet Sheshet ha-Yamim" [The Muslim Council in East Jerusalem and Judea and Samaria since the Six Day War]. *Ha-Mizrah he-Hadash* 28, no. 1–2 (1979), 3–21.

———. "Toshavei ha-Shtahim ve-'Emdoteihem ha-Politiyot" [The inhabitants of the territories and their political views]. In *Yom 'Iyun 'al ha-Mediniyut ha-Yisre'elit ba-Nose ha-Palastina'i* [A seminar on Israeli policy regarding the Palestinian issue], 15–26. Ef'al: Yad Tabenkin; Ha-Kibbutz ha-Me'uhad, 1976.

Gai, Karmit. *Bar-Lev.* Tel Aviv: 'Am 'Oved; Sifriyat Po'alim, 1998.

Galili, Yisrael. *El ve-'Al: Igrot u-Dmuyot* [To and on: Letters and personalities]. Ramat Ef'al: Merkaz Yisrael Galili, Yad Tabenkin; Ha-Kibbutz ha-Me'uhad, 1990.

Gan, Alon. *Ha-Si'ah she-Gava'?: "Tarbut ha-Sihim" ke-Nisayon le-Gabesh Zehut Meyahedet la-Dor ha-Sheni ba-Kibbutzim* [The discourse that faded away?: The "discourses culture" as an attempt to form a distinctive identity to the kibbutzim's second generation]. Ph.D. diss., Tel Aviv University, 2002.

Gazit, Shlomo. *Gibush ha-Mediniyut u-Dfusei ha-Irgun ba-Shtahim ha-Muhzakim (Dagesh 'al Yehudah ve-Shomron, 1967–1968)* [The consolidation of policy and organization patterns in the administered territories: Emphasis on Judea and Samaria, 1967–1968]. M.A. diss., Tel Aviv University, 1980.

———. *Ha-Makel ve-ha-Gezer: Ha-Mimshal ha-Yisre'eli bi-Yehudah ve-Shomron* [The stick and the carrot: The Israeli administration in Judea and Samaria]. Tel Aviv: Zmora, Bitan, 1985.

———. "Mediniyut Moshe Dayan bi-Yehudah, Shomron ve-'Azah" [Moshe Dayan's policy in Judea, Samaria, and Gaza], *'Iyunim ba-Bitahon ha-Le'umi* [Studies in national security], November 2003, 51–60.

———. *Ha-Shtahim ha-Muhzakim—Hamesh Shanim* [The administered territories—Five years]. Jerusalem: Misrad ha-Hinukh ve-ha-Tarbut, Merkaz ha-Hasbarah, Sherut ha-Pirsumim, 1972.

———. "Ha-Shtahim ha-Muhzakim—Mediniyut u-Maʿas" [The administered territories—Policy and practice], *Maʿarakhot* 204 (January 1970), 24–39.

Gilboʿa, Moshe. *Shesh Shanim Shishah Yamim: Mekoroteha ve-Koroteha shel Milhemet Sheshet ha-Yamim* [Six years, Six days: The origins and the history of the Six Day War]. Tel Aviv: ʿAm ʿOved, 1968.

Golan, Shimon. *Milhamah be-Shalosh Hazitot: Kabalat ha-Hahlatot ba-Pikud ha-ʿElyon shel Tsahal be-Milhemet Sheshet ha-Yamim* [A war on three fronts: The decision making by the IDF's Supreme Command in the Six Day War]. Tel Aviv: Maʿarakhot, 2007.

Goldstein, Yossi. *Eshkol: Biyographyah* [Eshkol: A biography]. Jerusalem: Keter, 2003.

———. *Rabin: Biyographyah* [Rabin: A biography]. Jerusalem: Schocken, 2006.

Gvati, Haim. *100 Shnot Hityashvut: Toldot ha-Hityashvut ha-Yehudit be-Eretz-Yisrael* [One hundred years of settlement: The history of Jewish settlement in the land of Israel]. Vol. 2. Tel Aviv: Ha-Kibbutz ha-Meʾuhad, 1981.

———. *Sipur Hayai* [The story of my life]. Tel Aviv: Ha-Kibbutz ha-Meʾuhad, 1985.

Haber, Eitan. *Hayom Tifrots Milhamah: Zikhronotav shel Tat-Aluf Yisrael Liʾor, ha-Mazkir ha-Tsvaʾi shel Rashei ha-Memshalah Levi Eshkol ve-Golda Meir* [Today war will break out: The reminiscences of Brigadier General Yisrael Liʾor, military aide de camp to Prime Ministers Levi Eshkol and Golda Meir]. Tel Aviv: ʿEdanim, 1987.

Herzog, Chaim. *Derekh Hayim: Sipuro shel Lohem, Diplomat ve-Nasi* [A way of life: The story of a warrior, diplomat, and president]. Tel Aviv: Yediot Ahronot—Sifrei Hemed, 1997.

Holzman, Haim. *Tehikat ha-Bitahon ba-Shtahim ha-Muhzakim* [The security legislation in the administered territories]. Givʿat Havivah: Center for Arabic and Afro-Asian Studies, 1968.

Huberman, Haggai. *Ke-Neged Kol ha-Sikuyim: 40 Shnot Hityashvut bi-Yehudah ve-Shomron, Binyamin ve-ha-Bikʿah, 5727–5767* [Against all odds: Forty years of settlement in Judea and Samaria, Binyamin, and the {Jordan} Valley, 1967–2007]. Vol. 1. [Jerusalem?]: Sifriyat Netsarim, 2008.

Israeli, Rafi, ed. *ʿEser Shnot Shilton Yisreʾeli bi-Yehudah ve-Shomron: 1967–1977* [Ten years of Israeli rule in Judea and Samaria, 1967–1977]. Jerusalem: Magnes, 1980.

———, ed. *Prahim le-David: Yad le-David Farhi* [Flowers to David: A memorial to David Farhi]. Jerusalem: 1981.

Itzchaki, Arieh. *Latrun: Ha-Ma'arakhah 'al ha-Derekh li-Yerushalayim* [Latrun: The battle on the road to Jerusalem]. Vol. 2. Jerusalem: Kanah, 1982.

Klieman, Aharon. "Ha-Diplomatyah ha-Yisre'elit—Hemshekhiyut u-Tmurah" [Israeli diplomacy—Continuity and change]. In *Ha-Sikhsukh ha-'Arvi-Yisre'eli: Gormim, 'Imutim, Sikuyim* [The Arab-Israeli conflict: Causes, confrontations, prospects], ed. Eytan Gilboa and Mordechay Naor, 43–59. Tel Aviv: Misrad ha-Bitahon—ha-Hotsa'ah la-Or, Matkal / Ktsin Hinukh Rashi, 1981.

Lifshitz, Yaacov. *Ha-Hitpat'hut ha-Kalkalit ba-Shtahim ha-Muhzakim, 1967–1969* [Economic development in the administered territories, 1967–1969]. Tel Aviv: Ma'arakhot, 1970.

Ma'oz, Moshe, and B. Z. Kedar, eds. *Ha-Tnu'ah ha-Le'umit ha-Falastinit: Me-'Imut le-Hashlamah?* [The Palestinian National Movement: From confrontation to reconciliation?]. Tel Aviv: Misrad ha-Bitahon—ha-Hotsa'ah la-Or, 1996.

Medzini, Meron. *Ha-Yehudiyah ha-Ge'ah: Golda Meir ve-Hazon Yisrael: Biyographyah Politit.* [The proud Jewess: Golda Meir and Israel's vision, a political biography]. Jerusalem: 'Edanim, Yediot Ahronot, 1990.

Nadel, Chaim. *Bein Shtei ha-Milhamot: ha-Pe'ilut ha-Bit'honit ve-ha-Tsva'it la-Konenut ve-ha-Hitkonenut shel Tsahal, mi-Tom Milhemet Sheshet ha-Yamim ve-'ad Milhemet Yom ha-Kipurim* [Between the two wars: IDF security and military action to achieve alertness and readiness, from the end of the Six Day War to the Yom Kippur War]. Tel Aviv: Ma'arakhot, 2006.

Netzer, Moshe. *Netzer mi-Shorashav: Sipur Hayim* [A branch from his roots: A life story]. Tel Aviv: Misrad ha-Bitahon—ha-Hotsa'ah la-Or, 2002.

Pedatzur, Reuven. Hashpa'atam shel "Mitbahei Hahlatah" bi-Kvi'at Mediniyut ha-Bitahon ha-Le'umi: Memshelet Eshkol ve-ha-Shtahim, 1967–1969 [The influence of "decision kitchens" on the formation of national security policy: The Eshkol government and the territories, 1967–1969]. Ph.D. diss., Tel Aviv University, 1992.

———. *Nitshon ha-Mevukhah: Mediniyut Yisrael ba-Shtahim le-ahar Milhemet Sheshet ha-Yamim* [The triumph of bewilderment: Israel and the territories after the Six Day War]. Tel Aviv: Bitan and Yad Tabenkin, 1996.

Pundak, Itzhak. *Hamesh Mesimot* [Five missions]. Tel Aviv: Yaron Golan, 2000.

Ronen, David. *Shnat Shabak: Ha-He'arkhut bi-Yehudah ve-Shomron, Shanah Rishonah* [The year of the *Shabak:* The deployment in Judea and Samaria, first year]. Tel Aviv: Misrad ha-Bitahon—ha-Hotsa'ah la-Or, 1989.

Rosenthal, Ruvik. "Me'ah ha-Yamim ha-Rishonim" [The first hundred days], *Panim* 39 (June 2007), 38–48.

Sasson, Moshe. "'Al ha-Masa'im ve-ha-Matanim le-Shalom 'im Shkheneinu: (Histaklut Ishit)" [On the peace negotiations with our neighbors: A personal observation]. In *Misrad ha-Huts, 50 ha-Shanim ha-Rishonot* [The Foreign Ministry, the first fifty years], ed. Moshe Yegar, Yosef Govrin, and Arye Oded, 104–30. Jerusalem: Keter, 2002.

———. *Le-lo Shulhan 'Agol* [Without a roundtable]. Or Yehudah: Sifriyat Ma'ariv, 2004.

Schiff, Zeev, and Eitan Haber, eds., Arie Hashavya, assoc. ed. *Leksikon le-Vit'hon Yisrael* [A lexicon of Israel's security]. Tel Aviv: Zmorah, Bitan, Modan, 1976.

Segev, Shmuel. *Milhamah ve-Shalom ba-Mizrah ha-Tikhon* [War and peace in the Middle East]. Tel Aviv: N. Tverski, 1968.

Segev, Tom. *1967: Ve-ha-Aretz Shintah et Paneha* [1967: And the land changed its face]. Jerusalem: Keter, 2005.

Shaham, David. *Yisrael—40 ha-Shanim* [Israel—The forty years]. Tel Aviv: 'Am 'Oved, 1991.

Shapira, Anita. *Yigal Allon: Aviv Heldo: Biografyah* [Yigal Allon: The spring of his life, a biography]. Tel Aviv: Ha-Kibbutz ha-Me'uhad, 2004.

Shashar, Michael. *Milhemet ha-Yom ha-Shvi'i: Yoman ha-Mimshal ha-Tsva'i bi-Yehudah ve-Shomron (Yuni–Detsember 1967)* [The seventh-day war: The diary of the Military Government in Judea and Samaria, June–December 1967]. Tel Aviv: Sifriyat Po'alim, 1997.

———. *Sihot 'im Rehav'am-Gandi-Ze'evi.* [Conversations with Rehav'am-Gandi-Ze'evi]. Tel Aviv: Yediot Ahronot; Sifrei Hemed, 1992.

Shemesh, Moshe. *Me-ha-Nakbah la-Naksah: Ha-Sikhsukh ha-'Arvi-Yisre'eli ve-ha-Be'ayah ha-Le'umit ha-Falastinit 1957–1967; Darko shel Nasser le-Milhemet Sheshet ha-Yamim* [From the *Nakbah* to the *Naksah:* The Arab-Israeli conflict and the Palestinian national problem, 1957–1967; Nasser's road to the Six Day War]. Sede Boker: Ben-Gurion Institute and Ben-Gurion University Press, 2004.

Shem-Tov, Victor. "Ha-Tvusah ba-Nitsahon" [The defeat within the victory]. In *Kovshim 'Atsmam la-Da'at: 67–87: Kovets Ma'amarim Sipurim ve-Shirim* [Occupying themselves to death, 67–87: A collection of articles, stories, and poems], ed. 'Amit Anter and David Bender, 53–56. Tel Aviv: Mapam and 'Al ha-Mishmar, 1987.

Shifris, Amos. *Yisrael Galili: Shomer ha-Masad ve-Noteh ha-Kav* [Yisrael Galili: The guardian of the foundations and establisher of the line]. Ramat Ef'al: Yad Tabenkin, 2010.

Shiloah, Zvi. *Ashmat Yerushalayim* [The guilt of Jerusalem]. Tel Aviv: Karni, 1989.

Steinberg, Matti. *'Omdim le-Goralam: Ha-Toda'ah ha-Le'umit ha-Falastinit, 1967–2007* [Facing their fate: The Palestinian national consciousness, 1967–2007]. Tel Aviv: Yediot Ahronot; Sifrei Hemed, 2008.

Stendel, Ori. "Ha-Ukhlusiyah ha-'Arvit be-Mizrah Yerushalayim, Manhigut u-Kvutsot Motsa" [The Arab population in East Jerusalem, leadership and origin groups]. In *Yehudah ve-Shomron: Prakim be-Ge'ografyah Yishuvit* [Judea and Samaria: Studies in settlement geography], vol. 2, ed. Avshalom Shemu'eli, David Grossman, and Rehav'am Ze'evi, 489–502. Jerusalem: Kna'an, 1977.

———. "Ha-Ukhlusiyah ha-'Arvit bi-Yehudah u-ve-Shomron" [The Arab population in Judea and Samaria], *Skirah Hodshit* 35, no. 8 (22 August 1988), 3–19.

Susser, Asher, ed. *Shishah Yamim—Shloshim Shanah: Mabat Hadash 'al Milhemet Sheshet ha-Yamim* [Six days—thirty years: A new look at the Six Day War]. Tel Aviv: Merkaz Rabin le-Heker Israel; 'Am 'Oved, 1999.

Sutton, Rafi. *Ha-Hahmatsot ha-Gdolot: Hizdamnuyot Mediniyot ve-Yozmot le-Shalom she-Yisrael Hehmitsah* [The great missed opportunities: Political opportunities and peace initiatives that Israel missed]. Or Yehudah: Sifriyat Ma'ariv, 1994.

Sutton, Rafi, and Yitzhak Shoshan. *Anshei ha-Sod ve-ha-Seter: Me-'Alilot ha-Modi'in ha-Yisre'eli me-'Ever la-Gvulot* [Men of secret and stealth: Tales of Israeli intelligence ventures beyond the borders]. Tel Aviv: 'Edanim, Yediot Ahronot, 1990.

Warhaftig, Zerah. *Hamishim Shanah ve-Shanah: Pirkei Zikhronot* [Fifty years from year to year: Memoirs]. Jerusalem: Yad Shapira, 1998.

Weitz, Yosef. *Yomani ve-Igrotai la-Banim* [My diary and letters to my sons]. Vol. 3, *Mishmar Homot (1945–1948)* [Walls' guard, 1945–1948]. Tel Aviv: Masadah, 1965.

———. *Yomani ve-Igrotai la-Banim.* Vol. 6, *Prishati (1964–1970)* [My retirement, 1964–1970]. Tel Aviv: Masadah, 1973.

Ya'acobi, Gad. *Hesed ha-Zman: Pirkei Biografyah* [The grace of time: A biography]. Tel Aviv: Yediot Ahronot; Sifrei Hemed, 2002.

———. *Ke-Hut ha-Sa'arah: Eikh Huhmats Hesder bein Yisrael le-Mitsrayim ve-Lo Nimne'ah Milhemet Yom-ha-Kipurim* [By a hair's breadth: How a settlement between Israel and Egypt was missed and the Yom Kippur War was not prevented]. Tel Aviv: 'Edanim, Yediot Ahronot, 1989.

———. *Pgishot be-Maslul Hayai* [Encounters in the course of my life]. Jerusalem: Carmel, 2009.

Yadlin, Rivkah. *'Amadot ve-De'ot be-kerev 'Arviyei ha-Gadah* [Attitudes and viewpoints among the {West} Bank Arabs]. Jerusalem: Hebrew University, 1973.

Zak, Moshe. *Hussein 'Oseh Shalom* [Hussein makes peace]. Ramat Gan: Bar Ilan University Press, 1996.

Index

'Abdallah, Radhi, 125

'Abdallah I, King of Jordan, xxxi, 31

'Abd al-Nasser, Gamal. *See* Nasser, Gamal 'Abd al-

'Abdu, Saleh, 31, 122

Abna' al-Quds al-Ahrar (The free sons of Jerusalem), 84

Abu al-Rish, Ibrahim, 306n36

Abu al-Zuluf, Mahmoud, 148

Abu Ghosh, Hasan Ahmad Hasan, 107

Abu Hijleh, 'Abd al-Majid, 28–29

Abu 'Itah, Nikola, 239

Abu Mayzar, 'Abd al-Muhsin, 89

Aburish, Said, 5

Accidental Empire, The (Gorenberg), xvii

Adams, Philip, 69

Ahdut ha-'Avodah, 18

Ahituv, Avraham, 100, 180

Aircraft sales, to Israel, 4, 23, 182, 189, 205, 227, 247, 252, 258, 259–60, 279

Akhbar al-Usbu', 201, 241

'Ala' al-Din, Sa'id, 92, 318n60

al-'Alami, Musa, 228–30, 244, 361n11

Albeq, Shmuel, 34

Alignment (of *Mapai* and *Ahdut ha-'Avodah*), 18–19. *See also* Political Committee

Allenby Bridge, 99, 104, 108, 118, 121, 185, 203; designated point of entry/exit into/from Israel, 222; dynamiting of, 322n8; meetings at, 126, 127, 197, 204, 208

Allon, Yigal, 38, 67, 199, 232, 249, 362n22; on Arab emigration, 44–45; biography of, xxvi; in coalition government, 19; expansionist views of, 247, 269; on historical association concept, 271; -Hussein meetings, (27 September 1968), 17, 256–57, (19 November 1968), 269; and Jewish settlements, 140, 200, 224–25, 348n81; on Palestinian alternative stratagem, 157; personal hostility to Hussein, 17, 191; proposal to transfer of Palestinian refugees, 114; on return of new refugees, 125

Allon Plan, xxvi, 44, 67, 221, 245–50, 246 (map), 254, 256, 257, 259, 261, 271, 272, 273, 370n144

All-Palestine Government (1948), xxx, 33

American University of Beirut (AUB), xxix, 58

Amery, Julian, 50, 159, 191, 341n102, 343n126

Amit, Meir, 41, 276

Amitai, Eliezer, 110, 122

Amman Bar Association, 94

Amman Radio, 36, 91, 93, 94, 97, 120–21, 145, 175, 240–41, 320n90, 320n93

'Anabta, expulsions from, 114

Anderson, Robert, 154, 341n100

Angleton, James Jesus, 72, 310n93

Antonius, George, xvi

Aqaba, Gulf of (Aqaba Bay), 39–40, 45, 289n2, 369n138

'Aql, 'Isa, 59, 60, 61, 93, 168, 306n36

Al-Aqsa Mosque, 56, 62, 88

Arab Awakening, The (Antonius), xvi

Arab Civil administration: Dayan's practice (late 1967), 171; Israel's project of (summer of 1968), 8, 225, 229, 234–45, 249, 260, 273, 363n35; Ja'bari-Di'mas's plan of, 233; Ja'bari's request from Eshkol, 231; Nablus's plan of, 170–71, 172, 177, 179–80, 210, 228–29, 265

Arab-Israeli war: terminology for, xx–xxi. *See also* June 1967 War; 1948 War; Sinai Campaign, 1956; War of Attrition; Yom Kippur War

Arab League, 66, 136, 149, 151, 192, 233, 283. *See also* Khartoum Summit; Saudi peace initiative

Arab Legion, 108, 140

Arab Nationalism, 14, 16, 149–50

Arab Revolt of *1916*, xxx–xxxi

Arab Revolt of *1936–39*, xxix, 86, 174

Arabs, Israeli. *See* Palestinians

Arabs, Israeli view of, 19

'Arafat, Yasir: assassination plot against Shehadeh and Janho, 202, 353–54n34; -Dayan meeting proposal, 265–66; and escapes from Israeli raids, 206,

253; -Rabin historic handshake, 281; takeover of PLO, 3, 265

'Ariqat, Rashad, 306n36

Armistice agreement of *1949*, 7, 10 (map), 12, 159, 266, 290n16, 301n95

Arms embargo, French, 4, 182, 279

Aron, Raymond, 187

Arrane, Zalman, 96

al-Ashhab, Na'im, 84–85, 91–92, 102, 146, 317n46;n57

Ashkenazi-Landau, Dalia, xi–xii

Ashton, Nigel, 73, 274, 310n93

'Atallah, Antoun, 31, 37, 60, 74, 92, 94, 96, 167, 173, 178, 306n36; banishment by Israel, 175–76, 202, 346n44; swearing in as Jordanian Senator, 174–75, 202

al-Atasi, Nur al-Din, 151

Athens airport, attack on El Al airliner, 279

Avnery, Uri, 330n128

a'yan. See Urban notables class

Azoury, Nagib, 8

Badras, destruction in, 109

Bakr, Ibrahim: and civil disobedience, 86; in Committee of Four talks, 58, 59, 61, 62, 306n36; deportation of, 172–73, 174, 175–76, 177; intimidation of moderates, 173, 174; and Rabat summit delegation initiative, 177–78; and revision of the Palestinian National Charter, 365n68; three-month internal exile of, 89

Ball, George, 249–52, 255, 363n38

al-Bandak, Elias, 144, 235, 237, 238, 240

Barbour, Walworth, 68, 69–70, 126–27, 128, 132, 164, 175, 183, 184, 191, 197, 206, 225, 250, 251–52, 295–96n21, 307n44, 308n62, 357n98

Bar-Haim, Shaul, 80, 173, 197, 327n78, 353n27, 356n74; in Committee of Four,

49, 57, 58, 60–65, 74–75, 306n33,
  307n49
Bar-Lev, Baruch ("Borka"), 107, 111
Bar-Lev, Haim, 184, 203, 220
Barzilai, Yisrael, 240
Bashiti, Muhammad Nasir al-Din, 74–75
Bassiouny, Saleh, 46
Bastuni, Rustum, 147
al-Ba'th party, 20, 58, 86, 89, 147, 151, 172–73
Battle, Lucius, 126, 141
Bavly, Dan, 26–31, 32, 41, 57, 60, 295n17,
  311n101
Bayh, Birch, 306n39
Bayt 'Awa, destruction of, 109, 110–11
Bayt Illo, destruction in, 109
Bayt Jalla, and civil administration
  project, 233, 238, 239, 240
Bayt Mirsim, destruction of, 109, 110–11
Bayt Nuba: destruction of, 107–8,
  324n36; Jewish settlement at, 109. See
  also Latrun Salient
Bayt Sahour, and civil administration
  project, 233, 239, 240
Bazooka attack, on Farouqi's house, 173,
  174, 175
Bedouins, removal of, 187
Beersheba (Bi'r al-Sab'; Be'er Sheva), 75
Begin, Menachem, 18, 44, 47, 48, 130,
  204, 240, 247, 303n124, 359n113, 374n68
Beilin, Yossi, 271
Beirut airport, Israeli raid on, 279–80
Bellow, Saul, 213
Ben-Eliezer, Aryeh, 280, 374n65
Ben-Gurion, David, xxv, 18, 38, 39–40,
  228
Ben-Horin, Elyashiv, 76
Bennet, Sir Erik, 343n126
Bentov, Mordekhai, 75, 112, 121
Bethlehem: annexed areas of, 53; and
  civil administration project, 233, 235,
  236, 237, 238, 239–40; detached from
  Arab Jerusalem, 55; expulsion from,
  104; refugee return, ban on, 129, 131

Borders: in Allon Plan, 67, 245, 246
  (map); Armistice Agreement of 1949
  (Green Line), 10 (map), 12, 105, 110, 139,
  187–88, 290n16; Cabinet Resolution
  95 of 31 October 1968, 259; Cabinet
  Resolution 563 of 19 June 1967, 44,
  45–47, 139, 188, 259; ceasefire lines of
  June War, 139–40; Hussein on, 160,
  199; Jerusalem, 52 (map); and Johnson-
  Eshkol summit, 186, 188, 189; Jordan
  River as, 43, 44, 66, 153, 162, 186, 281,
  308n52; of occupied territories, 11
  (map), 12; pre–June War, return to, 17,
  283; UN Partition Resolution of 1947,
  8, 9 (map), 12; West Bank, 106 (map)
Bourguiba, Habib, 228
Bride-and-dowry metaphor, 3, 39,
  51, 53, 125, 162, 225–26, 272, 299n71,
  343n129
Britain (United Kingdom), xx; and
  annexation of Arab Jerusalem, 310n85;
  and first shot of June War, 22; and
  Hussein-Israel settlement efforts, 49,
  180, 309n72; and Jordan's annexation
  of West Bank, 12; in 1956 War, 13; and
  Palestinian option, 35, 298n49; on
  return of new refugees, 125, 131; and
  Suez Canal, 309n72; and UN Resolution 242, 162
British Mandate, xxviii, xxx, 5–6, 20, 28,
  86, 303n124. See also Mandatory
  Palestine
Brown, George, 54, 71, 125, 131–32, 137,
  310n85
Bull, Odd, 208, 299n61
Bundy, McGeorge, 39, 41, 72
al-Burj, destruction in, 109
Burns, Findley, 72, 130–31, 333n176

Cabinet Resolution 95 of 31 October
  1968, 259
Cabinet Resolution 563 of 19 June 1967,
  44, 45–47, 139, 188, 259, 270, 302n111

Califano, Joseph, 278, 373n56
Capucci, Hilarion, 94, 229, 298n56,
    320n95, 356n78, 359n116
Caradon, Lord (Hugh Foot), 163
Carmon, David, 309n73
Carrot and the Stick, The (Gazit), xvii,
    xviii, 288n9, 314n22
CIA (Central Intelligence Agency), 17,
    70, 71, 72, 292n41, 310n93, 335n10
Civil administration. *See* Arab civil
    administration
Civil disobedience: appeals to inter-
    national bodies, 96; deportation of
    leaders, 89–90, 98–99; education
    issues in, 94–95, 96; general strike, 91,
    93, 98; Israeli response to, 89–90,
    93–94, 98–102, 172–73; Jordanian
    incitement of, 97, 320n90; and King
    Hussein, 93, 97; petitions and declara-
    tions, 90–91, 93, 98; precipitating
    factors in, 79–80, 83–84, 99; religious
    issues in, 86, 88, 96; and shift in
    political mood, 75, 84, 97–98; 24 July
    Assembly, 86–87, 88, 89; violent
    insurgency rejected, 96–97
Cohen, Amnon, 313n3
Cohen, Victor, 82–83, 94, 314n17
Cold War, 13, 39, 276–77
Collaborationist leaders (quislings),
    Israeli cultivation of, xiv, 2, 80–84, 161,
    179, 232, 264, 313n3, 314n16
Comay, Michael, 120
Committee of Four, 48–49, 57–65, 73, 76,
    77, 80, 83–84, 158, 303n128
Committee of Heads of the [intelligence]
    Services (*Varash*), 49, 65
Communist Party; Communists, 20, 30,
    58, 147, 192, 315n27, 338n55; deporta-
    tion of leaders, 89, 172, 317n46; and
    Interim National Covenant, 146;
    intimidation of moderates, 173;
    resistance to occupation, 84–85, 86,
    91–92, 96–97

Confederation/federation idea, 31, 32, 33,
    34, 36, 41, 42, 50, 60, 61–62, 64, 147–48,
    214, 219
Contacts Committee. *See* Political
    Contacts Committee
Counterterrorist activity, Israeli, in
    Jordan, 197, 202–7, 252–53, 281

al-Dajani, Kamal, 92
al-*Dakhil*, ("inside" of occupied
    territories), shift from, 207, 265
Darwish, Muhammad, 144, 174, 338n53
Daud, Muhammad, 196–97, 198, 204, 208
Dayan, Moshe: and ʿAlami's visit, 229;
    and Allon Plan, 247; annexation of
    Arab Jerusalem, 54, 307n40; -Arab
    contacts, xxviii, 19; –ʿArafat meeting
    proposal, 265–66; biography of,
    xxv–xxvi; and CIA-brokered meeting
    with Hussein, 310–11n93; and civil
    administration project, 171, 179, 236,
    238, 239, 240, 241; on civil disobedi-
    ence, 90, 95–96, 100; in coalition
    government, 18, 19; and deportation
    policy, 172, 175, 224, 346n44; and
    destruction of Harat al-Magharibah,
    113; and destruction of villages and
    towns, 107, 110–12, 326n55; emigration
    encouraged by, 104, 325n42; -Eshkol
    rivalry, 48, 83; five "fists" plan of,
    66–67; on guerrilla movement, 265;
    injured in cave-in, 205; on Jewish
    settlements, 185; on Jordan coup, 211,
    217; and Jordanian-Israeli dialogue,
    49, 165, 252, 255–56; and Karameh raid,
    204; on killing returning refugees,
    123–24, 330n127; "living space" remark
    of, 142, 333n176; no aim of conquest
    declaration of, 25; occupation policy
    of, 75, 79, 94, 100; on Palestinian
    alternative stratagem, 157–58, 161, 191;
    on Palestinian capital, 216; on
    Palestinian collaborators (quislings),

83, 232; on Palestinian-Israeli
dialogue, xix, 77, 232; and Palestinian
option, 42–43, 74, 211–12, 215–17,
357n84; on peace settlement, 43–44, 51,
161, 187–88, 199–200, 250, 255, 275–76,
300–301n90, 373n48; press ban favored
by, 76; and Rabat summit delegation
initiative, 176–77; and refugee policy,
116, 117, 120, 122, 215; retaliation for
petition of West Bank leaders, 243; on
retaliatory raids, 203, 279; on victory
in June War, 38
Dayan, Yaël, 304–5n10
al-Dazdar, Ishaq, 89–90, 317n46
Deception, Israeli foreign policy of, 7–8;
and Allon Plan, 247–48, 249–50,
273; and Eban's devious approach
(*takhsisanut*), 183, 212, 247, 248, 255,
257, 273–74; and Eban's dossier
diplomacy, 180–82, 212; Hussein on,
273, 274–75; Meir on, 255, 260; and
Palestinian alternative stratagem,
156–58, 160–62, 163–64, 172, 176,
256–57; pretext for June War, 21–23,
294n67; prevarication strategy, 4, 73,
274, 247–48; and US relations, xiv–xv,
2, 4–5, 183, 249–50, 273, 274
Defiance, Israeli foreign policy of, 279
Deganyah Bet (kibbutz), 262
de Gaulle, Charles, 23
Demographic danger, 6, 39, 47–48, 125,
133–34, 162, 232, 248, 268
Deportation of West Bank leaders, xxix,
89–90, 98–99, 100–101, 147, 172–73,
174–76, 177, 202, 224, 264, 288n13,
321nn96,97,98, 339n69, 346n38,
360n123, 365n68
Devious tactics, Israeli. *See* Deception,
Israeli foreign policy of
Di'mas, Wadi', and civil administration
project, 233, 234, 235–36, 237, 238, 241
Dome of the Rock, 56
Dossier diplomacy, 180–82, 212

East Jerusalem. *See* Jerusalem, Arab
Eban, Abba: and Allon Plan, 249–50; on
annexation of Arab Jerusalem, 54, 55;
biography of, xxvi; and Cabinet
Resolution 563 of 19 June *1967*, 46, 47,
139, 142; in coalition government, 19;
on delaying tactics, 200–201; on
demographic danger, 133–34, 268;
devious approach (*takhsisanut*) of, 183,
212, 247, 248, 255, 257, 273–74, 284;
dossier diplomacy of, 180–82, 212; and
emissaries to Hussein, 198–99, 200,
249–51, 255; on Gaza Strip, 269; global
image concerns of, 227; on guerrilla
movement, 265; -Hussein meetings, (3
May 1968) 220–21, 250, (27 September
1968) 256–57; on Hussein-Nasser
peace proposal, 154; and Hussein's
peace initiatives, 66, 67, 68–69, 70–71,
155, 156, 190–91; Hussein's view of, 159;
on Jewish settlements, 140–41, 225; on
Johnson's support, 257–58; -Johnson
talks, 153, 156, 341–42n109; and
Karameh raid, 203, 205, 208; on
Khartoum resolutions, 138; on missed
opportunity for peace, 282–83, 284; on
modus vivendi concept, 232; nine-
point peace plan of, 260; and no aim
of conquest declaration, 25, 142; and
Palestinian-Israeli contacts, 303n128;
and Palestinian option, 41, 145, 199,
212, 213; pretext for June War, 22,
294n67; on prewar border, 7; publications of, xvii–xviii; and Rabat summit
delegation initiative, 177; and refugee
policy, 45, 119, 121, 122; and return of
new refugees, 126, 127, 128, 130, 132–33,
134; -Rusk meetings, 46, 67, 71, 145, 258,
302n114;n120; on territorial requirements, 153–54, 250, 255, 267; on
trade-off formula, 1–2; and UN
resolution on Israeli withdrawal,
152–53

Economist, 29

Education system, Palestinian, Israeli interference in, 94–95, 96, 319n74

Egypt (United Arab Republic; UAR): armistice agreement of *1949,* 10 (map), 12; and Cabinet Resolution 563 of 19 June *1967,* 46, 47, 270; -Israel peace accord of *1979,* 281; losses in June 1967 War, 1, 5; *1956* Arab-Israeli War, 13; outbreak of June War, 21–22; peaceful coexistence proposal of, 154; and peace settlement, 272; and Rabat summit, 176; Sadat's offensive against Israel in October *1973,* 281; and Soviet Union, 276; War of Attrition, 3, 281, 289n10. *See also* Nasser, Gamal 'Abd al-

El Al airliner, attack on, 279

Ellis, Harry, 295–96n21

Elon, Amos, 96

Emigration of June 1967 War: demographic danger reversed by, 6, 114, 133–34, 268; and destruction of villages and towns, 107–12, 185–86; expulsion, 104–5, 107, 113–15; free transport to Jordan River, 115–16, 118–19, 185; from Gaza Strip, 6, 44–45, 64, 117, 124, 129, 269–70; information campaign and counter-propaganda on, 119–20; Israeli encouragement of, 2, 5, 65, 77, 103–4, 115, 117–18, 121–22, 185, 269; motives for, 115, 270, 327n74; from refugee camps, 20, 114–15, 117; size of, 5, 103, 118, 125, 133, 328n96. *See also* Refugees, new (of June 1967 War)

Encounter, 368n8

Entity movement. *See* Palestinian entity movement

Eshkol, Levi: and 'Alami's visit, 229; and Allon plan, 245, 249, 370n144; annexation of Arab Jerusalem, 54; and anti-Hussein campaign, 155; on Beirut airport raid, 279; biography of, xxv; bride-and-dowry metaphor of, 39, 125,

225–26, 272, 299n71; and civil administration project, 225–26, 234, 235, 237, 238, 239, 243; on civil disobedience, 88; coalition government of, 18–19; and Committee of Four, 48–49, 57; -Dayan rivalry, 48, 83; death of, 3, 262, 280, 370n2; on demographic danger, 162, 232, 248; and destruction of Harat al-Magharibah, 113; and destruction of villages and towns, 108, 112; Hussein's July 1967 peace initiative, reaction to, 68, 154–55; -Ja'bari talks, 231, 241–42; and Jewish settlements, 140, 142, 184, 225; -Johnson summit, 179, 182, 186, 188, 189–90; Jordanian dialogue favored by, 247–48; and Jordanian option, 66, 68, 200, 232; and Jordan-Israel September 1968 summit, 255–56; and Karameh raid, 204, 205, 206; modus vivendi concept of, 231, 232, 233; on Palestinian alternative stratagem, 162; and Palestinian-Israeli dialogue, 32, 48, 49, 158, 194–96, 201, 217–19; and Palestinian option, 66, 168–69, 187, 214–15, 218, 232, 265; on Palestinian peoplehood, 263; peace policy of, 43, 64, 66, 182–83, 186–87, 223, 247–48, 250, 255, 282; pledge of no aim of conquest, 25; and Rabat summit delegation initiative, 177, 179; and refugee relocation, 44, 237, 241–42, 270; and Resolution 563 of 19 June *1967,* 45, 139; and return of new refugees, 123, 124, 125, 128, 130, 131, 134, 217–18, 268; on US-Israeli relations, 301–2n110; on victory in June War, 38

Etzion Block, 110; Jewish settlements in, 140, 141

Evron, Ephraim ("Eppie"), 71, 209, 214, 278, 356n76

Exodus from West Bank/occupied territories. *See* Emigration of June 1967 war

Fahmi, Isma'il, 47

Farhi, David: biography of, xxvii; and civil disobedience, 89, 92, 93–94; contacts with West Bank leaders, 148–49, 166, 210, 217, 219, 298n56, 339–40n81, 363n30; and deportation of West Bank leaders, 89; on Farouqi, 151; on return of new refugees, 132, 333n182; on Shehadeh, 216; on West Bank political mood, 230

Farid, 'Abd al-Majid, 357n94

al-Farouqi, Hamdi al-Taji, 150; bazooka attack on residence, 173–74, 175; "Proposed Palestinian State" plan, 151

al-Fateh, 109, 192, 210, 211, 254, 291n33; activities against Israeli targets, 15, 16, 176, 195; attacks on West Bank leaders, 173–74, 202; and autonomous Palestinian entity, 15; Dayan- 'Arafat contact attempt, 265–66; formation and development of, 14–15, 264; Karameh raid, 203–8; Israeli raids against, 15, 16, 176, 203–7, 220, 251, 252–53, 355n52; takeover of PLO, 3, 207, 244, 265. *See also* Guerrilla movement

Fida'iyyun. See al-Fateh; Guerrilla movement; Palestine Liberation Organization (PLO)

Foreign policy of deception. *See* Deception, Israeli foreign policy of

France, arms embargo of. *See* Arms embargo, French.

Galili, Yisrael, 153, 155, 284

Gavish, Yesha'yahu, 124

Gaza Strip, 1, 2, 12, 13, 25, 48, 51; and civil administration project, 234, 235; demographics, 5, 20; designated for annexation, 44, 51, 124, 268–69; disengagement from, 283; emigration from, 6, 44–45, 64, 103, 104, 117, 124, 129, 133, 269–70; lack of political leadership in, 19–20; National Front in, 145; and Rabat Summit delegation initiative, 177; refugee camps in, 6, 12, 20; refugee relocation plan for, 44–45, 64, 177, 237, 241–42, 269

Gazit, Mordechai, 357n98

Gazit, Shlomo, xvii, xviii, 40, 76, 77, 96, 99, 111, 175, 288n9, 299–300n78, 313n3, 343n128, 346n47

General Security Service. *See* GSS (General Security Service; *Shabak*)

General strike, 91, 93, 98

Geneva Conventions; Forth Geneva Convention (1949), 54, 110, 140, 141, 325n48

Ghana Airways, 279

Golan Heights (Syrian Plateau), 1, 45, 46, 48, 139, 163, 187, 225, 267; inhabitants' flight from, 103, 322n2; Jewish settlements in, 140, 141, 267

Goldberg, Arthur, 69, 154, 251, 252, 269, 278, 302n120

Goren, Moshe, 124

Gorenberg, Gershom, xvii

Greater Israel, ideology of, 18, 47, 272. *See also* Whole Land of Israel

Green Line (Armistice Demarcation of 1949), 7, 10 (map), 12, 27, 67, 75, 105, 108, 109–10, 113, 114, 139, 187–88, 248, 290, 335n19

Gromyko, Andrei, 39, 302n120

GSS (General Security Service; *Shabak*), xiii, xiv, 40, 143, 145, 146, 173; and civil administration project, 242; and civil disobedience, 87–88, 89, 94, 100; and cultivation of collaborationist leaders, 80, 81; in expulsion from Gaza, 124; and Operation Sadducees, 82–84; and Rabat summit delegation initiative, 178, 179–80

Guardian, 125–26

Guerrilla movement: Athens airport raid, 279; attacks from Jordanian soil, 195, 196, 202, 280–81; bus incident,

Guerrilla movement (continued)
203; formation of, 14; in Gaza Strip, 20; growth of, 15, 207, 264–65; and Hussein, 197, 209, 253, 280; Israeli belittlement of, 265; Israeli reprisal raids against (*See* Reprisal raids); Jordan-Israeli talks on, 220; and Palestinian option, 210–11, 265, 266; as pretext for Jewish settlements, 200; and West Bank leadership, 244–45. *See also* al-Fateh; Palestine Liberation Organization (PLO)

Gur, Mordechai, 371n25

Gussing, Nils-Göran, 103, 111–12

Gvati, Haim, 348n81

Hablah, destruction in, 109

Hadow, Michael, 1, 18, 70, 134, 276

Hague Regulations (1907), 110

d'Halloy, Christian, 228, 229

Hammudah, Yahya, 192, 211

Hanadiv Fund, 239

Hanoun, Hilmi, 114, 149

al-Haram al-Sharif (Noble Sanctuary), 56

Harat al-Magharibah (Moroccan quarter, Jerusalem), destruction of, 112–13

Harb, Jalil, 62, 306n36

Harman, Avraham, 67, 342n109

Harmelin, Yosef, 80, 81, 82, 83

al-Hasan, Khalid, 15

Hasbarah (information campaign; propaganda), 119, 120, 150, 279, 329n104

Al-Hayat (Beirut), 146

Hebron: capture of, 114; in civil administration project, 233, 236 237; Jewish settlements in, 224–25, 247, 267

Heikal, Muhammad, 137, 278, 279

Herbert, Emanuel, 50, 159, 161, 220, 253, 256

Herzog, Chaim, xxvii, 33, 34–35, 42, 48, 81, 297n42; in Committee of Four, 49,

57, 64, 306n33, 308n52; on destruction of Harat al-Magharibah, 113; and Palestinian exodus from the West Bank, 115–16, 117–18, 120, 328n96

Herzog, Ya'acov: on Allon Plan, 254; and ban on political organization, 75; biography of, xxvi–xxvii, 19; and civil administration project, 239, 245; and Committee of Four, 57, 65; on delaying tactics, 260; and Eshkol-Johnson summit, 186, 189; historical association concept of, 160, 188, 254, 271–72; in Hussein–Eban and Allon meeting (27 September 1967), 256; in Hussein-Eban meeting, (3 May 1968), 220, 221; -Hussein meetings, (2 July 1967) 49–50, 70, (19, 20 November 1967) 159–61, (22 August 1968) 271–72, (25 April 1969) 275; on Hussein's July 1967 peace initiatives, 71–72; on Hussein's willingness to negotiate, 155, 158–59; on Khartoum resolutions, 138; minutes of secret talks, xix; on modus vivendi concept, 232; and Palestinian option, 40, 156–57; on refugee policy, 121–22; and refugee repatriation program, 131; -Rifa'i meetings, 222–23, 245, 248–49, 252–53; on 24 July Assembly, 87; and West Bank leaders, cultivation of, 81

Herzog, Yitzhak HaLevi, xxvi–xxvii

Hillel, Shlomo, 41

Historical association concept, 4, 159–60, 188, 221, 254, 271–72

Holocaust, memory of, 7, 268

Hourani, Albert, 292–93n52

Hourani, Cecil, 228–30, 244, 361nn8,11

Humphrey, Hubert, 278

Hussein Bin Talal, King of Jordan: -Allon meeting (19 November 1968), 269; and Allon plan, 245, 247; Ball and Sisco as emissaries to, 249–51;

biography of, xxx–xxxi; and border issues, 186, 188, 199; ceasefire offer rejected by, 38; and CIA-brokered meeting, 71–72, 310–11n93; civil administration proposal of, 180; and civil disobedience, 93, 97; on collaboration of West Bank leaders, 142, 143; and coup plots against, 209, 211, 217, 254, 358n102; –Eban and Allon meetings, (27 September 1968), 256–57; -Eban meeting (3 May 1968), 220–21, 250; Eban's ultimatum to, 213; and guerrilla movement, 197, 209, 253, 280; -Herzog meetings, 16, (2 July 1967) 49–50, 70, (19, 20 November 1967) 159–61, 221, (22 August 1968) 271–72, (25 April 1969) 275, (21 November 1967) 343n126; on incitement of refugees charge, 130; and Interim National Covenant, 147; -Israeli dialogue characterized, 8; on Israeli duplicity, 273, 274–75; on Israeli peace terms, 284; Israeli publicity campaign against, 155–56; Israeli view of, 17, 191, 209; and Khartoum Summit, 136–37, 142–43; motives for peace initiatives, 254; -Nasser defense pact, 16–17; -Nasser peace concessions, 154; Palestinian alternative stratagem directed to, 157–58, 160–62, 163–64, 172, 273; and Palestinian option, 31, 158, 166, 221; as Palestinian spokesman, 6, 201; peace initiative (July 1967), 67–73; and Rabat summit initiative, 176; relations with Jews, 16, 17; on reprisal raids, 208–9, 254; Washington visit of, 154; and West Bank leaders, xxix, 21, 201–2; willingness to negotiate, 50, 51, 67–68, 70, 156, 158–59, 181, 190, 191, 223, 245, 271, 274. See also Jordanian-Israeli dialogue

al-Husseini, Daud, 89
al-Husseini, Muhammad Amin, xxviii, 86

Idna, destruction in, 109
Al-Ikhwan al-Muslimun (Muslim Brotherhood), 20
'Imwas, destruction of, 107–8. See also Latrun Salient
Interim National Covenant (al- Mithaq al- Watani al-Marhali), 146–47, 148, 149–50, 169, 190, 230
Intifadah (first), 282
Intifadah (second), 282, 300n84
al-'Isa, Daud, 26, 60, 62, 63, 201, 306n36
Islamic Council (al-Hay'ah al-Islamiyyah), 86–87, 88, 90, 91, 93, 100, 315–16n34, 317n54
Islamic religious affairs, Israel interference in, 86, 87–88, 96
Israeli Arabs. See Palestinians
Al-Ittihad, 238

al-Ja'bari, Muhammad 'Ali: biography of, xxviii; and civil administration project, 233, 235–36, 237, 239, 240, 241, 243–44; collaboration charge against, 145, 146; corruption of, 237, 243, 314n19; -Eshkol talks, 231, 241–42; intimidation of, 174; Israeli cultivation of, 81, 82; in Jericho Congress of 1948, 32; and Palestinian-Israeli dialogue, 32–33, 59, 306n36; and Palestinian option, xiii, 144, 145, 149, 209, 231; and resettlement of Gaza refugees, 241–42
al-Ja'bari, Sidqi, 306n36
Jackson, Harold, 125–26, 225
Janho, 'Abd al-Nur, 74, 150, 166–67, 168, 202
Jarring, Gunnar, peace mission of, 3, 4, 163, 180–81, 182, 190, 193, 198–99, 204–5, 208, 212, 213, 221, 222, 223, 227,

Jarring, Gunnar (continued)
229, 237, 248, 251, 252, 254, 255, 260–61,
264, 265, 272, 277, 334n195, 355n68
Jericho, emigration from, 104
Jericho Congress of 1948, xxviii, 31, 144
Jerusalem: emotional attachment to Old
City, 77; and Hussein's July 1967 peace
initiative, 69, 77; internationalization
proposal for, 75; Israeli intransigence
over, 69–70; Municipal Council of,
85–86; requisition of Palestinian-
owned land, 195; as seat of government, 56, 167
Jerusalem, Arab, xxi, 1; annexation of, 2,
4, 6, 34, 51, 52 (map), 53–56, 79, 195,
267; ban on return of new refugees,
129, 270; and Bethlehem, status of, 55;
and civil administration project, 234,
235; civil disobedience in, 94–95;
destruction of Harat al-Magharibah,
112–13; dissolution of municipal
government, 85; emigration of June
1967 war, 115–16, 117, 124; evictions of
Arabs, 112; Judaization of, 54, 224,
267; as Palestinian capital, 216;
Palestinian leadership in, 20;
resistance to annexation, 86, 99; as
spiritual capital, 56
Jerusalem District Electricity Company,
224
Jerusalem Liberation Day, 224
Jerusalem syndrome, 77, 312n123
Jewish settlements in occupied territories, xv; expansion of, 267, 280, 282;
foreign criticism of, 140–41; government authorization for, 109, 140–42;
in Hebron, 224–25, 247, 267; military
pretext for, 4, 141, 184–85, 200, 267; on
refugees' land, 185–86; and water
sources, 185, 349n88
al-Jiftlik, destruction of, 185–86
Johnson, Lyndon, 39, 66, 72; and aircraft
sales, 205, 227; -Eban talks, 153, 156,

341–42n109; -Eshkol summit, 179, 182,
186, 188, 189–90; and Hussein, 154; and
Hussein-Israeli dialogue, 223, 252,
257–58, 274; and Israeli duplicity, 274;
Jewish ties of, 278; Karameh raid
opposed by, 206; on Khartoum
Summit, 137; and outbreak of June
War, 14, 22, 25; and Palestinian option,
36; pro-Israel attitude of, 189, 277–79;
on refugee problem, 116
Jordan: annexation of West Bank, 12, 31;
Armistice Agreement of 1949, 10
(map), 12, 301n95; and civil administration project, 240–41, 244, 245;
-Egypt defense pact, 16–17; expulsion
of guerrillas from, 281; fighting on
ceasefire line, 197; guerrilla attacks
from, 195, 196, 202, 280–81; incitement of civil disobedience charge
against, 97, 320n90; incitement of
refugees charge against, 130–31; -Israel
Armistice agreement of 1949, 10
(map), 12, 290n16; -Israel peace treaty
of 1994, 281; June War attack by, 37–38;
losses in June 1967 War, 1, 6, 17;
peaceful coexistence proposal of, 154;
peace settlement supported in, 69;
population of, 17, 292n42; refugees of
June War in, 114, 120–21, 133, 197, 223;
reprisal raids against guerrillas in, 15,
16, 203–9, 252–53, 264–65; and return
of new refugees, 126, 127, 130; West
Bank leaders' support for rule of,
59–60, 62, 63, 64, 65, 73, 94, 144. See
also Hussein Bin Talal, King of
Jordan; Jordanian-Israeli dialogue;
Jordanian option; Peace settlement
Jordanian civil administration,
Hussein's idea of, 180
Jordanian Communist Party (JCP). See
Communist Party
Jordanian-Israeli dialogue, xvii, xviii, 3,
4, 8, 369n138; agreement to negotiate,

51; and Allon Plan, 249–50, 254, 256, 257, 261; Ball and Sisco as emissaries for, 249–51; and CIA-brokered meeting, 71–72, 310n93; Daud's mission, 196–97, 204, 208; delaying tactics in, 247–48, 251, 183, 260; on Gaza Strip, 269; Hussein-Allon meeting (19 November 1968), 269; Hussein–Eban and Allon meeting (27 September 1968), 255–59; Hussein-Eban talk (3 May 1968), 220–21; Hussein-Herzog talks, 16, (2 July 1967) 49–50, 70, (19 November 1967) 159–61, 221, (22 August 1968) 271–72, (25 April 1969) 275, (19, 20 November 1967) 343n126; and Jerusalem question, 69–70, 195–96; Rifa'i-Herzog talks, 222–23, 245, 252–53; Rifa'i's role in, 17–18; unequal parties in, 15–16; US role in, 68, 71–72, 252, 257–60; West Bank emissaries in, 170, 195, 196, 198–99, 200, 201, 212–14, 253, 255, 264; West Bank leaders' view of, 59–60, 63

Jordanian option, 2; and Committee of Four, 73; Hussein-Eban talks on, 221; and Interim National Covenant, 146–47, 149–50, 230; Israeli view of, 66, 67, 68–69, 200, 273; and Jerusalem question, 150, 273; and refugee problems, 223; West Bank support for, 59–60, 62, 63, 65, 73, 94, 144, 166, 190, 337n51

Jordan River, as border, 43, 44, 66, 153, 162, 186, 281, 308n52

Jum'ah, Sa'd, 31, 36, 63, 72, 130, 145

June 1967 War (Six Day War): Arab threats prior, 7; archival and other sources on, xvi–xx; calamity for Palestinians, 5–6, 56; destruction of villages and towns following the fighting, 105–13, 77; and Egypt-Jordan defense pact, 16–17; historical background and setting to, 8–17, 18;

Israeli euphoria and hubris in victory, 38, 71, 267, 276; Israeli pretext for, 21–23, 294n67; Israeli warnings to Hussein, 37–38; and Jewish nationalism, 6; Jordan's attack in, 38; Jordan's losses, 6, 17; no aim of conquest pledges, 25, 142; official map featuring ceasefire lines of, 139–40; Palestinian reaction to occupation, 25–26; refugee camps bombed in, 114–15; refugees of, 103 (see also Refugees, new [of June 1967 War]); significance of, 1, 5, 268; Soviet Union's motion at UN in response to, 39, 47, 54; superpowers' involvement in and after, 13–14, 276–77; terminology of, xxi; territorial gains from, 1–2, 11 (map); "waiting period" preceding, 7. See also al-Naksah; Peace settlement

Kalyah (Nahal settlement), 184
Kan'an, Hamdi: biography of, xxviii; and civil administration project, 238, 242–43; and civil disobedience, 94; -Dayan meetings, 211, 123–24, 215–16, 357n84; intimidation of, 174; Israeli cultivation of, 82, 232; and killing of returning new refugees, 123–24; and Kimche-Bavly talks, 29, 30; and Palestine entity initiative, 146, 148–49; and political contacts with Israel, 164, 170, 219, 230; and Rabat summit delegation initiative, 176, 177–78, 347n50
Kan'an, Tiyasir, 36, 37, 74, 92, 210, 356n78, 356n101; -Eshkol meeting, 217–19
Karameh, Israeli raid on, 203–9, 214, 244, 254, 264–65, 279, 355n52
Karman, 'Izzat, 150, 173, 311n101
Katzenbach, Nicholas, 118, 121, 153, 156, 189, 258
Kenan, Amos, 324n36
Kennedy, John F., 277

Kerr, Malcolm, 13
Kfar Etzion (civilian settlement), 140, 141
Khafaqat Dhakirah: Qissah (Khayri), xii
Khalaf, Salah (Abu Iyad), 291n33
Khalidi, Rashid, 206–7
Khamis, Edward, 93
Khamis, Jabara, 238, 239, 241, 364n50
Khammash, ʿAmer, 220
Kharas, destruction of, 109
al-Kharij ("outside" of occupied
   territories), shift to, 207, 265
Khartoum Summit of *1967*, 47, 136–38,
   140, 142–43, 223, 297n42, 335nn10,12,
   337n47
al-Khatib, Anwar, 74, 85, 92, 232, 260,
   288n13; biography of, xxviii–xxix;
   deportation of, 89, 90, 147, 316n34,
   360n123; -Eshkol meeting, 217, 218;
   and Jordanian-Israeli dialogue, 33,
   59–60, 63, 170, 219; and Palestinian-
   Israeli dialogue, 34, 36–37, 56, 306n36;
   and Palestinian option, 147–48, 142,
   296n31; and Rabat summit delegation
   initiative, 176, 177; transport request
   for Jordanian nationals, 115; at 24 July
   Assembly, 86; and UN trusteeship
   plan, 229; willingness to cooperate, 42
al-Khatib, Rashad, 59, 306n36
al-Khatib, Ruhi, 96; and annexation of
   Jerusalem, 56; biography of, xxix;
   deportation of, 224; deportation
   threat against, 172; on emigration
   from Arab Jerusalem, 124; and general
   strike, 91; at July 24 Assembly, 86; and
   National Guidance Committee, 92,
   100; in Palestinian-Israeli dialogue,
   34–35, 306n36; and Palestinian option,
   33; participant in conference proposal,
   74; and Rabat summit delegation
   initiative, 177–78; willingness to
   cooperate, 85
Khayri, Bashir, xi–xii
al-Kilani, Muhammad Rasul, 84

Kimche, David: in Committee of Four,
   48–49, 57, 64–65, 306n33, 307nn50,51;
   and cultivation of collaborationist
   Palestinian leaders, 80, 81; on
   Palestinian state, 30, 35, 41, 64–65,
   307n50; and survey of Palestinian
   political thinking, 26–31, 32, 35, 41, 57,
   60, 295nn17,18, 296n26, 311n101
Kimche, Jon, 35, 64, 307n50
Kiryat Arbaʿ, 225
Kissinger, Henry, 374n66
Kollek, Teddy, 81, 85, 314n15; and
   destruction of Harat al-Magharibah,
   113, 326n61
Kol Yisrael, 21, 115
al-Kony, Muhammad, 278
Korn, David, 302n115
Kosygin, Aleksey, 25

Labor Party, 18–19, 224, 267, 271, 280. *See
   also* Political Committee
Lahat, Shlomo ("Chich"), 34, 112–13, 116
Latrun Salient, 40, 324n29; destruction
   of villages in, 107–9, 110–12, 115, 248,
   324n37, 326n55. *See also* Bayt Nuba;
   ʿImwas; Yalu
Lausanne Conference of *1949*, xxx, 26,
   27, 210
League of Nations, 5–6
Lebanon, armistice agreement of *1949*, 10
   (map), 12
Lebensraum ("living space"), 130, 142,
   333n176
Leibowitz, Yeshayahu, 276
Lemon Tree, The (Tolan), xii
Lewis, Bernard, 263–64
Liberated Bride, The (Yehoshua), xv
Lies and lying, in international relations,
   22, 275
Life magazine, 100
"Lily North" (*Havatselet Tsafon*)
   resolution, 262
Liʾor, Yisrael, 123

Living space. *See Lebensraum*

Lurie, Ra'anan, 114, 327n68

Mahjub, Mohammad, 138

Majali, 'Abd al-Wahab, 130

Mandatory Palestine, xxvi, xxvii, 2, 8, 12, 14, 15, 61, 66. *See also* British Mandate

Manor, Amos, 81

Mapai party, 18, 44, 183

Marie Thérèse, Sister, 104, 110

Masakh shel Hol (A Curtain of Sand; by Allon), 271

al-Masri, Hajj Ma'zuz, 28

al-Masri, Hikmat, 59, 94, 147, 151, 198, 306n36, 357n94, 359n116; biography of, xxix; and civil administration project, 171, 242, 243; in civil disobedience, 90, 94; -Eban meeting, 212–13, 357n93; -Eshkol meeting, 201; -Hussein meeting, 201–2, 211; Israeli cultivation of, 232; and Nablus's proposal for self rule, 171, 209, 210; -Nasser meeting, 222; and UN trusteeship plan, 228–29

Matri, Laurent, 125

McPherson, Harry, 66

Mearsheimer, John, 22, 275

Meholah (*Nahal* settlement), 184, 185

Meir, Golda: and contacts with Hussein, 3, 183, 219, 248, 255; and contacts with Palestinians, 3; denial of Palestinian peoplehood, 262–63; and the future of the occupied territories, 44, 183, 248, 271; -Hussein meeting (1965), 16; and objection to Allon Plan, 248; premiership, 61, 262, 280; on President Johnson, 277; and support of foreign policy of *takhsisanut*, 248, 255, 260

Meron, Theodor, 140

Mevo Horon (civilian settlement), 109

Michael, Michael, 197, 357n98

Ministerial Committee for Security Affairs, 43–44, 45, 117, 123, 172–73, 187–88, 203, 204, 205–6, 229, 240, 243, 279, 359n120

Mirage fighter jets, 4, 23, 182, 279.

Moda'i, Yitzhak, 124

Moledet party, 300n84

Le Monde, 66, 308n60

Moroccan quarter. *See* Harat al-Magharibah

Mossad, 26, 30, 41, 49, 57, 71, 72, 80, 269, 276, 313n7

Movement for the Whole Land of Israel, 157, 184

Mu'ammar, Nabih, 92

al-Muhtasib, Hilmi, 100

Musallam, Ayub, 144; and civil administration project, 235, 236, 237, 238, 241; -Eshkol meeting, 194–95

Muslim Brotherhood. See *Al-Ikhwan al-Muslimun*

Mustafa, Ribhi, 241

Mutawi, Samir A., 291n32

al-Nabi Samwil, destruction in, 109

Nablus, self rule proposal in, 170–71; opposition to entity movement in, 150–51

Nahal military settlements, 109, 141, 184–85

Al-Nahar (Beirut), 368n8

al-Nakbah, xxi, 5, 102. *See also* 1948 War

al-Naksah, 5, 14, 270. *See also* June 1967 War

Narkiss, Uzi: destruction of Harat al-Magharibah, 113; destruction of villages and towns, 104, 105, 107, 108, 110, 111, 112, 326n51; and free transport to Jordan River, 116, 118–19; on killing of returning new refugees, 122; and Operation Sadducees, 83; and Palestinian autonomy, 42, 74

al-Nashashibi, Nasser al-Din, 233,
    362n24
Nashashibi, Rashid, 148, 297n45
Nasir, Kamal: in Committee of Four
    talks, 58, 59, 61, 62, 306n36; deporta-
    tion of, 172–73, 174, 175–76, 177;
    intimidation of moderates, 173, 174;
    and Rabat summit delegation
    initiative, 177–78
Nasir, Musa, 200, 306n36
Nasser, Gamal ʿAbd al-, 21, 37, 69, 114,
    151, 161, 169, 171, 202, 209, 212, 233,
    264, 278, 281, 289n10, 357nn93,94;
    consent to peace settlement, 214, 221,
    248, 366nn79,80; Eban's ultimatum
    to, 213, 357n93; -Hussein defense pact,
    16–17; -Hussein peace concessions,
    154, 159; and Hussein peace efforts,
    68, 142; at Khartoum Summit,
    137–38, 143, 335n10; negotiating role
    for, 60; and Palestinian option, 210;
    reversal of Tiran blockade, 13; and
    UN trusteeship plan, 229; unwilling-
    ness to negotiate, 70–71, 137, 222,
    359n116
National Front (Gaza Strip), 145
National Guidance Committee (Lajnat
    al- Tawjih al- Watani), xxix, xxx, 85,
    92–93, 96, 98, 100, 144, 145–46, 147, 172,
    177–78, 224, 317n57, 321nn98,111
Nationalism: Arab, 14, 16, 149–50;
    Jewish, 6, 14, 16
National Unity Government; National
    Unity coalition, 18–19, 156–57, 224,
    267
Ne'eman, Yuval, 40–41, 300n79
Neff, Donald, 153
Netanyahu, Benjamin, 284
Newsweek, 263, 324n37
New York Times, 87, 132, 253
Al-Nidal al-Shaʿbi al-Quds (The popular
    struggle, Jerusalem), 84
al-Nimr, Rashad, 32, 296n26

1948 War, xi, xiv, xxi, xxx, 5, 12, 14, 38,
    103, 104, 108, 110, 111, 116, 140, 185, 228,
    290n16. See also al-Nakbah
1967 (Segev), xvi–xvii, 287n6, 302n113,
    349n97
Nixon, Richard, 54, 247, 274, 277, 280,
    374n66
Notables class. See Urban notables
    class
NPT. See Treaty on the Non-
    Proliferation of Nuclear Weapons
Nuseibeh, Anwar, 29; absence from
    notables meetings, 87, 316n36;
    biography of, xxx; and civil adminis-
    tration project, 235; and civil disobedi-
    ence, 96; in Committee of Four talks,
    306n36; and conference of West Bank
    leaders, 74, 75; emissary to Hussein,
    195, 196, 198–99, 248, 253, 255; -Eshkol
    meeting, 195–96; -Herzog talks, 34–35,
    297n42; Israeli cultivation of, 81, 232,
    314n15; on Jarring peace mission, 190;
    Jordanian post offered to, 201–2;
    manifesto on Jerusalem occupation,
    231; in National Guidance Committee,
    92; negotiating tenets of, 167–68, 169;
    and Palestinian option, 29, 33–34,
    94, 145, 148, 175, 306–7n39; on peace
    settlement, 59, 60, 62; and Rabat
    summit delegation initiative, 178;
    on refugee problem, 193; and 24 July
    Assembly, 87, 316n36; and UN
    trusteeship plan, 229
Nuseibeh, Muhammad, 297n42
Nusseibeh, Sari, 87, 265, 297n36, 314n15
Nusseibeh, Zaki, 314n15

Occupied territories: administrative
    decrees on, 222; annexation of, 38–39;
    annexation of Arab Jerusalem, 2, 4, 6,
    34, 51, 52 (map), 53–56; ban on political
    activity in, 74–77, 179; ban on press
    contacts in, 76; and bride-and-dowry

metaphor, 3, 39, 125, 225–26, 272, 299n71; civil administration project for (*see* Arab Civil administration); civil disobedience in (*see* Civil disobedience); Dayan's indirect rule policy in, 79; and demographic danger, 6, 39, 47–48; destruction of villages and towns in, 2, 107–12, 185–86; emigration from (*see* Emigration of June 1967 War); Israeli infatuation with, 267–68, 272; Jewish settlements in (*see* Jewish settlements in occupied territories); legal status of, 12, 290n23; Palestine Authority in, 282; PLO influence in, 281; popular sentiment for retention of, 157, 184; refugee camps in, 20; relocation plan for, 64, 65, 66; retaliatory measures in, 176; and *sumud* (steadfastness) strategy, 270; terminology for, xxi; travel permits in, 81, 243; UN trusteeship proposal for, 228–30; uprising (*Intifadah*) in, 282; water resources in, 185, 349n88. *See also* Gaza Strip; Jerusalem, Arab; Palestinian option; West Bank leaders

Ohman, Yosef, 108

Olmert, Ehud, 282, 284

Operation Excrement 2 (*Mivtsa' Peresh*), 98–99, 321n97

Operation Excrement 3 (*Mivtsa' Peresh*), 173, 321n97

Operation Refugee (*Mivtsa' Palit*), 125–35, 270, 275

Operation Sadducees (*Mivtsa' Tsdokim*), 82–84, 314n17

Operation *Tofet*, 206, 207

Oren, Michael, 330n127

Ottoman Turkey, 5

Owen, Roger, 207

Pa'il, Meir, 324n29

Pakistan, 12

Palestine: Arab-Israeli War of *1948*, 12; foreign rulers of, 5–6; in late nineteenth and early twentieth centuries, 263; partition of, 8, 12; Zionist view of, 262–63

Palestine Liberation Army (PLA), 124

Palestine Liberation Organization (PLO), 69, 86, 147; formation of, xxix, 14; growth in influence, 14–15, 192; influence in occupied territories, 281; Israeli recognition of, 281–82; and Khartoum summit, 137; and Palestinian option, 34, 210–11; Shuqayri's dismissal from, 192; takeover by al-Fateh, 3, 207, 244, 265; West Bank leaders in, xxix, 58. *See also* 'Arafat, Yasir; Guerrilla movement

Palestinian alternative stratagem, Israeli, 156–58, 160–62, 163–64, 172, 176, 256–57, 273

Palestinian Authority, 282

Palestinian entity movement: Arab opposition to, 145–47, 148, 150–51, 166, 340n87; decline of, 230–31; Hussein's response to, 166; intimidation by extremists, 173–74; Israeli response to, 144–45, 209–10, 273; and al-Khatib (Anwar), 148; and Nuseibeh, 148; political program of, 149–50, 166; revival of, 209; Sasson's meetings with, 166–69, 175; Shehadeh's creation of, 143–44, 145; support for, 149. *See also* Palestinian option

Palestinian-Israeli dialogue: Arab opposition to, 36; archival sources on, xviii–xix; on civil administration project, 170–71, 179, 225–26, 231, 233–45; Committee of Four talks, 57–65, 74–75, 305–6n33; Dayan-'Arafat initiative, 265–66; Dayan in, 215–17; entity movement in, 166–69; Eshkol in, 194–95, 231, 217–19; and guerrilla

Palestinian-Israeli dialogue (continued)
movement, lack of contact, 265–66;
Herzog (Ya'acov) in, 34–35, 297n42;
impact of annexation on, 56–57;
Israeli participants in, xxv–xxvii;
Kimche-Bavly talks, 26–31, 57, 60,
294n5; Meir's rejection of, 3; minutes
of, xix; modus vivendi concept in, 231–
34; Palestinian alternative stratagem
in, 156–58, 160–62, 164; Palestinian
participants in, xxviii–xxx, 58; phases
of, 7–8; press reports on, 35–36, 230;
and Rabin, 32; Sasson-entity proponents talks, 167–72; Sasson's preparation for, 57–58, 60, 62–63; Sasson's
reports on, 63–65, 191–93; unequal
parties in, 15, 62
Palestinian National Charter, 244,
365n68
Palestinian National Council (PNC), 58,
244–45
Palestinian National Liberation
Movement. See al-Fateh
Palestinian option, 2; Committee of
Four's rejection of, 64–65; and Dayan,
42–43, 74, 211–12, 215–16, 357n84; and
Eban, 41, 145, 199, 212, 213; and Eshkol,
66, 187, 214–15, 218, 232, 265; experimental autonomy plan, 74; Farouqi's
proposal for, 151; and fear of Israeli
control, 62–63; Hussein's view of, 31,
158, 166–67; Israeli proposals for,
29–30, 40–42, 187, 214–15; Israeli view
of, 36, 144–45, 152, 209–11, 273; and
Jerusalem question, 61–62, 216;
Shak'ah's initiatives, 210–11, 265, 266;
Shehadeh's proposal of June 1967,
26–29, 30; and United States, 17, 35–36;
West Bank views of, 29–31, 33–35, 41,
73–74, 230, 296n69, 306–7n39, 337n51.
See also Palestinian entity movement
Palestinians: Israeli citizens ("Israeli
Arabs"), 5, 32–33, 81; nationalism, 14,

16, 149–50; as people, 262–63; written
culture of, xviii–xix. See also Refugees, new (of June 1967 War); Refugees
of 1948; West Bank leaders
Palmah, xxvi, 110
Partition Resolution of 1947 (Partition
Plan; UN Resolution 181), 8, 9 (map),
26, 27, 32, 34, 35, 55–56, 60, 140, 151, 167,
168, 172, 190, 273, 306n309
Peace settlement: Allon Plan, xxvi, 44,
67, 245, 246 (map), 247–48, 249–50,
254, 257, 272; anti-Hussein campaign,
155–56; Arab League initiative of 2002,
283–84; Arab states' rejection of, 2;
Cabinet Resolution 563 of 19 June 1967,
44, 45–47, 139, 142; confederation/
federation plan, 31, 33, 60–61, 147–48;
Dayan's proposal for, 43–44; direct
negotiations as Israeli condition, 7,
77–78, 139, 159, 161, 168, 169, 266; and
Eban's dossier diplomacy, 180–82, 212;
Eban's threat of force, 213, 357n93;
Egypt-Israel treaty of 1979, 281; and
historical association concept, 4, 160,
188, 221, 254, 271–72; Hussein-Nasser
agreement on concessions, 154, 159;
Hussein's peace initiative (July 1967);
Hussein's willingness to negotiate, 50,
51, 67–68, 70, 158–59, 201, 223, 245, 274;
Israeli agenda in, 65–66, 266–70, 272,
282; and Israeli anti-Hussein campaign, 155–56; and Israeli deception
(see Deception, Israeli foreign policy
of; Takhsisanut); and Israeli delaying
tactics, 73, 201, 247–48, 260; and Israeli
hardened stance, 72, 78, 138–39, 225,
251; Israeli indecision on, 64, 182–83,
186–93, 200–201, 223–24, 267, 271;
Israeli territorial requirements in, 7,
153–54, 255, 267–69; Israeli unwillingness to negotiate, 43, 72–73, 77, 180, 219,
223, 230; Jarring mission, 3, 163, 180–81,
190, 252; and Jerusalem question, 62,

69–70, 77, 195–96, 216; Jordan-Israel treaty of *1994*, 281; and Khartoum resolutions, 47, 137–38, 142–43; and lesson of *1956*, 13; missed opportunities for, xiii, 4, 284; Nasser's consent in, 214, 221; and Palestinian alternative stratagem, 156–58, 160–62, 163–64, 172, 176, 256–57; Palestinian negotiating principles, 167–68, 169; and Palestinian willingness to negotiate, 30–32, 34, 35–37, 63, 230, 274; trade-off formula in, 1–2; unequal parties in, 15–16, 284–85; UN resolution on withdrawal, and Israeli strategy, 3–4, 152–53, 155, 162–63; UN Resolution 242, 4, 162–63, 176, 180, 270; US pressure for, 43, 68, 72, 153, 227, 251–52, 258–59. *See also* Borders; Jordanian-Israeli dialogue; Jordanian option; Palestinian entity movement; Palestinian-Israeli dialogue; Palestinian option

Pedatzur, Reuven, xvii, 272–73, 372n39

Personal Witness (Eban), 47

Phantom (F-4) fighter bomber, 4, 182, 189, 205, 227, 247, 252, 258, 260–61

Piterberg, Gabriel, 134–35

Political Committee: of the Alignment, 19, 44, 66, 88, 125, 128, 142, 183; of the Labor Party, 19, 199–200, 220, 234, 247–48, 255–56

Political Contacts Committee, 231, 236, 237–38, 239, 240, 249, 362n22

Politics of notables, 20, 264, 292–93n52. *See also* Urban notables class

Popular Front for the Liberation of Palestine (PFLP), 195, 279

Press: Arabic, xx; ban on Palestinian contact with, 76; on civil administration project, 238; on civil disobedience movement, 87; on Palestinian-Israeli dialogue, 35–36, 230; on refugee problem, 119

Pryce-Jones, David, 104

Qaddumi, Faruq, 15

Qalqilyah, expulsion from and destruction in, 105–7, 108, 110, 111, 112, 114, 115

al-Qawmiyyun al-'Arab (the Arab Nationalists), 20, 86, 147

Quba'in, Najib, 173

Al-Quds, xx

Quislings. *See* Collaborationist leaders

Rabat summit (scheduled for January 1968): Palestinian delegation to, 176–79; postponement of, 178, 190, 191

Rabin, Yitzhak, 32, 75, 76, 184; as ambassador to Washington, 182, 212, 252, 256, 258, 259; –'Arafat historic handshake, 281; and Cabinet Resolution 563 of 19 June *1967*, 46, 302n11; on civilian casualties, 254; critical of occupation policy, 89; and departure from West Bank, 3, 104, 322n7; on deportation of West Bank leaders, 89, 174; and destruction of villages and town, 105, 107, 108, 111; on Hussein's readiness for peace, 248; and killing of returning new refugees, 123, 330n128; and Palestinian state, 187; pretext for June War, 22; and refugee repatriation, 129

Rafael, Gideon, 19, 119, 153, 232, 354n45, 366n79

Rafi party, 18–19

Rakah (Israeli Communist Party), 238.

Ramla; al-Ramla, xi–xii

Red Cross, 124, 125, 126, 127, 131

Refugees, new (of June 1967 War): barriers to repatriation, 102, 116–17, 215, 270; Bedouins, 185; conditions in Jordan, 120–21; incitement charge against Jordan, 130–31; relocation plan for, 44–45, 64, 65, 66, 237, 241–42; repatriation program (Operation Refugee), 125–35; return, authorization of, 124–25; Rifa'i-Herzog talks on, 223;

Refugees, new (continued)
UN resolution on, 12–13; violence against returning refugees, 122–24, 330n127;n128. *See also* Emigration of June 1967 war

Refugees of *1948*, xxx, 12–13, 20, 26, 85, 103, 111, 115, 116, 117, 120, 124, 129, 185, 188, 193, 268, 269, 300–301n90, 371n25

Religious affairs, Israel interference in. *See* Islamic religious affairs, Israel interference in

Remez, Aharon, 131–32, 303n134

Reprisal raids: on Beirut airport, 279; impact on guerrilla movement, 15, 207, 264–65; international reaction to, 279–80; on Karameh, 203–9, 254, 264–65, 279; in occupied territories, 281; on al-Safi, 355n52; on Salt, 253, 254; on Samu', 15, 16, 203; UN condemnation of, 207–8, 254, 279

Resolution 95 of 31 October 1968. *See* Cabinet Resolution 95

Resolution 181, United Nations. *See* Partition Resolution of 1947 (Partition Plan; UN Resolution 181)

Resolution 194, United Nations, 28, 283, 291n25

Resolution 242, United Nations, 4, 73, 162–63, 176, 180, 182, 190, 202, 212–13, 222, 228, 250, 257, 272, 277, 343nn126,130

Resolution 563 of 19 June 1967, Israeli. *See* Cabinet Resolution 563

"Retroactive transfer," 134

al-Rifa'i, 'Abd al-Mun'im, 250

al-Rifa'i, Samir (1901–65), xxxi

Rifa'i, Samir (b. 1966), xxxi

al-Rifa'i, Zayd: on Allon Plan, 248–49, 254, 257; biography of, xxxi; on civil administration project, 245; -Herzog meetings, 222–23, 245, 248–49, 252–53, 257, 367–68n102; in Hussein's meetings with Israelis, 220, 221, 256, 271, 359n115,

369n138; on Israel's attitude, 250, 255; in meeting of Israel and Jordan's chiefs of staff, 369n138; role in Hussein-Israelis meetings, 17–18

Riyadh Summit of *2007*, 283

Ronen, David, xiii, xiv, 314n17

Rostow, Eugene, 35, 67, 131, 153, 156, 208, 278, 298n48

Rostow, Walt, 153, 251, 256, 258–59, 277

Rothschild, Lord, 239

Rusk, Dean: -Eban meetings, 45, 46, 67, 71, 142, 145, 258, 302n120, 309n76, 336–37n42; on Israeli foreign policy of deception, 275; on Israeli inflexibility and playing for time, 183, 189, 256; on Israeli talk about toppling Hussein, 209; and Jordan, 152, 258; on Jordanian-Israeli peace negotiations, 68, 70, 251–52, 256; on new refugees and their return, 116–17, 118, 126, 132, 133; and Palestinian option, 17, 145; and Resolution 563 of 19 June, 46–47; on UN Resolution 242, 162–63; on who started June War, 22, 293n63

Saba, Bulus, 143

Sabri, Hussein, 105

al-Sadat, Anwar, 281

al-Safi, Israeli raid on, 355n52

Sahliyeh, Emile, 92–93

Said, Edward, 287n4

Sa'ih, 'Abd al-Hamid al-: and civil disobedience, 86, 90, 91–92, 93, 94, 96–97, 100–101, 316n36, 320n95, 338n63; and conference on West Bank future, 74; deportation of, xxix, 98–99, 100–101, 147, 175, 224; and Rabat summit delegation initiative, 178

Saleh, 'Abd al-Jawad, 61, 108, 150, 174, 306n36, 339–40n81

Salt, Israeli attack on, 253–54

Samu', Israeli raid on, xxviii, 15, 16, 203

Sapir, Pinhas, 119

Sapir, Yosef, 18, 225, 359n113

Sasson, Eliyahu, xxvii, 99, 104, 161, 232, 236–37, 314n19, 342nn120,122

Sasson, Moshe: biography of, xxvii; and civil administration project, 233, 234–35, 236, 237, 238, 239–40, 241, 242, 244, 260; in Committee of Four, 49, 57; and conference of West Bank leaders, 75, 242; and cultivation of collaborationist West Bank leaders, 81; and entity movement, 166–69, 175; in Eshkol-Palestinian meeting, 194; on extremists, 172; inflexible attitude of, 170; on intimidation of West Bank moderates, 173; and Jordanian option, 63, 64; minutes of secret talks, xix; Palestinian-Israeli contacts handled by, 19, 158, 164, 165; and Palestinian option, 209–11, 214, 215; -Palestinian talks, 60–63, 74–75, 165–66, 167–72, 190, 191–93, 242, 305–6n33; and PLO links, 211; on political mood in West Bank, 77, 230; preparation for Palestinian-Israeli talks, 57–58, 60, 62–63; and Rabat summit delegation initiative, 176, 177, 179; Saleh on meetings with, 61; and Shehadeh peace initiative of June 1967, 26; on West Bank leadership, 21, 169, 171–72, 288n18

Saudi Arabia, losses in June 1967 War, 1, 2

Saudi peace initiative of 2002, 283–84

Saunders, Harold, 205, 209, 214, 251, 258, 259, 277

Sayigh, Yezid, 207

Schleifer, 'Abdullah, 37

School curriculum, Palestinian, Israeli interference in, 94–95, 319nn74,75

School strike, 87, 90, 95, 319n80

Scranton, William, 247, 274

Segev, Tom, xvi–xvii

Settlements in occupied territories. See Jewish settlements in occupied territories

Shabak. See General Security Service (GSS)

Shaham, Ze'ev, 105–7, 114

al-Shak'ah, Walid, 74, and civil administration project, 235, 242; in Committee of Four, 306n36; -Eshkol meeting, 201; and Kimche-Bavly talks, 28–29; and Nablus's proposal for self rule, 170–71, 228–29; opposition to entity movement, 151; and proposal for Palestinian state, 210–11, 265, 266

Shapira, Hayyim Moshe, 254

Shapira, Ya'acov Shimshon, 45, 53–54, 113, 140, 304n5

al-Sharif, 'Ali, 211

al-Sharif, Salim, 201

Sharm al-Sheikh, 259, 267, 281

Sharon, Ariel, 99, 283, 284, 310–11n93

Shashar, Michael, 75

Sha'th, Nabil, 207

Shehadeh, 'Aziz: assassination attempt on, 202, 353–54n34; and civil administration project, 235, 236; confederation plan of, 60–61; and conference of West Bank leaders, 74; -Dayan meeting, 215–16; emissary to PLO, 211; and entity movement, 143–44, 145, 146, 148, 149, 150–51, 166, 167, 273; Eshkol's meeting with, 194–95; experimental autonomy plan of, 74; intimidation of, 173, 174; Israeli cultivation of, 83, 84; on Jerusalem, 307n42; Palestinian option initiative of June 1967, 26–29, 30, 51; on peace settlement prospects, 284; on PLO, 192; and Rabat summit delegation initiative, 178; Sasson's meetings with, 209–10, 168, 169, 306n36

Shlaim, Avi, 254, 280, 302n114

Shnat Shabak (Ronen), xiii, xiv

al-Shu'aibi, 'Isa, 173

al-Shuqayri, Ahmad, 42, 137, 151, 176, 192, 211, 333n182, 347n50

Shweikah, destruction of, 109

Sinai Campaign (1956), xxvi, 13, 39–40

Sisco, Joseph, 249–52, 363n38

Six Day War. *See* June 1967 War

Sourif, destruction in, 109, 110, 111

Soviet Union (USSR), 13, 14, 22, 39, 40, 47, 54, 147, 163, 183, 189, 192, 227, 258, 276, 277

Spiegel, Steven, 277

Stewart, Michael, 223

Strike, general, 91, 93, 98

Suez Canal, 3, 45, 65, 103, 114, 154, 276, 281, 309n72

Sumud (steadfastness) strategy, 270

Sutton, Rafi, 31, 43

Symmes, Harrison, 198, 250

Syria, 13, 14, 16, 336–37n42; armistice agreement of *1949*, 10 (map), 12; and Cabinet Resolution 563 (19 June 1967), 45, 46, 47, 51, 78, 139, 259, 270; -Egypt offensive of October *1973*, 281; and Khartoum Summit, 137; losses in June War, 1, 5; and Rabat summit, 178; rejectionist attitude to Israel, 2, 272; and Soviet Union, 276

Syrian Plateau. *See* Golan Heights

Tahbub, Hajj Fatin, 306n36

Tahbub, Hasan, 93

Takhsisanut, 183, 212, 247, 248, 255, 257, 260, 273, 274, 275, 284. *See also* Deception, Israeli foreign policy of

al-Takruri, Yusuf, 306n36

al-Talhuni, Bahjat, 152, 175, 176, 198, 201, 204, 211, 222, 240–41, 244, 245, 357n94, 359n116, 364n46

al-Tall, Wasfi, 218, 219, 291n32, 358n109

al-Tarifi, Ahmad, 353n34

Taybeh, destruction in, 109

Tcherniakov, Yuri, 298n48

Tekoah, Yosef, 127, 348n62

Terrorism. *See* Guerrilla movement

Thalmann, Ernest, 96, 98

Thant, U, 39, 55, 223, 260–61, 355n68

Al-Thawrah, (Damascus), 36

Three "no"s of Khartoum, 47, 137, 138, 223. *See also* Khartoum Summit

Time magazine, 245

Times of London, 228, 229

Tiran, Island of, 1, 2, 39–40, 289n2

Tiran, Straits of, 13, 45, 65, 289n2

Tolan, Sandy, xii

Toledano, Shmuel, 80–81

Touqan, Fadwa, 266, 276

Touqan, Qadri, 95, 151, 242–43, 306n36

Travel permits, 81, 241, 243

Treaty on the Non-Proliferation of Nuclear Weapons (NPT), 205

Troyon, Roland, 127

Truman, Harry, 277

Tsur, Zvi, 29, 187, 256, 295n10

Tulkarm, destruction in, 111; expulsion from, 113–14

Turkey. *See* Ottoman Turkey

24 July Assembly, 86–87, 88, 89, 90

'Udwan, Kamal, 15

United Arab Republic (UAR). *See* Egypt

United Kingdom. *See* Britain

United Nations: and annexation of Arab Jerusalem, 55; condemnation of retaliatory attacks, 207–8, 254, 279; Eban's nine-point peace plan, speech in, 260; fabricated story on outbreak of war in, 22; Jarring peace mission (*see* Jarring, Gunnar, peace mission of); Partition Resolution of 1947 (*see* Partition Resolution of 1947 [Partition Plan; UN Resolution 181]); and refugee problem, 12–13, 103, 116, 119; Resolution 194 (*see* Resolution 194, United Nations); Resolution 242 (*see* Resolution 242, United Nations); Soviet demand for Israeli withdrawal, 39, 47, 54; and trusteeship proposal,

228–30; withdrawal resolution and
Israeli strategy, 3–4, 152–53, 155,
162–63
United Nations Relief and Works
Agency (UNRWA), 103, 104, 108,
109, 117, 120, 121, 124, 126, 129, 131, 133,
270
United Press International (UPI), 118
United States–Israel relations: and
aircraft sales, 182, 189, 205, 227, 247,
258, 260; and Allon Plan, 247, 249–50,
259; and border issue, 189; CIA-
brokered meeting with Hussein,
71–72, 310n93; and Israeli anti-Hussein
campaign, 155–56; Israeli duplicity
in, xiv–xv, 2, 4–5, 183, 249–50, 273,
274; Israeli objectives in, 182; and
Jordanian-Israeli dialogue, 68,
71–72, 223, 252, 257–60, 259; and 1956
Arab-Israeli war, 13; and 19 June
Resolution, 46, 47; and outbreak of
June War, 13–14, 22, 25; and Palestinian option, 17, 35–36; pressure for
peace settlement, 39, 43, 188, 251–52,
258–59; and refugee problem, 116–17,
118–19, 121; and reprisal attacks, 198,
203, 204, 205, 206; and return of new
refugees, 126, 129, 131, 132, 133, 270; and
territorial expansionism, 141–42,
336n38, 337n42; and UN resolution on
withdrawal, 39; US acquiescence to
Israel, 205, 258–60, 275, 276–79, 280;
and withdrawal from occupied
territories, 153, 184. See also Johnson,
Lyndon; Rusk, Dean
Urban notables class (a'yan), Arab
Jerusalem and West Bank, 20, 21. See
also Politics of notables
USSR. See Soviet Union

Van Creveld, Martin, 66
Varash. See Committee of Heads of the
[intelligence] Services

Vardi, Raphael, 74–76, 83, 91, 96, 99, 243,
293n55, 315n34, 321n100
Vatikiotis, P.J., 34, 306–7n39

Waqf (Islamic endowment), 93, 112
War crimes, 110
Warhaftig, Zerah, 88, 113
War of Attrition (1969–70), 3, 281, 289n10
Warrad, Fa'iq, 172, 173
Wasserstein, Bernard, 360n123
Water resources, in occupied territories,
6, 185, 241–42, 299n71, 349n88
Weitz, Yosef, 134
West Bank, xxi, 1, 2, 6, 12, 25, 106 (map).
See also Occupied territories;
Palestinian option; West Bank leaders
West Bank Committee, 80–81, 87–88
West Bank leaders: and ban on political
organization, 77, 264; biographies of,
xxviii–xxx; and civil administration
project, 170–71, 231, 233, 234–44, 260,
273; collaboration attacked by Arabs,
142, 143, 145–46, 150; conference of,
74–75, 242; -Dayan meeting, 211,
215–17; deportation of, 89–90, 98–99,
172–73, 174–76; divisions among, 264,
289n18; education of, 58; as emissaries
to Hussein, 170, 192, 195, 196, 198, 200,
201, 212–14, 264; in entity movement
(see Palestinian entity movement); in
Gaza Strip, 19–20; and guerrilla
movement, 244–45; intimidation of
moderates, 173–74; in Islamic Council,
86–87, 88, 90, 91, 93; Israeli alienation
of, 75, 84, 101, 230–31, 242; Israeli
cultivation of, xiv, 80–84, 143, 232, 243,
264, 313n3, 314nn15,16; Israeli view of,
264; and Jerusalem municipal council,
refusal to participate in, 85–86, 87;
and Jordanian cabinet appointments,
201–2, 357n94; Jordanian rule
supported by, 59–60, 62, 63, 64, 65, 73,
94, 144, 190, 230; in Nablus, 150–51,

West Bank leaders (continued)
170–71; in National Guidance
Committee, 92–93, 145–46; negotiating principles of, 167–68, 169; from
notables class, 20, 21; petition of,
242–43; political affiliations of, 58,
171–72, 306n36; and Rabat summit
delegation initiative, 176–79; radical
activists, 20–21; and refugee problem,
135, 193; Sasson's talks with, 60–63,
74–75. 167–72, 190, 191–93, 242; shift
from *dakhil* ("inside") to *kharij*
("outside"), 207, 265; and UN
trusteeship plan, 228–30; willingness
to negotiate, 30–32, 34, 35–37, 63, 274.
See also Palestinian-Israeli dialogue
Western Wall (*ha- Kotel ha- Ma'aravi*),
54, 113
Whole land of Israel (*Eretz Yisrael
ha-Shlemah*), 18, 247. *See also* Greater
Israel
Wilson, Evan, 37, 87, 122

Wilson, Harold, 304n137, 366n79
Woodward, Bob, 292n41

Ya'ari, Ehud, 174
Ya'bed, destruction in, 109
Yafeh, Avi'ad, xxvii, 65, 119–20, 132, 184,
197, 218, 225, 232, 342n122, 359n38
al-Yahya, Tawfiq, 27, 28
Yalu, destruction of, 107–8. *See also*
Latrun Salient
Yariv, Aharon, 19, 138
Yehoshua, A. B., xv
Yehoshu'a, Ya'acov, 88
Yom Kippur War (October 1973), xxvi,
181, 271, 276, 280, 281

Zahni, Yusif, 127
al-Zaru, Nadim, 59, 60, 61, 108, 161, 174,
306n36, 346n38
Ze'evi, Rehav'am, 41, 80, 300n84
Zeita, destruction of, 109
Zionism, 8, 14, 95, 96